RIGHTS AND PRIVATE LAW

In recent years a strand of thinking has developed in private law scholarship which has come to be known as 'rights' or 'rights-based' analysis. Rights analysis seeks to develop an understanding of private law obligations that is driven, primarily or exclusively, by the recognition of the rights we have against each other, rather than by other influences on private law, such as the pursuit of community welfare goals. Notions of rights are also assuming greater importance in private law in other respects. Human rights instruments are having an increasing influence on private law doctrines. And in the law of unjust enrichment, an important debate has recently begun on the relationship between restitution of rights and restitution of value.

This collection is a significant contribution to debate about the role of rights in private law. It includes essays by leading private law scholars addressing fundamental questions about the role of rights in private law as a whole and within particular areas of private law. The collection includes contributions by advocates and critics of rights-based approaches and provides a thorough and balanced analysis of the relationship between rights and private law.

Rights and Private Law

Edited by
Donal Nolan
and
Andrew Robertson

·HART·
PUBLISHING

OXFORD AND PORTLAND, OREGON
2014

Published in the United Kingdom by Hart Publishing Ltd
16C Worcester Place, Oxford, OX1 2JW
Telephone: +44 (0)1865 517530
Fax: +44 (0)1865 510710
E-mail: mail@hartpub.co.uk
Website: http://www.hartpub.co.uk

Published in North America (US and Canada) by
Hart Publishing
c/o International Specialized Book Services
920 NE 58th Avenue, Suite 300
Portland, OR 97213-3786
USA
Tel: +1 503 287 3093 or toll-free: (1) 800 944 6190
Fax: +1 503 280 8832
E-mail: orders@isbs.com
Website: http://www.isbs.com

Hart Publishing is an imprint of Bloomsbury Publishing plc.

British Library Cataloguing in Publication Data

Data Available

ISBN: 978-1-84946-142-9 (Hardback)
ISBN: 978-1-84946-656-1 (Paperback)

Typeset by Forewords, Oxford
Printed and bound in Great Britain by
Lightning Source UK Ltd

Acknowledgements

This book had its origins in the Fifth Biennial Conference on the Law of Obligations (Obligations V), which was co-hosted by the Faculty of Law at the University of Oxford and Melbourne Law School and was held at St Anne's College, Oxford from 14–16 July 2010.

We would like to express our gratitude to the Faculty of Law at the University of Oxford and to Melbourne Law School for supporting the conference, and particularly to Timothy Endicott, Dean of the Faculty of Law at the University of Oxford and to Michael Crommelin and James Hathaway, former Deans of Melbourne Law School. For their work in connection with the conference, we are grateful to Marianne Biese, Maureen O'Neill, Steve Allen, Sadie Slater, Anne Currie and Bento De Sousa in Oxford, as well as to Mardi Richardson, Genevieve Allan and Jessica Sullivan in Melbourne. We are particularly grateful to James Goudkamp for the enormous amount of time and energy which he put into assisting us with the organisation of the conference, and to the Oxford graduate students who helped to ensure the smooth running of the conference sessions: Carmine Conte, Andrew Lodder, Aruna Nair, Jaani Riordan, Guy Sela and David Winterton. Finally, we would like to thank Hart Publishing, Cambridge University Press and Freshfields Bruckhaus Deringer for their sponsorship of the conference, and Allan J Myers AO, QC for his generous financial support of the conference.

Our collaboration on the introductory chapter was facilitated by Melbourne Law School's International Research Visitors Scheme, and we are grateful to Melbourne Law School for its support. Finally, we are enormously grateful to Julia Wang for her extremely careful and thorough editing of the manuscript.

Donal Nolan and Andrew Robertson
May 2011

Contents

Contributors

TT Arvind is a Lecturer at York Law School, University of York.

Roderick Bagshaw is a Fellow and Tutor in Law at Magdalen College, Oxford and a Lecturer at the Faculty of Law, University of Oxford.

Elise Bant is an Associate Professor of Law at the University of Melbourne.

Allan Beever is a Professor of Law at the University of South Australia.

Andrew Burrows is Professor of the Law of England at the University of Oxford and a Fellow of All Souls College, Oxford.

Peter Cane is Distinguished Professor of Law and the Director of Research at the College of Law, Australian National University.

Erika Chamberlain is an Associate Professor at the Faculty of Law, University of Western Ontario.

Helge Dedek is an Assistant Professor at the Faculty of Law, McGill University.

François du Bois is an Associate Professor and Reader in Private Law at the University of Nottingham.

John CP Goldberg is a Professor of Law at Harvard Law School.

Sarah Green is a Fellow and Tutor in Law at St Hilda's College, University of Oxford.

Gregory C Keating is the William T Dalessi Professor of Law and Philosophy at the Gould School of Law, University of Southern California.

Nicholas J McBride is a Fellow of Pembroke College, Cambridge.

Ben McFarlane is a Reader in Property Law at the University of Oxford and a Fellow and Tutor in Law at Trinity College, Oxford.

JW Neyers is an Associate Professor at the Faculty of Law, University of Western Ontario.

Donal Nolan is the Porjes Foundation Fellow and Tutor in Law at Worcester College, University of Oxford.

Andrew Robertson is a Professor of Law at the University of Melbourne.

Stephen A Smith is James McGill Professor at the Faculty of Law, McGill University.

Robert Stevens is Professor of Commercial Law at University College London.

Richard W Wright is a Distinguished Professor of Law at the Chicago-Kent College of Law, Illinois Institute of Technology.

Benjamin C Zipursky is the Associate Dean for Research and holds the James H Quinn '49 Chair in Legal Ethics at Fordham Law School.

Table of Cases

Australia

Canada

European Court and Commission of Human Rights

Germany

Israel

Netherlands

New Zealand

Republic of Ireland

South Africa

Uganda

United Kingdom

United States of America

Table of Legislation

Canada

European Union

France

Germany

Italy

New Zealand

South Africa

Soviet Union

United Kingdom

Secondary legislation

United States of America

Table of Treaties

1

Rights and Private Law

DONAL NOLAN AND ANDREW ROBERTSON*

I. INTRODUCTION

IN RECENT YEARS a strand of thinking has developed in private law scholarship which has come to be known as 'rights' or 'rights-based' analysis. This kind of analysis seeks to develop an understanding of private law obligations which is driven, primarily or exclusively, by the recognition of the rights we have against each other, rather than by other influences on private law, such as the pursuit of community welfare goals. Rights-based theories of contract,[1] torts[2] and unjust enrichment[3] have been developed. A number of doctrines within the law of tort have been subjected to rights analysis.[4] Thinking on the law of property has been informed by innovative analysis of the nature of property rights.[5] The relationship between primary rights and the second-

* We are grateful to Allan Beever, Peter Cane, Helge Dedek, Gregory Keating, Jason Neyers and Robert Stevens for their helpful comments on an earlier draft. The usual caveat applies.

[1] See, eg, P Benson, 'The Unity of Contract Law' in P Benson (ed), *The Theory of Contract Law* (Cambridge, Cambridge University Press, 2001) 118. On rights-based theories of contract more generally, see SA Smith, *Contract Theory* (Oxford, Oxford University Press, 2004) 140–58.

[2] R Stevens, *Torts and Rights* (Oxford, Oxford University Press, 2007).

[3] See, eg, EJ Weinrib, 'The Normative Structure of Unjust Enrichment' in C Rickett and R Grantham (eds), *Structure and Justification in Private Law: Essays for Peter Birks* (Oxford, Hart Publishing, 2008) 21.

[4] See, eg, A Beever, *Rediscovering the Law of Negligence* (Oxford, Hart Publishing, 2007); P Benson, 'Should *White v Jones* Represent Canadian Law: A Return to First Principles' in JW Neyers, E Chamberlain and SGA Pitel (eds), *Emerging Issues in Tort Law* (Oxford, Hart Publishing, 2007) 141; JW Neyers, 'Rights-Based Justifications for the Tort of Unlawful Interference with Economic Relations' (2008) 28 *Legal Studies* 215; JW Neyers, 'The Economic Torts as Corrective Justice' (2009) 17 *Torts Law Journal* 162; D Nolan, '"A Tort Against Land": Private Nuisance as a Property Tort' ch 16 of this book; E Chamberlain, 'Misfeasance in a Public Office: A Justifiable Anomaly within the Rights-Based Approach?' ch 19 of this book.

[5] Notably B McFarlane, *The Structure of Property Law* (Oxford, Hart Publishing, 2008).

ary rights triggered by their infringement has been the subject of ongoing debate.[6] Notions of rights are also assuming greater importance in private law in other respects. Human rights instruments are having an increasing influence on private law doctrines in a number of jurisdictions, and increasingly attention is being paid by private law scholars to the rights that claimants have to particular court orders, and to the rights arising from the making of those orders.[7] A debate has also arisen in the law of unjust enrichment as to whether there is an obligation to make restitution of rights which is distinct from the obligation to make restitution of value.[8]

While thinking about rights has been influential across the whole spectrum of private law, the law of torts has been the primary focus of much recent rights analysis and the field of the most intense debate. Rights analysis in tort law is strongly associated with anti-instrumentalism and the idea that the law of torts is and should be concerned primarily or exclusively with notions of interpersonal morality, rather than the pursuit of community welfare goals. Because tort law has become the primary site of contest between instrumentalist and non-instrumentalist conceptions of private law, rights analysis has been at its most provocative and vociferous in relation to tort law, and has attracted an equally vehement response from its critics. While the chapters in this collection concern the role of rights analysis in a number of different areas of private law, tort law inevitably attracts the most attention.

II. WHAT IS RIGHTS ANALYSIS?

Since private law is generally understood to concern the rights and duties which we owe each other, at first blush it seems unlikely that analysis of private law in terms of rights will prove to be particularly insightful or illuminating. First impressions can, however, be misleading, and closer inspection reveals that what has come to be known as rights (or 'rights-based') analysis of private law does offer a distinctive and important take on private law, both at a general level, and with reference to particular private law doctrines. What, then, *is* 'rights analysis'? The central claim of rights analysis is perhaps best summed up by Robert Stevens when he says that 'Private law is simply about the rights we have one against another'.[9]

---

[6] See, eg, R Zakrzewski, *Remedies Reclassified* (Oxford, Oxford University Press, 2005).

[7] SA Smith, 'The Rights of Private Law' in A Robertson and HW Tang, *The Goals of Private Law* (Oxford, Hart Publishing, 2009) 113; SA Smith, 'Rule-Based Rights and Court-Ordered Rights' ch 8 of this book.

[8] This issue is explored by B McFarlane, 'Unjust Enrichment, Rights and Value' ch 20 of this book; E Bant, 'Rights and Value in Rescission: Some Implications for Unjust Enrichment' ch 21 of this book.

[9] R Stevens, 'The Conflict of Rights' in A Robertson and HW Tang, *The Goals of Private Law* (Oxford, Hart Publishing, 2009) 139, 141.

Similarly, Ernest Weinrib has written that 'The various branches of civil liability work out the circumstances under which the defendant can be said to have or to have done something that is inconsistent with a right of the plaintiff'.[10] Rights theorists also frequently define rights analysis by reference to what it is *not*. Hence Stevens contrasts his conception of torts as 'infringements of primary rights'[11] with what he refers to as the 'loss model', according to which 'the defendant should be liable where he is at fault for causing the claimant loss unless there is a good reason why not',[12] and similarly Nicholas McBride contrasts his rights-based view of tort law with the belief that the function of tort law is to determine when a claimant is able to claim compensation for a loss that the defendant has caused the claimant to suffer.[13] In a similar vein, rights theorists based in the United States frequently contrast their conception of private law with a rival conception grounded in the American legal realist tradition, according to which liability is not a response to violations of rights but instead 'a state-imposed sanction for undesirable conduct', with the result that private law is 'a "mere" means by which governmental officials in given historical periods have pursued certain policy objectives'.[14] On this conception, although private law may be conventionally formulated in terms of rights and duties, these rights and duties are merely devices 'for signifying a condition for a claim to arise and the person in whose favor it arises'.[15]

If, then, we pose the question of what private law is about if it is *not* about rights and duties, we can see that at least two responses are possible. The first is that private law is regulatory law, and is largely composed of liability rules designed by the state to incentivise us to act in ways which the state considers to be in the public interest. Under this approach, the central normative message of private law is frequently conceptualised in 'either/or' terms: *either* you conform with the (apparent) norm *or* you pay for not doing so—the choice is yours. The second response is that large tracts of private law—particularly, but not exclusively, the law of tort—are concerned not with the protection of primary rights but with compensation for loss. Like the former view, this conception of (elements of) private law may also embody the legal realist claim that 'private law

---

[10] EJ Weinrib, 'Corrective Justice in a Nutshell' (2002) 52 *University of Toronto Law Journal* 349, 353. See also S Perry, 'The Role of Duty of Care in a Rights-Based Theory of Negligence Law' in A Robertson and HW Tang (eds), *The Goals of Private Law* (Oxford, Hart Publishing, 2009) 79, 81 ('the core of tort law concerns certain fundamental moral duties and their correlative rights').

[11] Stevens, *Torts and Rights*, above n 2, at 3.

[12] ibid, at 1.

[13] NJ McBride, 'Rights and the Basis of Tort Law' ch 12 of this book, text accompanying n 13.

[14] JCP Goldberg and BC Zipursky, 'Rights and Responsibility in the Law of Torts' ch 9 of this book, text accompanying n 3.

[15] P Jaffey, 'Liabilities in Private Law' (2008) 14 *Legal Theory* 233, 244.

is public law', with loss compensation being justified by reference to concerns of distributive justice or the social desirability of 'loss-spreading'. If, however, private law is limited on this loss compensation approach to the compensation of *wrongful* losses, then that might be thought to move it closer to the realm of interpersonal justice. At this point, the contrast with a rights-based approach becomes less distinct, since while 'wrongful' could simply connote 'unjust' (or the breach of a duty 'in the air'), it might also be thought to entail a 'wrong', which would in turn entail a violation of a right.[16]

The nature of rights analysis can also be explored by identifying a number of central characteristics of this approach to private law. One such characteristic is that rights analysis is *structural*, in the sense that rights theorists have a particular interest in the structures which underlie private law. Hence Allan Beever claims in his rights-based account of the law of negligence that when viewed in the right light, negligence law can be seen to possess 'a conceptually coherent, indeed conceptually *unified*, structure',[17] while Stevens describes his book *Torts and Rights* as 'foundational, trying to make clear the structure of the law',[18] a claim endorsed in two critical assessments of his work.[19] Another leading rights theorist, Weinrib, describes the Aristotelian concept of corrective justice as the 'form of the private law relationship'[20] and 'the unifying structure that renders private law relationships immanently intelligible'.[21] A corrective justice approach, therefore, 'attempts to bring to the surface the structure of normative thought latent in the institutions and concepts of a liability regime'.[22]

A connected characteristic of rights analysis is that it is *monist* rather than pluralist: the claim of rights theorists is not therefore that some parts of private law—or of the particular area of private law under scrutiny— are best understood in terms of rights, but that all (or almost all[23]) of

---

[16] For an argument that not all wrongful losses result from wrongs, see J Coleman, *Risks and Wrongs* (Cambridge, Cambridge University Press, 1992) ch 17.

[17] A Beever, *Rediscovering the Law of Negligence*, above n 4, at 30 (emphasis in original). See also at 515 ('The law of negligence has a structure, and it is our primary role as academics to discover what that structure is').

[18] Stevens, *Torts and Rights*, above n 2, at vii.

[19] See J Murphy, 'Rights, Reductionism and Tort Law' (2008) 28 *Oxford Journal of Legal Studies* 393, 394 ('an attempted reductionist account of the way in which *the structure* of tort law can best be understood') (emphasis in original); P Cane, 'Robert Stevens, *Torts and Rights*' (2008) 71 *Modern Law Review* 641, 644 ('Stevens' account is structural').

[20] EJ Weinrib, *The Idea of Private Law* (Cambridge MA, Harvard University Press, 1995) 75.

[21] ibid, at 19.

[22] Weinrib, 'Corrective Justice in a Nutshell', above n 10, at 356. On the relationship between rights and corrective justice, see part IX below.

[23] See, eg, Stevens, *Torts and Rights*, above n 2, at 242 (describing the tort of misfeasance in a public office as 'an exception to the rule that the deliberate infliction of loss, absent the violation of a right, is not actionable').

it is. Hence Beever's reference to the 'conceptually *unified*' structure of negligence law,[24] and Peter Cane's characterisation of Stevens' account of the law of torts as 'unitary in that it understands all torts to be protective of specific primary rights'.[25] Similarly, John Murphy describes Stevens' account as 'reductionist', in the sense that it 'seeks to identify a single norm, goal, principle or feature that explains or underpins the disparate causes of action that comprise tort law',[26] while in his book *Contract Theory* Stephen Smith presents rights-based theories of contract law as a unitary explanation of 'the entirety of contract law'.[27] This concern with presenting a unitary account of private law has given rise to a number of contributions by the rights theorist Jason Neyers, in which he has sought to reconcile private law doctrines which at first sight seem difficult to explain in terms of rights with the rights-based approach.[28]

Rights theorists themselves are also keen to emphasise that their goal is an *interpretive* one: to give the 'best account' of private law or particular private law doctrines. According to Stevens, for example, the 'first task of the academic lawyer is to explain the law so that it makes coherent sense and to account for it in the best possible light'.[29] Similarly, Beever describes his account of negligence law as an 'interpretive theory', by which he means an attempt to 'help us to make sense of the law and to see it in a coherent and meaningful light'.[30] Smith plausibly distinguishes interpretive accounts of the law from what he calls descriptive accounts, historical accounts and prescriptive accounts.[31] When rights theorists self-identify as interpretivists therefore, they are telling us that they are not setting out simply to describe the current law, nor to explain how and why the law has developed as it has, nor to put forward an account of

---

[24] Beever, *Rediscovering the Law of Negligence*, above n 4, at 30. By this, Beever says that he means that 'the various stages of the negligence enquiry ... are seen as parts of a conceptually integrated whole' and not as 'a series of conceptually separate questions' (ibid).

[25] Cane, 'Robert Stevens, *Torts and Rights*', above n 19, at 644. This should perhaps be 'almost all': see above n 23. Although Stevens says that 'there is little underlying unity' to the *law of torts* (*Torts and Rights*, above n 2, at 299), Cane's point is that *Stevens' account* of the law of torts is unitary in that he conceives of all (or almost all) torts as violations of primary rights.

[26] Murphy, above n 19, at 394.

[27] Smith, *Contract Theory*, above n 1, at 107.

[28] See JW Neyers, 'A Theory of Vicarious Liability' (2005) 43 *Alberta Law Review* 287; Neyers, 'Rights-Based Justifications', above n 4; Neyers, 'The Economic Torts as Corrective Justice', above n 4; JW Neyers, 'Explaining the Inexplicable? Four Manifestations of Abuse of Rights in English Law' ch 11 of this book. See also E Chamberlain, 'Misfeasance in a Public Office', above n 4, in which Erika Chamberlain argues that the tort of misfeasance in a public office can be reconciled with the rights-based approach.

[29] R Stevens, 'Damages and the Right to Performance: A *Golden Victory* or Not?' in JW Neyers, R Bronaugh and SGA Pitel (eds), *Exploring Contract Law* (Oxford, Hart Publishing, 2009) 171, 198. See also Stevens, *Torts and Rights*, above n 2, at vii ('This book seeks to paint the best picture of the common law of torts which can be rendered').

[30] Beever, *Rediscovering the Law of Negligence*, above n 4, at 21.

[31] Smith, *Contract Theory*, above n 1, at 4–5.

what the ideal law would be. Instead, their aim is to provide the most plausible, coherent and appealing account of the law *as it stands*. This of course imposes significant constraints on these theorists, as well as giving us criteria—fit, coherence, morality and transparency, according to Smith[32]—by which we can evaluate their analysis of private law on its own terms, with the caveat that of course opinions may differ both as to the criteria to be used in the evaluative process and as to the relative weight to be attached to them.[33]

The work of rights theorists of private law can also be described as *formalist*.[34] We mean by this that rights theorists believe that 'the general, structural concepts of private law ... determine the result (or the rule) to be applied in particular (types of) cases'.[35] In this sense, formalism can be contrasted with the realist view that private law cases are entirely or largely determined by policy determinations, for which general, structural concepts merely provide a foil. As Christian Witting puts it in his discussion of Beever's work on negligence law:

> The argument of the formalists is against the idea that much of tort law is to be explained in terms of policy choices and that various tort doctrines do no more than 'mask' policy-based decision-making.[36]

In place of policy, we find 'principle', with Beever describing his work on the law of negligence as a project 'to re-establish general principle in our understanding of the law of negligence',[37] its aim 'to show that the law of negligence can be understood in a principled way without appeal to policy'.[38] While acknowledging the difficulty of distinguishing the two, Beever defines 'principle' as 'the rules and the doctrine of the law itself', and 'policy' negatively as 'everything apart from principle'.[39] This *internalist* perspective[40] is also apparent in the work of other rights theorists, such as Weinrib, who contrasts his 'internal' account of private law with what he terms 'functionalist' analysis,[41] and Stevens, who argues that it is

---

[32] ibid, at ch 1.

[33] Some rights theorists appear to attach particular significance to the criterion of coherence, for example (see, eg, Beever, *Rediscovering the Law of Negligence*, above n 4, at 22–25; Weinrib, *The Idea of Private Law*, above n 20, at 29–46), while Beever argues that the criterion of transparency 'requires special treatment when applied to the law of negligence' (*Rediscovering the Law of Negligence*, above n 4, at 28). See further A Robertson, 'Rights, Pluralism and the Duty of Care' ch 15 of this book.

[34] See, eg, Weinrib, *The Idea of Private Law*, above n 20, at ch 2.

[35] M Stone, 'Formalism' in J Coleman and S Shapiro (eds), *The Oxford Handbook of Jurisprudence and Philosophy of Law* (Oxford, Oxford University Press, 2002) 166, 189.

[36] C Witting, 'The House that Dr Beever Built: Corrective Justice, Principle and the Law of Negligence' (2008) 71 *Modern Law Review* 621, 623.

[37] Beever, *Rediscovering the Law of Negligence*, above n 4, at 39.

[38] ibid, at 71.

[39] ibid, at 3.

[40] ibid, at 34–35.

[41] Weinrib, *The Idea of Private Law*, above n 20, at 11.

illegitimate for judges to decide tort cases by reference to considerations of public policy, and who explicitly distinguishes his approach from that of other tort scholars whom he describes as legal realists.[42] Rights theorists' internalist perspective is closely tied to the fact that their work is characteristically *non-instrumentalist*, in other words that it 'construes law as being internally intelligible and thus requiring no reference to purposes external to itself'.[43] Weinrib's account of private law is radically non-instrumentalist in this sense, so much so that he describes both Charles Fried's promise theory of contract[44] and George Fletcher's account of tort law[45] as instrumentalist on the grounds that they treat private law as a servant of, or means of implementing, a non-instrumental morality.[46] Similarly, Smith characterises rights-based theories of contract as 'concerned with duties that contracting parties owe to each other rather than any broader social goal',[47] and both Stevens and Beever deny that the law of torts is an instrument of social policy, claiming instead that it is founded on a base of 'fundamental' or 'moral' rights.[48]

We should note, however, that not all rights theorists are opposed to the use of policy arguments and instrumentalist reasoning in private law adjudication. When it comes to the law of tort, for example, there is a clear division between rights theorists, such as Beever and Stevens, who maintain that judges should avoid policy-based reasoning altogether, and others, such as McBride, who, while acknowledging that arguments from principle should take centre stage, reject the notion that 'considerations of what is in the public interest are *never* relevant to claims in tort'.[49] While it is possible, therefore, to identify certain distinguishing features which appear to characterise the work of all those who self-identify as rights theorists, some take a more uncompromisingly non-instrumentalist position than others.

III. WHAT IS MEANT BY 'RIGHTS'?

Since our focus is on private law, the rights which we are primarily interested in are rights against others, as opposed to rights against the state

---

[42] Stevens, *Torts and Rights*, above n 2, at ch 14.

[43] Weinrib, *The Idea of Private Law*, above n 20, at 50–51.

[44] C Fried, *Contract as Promise* (Cambridge MA, Harvard University Press, 1981).

[45] GP Fletcher, 'Fairness and Utility in Tort Theory' (1972) 85 *Harvard Law Review* 537.

[46] Weinrib, *The Idea of Private Law*, above n 20, at 48–55.

[47] Smith, *Contract Theory*, above n 1, at 140–41.

[48] See, eg, A Beever, 'Our Most Fundamental Rights' ch 3 of this book; Stevens, *Torts and Rights*, above n 2, at 329–37.

[49] McBride, 'Rights and the Basis of Tort Law', above n 13, text accompanying n 29. See also Perry, 'The Role of Duty of Care', above n 10, at 83 (refusing to 'rule out the possibility that the best moral theory of rights has a consequentialist dimension').

(such as 'human rights').[50] At least three different general meanings of the word 'right' are discernible in the private law context.[51] The first is what Wesley Hohfeld called a 'claim', by which he meant a legal right which correlates with a legal duty.[52] An example of a 'claim right' of this kind is a right not to be battered or a right not to have others trespass on your land. Claim rights are in their very nature fully specified, absolute and conclusive, with the full specification providing 'for all possible contingencies, so that the right is absolute or conclusive in that it can never be justifiably overridden'.[53] It follows that it is logically impossible for claim rights to conflict. The assertion of a claim right in this sense is no more than a positivistic assertion as to the import of the law—a conclusion to a legal question[54]—from the standpoint of the beneficiary of the rule in question. Primary claim rights, which correlate with primary duties or obligations, can be distinguished from secondary claim rights, which are triggered by the violation of primary claim rights, and which correlate with secondary duties or obligations to make reparation.

Some rights theorists believe that there are also such things as 'moral rights', which exist quite apart from the state.[55] These moral rights can in a sense therefore be described as 'extra-legal', although they may of course ground 'legal' claim rights which the state will enforce.[56] According to Stevens, these moral rights 'are capable of being deduced from the nature and experience of ourselves, and the world and society in which we live'.[57] The nature of moral rights of this kind has been the subject of extensive philosophical debate, which it is not possible to do justice to here. Nevertheless, Stevens does make it clear that in his view moral rights share at least one characteristic of legal claim rights, in that the violation of a moral right triggers a secondary moral right to reparation.[58] Needless to say, not everyone agrees that there are such things as moral rights at all. On the contrary, it can be argued that the assertion of a 'moral right' is no more than a subjective opinion as to what the moral position is, and (perhaps) what the legal position ought to be. On this sceptical view, rights 'cannot, therefore, have a real objective existence outside the

---

[50] See further Stevens, 'The Conflict of Rights', above n 9, at 146–49.

[51] There are also other, more specific meanings, such as 'rights of action', but where appropriate these are dealt with in later parts of this chapter.

[52] WN Hohfeld, 'Some Fundamental Legal Conceptions as Applied in Judicial Reasoning' (1913) 23 *Yale Law Journal* 16, 32.

[53] P Jaffey, 'Duties and Liabilities in Private Law' (2006) 12 *Legal Theory* 137, 141.

[54] Stevens, 'The Conflict of Rights', above n 9, at 143.

[55] See, eg, Stevens, *Torts and Rights*, above n 2, at 329–37; Beever, 'Our Most Fundamental Rights', above n 48.

[56] This is something of a terminological minefield, because as Beever points out ('Our Most Fundamental Rights', above n 48, text accompanying n 37 ff) some philosophers have taken the view that private *law* is 'conceptually prior to the state'.

[57] Stevens, *Torts and Rights*, above n 2, at 330.

[58] ibid, at 336.

law', and so cannot be used as justificatory concepts that determine the content of the law.[59]

In any case, it is obviously important that those writing about rights and private law distinguish clearly between the legal and the moral meaning of the word 'right':

> Because the two senses of the word [are] so closely intertwined in common parlance, there [is] a strong tendency for the one to collapse into the other ... and for legal scholars to base their ostensibly objective descriptions of the law on their own subjective moral evaluations.[60]

The risk of slippage of this kind is most acute when reference is made to more general rights, such as the 'right to bodily integrity' or the 'right to reputation'. General rights of this kind have been aptly described by James Penner as a device for describing constellations of norms which organises them on the basis of the interests which the various norms in the system reflect.[61] Note, however, that this tells us nothing about what *kind* of norms we are dealing with, nor *which* system the norms are to be found in. It follows that references to general rights of this kind could be references either to a constellation of *legal* norms which protect a particular interest[62] or to a constellation of *moral* norms which protect a particular interest. As McBride emphasises, on the first of these two meanings, general rights of this kind—which he calls 'liberty/interest rights'—are merely expressive, so that when we refer to the (general legal) 'right to freedom of expression' all we are saying is

> that the law takes some steps to protect my freedom of speech from being interfered with by other people by, for example, granting me coercive rights [claim rights] requiring other people not to interfere with my freedom of speech, or by granting me exemptions [immunities] from certain legal rules that would otherwise allow other people to interfere with my freedom of speech ... My freedom of speech is not protected because I have 'a right to freedom of expression'. Rather, I have a 'right to freedom of expression' because my freedom of speech is protected.[63]

By contrast, on the second of these two meanings, where what is meant is a general *moral* right, the assertion of the right is expressive not of what the legal position is, but of what the speaker considers the moral position to be (and therefore, perhaps, what the legal position *should* be). This inherent ambiguity in the terminology of general rights means that it is particularly important that all those who write on the role of

---

[59] TT Arvind, 'Beyond "Right" and "Duty": Lundstedt's Theory of Obligations' ch 6 of this book, text following n 31.

[60] ibid, text accompanying n 56 (referring to the views of Anders Vilhelm Lundstedt).

[61] JE Penner, 'The Analysis of Rights' (1997) 10 *Ratio Juris* 300, 312.

[62] As McBride points out ('Rights and the Basis of Tort Law', above n 13, text accompanying n 34), these legal norms may include Hohfeldian immunities as well as claim rights.

[63] ibid, text accompanying nn 40–41 (footnotes omitted).

rights in private law make it clear precisely what they mean when they refer to general rights of this kind. Finally, we should note that those who deny the existence of moral rights ought logically to refer to general rights only in the legal sense, but that in practice even moral rights sceptics sometimes use the language of general rights rhetorically when what they actually mean are the *interests* which they believe justify legal claim rights. This slippage is unfortunate, because of course rights and interests are not the same thing.[64]

IV. IS RIGHTS ANALYSIS DISPOSITIVE?

To the extent that rights-based analysis of private law is concerned only with identifying and understanding the primary rights that underlie private law, it does not offer any direct guidance as to what the law should be. As John Goldberg and Benjamin Zipursky observe in chapter 9 of this book, rights theory is primarily concerned with understanding the structure of the law, and in this respect does analytical rather than normative work. The main focus of Stevens' book *Torts and Rights*, for example, is on understanding the structure and operation of the law of torts through the identification and analysis of categories of 'claim rights' in the Hohfeldian taxonomy. And as we have seen, the identification of a legal claim right is merely a description of what the law *is*, and cannot tell us what the law *should be* on a particular issue.

It would, however, be a mistake to suppose that rights-based accounts of private law are devoid of normative implications. There are at least three reasons for this. The first is that rights theorists believe that the system of private law rights should be consistent and coherent (or at least that it should be *interpreted* in as consistent and coherent a manner as possible). It follows that the recognition of a particular claim right is questionable if it does not fit within a broader, coherent set of recognised claim rights or with what Beever calls 'general features of the common law'.[65] The identification of bundles or categories of claim rights, and the insistence on coherence and consistency within and between those categories, therefore give rights analysis a limited normative agenda. To say, then, that *x* has no claim against *y* because *y* has infringed no right held by *x* may mean that any authority that exists in the case law to support such a claim must be wrong because any claim right held by *x* against *y* could not be accommodated within a coherent framework of rights. Thus, for example, Beever argues that the decision of the House of Lords in *White v Jones*[66] (allowing disappointed beneficiaries to recover damages from the

---

[64] Penner, above n 61, at 306.
[65] Beever, *Rediscovering the Law of Negligence*, above n 4, at 62.
[66] *White v Jones* [1995] 2 AC 455 (HL).

testator's negligent solicitor) was incorrect because any right of the beneficiaries would have to be based on the intentions of the testator with respect to his estate, but rights of this kind are governed by the law of wills, and according to the law of wills on the facts no such right existed.[67] Stevens observes that the decision in *White v Jones* 'appears anomalous' because 'We do not have rights good against the rest of the world to be assisted in inheriting wealth', but justifies the outcome as 'a controversial attempt to vindicate the testator's contractual right against the solicitor to performance.'[68] The requirements of consistency and coherence demand not only that the courts deny rights which do not fit within established categories or bundles of rights, but also that the courts do not impose arbitrary or anomalous limits on established categories of rights. Thus, Stevens criticises the restrictions on the recognition of duties of care not to cause psychiatric illness to secondary victims imposed by the House of Lords in *Alcock v Chief Constable of South Yorkshire Police*[69] on the basis that if arbitrary limits are to be imposed on the right 'that each of us has ... good against others that they take care not to damage our mental, as well as physical, health', this is something that ought to be done by the legislature, rather than the courts.[70]

The second reason why rights analysis may have normative implications is the claim of some rights theorists that the private law rights recognised at common law should be determined solely by reference to interpersonal moral rights. Theorists of this stripe do not always agree on the precise nature of the relationship between moral rights and private law. Weinrib argues, for example, that moral rights do not underlie or provide an external justification for private law, but are inherent in it. On this view, 'Kantian right supplies the moral standpoint' that is immanent in the structure of the private law relationship, and it is a mistake to suppose that private law is in the service of moral arguments that are 'external to the law's self understanding'.[71] For Stevens, on the other hand, it is the decisions of common law judges that give certain moral rights the force of law.[72] Nevertheless, Weinrib and Stevens agree that moral rights provide the only legitimate justification for common law judges to recognise private law rights. A corollary of the claim that common law rights should be derived solely from interpersonal moral rights is that the existence or otherwise of a common law right cannot and should not be determined by reference to considerations of policy or community welfare. Since this rejection of policy-based reasoning in private law adjudication has been

---

[67] Beever, *Rediscovering the Law of Negligence*, above n 4, at 266.
[68] Stevens, *Torts and Rights*, above n 2, at 178–81.
[69] *Alcock v Chief Constable of South Yorkshire Police* [1992] 1 AC 310 (HL).
[70] Stevens, *Torts and Rights*, above n 2, at 54–55.
[71] Weinrib, *The Idea of Private Law*, above n 20, at 19, 49.
[72] Stevens, *Torts and Rights*, above n 2, at 330–32.

such a strong feature of recent rights analysis, this issue will be discussed further in part VIII below.

The third reason why rights analysis may have normative implications is that it is clear that at least some rights theorists think that there are limits on what can count as a private law right. Stevens has identified at least three such limits. First, he argues in his chapter in this book that because a 'wrong, or injury, occurs in a moment of time', it is 'meaningless to talk of a right not to be caused loss',[73] in other words that such a right is (as McBride puts it) 'conceptually impossible'.[74] Secondly, Stevens argues that 'courts cannot create rights which require the answer to questions they cannot give',[75] and that since in his view courts are not entitled to engage in policy reasoning, it follows that courts cannot recognise rights (such as a right not to be insulted) which would be so broad in their prima facie scope that they would have to be cut back by reference to countervailing policy considerations. Finally, Stevens argues that the rule of law requires that the rights we have are capable of being determined in advance,[76] and that this explains why the list of recognised property rights is 'closed and determinate' so that, for example, parties cannot create any form of property right 'good against everyone that they choose'.[77] Other theorists have also placed limits on what they perceive to be acceptable as private law 'rights'. According to Weinrib, for example, there can be no right not to be exposed to risk, because on his Kantian approach to corrective justice, rights are 'juridical manifestations of the will's freedom', and the 'absence of the prospect of injury is not itself a manifestation of the plaintiff's free will'.[78] Richard Wright also relies upon Kantian right to argue in his defence of the objective standard of care in negligence that our rights in our person and property 'must be defined by an objective level of permissible risk exposure by others which ... must be equally applicable to all and objectively enforced'.[79] This question of what limits there might be on the recognition of particular rights is further explored by Roderick Bagshaw in his chapter in this book.[80]

Careful attention to the normative claims of rights theorists may, however, distract attention from a significant feature of rights analysis, which is its powerful rhetorical and, some would say, ideological effect.[81] Rights talk holds out the promise of an attractively simple understanding of com-

---

[73] R Stevens, 'Rights and Other Things' ch 5 of this book, text accompanying n 12.

[74] For criticism of this idea, see McBride, 'Rights and the Basis of Tort Law', above n 13, part VI(D).

[75] Stevens, *Torts and Rights*, above n 2, at 338.

[76] ibid, at 339.

[77] ibid, at 340.

[78] Weinrib, *The Idea of Private Law*, above n 20, at 157.

[79] RW Wright, 'The Standards of Care in Negligence Law' in DG Owen (ed), *Philosophical Foundations of Tort Law* (Oxford, Oxford University Press, 1995) 249, 259.

[80] R Bagshaw, 'The Edges of Tort Law's Rights' ch 14 of this book.

[81] See Arvind, 'Beyond "Right" and "Duty"', above n 59.

plex legal phenomena, and offers us an appealing image of ourselves as the powerful bearers of rights. But the principal rhetorical power of rights discourse lies in the space between the positive and normative claims, between legal rights and moral rights. As we have seen, the inherent ambiguity of the term 'rights' allows for an effective slippage between the positive and the normative. Claims about rights can therefore acquire a justificatory force through uncertainty as to whether reference is being made to the content of the law or its conceptual underpinnings. In the space between positive and normative claims as to whether we do or do not have particular rights, there is a danger that particular conclusions and outcomes may come to appear self-evident rather than argued for. This matters because, while rights theorists may be on relatively solid ground when making claims about the positive legal rights individuals have against each other, the terrain of underlying moral rights is highly contestable and contested.[82]

V. RIGHTS AND DUTIES

Claim rights correlate with duties, and so the claim rights instantiated by private law are mirrored by duties (or obligations) which enjoin conduct. This is true both of primary claim rights, which correlate with primary duties, and secondary claim rights, which correlate with secondary duties. Rights in this sense cannot exist without duties. Duties (such as the duty not to possess illegal drugs) can exist without correlative rights,[83] but in the Hohfeldian scheme duties owed to others cannot. Attempts have been made to show that there are exceptions to the Hohfeldian correlativity thesis, though it is questionable whether these have been successful.[84] The matter need not detain us here. For our purposes, it is enough to say that rights and duties to others are always (or almost always) just two different ways of looking at the same jural relationship, with the 'right' perspective that of the person who benefits from the relationship, and the 'duty' perspective that of the person burdened by it.[85] It follows that rights and

---

[82] See ibid.

[83] See further Goldberg and Zipursky, 'Rights and Responsibility', above n 14, part II(A).

[84] See, eg, N MacCormick, *Legal Right and Social Democracy* (Oxford, Clarendon Press, 1982) 161–62, critiqued by Penner, above n 61, at 309–10. See also the disagreement as to whether private law duties can be owed to foetuses who lack legal personality: compare Beever, *Rediscovering the Law of Negligence*, above n 4, at 386 with R Perry, 'Correlativity' (2009) 28 *Law and Philosophy* 537.

[85] See J Finnis, *Natural Law and Natural Rights* (Oxford, Clarendon Press, 1980) 205: 'In short, the modern vocabulary and grammar of rights is a many-faceted instrument for reporting and asserting the requirements or other implications of a relationship of justice *from the point of view of the person(s) who benefit(s) from* that relationship' (emphasis in original).

duties to others are 'interdefined: neither is prior to the other';[86] they are 'the same thing, just viewed through different ends of the telescope'[87]—hence Stevens' observation that he could just as easily have given his book *Torts and Rights* the title *Torts and the Duties We Owe One to Another*, 'though that wouldn't have been quite so snappy'.[88]

Despite the simplicity of the duty/right relationship when seen in these terms, the correlativity thesis gives rise to at least two possible complications for rights theorists. The first, which is more apparent than real, relates to strict liability. Superficially, there might appear to be a difficulty with identifying the duty which is breached when a tort of strict liability is committed. There is in fact no problem here, however, once it is understood that when it comes to strict liability wrongs (including many instances of breach of contract) the duty is a duty not to bring about a particular outcome, as opposed to a duty to take reasonable steps not to bring about a particular outcome.[89] The correlativity thesis therefore poses no barrier to a rights-based analysis of strict liability torts such as battery and trespass to land. A distinction must however be drawn between torts like these, which impose primary norms enjoining certain conduct (battering, trespassing, etc) and liability rules which do not enjoin conduct at all, but simply lay down that in eventuality x, y has a claim against z. These kinds of liability rules are considered in part VI of this chapter.

The second possible complication relates to negligence law. Here, the difficulty is that although rights theorists have been anxious to emphasise that the duty of care element of the negligence inquiry is a real requirement, grounded in considerations of interpersonal justice, and not just a policy-driven 'control device',[90] they have arguably given insufficient consideration to the implications which their analysis of the duty issue has for the nature of the right or rights which underlie liability in negligence. After all, if rights theorists believe that the duty of care is a duty in the

---

[86] J Finnis, 'Natural Law: The Classical Tradition' in J Coleman and S Shapiro (eds), *The Oxford Handbook of Jurisprudence and Philosophy of Law* (Oxford, Oxford University Press, 2002) 1, 24. Note that while BC Zipursky, 'Rights, Wrongs and Recourse in the Law of Torts' (1998) 51 *Vanderbilt Law Review* 1, 64, describes relational legal rights as 'just the analytical reflex' of relational legal duties, Weinrib (*The Idea of Private Law*, above n 20, at 123–24) argues that when right and duty operate as correlatives, 'they constitute an *articulated* unity' (emphasis in original), and that they should not therefore be regarded 'as analytic reflexes of each other'.

[87] McBride, 'Rights and the Basis of Tort Law', above n 13, text accompanying n 33.

[88] Stevens, 'Rights and Other Things', above n 73, text accompanying n 4.

[89] Note that *pace* John Gardner, this is emphatically *not* a distinction between a 'duty to try' and a 'duty to succeed' (J Gardner, 'Obligations and Outcomes in the Law of Torts' in P Cane and J Gardner (eds), *Relating to Responsibility: Essays in Honour of Tony Honoré on His 80th Birthday* (Oxford, Hart Publishing, 2001) 111). Both are duties to succeed, but while one is a duty to succeed in not bringing about a particular outcome, the other is a duty to succeed in not bringing about a particular outcome through falling short of an objective standard of reasonable conduct.

[90] See, eg, JCP Goldberg and BC Zipursky, 'The *Restatement (Third)* and the Place of Duty in Negligence Law' (2001) 54 *Vanderbilt Law Review* 657; NJ McBride, 'Duties of Care—Do They Really Exist?' (2004) 24 *Oxford Journal of Legal Studies* 417.

Hohfeldian sense,[91] then it follows that the correlative right must be a right not to be exposed to unreasonable risks of certain kinds of interference with one's bodily integrity, personal property and so forth. As well as being both counter-intuitive and philosophically problematic,[92] this conclusion would be at odds with the well-established principle that actions in negligence arise only when the defendant's unreasonable conduct results in damage to a protected interest of the claimant. One rights theorist who has addressed this issue head-on is Stephen Perry, who identifies the true duty in negligence cases as a duty 'not to harm others as a result of acting negligently towards them', as opposed to a duty of care.[93] If this is correct, however, then the claim that the duty of care is not a real duty (a claim apparently anathema to many rights theorists) turns out to be true after all, at least if the word 'duty' is understood in Hohfeldian terms.[94] Nor can the duty of care concept be rescued by reformulating it (as Stevens does in his chapter in this book[95]) as a 'duty of care not to injure', because that formulation of the 'duty of care' concept is clearly not the one employed by lawyers, who mean by 'breach of (the) duty (of care)' sub-standard conduct which *may foreseeably* cause the claimant injury, not sub-standard conduct which *does in fact do so*.[96] Of course, none of this means that a negligence standard is in any way incompatible with rights analysis, and it is difficult to see the force in Cane's claim that strict liability 'is a necessary corollary of a system of rights',[97] since it is hard to see why a system of rights not to suffer injury through negligent conduct would not be a system of rights nonetheless.

VI. RIGHTS AND LIABILITIES

Where a private law right is violated, this will usually[98] trigger a right of action, which in Hohfeldian terms is a power in the person wronged to bring an action against the wrongdoer. This power correlates with

---

[91] As Stevens certainly does: 'The duty of care reflects a correlative right. This right is a real right' (*Torts and Rights*, above n 2, at 291).

[92] On the philosophical difficulties, see Perry, 'The Role of Duty of Care', above n 10, at 92–107.

[93] ibid, at 101. Weinrib appears also to take the view that the duty is one of non-injury: see 'Corrective Justice in a Nutshell', above n 10, at 353 ('freedom from the injury of which the plaintiff is complaining is both the content of the plaintiff's right and the object of the defendant's duty').

[94] For discussion of this issue with reference to Beever's rights-based account of negligence, see P Cane, 'Rights in Private Law' ch 2 of this book, text accompanying n 35 ff.

[95] Stevens, 'Rights and Other Things', above n 73, text accompanying n 8 ff.

[96] See, eg, WVH Rogers, *Winfield and Jolowicz on Tort*, 18th edn (London, Sweet & Maxwell, 2010) para 5-1 ('Negligence as a tort is a breach of a legal duty to take care which results in damage to the claimant').

[97] P Cane, *Responsibility in Law and Morality* (Oxford, Hart Publishing, 2002) 198.

[98] For the argument that it does not always do so, see Stevens, 'The Conflict of Rights', above n 9, at 150.

a 'liability' of the wrongdoer, in the sense that the wrongdoer is now susceptible to legal action. It follows that private law 'both recognises Hohfeldian claim rights ... and grants to those whose rights have been violated a Hohfeldian power'.[99]

Private law liabilities are not always triggered by wrongs, however. Examples are obligations arising in the law of unjust enrichment and according to the principles relating to salvage and general average. In these cases the defendant is not susceptible to legal action because he or she has violated a right of the claimant, but simply because the law has laid down that in circumstance x, y has a claim against z.[100] Liabilities like this are distinguishable from strict liability wrongs such as battery because the legal norm in question does not *prohibit* anything, so that the obligation to pay money is a primary obligation, as opposed to a secondary one triggered by a breach of duty (a wrong) on the part of the defendant.[101]

Some liabilities of this kind are traditionally classified as falling within the law of tort. A good example is the liability that arises under the Consumer Protection Act 1987 (UK) where damage is caused by a defective product. The central provision of the 1987 Act, section 2(1), states simply that 'where any damage is caused wholly or partly by a defect in a product, every person to whom subsection (2) below applies shall be liable for the damage'. The legislation therefore imposes no duty, but only a liability.[102] As a result, a variety of actors involved in the production and distribution of the defective product are made potentially liable, with none of the constraints to which a duty-imposing norm would be subject. Another example may be the rule in *Rylands v Fletcher*:

> We think that the true rule of law is, that the person who for his own purposes brings on his lands and collects and keeps there something likely to do mischief if it escapes, must keep it in at his peril, and, if he does not do so, is prima

---

[99] Goldberg and Zipursky, 'Rights and Responsibility', above n 14, text following n 34 (referring specifically to tort law).

[100] As Peter Jaffey says, in such cases 'C acquires a claim against D if a certain contingency materializes, but D does not have a duty to prevent it from materializing': 'Duties and Liabilities in Private Law', above n 53, at 146. See also Stevens, *Torts and Rights*, above n 2, at 100 ('a primary obligation triggered by the fulfilment of a condition').

[101] As Zipursky points out ('Rights, Wrongs and Recourse', above n 86, at 59), a legal wrong means that there is 'a directive legal norm enjoining people from engaging in that act'. We therefore disagree with Gregory Keating when he says that 'Strict liability in tort ... attaches to conduct that is ... not wrongful' and that in the case of strict liability 'the primary obligation is to make reparation for harm fairly attributed to one's *justified or faultless* conduct': GC Keating, 'Is the Role of Tort to Repair Wrongful Losses?' ch 13 of this book, text following n 83 (emphasis in original). In our view, this is true of liability rules of the kind under discussion, but not of strict liability wrongs such as breach of contract, trespass to land, etc.

[102] cf, eg, Occupiers' Liability Act 1957 (UK), s 2(1): 'An occupier of premises owes the same duty, the "common duty of care", to all his visitors'.

facie answerable for all the damage which is the natural consequence of its escape.[103]

Although the word 'must' in this passage might be thought to impose a duty, the qualification 'at his peril' could be taken to mean that the person who makes the accumulation is not under a duty to 'keep it in', but simply that if he does not do so he will be liable for the damage which it causes. This interpretation is reinforced by the fact that liability under the rule attaches to the person who accumulates the thing that escapes, not the person who causes the escape to occur.[104] It could therefore be argued that a claim under the rule in *Rylands v Fletcher* 'arises from a primary-liability relation that allocates to D the risk of loss to C without imposing on him a duty to prevent it'.[105]

The existence of liability rules of this kind would only pose a problem for rights theorists if they were making the implausible claim that *all* private law actions arise out of rights violations. Nevertheless, such rules would appear to have taxonomical implications for rights theorists, since if as they argue a tort is a wrong and the law of 'torts' is the law of wrongs, then liabilities of this kind are no more the business of tort law than are mistaken payments or claims to general average.[106] If, by contrast, the law of 'tort' is thought to concern not only rights violations but also 'compensation for loss', then since these are liabilities to make good damage done, they can be seen as falling within the ambit of tort law as so conceived. In addition, the fact that liability rules of this kind are not the result of wrongs may have implications when it comes to substantive questions such as causation and the assessment of compensation. Although the courts sometimes bend the rules on causation to hold a wrongdoer liable, it does not necessarily follow that they should do the same when the defendant is innocent of any wrongdoing. Similarly, the principle that a wrongdoer should make good all the losses flowing from his or her wrong (subject to remoteness principles) does not apply, and more generally the courts should not feel bound in such cases by general principles of compensation which presuppose the existence of a wrong. As Peter Birks pointed out, 'not-wrongs ... offer no general licence to mistreat the defendant'.[107]

---

[103] *Fletcher v Rylands* (1866) LR 1 Ex 265 (Exch Cham) 279–80 (Blackburn J).

[104] See K Oliphant (ed), *The Law of Tort*, 2nd edn (London, LexisNexis Butterworths, 2007) para 23-35.

[105] Jaffey, 'Liabilities in Private Law', above n 15, at 240. See also Murphy, above n 19, at 400.

[106] Hence, in NJ McBride and R Bagshaw, *Tort Law*, 3rd edn (Harlow, Pearson Education, 2008), the discussion of the rule in *Rylands v Fletcher*, liability under the Consumer Protection Act 1987 (UK) and civil liability for public nuisance is to be found not in the part of the book entitled 'Torts', but in the part entitled 'Alternative sources of compensation'.

[107] P Birks, 'Rights, Wrongs, and Remedies' (2000) 20 *Oxford Journal of Legal Studies* 1, 33.

We should not leave the topic of rights and liabilities without advert-ing to the lawyer economists who conceive of the law of tort as *largely composed* of liability rules.[108] As we saw earlier, this conception of tort law is radically at odds with rights analysis, since while rights theorists believe that the duties imposed by private law are duties enjoining 'citizens to behave in certain ways and to refrain from behaving in other ways'[109] (and conversely that rights conferred by private law are rights that others behave in certain ways and refrain from behaving in other ways), under the liability rule analysis, to say that the defendant has a 'duty' to do x is just to say that he or she will have to pay a sum of money if they do not, and to say that the claimant has a 'right' is just to say that they will have a claim for compensation if they suffer a particular kind of injury.[110] One thing which unites all rights theorists, therefore, and which distin-guishes them from the economists, is the belief that rights and duties in private law are *real*, that they are what they appear or claim to be.[111]

VII. RIGHTS AND REMEDIES

Scholars working in private law commonly draw a distinction between the primary rights that we have against others that they behave in par-ticular ways (eg, that they perform contractual obligations owed to us and do not batter us) and the secondary, remedial rights that arise from the violation of those primary rights (eg, the right to damages for breach of contract or battery). In addition, there is increasing attention being paid in private law scholarship to the nature of the power enjoyed by a person whose rights have been violated to 'have the state alter the legal relationship between the parties'[112] by instituting legal proceedings, and the correlative liability on the part of the wrongdoer.[113] According to Murphy, Hohfeld would have considered the relationship brought about by the violation of a primary right to be a power/liability relation of this sort, and not a claim right/duty relation, and Murphy himself argues that

---

[108] See, eg, RA Posner, 'A Theory of Negligence' (1972) 1 *Journal of Legal Studies* 29; G Calabresi and AD Melamed, 'Property Rules, Liability Rules and Inalienability: One View of the Cathedral' (1972) 85 *Harvard Law Review* 1089.

[109] Zipursky, 'Rights, Wrongs and Recourse', above n 86, at 58.

[110] ibid, at 55–56.

[111] See, eg, Weinrib, *The Idea of Private Law*, above n 20, at 143 ('liability reflects the defendant's commission of an injustice. Liability is not therefore the retrospective pricing or licensing or taxing of a permissible act'); Goldberg and Zipursky, 'Rights and Responsibil-ity', above n 14, text following n 30 ('the duties of tort law are not disjunctive duties to forbear or pay ... They are duties of conduct').

[112] BC Zipursky, 'Philosophy of Private Law' in J Coleman and S Shapiro (eds), *The Oxford Handbook of Jurisprudence and Philosophy of Law* (Oxford, Oxford University Press, 2002) 623, 633.

[113] See the work of Zipursky, ibid and below n 115, and Smith, above n 7.

a person who has been wronged does not have a claim right against the wrongdoer that is correlative to a duty on the part of the wrongdoer to pay damages, but only a power to sue, which is correlative to a liability on the part of the wrongdoer that is contingent on the making of a court order.[114] Similarly, Zipursky has argued that it makes no sense to say that a tortfeasor has a duty to pay damages which exists prior to being sued and which is somehow waived if the victim fails to sue.[115]

In fact, however, Hohfeld explicitly distinguished what he called the secondary or remedial right/duty relation from the power/liability relation which we call a right of action. In an article on the nature of stockholders' individual liability for the debts of a corporation, Hohfeld made it clear that in his view the infringement by X of a primary right held by A gives rise to a new legal relationship between X and A in which X is under a secondary or remedial duty to pay damages to A, and that if '*X fails to act under his remedial duty*, A has ab initio the power, by action in the courts, to institute a process of compulsion against X.'[116] In other words, although Hohfeld accepted that the right of action itself was a power/liability relation, he regarded this as complementary to, rather than inconsistent with, the notion that the victim of a wrong has a claim right to damages against the wrongdoer which subsists from the time the wrong is committed until the making of a court order.[117] This is also the view of Stevens, who argues that the fact that the right to damages arises immediately upon commission of the wrong, and is not contingent upon the making of the court order, is demonstrated by, for example, the rules governing payments before action and interest on damages awards.[118]

Because we naturally conceive of the law of 'torts' as a law of 'wrongs', it is 'wrongs' that tend to capture our attention and organise our understanding of the subject. Rights analysis offers a valuable corrective to this pattern of thought by forcing us to consider on what, if any, primary rights the notion of wrongdoing depends. Paradoxically, however, the most striking claims of rights theorists, and the most significant implications of rights analysis, may well be those that concern secondary or remedial

---

[114] Murphy, above n 19, at 397.

[115] BC Zipursky, 'Civil Recourse, Not Corrective Justice' (2003) 91 *Georgetown Law Journal* 695, 720.

[116] WN Hohfeld, 'Nature of Stockholders' Individual Liability for Corporation Debts' (1909) 9 *Columbia Law Review* 285, 293–94. We are grateful to TT Arvind for bringing this passage to our attention.

[117] In his chapter in this book, Helge Dedek argues that William Blackstone also recognised the existence of a remedial right distinguishable from the right of action, although in Blackstone's view this right was an incomplete or inchoate one until it was rendered complete and determinate by the intervention of the law, so that the natural remedial right could 'only come into its own with the help of the state': H Dedek, 'Of Rights Superstructural, Inchoate and Triangular: The Role of Rights in Blackstone's *Commentaries*' ch 7 of this book, text following n 201.

[118] Stevens, 'Rights and Other Things', above n 73, text accompanying nn 79–80.

rights, rather than primary rights. That is because it is in the approach to remedies that the contrast between the rights-based model and rival models of private law is at its most stark. According to Andrew Burrows, the rights-based approach to remedies 'constitutes a radical and novel reinterpretation of the law'[119] and offers explanations of legal rules that are otherwise difficult to justify. As a result, rights-based analysis has ignited debate on a number of significant remedial issues in private law.[120]

There is no difficulty in explaining specific remedies on the rights-based approach: they directly enforce the primary right by giving the claimant the very thing to which he or she is entitled. Indeed, as Stevens has pointed out, the fact that damages are considered inadequate and specific performance justified where the claimant suffers no loss as a result of a breach of contract would seem to indicate that the law is concerned with giving effect to contractual rights, rather than preventing loss.[121] In Stevens' view, where the primary right cannot or should not be specifically enforced, the claimant is entitled to an award of damages in substitution for the right. These 'substitutive damages' represent the value of the right infringed. In this way, the law of damages aims, not to compensate loss, but to give the claimant the 'next best' thing to not having the right violated. Stevens substantiates this claim by setting out numerous examples in contract and tort where the law awards damages even though the claimant suffers no loss, in the sense of being 'factually worse off', as a result of the violation of his or her rights.[122] It does not follow, however, that the claimant's loss is irrelevant to the assessment of damages under Stevens' approach. On the contrary, he makes it clear that in addition to an amount representing the value of the right, a damages award may include consequential loss arising from the infringement of the right.[123]

Determining the value of a right that has been infringed is, in many instances, quite straightforward and simply another way of understanding what courts routinely do. The value of a right can often be assessed by reference to the market price of the thing that is the subject of the right. The value of a contractual right to buy goods at a particular price, for example, is the difference between the contract price and the market price at the time of the breach. In other cases, such as those involving the right to reputation or bodily integrity, the value of a right does not have any 'naturally correct quantification', and in these instances 'the courts have no choice but to set out guidelines' for its assessment.[124]

---

[119] A Burrows, 'Damages and Rights' ch 10 of this book, text following n 11.
[120] See Burrows, above n 119.
[121] Stevens, *Torts and Rights*, above n 2, at 57.
[122] ibid, at 59–91; Stevens, 'Damages and the Right to Performance', above n 29, at 198.
[123] Stevens, *Torts and Rights*, above n 2, at 60–61.
[124] ibid, at 78–79.

Stevens' rights-based approach to damages raises a number of important and controversial issues. He argues, for example, that most examples of 'gain-based' damages awards are better understood as awards in substitution for the right infringed.[125] Nominal damages appear anomalous under a loss-based approach, but can be justified under a rights-based approach on the basis that they are awarded in substitution for a right that is valueless, or that is infringed in an insignificant way.[126] Moreover, Stevens argues that punitive damages are justified not by deterrence considerations, but on the basis that 'the contumacious infringement of a right is more serious' than a less culpable infringement, notwithstanding the fact that the degree of culpability does not affect the value of the right infringed.[127] Damages awarded in substitution for the right therefore depend not only on the value of the right, but also on the manner and circumstances in which the right is infringed. If a rights-based approach requires a person who has infringed a right to restore the value of the right infringed to the victim, however, it is not immediately obvious why the quantum of the award should be affected by the nature of the infringement. It is also noteworthy that other rights theorists, such as Weinrib, have taken the view that exemplary damages have no place in private law, since they 'are geared, not to restoring the plaintiff's rights, but to punishing the defendant'.[128] A number of other objections have been made to Stevens' analysis of damages, and these are dealt with in some detail in the chapters by Burrows (a leading critic of the analysis) and Stevens in this book. Whatever conclusion is reached on the validity of Stevens' approach, there is no denying that it is a good illustration of the profound implications that rights analysis may have for our understanding of particular doctrines of private law.

VIII. RIGHTS AND POLICY

A significant feature of contemporary rights analysis is a sustained attack on policy-based reasoning. Positive claims about the role of rights in private law often go hand in hand with negative claims about the illegitimacy of policy or community welfare considerations. Indeed, one of the primary motivations behind rights analysis seems to be a desire to rid private law of policy considerations. According to Cane, 'Rights, not policy' is the

---

[125] ibid, at 79–84; Stevens, 'Rights and Other Things', above n 73.

[126] Stevens, *Torts and Rights*, above n 2, at 84–85; Stevens, 'Damages and the Right to Performance', above n 29, at 194–95. Burrows challenges this rationalisation of nominal damages in 'Damages and Rights', above n 119.

[127] Stevens, *Torts and Rights*, above n 2, at 86.

[128] EJ Weinrib, 'Two Conceptions of Remedies' in CEF Rickett (ed), *Justifying Private Law Remedies* (Oxford, Hart Publishing, 2008) 3, 24. See also A Beever, 'The Structure of Aggravated and Exemplary Damages' (2003) 23 *Oxford Journal of Legal Studies* 87.

message of what he terms 'rights fundamentalism' reduced to its 'bare essentials'.[129] While Hohfeld suggested that whether there should be claim rights in a particular situation or relationship was 'ultimately a question of justice and policy',[130] this is not a view shared by most contemporary rights theorists. If one takes the view that legal rights are derived from or give effect to moral rights, then policy considerations are irrelevant to the identification or determination of private law rights. For Weinrib, therefore, the illegitimacy of policy considerations is a necessary implication of the idea that moral rights are immanent in the very structure and nature of private law. And while Stevens accepts that the legislature can legitimately create private law rights for policy reasons, he argues that judges can only derive legal rights from moral rights.[131] On these understandings of private law, community welfare considerations can have no role to play in determining the rights that individuals have against each other. Nor can policy considerations serve as a justification for a court not recognising a private law right. To deny the existence of private law rights for reasons of community welfare is to confiscate what is due to the claimant and to treat him or her as a means to the ends of others.[132]

On the views of rights theorists such as Weinrib and Beever, policy considerations are simply irrelevant to the judicial task of identifying private law rights because such rights are based entirely on the considerations of interpersonal morality that are inherent in the principle of corrective justice. Beever himself says that 'policy concerns are *irrelevant* to the conception of justice that informs the law of negligence'.[133] Nevertheless, Beever has made a very strong collateral attack on policy-based reasoning, and in doing so has put forward arguments similar to those made by Stevens. Beever and Stevens argue that judges lack both the technical competence to determine whether a particular decision is likely to be beneficial or detrimental to the community, and the political legitimacy to make such determinations.[134] Moreover, they say, reasoning by reference to community welfare makes decision-making more difficult, since policy arguments can often be advanced both for and against a particular rule or decision, and require the weighing of incommensurable considerations.[135]

---

[129] Cane, 'Rights in Private Law', above n 94, text following n 26.

[130] Hohfeld, 'Some Fundamental Legal Conceptions', above n 52, at 36.

[131] Stevens, *Torts and Rights*, above n 2, at 331.

[132] EJ Weinrib, 'Does Tort Law Have a Future?' (2000) 34 *Valparaiso University Law Review* 561, 566; Beever, *Rediscovering the Law of Negligence*, above n 4, at 176–77. See further the discussion in A Robertson, 'Constraints on Policy-Based Reasoning in Private Law' in A Robertson and HW Tang (eds), *The Goals of Private Law* (Oxford, Hart Publishing, 2009) 261, 277–79.

[133] Beever, *Rediscovering the Law of Negligence*, above n 4, at 29.

[134] ibid, at ch 5; Stevens, *Torts and Rights*, above n 2, at ch 14. See further Robertson, 'Rights, Pluralism and the Duty of Care', above n 33.

[135] Beever, *Rediscovering the Law of Negligence*, above n 4, at 173–75; Stevens, *Torts and Rights*, above n 2, at 310.

Although, for the reasons given above, these collateral attacks on policy reasoning may not be necessary for some rights theorists, the vociferousness and persistence of arguments of this kind are significant features of much contemporary rights analysis of private law.

As noted above, the analysis of private law and private law doctrines by reference to rights does not necessarily involve a complete rejection of policy-based reasoning. Some rights theorists accept that collective interests have a legitimate role to play in determining what private law rights should be recognised by the courts. In chapter 12 of this book, for example, McBride argues that it is not a necessary feature of a rights-based theory of tort law that it makes no reference to the public interest. For McBride, the function of tort law is to make the world a better place by granting people rights that they can assert against others, and remedies to uphold those rights, and it would be irresponsible for the courts to disregard the public interest when deciding what rights should be recognised.[136] Perry has also advocated a pluralist rights-based understanding of tort law. This pluralism, Perry suggests, could take the form of a 'lexically ordered hierarchy' in which interpersonal moral considerations are given priority, but instrumental considerations such as deterrence or loss-spreading are brought into play when 'indeterminacy strikes' in the application of those lexically prior considerations.[137] Rights-based pluralism can also take the form of a relational approach to the identification of prima facie rights, which are defeasible on community welfare grounds. Pluralism of this kind is exemplified by the two-stage approach to the duty of care in negligence, which focuses primarily on relational considerations, but allows a prima facie duty to be overridden by policy considerations where recognition of the duty would be detrimental to community welfare.[138]

IX. RIGHTS AND CORRECTIVE JUSTICE

The relationship between rights and corrective justice in private law theory is a complex one. As Cane points out in his chapter in this book, corrective justice theories were developed from the 1970s on in response to economic analysis of private law which was forward-looking and instrumentalist.[139] By contrast, corrective justice theorists adopted a backward-looking internalist conception of private law as a form of interpersonal morality

---

[136] McBride, 'Rights and the Basis of Tort Law', above n 13, text accompanying n 29, citing R Bagshaw, 'Tort Law, Concepts and What Really Matters' in A Robertson and HW Tang (eds), *The Goals of Private Law* (Oxford, Hart Publishing, 2009) 239.

[137] SR Perry, 'Professor Weinrib's Formalism: The Not-So-Empty Sepulchre' (1993) 16 *Harvard Journal of Law and Public Policy* 597, 618–19.

[138] See Perry, 'The Role of Duty of Care', above n 10, at 83–91 and the discussion in Robertson, 'Rights, Pluralism and the Duty of Care', above n 33.

[139] Cane, 'Rights in Private Law', above n 94, text accompanying n 22.

concerned with the *relationship between the parties*, as opposed to the parties 'as solitary individuals or as members of a wider community'.[140] A narrow and a broad conception of corrective justice can be identified.[141] The narrow version of corrective justice conceives it as concerned solely with the *rectification* of injustices inflicted by one person on another.[142] This conception of corrective justice is of limited significance for private lawyers, since it purports to explain only the secondary obligations or duties of repair generated by breaches of primary obligations, and not the primary obligations themselves.[143] The second conception of corrective justice is broader, and conceives it as concerned with the 'justice of interactions between individuals' more generally.[144] On this conception, corrective justice not only tells us how the law should respond to an interpersonal injustice but also what amounts to an interpersonal injustice in the first place.[145] Since the terminology of 'corrective' justice implies the narrower conception, adherents of the broader conception have suggested that terms such as 'interactive justice'[146] or 'interpersonal justice'[147] could be used instead. Corrective justice on either conception can be distinguished from distributive justice, which, according to Weinrib, 'deals with the sharing of a benefit or burden' and 'involves comparing the potential parties to the distribution in terms of a distributive criterion'.[148]

Some of the most prominent corrective justice theorists explicitly rely upon the idea of correlative rights and duties in their analysis of private law. According to Weinrib, for example, 'Corrective justice links the doer and sufferer of an injustice in terms of their correlative positions',[149] and in sophisticated systems of private law, 'the overarching justificatory categories' expressive of this correlativity 'are those of the plaintiff's rights and the defendant's corresponding duty not to interfere with that right', with the injustice that liability rectifies consisting in the defend-

---

[140] Beever, *Rediscovering the Law of Negligence*, above n 4, at 46. For a useful summary of the corrective justice idea, see Weinrib, 'Corrective Justice in a Nutshell', above n 10.

[141] See Stevens, *Torts and Rights*, above n 2, at 327–28.

[142] See, eg, J Coleman, *The Practice of Principle: In Defence of a Pragmatist Approach to Legal Theory* (Oxford, Oxford University Press, 2001) 32.

[143] See Stevens, 'Rights and Other Things', above n 73, text accompanying n 114, describing this 'weak or thin' version of corrective justice as 'a trite claim of little importance'.

[144] See, eg, RW Wright, 'Substantive Corrective Justice' (1992) 77 *Iowa Law Review* 625; Beever, *Rediscovering the Law of Negligence*, above n 4, at ch 2.

[145] See, eg, Beever, *Rediscovering the Law of Negligence*, above n 4, at 59 (defining corrective justice as 'that area of morality that determines how individuals should behave with respect to each other as individuals'). See also Smith, 'The Rights of Private Law', above n 7, at 115 (referring to the argument that 'the idea of rectification contains within it, or at least is predicated upon, a particular understanding of wrongs and injustices and thus of the kinds of non-rectificatory duties the law should uphold').

[146] RW Wright, 'Private Nuisance Law: A Window on Substantive Justice' ch 17 of this book, text accompanying n 4.

[147] Beever, *Rediscovering the Law of Negligence*, above n 4, at 61.

[148] Weinrib, 'Corrective Justice in a Nutshell', above n 10, at 351.

[149] ibid.

ant's 'having something or having done something that is incompatible with a right of the plaintiff'.[150] Rights, he argues, are therefore 'the normatively decisive components of the relationship between the parties in private law'.[151] The relationship between corrective justice and rights is also particularly marked in the work of Beever, whose rights-based theory of negligence law is expressly founded on the idea of corrective justice in the broad sense, which he defines as 'an area of interpersonal morality that both defines rights persons possess against each other as individuals and elucidates how one should respond to violations of those rights'.[152] As Goldberg and Zipursky point out, therefore, corrective justice theorists 'invoke the concept of right to fill out the key notions of wrongdoing, duty, and repair'.[153]

The strength of the relationship between rights and corrective justice is also indicated by the fact that some liability rules which do not embody a right/duty relation may be difficult to analyse in corrective justice terms, and may be better understood as being grounded in *distributive* justice. As Weinrib makes clear, one of the defining characteristics of corrective justice is that 'it links two parties and no more because a relationship of correlativity is necessarily bipolar',[154] whereas distributive justice 'admits any number of parties because, in principle, no limit exists for the number of persons who can be compared and among whom something can be divided'.[155] It follows, therefore, that a liability rule such as the one laid down by section 2 of the Consumer Protection Act 1987 (UK)—which imposes liability on a range of parties involved in the production and distribution of a defective product—may be more easily explicable as instantiating distributive, rather than corrective, justice. It does not necessarily follow, however, that all injustices which require correction are rights violations. Hence while the law of unjust enrichment has been explained in terms of corrective justice,[156] the orthodox view is that liability in unjust enrichment is not grounded on the violation of a primary right.[157]

---

[150] ibid, at 352. See also Weinrib, *The Idea of Private Law*, above n 20, at 144 ('the intrinsic unity of the private law relationship can be seen in private law's embodying in its structure, procedure, and remedy the correlativity of right and duty').

[151] Weinrib, 'Two Conceptions of Remedies', above n 128, at 11. See also Weinrib, 'Corrective Justice in a Nutshell', above n 10, at 352, where he states that in negligence it is not enough that the defendant's negligent act resulted in harm to the plaintiff, since the 'harm has to be to an interest that has the status of a right'.

[152] Beever, *Rediscovering the Law of Negligence*, above n 4, at 56.

[153] Goldberg and Zipursky, 'Rights and Responsibility', above n 14, text accompanying n 20.

[154] Weinrib, 'Corrective Justice in a Nutshell', above n 10, at 351.

[155] ibid, at 351–52.

[156] See, eg, EJ Weinrib, 'Restitutionary Damages as Corrective Justice' (2000) 1 *Theoretical Inquiries in Law* 1; L Smith, 'Restitution: The Heart of Corrective Justice' (2001) 79 *Texas Law Review* 2115.

[157] Although note that Weinrib, *The Idea of Private Law*, above n 20, at 141, describes the *retention* of the enrichment by the defendant as 'an infringement of the plaintiff's right'.

Similarly, Stevens describes the general liability clause of the French *Code Civil*, Article 1382, as 'a principle of corrective justice' even though the article makes no mention of any rights violation.[158]

If Stevens is right, then it would seem to follow that a commitment to private law as a form of corrective justice does not *necessarily* entail reliance on rights and duties as fundamental elements of the private law mosaic, even if in practice corrective justice theorists do tend to treat them as such. Conversely, not all 'rights theorists' rely on the concept of corrective justice in their scholarship, and some are explicitly critical of it. Stevens, for example, dismisses the narrow conception of corrective justice as 'trite',[159] and describes the broad conception as 'implausible', because the 'scope of our rights is not solely determined by considerations of what is fair as between claimant and defendant, ignoring all others'.[160] Similarly, although Goldberg and Zipursky are rights theorists who argue in their chapter in this book that thinking about 'torts in terms of rights ... will provide a more accurate account of tort law's structure' and will also 'enable us to attain a greater appreciation of tort law's normative underpinnings',[161] they reject 'the central metaphor of corrective justice' on the grounds that it suggests that the state is 'aiming to achieve justice by itself rectifying private wrongs'; in their view, by contrast, 'the state, through tort law, empowers private parties to redress wrongs done to them, if they so choose'.[162] While, therefore, the linkages between rights and corrective justice in private law theory are undoubtedly strong ones, and many rights theorists could also be described as corrective justice theorists, it would be a mistake to treat rights theories of private law and corrective justice theories of private law as synonymous.

X. RIGHTS AND TAXONOMY

There are always different ways of categorising and organising the norms which exist within any normative system,[163] and private law is a case in point. What implications, if any, does rights analysis have for the taxonomy of private law? As we saw earlier, general rights such as the 'right to reputation' and the 'right to bodily integrity' are themselves taxonomic devices, ways of organising norms on the basis of the interests which the various norms in the system reflect.[164] Because rights theorists are anxious to emphasise the centrality of rights in private law, they tend to favour

---

[158] Stevens, 'Rights and Other Things', above n 73, text following n 112.
[159] See above n 143.
[160] Stevens, *Torts and Rights*, above n 2, at 328.
[161] Goldberg and Zipursky, 'Rights and Responsibility', above n 14, text following n 1.
[162] ibid, text following n 48.
[163] Penner, above n 61, at 311.
[164] ibid, at 312.

a rights-based classification of private law. A good example of this is Stevens' view that the law of torts should be classified according to the primary right which has been infringed.[165] It is clear that by 'primary right', Stevens does not mean what he calls 'specific claim rights'[166] (such as the right not to battered) but what he calls 'the claim rights which arise together for a common reason and which are specific to a larger bundle of different species of rights',[167] such as the rights to 'bodily safety', 'freedom of movement', 'reputation' and so on.[168] In practice, common law systems have tended to adopt a mixed approach, with a series of discrete nominate torts which are consistent with Stevens' taxonomy (the various forms of trespass, private nuisance, defamation, deceit, conversion, etc) operating alongside the tort of negligence, the scope of which is determined solely by the nature of the defendant's conduct. Unsurprisingly, therefore, Stevens favours the dismantling of what he calls the '*über*-tort' of negligence,[169] with cases of negligently caused personal injury being classified with battery, cases of negligently caused damage to personal property with conversion and trespass to goods, and so on.

In his chapter in this collection, Stevens makes what appears to be a stronger taxonomic claim, namely that:

> [W]here the reason for the existence of the right is the same, the same wrong is committed. Infringements of the same right involve the same kind of wrong ... Conversely where different rights are infringed, different wrongs are committed.[170]

Again, here Stevens is obviously referring to rights in his general sense, but this time he is using the 'reason for the existence of the right' not only as a way of classifying different torts but as a way of defining what a tort is in the first place. In other words, whereas previously he seemed to be saying that we should classify the *wrongs* of conversion, trespass to goods and negligently causing damage to personal property together, he now seems to be saying that there is just one *wrong* of 'wrongful interference with personal property'. Furthermore, since the only example he gives of a reason for the existence of a general right is 'possession' as the reason for the existence of property rights,[171] it seems to follow that in his view even this approach would be overly specific, as there is just one general 'right to property' and hence just one wrong of 'violation of the

---

[165] Stevens, *Torts and Rights*, above n 2, at 299.

[166] ibid, at 4.

[167] ibid.

[168] See ibid, at 303, for the full list. Note that Stevens is careful not to refer to protected interests here, since he takes the view that 'one right may protect a number of different interests' and that 'one interest can be concurrently protected by a variety of different rights' (at 290).

[169] ibid, at 295.

[170] Stevens, 'Rights and Other Things', above n 73, text following n 91.

[171] ibid.

general right to property'. Quite where that leaves the traditional division between real and personal property rights, not to mention the various different 'torts' on either side of the divide, is unclear.[172]

If we step back from the classification of torts to consider the 'law of torts' as a category in itself, we can see that the taxonomic implications of rights analysis are perhaps more radical than some rights theorists themselves appear to realise. Stevens, for example, defines the law of torts as 'concerned with the secondary obligations generated by the infringement of primary rights'.[173] This definition is, however, both over- and under-inclusive. It is over-inclusive because it follows that breaches of contract fall within the law of torts, and yet Stevens accepts that this is not the general understanding, and himself distinguishes breach of contract from torts.[174] More significantly, Stevens' definition is radically under-inclusive because it takes no account of the important role which the law of torts plays in determining the content of our primary rights.[175] This role is most obvious when it comes to those innate primary rights which we are owed simply by virtue of residing in a particular jurisdiction, such as claim rights protecting bodily integrity, freedom of movement, reputation and so forth. However, tort law also plays an important role when it comes to determining the content of acquired primary rights, such as property rights. This is because the law of trespass to land, private nuisance, conversion and so forth to a considerable extent tells us what the content of our primary property rights *actually is*.

Moving out to consider the relationship between tort and contract, again it becomes clear that rights analysis has significant taxonomic implications. Prominent rights theorists take the view that assumptions of responsibility which fall short of contract nevertheless create new primary rights and duties. They argue that this explains why although there is no general right not to suffer negligently inflicted economic loss, and no general right that others take reasonable steps to confer benefits on us, nevertheless liability can sometimes arise where the defendant has negligently inflicted economic loss or failed to confer a benefit by, for example, failing to take reasonable steps to rescue a claimant in peril. In these cases, it is argued, the source of the right is a prior assumption of responsibility by the defendant towards the claimant.[176] If this is correct,

---

[172] Perhaps sensing the radical implications of this analysis, Stevens seems to backtrack slightly, referring to the negligent and deliberate smashing of a car not as the same wrong, but as the *same sort of* wrong: ibid, text following n 92. As a result, the taxonomic implications of his analysis are rendered even less clear.

[173] Stevens, *Torts and Rights*, above n 2, at 2.

[174] ibid, at 11.

[175] While this is true of Stevens' definition of the law of torts at the start of his book, it is not true of his work as a whole. For a more nuanced analysis, which highlights the ambiguous scope of 'the law of torts', see the discussion in ibid, at 300.

[176] See, eg, Beever, *Rediscovering the Law of Negligence*, above n 4, especially at ch 8; Stevens, *Torts and Rights*, above n 2, especially at 9–14, 114–24.

then the primary right created by the assumption of responsibility would appear to have more in common with contractual rights than with innate 'personal rights' such as the right not to be battered.[177]

When it comes to classifying primary legal rights, arguably the two most fundamental distinctions are between rights that are innate and rights that must be acquired, and between rights that are good against everyone and rights which are good only against particular persons (in Hohfeld's terminology, 'paucital' rights and 'multitial' rights[178]). 'Personal' rights and rights created by an assumption of responsibility fall on different sides of *both* these dividing lines. It follows that although on a conduct-based classification it may make sense to categorise fault-based obligations arising out of assumptions of responsibility along with other fault-based obligations, on the rights-based view of private law it seems more logical to classify primary rights which arise out of contracts, undertakings and other consensual acts (including assumptions of responsibility) separately from primary rights which do not.

That brings us to the novel and interesting taxonomy of private law in Beever's book *Rediscovering the Law of Negligence*.[179] As far as property rights are concerned, Beever argues that the law of tort only 'enforces' primary property rights which are 'recognised by' property law, saying for example that 'in conversion, the claimant's primary right is a matter determined entirely by the law of property and about which tort law is silent'.[180] On its face, this appears to suggest that both the existence *and the content* of primary property rights are determined entirely by the law of property, which we have seen cannot be true, because the content of such rights must also be determined by reference to the causes of action that lie for their violation.[181] In any case, when it comes to personal rights such as the right to bodily integrity, Beever acknowledges that tort law both 'recognises' and 'protects' the right,[182] and this insight means that he is able to develop a classificatory scheme which seems better suited to the rights-based approach to private law than previous schemes based on Roman law taxonomies which did not even acknowledge the distinction between primary and secondary rights.[183]

Beever's scheme is organised around three main categories: Property, the Law of Persons and Consents.[184] An alternative way of expressing

---

[177] See Beever, *Rediscovering the Law of Negligence*, above n 4, at 282.

[178] WN Hohfeld, 'Fundamental Legal Conceptions as Applied in Judicial Reasoning' (1917) 26 *Yale Law Journal* 710, 716.

[179] Beever, *Rediscovering the Law of Negligence*, above n 4.

[180] ibid, at 213.

[181] See further on this point (in the context of private nuisance) Nolan, above n 4.

[182] Beever, *Rediscovering the Law of Negligence*, above n 4, at 213.

[183] See, eg, P Birks, 'Equity in the Modern Law: An Exercise in Taxonomy' (1996) 26 *University of Western Australia Law Review* 1.

[184] The most fully developed version of Beever's scheme is to be found in Beever, *Rediscovering the Law of Negligence*, above n 4, at 311, although he acknowledges that even this version is not complete. It does not, for example, include unjust enrichment.

this threefold classification would be by reference to the primary rights themselves: for this, we could use the labels personal rights, property rights and consensual rights. In the light of the two apparently fundamental distinctions identified above, we might then define these rights as innate rights which we enjoy simply by virtue of residing within a particular jurisdiction[185] (*personal* rights, tracking a 'law of persons'), acquired rights good against everyone (*property* rights, tracking a 'law of property'), and acquired rights good only against particular persons (*consensual* rights, tracking a 'law of consents'). On this approach, it is hard to see the need for any separate distinction between rights in rem and rights in personam (although Beever himself is reluctant to let it go) and the civilian distinction between the law of property and the law of obligations collapses.[186] Of course, not everyone will agree that even on the rights-based approach this is the best way of classifying private law, and rights sceptics are most unlikely to think that it is. The fact remains, however, that taking rights analysis seriously would appear to have very significant taxonomic implications.

XI. RIGHTS AND THE STATE

We must finally consider the role of the state in a rights-based understanding of private law. Some rights theorists, such as Beever, argue that private law rights exist independently of the state.[187] The more orthodox view is that private law rights exist only if and to the extent that the state is willing to recognise and enforce them. This gives rise to the question of whether a person has a right against the state that the state realise that person's private law rights against other individuals. This question can be answered at three levels: first, at the level of claim rights or ordinary domestic law; secondly, at the level of constitutional rights; and thirdly, at the level of moral rights.

First, as a matter of positive law, an individual could be said to have a right against the state that the state give effect to rights against other individuals through the granting of those remedies that are available as of

---

[185] See Smith, 'The Rights of Private Law', above n 7, at 133. As Birks pointed out, 'Most of us enter the jurisdiction by birth' ('Rights, Wrongs, and Remedies', above n 107, at 22).

[186] This is most clearly observable when torts such as private nuisance and conversion are analysed in rights terms: see Nolan, above n 4, part XI; S Green, 'Rights and Wrongs: An Introduction to the Wrongful Interference Actions' ch 18 of this book, text accompanying n 77 (criticising a purported bright line distinction between 'torts' and 'property').

[187] Beever, 'Our Most Fundamental Rights', above n 48. This was also Immanuel Kant's view, although for Kant private law in the state of nature remained 'necessarily imperfect' because of the 'inherent defects, the lack of concreteness of the regulations of natural law': Dedek, above n 117, text accompanying n 207.

right.[188] This could be characterised as something analogous to a Hohfeldian claim right in the sense that it is correlative to a duty owed by the state to provide those remedies. Smith suggests that claimants hold 'action rights' of this kind against courts: 'When claimants argue that they have a right to a particular "remedy" from the court, they are arguing that the law requires that the *court* do something—namely, make an order against the defendant.'[189] To the extent that this can accurately be characterised as an obligation on the part of the state, it is an obligation that is limited to redressing such wrongs as are recognised by the state through the granting of remedies that the state recognises as being available as of right. This obligation does not, therefore, require the state to recognise or give effect to any particular rights other than those recognised by the legal system in question.

The second kind of right that an individual may be said to have against the state is a constitutional right, or right under a human rights instrument, that the state recognise certain private law rights against other individuals. In most instances such rights against the state are procedural, and require only that the state provide access to a court and due process in the realisation of whatever private law rights are recognised under domestic law. Article 6 of the European Convention on Human Rights, for example, provides that everyone is entitled to a fair, public and timely hearing before an independent tribunal '[i]n the determination of *his civil rights and obligations*'.[190] Although in *Osman v United Kingdom*[191] the European Court of Human Rights appeared to interpret Article 6 as creating more than a merely procedural entitlement, the Court subsequently confirmed that Article 6 'does not itself guarantee any particular content for (civil) "rights and obligations" in the substantive law of the Contracting States'.[192] In some instances a constitutional right against the state can affect the content of private law rights, and oblige the state to maintain or implement a regime of private law rights that conforms to particular constitutional norms.[193] In chapter 4 of this book, François du Bois gives the example of the '*Bürgschaft*' decision in Germany, in which an 'ordinary' court upheld an exceptionally onerous guarantee contract on the basis that the creditor was not obliged to inform the surety of the risk she was running or to ensure that she understood the obligations she was

---

[188] The situation is of course more complicated with remedies that can be characterised as discretionary: see Smith, 'The Rights of Private Law', above n 7, at 119.

[189] ibid (emphasis in original).

[190] European Convention for the Protection of Human Rights and Fundamental Freedoms (1953), art 6(1) (emphasis added).

[191] *Osman v United Kingdom* (2000) 29 EHRR 245.

[192] *Z v United Kingdom* (2002) 34 EHRR 3 [87].

[193] See JCP Goldberg, 'The Constitutional Status of Tort Law: Due Process and the Right to a Law for the Redress of Wrongs' (2005) 115 *Yale Law Journal* 524.

undertaking.[194] This decision of the ordinary court was later found by the German Constitutional Court to have infringed the surety's constitutional right to autonomy and the principle of the 'social state'. In cases such as this, the state is required to recognise and give effect to such private law rights as are necessary to ensure compliance with individuals' constitutional rights.

At the third level, an individual may be said to have a moral right against the state that the state realise his or her private law rights. Zipursky and Goldberg have suggested that we do enjoy such a moral right.[195] Their argument is based in part on John Locke's *Second Treatise on Civil Government*,[196] and can relevantly be summarised as follows. In the state of nature, individuals have a right of self-preservation, which includes an entitlement to retaliate or seek reparation for wrongs done to them by others. By entering into civil society, individuals entrust to the state the power to redress injury caused by wrongdoing. In social contract terms, individuals are said to relinquish their entitlement to retaliate for wrongs in return for the state's commitment to provide an avenue of civil recourse. To put it another way, if the state insists that individuals do not retaliate in response to wrongs, then the state has an obligation to provide an avenue of redress, and an individual who is wronged has a correlative right, grounded in natural law or political morality, against the state. This argument therefore depends on the existence of two particular moral rights: a moral right to reparation from wrongdoers in a state of nature; and a moral right of civil recourse against the state if the freedom to seek reparation directly is taken away. As with all alleged moral rights, the existence of these two rights is inevitably contestable. It should also be apparent that Goldberg and Zipursky's theory of civil recourse differs markedly from corrective justice theories of private law, because while the latter are theories of interpersonal justice, their civil recourse theory is primarily concerned not with interpersonal justice per se, but with the obligation of the state 'to provide a body of law that defines wrongs and empowers victims of wrongs to respond to those who have wronged them'.[197]

Goldberg and Zipursky's idea that the state has an obligation to provide an avenue of civil recourse to a person who has been wronged

---

[194] Bundesverfassungsgericht [German Constitutional Court], 1 BvR 567/89, 1 BvR 1044/89, 19 October 1993 reported in (1993) 89 BVerfGE 214 (cited by F du Bois, 'Social Purposes, Fundamental Rights and the Judicial Development of Private Law' ch 4 of this book, text accompanying n 64).

[195] Zipursky, 'Philosophy of Private Law', above n 112, at 637–40; Goldberg, above n 193, 541–44; Goldberg and Zipursky, 'Rights and Responsibility', above n 14.

[196] J Locke, *Two Treatises of Government* (London, 1690) book 2.

[197] Goldberg and Zipursky, 'Rights and Responsibility', above n 14, text accompanying n 44.

also draws support from William Blackstone's *Commentaries*.[198] As Helge Dedek shows in his chapter in this book, this focus on the triangular relationship between the victim of a wrong, the wrongdoer and the state was a marked feature of Blackstone's seminal work on English private law.[199] Dedek argues that for Blackstone the very purpose of forming societies and states was to safeguard those rights which antedate societies, so that the 'principal aim and sole justification' of the state was the protection of rights.[200] It followed that for Blackstone citizens did indeed have a right to the establishment of institutions which ensured effective protection of their rights, and that government had a correlative duty to 'take the measures and create the institutional framework' that would guarantee such protection.[201] According to Dedek, Blackstone recognised that the citizen has a right against the state not only to an institutional framework for the protection of what we now call primary rights, but also to a particular remedial response from the state to the infringement of those rights. For Blackstone, from the moment of injury the victim of a wrong has an inchoate right against the wrongdoer to compensation, and that right is perfected only through the intervention of the state.[202] Dedek's chapter, along with others in this book, suggests both that private law rights have an important role to play in any fully developed theory of the state, and that the state has an important role to play in any fully developed theory of private law.

---

[198] Zipursky, 'Philosophy of Private Law', above n 112, at 641–42; Goldberg, above n 193, 545–59.
[199] Dedek, above n 19.
[200] ibid, text accompanying n 151.
[201] ibid, text accompanying n 174.
[202] ibid, text accompanying n 183.

2

Rights in Private Law

PETER CANE*

I. PRIVATE LAW AND RIGHTS

WHAT IS THE role of the concept of 'rights' in private law? An answer to this complex and difficult question must begin with some reflection on both main terms of the question: 'private law' and 'rights'. Within private law there is a major, traditional division between, on the one side, the law of obligations and, on the other, the law of—what? Here we immediately confront a problem of naming. If we call it the law of private 'rights', we beg the very question we are asking. However, calling it 'the law of property' is unsatisfactory because not everything on this 'other side' of private law is 'property' in the technical sense. The term 'interests' is broader, but has no technical legal meaning. Moreover, its use to describe a particular theory of rights— the interest theory—makes it unsuitable for my purposes. So, for want of a better term, I will refer to 'the law of entitlements'. Private law, we may say, has two interrelated elements: a law of entitlements and a law of obligations. Property law, for instance, is primarily concerned with the creation, transfer and extinguishment of certain sorts of entitlements. The law of contract, by contrast, is concerned both with the creation, transfer and extinguishment of entitlements and also with enforcement of obligations that protect those entitlements. Tort law, it is sometimes suggested, is not concerned with the creation of entitlements but is purely a law of obligations. And so on. The distinction between the law of entitlements and the law of obligations does not map neatly onto the traditional substantive categories of private law.

However, the fact that private law has two elements (a law of entitlements and a law of obligations) does not distinguish it from the other major division of the law—public law—because both these legal categories

* Donal Nolan, Andrew Robertson and Jane Stapleton made very perceptive comments on earlier drafts that helped me to improve the argument significantly. Its weaknesses are definitely my responsibility.

are concerned (at least partly) with both entitlements and obligations. Central to the distinction between public law and private law is another distinction between public functions and private activities or, more colloquially and less precisely, between public life and private life. Private law is the law of private activities, whether engaged in by citizens or government. In other words, it is the law that regulates private life, whether the private life of citizens or of government.

This conclusion creates more problems of categorisation. For instance, tort law is one of the main departments of private law. However, there is one tort—misfeasance in a public office—that regulates public life, not private life. Moreover, there are rules that modify or qualify the operation of torts, such as negligence and nuisance, in their application to the performance of public functions. Such rules might more appropriately be classified as part of public law than private law.

In the common law, three departments of private law—the law of property (both legal and equitable), contract law and tort law—together, arguably, with the law of restitution and the law of trusts—are foundational in the sense that their central concepts provide important building blocks for what we might call 'social legal categories' such as environmental law, employment law, family law, corporations law, and so on. However, such categories may have public law components as well as private law components—environmental law is an obvious example.

These various points about the concept of private law only go to confirm the complexity and difficulty of the question I am addressing. This chapter only scratches the surface of the topic. In fact, it focuses on the work of a small number of theorists of private law, particularly Allan Beever and Robert Stevens, and on the areas of private law with which they are concerned.

Concerning rights, we may identify three different questions: what does it mean to say that we have rights? What are rights for? And, what rights do we have? The most famous answer to the first question is that of Wesley Hohfeld in *Fundamental Legal Conceptions as Applied in Judicial Reasoning*.[1] As his title implies, Hohfeld was interested in the use of the word 'right' in legal discourse. By contrast, much of the theoretical literature on rights is less focused on legal usage, and writers typically do not explore in any detail the similarities, differences and interactions between legal and extra-legal usages of the term 'right'.[2] Nevertheless,

---

[1] The edition I used in preparing this paper is WN Hohfeld, *Fundamental Legal Conceptions as Applied in Legal Reasoning* (D Campbell and P Thomas eds, Aldershot, Ashgate Dartmouth, 2001).

[2] For a careful argument that comparing and contrasting legal and extra-legal usage of a word such as 'right' is preferable to 'conceptual analysis' as a way of understanding law see AWB Simpson, 'The Analysis of Legal Concepts' (1964) 80 *Law Quarterly Review* 535. I have much sympathy with this argument but have decided, in this chapter, to engage with rights theorists of private law on their own (conceptual) turf.

Hohfeld's analysis has been influential well beyond legal theory. Hohfeld's basic claim was that 'jural interests' recognised in areas of law such as contract, tort and property can be analysed in terms of a set of 'fundamental jural relations' of correlation and opposition amongst concepts that he called 'rights' (or 'claims'), 'privileges' (or 'liberties'), 'powers' and 'immunities',[3] and their respective correlates, 'duties', 'no-rights', 'liabilities' and 'disabilities'.[4]

Amongst theorists concerned to answer the second question (what are rights for?), there is a long-standing and unresolved debate between those who say that the function of rights is to protect individuals' interests (the 'interest theory of rights') and those who counter that the function of rights is to promote individual choice (the '"choice" or "will" theory of rights'). The debate is unresolved because neither theory can plausibly explain all common uses of the term 'right'. Leif Wenar argues that each right has one or more of six specific functions, which he respectively calls 'exemption', 'discretion', 'authorisation', 'protection', 'provision' and 'performance'.[5] His account makes clear the connection between answers to the first and second questions. For instance, he argues that the species of right that Hohfeld called a 'claim' 'can entitle its bearer to *protection* against harm ... or to *provision* in case of need, or to ... *performance* of some agreed-upon ... or legally or conventionally specified action'.[6]

The third question (what rights do we have?) can be answered in various ways. We may usefully distinguish between three types of answers: descriptive, interpretive and prescriptive. Answers of the first type typically purport to give an account of what we might call 'social rights-generating practices', whether legal or extra-legal, while answers of the third type typically give an account independent of social practice. Answers of the second, interpretive type purport to bridge the gap between description and prescription. Many 'interpretivists' are inspired by Ronald Dworkin's argument that determining what the law *is* involves presenting it 'in the best possible light'.[7] Whereas the positivist would draw a sharp distinc-

---

[3] All of which, he said, are indiscriminately referred to as 'rights'.

[4] For a debate about whether the Hohfeldian concepts can explain tort liability for unauthorised but justified use of another's property see P Jaffey, 'Duties and Liabilities in Private Law' (2006) 12 *Legal Theory* 137; A Halpin, 'Rights, Duties, Liabilities and Hohfeld' (2007) 13 *Legal Theory* 23; P Jaffey, 'Liabilities in Private Law' (2008) 14 *Legal Theory* 233. For more general scepticism about the project of understanding rights-talk in terms of atomised jural relations see DN MacCormick, 'Rights in Legislation' in PMS Hacker and J Raz (eds), *Law, Morality and Society: Essays in Honour of HLA Hart* (Oxford, Clarendon Press, 1977) 189.

[5] L Wenar, 'The Nature of Rights' (2005) 33 *Philosophy and Public Affairs* 223. See also L Wenar, 'The Analysis of Rights' in MH Kramer et al (eds), *The Legacy of HLA Hart: Legal, Political, and Moral Philosophy* (Oxford, Oxford University Press, 2008) 251.

[6] Wenar, 'The Nature of Rights', above n 5, at 229 (emphasis in original).

[7] For a brief discussion see A Marmor, 'Interpretation, Law as' in P Cane and J Conaghan (eds), *The New Oxford Companion to Law* (Oxford, Oxford University Press, 2008) 628, 628–29.

tion between, for instance, legal statements about the rights we have and extra-legal statements about the (legal) rights we ought to have, an interpretivist would say that the question of what legal rights we have cannot be answered without making judgments of value because law is an essentially value-laden phenomenon.

Besides being a theory of what (the) law is, interpretivism is also a methodology used to develop and evaluate theories of what (the) law is *for*. According to a well-known account of interpretivist methodology,[8] there are four criteria for assessing such theories: fit, coherence, morality and transparency. The 'fit' criterion is concerned with how well the theory fits the data (ie, the set of legal rules and principles that it seeks to explain). The 'coherence' criterion asks whether the theory explains the data in a coherent way or, differently put, shows the relevant set of rules and principles to be internally coherent and also able to 'sit comfortably alongside other basic common law principles'.[9] The 'morality' criterion concerns the relationship between the law as presented by the theory and views about how people ought to behave independently of what the law requires. The 'transparency' criterion is primarily relevant to theories of the common law. Such theories are transparent to the extent that they take account of the reasons judges give for their decisions as well as the decisions themselves.

Each of these criteria can be understood and applied in various ways. Moreover, the various criteria may conflict with one another. For instance, because law is a social product of the activities of many actors over long periods of time, the theory that best fits the data or is most transparent may not score well on the criterion of coherence. By contrast, because a body of morally bad law may be perfectly coherent, a theory that is strong in terms of coherence may be weak in terms of morality. In developing a theory of law, the various criteria may need to be traded off against one another, and interpretivists may reasonably disagree about how to do this so as to produce the 'best' theory of law.

Our interest here is in theories that find the purpose of private law (or of some part of it) in the protection of rights. Such theories may be called 'singularist' in the sense that they attribute to the law only one purpose; and they may be contrasted with 'pluralist' theories that attribute to the law several purposes (such as compensation, deterrence and loss distribution in the case of tort law, for instance). It is a plausible hypothesis that singularists and pluralists will understand and apply the four interpretivist criteria differently. In particular, one would expect singularists to put greatest weight on coherence and to be inclined to resolve conflicts between coherence and the other criteria in its favour. Evidence support-

---

[8] SA Smith, *Contract Theory* (Oxford, Oxford University Press, 2004) 4–32.
[9] JW Neyers, 'The Economic Torts as Corrective Justice' (2009) 17 *Torts Law Journal* 162, 167.

ive of this hypothesis can be found in Beever's discussion of interpretivist methodology.[10] He sidelines what he calls 'moral intuitions'[11] as a counterpoint to a theory of law by substituting 'case law' for morality. In a later passage[12] Beever adopts a narrow view of morality, which he defines in terms of corrective justice. While acknowledging that this 'interpersonal morality' is only one aspect of a much larger set of practices, he asserts that it is the (only) aspect relevant to an interpretive analysis of negligence law, thus weakening the force of morality as an independent criterion of the success of his theory.

Beever makes short work of transparency by openly admitting that his theory ignores what he calls 'the modern case law' because 'no [general] theory could ever hope to provide a high degree of transparency'.[13] Indeed, he bases his theory on just 'five great cases',[14] which he considers to be 'central'[15] to the law of negligence. Nevertheless, he argues that the theory fits 'the vast majority of the case law'[16] — showing that his understanding of the criterion of 'fit' is at least as concerned with the results of cases as with judicial reasoning.

Most importantly, Beever opts for a strong version of coherence according to which 'a theory achieves coherence only if it shows that the law can be understood as a unified system perhaps under a single principle'.[17] Combined with his treatment of the other interpretivist values of fit, morality and transparency, this approach supports the hypothesis that interpretivists who are also singularists value coherence above all as a criterion for success in theory building. They seem prepared to pay a heavy price in terms of fit, transparency and even (it seems) morality to produce an account of the law that they consider 'coherent'.

Private law is saturated with rights-talk. However, as Wenar argues (following Hohfeld), the word 'right' is 'systematically ambiguous'[18] in the sense that, both within and outside the law, it is given 'various different meanings'.[19] Being alert to the ambiguity of the term 'right' (and, more deeply, of the concept of 'a right') is particularly important when considering arguments to the effect that private law (or some segment of private law, such as negligence law, tort law or contract law) is not only replete with rights but also built on a foundation of rights, and that every other concept found in private law is, in some sense, secondary to

---

[10] A Beever, *Rediscovering the Law of Negligence* (Oxford, Hart Publishing, 2007) 21–34.
[11] ibid, at 25.
[12] ibid, at 42–44.
[13] ibid, at 28.
[14] ibid.
[15] ibid, at 31.
[16] ibid, at 32.
[17] ibid, at 22.
[18] Wenar, 'The Nature of Rights', above n 5, at 236.
[19] ibid, at 237.

and derivative of the foundational concept of a right.[20] I shall refer to such arguments about the 'priority of rights' as 'rights-fundamentalist'—or 'fundamentalist' for short. Fundamentalism is reductionist: it sets out to explain all the features of a legal phenomenon such as private law—or, at least, the features that are considered to be the most significant—in terms of the single concept of a 'right'.[21] Furthermore, because the methodology of fundamentalism is a version of interpretivism that privileges coherence, fundamentalists have few qualms about dismissing aspects of the law as 'mistakes' if this is necessary to reveal it in the best light, as conceptually unified and internally coherent.

Rights-fundamentalism is particularly associated with corrective justice approaches to private law. Corrective justice theories were developed from the 1970s onwards in response to economic analyses of law. Economic analysis is concerned with the future and with the social consequences of law and legal phenomena. By contrast, although there is much disagreement amongst corrective justice theorists, all adopt a backward-looking, responsibility-based perspective on law.[22] In addition, central to all corrective justice accounts of private law is the concept of 'correlativity', which refers to a relationship between an agent on the one side and a person affected by conduct on the other, and entails that the law is equally concerned with the agent and the person affected. It is worth noting, however, that rights-fundamentalism does not seem to be a necessary corollary of the backward-looking approach or of correlativity. This suggests that we must look elsewhere to explain the association between corrective justice theories and rights-fundamentalism.

In what follows, the plan is to think about fundamentalism in terms of the three questions about rights identified above: what does it mean to say that we have rights? What are rights for? And, what rights do we have? In this way I attempt to place rights fundamentalism in a wider landscape of theorising about rights and thereby to understand it better. Finally, I will examine the fundamentalist concept of the priority of rights in private law. The main arguments developed in this chapter are (1) that fundamentalist, reductionist accounts of private law oversimplify and misrepresent

---

[20] In other words, that rights are not only necessary but also sufficient to explain the area of law being analysed. Such a claim of sufficiency is very ambitious.

[21] The fundamentalist concept of rights is explained in the text accompanying below n 45. Not all rights theories are fundamentalist: see, eg, JCP Goldberg and BC Zipursky, 'Rights and Responsibility in the Law of Torts' ch 9 of this book.

[22] Ironically, however, because economic analysts and corrective justice theorists both offer singularist accounts, they confront the common problem of what to say about cases that do not fit their theory. Characteristic moves involve concentrating on results and ignoring inconvenient judicial reasoning, and dismissing problem cases as 'mistakes'. Such strategies (which Jane Stapleton felicitously refers to as 'reverse engineering': J Stapleton, 'Evaluating Goldberg and Zipursky's Civil Recourse Theory' (2006) 75 *Fordham Law Review* 1529, 1538) are much more problematic for interpretivists than for functionalists, who value neither coherence nor transparency for their own sakes.

complex legal phenomena, and that they are historically implausible; and (2) that although fundamentalism is proffered as the best account of the 'internal' structure of private law,[23] it is motivated and driven by an 'external', individualist ideology of autonomy and an 'external' view about the proper role of judges. My basic point, unvarnished, is that fundamentalism is more prescriptive than descriptive.

II. WHAT DOES IT MEAN TO SAY THAT WE HAVE RIGHTS?

There is no single fundamentalist account of the role of rights in private law. However, if there is one proposition about which fundamentalists seem agreed it is that courts are ill-equipped to deploy 'policy' arguments to establish the limits of liability in private law and that it is illegitimate for them to do so.[24] A favourite target is the *Caparo*[25] three-stage test of duty of care in negligence: foreseeability, proximity, and fairness, justice and reasonableness (the last of which Beever describes as 'code for policy').[26] According to fundamentalists, it is the concept of 'rights' that courts should deploy to establish the grounds and bounds of liability in private law; and pragmatically, not being world-class equestrians, judges are well advised to choose the gentle pony 'rights' over the wild horse 'policy'. Moreover, say the fundamentalists, it is an account in terms of rights, not policy, which provides the best interpretation of the grounds and bounds of liability in the private law we actually have. 'Rights, not policy' is the fundamentalist message reduced to its bare essentials.

But what do fundamentalists mean by 'rights'? To the question 'what is a right?' an answer that might readily spring to mind—in the context of private law, at least—is Hohfeld's: a right—or what he called a 'claim'[27]—is the correlative[28] of a duty. In Hohfeld's scheme, the correla-

---

[23] See, eg, Beever, above n 10, at 34–36. Ernest Weinrib describes the internal approach as 'formalism': EJ Weinrib, *The Idea of Private Law* (Cambridge MA, Harvard University Press, 1995) ch 2.

[24] This view is neatly stated by Jason Neyers: 'in a liberal democracy it is impermissible for unelected judges to be implementing social policy from the bench' (JW Neyers, 'On the Right(s) Path' (2008) 19 *Kings Law Journal* 413, 413).

[25] *Caparo Industries plc v Dickman* [1990] 2 AC 605 (HL).

[26] Beever, above n 10, at 187. Indeed, Beever thinks that under the *Caparo* test, 'the duty of care is determined entirely by policy': at 187. Amongst final appeal courts in the major common law jurisdictions, the Canadian Supreme Court is a leading exponent of the three-stage, 'foreseeability-proximity-policy' approach to duty (see recently *Fullowka v Pinkerton's of Canada Ltd* [2010] SCC 5). It may, therefore, be no coincidence that many leading corrective justice and rights-fundamentalist theorists—such as Weinrib, Beever, Neyers and Peter Benson—live and work in Canada or have significant Canadian connections.

[27] Hohfeld argued that the word 'right' would ideally be used only to refer to a 'claim': above n 1, at 12–13. This is because his main project was to promote analytical clarity. Theorists with a different aim may reject this prescription: see, eg, MacCormick, above n 4.

[28] Note that Hohfeld's concept of 'correlativity' is different from that of corrective justice theory, in which the term refers primarily to a relationship between two individuals—a doer

tivity of claims and duties means that whenever one person has a claim, at least one other person has a (correlative) duty; and, conversely, that whenever one person has a duty, at least one other person has a (correlative) claim. In Hohfeldian terms, to say that C has a claim against D is just to say that C is owed a duty by D; and to say that D owes a duty to C is just to say that D is subject to a claim by C. For Hohfeld, claims are necessary and sufficient conditions of duties, and vice versa.[29] In this sense, Hohfeldian correlativity is purely formal and definitional.[30]

A logical precondition of this formal, definitional relationship between claims and duties is that a claim and its correlative duty must have the same substantive content. So, for instance, in Hohfeldian analysis the correlative of a duty to take care is a claim that care be taken; and the correlative of a claim not to be defamed is a duty not to defame. But note that Hohfeldian analysis can tell us nothing about the substantive content of claims and duties or, in other words, what claims and duties we have. All it tells us is that the corollary of a claim with a particular substantive content is a duty with the same substantive content and that the corollary of a duty with a particular substantive content is a claim with the same substantive content.

Stevens explicitly says that he is using the term 'right' in the Hohfeldian sense of a 'claim',[31] and he apparently understands claims as being correlative to duties:

> A tort is a species of wrong. A wrong is a breach of duty owed to someone else. A breach of duty owed to someone else is an infringement of a right they have against the tortfeasor.[32]

---

and a sufferer of harm, in Weinrib's memorable phrase: above n 23, at 65. By contrast, in Hohfeld's scheme the term refers primarily to a relationship between legal concepts or 'positions': rights and duties, powers and liabilities, and so on.

[29] MacCormick, above n 4 rejects the Hohfeldian scheme on the basis that in law, at least, not only can there be rights without correlative duties, but also that rights can generate duties and, in this sense, be prior to them.

[30] For an illuminating discussion of Hohfeld's formalism see N Simmonds, 'Introduction' in Hohfeld, above n 1, ix–xxix. The various correlations and oppositions Hohfeld identified were not derived by descriptive or interpretive analysis of legal materials. By contrast, fundamentalists present their account of the relationship between rights and duties as the best interpretation of private law (or some part of it), although this does not involve describing and analysing how the term 'right' is actually used in legal materials. For a rigorous application of Hohfeld's approach to tort law see NJ McBride and R Bagshaw, *Tort Law*, 3rd edn (London, Pearson Longman, 2008) 6, 17. See also NJ McBride, 'Rights and the Basis of Tort Law' ch 13 of this book. Neyers wrongly implies that McBride and Bagshaw are rights-fundamentalists: JW Neyers, '*Tate & Lyle Food & Distribution Ltd v Greater London Council* (1983)' in C Mitchell and P Mitchell (eds), *Landmark Cases in the Law of Tort* (Oxford, Hart Publishing, 2010) 227, 227 n 4. McBride and Bagshaw do appear to adopt a corrective justice approach to tort law; but as observed earlier, rights-fundamentalism does not necessarily follow from that approach.

[31] R Stevens, *Torts and Rights* (Oxford, Oxford University Press, 2007) 4.

[32] ibid, at 2.

This statement could be rephrased in Hohfeldian terms as follows: a tort is a breach of a duty and (by definition) the infringement of a correlative right. However, there are two major obstacles to adopting this rephrasing as an accurate expression of Stevens' meaning. The first is that it deprives the fundamentalist argument that rights are conceptually basic to tort law of any real bite because it equally supports the proposition that duties are conceptually basic to tort law. On the basis of Hohfeldian analysis, it can no more be said that rights are fundamental to private law than that duties occupy that place. The second problem is that Stevens makes it clear in the very next sentence that whatever his understanding of the relationship between rights and duties, it is not Hohfeld's. 'Before a defendant can be characterized as a tortfeasor', he continues, 'the anterior question of whether the claimant had a right against him must be answered.'[33] In Hohfeld's scheme, rights are not 'anterior' to duties but correlative with them: if a person has a right they are owed a duty of the same substantive content, and vice versa.[34] We must conclude that even if Stevens accepts that rights are correlatives of duties, he is not using the term in this sense when he says that rights are conceptually basic to tort law.

Beever's position is rather more complex. As far as I can see, the closest he comes to acknowledging Hohfeld is the statement that '[o]bligations are, of course, the concomitants of rights'.[35] But since this statement is made incidentally in a footnote, we are justified in concluding that it is not central to Beever's analysis of the tort of negligence. In Hohfeldian terms, the most straightforward way to analyse that tort (at least for starters) would be to say that the duty to take care is correlative to a claim that care be taken. However, Beever's analysis is very different. In his account, negligence liability has five components: (1) negligent conduct that breaches a (2) duty of care (3) causing 'deprivation'[36] that (4) is not too remote and (5) constitutes 'injury', not merely 'factual harm'. Negligent conduct consists in creating an unreasonable risk. C is owed a duty of care if he or she 'belonged to a class of persons put at reasonably foreseeable risk by the ... negligence'.[37] Similarly, the test of remoteness is reasonable foreseeability.[38] Injury is interference with or infringement of a right (such as a property right or a right of bodily integrity).[39] Harm that does not infringe a right is not an injury. For instance, economic loss to

---

[33] ibid.

[34] The argument that rights are conceptually prior is considered in more detail in part V of this chapter.

[35] Beever, above n 10, at 238 n 61.

[36] ibid, at 211.

[37] ibid, at 148.

[38] ibid, at ch 4. As I read ch 4, its aims are to establish reasonable foreseeability as *the* test of duty and remoteness, to link both to the concept of negligent conduct and to demonstrate the irrelevance of 'policy' to all three.

[39] ibid, at 211–12, 218–19. The relationship between 'right' and 'injury' is definitional. But note that according to Beever, the duty component of the tort of negligence is not a

C resulting from physical damage caused negligently by D to the property of a third party is harm but not injury.[40] Without injury, there can—or so it would seem—be no liability even if all other elements of the tort are present—that is, even if D created an unreasonable risk (and so was negligent), C was foreseeably at risk (and so was owed a duty of care) and the harm to C that resulted was foreseeable (and so not too remote).

It might seem to follow from this analysis that there could be a duty (ie, an obligation not to create an unreasonable risk)[41] without a corresponding right (not to be injured)[42] and a breach of duty (not to create an unreasonable risk) without infringement of a right (not to be injured). In this interpretation, to say that someone is owed a duty of care is not to say that they have a right not to be injured because to be owed a duty of care is merely to be put foreseeably at risk by unreasonable conduct. However, it is not clear that this is what Beever actually means to say. In a passage discussing liability of D for 'foreseeably damaging' a car, he suggests that whether D owes C a 'duty of care' depends on whether or not C 'has a right to the car'. If so, he says, D owes C a duty of care; but if not, D owes C no duty of care 'whether or not ... damage of the car is reasonably foreseeable' by D.[43] Similarly, in his discussion of wrongful birth claims, Beever says that 'foetuses possess no rights' and that being born with disabilities resulting from harm suffered in the womb 'cannot be regarded as arising from the violation of the claimant's rights'[44]—regardless (it seems) of whether or not harm to the foetus was foreseeable.

---

duty not to injure but a duty to take care. There is no definitional correlation between the right interference with which constitutes an injury and the duty to take care.

[40] ibid, at ch 7.

[41] Or, put positively, to comply with the standard of reasonable conduct.

[42] Throughout I will use the term 'right not to be injured' as a shorthand for a more accurate but much more cumbersome phrase such as 'an entitlement belonging to the species of entitlements interference with which, or infringement of which, constitutes an injury as opposed to mere harm'.

[43] Beever, above n 10, at 238.

[44] ibid, at 386. However, by way of contrast, consider his discussion of what he calls the 'not-yet-existent claimant': at 148. In that passage, he is concerned with a case in which a claimant was born with disabilities after suffering harm in the womb as a result of pre-conception negligence. Beever says that the Court rightly rejected the argument that no duty of care can be owed to a claimant who does not exist—apparently supporting the imposition of liability in such cases. Indeed, he adds, it 'flows from *Donoghue v Stevenson*' (at 149) that because the claimant 'belonged to a class of persons put at reasonably foreseeable risk' (at 148), the claimant was owed a duty of care. But on the basis that there can be no liability without a primary right not to be injured, it should follow from the fact that the claimant did not exist at the time of the negligence that C suffered no 'injury' and was owed no secondary duty, even though C belonged to a foreseeable class. Incidentally, Beever's treatment of this type of case also supports the interpretation of his account according to which there can be a duty of care without a right not to be injured. Ronen Perry argues that tort liability to claimants who were not legal persons at the time of the tortious conduct disproves the 'correlativity' of duties and rights in tort law: R Perry, 'Correlativity' (2009) 28 *Law and Philosophy* 537. Since legal non-persons have no legal rights, the secondary duty

Whichever interpretation of Beever's position is to be preferred, it seems clear that what Beever means by a 'right' is not the same as what Hohfeld means by a 'claim'. In the former interpretation, there can be a (breach of) duty without (infringement of) a right; and in both interpretations, the corresponding rights and duties are not correlative in the Hohfeldian sense because they do not have the same substantive content. In the case of damage to the car, for instance, the duty in question is to take care while the right is proprietary. In Hohfeldian terms, the correlative of a duty to take care is a right that care be taken; and the correlative of right to property is a duty not to interfere with the property. A 'right to a car' cannot correlate with a 'duty to take care'.

If fundamentalist rights are not correlatives of duties in the Hohfeldian sense, what are they? First (we are told), they are 'primary', not 'secondary'.[45] Loosely, secondary rights are remedial—the right to damages is the paradigm example. So fundamentalist rights are not secondary; and unlike fundamentalist rights, it seems, secondary rights do obey Hohfeldian logic by correlating with secondary duties. Secondly, infringements of primary rights 'give rise to'[46] or 'generate'[47] secondary rights and their correlative duties.[48] However, note, thirdly, that this generative relationship between primary rights and secondary duties is not formal or definitional or conceptual in the way that Hohfeldian correlativity of rights and duties is formal, definitional and conceptual. In the fundamentalist scheme, to say that C has a primary right is not (just) to say that C is owed a secondary duty; and it is obvious that primary rights and secondary duties do not have the same substantive content. We must, therefore, beware of the risk of thinking that when fundamentalists substitute 'rights' for 'policy' as a device for controlling the grounds and bounds of liability in private law, this move by itself creates a more logically coherent analytical scheme.[49]

---

owed to a claimant who lacked legal personality at the time of the alleged tort must arise from a breach of a primary duty, not interference with a primary right (Perry calls such duties 'abstract' and 'standalone'). However, it is not clear how legal non-persons can be owed legal duties if they cannot possess legal rights. Birth changes everything. Both legal duties and legal rights are acquired at birth and can provide the foundation for imposition of secondary duties even in relation to conduct that occurred before birth. The theoretical puzzle here is related to the temporal relationship between the relevant conduct and the acquisition of legal status, not to the conceptual relationship between rights and duties.

[45] Hohfeldian rights can, of course, be either primary or secondary.

[46] Beever, above n 10, at 212.

[47] Stevens, *Torts and Rights*, above n 31, at 2, 98.

[48] For example, Stevens states that 'the law of torts is concerned with the secondary obligations generated by the infringement of ... primary rights': ibid, at 2, 98. In this respect, fundamentalists agree with MacCormick, above n 4 that one of the functions of rights is to justify giving a remedy: *ubi ius, ubi remedium* (understood prescriptively rather than descriptively).

[49] I am not suggesting that failure to adopt the Hohfeldian approach is a defect but rather that Hohfeld is not the place to start trying to understand what fundamentalists are doing. This is so not only because fundamentalist rights are not Hohfeldian claims but also

Whatever 'coherence' means, it has nothing to do with the deontic logic of rights and duties. Fundamentalist 'rights' are the functional equivalents of 'policies' and the success of fundamentalism as a theory of private law must be judged in the light of that equivalence rather than in terms of conceptual analysis of rights and their relationship to duties.

How does fundamentalism appear in that light? Private law is saturated with talk of rights and duties; but the language of policy is also pervasive. It seems unlikely, therefore, that the interpretive superiority of one or the other approach could be conclusively established merely by textual analysis or simply in terms of the internal form and structure of private law. Like Hohfeldian conceptualism, interpretivism—especially of the variety practised by singularists—lacks the resources fundamentalists need in order to make the case that rights play the pivotal role in private law that they assign to them. As the first paragraph of this part suggests, they also need normative arguments about the functions of rights (discussed in the next part) and some account of where rights come from and what rights we have (discussed in part IV).

III. WHAT ARE RIGHTS FOR?

Asked in such general terms, this question is very tricky to answer. For present purposes it can be narrowed to refer to 'rights' in the sense in which fundamentalists use the term 'right'—namely a primary legal entitlement of one person (C) that attracts a secondary legal obligation of another (D). What is the point of legal rights in this sense (which hereafter I shall simply call 'legal rights')? Fundamentalists do not explicitly address this question. However, their accounts implicitly provide an answer, and the aim of this part is to draw it out. To do this, I take as a point of departure the two main accounts of the purpose of rights outlined earlier.

One theory about the purpose of rights says that rights protect interests and the other that rights promote individual choice. We can define a person's 'interests' in terms of what is good for them—their well-being. A person's legal rights protect their interests by providing others with strong reasons (in the form of legal duties) to act towards that person in such a way as to promote their protected interests as defined by their legal rights. Not everything that can be said to be in our interests is so protected; but provided we understand 'interests' objectively (rather than in terms of what people want or what they think will promote their well-being), it seems safe to say that one function of legal rights in private law is to protect interests (whatever else they might do).

because a foundational implication of Hohfeld's strategy is that the concept of a claim by itself is inadequate to explain tort law (for instance).

According to the choice account, the purpose of rights is to give people control over how other people behave towards them; or, more specifically, to give the holder of a legal right some measure of control over performance of the legal duty correlative to the legal right. According to HLA Hart, the chief proponent of this account,[50] the 'fullest measure' of such control has

> three distinguishable elements: (i) the right holder may waive or extinguish the duty or leave it in existence; (ii) after breach or threatened breach of the duty he may leave it 'unenforced' or may 'enforce' it by suing for compensation ... ; and (iii) he may waive or extinguish the obligation to pay compensation to which the breach of duty gives rise.[51]

Note that in this formulation, Hart distinguishes between primary and secondary duties. The first limb of the formulation relates to the primary duty. In Hohfeldian terms, the first limb can be expanded by saying that a primary right carries with it a power to change the legal position of the person under the correlative primary duty by waiving or extinguishing the duty, with the result that the person formally under the duty to act, or not to act, in a particular way in relation to the right-holder is now at liberty (as the case may be) not to act or to act in that way. The second limb relates to the liberty (and an associated power) to enforce the primary duty once breached, and the third limb relates to the secondary duty.

Wenar argues that the 'contest' between interest theorists and choice theorists of rights is a proxy for a debate about distributive justice between 'welfarists' and 'Kantians' respectively.[52] His point seems to be that the protagonists on each side understand rights in the way they do, not because they believe that their respective accounts are more faithful to social practice or better meet criteria of good conceptual analysis, but in order to 'preempt objections'[53] to their respective theories of distributive justice (based on well-being in the case of the welfarists and autonomy in the case of the Kantians) by enlisting the rhetoric of rights on their side. Similarly, Matthew Kramer argues that debates about the purpose of rights are motivated 'at least in part by considerations of political morality'.[54] For instance, there are obvious reasons (based on what we know about mental capacity) for an animal-rights campaigner to prefer the interest

[50] See especially HLA Hart, 'Bentham on Legal Rights' in AWB Simpson (ed), *Oxford Essays in Jurisprudence, Second Series* (Oxford, Clarendon Press, 1973) 171.

[51] ibid, at 192.

[52] Wenar, 'The Nature of Rights', above n 5, 250. Wenar also argues that both theories fail because they cannot account for all the functions of rights. He offers a 'pluralistic' theory in their place.

[53] ibid.

[54] M Kramer, 'Rights in Legal and Political Philosophy' in KE Whittington, RD Kelemen and GA Caldeira (eds), *The Oxford Handbook of Law and Politics* (Oxford, Oxford University Press, 2008) 414, 421.

theory to the choice theory regardless of analytical considerations such as explanatory clarity or parsimony.

Where do fundamentalists stand in these debates? Some explicitly identify themselves as Kantians. This is most obviously true of Ernest Weinrib. The concept he calls 'Kantian right' is central to his analysis of private law as corrective justice.[55] The Kantian 'principle of right', which governs relationships between individuals, says that 'the free choice of the one must be capable of coexisting with the freedom of the other' according to rules that apply equally to all.[56] The criterion of wrongfulness under the principle of right is exercising one's freedom inconsistently with the freedom of another. By contrast, failing (for instance) to meet the needs of another or to satisfy their wishes cannot be wrongful under that principle. For Weinrib, this explains the absence of a general legal duty to rescue. Stevens seems to go even further down this route. The fact that rights can be waived shows (he says) that what rights protect is not our well-being but rather each person's control over their life.[57] For Beever, 'rights are defined with reference to the right-holder's will',[58] and this (for instance) provides the basis for the defence of *volenti non fit injuria*.

In fact, there seems to be a particular association between fundamentalism and an ideology of individual freedom. Although fundamentalists argue that an analysis based on rights gives the best account of both liability and no-liability in private law, some seem to think that the biggest theoretical pay-off of the analysis is to explain cases of no-liability. Not surprisingly, perhaps, this is particularly clear in Beever's account of the law of negligence.[59] Liability in the tort of negligence, he says, is liability for causing injury by creating an unreasonable risk of the sort of injury suffered. Beever defines 'injury' as the violation of a legal right; and he goes on to use that concept of a legal right to explain various instances of no-liability for harm (to well-being) caused by negligence. The irony in this manoeuvre deserves to be articulated. Both the main theories of what rights are for see them as benefits—they either protect interests or promote the autonomy of their holders. By contrast, fundamentalists use rights as a tool for suppressing private law's interest-protecting instincts and for minimising the incidence of liability-creating duties.

There is another common feature of fundamentalist arguments that seems to me to be at least indirectly in tension with the interest theory of rights. As we have already observed, leading fundamentalists such as Weinrib, Beever and Stevens dislike judicial discretion and seek to limit the role of judicial choice in settling disputes and developing the common

---

[55] Weinrib, above n 23, at ch 4.
[56] ibid, at 104.
[57] Stevens, *Torts and Rights*, above n 31, at 339.
[58] Beever, above n 10, at 347.
[59] Beever, above n 10.

law. Beever associates discretion with a sort of free-wheeling balancing of interests, including social interests;[60] while Weinrib thinks of it in terms of the distinction between corrective justice and Kantian right (the province of law and courts) on the one side, and distributive justice (the province of politics and the legislature) on the other.[61] For these theorists, fundamentalism is the best theory of private law because rights limit judicial discretion. There are at least two significant problems with this strategy, both of which Weinrib and Beever avoid by ignoring them. The first problem becomes obvious as soon as we ask where rights come from or, put differently, what rights we have. Weinrib avoids this question largely by relegating it to the realm of politics—in other words, he says that it is primarily a matter of distributive, not corrective, justice. Beever, by contrast, argues that the idea of corrective justice can tell us what rights we have,[62] but he does not show how that can be done consistently with confining judicial discretion in the way he favours. To his credit, Stevens does attempt to explain how the rights-based account of tort law limits judicial discretion in identifying and protecting legal rights, and I will discuss his analysis later.

The second problem arises out of the possibility that legal rights, like interests, may conflict. The absence from Beever's account, as from Weinrib's, of significant discussion of conflicts of rights might suggest that he considers the Kantian account of legal rights to be free of the problem. It seems reasonable, at least in principle, to expect fewer conflicts of legal rights than conflicts of interests if only because, even according to the interest theory, rights are strongly protected interests, and not all interests are strongly protected. Moreover, in the fundamentalist account, legal rights (ie, primary entitlements that correspond to secondary obligations) protect only individualised interests, not interests of groups and society more generally. On the other hand, it seems implausible to think that courts, in deciding claims in private law, may not frequently be confronted by significant conflicts of rights that may be incommensurable. Stevens acknowledges as much and, once again, should be given credit for confronting the issue head-on.

As Stevens says, one way—in theory, at least—of resolving conflicts between values is by accepting a single master value, such as utility or efficiency, to break ties between equal or incommensurable values.[63] However, this strategy is not open to Kantian fundamentalists. Their master value is individual autonomy; but precisely because this is an individual rather than a social value, it cannot be used to resolve conflicts between individuals each seeking to exercise their autonomy. In Stevens' view,

---

[60] ibid, at 3–19, 142 ('policy-based free-for-all').
[61] Weinrib, above n 23, at ch 8.
[62] Beever, above n 10, at 62–63.
[63] Stevens, *Torts and Rights*, above n 31, at 337.

'there is no mathematical formula or single yardstick for the ordering of rights'.[64] Instead, Stevens suggests a procedure for resolving conflicts of rights, namely the exercise of 'judgment'.[65] This is also the procedure Weinrib recommends for bridging the gap between the dictates of corrective justice and 'the uniquely correct result for particular cases'.[66] Weinrib distinguishes permissible judicial judgment from impermissible appeals to 'political considerations' by associating judgment with the constraints imposed on judges by the existing body of legal materials,[67] their professional training and experience, 'the requirements of [the] judicial role' and the discipline of reasoning by analogy.[68]

In this light, we can see why fundamentalists are attracted to rights as the theoretical foundation for private law. The fundamentalists' rights are individualised: they protect interests of individuals, not of groups or of society more widely. As a result (so it is argued, however implausibly), the 'uniquely correct' application 'in particular cases'[69] of (what Stevens calls) 'general' as opposed to 'specified' rights[70] can be decided, and conflicts between rights can be resolved, without reference to social interests, otherwise called 'policies'. This is just as well because, according to Stevens, courts (at least as compared to the legislature) are not 'competent' to decide 'how the common good is best pursued'.[71] Because (so it is argued) the application of rights to particular cases can be determined and conflicts between rights can be adjudicated without reference to social interests, rights are compatible with the judgment model of judicial reasoning in a way that 'policy' is not. Put bluntly, for fundamentalists one of the main functions of rights in private law (apart, of course, from promoting individual autonomy) is to constrain judicial discretion.

I know that at least some fundamentalists will unequivocally reject this conclusion. As Stevens says, 'Private law is simply about the rights we have one against another.'[72] Or, as Weinrib might say, rights *just are* the building blocks of private law, intrinsic to its very form and structure; to adapt his famous mantra, the only function of rights is to be rights. So perhaps I should rephrase my conclusion to say that a significant motivation of fundamentalists for generating a rights-based account of private law is to limit judicial discretion in developing the law and resolving conflicts

---

[64] ibid.

[65] R Stevens, 'The Conflict of Rights' in A Robertson and HW Tang, *The Goals of Private Law* (Oxford, Hart Publishing, 2009) 139.

[66] Weinrib, above n 23, at 222–26. See also Beever, above n 10, at 49–50, 140–42.

[67] Thus, apparently, assuming what he sets out to prove, namely that on its best interpretation the law does not make reference to policy and that it does not allow or require judges to take account of social interests.

[68] Weinrib, above n 23, at 223–24.

[69] ibid, at 222.

[70] Stevens, *Torts and Rights*, above n 31, at 143.

[71] ibid, at 147.

[72] Stevens, 'The Conflict of Rights', above n 65, at 141.

between values. This conclusion is much harder to reject because leading fundamentalists have said as much; and it gives rise to two puzzles.

The first puzzle is this: it is not necessary to be a rights-fundamentalist to think that courts should be subsidiary to legislatures as law-makers and that judicial reasoning should be more constrained in various ways than that of legislatures.[73] Some version of the 'judgment' model of judicial choice is attractive to and, I imagine, accepted as appropriate by very many of those who have thought seriously about such matters. So it would be wrong for fundamentalists to think that a belief in the virtues of the judgment model sets them apart from non-fundamentalists. What fundamentalists seem to object to above all is the idea that non-individual ('social') interests may be relevant to determining the proper scope of legal protection for individual interests in particular cases, and to resolving conflicts between individual interests. According to them, it is legislatures, not courts, that should take account of non-individual interests when making law, not only for democratic reasons but also because courts are ill-equipped to promote social interests. If this is right, it seems to me that what really divides the fundamentalists from non-fundamentalists is not the fundamentalists' belief in the virtues of the judgment model of judicial reasoning but rather their insistence that in bridging the gap between general statements of individual interests and the resolution of particular disputes, and in resolving conflicts between individual interests, courts should be *prohibited* from taking account of social interests,[74] *even if* this is done in accordance with the judgment model. I deliberately phrase this statement in normative terms to make it clear that in my view, fundamentalism is not—contrary to what fundamentalists sometimes seem to suggest—a non-prescriptive project.[75] Fundamentalists think that when judges make private law and adjudicate private law disputes they have no business paying attention to or taking any account of social, as opposed to individual interests. They often present this position as an internal 'interpretation' of private law,[76] but it is simply an expression of external value.

Here is the second puzzle: fundamentalists purport to provide accounts of the role of rights 'in private law', or in some part of private law such as tort law or negligence law. Private law in the twenty-first century is a complex product of both judicial and legislative activity; and as we have seen, fundamentalists make much of the difference between the two

---

[73] For indisputable proof see P Cane, 'Taking Disagreement Seriously: Legislatures, Courts and the Reform of Tort Law' (2005) 25 *Oxford Journal of Legal Studies* 393.

[74] Beever, above n 10, at 103–06, 176.

[75] See, eg, Beever's disclaimer: ibid, at 21.

[76] See, eg, Beever's historically (M Lunney, 'Counterfactuals and Corrective Justice: Legal History and Allan Beever's *Reconstructing* [sic] *the Law of Negligence*' (2009) 17 *Torts Law Journal* 291) and doctrinally implausible interpretation of *Bolton v Stone*: ibid, at 96–106. See also Weinrib, above n 23, at 147–52.

institutions and their respective roles in making private law. If a major motivation for rights-fundamentalism is to constrain judicial choice, how can it convincingly be offered as the best understanding of an area of law which is only partly, and decreasingly, a product of judicial activity? Moreover, how can a theory that focuses on judicial activity be convincingly offered as a theory of the social phenomenon of private law claiming in which judicial activity plays only a very small role? This, surely, is an egregious instance of the tip of the iceberg being mistaken for the whole, on which the fundamentalist vessel must surely come to grief.[77]

In summary, according to rights-fundamentalism, rights in private law perform two main functions: they protect and promote individual autonomy and they constrain judicial discretion in resolving disputes and making law. Of course, it does not follow from this conclusion about the functions of rights that fundamentalism does not provide the best interpretation of private law. That is a separate issue to which we will return in part V.

IV. WHAT RIGHTS DO WE HAVE?

The main game for fundamentalists is establishing that a rights-based analysis provides the best interpretation of private law (or some part of it), not discovering what rights private law confers. However, they cannot dodge this latter question effectively. At least some fundamentalists apparently accept that the best explanation for a decision against a claimant can be that the claimant lacked a right against the defendant, even though this is not the reason given by the court. What is the basis, in such a case, for the assertion that the best explanation for the decision is rights-based unless it be some theory of the rights we have? Conversely, at least some rights-fundamentalists seem to think that the best explanation for a decision in favour of a claimant can be that the claimant had a right, even though this is not the reason given by the court. What can the basis be for such a view other than some theory of the rights we have? It is, of course, not open to the fundamentalist to argue that a finding of liability *entails* the presence of a right and that a finding of no-liability *entails* the absence of a right, because such an argument would beg the very question in issue and turn the fundamentalist thesis into a mere stipulation rather than an interpretation. Lurking beneath such arguments there must be a theory of where legal rights come from and what legal rights there are.

---

[77] In fact, we know that the tip of the private law iceberg is a very much smaller proportion of the whole than the tip of its natural counterpart (probably less than 1% even of private law claiming activity let alone of the social operation of private law, of which it is an infinitesimal proportion): see P Cane, *Atiyah's Accidents, Compensation and the Law*, 7th edn (Cambridge, Cambridge University Press, 2006) 201–06.

Such a theory cannot be 'descriptive' or 'positivistic' in any simple sense because of the lack of direct correlation, in the fundamentalist account, between the presence or absence of judicial rights-talk and the presence or absence of rights.

The most explicit and sustained fundamentalist attempt to provide such a theory of which I am aware is that of Stevens in *Torts and Rights*.[78] His (neo-Kantian) account goes somewhat as follows. Both legislatures and courts can create legal rights. Although such rights protect individual interests, policy considerations (also known as social interests) may be relevant to deciding what individual interests the law should protect. However, taking account of social interests is appropriately the task of legislatures, not courts. When courts create legal rights, they must not do so 'according to their own assessment of the weight to be given to a basket of frequently unarticulated policy concerns'.[79] Instead, by reflecting on 'the nature and experience of ourselves, and the world and society in which we live' judges will be able to deduce, by the power of reason, what 'moral rights' we have and which of those moral rights 'ought to be given the force of law'.[80] The legislature, Stevens says,

> has the power to create legal rights for any reason at all, unconnected with the moral rights we have against one another ... By contrast, the judiciary, in creating and changing over time our common law, sourced our legal rights one against the other in our moral rights.[81]

Moreover, judges are well equipped by 'their professional skills acquired from experience and reflection on justice' to 'decide moral questions'.[82]

Moral rights, says Stevens, 'do not change over time'[83] nor do they have 'functions or goals'[84] such as making the world a better place. We 'value moral rights for themselves'[85] not for any good they might do (and, presumably, regardless of any evil they may produce). However, Stevens is no philosophical realist. Moral rights, he says, 'do not just exist like stones to be picked up and observed' but are 'derived by human reflection'.[86] On the other hand, nor (unlike 'conventional morality') are

---

[78] Stevens, *Torts and Rights*, above n 31, at 329–40. I should preface this discussion by saying that my focus on Stevens' work should not be taken to imply that I am critical of it in particular. On the contrary, as I have said, Stevens deserves credit and admiration for tackling such difficult issues. I think that his account raises many issues that any such account is likely to raise and faces many of the problems that any such account is likely to face.

[79] ibid, at 329. For a very different approach to the role of policy and social interests in a rights-based theory of tort law see NJ McBride, 'Rights and the Basis of Tort Law' ch 12 of this book.

[80] Stevens, *Torts and Rights*, above n 31, at 330. Cf Beever, above n 10, at 216.

[81] Stevens, 'The Conflict of Rights', above n 65, at 145.

[82] Stevens, *Torts and Rights*, above n 31, at 332.

[83] ibid.

[84] ibid, at 333.

[85] ibid.

[86] ibid, at 331.

they the product of social practice, for although discerning moral rights requires 'experience, reflection and discourse with others ... [u]ltimately ... we are each of us on our own'.[87] Still, rights derived by rational reflection on the human condition are 'peculiarly interesting and important' and 'we must be wary of such judicially recognized rights being cut back by legislation'[88] — presumably because legislation may not be the product of such reflection.

So much for Stevens' views about the moral source of such of our private law rights as have been (properly) recognised by judges. But what *are* our moral rights? 'In determining the minimum content of our moral rights, the starting point is the negative formulation of the golden rule':[89] do not do to others what you would not want done to you.[90] The criterion for whether particular interests should be strongly protected by a legal right is not whether doing so would make the world a better place but whether it would give effect to the (negative formulation of the) golden rule. Thus, for instance, murdering someone is 'wrong' not because murder makes the world a worse place but because no-one wants to be murdered.[91]

It might be expected that Stevens' account of the rights we do not have would simply mirror this account of the rights we have, but in fact it does not. His idea here is that besides having to be 'moral', legal rights must also be 'minimalist' rather than 'broad'.[92] The reason seems to be that in order to perform their function of protecting and promoting individual autonomy consistently with respect for others' autonomy, broad rights would have to be cut down, and this could only be done by reference to policy considerations, which judges are incompetent to assess.

This account bristles with difficulties. Consider Stevens' distinction between law and morality, which has two elements. First, for Stevens, morality strictly so-called is a product of individual reflection and reason ('in the end, each of us is alone') whereas law (like 'conventional morality') is a product of social practice. Although this characterisation of the two domains does not appeal to me, we may accept it for present purposes. The problem is this: if judicially created legal rights should reflect

---

[87] ibid, at 332.

[88] ibid, at 331.

[89] ibid, at 332.

[90] It is odd for a rights-fundamentalist to offer what sounds like a duty-based principle as the basis for rights. In Hohfeldian analysis, of course, duties and rights are formally correlative and, in that sense, equivalent. But as we have seen, the fundamentalist account of rights is quite different.

[91] In other places, Stevens makes statements that sit uneasily with this part of his analysis. For instance: 'In determining the rights we have ... a compromise is made between the interest we all have in liberty to act, and the interest we also all have in security from harm' (*Torts and Rights*, above n 31, at 107). Indeed, the negative formulation of the golden rule might itself seem to be based on the idea that moral rights protect interests.

[92] ibid, at 338.

our moral rights, and if our moral rights are the product of individual reflection and reason, why should our legal rights depend on what judges think our moral rights are? Although Stevens does not explicitly say so, I assume, on the basis of his individualistic account of the epistemology of moral rights, that he contemplates the possibility that reasonable judges may disagree about what our moral rights are. In that case, if there is a democratic objection to judges factoring social interests into decisions about what our legal rights are, surely there is also a democratic objection to their deciding, according to their own lights ('on their own'), what our moral rights are. Would it not be more 'democratic' for our legal rights to depend on legislators' views about morality?[93] Stevens might counter that judges are competent to determine what moral rights we have in a way that they are not competent to assess social policies. However, Stevens merely asserts the moral competence of judges and offers no evidence or argument in support; and anyway the reply does not explain how to resolve moral disagreements between equally competent judges.

The second element of Stevens' distinction relates to the role of social interests. In his account, 'morality' focuses on the individual whereas law encompasses society as well, and the individual's interactions with the collective. In his view, social interests may be relevant to legal rights[94] whereas moral rights are ultimately a matter of personal autonomy. It is acceptable, of course, for Stevens to understand morality and its relationship to law in this way, but it is not necessary. There is no reason to think that an individual's rational reflection on the human condition may not give weight to social as well as individual interests and no reason to deny that such reflection and its conclusions may have 'moral' status. The functions of the concept of morality in Stevens' account, like the functions of the concept of rights itself, are to protect and promote the value of individual autonomy and to limit judicial discretion.

There is good reason to think that the same is likely to be true of any fundamentalist account of the rights we have in private law. Weinrib's account, for instance, is based on the concept of Kantian right. In Beever's words, Kantian right is a 'conception of "personality"'[95] that rests on 'a very abstract account of the person'.[96] But the fact that it is very abstract does not mean that it is not value-laden—quite the opposite, in fact. It turns out that Kantian right entails a concept of the person as a self-contained, autonomous agent, without wants or needs, whose personhood is expressed entirely in action and whose only interactions are with

---

[93] It is, perhaps, ironical that while Stevens distrusts judges on issues of social policy, he is prepared to cast them as a sort of moral elite.

[94] At least those created by the legislature.

[95] Beever, above n 10, at 63.

[96] ibid, at 64.

other self-contained, autonomous, individual agents. As Beever explains,[97] Kantian right provides a possible corrective-justice account of the rights we have in private law because it informs what he calls 'that area of morality that determines how individuals should behave with respect to each other as individuals'.[98] This makes it clear that the function of rights in Weinrib's fundamentalist account of private law is to protect and pro-mote the value of human autonomy rather than other human values such as community and solidarity. Moreover, because, according to Weinrib, the institutional role of judges in relation to private law is to administer corrective justice,[99] Kantian right also functions to put consideration of social interests (or what he calls 'political considerations') beyond their province and into the domain of the legislature.

In summary, consideration of fundamentalists' approaches to the ques-tion of what rights we have confirms the earlier conclusion that despite internalist pretensions, fundamentalism is driven by an external ideology of individual autonomy and an external view about the sorts of arguments to which judges may give effect in resolving disputes and making law.

V. THE PRIORITY OF RIGHTS AND THE RELATIONSHIP BETWEEN WRONGS, RIGHTS AND DUTIES

As we have seen, in Hohfeld's account of legal rights there is no relation-ship of priority and subsidiarity between duties and rights in favour of one of these concepts or the other. Instead, Hohfeld conceptualises rights and duties as correlates. In his scheme, it is true by definition that where there is a legal duty, there is a correlative legal right and that where there is a legal right, there is a correlative legal duty. By contrast, fundamen-talists argue that in the best account of private law, the prime concept is that of a right: primary rights, not primary duties, regulate the incidence of secondary rights/duties,[100] and breach of a primary duty can attract a secondary right/duty only if it interferes with a primary right.

In so arguing, fundamentalists seem out of step with a very long tradi-tion in Western private law (Roman law, civil law and the common law) that (as Nils Jansen explains) views torts and other private law wrongs as *either* breaches of duty *or* interferences with rights.[101] Moreover, Jansen

---

[97] ibid, at 56–70.

[98] ibid, at 59.

[99] Weinrib, above n 23, at 105–07.

[100] Eric Descheemaeker, by contrast, argues that the concept of (primary) 'duty' regulates the incidence of secondary obligations: E Descheemaeker, *The Division of Wrongs: A His-torical Comparative Study* (Oxford, Oxford University Press, 2009).

[101] N Jansen, 'Duties and Rights in Negligence: A Comparative and Historical Perspec-tive on the European Law of Extracontractual Liability' (2004) 24 *Oxford Journal of Legal Studies* 443. Stevens thinks that these two approaches are 'incompatible': *Torts and Rights*, above n 31, at 1. Beever reads Jansen as supporting a rights-based interpretation of 'West-ern tort law': above n 10, at 216.

associates breach of duty with liability for fault (intention, recklessness or negligence) and infringement of rights with strict liability.[102] It is deeply ironical, then, that some fundamentalists argue that rights fundamentalism is inconsistent with strict liability. According to Weinrib, strict liability is inconsistent with Kantian right and corrective justice because it infringes individual autonomy by attaching sanctions merely to acting, which is the very core of personal autonomy. He maintains that examples of tort liability that appear on their face to be strict are in fact cases of liability for fault.[103] This rejection of strict liability creates numerous problems for Weinrib's analysis of private law, which must accommodate not only what appear to be instances of strict liability in tort law, such as liability for trespass to land,[104] but also contractual liability regardless of fault and, even more problematically, liability to restore a mistaken payment, which not only requires no fault on the part of the recipient, but no action either.[105]

Stevens' position is rather different. His choice of tort law as the subject of analysis needs to be viewed in the light of his admission that '"[t]orts" has no unity, other than that it is what is left after the other two categories of wrongs [ie, breaches of contract and equitable wrongs] are excluded'.[106] He finds no inconsistency between fundamentalism and strict tort liability. For instance, he accepts that 'the intentional torts' (by which he apparently means the various forms of trespass)[107] are actually torts of strict liability.[108] These torts are an easy case for the fundamentalist because they are most obviously explained as protecting (primary) rights. Much more difficult is (strict) vicarious liability. Beever deals with vicarious liability by categorising it as 'external to' or 'parasitic on' rather than part of 'tort law'.[109] By contrast, Stevens attempts to reconcile it with the fundamentalist dogma of 'no liability without infringement of

---

[102] In Descheemaeker's scheme, strict liability, like fault liability, is understood in terms of breach of duty—a duty not to harm as opposed to a duty to take care not to harm. For a theoretical argument in support of the idea of a duty not to harm (a 'duty to succeed' as opposed to a 'duty to try') see J Gardner, 'Obligations and Outcomes in the Law of Torts' in P Cane and J Gardner (eds), *Relating to Responsibility: Essays in Honour of Tony Honoré on His 80th Birthday* (Oxford, Hart Publishing, 2001) 111.

[103] Weinrib, above n 23, at 185–96.

[104] A person can be liable for trespass to land even if they did not know and had no reason to know that the land was not theirs. Stevens says that 'it is sufficient to show that I intended ... to walk where I did': *Torts and Rights*, above n 31, at 101. I doubt that deliberate entry is a requirement for liability for trespass to land; but even if it were, it would not introduce a fault element into the tort because there is no fault involved in entering what you reasonably believe to be your own land even if you do so deliberately.

[105] For a discussion of the way Weinrib deals with strict liability in various areas of private law see P Cane, 'Corrective Justice and Correlativity in Private Law' (1996) 16 *Oxford Journal of Legal Studies* 471, 485–87.

[106] Stevens, *Torts and Rights*, above n 31, at 286.

[107] This is confusing because there are torts such as deceit and intimidation that require an intention to harm and are, for that reason, accurately called 'intentional torts'.

[108] Stevens, *Torts and Rights*, above n 31, at 100.

[109] Beever, above n 10, at 35–36.

a primary right' by resurrecting the 'master's tort' theory, according to which what is attributed to the employer is not the employee's tort but the employee's act(s).[110] However, the theoretical basis on which he does this is less than clear. On the one hand, he claims that 'if ... words or acts [of the employee] amount to a tort, the [employer] to whom they are attributed ... is a tortfeasor'.[111] It follows (according to Stevens) that since the employee will be a tortfeasor only if the relevant acts infringe someone's rights, the employer to whom those acts are attributed will also have infringed the person's rights. In other words, vicarious liability is liability for infringement of a right by the employer. On the other hand, Stevens argues that the master's tort theory can explain vicarious liability in the absence of a tort by the employee[112] and also whether or not an employer can be vicariously liable for a breach of statutory duty by an employee.[113] In both instances, the explanation seems to be that vicarious liability depends on a *breach of duty by the employer* constituted by the acts of the employee that are attributed to the employer.[114]

This duty-based explanation supports an Hohfeldian interpretation of Stevens' position[115] according to which the employer's breach of duty is correlative to the injured person's right. However, since Stevens accepts that vicarious liability is strict, the duty he has in mind cannot be a duty of care. Instead, it must be what John Gardner calls a 'duty to succeed' as opposed to a 'duty to try'[116] or what we might also call a 'duty not to harm' as opposed to a 'duty to take care not to harm.' Because such a 'strict' duty would penalise conduct as such, Weinrib rejects the concept.[117] For Stevens, the major problem with the duty-based analysis of vicarious liability is that it appears to be inconsistent with the basic fundamentalist tenet that rights are prior to duties: in his theory of vicarious liability, the breach of duty by the employer seems to give rise to infringement of the injured person's rights. Moreover, both the rights-based analysis and the duty-based analysis of strict vicarious liability commit Stevens to the curious conclusion that a person can infringe another's rights or breach

---

[110] Stevens, *Torts and Rights*, above n 31, at 257–74. Despite significant support in the cases, Stevens dismisses the theory that vicarious liability involves attribution of the employee's tort as 'academic orthodoxy' that has led judges astray: at 274.

[111] ibid, at 260.

[112] ibid, at 263.

[113] ibid, at 264–65.

[114] See especially Stevens' explanation of *Twine v Bean's Express Ltd* [1946] 1 All ER 202 (KB): ibid, at 263 (occupier owed no duty to trespasser); and his discussion of *Majrowski v Guy's and St Thomas's NHS Trust* [2006] UKHL 34, [2007] 1 AC 224: ibid, at 265 ('the correct question is whether ... the duty is imposed on the employer').

[115] See above n 28 and accompanying text.

[116] Gardner, above n 102.

[117] Weinrib, above n 23, at 179.

a duty without doing anything that could constitute such an infringement or breach.[118]

Weinrib's choice to theorise private law and Stevens' choice to analyse tort law force them to confront the issue of strict liability head-on. By contrast, Beever's choice to focus on negligence enables him to steer clear of the Scylla of strict liability[119] but only at the risk of coming perilously close to his very own Charybdis. The snare is not difficult to spot: according to standard doctrine, negligence is breach of a duty of care owed to the victim. One might think that this would present a problem to an interpretivist and internalist, such as Beever,[120] who wants to argue that 'rights' constitute the 'base' of the tort of negligence.[121] As we have seen, Beever cannot escape by arguing that the primary duty of care is correlative (in a formal or definitional sense) to the primary rights that generate secondary duties. Precisely what fundamentalists *deny* about negligence is that the primary duty to take care generates a primary right to be treated with care that can generate a secondary duty.[122] The reason

---

[118] Stevens' answer to this objection probably would lie in the analogy he draws between vicarious liability and attribution to corporations of the acts of natural persons. However, the analogy is weak because the purpose of attribution in the two cases is quite different.

[119] Beever, above n 10, at 71. At one point Beever implies that strict liability is inconsistent with 'justice': at 81. See also Beever's statement that 'the thin skull rule ... is a restricted form of strict liability ... [and so] must not be permitted if the law is to be fair between the parties': at 166. However, he also argues (apparently with approval) that 'intentionally' using another's property without their consent may attract liability regardless of fault: at 35–36, 111–12.

[120] ibid, at 19–36. But compare Beever's startling admission that 'the law gets by in practice without much reference to primary rights' (at 217) with his recommendation that '[a]ttention must be paid to what the court actually said' (at 515). Neyers goes so far as to claim, on the basis of a single decision, that the tort of negligence 'requires a particular two-step analysis' which (as he acknowledges) finds no place in any of the general judicial expositions of the conceptual structure of the tort: '*Tate & Lyle Food and Distribution Ltd*', above n 30, at 234. Stevens argues (*Torts and Rights*, above n 31, at 306) that his rights-based account of tort law is both interpretively and normatively superior to what he calls the 'loss model', which he describes as 'probably dominant' (at 1) in the common law world. As Po Jen Yap points out, theories that are so removed from reality are unlikely to influence judicial reasoning: PJ Yap, 'Pure Economic Loss and Defects in the Law of Negligence' (2009) 17 *Tort Law Review* 80, 98.

[121] Beever, above n 10, at 210.

[122] Stevens, for instance, describes primary rights as 'specific claims' (*Torts and Rights*, above n 31, at 4) and (oddly) refers to the *duty* to take care as 'merely a shorthand for the potentially large number of primary *rights* which could be infringed' by negligent conduct (at 291). However, Stevens is not entirely consistent on this point, also stating that '[o]ne person's duty to take care not to do something correlates with another's right that they take such care': at 95. Note, too, Beever's view that assuming responsibility to be careful can generate a right to be treated with care, and that this right is correlative to a duty to take care: above n 10, at 301. In this approach, although a duty to take care does not generate a primary right to be treated with care, a primary right to be treated with care does generate a duty to take care. Stephen Perry adopts a rights-based approach but considers that 'the most fundamental right underlying negligence law is ... a right not to be harmed as a result of someone else acting negligently towards one': S Perry, 'The Role of Duty of Care in a Rights-Based Theory of Negligence Law' in A Robertson and HW Tang (eds), *The Goals of Private Law* (Oxford, Hart Publishing, 2009) 79, 101.

for this denial is clear enough: if a primary duty to take care generated a primary right to be treated with care, the concept of a primary right could not perform the function that Beever (like Stevens) attributes to it in his discussion of liability for economic loss (for instance) of limiting liability for failure to take care.

This can be seen clearly in Beever's analysis. As we have noted, he associates rights in the tort of negligence not with the conduct-related elements of the tort but with the 'consequence' element: the consequence of negligence that is the gist of the tort is the infringement of a right. If no right of the claimant has been infringed and the claimant has suffered only factual harm, there can be no liability; and this, according to Beever, explains instances of no-liability for negligence, such as that in cases of relational economic loss.[123] Indeed, Beever explains the general rule of no-liability for non-feasance in the law of negligence by defining non-feasance as conduct that does not infringe a primary right not to be injured.[124] In Beever's account, the duty of care element of the tort of negligence is concerned with whether the unreasonable risk that the defendant created (and which the defendant had a duty not to create) was foreseeably a risk *to the claimant*, not whether the defendant's conduct infringed a right of the claimant.[125] Rights are prior to duties in the fundamentalist account of the tort of negligence precisely because there can be no liability for negligence unless the claimant can identify a right not to be injured that was infringed by defendant's negligence. This right not to be injured is an independent element of the tort of negligence in addition to the other traditional elements—duty of care, negligent conduct, causation and remoteness of damage.

Why does Beever add this requirement of a right not to be injured to the traditional elements of the tort of negligence? Because, I would suggest, such a requirement is necessary to enable Beever to explain certain no-liability decisions without recourse to 'policy' arguments, and to label judicial explanations that appeal to such arguments as mistaken or, as Stevens would have it, a breach of judicial obligation.[126] Where do such rights not to be injured come from? Somewhat opaquely, Stevens calls them 'antecedent';[127] and as we saw in the previous part, he thinks that

---

[123] Beever, above n 10, at ch 7. See also Stevens, *Torts and Rights*, above n 31, at 20–43.

[124] Beever, above n 10, at 217–22. Thus, he describes causing relational economic loss as 'non-feasance': at 267. Neyers goes even further and defines 'pure economic loss' generally as harm that involves no infringement of a primary right: '*Tate & Lyle Food and Distribution Ltd*', above n 30, at 246–47.

[125] As Beever puts it, in the law of negligence the enquiry whether the claimant had a primary right is 'a proper *prerequisite* of the duty enquiry': above n 10, at 221 (emphasis in original).

[126] Stevens, *Torts and Rights*, above n 31, at 314: a judge who thinks recourse to policy is necessary should 'think again or ... resign'.

[127] ibid, at 349.

they are rooted in 'morality'. For Stevens, tort law is 'parasitic'[128] on what we might dub 'the law of rights'. Beever's position is more complex. On the one hand, he recognises that the role of tort law in relation to property rights (which are created in accordance with the rules of property law) is different from its role in relation to the right to bodily integrity: whereas tort law simply 'protects' property rights, it both 'recognises' and protects the right to bodily integrity.[129] On the other hand, he stops short of saying that tort law 'creates' the right to bodily integrity in the sense that 'property law' creates property rights. Rather he posits a 'law of persons'[130] to provide the rights base for torts such as battery, assault, defamation, false imprisonment and negligence.[131] An obvious problem with this approach is that while Roman law had such a legal category,[132] the common law does not.[133]

The reason for Beever's reluctance to say that tort law creates primary rights is, perhaps, that in his account of the tort of negligence (as we have seen), the agent's primary duty to avoid creating an unreasonable risk of the harm actually suffered by the plaintiff does not generate the primary rights that Beever identifies as constituting the base of the law of negligence, such as property rights and the right to bodily integrity. As Beever puts it, we can 'infer the existence' of the right to bodily integrity from successful claims for violation of the right[134]—in other words, from the existence of a *secondary* duty to compensate, *not* (we might add) from the existence of a *primary* duty not to create an unreasonable risk of bodily harm. In a real sense, the fundamentalists' primary rights are not found within tort law but are imposed on it by a process that Jane Stapleton graphically describes as 'reverse engineering'.[135]

---

[128] ibid, at 299.

[129] Beever, above n 10, at 212–14.

[130] ibid, at 214.

[131] Assumption of responsibility plays a central role in fundamentalist explanations of tort liability for economic loss: see, eg, P Benson, 'Should *White v Jones* Represent Canadian Law: A Return to First Principles' in JW Neyers, E Chamberlain and SGA Pitel (eds), *Emerging Issues in Tort Law* (Oxford, Hart Publishing, 2007) 141; Beever, above n 10, at ch 8. The basic argument is that assumption of responsibility creates a primary right even in the absence of contract. The obvious conclusion would seem to be that tort law 'creates' the right precisely because it can be found in no other area of the law, and Beever would apparently accept this conclusion (at 314), although he does contemplate a 'law of consents' analogous to the law of persons (at 333). However, this conclusion seems inconsistent with the feature of his analysis discussed in below n 133.

[132] See, eg, B Nicholas, *An Introduction to Roman Law* (Oxford, Clarendon Press, 1962) 60–97.

[133] It seems that in Beever's scheme, tort law cannot recognise rights in the nature of property, contractual or testamentary rights that are not recognised by the law of property, contract or wills, respectively: above n 10, at 267. This leads to the curious conclusion that tort law can recognise the right to bodily integrity only because there is no recognised category of law to which such a right belongs.

[134] ibid, at 213.

[135] Stapleton, above n 22, at 1538.

Although Beever seems satisfied that by positing various rights not to be injured he can shift the centre of gravity of negligence law from causation of harm to interference with rights and in that way force it into the Procrustean bed of fundamentalism, Stevens is not so sure that the negligence 'cuckoo'[136] can be so easily accommodated in tort law's capacious nest. This is because, unlike Beever, he finds the basic concept of the tort of negligence in faulty conduct (ie, breach of duty), not infringement of rights. His preference would be to dismantle the '*über*-tort'[137] of negligence and re-classify all torts according to the primary right(s) each protects.[138] As Stevens himself concedes, rigorous application of fundamentalist logic shows tort law to be a theoretically incoherent legal category in the sense that its various component parts are not held together by a single foundational concept, whether that be 'wrong', 'right', 'duty' or 'fault'.[139] About this he is surely correct; and in so conceding he supports the conclusion that despite claims that fundamentalism adopts an internal, interpretive perspective on tort law, in fact its prime motivations are externalist and revisionist.

VI. CONCLUSION

Because private law is riddled with rights and rights-talk, the concept of a right must figure in any adequate account of private law. However, contrary to what fundamentalists want to argue, private law is not 'all about rights' and the fundamentalist concept of a primary right is not sufficient adequately to explain the shape and scope of liability in private law. Protection of individual autonomy is certainly one of the values underpinning private law, but it also protects social interests. In this chapter I have argued that the fundamentalist insistence that primary rights provide a sufficient explanation of private law is ideologically based. The rights-fundamentalist account of private law is at least as much concerned with influencing the future of private law as with chronicling its past history and present condition, and at least as much concerned with what private law should be and do as with what it is and does.

---

[136] Stevens, *Torts and Rights*, above n 31, at 296. Interestingly, Descheemaeker uses the same metaphor: above n 100, at 232.

[137] Stevens, *Torts and Rights*, above n 31, at 295.

[138] By contrast, Beever is comfortable with the idea that 'negligence is protean and protects many types of primary rights': above n 10, at 214.

[139] Stevens, *Torts and Rights*, above n 31, at 300.

3

Our Most Fundamental Rights

ALLAN BEEVER*

I. INTRODUCTION

WHAT ARE OUR most fundamental rights? If one were to ask this question of lawyers or laypeople, the answers would be of a pattern. The English would refer to their important constitutional documents: the Magna Carta, the Bill of Rights 1689, and the Human Rights Act 1998. Scots might add the Union with Scotland Act 1706 and the Scotland Act 1998. Americans would refer to their Constitution and in particular to the Bill of Rights. Canadians would point to their Charter of Rights and Freedoms, New Zealanders to their Bill of Rights Act 1990, Germans to their Basic Law, and so on. Some in Britain and many others in Europe would mention the European Convention on Human Rights, officially called the Convention for the Protection of Human Rights and Fundamental Freedoms, and might now also point to the Charter of Fundamental Rights of the European Union.

The European documents just mentioned declare on their face that they contain rights that are fundamental. Also of significance is the doctrine of fundamental rights developed by United States courts, according to which some rights enshrined in the Constitution are to be afforded an especially high degree of deference when a court adjudicates conflicts between individual liberty and governmental intervention.

But what does it mean to say that a right is fundamental? First and most obviously, it means that the right is of great importance. Because of this, it is thought permissible to infringe the right only in exceptional circumstances. In other words, the right is at least relatively inviolable. But the claim means more than this. It means also that the right is, or ought to be recognised as, a foundational legal value. To say that a right is fundamental, then, means that it forms part of the bedrock of the legal

* Thanks to Charles Rickett and Jason Neyers. Thanks also to the Leverhulme Foundation for the Major Research Fellowship that facilitated the writing of this chapter.

system,[1] or that it should do so. We can summarise these ideas by saying that a right is fundamental to the extent to which it is both inviolable and foundational.

The idea that certain rights are fundamental lends itself to the notion that they should be enshrined in constitutional documents, protecting them from standard amendment procedures. Examples include the first 14 amendments of the United States Constitution and the Canadian Charter of Rights and Freedoms. These laws 'entrench' rights, reflecting the belief that the rights are inviolable. And the laws are constitutional—they are part of the constitution or basis of the law—reflecting the idea that the rights are foundational. This is particularly obvious with respect to the *Basic* Law of the Federal Republic of Germany.

This also explains why technically ordinary legislation that contains these rights is viewed as constitutional or quasi-constitutional. The Bill of Rights Act 1990 (NZ) and the Human Rights Act 1998 (UK) are not entrenched. In that sense, they are ordinary. Nevertheless, the legislation is understood to possess a quasi-constitutional character in virtue of the rights it contains.

This is evident even in the titles of the legislation, which would otherwise seem strangely imprecise. On its face, a Bill of Rights is a statute that presents all our rights: a Bill (ie, statute) of our rights. Similarly, a Human Rights Act would appear to be a piece of legislation that contains all the rights that human beings have. But, of course, these statutes possess only a minute subset of such rights. Why, then, do we feel no need to refer to these pieces of legislation as Bills of Some Rights, Partial Human Rights Acts, and Charters of a Few Rights and Freedoms? The answer is that these Acts are believed to contain, not all rights, but *the* rights: the fundamental rights in both senses of the term.

It is also widely held that these rights concern, at least in the first instance, the entitlements that individuals hold vis-a-vis the state. Typically, they are understood to demand legislative and other governmental restraint. For instance, the right to freedom of religion is conceptualised as a prohibition on governmental action that would prevent people holding and practising their preferred religious beliefs. It might also be thought to support certain forms of government action, for example action needed to protect minority religions.[2] These rights, then, belong to public law in the broad sense of that term.

As indicated earlier, this view is not unique to lawyers. In fact, it did not originate with lawyers. Rather, it is widely accepted that these ideas

---

[1] This claim is normative, not historical. Of course, the Human Rights Act 1998 (UK) did not exist before 1998. The idea, however, is that now that it is in force, it is foundational in the senses explained. Also, perhaps before it was in force, the norms it contains were also foundational.

[2] See, eg, the judgment of L'Hereux-Dubé J in *Adler v Ontario* [1996] 3 SCR 609.

received canonical formulations in the writings of influential political philosophers such as John Locke and Thomas Paine, who in the seventeenth and eighteenth centuries promoted the idea of fundamental human rights.[3] According to these theories, often said to lie at the heart of the liberal tradition,[4] certain rights are fundamental because they exist in the state of nature and so are preconditions of or are built into the social contract. They are fundamental, then, in that they are inviolable and in that they are the foundational values upon which our legal systems are built.

Though the views of modern political philosophers of course differ from those of seventeenth and eighteenth century thinkers, the basic pattern of modern thought is as outlined above. To take just one example, the picture painted here is clearly mirrored in the opening chapters of John Rawls' *A Theory of Justice*, about which I say more later.[5]

The view is also widely shared by the general public. Consider, for instance, this introduction to the Magna Carta written by a journalist for a general audience.

> Though it's been transformed somewhat, the Magna Carta that was signed in 1215 still forms the legal foundation of Great Britain today. Together with the Bill of Rights in the year 1791, it also became the basis for all the laws of the United States. The US Constitution draws to a large extent on the Magna Carta. And it wouldn't be an exaggeration to say that the Magna Carta provided the basis for every declaration that created the conditions for increased civil liberties and rights—at first, on the British isle, and later, on the European continent.[6]

One can fairly say that the general idea outlined above is the modern view. Almost nobody disagrees with it.

But that does not prevent it from being wrong. The rights contained in the documents mentioned above are important, of course. They may even be inviolable—I take no stand on that matter here. But they are certainly not foundational. Ironically, this idea can be illustrated by examining what many consider to be the most fundamental document of all: the Magna Carta.

---

[3] J Locke, *Two Treatises of Government* (London, 1689); T Paine, *Rights of Man; Common Sense; and Other Political Writings* (Oxford, Oxford University Press, 1995).

[4] See, eg, L Jaume, 'Hobbes and the Philosophical Sources of Liberalism' in P Springborg (ed), *The Cambridge Companion to Hobbes's Leviathan* (Cambridge, Cambridge University Press, 2007) 199, 202.

[5] It is neatly captured in the diagram in J Rawls, *A Theory of Justice*, rev ed (Cambridge MA, Harvard University Press, 1999) 94.

[6] M von Hellfeld, *The Great Charter of Freedoms: Magna Carta—June 15, 1215* (15 November 2009) Deutsche Welle, at www.dw-world.de/dw/article/1,,4621342,00.html, accessed on 19 April 2010.

II. THE MAGNA CARTA

The Magna Carta is unquestionably one of the most important documents of English law. Most significantly, it marks the transition from the idea that the king possessed arbitrary power to the notion that governmental authority can be exercised only through law. Along with other events and although special areas of prerogative power remained, it put an end to the idea that the king was above the law. As John Kelly explains:

> In the thirteenth century, above all in England, there was strong resistance to the idea that the king might be above the law; and the contrary proposition passed definitively from the realm of admonition and moral precept into that of a supposed positive constitutional rule. A famous milestone (even if one which requires interpretation in the light of its own special historical setting) is Magna Carta, the 'Great Charter' conceded by the English King John in 1215, chapter 39 of which provides that 'no free man shall be taken or imprisoned, or disseised, or outlawed or exiled or in any way ruined, nor will we go or send against him, except by the lawful judgment of his peers or by the law of the land (*per legem terrae*)'. ... '[T]he king was now under the law in the constitutional sense.'[7]

On the understanding outlined above, however, this was, quite literally, impossible.

The idea is meant to be this. Before he signed the Magna Carta, King John was (or at least could have been) above the law. However, after he signed, he was bound by the law because of the fact that he signed the Magna Carta.[8] That will not be news to anyone. The problem is that it is impossible for his signing to have had this effect on the modern view.

In order to see this, we must first understand what it meant to be above the law. Today, unfamiliar as we are with the concept, we are inclined to think that if a person is above the law, it means that there are no laws that bind that person. On this view, then, John was above the law just because, as it happened, there were no laws in effect that bound him. When he signed the Magna Carta, however, such a law came into effect and so he was no longer above the law. Simple.

But this is not what being above the law meant. The idea can be traced to Ulpian's bald assertion that 'The emperor is not bound by statutes'.[9] The claim that the king was above the law did not mean that there were no laws then in force that bound the king. It meant that even laws that

[7] JM Kelly, *A Short History of Western Legal Theory* (Oxford, Oxford University Press, 1992) 133, quoting JAP Jones, *King John and Magna Carta* (London, Longman, 1971) 105.

[8] As usual, things are much more complex than this. What we now call the Magna Carta was not the charter signed in 1215 but a later charter issued in 1225. Moreover, the actual document with which most people are familiar was not issued by John, but by Edward I. For the most part, I ignore these complications here.

[9] A Watson (tr), *The Digest of Justinian* (Philadelphia, University of Pennsylvania Press, 1998) book 1 ch 3 para 31.

claimed to bind the king were unable to do so. In other words, the idea was that no law, real or hypothetical, could bind the king, regardless of its content or origin. The king was above the law in the sense that he was immune to the law and able to govern without it.

Given this, John could not have bound himself to the rule of law in the way imagined. When John signed the Magna Carta he made a new law. He gave the Magna Carta the force of law. This law stated that John was subject to the law. But if John was above the law when he made this law, then he remained above this law too.

The point is a general one and is not focused on John or on the peculiar circumstances surrounding the Magna Carta. If a person is above the law, then she cannot make herself subject to the law. This is because one can become subject to law only through law, but a person who is not subject to the law cannot make herself subject to the law by making a law.

The point is perhaps most easily seen by imagining a defiant John violating the terms of the Magna Carta, replying to his critics by saying the following: 'When I made the law, I was above the law. Surely, the law states that I am subject to the law; but that is just a law and I am and remain above it.' What exactly is one to say to this?

Perhaps one might attempt to answer this question by pointing out that this law clearly applied to John. For instance, clause 39 of the original document states that '[n]o freeman shall be taken captive or imprisoned ... except by the lawful judgment of his peers or by the law of the land'.[10] This clearly implies that no person is entitled to seize a free man except in accordance with the rule of law. And, as John was a person, that rule applied to him.

But this argument cannot succeed as it relies on the wrong understanding of being above the law. On their face, there were other laws that applied to John. But his claim was that they did not in fact do so as he was above (immune to) the law. Accordingly, that John was captured by the terms of the Magna Carta is, in itself, irrelevant.

Perhaps the point is that John was actually named in the document and so the clauses clearly bound him. But that takes us no further. Yes, the document named him. Yes, the clauses applied to him. But they applied to him *as law* and if he were above the law when he made them then he remained above the law after he had done so. Again, that his name was used in the Magna Carta is not, in itself, relevant.

A more promising, and perhaps more obvious, answer to our question is found by focusing, not on the law itself, but on the fact that it was made by John. But again, what exactly is the significance of that point?

---

[10] This has become cl 29 of the current authorised version of the Magna Carta, which reads '[n]o Freeman shall be taken or imprisoned ... but by lawful judgment of his Peers, or by the Law of the Land'.

John made many laws and felt that he was above them all. Why not this law too?

The answer to that question is surely that John was bound by this law because, given its content and the context in which it was made, in making the law John *agreed* to be bound. This, I submit, is the silent premise that leads us to believe that the Magna Carta was binding on John. It is even suggested by the name of the law, which is usually translated as 'Great Charter' but could also be rendered 'Great Contract'.

I imagine that this appears quite unsurprising, perhaps even uninteresting. But what is remarkable is that the view is inconsistent with the modern understanding outlined in part I above. According to that view, remember, the Magna Carta is meant to be both inviolable and foundational. It is, we are told, 'the legal foundation of Great Britain'.[11] But we now see that it cannot be foundational. The Magna Carta can be of significance only if a more basic value is assumed: that people are bound by their agreements.

The reason the Magna Carta was binding, then, was not merely because it was promulgated by a person with legislative authority. As we have seen, a statute based on that alone would have had no effect on John whatsoever. The Magna Carta was binding because John agreed to be bound by it. And this is of crucial importance here because it shows that the Magna Carta is not grounded by considerations of legislative or prerogative power but by what has been called the principle of *pacta sunt servanda*, what I will call the sanctity of contract. And that means that the foundational value in operation in this context belongs to private rather than public law. It is the private element that grounds the public. The Magna Carta was important, no doubt, but it would have meant nothing without the norm that belongs to private law.

Some will object that my argument has been too legalistic. In particular, it has been put to me that the Magna Carta is not law but realpolitik. In support of this view, one might mention that the Magna Carta did little to limit the power of the monarchy before the Civil War of the seventeenth century, that indeed John felt ready to violate the Magna Carta as soon as he was out of the power of the Barons, and the in some ways corresponding desire of the Barons and others to have the Magna Carta reissued by John's successors, Henry III and Edward I.[12]

However, interesting as these historical details are, they are in the end irrelevant. The issue can be put bluntly: if I am wrong to think that the sanctity of contract is fundamental, then what was the point of getting John to sign the Magna Carta? Surely, the Barons were keen to ensure that John signed because they thought that there was some significance in

---

[11] von Hellfeld, above n 6.

[12] For an analysis of these issues, and many others, see JC Holt, *Magna Carta* (Cambridge, Cambridge University Press, 1992).

his doing so, a significance foundational enough to undercut his alleged absolute sovereignty. Certainly, this seems to have been the view of Pope Innocent III, who, concerning clause 61 of the Magna Carta that rendered John king in name only,[13] for once found himself on John's side and so was prepared to release John from his oath—an action that would have been pointless if the Magna Carta were a mere piece of realpolitik. Moreover, if I am wrong to think that the sanctity of contract was considered important, then what was the point of having John's successors agree also? Why waste time trying to secure their assent?

Furthermore, while there can be no doubt that the Magna Carta of today is in no small measure the creation of jurists such as Sir Edward Coke, it remains the case that the reason these people were so drawn to the Magna Carta was because it had been agreed to. Compare this with the United States Declaration of Independence. This, it might be thought, is another fundamental document and a piece of realpolitik. But though it is addressed in part to the British Crown (ie, King George), no one has thought that it binds the Crown. There are no modern Cokes in English courts appealing to the Declaration. In the United States it is, of course, another matter, and that is because the Declaration was there agreed to.

Naturally, the Magna Carta was a political event, but it was the political event that it was because John agreed to it. And that is possible only if the sanctity of contract is a foundational value.

Another way of putting this is to say that, whatever John and his Barons may have believed in fact, their views were inconsistent with the idea that John was ever above the law *tout court*. Moreover, whatever we believe in fact, our views are inconsistent with that idea also. This is because, like John and his Barons, we think that the sanctity of contact had sufficient purchase on John so that, when he agreed to be bound by the law, he was so bound. The best way of making sense of this is to say that, on reflection, John was above the public, but not the private, law.[14]

It is interesting to note that a similar view was enunciated by John's equally notorious successor, James I. In an infamous passage, James claimed that it was

> sedition in subjects to dispute what a king may do in the height of his power, but just kings will ever be willing to declare what they will do, if they will not incur the curse of God. I will not be content that my power be disputed upon, but I shall ever be willing to make the reason appear of all my doings, and rule my actions according to my laws.[15]

[13] The clause in question applied the practice of distraint to the monarch. This meant that the king could at any time be overruled by a 'committee' of 25 barons.

[14] Strictly speaking, as will be stressed in part IX, the claim is only that John was not above *the relevant aspect of* the private law.

[15] JP Kenyon, *The Stuart Constitution, 1603–1688: Documents and Commentary* (Cambridge, Cambridge University Press, 1966) 14.

This is often taken to mean that James thought himself above the law in the full sense.[16] In fact, however, James accepted that he was legally obliged to rule according to law. If he did not so rule then he would incur the curse of God, not merely because he would have acted unethically, but because he would have violated the natural law. Hence, James accepted that he was bound by law, or to put this another way, that it was possible for him to perform actions that were illegal. But his point was that, even so, his subjects were not entitled to pursue that illegality in court. His claim was that it is sedition to dispute what a king may do—that is, to bring court actions and the like—not that kings can do no wrong. In other words, James did not hold himself to be above the law; he did not claim that he was immune from law. Rather, he maintained merely that he was immune from suit.[17]

With our modern, largely positivist mindset, this appears to be a distinction without a difference; but it is not. On the view taken by James, it is possible for a king to waive or even abolish his immunity. He does so if he utilises the legal norms by which he is bound to give his subjects a right to pursue actions in court. Here, then, the 'paradox' examined above does not arise.

A different reply to the argument presented here holds that the sanctity of contract is a moral rather than a legal value. On this view, John's promise was binding because of the moral sanctity of agreements, a norm distinct from contract law. But this reply is misconceived. The claim is not that John was bound by his promise because of the decisions of medieval courts in cases dealing with what we now call the law of contract. Naturally, the sanctity of contract is a moral norm. But the issue is where the norm finds legal recognition. In fact, all the norms in question are moral. The legal principle of habeas corpus is said to be fundamental, because it is thought to relate to a moral norm both (relatively) inviolable and foundational. The point is this. The general view is that the most foundational area of law is the public, because that area of the law reflects those moral values that are most foundational. My argument is that this is wrong. The most foundational values are found in the private law. For instance, in English law, the origin of the principle of habeas corpus is the Magna Carta, but that document has the legal significance it does only because of a norm that underlies private, not public, law.

It is also worth stressing that when John signed the Magna Carta, the result was held to be a legally binding agreement—ie, a contract—because of the moral norm in question. The result was not a mere 'gentleman's agreement', binding in morality 'only', between John and the Barons. In other words, there was 'intent to create legal relations' and that intent

---

[16] See, eg, Kelly, above n 7, at 232–33.
[17] This idea prevailed, at least in theory, until the passage of the Crown Proceedings Act 1947 (UK).

(eventually) succeeded. The relevant norm, then, is not moral *rather than* legal. Also of significance is that James' apparent attempt to resurrect the notion that the king was above the law was widely understood to be an attack on the legal values enshrined in the Magna Carta. Hence, when Coke CJ famously criticised James' view, he appealed to that document.[18] In other words, for Coke CJ as for many others, the agreement contained in the Magna Carta had positive legal effect. That is surely also the current view. If not, then we would not think of the Magna Carta as a legal document at all, much less the most fundamental one.

In summary, then, though it is widely believed that the Magna Carta is perhaps the most fundamental legal document of all, its significance relies on a largely unnoticed value. This value is so foundational that it usually passes without notice. It is the sanctity of contract and it receives recognition in the private law.

III. HOBBES AND THE SOCIAL CONTRACT

It is instructive to note that an exact parallel of this issue is found in the work of Thomas Hobbes. And it is no coincidence that this philosopher is the progenitor of the modern view. As is well known, Hobbes presents a social contract argument for the authority of the sovereign. I briefly summarise it now.

Hobbes maintains that life without sovereign authority—ie, life in the state of nature—is 'solitary, poor, nasty, brutish, and short'.[19] This is both because human beings lack security in the state of nature and are thus always threatened with violence and because, due to the lack of security, there is no incentive to industry in that state.[20] This entails that the state of nature 'is a condition of war of every one against every one' and that in such a state no one owes any duties to others. Because of this, 'every man has a right to every thing; even to one another's body'.[21] This means that everyone has a *liberty* to the use of others' bodies, as Hobbes maintains that there are no rights—ie claim rights—in the state of nature.[22] The situation is intolerable. Therefore, when conditions make this possible, one must form a social contract that gives power to a sovereign to create and enforce law. This is the only way to achieve peace or provide the conditions that permit life to be better than solitary, poor, nasty, brutish and short.[23]

---

[18] *Prohibitions del Roy* (1607) 12 Co Rep 64, 77 ER 1342.
[19] T Hobbes, *Leviathan* (Oxford, Oxford University Press, 1996) ch 13 para 9.
[20] ibid, at ch 13 para 14.
[21] ibid, at ch 14 para 4.
[22] ibid, at ch 14 paras 1–4.
[23] ibid, at ch 14 para 5.

There are notorious difficulties with this approach. For instance, it is not clear that the state of nature is as bad as Hobbes depicts.[24] Another problem is that few have ever entered into such a contract. Perhaps those difficulties can be solved. But I wish to focus on a less noticed difficulty, though it is one detected by Hobbes himself.

The problem is simply this: why is the social contract binding? Even for a person who has freely signed the social contract, why is that contract binding? As we have seen, Hobbes maintains that there are no rights (ie, claim rights) in the state of nature. That state is a war of all against all. It is a state void, not only of positive law, but of legal norms. How, then, does the social contract bind? To put this problem a different way: Hobbes maintains that all political obligations and all law is the product of the sovereign. But if that is so, then how can the social contract bind when it is not, and cannot be, the *product of* the sovereign (it is the social contract, remember, that produces the sovereign)?

Hobbes recognises that this is a pertinent question, but he gives it a rather odd answer:

> From that law of nature, by which we are obliged to transfer to another, such rights, as being retained, hinder the peace of mankind, there followeth a third; which is this, *that men perform their covenants made*: without which, covenants are in vain, and but empty words; and the right of all men to all things remaining, we are still in the condition of war.[25]

What is the claim here?

One might argue that it involves an appeal only to prudence. On this view, the idea is that we will end up back in the state of nature if we do not keep our promise.[26] But that argument does not work. It is plausible to think that people will not leave the state of nature unless everyone agrees to form the social contract. It is perhaps even right to say that people must promise sincerely. If so, then prudence demands that individuals in the state of nature sincerely promise to obey the sovereign. But that does not mean that prudence demands that individuals keep their sincerely made promises when the transition to the civil condition has been achieved. Prudence makes that demand only if there is a strong connection between one person breaking his promise and others doing so also, hence leading to a slide back to the state of nature. But there is no reason to think that that connection exists.

---

[24] Samuel Pufendorf and Jean-Jacques Rousseau thought not. See, eg, S Pufendorf, *Of the Law of Nature and Nations* (HC Oldfather and WA Oldfather trs, Oxford, Clarendon Press, 1934) book 2 ch 2 § 7; J Rousseau, 'Discourse on the Origin of Inequality' in J Rousseau, *Basic Political Writings* (DA Cress tr and ed, Indianapolis, Hackett Publishing, 1987) 25.

[25] Hobbes, *Leviathan*, above n 19, at ch 15 para 1.

[26] R Tuck, 'Hobbes's Moral Philosophy' in T Sorrell (ed), *The Cambridge Companion to Hobbes* (Cambridge, Cambridge University Press, 1996) 190.

Consider again Hobbes' claim: 'that men perform their covenants made: without which, covenants are in vain, and but empty words'.[27] That claim is literally true only if 'men' refers to all or at least many men. But that is not the question. The passage states, not that people in general must keep their promises, but that each and every one of us must do so. Considerations of prudence are incapable of establishing this.

The passage, then, must appeal to an obligation to keep our covenants.[28] The appeal is to the kind of thought: 'but imagine if everyone did that'. As not everyone does that, the appeal must involve an appeal to morality. To put this in other terms, the problem we are grappling with is a version of the free rider problem. The question is: why should an individual not free ride on others' adherence to the rules of the civil condition? No appeal to prudence will be able to answer this question. Hobbes' rhetorical genius is revealed in the fact that his formulation is almost perfectly ambiguous as between the prudential and moral interpretation of his theory, but only the latter is able to make sense of his claims.

Accordingly, though much is opaque, what is clear is that Hobbes' argument relies on the idea that one has an obligation to obey one's covenants in the state of nature.[29] And as that obligation must exist prior to the sovereign, it binds regardless of external authority. And that means that it is foundational. It is the norm upon which the social contract and the state are based.

A different, though no less important, problem with Hobbes' theory is this: if the sanctity of contract is recognised to be a foundational value that exists prior to the state, then why would one think that it is the only such value? Surely, it is very odd to think that you have a right in the state of nature that others keep their agreements with you, but no right that they refrain from killing, maiming or wounding you. If sanctity of contract is a foundational value, then there are surely other such values. A right to bodily integrity is an obvious candidate. In other words, it is unclear why one would accept Hobbes' commitments without also being prepared to accept other foundational principles that also belong to the private law.[30] This in turn can be demonstrated by a discussion of modern political thought.

---

[27] Hobbes, *Leviathan*, above n 19, at ch 15 para 1.

[28] See also T Hobbes, *Man and Citizen (De Homine and De Cive)* (B Gert ed, Indianapolis, Hackett Publishing, 1998) ch 2 para 22, ch 3 paras 1–3, ch 6 para 20.

[29] Against this, Hobbes explicitly maintains that unperformed contracts do not obligate in the state of nature: ibid, at ch 2 para 11; Hobbes, *Leviathan*, above n 19, at ch 14 para 18. According to Hobbes, this is because, since in that state there is no guarantee that the other party will perform, there can be no obligation on one to perform. But this argument operates on the assumption that contracts create obligations per se; it is just that in the state of nature further considerations undermine that obligation, considerations that do not apply to the social contract. Again, then, we see Hobbes' account of contract covertly incorporating moral notions.

[30] For the idea that the norms are found in the criminal law, see part VII below.

IV. PRIVATE LAW NORMS IN MODERN POLITICAL PHILOSOPHY

Let us return to Rawls' theory. As is well known, Rawls argues that questions of political justice can be approached via a thought experiment in which people imagine themselves to be in what he calls the original position. This is the idea that people are to think of themselves in the state of nature—ie, a situation that is void of political and legal norms—and picture themselves coming together to form a two stage agreement. First, they are to agree on principles of justice that will govern their further deliberations and interactions.[31] Secondly, they are to agree on a constitution.[32] Later, once the first two steps have been completed, a 'fully political' stage begins in which the laws of the society are determined in accordance with the principles of justice and the constitution.[33]

Rawls recognises that a problem with this strategy is that people are likely to choose principles that benefit them unfairly. To counteract this, he insists that the deliberations be done from behind a 'veil of ignorance'. This is the idea that people will be unaware of the positions that they will hold, the kind of lives they will wish to lead, etc, in the society that they create.[34] These people, then, sit down in a convention, behind a veil of ignorance, to determine the structure of their society.

A similar theory is presented by Ronald Dworkin, whose version of the original position imagines people given the same number of clam shells that they use to bargain for the society's resources. On both of these views, the resulting principles of (distributive) justice are meant to be foundational. It is from these principles that other norms, such as those relevant to private law, are to be derived.[35]

But this is an illusion of the kind examined above. Take Dworkin's account. As noted, Dworkin asks us to imagine ourselves in the original position using clam shells to bargain for resources. But what is to stop me simply thumping you and taking your shells? And what is to prevent me agreeing to a particular distribution but then reneging on my agreement? Why am I not able to kill you in Rawls' original position or walk away from any agreement that I make? Of course, the social contract is only a thought experiment, a 'device of representation' in Rawls' words.[36] But the point is this. Rawls and Dworkin claim to be using these thought experiments to generate fundamental political and legal values. It is from

---

[31] Rawls, *A Theory of Justice*, above n 5, at 11.

[32] ibid, at 12, 172.

[33] ibid, at 174–76.

[34] ibid, at 10–11.

[35] R Dworkin, *Sovereign Virtue: The Theory and Practice of Equality* (Cambridge MA, Harvard University Press, 2000). The best account of this of which I am aware—though I am forced to disagree with it—is A Ripstein, 'The Division of Responsibility and the Law of Tort' (2004) 72 *Fordham Law Review* 1811.

[36] J Rawls, *Political Liberalism* (New York, Columbia University Press, 1993) 24.

these values that, at the end of a long chain of reasoning, we are meant to arrive at the norms of private law. In fact, however, their thought experiments *presuppose* (some of) the norms of private law. Rawls' original position does not only overtly import the veil of ignorance, it covertly imports rights to bodily integrity, to performance of a contact and (as Dworkin's version helps to make clear) property rights (or I could just take your shells). These norms, and not the ones generated by Rawls' and Dworkin's thought experiments, are foundational.

V. THE TRADITIONAL VIEW

It is interesting to note that the position being argued for was the traditional view before Hobbes, and it was even common after Hobbes, especially on the Continent amongst political philosophers who were interested in law. The view has its origin in Aristotle's *Nicomachean Ethics*. In the fifth book of that work, Aristotle distinguishes between distributive and corrective justice. The former concerns the allocation of benefits and burdens throughout society as a whole, the latter the justice of interactions between individuals. Moreover, Aristotle maintains that both forms of justice rely on a conception of equality, but that that conception is politically controversial only in the case of distributive justice.[37]

Unsurprisingly, this means that distributive justice is political and is essentially connected with the state. More surprisingly, however, it means that corrective justice is not political and, as a value, is entirely independent of the state. Consequently, corrective justice generates rights that depend on the state only for their enforcement, and those rights include a right to have contractual promises performed and a right to bodily integrity.[38] These rights, then, are more foundational than those that arise in the political context.

Unsurprisingly, a very similar view is found in Thomas Aquinas.[39] Our right to life, to bodily integrity, to contractual performance and to property are, he argues, based on commutative justice.[40] These rights pre-exist the sovereign.

Hugo Grotius also bases the same rights on what he calls expletive

---

[37] Aristotle, *Nicomachean Ethics* (T Irwin tr, Indianapolis, Hackett Publishing, 1999) paras 1131a–1134a.

[38] For discussion, see A Beever, *Rediscovering the Law of Negligence* (Oxford, Hart Publishing, 2007) 56–61 and A Beever, 'Justice and Punishment in Tort: A Comparative Theoretical Analysis' in CEF Rickett (ed), *Justifying Private Law Remedies* (Oxford, Hart Publishing, 2008) 249, 253–56, where I show that corrective justice is concerned with far more than merely correcting injustices.

[39] T Aquinas, *Summa Theologica* (Fathers of English Dominican Province trs, New York, Benziger Bros, 1947) part 2(2) question 61 art 3.

[40] ibid, at part 2(2) question 61 art 1 reply 5, part 2(2) questions 64–66.

rather than attributive justice and makes clear that expletive justice is prior to the political.[41] The consequence of this view finds very explicit expression in Samuel Pufendorf, who in his eight-book *Of the Law of Nature and Nations* discusses the justification of bodily integrity in the first chapter of book three, the right to contractual performance in the fifth to eighth chapters of that book, and property rights in the fourth to the ninth chapters of book four; but does not concern himself with the justification of the state until book eight. The same can be said of Immanuel Kant, who in the *Rechtslehre* examines private law before public law, arguing that the latter is dependent on the former.[42] The view is also clearly found in GWF Hegel, for whom private law is conceptually prior to the state.[43]

Though other events are also responsible, it is largely because of the influence of Hobbes that we find these views so difficult to understand today. In fact, they are so foreign to the modern way of thinking that they are frequently ignored.[44]

VI. LOCKE, PRIVATE LAW AND CONSTITUTIONAL RIGHTS

As indicated above, Locke is usually thought to be a progenitor of the modern view. But this is wrong. In fact, Locke is a proponent of the traditional view.

According to Locke:

> The state of nature has a law of nature to govern it, which obliges every one: and reason, which is that law, teaches all mankind, who will but consult it, that being all equal and independent, no one ought to harm another in his life, health, liberty, or possessions ...[45]

Because Locke maintained that these rights are retained on entry into society,[46] the rights are also held against the sovereign. This idea played an enormous role in the development of many of the documents considered to contain our most fundamental rights.

For Locke, the problem with the English political situation in the latter

---

[41] H Grotius, *De Jure Belli ac Pacis Libri Tres* (FW Kelsey tr, Oxford, Clarendon Press, 1925) book 2 ch 12, book 2 ch 17.

[42] I Kant, *Practical Philosophy* (MJ Gregor tr and ed, Cambridge, Cambridge University Press, 1996) paras 6:307–6:308.

[43] GWF Hegel, *Elements of the Philosophy of Right* (HB Nisbet tr, AW Wood ed, Cambridge, Cambridge University Press, 1991) §§ 41–104, §§ 257–329.

[44] For instance, even a work as fine as Kelly, above n 7 makes no mention of the fact that the vast majority of the thinkers it examines held that the norms of private law were more foundational than those of public law and that the authority of the state is somehow based upon the former norms.

[45] Locke, above n 3, at book 2 § 6.

[46] ibid, at book 2 chs 11–13.

seventeenth century, the problem that led him to write the *Two Treatises of Government*, was not that these rights received inadequate legal recognition. It had long been the law that 'no one ought to harm another in his life, health, liberty, or possessions'. The problem was that, in Locke's view, Charles II had begun to interfere with these rights (illegally) in certain areas and that the future James II was bound to extend this. In other words, the point of insisting on these fundamental rights was not to maintain that they ought to receive legal recognition, it was to insist that Charles II respect them.

Similar ideas are found in the battles between James I and Coke. Coke's allegations were not that James ought to recognise rights that did not before exist. They were that James ought to respect the rights long recognised by the common law.

Returning to Locke, his position was that rights to life, health, liberty, and possessions had long been recognised. The problem was that they were under threat from the actions of Charles II. Where did they exist? Predominately, in the private law. Where was the threat? From the prerogative and legislative power of the king; in other words, from public law.

Hence, Locke's position in this regard is the exact reverse of the modern one. We think that the public law contains and protects our fundamental rights. But Locke thought that the public law contained the most significant threat to our fundamental rights, rights found (predominantly) in the private law.

In the hands of later theorists, Locke's ideas were translated into the notion that fundamental rights ought to be protected by public law (eg, by the constitution). Though it is common to attribute these ideas to Locke, they are found nowhere in his works. In fact, if the modern view is not to depart altogether from Locke's, it must hold that public law (via constitutional and quasi-constitutional rights) provides the answer to the threat that it itself poses (via prerogative and legislative power).[47] Though we are oblivious to it, this view is perfectly consistent with the notion that our foundational rights are at least primarily a matter of private law. Moreover, as I now suggest, we can see on reflection that this is how our constitutional or quasi-constitutional law operates.[48]

Consider, for instance, the protection for freedom of religion provided by section 2(a) of the Canadian Charter of Rights and Freedoms. The case law based on this section deals with issues that would come as a

---

[47] In fact, this was the view of the United States founding fathers who feared, perhaps more than anything else, the tyranny of the majority (ie, the legislative power of the plebs).

[48] The general point of the arguments that follow was also made, though in a very different fashion, by AV Dicey, *Introduction to the Study of the Law of the Constitution* (Indianapolis, Liberty Fund, 1982) chs 4–10.

surprise to those inexperienced in law. The most important cases examine prohibitions on trading on the Christian Sabbath;[49] the funding, oversight and regulation of religious education in schools;[50] and medical treatment of minors against the religious beliefs of their parents.[51] These issues are important, but they are hardly the ones for which millions of people died in the Thirty Years' War.[52]

What are the most fundamental aspects of freedom of religion? They are, surely, the right to hold one's own religious views and to gather with others in order to practise that religion. Why, then, is there no case law in Canada dealing with those issues? The answer is obvious; indeed so obvious that it often escapes notice. Those aspects of freedom of religion are protected by other areas of the law and were so protected long before the Charter came into effect.

How can freedom of religion be violated? If I wished to violate your freedom, I could physically restrain you from attending your place of worship or threaten you so that you feel unable to attend. I could constrain you so that you are unable to leave your house to attend. Or I could lie about you or spread stories about you so that you are unwelcome amongst your coreligionists. All of these would constitute torts: battery, assault, false imprisonment, injurious falsehood and defamation respectively. Moreover, I could violate your freedom of religion by destroying your places of worship or by preventing you from accessing them (without imprisoning you). These actions would also be torts: they are trespasses to property or nuisances.

Similarly, it is common to claim that freedom of movement is protected by the Privileges and Immunities Clause of the United States Constitution, which states that '[t]he Citizens of each State shall be entitled to all Privileges and Immunities of Citizens in the several States'.[53] In *Corfield v Coryell*,[54] the Court found a right to freedom of movement in this clause. In *Paul v Virginia*, the Supreme Court defined this right as the 'right of free ingress into other States, and egress from them'.[55] Since then, court action has focused in two main areas. First, there has been dispute as to whether the entitlement to protect this right falls to the State or federal

---

[49] *R v Big M Drug Mart Ltd* [1985] 1 SCR 295; *Edwards Books and Art Ltd v The Queen* [1986] 2 SCR 713.

[50] *Zylberberg v Sudbury Board of Education (Director)* (1988) 52 DLR (4th) 577 (Ontario Court of Appeal); *Trinity Western University v British Columbia College of Teachers* [2001] SCC 31, [2001] 1 SCR 772; *Re Corporation of the Canadian Civil Liberties Association* (1990) 65 DLR (4th) 1 (Ontario Court of Appeal); *Reference Re Bill 30, an Act to Amend the Education Act (Ontario)* [1987] 1 SCR 1148; *Adler v Ontario* [1996] 3 SCR 609.

[51] *B (R) v Children's Aid Society of Metropolitan Toronto* [1995] 1 SCR 315.

[52] Estimates for deaths during the war range from about 3 million to nearly 12 million.

[53] US Constitution, art IV § 2.

[54] *Corfield v Coryell* 6 Fed Cas 546 (ED Pa 1823).

[55] *Paul v Virginia* 75 US 168 (1869) 180 (Field J for the Court).

governments.[56] Secondly, there has been argument about whether the federal government is entitled to refuse passports to those it believes will act abroad in ways of which it disapproves[57] or to those who have failed to pay child support.[58] Again, these issues are important, but they are not ones a political philosopher would or should use to illustrate the fundamental importance of the right to freedom of movement. Being placed under house arrest or being wrongly imprisoned would be more appropriate. Again, the reason United States constitutional law has not concerned itself with these issues is that these aspects of freedom of movement are protected by other areas of the law, in particular by the law of tort.

Frequently, then, in a way that mirrors the discussion of Locke above, the force of the legal recognition of constitutional or quasi-constitutional rights is not, 'recognise these heretofore unrecognised rights', but 'stop interfering with the rights recognised in the private law'.

VII. THE CRIMINAL LAW

Of course, the rights mentioned above are not protected exclusively by the law of tort. Many are also secured by the criminal law. And that law is, of course, public rather than private. I have insufficient space to deal with this issue fully here, but the following comments are pertinent.

In general, criminal lawyers argue that the concept of crime is essentially connected with the state and community. According to Andrew Ashworth, for example:

> The idea of crime is that it is something that rightly concerns the State, and not just the person(s) affected by the wrongdoing. Many crimes are civil wrongs as well (torts or breaches of contract, for example), and it is for the injured party to decide whether or not to sue for damages. But the decision to make conduct into a crime implies that there is a public interest in ensuring that such conduct does not happen and that, when it does, there is the possibility of State punishment.[59]

On this view, then, while it is true to say that battery is a crime because of a concern for individuals' bodily integrity, that concern is not in itself a sufficient justification or explanation. Instead, there is also a need to refer to the public interest. My claim is that, if true, that fact demonstrates that the criminal law is less foundational (but not less important) than private law.

---

[56] See, eg, *Ward v Maryland* 79 US 418 (1871); *United States v Guest* 383 US 745 (1966).

[57] See, eg, *Aptheker v Secretary of State* 378 US 500 (1964).

[58] See, eg, *Weinstein v Albright* 261 F 3d 127 (2nd Cir 2001).

[59] A Ashworth, *Principles of Criminal Law*, 6th edn (Oxford, Oxford University Press, 2009) 2.

VIII. FUNDAMENTAL RIGHTS AND FUNDAMENTAL REMEDIES

It might be said, however, that attention to the mechanisms by which the private law operates reveals that it cannot be fundamental in the sense under examination. Two issues are of crucial importance. First, actions in private law concern individuals. They pit one person against another. Not only does this leave out the state, it also omits every other individual. Nothing fundamental would do so. Secondly, when the private law detects a wrong, it responds only by requiring the wrongdoer to make good the wrong committed, typically through compensation. There is nothing fundamental about that. I examine these arguments in turn.

As indicated in part III above, Hobbes has had an enormous influence on our understanding of the political and the legal. His ideas that the foundational political norms are obligations owed to the state (coupled, perhaps with the un-Hobbesian thought that the state might also owe obligations to us) and that legal norms are created by the sovereign or by those to whom the sovereign has delegated authority (eg, judges) are held by many to be axiomatic. But it need not be so. Surely, on reflection, there is nothing odd in the idea that our fundamental political obligations[60] are owed to each other as individuals, obligations out of which our obligation to the state is generated.

In short, if it is plausible to think that the most basic political norms run between individuals, then we need not think that the private law cannot deal in foundational values merely because it deals with interactions between individuals. On the contrary, we may think that the private law is foundational because of that very feature. And the fact that an individual case deals with only two individuals does not undermine its foundational status. *A v B* is itself about only A and B, but it lays down a principle relevant to anyone similarly situated. It is, in that sense, relevant to all.[61]

What, then, should we say about the private law's responses to wrongdoing? The first thing to say is that the traditional thinkers mentioned earlier very definitely did not share the view that because the private law responds in a (largely) remedial fashion it cannot be foundational. All

---

[60] By 'political obligations', I here refer to obligations that legitimate coercion. Of course, one might define 'political' to refer only to the state. But the debate is not about the best use of terminology.

[61] And note that, the fact that *A v B* is relevant to all in this way does not mean that *A v B* should be decided by considering the interests of all. In fact, that the principle enunciated in *A v B* is relevant to all who are similarly situated shows that *there is no point whatsoever* in considering the interests of anyone other than A and B. If the decision is just as between A and B, then it will be just as between anyone similarly situated in the relevant way. Or to put this another way, as the decision only applies to others if they are similarly situated, as long as A and B's interests are properly taken into account, the ratio of *A v B* will respect others' interests as well.

of these thinkers regard a duty to repair[62] as secondary but nevertheless fundamental. In other words, the duty is consequent to the violation of a primary right, but it does not depend on other notions. For Aristotle, as we have seen, distributive and corrective justice are the two forms of justice and the latter has immediate, non-political content. Hence, the duty to repair violations of foundational rights is itself foundational in the relevant sense. For instance, the duty to compensate for harm is not the product of a social policy designed to promote some social end. It is a basic principle of justice.[63] Aquinas' view is the same.[64] Similarly, Grotius and Pufendorf argue that a duty not to harm—which as we have seen is foundational—immediately entails a duty to remedy any harm caused.[65] In the words of Pufendorf—and here one should note the connection between the primary and the secondary duty and the absence of policy-type reasoning:

> *If anyone has done another some hurt, and has caused him in any way some loss, which can properly be imputed to the aggressor, the aggressor must, so far as he can, make good the loss.* For it is surely a vain thing to have given orders that a person receive no hurt, if, when such hurt befalls him, he must accept the loss at his own cost, while the man who offered him the hurt may enjoy the fruit of his injury in peace and without making restitution.[66]

Moreover, if we put aside our modern legal indoctrination for a moment, it is easy to see why these thinkers held that view. There is surely no remedy more basic than the repair of a wrong. If I wrongly injure you, the most immediate duty I have is to repair that injury. If I promise to do something for you, the fundamental duty I have is to perform that promise. If I do not, then my immediate duty is to make good my failure to do so. These are common sense notions that clash with the lawyer's 'common sense' only because of the pernicious influence of her training.[67] Who apart from a lawyer would have thought that the duty to compensate for a wrongly caused injury must be explained in terms of social policy or that there is no natural duty to keep a promise or, failing that, to put the promisee in the position in which he would have been had the promise been kept?[68]

---

[62] As I use the term, it is meant to include compensation, disgorgement, restitution, and so on.

[63] Aristotle, above n 37, at paras 1131b–1134a.

[64] Aquinas, above n 39, at part 2(2) question 62 arts 1–3.

[65] Grotius, above n 41, at book 2 ch 17 para 1; Pufendorf, above n 24, at book 3 ch 1 § 2.

[66] Pufendorf, above n 24, at book 3 ch 1 § 2 (emphasis in original).

[67] See also EJ Weinrib, 'Can Law Survive Legal Education?' (2007) 60 *Vanderbilt Law Review* 401.

[68] cf LL Fuller and WR Perdue Jr, 'The Reliance Interest in Contract Damages' (1936) 46 *Yale Law Journal* 52. Cf also J Gardner, 'The Purity and Priority of Private Law' (1996) 46 *University of Toronto Law Journal* 459, 474 who speaks of the 'well-known mystery of how reparation or restitution may serve to correct [wrongdoing]'. If there is such a mystery, however, it is not well-known and it is notable that Gardner does not cite any discussion

IX. FOUNDATIONAL RIGHTS

In part I of this chapter, we saw that rights can be fundamental in two senses. They can be inviolable and they can be foundational. We have also seen that our foundational rights are found, at least primarily, in the private law. It is important to spell out just what this does and does not mean.

First, it does not mean that private law rights are inviolable. I have argued that they are foundational, but there is no need to think that foundational rights need be inviolable. To think in that way is to make a mistake of the kind made by the United States Supreme Court in *Lochner v New York*,[69] a case that receives no support from the argument here. I do not, therefore, support a sort of human rights-isation of the private law. In fact, the argument here is not committed to the desirability of modern human rights law at all. Secondly, I have not argued that all of the rights found in the private law are foundational. Demonstrating the truth or falsity of that view would require more space than I have available here (for the record, I think the claim false, though much depends on what one means by 'private law'). Thirdly, there is no suggestion that all of our foundational rights and obligations are found in the private law. Finally, it is not claimed that private law is more fundamental than public law. The view is that neither area of the law can accurately be described as more fundamental than the other. One is more fundamental in one way, the other is more fundamental in the other.

X. PRIVATE LAW RIGHTS AND THE MODERN APPROACH TO PRIVATE LAW

So far, the thrust of this chapter may appear to be that public lawyers, particularly human rights lawyers, should get off their high horse (to the extent that they are on one) and recognise that other areas of the law are equally as fundamental as theirs. That is part of the message, but it is not central. The thrust is rather aimed at private lawyers themselves. The principal idea is that mainstream private law scholarship, though often informative and advantageous, frequently misunderstands the nature of its subject.

---

of it. (There is a well-known mystery about the purpose of criminal punishment, a mystery that goes back to at least Plato's *Gorgias*, but that is a different matter.) Of course, the common sense notion may be philosophically suspect and require proper analysis, but that does not justify presenting it as if it were in violation of common sense.

[69] *Lochner v New York* 198 US 45 (1905).

It seems that few modern lawyers think that there is anything fundamental about the private law. Rather, the modern view understands the private law to be an aspect of the state's management of society. On this picture, the norms of private law belong on a level with the government's economic and social policies. The ultimate expression of this idea is, of course, law and economics, but it is reflected in many other approaches. Consider, for instance, the nearly ubiquitous reference to 'policy'. The general thought is nicely captured in the title of a recent article by Lord Bingham, 'The Uses of Tort',[70] which indicates that tort law is an instrument to be used for achieving desirable ends in the same sort of way as, say, monetary or fiscal policy.

This approach finds its zenith in the law of tort, but it is not so restricted. Consider the claim that contract law is best understood by focusing on its 'core purpose', which is held to be the delivery of 'a regulatory framework within which exchange can take place',[71] and three subsidiary functions: facilitating exchange, protecting vulnerable parties and the public interest from improper use of the law of contract, and providing a contractual dispute resolution mechanism.[72] My point in drawing attention to these claims is not to deny that contract law does these things or that it is valuable because it does so. The point is that this misses the 'core' of the law.

One way to reveal this is to consider a parallel case. Imagine a human rights lawyer describing her area of law as follows: 'The core purpose of human rights law is to provide a regulatory framework within which human rights can be respected, to facilitate respect for human rights, to protect persons and the public interest from misuse of human rights, and to provide a resolution mechanism for disputes about human rights.' The key thing to notice is that, although human rights law indeed possesses these features, the description is odd nonetheless. Human rights law is not (or is not meant to be) a mere method of regulation. It is meant to be, at its heart, concerned with the recognition and protection of fundamental values.

And so too is the law of contract. The 'core purpose' of contract law is not regulation (though contract law regulates, of course) but the recognition and enforcement of binding agreements. That is fundamental. Ironically, the claim may appear bland precisely because the value is so fundamental.

---

[70] Lord Bingham, 'The Uses of Tort' (2010) 1 *Journal of European Tort Law* 3.
[71] R Brownsword, *Contract Law: Themes for the Twenty-First Century* (London, Butterworths, 2000) 23.
[72] ibid, at 24–25.

Witness also this passage that opens one of English law's leading tort textbooks: 'Today the law of tort is mainly, though by no means exclusively, concerned with "accidents" arising in countless ways'.[73] The book then examines the nature and frequency of these accidents before exploring the attitudes of various persons to the way in which the law responds to them.[74] Of course, no one denies that tort law deals with losses and that it is valuable in part because it does so. But this is a strange way to begin a book aimed to describe an area of law that deals with some of our most fundamental rights.

The view under examination is also found in the notion that the key to understanding tort law is found in a list of policy concerns of a kind that would interest a legislator. For instance, it has been suggested that tort law is best understood as one of society's ways of achieving various policy goals, including compensation, relieving individuals of the financial costs of injuries, deterrence of harmful conduct, minimising harmful conduct, education, appeasement and an 'ombudsman function'.[75] Such claims are routine. However, I suggest that at the very least they miss what is central to the law.

Most significantly, there is surely no right more fundamental—foundational and inviolable—than bodily integrity, and yet tort lawyers frequently deal with it as if it were a mere concern of social policy, to be placed alongside other concerns such as economic efficiency, the public interest, and administrative judicial convenience.

The deleterious consequences of the modern approach are practical as well as theoretical (to the extent to which the practical and the theoretical can be separated in law). A good example of the former has been pointed out by Tony Weir (incidentally, no champion of so-called 'corrective justice' or 'rights based' theories). Speaking of cases such as *Percy v Hall*[76] and *McGrath v Chief Constable of the Royal Ulster Constabulary*,[77] cases involving alleged false imprisonment, Weir complains that they 'illustrate how the salutary rules of trespass are being invaded by negligence-type thinking: the police were excused because what they did was perfectly reasonable, they were not at fault. But rights must be protected even against reasonable conduct which infringes them'.[78] Weir does not tell us why these rights must be so protected. He does not need to. The answer

---

[73] S Deakin, A Johnston and B Markesinis, *Markesinis and Deakin's Tort Law*, 6th edn (Oxford, Clarendon Press, 2008) 3.

[74] ibid, at 3–16.

[75] This view is presented, though not endorsed, in A Robertson, 'Introduction: Goals, Rights and Obligations' in A Robertson and HW Tang (eds), *The Goals of Private Law* (Oxford, Hart Publishing, 2009) 1, 3–4.

[76] *Percy v Hall* [1996] 4 All ER 523 (CA).

[77] *McGrath v Chief Constable of the Royal Ulster Constabulary* [2001] UKHL 39, [2001] 2 AC 731.

[78] T Weir, *An Introduction to Tort Law*, 2nd edn (Oxford, Oxford University Press, 2006) 139–40.

is clear: they are fundamental. And one of the reasons these rights have not been properly protected is because tort lawyers have come to think of the law as nothing more fundamental than a system of regulation for the public interest.

XI. OUR MOST FUNDAMENTAL RIGHTS AND THE ROLE OF PRIVATE LAW

As we saw in part III above, Hobbes' political philosophy has the following structure. First, he maintains that there are no legal or political obligations in the state of nature. Secondly, he argues that people must leave that state and enter a society with political authority. Third, he maintains that that authority creates political and legal norms. Though many aspects of Hobbes' account are unpopular today, almost all agree that political philosophy must share that basic structure. It is deeply ingrained in our perception of the political world.

But it is just the modern view. It was not the view of the thinkers examined in part V above. And we need not adopt it. Of course, this topic is too big to be examined here. I can end only with some brief comments.

Our understanding of politics and law is grounded on a distinction between what we might call political and mere moral values. Kant made this distinction by contrasting the juridical with the ethical aspects of morality: the *juridisch* with the *ethisch*, *das Recht* with *die Ethik*.[79] Similarly, Rawls distinguishes between right on the one hand and the concepts of value and moral worth on the other.[80] The main point of these distinctions is to draw a line between the obligations that legitimate coercion and those that do not. Politics, it is held, is about the former.

But if that is true, then, despite the pervasiveness of the idea in the modern world, is there any reason to believe that our fundamental political obligations are a creation of political authority as Hobbes thought? Is it not more likely that our most foundational political obligations are owed to others as individuals? Think about it this way. Which is the most plausible view: that the most basic reason I should not hit you, *and can be prevented from hitting you*, is because the state, for its good reasons, says that I must not; or because I owe you, directly, an obligation not to? Your legal training inclines you to say the former but, even despite the influence of the modern view, it is recognisably less attractive than the latter.

---

[79] Kant, above n 42, at paras 6:218–6:221.
[80] Rawls, *A Theory of Justice*, above n 5, at 94.

And if our fundamental political obligations are in personam in this way, then which institutions in our societies deal with them? Not the legislature and not public law, but private law. That area of the law deals with our most foundational political obligations.

As we have seen, that is not how matters are generally thought of today. To many, the view will appear outlandish. But it is, as I have argued above and hope to show in more detail in future, the traditional one. That is why it was routine to examine private law before public law or politics in works of political philosophy.

There are many reasons why this view has been forgotten. And in areas such as this, it is always difficult to separate cause and effect, in part because an effect soon becomes itself a cause. As I have argued, we live in an age in which the fundamental values that are found in private law are largely ignored. This is in part because modern lawyers ignore those values or treat them as mere policy concerns. The result is that individuals do not receive the moral respect from the private law that they deserve. A further consequence is that individuals are encouraged by the law to think of other individuals as resources to be used for their ends. After all, that was very clearly how the House of Lords used the claimant in *Hill v Chief Constable of West Yorkshire Police*[81] and how many courts have used many parties. But the influence runs in both directions. It is because we live in an age in which there is little respect for individuals as such (despite the contrary rhetoric), where governments routinely frame their policies 'for the good of society' as if society were a single organism, an age where we speak unabashedly of human resources as if human beings were things to be used up, that private lawyers have so easily and so apparently naturally treated the law as they have. For most private lawyers, though they would wish to reject the description, the parties are to be treated as means for realising some social end. Some of these ends are good for the parties and even wanted, such as compensation for plaintiffs, but one does not escape the charge of treating people as means simply by pointing to the fact that the ends are good or desired.

We might summarise these thoughts in language already introduced by saying that this is the age of human resources. And we should note that, in Commonwealth jurisdictions such as Canada, New Zealand and the United Kingdom, we have felt the need for legislation of the kind examined at the beginning of this chapter for precisely that reason. Human rights law is the ambulance at the bottom of the cliff. We need it in part because the fence at the top, constructed in no small part by the private law, has been torn down. But it is worse than this, as that law now encourages people to fall down. The claim is exaggerated but it will

---

[81] *Hill v Chief Constable of West Yorkshire Police* [1989] 1 AC 53 (HL). For analysis, see Beever, *Rediscovering the Law of Negligence*, above n 38, at 180–81.

serve as a conclusion to this chapter: human rights law is what we get when conditions are such that private lawyers ignore the foundations of their discipline.[82]

---

[82] Because of criticisms raised against my work by Peter Cane in 'Rights in Private Law' ch 2 of this book, it is necessary briefly to clarify the relationship between this investigation and the material Cane attacks. Unlike much of my previous work, this is not a piece of interpretive legal theory. It belongs to the study of political philosophy, broadly conceived. The project to which it belongs, then, is not the same project as that found in *Rediscovering the Law of Negligence* (above n 38) and the like. Though this is not the place to respond to Cane's criticisms in detail, the following remarks are pertinent.

In general, the basic problems with Cane's criticisms are these. First, he treats *Rediscovering the Law of Negligence* and similar works—particularly R Stevens, *Torts and Rights* (Oxford, Oxford University Press, 2007)—almost as if they were reruns of positions that he might have studied as a student. Because of this, his objections to these works repeat arguments—or rather, to be more accurate, assert conclusions—relevant only in a different context. As a result, Cane does not confront the positions advanced in the works he criticises, nor does he get to grips with them, but instead shoehorns those positions into pigeonholes with which he is more familiar. This is why Cane must so often speculate on the content of and motivations for the positions that he ascribes to his opponents, often attributing to them views that they explicitly reject. The result is that it is difficult for the authors of those views to recognise their ideas in Cane's presentations of them. In fact, in attributing to his opponents motivations and drives that they claim not to have, Cane's approach has more than the air of a conspiracy theory. Moreover, a fact that helps to explain the first error, in common with many others Cane virtually ignores the arguments presented in these works, preferring merely to assert his dissatisfaction with their conclusions. There is little to be learnt from this.

This chapter is intended to be politically transformative. What is more, the position advanced here expresses a concern for individuals and it insists on treating individuals as such rather than merely as elements in the collective. That is a position for which no liberal need apologise.

4

Social Purposes, Fundamental Rights and the Judicial Development of Private Law

FRANÇOIS DU BOIS*

I. INTRODUCTION

WORLDWIDE, PRIVATE LAW is increasingly subjected to the influence of rights laid down in international and constitutional charters. Since these fundamental rights have their origin in attempts to control the actions of state institutions, this is a striking development. It is also an important one, as such horizontal application of fundamental rights is present in a rising number of countries and a growing range of areas of private law.[1] However, there is equally widespread uncertainty and debate about the nature of this interaction. In Germany, where this development goes back more than 50 years, the rival theories of 'direct third-party effect' and 'indirect third-party effect' still have their supporters, now vying with those who find the roots of this interaction in the state's duties to protect individuals against one another.[2] Even as

* This chapter is part of a project on human rights and private law funded by a British Academy grant. Early versions were presented at the Obligations V conference in Oxford and at the Max Planck Institute for Comparative and International Private Law in Hamburg, and I thank participants at both events for helpful comments and advice. Antje du Bois-Pedain generously shared ideas and helped to improve their expression. I am very grateful to the British Academy and the German Academic Exchange Service (DAAD) for financing my research stay in Hamburg and to Professor Reinhard Zimmermann for hosting me.

[1] See D Friedman and D Barak-Erez (eds), *Human Rights in Private Law* (Oxford, Hart Publishing, 2001); A Sajó and R Uitz (eds), *The Constitution in Private Relations* (Utrecht, Eleven International Publishing, 2005); D Oliver and J Fedtke (eds), *Human Rights and the Private Sphere* (Abingdon, Routledge-Cavendish, 2007).

[2] See G Brüggemeier, 'Constitutionalisation of Private Law—The German Perspective' in T Barkhuysen and SD Lindenbergh (eds), *Constitutionalisation of Private Law* (Leiden, Martinus Nijhoff Publishers, 2006) 59 and the literature there cited. The theory of direct effect treats private persons as addressees of fundamental rights and thus directly bound by them, while the theory of indirect effect holds that private persons are not so bound

the Human Rights Act 1998 is making its presence felt in all corners of the legal system of the United Kingdom, the issue is mostly fudged and avoided in the upper reaches of the judiciary, aided and abetted by an academic literature in which all positions find support.[3] And South Africa's Constitutional Court, often cited as a leader in this field, stands accused of failing to give effect to a clear constitutional choice favouring direct application.[4]

This state of affairs should not surprise anyone. So far, discussion of this trend has overwhelmingly proceeded from the perspective of international and constitutional law. The arguments dominating this discussion are usually technical and dogmatic in tone, being rooted in specific documents and doctrines. However, the broad language of fundamental rights documents, which typically leave open the precise manner in which they are to be complied with, inevitably renders them inconclusive.[5] The surprisingly popular argument that it follows from the status of courts as state institutions or public authorities subject to fundamental rights that they are compelled to apply these rights when adjudicating disputes between private persons[6] does not take us any further. Everything depends on the content of the right in question.[7] If a right imposes duties only on public authorities, then the duty of a court to give effect to the right cannot compel the court to apply it against a private person. Perhaps in order to avoid this conundrum, courts in several countries have insisted that fundamental rights also constitute a system of values or principles suffusing the legal order as a whole, and have then proceeded to apply these values to disputes among private persons.[8] But the same challenge

---

but are affected indirectly since fundamental rights represent core values that 'radiate' into every part of the legal system.

[3] See the overview by A Young, 'Horizontality and the Human Rights Act 1998' in KS Ziegler (ed), *Human Rights and Private Law: Privacy as Autonomy* (Oxford, Hart Publishing, 2007) 35. On Scotland specifically, see H MacQueen and D Brodie, 'Private Rights, Private Law, and the Private Domain' in A Boyle et al (eds), *Human Rights and Scots Law* (Oxford, Hart Publishing, 2002) 141.

[4] See S Woolman, 'The Amazing, Vanishing Bill of Rights' (2007) 124 *South African Law Journal* 762.

[5] Even the South African Constitution, which addresses this issue directly, says no more than that '[a] provision of the Bill of Rights binds a natural or a juristic person if, and to the extent that, it is applicable, taking into account the nature of the right and the nature of any duty imposed by the right': s 8(2).

[6] See, eg, *Shelley v Kraemer* 334 US 1 (1948); *Campbell v MGN Ltd* [2004] UKHL 22, [2004] 2 AC 457 (*Campbell*) [114] (Lord Hope), [132] (Lady Hale); C-W Canaris, *Grundrechte und Privatrecht* (Berlin, Walter de Gruyter, 1999), especially at 31, 93.

[7] See also K Doehring, *Das Staatsrecht der Bundesrepublik Deutschland*, 3rd edn (München, Beck, 1984) 209. This is the fundamental reason why the approach to the US state action doctrine inaugurated by *Shelley v Kraemer* 334 US 1 (1948) has proven so unsatisfactory: see the criticism by Aharon Barak of 'the application to judiciary model' in A Barak, 'Constitutional Human Rights and Private Law' in D Friedman and D Barak-Erez (eds), *Human Rights in Private Law* (Oxford, Hart Publishing, 2001) 13, 27–28.

[8] Germany's *Bundesverfassungsgericht* showed the way in *Lüth*, Bundesverfassungsgericht

exists here—everything depends on the content of the value. Both lines of argument presuppose what they are meant to establish, which is that private persons are obligated alongside public institutions. There is no a priori reason why the same rights, principles or values should govern both relationships between individuals and the state and relations among individuals. A division of labour between constitutional and human rights law on the one hand, and private law on the other, is easily conceivable and perhaps indispensable.[9] Ultimately, therefore, the issue turns on what rights and duties (or values and principles) exist among private persons. That is inescapably a question of private law.

My aim in this chapter is therefore to explore the horizontal application of fundamental rights from the perspective of private law, asking whether and to what extent this practice might assist or frustrate private law in its task of regulating the relations among private persons. The manner in which private law discharges that task is in my opinion best captured by a rights-based analysis of private law. On this view, 'private law is concerned not with whether an act has increased or diminished welfare, but with whether that act can coexist with the freedom of another in accordance with practical reason'.[10] However, contrary to the accompanying claim that private law also repudiates 'the promotion of social purposes extrinsic to the relationship between the parties',[11] I show that it serves the common good in a manner that is fully compatible with its freedom-enhancing function. In fact, this additional service is vital to the legitimacy of private law in a world no longer governed by the authority of tradition and religion. It is this additional service that benefits from fundamental rights. This benefit, I argue, obtains when these rights are applied indirectly via the concepts and categories of private law, rather than directly.

The analysis commences with a discussion of the idea that fundamental rights support private law reasoning by facilitating a process of public

---

[German Constitutional Court], 1 BvR 400/51, 15 January 1958 reported in (1958) 7 BVerfGE 198. See also *Retail, Wholesale and Department Store Union, Local 580 v Dolphin Delivery Ltd* [1986] 2 SCR 573 (*Dolphin Delivery*) [39] (McIntyre J for Dickson CJ, Estey, McIntyre, Chouinard and Le Dain JJ); *Carmichele v Minister of Safety and Security* [2001] 4 SA 938 (Constitutional Court of South Africa) [54] (Ackermann and Goldstone JJ); *Campbell* [2004] UKHL 22, [2004] 2 AC 457 [17]-[18] (Lord Nicholls).

[9] Thus it is usual for societies to assign the discharge of socioeconomic duties, such as the duty to relieve poverty, to mechanisms of collective provision via the taxation and spending powers of the state, and to leave private persons free to spend their net income as they wish and to enter into transactions on the basis of their self-interest. For an explanation and justification of such a division, see EJ Weinrib, *The Idea of Private Law* (Cambridge MA, Harvard University Press, 1995) 208–14.

[10] ibid, at 131. As Ernest Weinrib makes clear, private law also does not pursue ethical duties: at 110–13.

[11] EJ Weinrib, 'Restitutionary Damages as Corrective Justice' (2000) 1 *Theoretical Inquiries in Law* 1, 37.

reason. In part II of this chapter, it is concluded that such a contention cannot account for the use of fundamental rights in the judicial development of private law. Proceeding from the view that the blame for this failure lies with a picture of private law that restricts its function to bilateral corrective justice, part III seeks a fresh start in the role that private law plays in constructing communities and their institutions. Part III demonstrates that it is the social construction role of private law, rather than its corrective justice function, that explains and justifies the use of fundamental rights in private law. Drawing on this argument, part IV explores the limits of the service so rendered by fundamental rights, concluding that the direct horizontal application of fundamental rights endangers the capacity of private law to play its distinctive role in the legal order.

II. FUNDAMENTAL RIGHTS AND PUBLIC REASON

Being concerned with whether one person's act 'can coexist with the freedom of another in accordance with practical reason',[12] private law reasoning is ultimately anchored in an understanding of human freedom, of what it is to function as a self-determining agent interacting with other self-determining agents and operating in the empirical circumstances of the world. But it also consists of much more than this. Rigorous reflection on what is needed to realise the human capacity for purposive agency in a world of social interactions reveals the need for the basic rights (and correlative duties) that make up the structure of private law, such as the rights to bodily integrity, property and contractual performance.[13] However, such rights are very abstract and still far removed from the actual content of private law.[14] They provide a framework which leaves open most of the answers to the concrete questions that private law concerns itself with. These questions revolve around issues such as how far those rights stretch, what happens when they conflict, and how they are acquired and lost: 'Does physical integrity, for instance, include protection against an apprehended contact or merely an actual one (that is, is there a tort of assault)?'[15] All developed systems of private law are intricate and technical in nature, being constructed of concepts, rules and principles that can be understood as providing detailed content to the abstract rights revealed by philosophical reflection but which extend well beyond what

---

[12] Weinrib, *The Idea of Private Law*, above n 9, at 131.

[13] See especially Weinrib, *The Idea of Private Law*, above n 9.

[14] A point most wittily made already in the nineteenth century by R von Jhering, *Scherz und Ernst in der Jurisprudenz* (first published 1885, M Leitner ed, Vienna, Linde Verlag, 2009), especially at 245–316 ('Im juristischen Begriffshimmel').

[15] LE Weinrib and EJ Weinrib, 'Constitutional Values and Private Law in Canada' in D Friedman and D Barak-Erez (eds), *Human Rights in Private Law* (Oxford, Hart Publishing, 2001) 43, 48.

can merely be inferred from these. This is as it should be, for private law must occupy itself with asking and answering such concrete questions if it is to provide the guidance to behaviour on which its claim to authority ultimately rests. It must—and does—seek to bring determinacy where moral philosophy underdetermines how we should act.[16]

But this generates a difficulty for the idea that private law serves to actualise freedom through law. This is that such private law determinations appear ineluctably heteronomous, at least when they are produced by the activities of courts. In a well-ordered—and thus democratic—society, the development of private law through legislation is in principle compatible with individual freedom since individuals can be thought of as participating therein via a representative legislature. However, it is a very different matter when it comes to the development of the law by the courts. It is no accident that the French revolutionaries both favoured legislative codification of the law and prohibited judges from announcing general principles when deciding cases.[17] Once tradition and religion have been discarded as sources of guidance for right action and replaced by the reason of self-determining individuals, it is no longer possible to think of judicial determinations as reflecting an expertise greater than that of individual citizens conscientiously pursuing their own conclusions. In combination, the legitimate diversity of convictions about what constitutes a good life, and the abstract nature of the rights specifying 'the sum of conditions under which the choice of one can be united with the choice of another in accordance with a universal law of freedom',[18] result in a situation where a wide range of concrete determinations of rights are all equally permissible. In a world of morally self-determining agents, the concrete content given to an abstract right by one notion of the good is neither superior nor inferior to the content arrived at by someone committed to a different notion of the good. Crudely expressed, in such a world—which is our world—one conscientious person's private law is as good as another's. A judge may be impartial between the parties, thus preventing one party from dominating the other, but this comes at the price of both parties having to submit to convictions that carry no recommendation other than that they are those of a third person. Against

---

[16] On the need for *determinatio* (implementation, concretisation or specification), see especially J Finnis, *Natural Law and Natural Rights* (Oxford, Clarendon Press, 1980) 281–90 and J Finnis, 'The Truth in Legal Positivism' in RP George (ed), *The Autonomy of Law: Essays on Legal Positivism* (Oxford, Oxford University Press, 1996) 195, 200–03.

[17] See AT von Mehren and JR Gordley, *The Civil Law System*, 2nd edn (Boston, Little, Brown and Co, 1977) 217–20. Article 5 of the Code Civil still forbids judges to decide cases submitted to them by way of general and rule-making dispositions.

[18] I Kant, *The Metaphysics of Morals* (M Gregor tr and ed, Cambridge, Cambridge University Press, 1996) para 6:230.

this background, judicial development of private law appears as nothing more than the exercise of pure power.[19]

Fundamental rights might, however, come to private law's rescue. Acknowledging that working out the concrete content of private law does not take place 'through philosophical speculation' but involves determinations of the kind just sketched, Lorraine Weinrib and Ernest Weinrib contend that this undertaking is rendered legitimate by a process of 'public reason' proceeding 'through reference to beliefs, values, and modes of reasoning that have public plausibility'.[20] In their view, the horizontal application of fundamental rights greatly facilitates this process. Describing such rights as 'society's authoritative repository of legally supreme and publicly accessible values concerning human dignity', they see them as having 'systemic normative significance within private law'.[21] On the one hand, there is a basic affinity between fundamental rights and private law rights, which are 'themselves the juridical embodiment of the dignity inherent in self-determining agency'.[22] On the other hand, fundamental rights bring something extra to private law reasoning since they are 'uniquely conspicuous' crystallisations of the social meaning of dignity.[23] Indeed, 'self-determining agents contracting to enter a constitutional democracy could not reasonably acknowledge a specification of private rights that is inconsistent with the indicia of dignity to which the citizens have accorded constitutional recognition'.[24]

This account fits well with the manner in which fundamental rights have been employed by courts in private law reasoning, for there is a notably widespread tendency to describe fundamental rights documents as charters of values and principles that 'radiate' throughout the law.[25] In this way, fundamental rights are indeed used to supply a vocabulary and framework of justification for the development of private law. A good practical illustration is provided by Lord Hoffmann's speech in *Campbell v MGN Ltd*,[26] which remains an outstanding example of the impact of fundamental rights on private law. This speech is particularly illuminating in the present context, since two features of *Campbell* indicate that the

[19] See especially D Kennedy, 'Form and Substance in Private Law Adjudication' (1976) 89 *Harvard Law Review* 1685; D Kennedy, *A Critique of Adjudication (fin de siècle)* (Cambridge MA, Harvard University Press, 1986); RM Unger, *The Critical Legal Studies Movement* (Cambridge MA, Harvard University Press, 1986); RM Unger, *What Should Legal Analysis Become?* (London, Verso, 1996); S Veitch, *Moral Conflict and Legal Reasoning* (Oxford, Hart Publishing, 1999).

[20] Weinrib and Weinrib, above n 15, at 49.

[21] ibid, at 50.

[22] ibid.

[23] ibid, at 48.

[24] ibid, at 50.

[25] The cases cited in above n 8 are representative. See also the literature referred to in above n 1 and T Rensmann, *Wertordnung und Verfassung* (Tübingen, Mohr Siebeck, 2007).

[26] *Campbell* [2004] UKHL 22, [2004] 2 AC 457.

Law Lords' decision in this case to develop a broad remedy for misuse of private information was animated less by a sense of legal compulsion than by the conviction that private law would benefit from the influence of fundamental rights. Not only did their Lordships draw on the European Convention of Human Rights (ECHR) even though the European Court of Human Rights (Strasbourg Court) had not yet decided that the Convention covered infringements by private persons with the right to private life,[27] Lord Hoffmann did so despite taking the view that Convention rights did *not* apply between private persons.[28]

Explaining the development affirmed by *Campbell*, Lord Hoffmann stated that:

> Instead of the cause of action being based upon the duty of good faith applicable to confidential personal information and trade secrets alike, it focuses upon the protection of human autonomy and dignity—the right to control the dissemination of information about one's private life and the right to the esteem and respect of other people.[29]

This both associated the cause of action with rights to autonomy and dignity, and gave specific concrete content to these abstract rights. Lord Hoffmann derived this content from human rights law. 'What human rights law has done', he observed, 'is to identify private information as something worth protecting as an aspect of human autonomy and dignity.'[30] In this way, Lord Hoffmann linked private law to human rights law via the concept of human dignity and then used human rights law to justify injecting particular concrete content into private law.

Nevertheless, the combination of public reason and fundamental rights constructed by Lorraine Weinrib and Ernest Weinrib fails to stave off concerns about the legitimacy of judicial elaboration of private law rights. Justifying conclusions 'in a manner that appeals to considerations that their addressees can reasonably acknowledge'[31] can only overcome these concerns if the addressees are unanimous in endorsing those considerations. In the absence of unanimity, public reason is the reason of merely *some* of the public, even if the section of the public concerned is sufficiently large and dominant to have ensured that its convictions are generally and correctly regarded as the values characteristic of that political community. Yet, at least in the contemporary world, genuine unanimity on moral matters does not exist within political communities. In these circumstances public reason cannot save judicial development of the law from unravelling into a pure exercise of power. True, a judiciary

---

[27] That was to happen soon after, in *Von Hannover v Germany* (2005) 40 EHRR 1 (*Von Hannover*).

[28] *Campbell* [2004] UKHL 22, [2004] 2 AC 457 [50].

[29] ibid, at [51].

[30] ibid, at [50].

[31] Weinrib and Weinrib, above n 15, at 48.

that decides in accordance with public reason does not stand alone; but ganging up against a minority is no less offensive to their freedom than the act of a lone bully.

Matters are not improved by the presence of a charter of fundamental rights. Fundamental rights are specified in such broad and general language that they convey very little indeed about the notion(s) of dignity endorsed by a given society, and definitely too little to tell a judge with any certainty whether, for example, newspapers should be free to publish reports about the sex lives of celebrities, let alone whether assault should be a tort in addition to battery. Moreover, such documents seldom enjoy universal support in all respects and are typically the object of at least some debate and proposals for reform. Even when this is not the case, and an existing charter is supported without any dissent at all, serious disagreement about the meaning of rights, their limits and relative significance is common. Hence this argument does not succeed in accounting for the use of fundamental rights in the judicial development of private law.

III. BEYOND CORRECTIVE JUSTICE

The doubts about the legitimacy of judicial concretisation of private law rights highlighted in part II arise from a specific vision of private law. This is one that sees the function of private law as limited to the resolution of conflicts between morally self-determining agents. On this account of private law, its sole task is corrective justice—determining 'the right' that is to resolve the conflicts resulting from the pursuit of individual conceptions of 'the good'. But compliance with 'the right' is no less the duty of every individual than is the quest for 'the good'.[32] Judicial decision-making appears dubious because the concrete requirements of 'the right' cannot be inferred through mere deduction from moral premises, but must be determined, decided—and among moral equals there is no a priori reason to regard the determination preferred by one person as better than that of another. A judge does no more than each of the parties can, and should, do; because his or her determination adds nothing to theirs, it competes with them on an equal footing.[33]

---

[32] This is so even when one agrees with Kant, above n 18, at para 6:231 (emphasis in original) that '[w]hen one's aim is not to teach virtue but only to set forth what is *right*, one may not and should not represent that law of right as itself the incentive to action.'

[33] See also J Raz, *The Authority of Law: Essays on Law and Morality* (Oxford, Clarendon Press, 1979) 233–49; J Raz, *Ethics in the Public Domain: Essays in the Morality of Law and Politics* (Oxford, Oxford University Press, 1994) 341–54. Kant, above n 18, at para 6:232 (emphasis in original) insisted that '[o]nly a completely external right can ... be called *strict* (right in the narrow sense).' But this merely means that 'strict right ... requires only external *grounds* for determining choice' (at para 6:232 (emphasis added)), not that the person making the decision has to be external. Ernest Weinrib's justification of judicial decision-making in *The Idea of Private Law*, above n 9, at 105–107 elides the distinction between external grounds for a decision and an external decision-maker.

But this is a mistaken picture of private law. Its role is not so constrained. A further function can be identified which is not only compatible with corrective justice but a necessary complement thereof. This may be termed the social construction role of private law. It arises in the course of the concretisation of abstract rights. For the reasons explained by Lorraine Weinrib and Ernest Weinrib, this process draws on the values endorsed by the community concerned.[34] However, contrary to their account thereof, private law's relationship to social values is not a unidirectional, passive one. In fleshing out the skeleton of rights produced by philosophical reflection, private law reasoning does not just draw on its social environment. It also helps to constitute it. Consequently, the private law of a community not only enables compliance with the requirements of interpersonal justice by its members, but also helps construct that community and its institutions.

Campbell[35] again provides a telling illustration. In holding that there is a right to private information enforceable against the press, the House of Lords provided legal support to a particular view about the extent to which everyone—including someone who, like the claimant Naomi Campbell, makes a living out of courting publicity—is entitled to draw boundaries around parts of their lives. That this view was not universally shared, or at least was one with uncertain contours, is evident from the vigour with which the newspaper defended itself in court, as well as from the wide readership enjoyed by press reports of this kind. Plainly, many people regard the dissemination and consumption of details and photographs about celebrities' social lives as perfectly respectable; it is certainly treated very differently from pornography. Admittedly, the decision in *Campbell* did not emerge out of the blue, but rather represented the culmination of a judicial approach that had been developing incrementally through several cases.[36] However, in deciding as it did, the House of Lords came down in favour of one side of a divide in social opinion, and provided it with the stabilising support of the legal system. In that way, it contributed to the character of British society as one in which there is (now) a certain boundary that delimits a sphere of privacy beyond which the press may not venture without permission. Of course, the precise contours of that boundary remain under construction, and might never acquire full acceptance or entirely sharp outlines.[37] But it is clear that

---

[34] See Weinrib and Weinrib, above n 15, at 47–51.

[35] *Campbell* [2004] UKHL 22, [2004] 2 AC 457.

[36] See G Phillipson, 'Transforming Breach of Confidence? Towards a Common Law Right of Privacy under the Human Rights Act' (2003) 66 *Modern Law Review* 726.

[37] See especially cases such as *CC v AB* [2006] EWHC 3083 (QB), [2007] EMLR 11 (which was 'subjected to a number of criticisms, the more restrained of these being directed to its "moral relativism"', according to Eady J in *Mosley v News Group Newspapers Ltd* [2008] EWHC 1777 (QB), [2008] EMLR 20 [129]); *Murray v Express Newspapers* [2008] EWCA Civ 446, [2009] Ch 481; *Terry v Persons Unknown* [2010] EWHC 119 (QB), [2010] EMLR 16.

while referring to 'beliefs, values, and modes of reasoning that have public plausibility' (rightly identified by Lorraine Weinrib and Ernest Weinrib as necessary to give concrete content to the parties' abstract rights[38]), the courts simultaneously help to shape those very features of society.

Where to draw the line between the public and private dimensions of the lives of individuals has been a matter of some controversy in all societies where growth in media profits and a celebrity culture have fed off each other.[39] Cases like *Campbell* and its equivalents in other jurisdictions therefore show particularly clearly that courts may have to make choices among rival social values and beliefs when giving concrete content to private law rights. But they are not exceptional. Cultures are not unitary or monolithic and no community is without some conflict.[40] Moreover, the pull of the familiar should not be mistaken for the compulsion of morality. Private law also endorses a particular social understanding when the issue is sufficiently uncontroversial to enable legal reasoning to restrict itself to identifying and applying existing social practices and convictions. Since these are in principle always open to challenge and change, giving effect to them always involves a choice in favour of one constellation of practices and convictions in preference to another. Private law is therefore never truly passive in respect of community values but always participates in the constitution of the social order within which it gives concrete content to individuals' rights and duties in respect of one another. And it does this over a broad swathe of human activities, of which cases like *Campbell* represent but a small corner. Thus the law of contract constitutes markets, and together with the law of property establishes a very particular type of market society. Family law by itself, and also often in association with the law of succession, shapes particular forms of intimate association. Tort law and the law of unjustified enrichment provide support and protection to these various social institutions, as well as to a society's convictions about the contours of individual autonomy. And the way in which this is done in a particular society—the nature of its markets, the forms of its family relationships and so on—help to give that society its particular character and identity.[41]

Private law therefore reaches beyond the correction of bilateral injustice between individuals to encompass also the stabilisation of many social institutions and of society as such. This is a complex process, involving

---

[38] Weinrib and Weinrib, above n 15, at 49.

[39] See H Beverley-Smith, A Ohly and A Lucas-Schloetter, *Privacy, Property and Personality: Civil Law Perspectives on Commercial Appropriation* (Cambridge, Cambridge University Press, 2005); AT Kenyon and M Richardson (eds), *New Dimensions in Privacy Law: International and Comparative Perspectives* (Cambridge, Cambridge University Press, 2006).

[40] See LA Coser, *The Functions of Social Conflict* (London, Routledge & Kegan Paul, 1956); E Durkheim, *The Division of Labour in Society* (London, Macmillan, 1984).

[41] See also O Kahn-Freund, 'Introduction' in K Renner, *The Institutions of Private Law and Their Social Functions* (A Schwarzchild tr, O Kahn-Freund ed, London, Routledge & Kegan Paul, 1949) 1.

an ongoing flow of influence in both directions between law and society, and an intricate and changing pattern of legal impact, ranging from the transformation of social institutions to their protection and maintenance. The relationship between law and society is, of course, hardly straightforward and is a matter of intense debate.[42] But however minimal sociologists may consider private law's contribution to social processes to be, it is one that serves the common good. This is so because the actualisation of purposive agency—the leading of a full and free human life—requires an array of social institutions in which individual identities can be formed, developed and expressed through interaction with others.[43] These enable individuals to develop, and to exercise, self-determining agency, as well as to form social bonds and to pursue common projects. Since they are therefore valuable to all members of a community regardless of individuals' own conceptions of a good life, they may be described as serving the 'common good'.[44] Because views may and do differ as to the social institutions necessary or desirable to this end, and the law of a given place and time may get it wrong, private law's pursuit of the common good may be neither uncontroversial nor invariably successful. The crucial point, however, is that it takes place. Private law accordingly plays a dual role, simultaneously pursuing social purposes and corrective justice.[45]

In the contemporary world, this dual role is mostly given effect via legislation regulating the social institutions that are private law's concern, such as property, the market and the family; however, as *Campbell* reminds us, judicial determination not infrequently features as well. It is this further function of the judicial specification of rights that provides an answer to the objections that can plausibly be raised as long as private

---

[42] For an overview, see R Cotterell, *The Sociology of Law: An Introduction*, 2nd edn (London, Butterworths, 1992) chs 2–3.

[43] See generally J Raz, *The Morality of Freedom* (Oxford, Oxford University Press, 1986).

[44] See Finnis, *Natural Law and Natural Rights*, above n 16, at 134–60 on this notion. GWF Hegel, *Elements of the Philosophy of Right* (TM Knox tr, Oxford, Oxford University Press, 1952) § 218 observes that once

> property and personality have legal recognition and validity in civil society, wrongdoing … becomes an infringement, not merely of what is subjectively infinite, but of the universal thing which is existent with inherent stability and strength. Hence a new attitude arises: the action is seen as a danger to society.

[45] See also H Dagan, 'The Limited Autonomy of Private Law' (2008) 56 *American Journal of Comparative Law* 809; H Dagan, 'Just and Unjust Enrichments' in A Robertson and HW Tang (eds), *The Goals of Private Law* (Oxford, Hart Publishing, 2009) 423, 432–35. However, this is not an instantiation of distributive justice, *contra* H Dagan, 'The Distributive Foundation of Corrective Justice' (1999) 98 *Michigan Law Review* 138; P Cane, 'Distributive Justice and Tort Law' [2001] *New Zealand Law Review* 401; J Gordley, *Foundations of Private Law: Property, Tort, Contract, Unjust Enrichment* (Oxford, Oxford University Press, 2006) 11. Private law specifies rights to property, contractual performances etc, thereby making it possible for people to acquire such rights; it does not *distribute* these rights (ie, determine who has how much property etc).

law is thought of as serving only the purpose of corrective justice. This is so because this additional role is one that could not be undertaken by individual agents, even though it serves the good of all individuals and its realisation makes demands upon all. The reason for this lies in the limited capacity of self-determining agents. As Garrett Hardin's famous example of the 'tragedy of the commons' reminds us, the uninhibited pursuit of individual aims leads to the collapse of resources serving the common good.[46] Such a result may be prevented by the moderating influence of community mores which socialise individuals into voluntarily restraining their behaviour, but this is no longer a meaningful inhibition in modern societies marked by the liberating collapse of the bonds of tradition and religion. The effects of this individualisation of society are reinforced by a further consequence of the processes of industrialisation and urbanisation which are its underlying cause.[47] This is the complexity of the social relations to which these processes give rise, including the development of vast networks of economic and social connections that individuals are drawn into without choice, or even knowledge, of those to whom they become connected. The result is a world in which every individual act can have far-reaching consequences that cannot be known to or controlled by individual agents, alone or in collaboration, and in which there is accordingly an even greater need for structures that work towards a common good independently of individual moral choice and determination.[48]

In these circumstances, as GWF Hegel showed, there is a pressing need for 'an institution ... [that] embodies the mutual recognition of moral agents as ends',[49] a need fulfilled by the well-functioning state.[50] Its function is not limited to securing the 'negative' freedom of agents to pursue their own ends, for its existence is necessitated by the destructive impact of such freedom on the very conditions for its own existence.[51] Instead, the state *determines* what the demands of mutual respect are and enforces these. In this context private law fosters the common good in situations involving interactions among individuals rather than between individuals

---

[46] G Hardin, 'The Tragedy of the Commons' (1968) 162 *Science* 1243.

[47] See A Giddens, *The Consequences of Modernity* (Cambridge, Polity Press, 1990); A Giddens and C Pierson, *Conversations with Anthony Giddens: Making Sense of Modernity* (Stanford CA, Stanford University Press, 1998) 94; G Delanty, 'Modernity', *The Blackwell Encyclopedia of Sociology* (Oxford, Blackwell Publishing, 2007).

[48] See Hegel, above n 44, at § 258.

[49] A Brudner, *The Unity of the Common Law: Studies in Hegelian Jurisprudence* (Berkeley CA, University of California Press, 1995) 72.

[50] See Hegel, above n 44, at §§ 258, 260, 268. For a broadly compatible account of the social role of law, see N Luhmann, *A Sociological Theory of Law* (E King-Utz and M Albrow trs, London, Routledge & Kegan Paul, 1985).

[51] See the remarks by Hegel, above n 44, at § 258 on the French Revolution and its aftermath. See also S Koslowski, 'Hegel als Theoretiker der bürgerlichen Gesellschaft und des modernes Staates?' (2008) 94 *Archiv für Rechts- und Sozialphilosophie* 86. For a careful and thorough development of this approach in relation to private law, see Brudner, above n 49.

and the state. A democratic representative legislature plays the leading role in such determinations, for reasons that are straightforwardly connected to the overall aim of maximising individual freedom, but it is complemented by the equally essential executive administration as well as courts.[52] For this reason judicial determination fulfils a task that cannot be carried out by individual agents, singly or in concert.[53] It follows that individual agents have nothing to complain about when the courts fulfil this role. They are not oppressed but liberated by judicial concretisation of private law rights.

It is also this social construction role of private law, rather than its corrective justice mission, that makes fundamental rights valuable to private law reasoning. Whether seen as embodying the aims of the state, as in revolutionary France, or as limitations on the state's ambitions, as in the United States, fundamental rights emerged in order to keep the state focused on its mission of pursuing the common good.[54] They flourished in both national and international legal orders because of the growing social prominence of the state, and as both the advantages and the risks inherent in such an institution became ever clearer over the course of the twentieth century. Fundamental rights developed into a powerful tool to structure the activities of the state, specifically in order to mediate between the conception of the common good held by state functionaries and the interests of the individuals whose good the state is meant to serve. They are not merely 'the modern idiom for moral rights',[55] but are rights regarded as sufficiently important to bind even those institutions and individuals that have been endowed with authority over the general population. In content and process, fundamental rights aim to ensure that the state indeed 'embodies the mutual recognition of individuals as ends' and does not become the instrument by which the good of some is advanced at the expense of others. They do so by allowing members of weak groups—groups that have insufficient economic power, or little social prestige, or for some other reason find it difficult to make an impact

---

[52] See Hegel, above n 44, at §§ 272–320, on the internal organisation of the state. Hegel describes a constitutional monarchy where power is divided between the Crown, legislature and executive, assigning the courts to the latter category: at § 287.

[53] ibid, at § 219:

The administration of justice must be regarded as the fulfilment of a duty by the public authority, no less than as the exercise of a right; and so far as it is a right, it does not depend upon an optional delegation to one authority by the individual members of society.

[54] For the French understanding, see M Troper, 'Who Needs a Third Party Effect Doctrine? The Case of France' in A Sajó and R Uitz (eds), *The Constitution in Private Relations* (Utrecht, Eleven International Publishing, 2005) 115, 119–23. The US vision is evident from *DeShaney v Winnebago County Department of Social Services* 489 US 189 (1989).

[55] R Stevens, 'The Conflict of Rights' in A Robertson and HW Tang (eds), *The Goals of Private Law* (Oxford, Hart Publishing, 2009) 139, 146.

on legislative politics—easier access to centres of power.[56] Their role is therefore to ensure that, 'in this association with other particulars, my particular welfare too shall be promoted' through the state's pursuit of the universal interest.[57] For, as Hegel realised:

> The maintenance of the state's universal interest, and of legality, in this sphere of particular rights, and the work of bringing these rights back to the universal, require to be superintended ... Just as civil society is the battlefield where everyone's individual private interest meets everyone else's, so here we have the struggle (a) of private interests against particular matters of common concern and (b) of both of these together against the organisation of the state and its higher outlook.[58]

Because the common good is fostered not only through the state's direct management of collective life via the instruments of public law, and of individual behaviour through the means of criminal law, but, as explained, also through private law, the service provided by fundamental rights is crucial here as well. If private law is to serve the common good, then it too must avoid being reduced to an instrument of domination. This may as often necessitate restraining the pursuit of individual goals in the interest of the common good as it may require moderating collective purposes in the interest of individuals. But in both instances it calls for the sort of mediation between individual goods and the common good that fundamental rights have since their inception been designed to provide.

Thus it is precisely in cases where the duality of private law's social role is clearest that courts have drawn on fundamental rights in private law reasoning. British experience in *Campbell* and its predecessors echoes what has happened elsewhere. Virtually without exception, freedom of expression, especially of the press, has been in the vanguard of the growing influence of fundamental rights over private law.[59] Perhaps most noteworthy here is the position in the United States, where the constitutional right to freedom of speech was used in *New York Times v Sullivan*[60] to revolutionise the law of defamation by requiring actual malice when claims are brought by public officials—despite the United States Supreme Court's adherence to the principle that the Constitution applies to state action

---

[56] J Raz, 'Rights and Politics' in J Tasioulas (ed), *Law, Values and Social Practices* (Aldershot, Dartmouth, 1997) 75, 96. See also Raz, *Ethics in the Public Domain*, above n 33, at 55–58.

[57] The quotation is from Hegel, above n 44, at § 229. See also at § 230.

[58] ibid, at § 289. At § 301, Hegel adopts the view that 'public welfare and rational freedom' are guaranteed 'far more effectively' by the judicial system than by the legislature ('the Estates').

[59] See *Schacht-Briefe*, Bundesgerichtshof [German Federal Court of Justice], I ZR 211/53, 25 May 1954 reported in (1954) 13 BGHZ 334; *Lüth*, Bundesverfassungsgericht [German Constitutional Court], 1 BvR 400/51, 15 January 1958 reported in (1958) 7 BVerfGE 198; *Hill v Church of Scientology of Toronto* [1995] 2 SCR 1130; *Du Plessis v De Klerk* [1996] 3 SA 850 (Constitutional Court of South Africa).

[60] *New York Times v Sullivan* 376 US 254 (1964) (*Sullivan*).

only.[61] The obvious concern in *Sullivan* and comparable cases elsewhere was that the protection of an individual's reputation through the law of defamation could harm the common good, as good governance depends on the free expression of political opinions. *Campbell* and other decisions developing a private law right to private information on the basis of fundamental rights similarly grapple with the demands of press freedom as a common good, albeit here in order to establish its boundary with personal privacy.[62] An important concern here is whether (and to what extent) this common good may be used to further the commercial interest of one person at the cost of the privacy interest of another.[63]

These cases provide a good illustration of the connection between the social construction role of private law and recourse to fundamental rights in judicial reasoning. The courts were not merely concerned with the interests of the parties, concretely or as representatives of all others similarly situated. The outcomes of these cases affected the common good of free expression and were seen to do so by the courts deciding them, and it was this feature that led the courts to draw fundamental rights into their reasoning. The significance of this to understanding the role of fundamental rights in private law adjudication is underlined by the fact that the same is true in other areas of private law affected by fundamental rights reasoning. Two brief examples must suffice, as a full survey cannot be given here.

The first comes from the German law of contract. In the famous *Bürgschaft* decision,[64] the *Bundesverfassungsgericht* limited the capacity of lenders to enforce loan guarantees provided by particularly vulnerable persons. A naive young woman with little education, a low income and no property had at the request of a bank stood surety for a large loan to her father for his business activities, and upon his default was ordered by the civil courts to pay the sum due under the suretyship contract. The *Bundesgerichtshof*, the highest 'ordinary' court, held that a creditor was not obliged either to inform a surety of the risk involved in the transaction or to satisfy itself that the surety understood the obligations involved.[65] The young woman then brought a constitutional complaint, arguing that the *Bundesgerichtshof* had violated her constitutional rights. Her complaint was successful. Relying on the constitutional protection

[61] On this principle, see E Chemerinsky, 'Rethinking State Action' (1985) 80 *Northwestern University Law Review* 503.

[62] See, eg, *Bartnicki v Vopper* 532 US 514 (2001).

[63] See EJ Bloustein, 'Privacy as an Aspect of Human Dignity: An Answer to Dean Prosser' (1964) 39 *New York University Law Review* 962; T Hoppe, 'Privatleben in der Öffentlichkeit' (2005) 13 *Zeitschrift für Europäishes Privatrecht* 656.

[64] *Bürgschaft*, Bundesverfassungsgericht [German Constitutional Court], 1 BvR 567/89, 1 BvR 1044/89, 19 October 1993 reported in (1993) 89 BVerfGE 214.

[65] *Bürgschaft*, Bundesgerichtshof [German Federal Court of Justice], IX ZR 171/88, 16 March 1989 reported in [1989] NJW 1605.

of autonomy in Article 2(1) of the *Grundgesetz*, and the principle of the 'social state' in Articles 20(1) and 28(1), the *Bundesverfassungsgericht* held that when a 'structural inequality' in bargaining power has resulted in a contract that is exceptionally onerous to the weaker party, the civil courts are obliged to intervene.[66]

The *Bundesverfassungsgericht* saw private law as a distinctive system that contributes to the indispensable legal structuring of private autonomy, understood as individual self-determination.[67] The Court observed that private law is concerned with interactions among bearers of constitutional rights who enjoy equal status and pursue different interests as well as frequently conflicting goals. Since all participants in private law transactions enjoy the protection of Article 2(1) and are equally entitled to the constitutional protection of their private autonomy, the right of the stronger party must not predominate. In contract law, the appropriate balance of interests is achieved through the agreement between the parties. But when the greater bargaining power of one party enables him or her as a matter of fact to determine the content of the contract unilaterally, then the other party is subjected to domination (*Fremdbestimmung*). Although the law cannot deal with every single case, not least because of considerations of legal certainty, private law must react and make it possible to set things right when one is dealing with a general type of case which is characterised by structural inequality between the parties and the consequences of the contract are exceptionally onerous for the weaker party. The Court observed that this could be achieved via the so-called 'general clauses' in the *Bürgerliches Gesetzbuch*, which refer to public policy/morality (*gute Sitten*, § 138) and good faith (*Treu und Glauben*, § 242). It held that, when interpreting and applying these general clauses, the civil courts are duty-bound to ensure that contracts are not used as instruments of domination.[68] When a contract is exceptionally onerous to one party and the balancing of interests evidently inappropriate, the courts are therefore not permitted simply to satisfy themselves with the assertion that a contract is a contract. Accordingly, when the case was returned to the *Bundesgerichtshof*, the Court promptly declared the suretyship void for infringing § 138.[69]

The *Bundesverfassungsgericht* here treated contract law as an aspect of the common good, serving the interest of both contracting parties, and thus to be safeguarded against one party's attempt to use it exclusively for his or her own purposes. The manner in which contract law pro-

---

[66] *Bürgschaft*, Bundesverfassungsgericht [German Constitutional Court], 1 BvR 567/89, 1 BvR 1044/89, 19 October 1993 reported in (1993) 89 BVerfGE 214.

[67] For the parts of the judgment paraphrased in this paragraph, see ibid, at 231–34.

[68] In doing so, the Court gave effect to *Lüth*, Bundesverfassungsgericht [German Constitutional Court], 1 BvR 400/51, 15 January 1958 reported in (1958) 7 BVerfGE 198.

[69] *Bürgschaft*, Bundesgerichtshof [German Federal Court of Justice], IX ZR 227/93, 24 February 1994 reported in [1994] NJW 1341.

motes the common good was determined by reference to constitutional fundamental rights, and this was then used to work out how the law should resolve conflicts between the parties' pursuit of their individual objectives. Because contract law was seen as an institution for fostering self-determination (*Selbstbestimmung*), it was considered justified to limit freedom of contract and to interfere with the bargain made by the parties when doing so was necessary to prevent the contract from being turned into an instrument of domination (*Fremdbestimmung*). In this way the Court simultaneously concerned itself with corrective justice and with the maintenance of the common good: the parties' bilateral relationship was regulated in a manner that preserved the integrity of the common good, fundamental rights providing the bridge between the two.

The second example consists of a series of property law cases. Here courts used fundamental rights to determine the limits of the legal powers of property owners. In *Shelley v Kraemer* the United States Supreme Court unanimously held that the prohibition on discrimination in section 1 of the Fourteenth Amendment of the Constitution prevented courts from enforcing a restrictive covenant stipulating that a property could be sold only to whites.[70] Thus the common law of property could not be used to exclude African Americans from access to the common good of property. Elsewhere, fundamental rights have been used to determine uses of residential property from which persons may not be excluded. Thus the right to religious freedom in the Quebec Charter of Human Rights and Freedoms led the Supreme Court of Canada in *Syndicat Northcrest v Amselem* to deny an injunction to a syndicate of co-owners seeking to enforce a by-law, binding on all co-owners of an apartment complex, against two co-owners who would thereby be prevented from constructing a *succah* (a small enclosed temporary hut required for the Jewish religious festival of *Succot*) on their balconies.[71] This decision prevented property law from being used to deprive the Jewish residents of the complex from full enjoyment of their property. Similarly, the *Bundesverfassungsgericht* held, in reliance on the constitutional right to freedom of information in Article 5 of the *Grundgesetz*, that a landlord must tolerate the installation of a satellite TV dish by a tenant when no cable connection is available and a foreign tenant would otherwise not be able to receive broadcasts from his country of origin.[72] Here fundamental rights were employed to ensure that private law structures property arrangements in a manner that enables everyone to use and enjoy their homes in accordance with their legitimate needs. In all three cases the use of fundamental rights in

---

[70] *Shelley v Kraemer* 334 US 1 (1948).
[71] *Syndicat Northcrest v Amselem* [2004] SCC 47, [2004] 2 SCR 551.
[72] *Parabolantennen*, Bundesverfassungsgericht [German Constitutional Court], 1 BvR 1687/92, 9 February 1994 reported in (1994) 90 BVerfGE 27, 33 ff.

private law adjudication served to maintain the common good of property as common.

IV. THE LIMITS OF HORIZONTAL APPLICATION

The conclusion reached in part III may be summed up as follows. Because it fosters the common good in addition to pursuing corrective justice, private law not only engages the rights and duties persons owe directly to each other, but also their rights and duties in respect of the organisation of collective life. For example, the decision to protect private information against publication in the press requires not only bilateral justification in terms of the relationship between the two parties, but, because it helps to constitute the social boundaries of press freedom as a common good, also raises the question of the extent to which, as it was put in older cases, freedom of the press is in the public interest.[73] That is a question about the organisation of communal life, specifically the proper balance between the common good and individual self-determination. Since this is the very issue that fundamental rights are designed to address, private law reasoning here benefits from drawing on fundamental rights.

This explanation of the 'horizontal' application of fundamental rights also delineates its boundaries. That is, in the technical vocabulary normally used to discuss this topic, it helps to settle the dispute between 'direct' and 'indirect' horizontal application. Given the reason for referring to fundamental rights in private law reasoning, this question can now be seen to turn on which alternative fits best with private law's contribution to the common good. That contribution lies in structuring direct interactions among persons rather than relations between persons and the state. Importantly, such interactions may be motivated by a broad—indeed unlimited—range of purposes on either side, many of which are not open to the state. This is so because private persons are normative equals whereas the state claims normative authority. As normative equals, all private persons enjoy the same freedom to set their own goals and thus are also constrained from prescribing the goals of others. However, since the 'role and primary normal function' of an authority, as Joseph Raz points out, 'is to serve the governed',[74] its instructions 'should require action which is justifiable by the reasons which apply to the subjects'.[75] This certainly covers a very wide field, but it does constrain the state, as

---

[73] See, eg, *Fraser v Evans* [1969] 1 QB 349 (CA) 360 (Lord Denning MR); *A-G v Observer Ltd* [1990] 1 AC 109 (HL) 282 (Lord Goff). Such statements highlight that the issue is not new: private law has always played such a 'social construction' role. What is new is the existence of fundamental rights that can give direction and content to the investigation of the 'public interest'.

[74] Raz, *The Morality of Freedom*, above n 43, at 56.

[75] ibid, at 51.

a political authority, to purposes which broadly speaking serve the collective interests of society. Hence the answer to the question depends on which of the alternatives is best suited to the normative equality of the subjects of private law.

To illustrate this point it is again helpful to turn to the cases on privacy, and more specifically to the contrast between the positions taken by, on the one hand, the Strasbourg Court, and, on the other hand, national courts in England and Germany. In *Von Hannover v Germany*, the Strasbourg Court upheld a complaint stemming from the German courts' refusal to hold that a number of published photographs showing various innocuous non-official activities of Princess Caroline von Hannover in public spaces violated her rights.[76] *Von Hannover* is strictly speaking not an instance of horizontal application, as the Strasbourg Court can only adjudicate claims against states; however, it set out the approach to be followed by national courts when deciding cases between private parties, thus laying down the horizontal implications of the pertinent Convention articles. Since the Court balanced the Article 8 rights of the applicant directly against the Article 10 rights of the press, this approach involves the direct application of the Convention to private persons. The central feature of the balance struck by the Court is its insistence that

> a fundamental distinction needs to be made between reporting facts ... capable of contributing to a debate in a democratic society relating to politicians in the exercise of their functions, for example, and reporting details of the private life of an individual, who, moreover, as in this case does not exercise official functions.[77]

In the latter case the press is not exercising 'its vital role of "watchdog" in a democracy'.[78] In the Court's view

> the public does not have a legitimate interest in knowing where the applicant is and how she behaves generally in her private life even if she appears in places that cannot always be described as secluded and despite the fact that she is well known to the public.

> Even if such a public interest exists, as does a commercial interest of the magazines in publishing these photos and these articles, in the instant case those interests must, in the Court's view, yield to the applicant's right to the effective protection of her private life.[79]

This is a very narrow conception of the interests in speech that are worth protecting. It stands in marked contrast with the observation by Lady Hale in *Campbell* that:

---

[76] *Von Hannover* (2005) 40 EHRR 1.
[77] ibid, at [63].
[78] ibid.
[79] ibid, at [76]–[77].

We have not so far held that the mere fact of covert photography is sufficient to make the information contained in the photograph confidential. The activity photographed must be private. If this had been, and had been presented as, a picture of Naomi Campbell going about her business in a public street, there could have been no complaint. She makes a substantial part of her living out of being photographed looking stunning in designer clothing. Readers will obviously be interested to see how she looks if and when she pops out to the shops for a bottle of milk. There is nothing essentially private about that information nor can it be expected to damage her private life. It may not be a high order of freedom of speech but there is nothing to justify interfering with it.[80]

Von Hannover contrasts equally sharply with the principles applied by the German courts in the decisions complained of by Princess Caroline.[81] The *Bundesverfassungsgericht* has consistently refused to restrict the protection of press freedom to publications or reports passing some test of quality or significance, regarding such a ranking as a form of 'statism' that would undermine the core of this right.[82] This protection is therefore not limited to political reports but also encompasses speech pursuing a commercial interest, such as advertisements[83] and entertainment,[84] and covers the formation of public opinion through entertaining publications on the activities and lifestyles of celebrities, including exposés of incongruities between public image and private behaviour.[85] Only at the stage of balancing freedom of the press against conflicting personality rights 'will it be relevant whether questions that are of significant concern to the public are discussed in a serious and factual manner or whether only private matters that serve only to satisfy curiosity are covered'.[86] On such

---

[80] *Campbell* [2004] UKHL 22, [2004] 2 AC 457 [154]. This contrast is confirmed in *McKennitt v Ash* [2006] EWCA Civ 1714, [2008] QB 73 [39] (Buxton LJ; Latham and Longmore LJJ agreeing). However, greater weight is attached to political speech than other forms of expression: *Campbell* [2004] UKHL 22, [2004] 2 AC 457 [117] (Lord Hope), [148] (Lady Hale).

[81] Excellent accounts of German law up to *Von Hannover* are found in KS Ziegler, 'The Princess and the Press: Privacy after *Caroline von Hannover v Germany*' in KS Ziegler (ed), *Human Rights and Private Law: Privacy as Autonomy* (Oxford, Hart Publishing, 2007) 189 and Beverley-Smith, Ohly and Lucas-Schloetter, above n 39, at 94–146.

[82] *Wallraff*, Bundesverfassungsgericht [German Constitutional Court], 1 BvR 272/81, 25 January 1984 reported in (1984) 66 BVerfGE 116, 134.

[83] *Marlene Dietrich II*, Bundesgerichtshof [German Federal Court of Justice], VI ZR 220/01, 14 May 2002 reported in (2002) 151 BGHZ 26 (use of a news clip featuring Marlene Dietrich permitted in a TV advert for a newspaper).

[84] *Lebach*, Bundesverfassungsgericht [German Constitutional Court], 1 BvR 536/72, 5 June 1973 reported in (1973) 35 BVerfGE 202, 222; *Caroline von Monaco II*, Bundesverfassungsgericht [German Constitutional Court], 1 BvR 653/96, 15 December 1999 reported in (1999) 101 BVerfGE 361, 390.

[85] *Caroline von Monaco II*, Bundesverfassungsgericht [German Constitutional Court], 1 BvR 653/96, 15 December 1999 reported in (1999) 101 BVerfGE 361, 390.

[86] *Soraya*, Bundesverfassungsgericht [German Constitutional Court], 1 BvR 112/65, 14 February 1973 reported in (1973) 34 BVerfGE 269, 283; ibid, at 391. Something similar is hinted at in *Murray v Express Newspapers* [2008] EWCA Civ 446, [2009] Ch 481 [56]

an approach, a minor impact on privacy might well be outweighed by something less lofty than the 'debate in a democratic society relating to politicians in the exercise of their functions' required in *Von Hannover*.

Significantly, the highest German courts have continued to reaffirm the essentials of this approach after *Von Hannover*. The *Bundesgerichtshof* and *Bundesverfassungsgericht* have admittedly sought to give effect to *Von Hannover* by replacing their own long-standing distinction between 'absolute persons of contemporary history' and 'relative persons of contemporary history' with one that follows the Strasbourg Court's own differentiation between politicians, public figures and ordinary persons, and by requiring photographs to be connected to at least some potential debate of social significance.[87] But their approach remains closer to that of Lady Hale in *Campbell* than to that of the Strasbourg Court. The German courts not only continue to refuse to condemn press reports for being merely entertaining,[88] but also employ a notion of what constitutes a debate of social significance that stretches well beyond the sphere of official politics that the *Von Hannover* judgment confined itself to.[89] It includes, for example, debating the propensity of Princess Caroline's husband, Prince Ernst August von Hannover, to break speed limits and the lessons that can be learnt about thrift in lean times from the willingness of this couple and other celebrities to let their holiday homes.[90]

(Sir Anthony Clarke MR for the Court), where it is observed that: 'We do not share the predisposition ... that routine acts such as a visit to a shop or a ride on a bus should not attract any reasonable expectation of privacy. All depends upon the circumstances.' The Court went on to hold that the taking and publication of photographs infringes the privacy of a very young child taken on shopping expedition by a famous parent (here, the writer JK Rowling) who had consistently kept the child out of the public eye.

[87] See *Caroline von Hannover*, Bundesgerichtshof [German Federal Court of Justice], VI ZR 51/06, 6 March 2007 reported in [2007] NJW 1977; *Caroline von Hannover*, Bundesverfassungsgericht [German Constitutional Court], 1 BvR 1602/07, 1 BvR 1606/07, 1 BvR 1626/07, 26 February 2008 reported in [2008] NJW 1793, especially at [80]–[82], [99]; *Heide Simonis*, Bundesgerichtshof [German Federal Court of Justice], VI ZR 156/06, 24 June 2008 reported in [2008] NJW 3134, [18].

[88] See *Freundin des Ex-Mannes von Uschi Glas*, Bundesverfassungsgericht [German Constitutional Court], 1 BvR 2606/04, 1 BvR 2845/04, 1 BvR 2846/04, 1 BvR 2847/04, 21 August 2006 reported in [2006] NJW 3406, 3407: 'The protection afforded [to freedom of speech] by Article 5(1) of the *Grundgesetz* does not cease to exist just because a media report is of a purely entertaining nature' (my translation). See also *Caroline von Hannover*, Bundesverfassungsgericht [German Constitutional Court], 1 BvR 1602/07, 1 BvR 1606/07, 1 BvR 1626/07, 26 February 2008 reported in [2008] NJW 1793, [42], [62]–[65].

[89] 'When assessing the interest in information, the courts must refrain from evaluating the content of the pertinent report as valuable or valueless, as serious and worthy or flippant, and are limited to examining and determining to what extent the report may contribute to the process of shaping public opinion': *Caroline von Hannover*, Bundesverfassungsgericht [German Constitutional Court], 1 BvR 1602/07, 1 BvR 1606/07, 1 BvR 1626/07, 26 February 2008 reported in [2008] NJW 1793, [67] (my translation).

[90] See *Ernst August von Hannover*, Bundesgerichtshof [German Federal Court of Justice], VI ZR 286/04, 15 November 2005 reported in [2006] NJW 599; *Ernst August von Hannover*, Bundesverfassungsgericht [German Constitutional Court], 1 BvR 565/06, 13 June 2006 reported in [2006] NJW 2835; *Caroline von Hannover*, Bundesverfassungsgericht [German

No wonder that the von Hannovers have returned to Strasbourg, where a Grand Chamber decision is currently pending in respect of this latest round of German decisions.[91]

Although it is less clear whether the English courts are also sticking to their guns,[92] it is important to note that the contrasting attitude to the purposes that may legitimately be pursued by the press coincides with another noteworthy difference between *Von Hannover* and these domestic decisions. This is that the approach of the English and German courts was forged in the course of the *indirect* horizontal application of fundamental rights. In *Campbell* Lady Hale expressly (and, arguably, the remainder of their Lordships implicitly) gave indirect horizontal effect to the relevant Convention rights by drawing on them to reform the existing doctrine of breach of confidence and then applying the reformed doctrine to resolve the dispute.[93] The German cases, which draw primarily on the fundamental rights in the *Grundgesetz*, also exemplify indirect rather than direct application. In classical indirect fashion, these constitutional rights were used to interpret the legislative provisions relied on by Princess Caroline and others complaining of the publication of their pictures without their permission,[94] and to develop privacy protection within the framework of the *Bürgerliches Gesetzbuch*'s tort provisions.[95] Because the two contrasts map onto each other, the divergence of the approaches adopted by the Strasbourg Court and these national courts illuminates the difference between direct and indirect horizontal application.

The essence of that difference lies in the domestic courts' refusal to reduce the legitimate purposes of press reports to the furtherance of a

---

Constitutional Court], 1 BvR 1602/07, 1 BvR 1606/07, 1 BvR 1626/07, 26 February 2008 reported in [2008] NJW 1793; *Heide Simonis*, Bundesgerichtshof [German Federal Court of Justice], VI ZR 156/06, 24 June 2008 reported in [2008] NJW 3134.

[91] *Von Hannover v Germany*, Cases 40660/08 and 60641/08 (hearing held on 13 October 2010).

[92] In *McKennitt v Ash* [2006] EWCA Civ 1714, [2008] QB 73, [66] the Court of Appeal repeated 'the long-standing view that what interests the public is not necessarily in the public interest', and quoted Lady Hale's assertion in *Jameel v Wall Street Journal Europe Sprl* [2006] UKHL 44, [2007] 1 AC 359 [147] that 'the most vapid tittle-tattle about the activities of footballers' wives and girlfriends interests large sections of the public but no-one could claim any real public interest in our being told all about it'. On the other hand, in *Terry v Persons Unknown* [2010] EWHC 119 (QB), [2010] EMLR 16 [100]–[104], Tugendhat J rejected the argument that public disclosure of private conduct (here, a professional footballer's extramarital relationship) would only be capable of contributing to a debate in a democratic society if it was unlawful, and insisted that, 'the freedom to criticise ... the conduct of other members of society as being socially harmful, or wrong' is 'one of the most valuable freedoms'.

[93] See *Campbell* [2004] UKHL 22, [2004] 2 AC 457 [16]–[18] (Lord Nicholls), [50]–[51] (Lord Hoffmann), [114] (Lord Hope), [132] (Lady Hale).

[94] Gesetz betreffend das Urheberrecht an Werken der bildende Künste und der Photographie 1907 (Act on Copyright in Works of Art and Photography) s 22.

[95] The *allgemeines Persönlichkeitsrecht* (general personality right). On this, see Beverley-Smith, Ohly and Lucas-Schloetter, above n 39, at 100 ff.

political 'watchdog' function.[96] Although both the German and English courts have tightened their protection of privacy against press intrusions, they have also continued to maintain a broad understanding of what constitutes information of public value and to regard not only political discourse as valuable but also discussion of topics traversing a much broader front of general social significance. The difference, then, is between an approach that mediates between the interest of the individual and the community as a politically organised entity and one that mediates between the interest of the individual and a wider conception of communal life as encompassing also matters such as social mores and economic activities.[97] Crucially, this divergence is of a piece with the origin of fundamental rights in concerns about the relationship between individuals and the management of the common good via the state. At heart, fundamental rights are focused on persons as participants in a political community and their direct gaze is limited accordingly to those human interests that are engaged in the common regulation of social life via the state. This stretches very far indeed, and does, as *Von Hannover* demonstrates, also direct attention to interactions among private persons that are not mediated by the state. But, as is also evident from *Von Hannover*, such attention retains its focus on the political dimensions of community life.

In this way, *Von Hannover* reveals a danger posed by direct horizontality. This is that the direct application of a fundamental right brings with it the concerns wrapped up in its origins and, in doing so, limits the purposes legitimated by that right to those which feature in the relations between individuals and the state.[98] Such a restriction is incompatible with the normative equality of individuals, since it follows from this principle that private persons may not prescribe to each other what purposes are to be followed.[99] The normative environment in which fundamental rights operate therefore changes when the state is replaced as counterparty by a private person.[100] Because all that one individual may rightly demand

---

[96] As Lord Cooke put it in *Reynolds v Times Newspapers Ltd* [2001] 2 AC 127 (HL) 220: 'Matters other than those pertaining to government and politics may be just as important in the community'.

[97] Since *Von Hannover*, the Strasbourg Court has held that Article 10 of the ECHR supports publication of reports on the activities of influential members of the worlds of business, culture or journalism; however, the significance of such reports was still seen to lie in their contribution to politics. See *Tønsbergs Blad AS and Haukom v Norway* App no 510/04 (ECHR, 1 March 2007); *Verlagsgruppe News GmbH v Austria* App nos 76918/01 and 10520/02 (ECHR, 14 December 2006); *Minelli v Switzerland* App no 14991/02 (ECHR, 14 June 2005); *Karhuvaara and Iltalehti v Finland* App no 53678/00 (ECHR, 16 November 2004).

[98] Revealingly, the Strasbourg Court has held that statements made in a commercial context fall outside the 'basic nucleus protected by freedom of expression': *Markt Intern and Beerman v Germany* (1990) 12 EHRR 161, 173.

[99] On the notion of normative equality and its link to corrective justice, see Weinrib, *The Idea of Private Law*, above n 9, at 76–83.

[100] Another dimension of this is that individuals are entitled to more wide-ranging pro-

from another is for the other to moderate the pursuit of their purposes in light of the first person's equal entitlement to pursue their own purposes, private law may assess the importance of an objective, but may not exclude the pursuit of that objective altogether. In the context of the privacy cases, this means that the pursuit by the press of non-political objectives must be accepted as legitimate, although the relative social value of a purpose—its relationship to the common good—may (indeed, must) feature in the balancing of the conflicting interests at stake. As both the German and the English cases discussed above show, this is exactly what is involved in the indirect horizontal application of fundamental rights. Because it absorbs fundamental rights into a balancing exercise that has the specific objective of determining what one individual may demand from another, indirect horizontality allows private law to relate these rights to the full complexity of interpersonal interactions.

For this reason, the horizontal application of fundamental rights is best treated as indirect rather than direct, such rights functioning as values and principles that leave room for the legal recognition of further interests.[101] Private law serves the common good by structuring direct interactions among persons. In doing so, it 'expresses the moral bonds that hold directly between citizens, without the mediation of the state', whereas public law 'concerns relations that are so mediated'.[102] This duality enables the legal order to recognise and support individual moral agency while simultaneously facilitating the collective pursuit of goals.[103] By enabling individuals to acknowledge each other as moral equals and to co-operate on this basis, private law fosters the development of the shared ethical life that provides the indispensible moral foundation for common citizenship and the joint pursuit of projects via the state.[104] As such, private law

tection against interference by other individuals than by the state. Thus, according to the *Bundesverfassungsgericht*, the range of personality interests afforded protection is narrower in constitutional law than in private law. See *Caroline von Hannover*, Bundesverfassungsgericht [German Constitutional Court], 1 BvR 1602/07, 1 BvR 1606/07, 1 BvR 1626/07, 26 February 2008 reported in [2008] NJW 1793, [88]. This appears also to be the case in the US: see Beverley-Smith, Ohly and Lucas-Schloetter, above n 39, at 54.

[101] This appears to be the significance of the distinction between fundamental rights functioning as 'rights' and as 'values' in both Germany, where it originated, and in Canada, where it was most prominently taken up. See *Lüth*, Bundesverfassungsgericht [German Constitutional Court], 1 BvR 400/51, 15 January 1958 reported in (1958) 7 BVerfGE 198; *Dolphin Delivery* [1986] 2 SCR 573.

[102] NE Simmonds, 'The Possibility of Private Law' in J Tasioulas (ed), *Law, Values and Social Practices* (Aldershot, Dartmouth, 1997) 129, 155.

[103] ibid.

[104] This is a major theme of Hegel, above n 44. Thus, 'Hegel details how through the institutions of private property and contract, individuals objectify their wills and are recognized by others in a common will; how through marriage, an individual comes to be an ethical being; how in civil society, by working in corporations, we work for still a greater objective; and how all of these stages prepare us to be citizens at home in the state and satisfied in carrying out the duties of citizenship': M Tunick, 'Hegel on Justified Disobedience' (1998) 26 *Political Theory* 514, 524–25.

makes a particular contribution to the legal order, but is also constrained in the manner that it contributes to the maintenance of the common good. It can only give effect to individuals' rights and duties in respect of collective life to the extent that these rights and duties can be translated into obligations compatible with the normative equality of interacting individuals. If more is required—if, for instance, particular purposes are to be prohibited altogether in the interest of the common good—then recourse should be had to legal techniques that mediate directly between individuals and society.[105]

V. CONCLUSION

Private law mediates interactions among individuals by providing a facility whereby one individual may prevent another individual from violating or continuing to violate his or her rights or may obtain redress for such a violation. It also specifies what these rights are, and how they are acquired, transferred and lost. It is therefore bilateral in structure. Because individuals are morally self-determining agents, and enjoy this status in equal measure, private law's remedies are available only where individuals transgress the boundaries of rightful action. Private law is thus specifically concerned with the rights and duties that govern bilateral relationships, and in that way functions as a mode of corrective justice. However, the cases surveyed in this chapter show that it also fulfils the additional role of helping to construct the social good. Contrary to the claim of Ernest Weinrib, private law does serve 'the promotion of social purposes extrinsic to the relationship between the parties'.[106] In fact, as we saw, this social construction role is crucial to the legitimacy of private law, as it justifies the authority of courts to determine the concrete content of private law rights.

As a powerful tool for mediating between the common good and the pursuit of individual aims, fundamental rights can assist private law reasoning in this further function. In this regard, they provide a more systematic, transparent and coherent articulation of the concerns that have long bubbled to the surface in the guise of 'public policy' and its cognates, such as 'good faith'. Concepts such as these attest to the role that private law plays in constructing social practices and institutions. It is therefore unsurprising that fundamental rights are typically drawn on in private law reasoning in contexts where 'public policy' (or comparable open-ended terms in civil codes) features prominently. Here fundamental rights assist the courts in determining how private law serves the common good and

---

[105] For example, criminal law and other forms of public control and regulation.
[106] Weinrib, 'Restitutionary Damages as Corrective Justice', above n 11, at 37.

in ensuring that it is not twisted into an instrument of domination. However, when absorbed into the framework of private law, fundamental rights can only perform these functions in a manner that is compatible with the normative equality of individuals, in particular their equal freedom to pursue their own projects. The horizontal application of fundamental rights must therefore be indirect if society is to continue to benefit from private law's particular contribution to the legal order.

Of course, very many cases of this kind are decided without reliance on fundamental rights. For instance, the courts in both England and the Netherlands made no reference at all to fundamental rights when confronted with the plight of people who had stood surety for loans taken out by family members, although they afforded much the same protection to such sureties as the *Bundesverfassungsgericht* in its *Bürgschaft* decision.[107] This contrast is part of a wider trend, with some jurisdictions and some areas of law displaying more extensive use of fundamental rights reasoning than others.[108] This pattern confirms the analysis put forward in this chapter, for it supports the notion that the value of fundamental rights to private law reasoning is rooted in concerns about the legitimacy of the judicial development of the law. It is precisely in those fields of law and those countries where this concern is most noticeable that recourse to fundamental rights reasoning is most prevalent. Thus in England, it is to be found in the law of confidence/privacy, where social concerns rubbed up against the existing conceptual structure, but not in contract law, which could accommodate these concerns within existing concepts. Similarly, fundamental rights reasoning is much less prominent in established common law systems, where judicial decisions are recognised as a source of law, than in civilian systems where judges are meant merely to interpret and apply enacted law, or in systems, like that in South Africa, which have experienced a constitutional revolution.[109]

---

[107] See *Royal Bank of Scotland plc v Etridge (No 2)* [2001] UKHL 44, [2002] 2 AC 773; *Van Lanschot v Moeder Brink*, Supreme Court of the Netherlands, HR 1 June 1990, [1991] NJ 759.

[108] See the books cited in above nn 1–3.

[109] See LWH Ackermann, 'The Legal Nature of the South African Constitutional Revolution' [2004] *New Zealand Law Review* 633.

5

Rights and Other Things

ROBERT STEVENS*

I. INTRODUCTION

D
IFFERENTIATING DISTINCT CONCEPTS is a constant battle. When I first started as a law tutor I was given the task of teaching criminal law, a subject I then had little interest in. One session was devoted to elucidating the difference between the concepts of *mens rea* and *actus reus*. During one tutorial with a particularly dense pair of undergraduates almost the entire hour had elapsed and I had spectacularly failed to get them to understand that bodily movement was not the same thing as the *actus reus* of an offence. In despair, I got up, firmly grasped one student's hand and used it to hit his colleague.

Tutor (hopeful): 'Now, who was it who hit you?'
Student (outraged): 'You!'
Tutor (triumphant): 'See!'

He did not.

The distinction between rights and other things can seem similarly elusive. Moral rights cannot be seen or touched. Like mathematical propositions they only exist in our heads, although I think they are no less important or real for that. If we adopt the perspective of Oliver Wendell Holmes' bad man,[1] which is no more obviously incorrect as a perspective than is mine, yours, a judge's or a legislator's, it would seem to make sense within private law to cut to the chase and start talking directly about the conditions under which the law will force someone to do something, such as pay money. A person who insists upon talking about 'rights' may be thought to be making an uninteresting formal claim about the structure of those conditions of liability, a claim of little interest to Holmes'

* I am very grateful for comments from Professors Allan Beever, Paul Mitchell, Jason Neyers, Ernest Weinrib and Richard Wright, and Dr George Letsas. All errors are mine. All comments gratefully received at robert.stevens@ucl.ac.uk.

[1] OW Holmes, 'The Path of Law' (1897) 10 *Harvard Law Review* 457.

bad man as the law could be structured in such a way as to do away with 'rights' talk altogether. Alternatively, lawyers who talk about moral rights may be thought to be trying to forestall argument about what those conditions ought to be, by introducing a concept with a rhetorical pull. Further, in our relativistic age, questions of morality may be perceived to be questions for the personal judgement of each of us, rather than matters of objective truth. The hard-headed lawyer, who vaguely remembers the legal positivism he or she learnt as a student, may take the view that as there is no necessary connection between law and morality the language of rights simply obscures what the law is for. Private law, it may be thought, should not be about enforcing one subjective view of morality or another, but rather just about making the world an objectively better place by deterring accidents or facilitating commerce or compensating the injured.

This chapter is a conservative one. I shall try to distinguish rights from other things with which they are frequently confused. I hope thereby to contribute to a defence of the view that rights talk is not mere surplusage, but is indispensable to understanding what private law is, and why it is important. I shall try to do so without committing a criminal offence.

In what follows rights are distinguished from six distinct things: Loss, Gains, Interests, Deontology, Corrective Justice, and Private Law. Whilst the parts are related, each contains a free-standing argument.

II. RIGHTS AND LOSS

Suppose that as Smith is travelling to the airport to catch an aeroplane, she is negligently injured by Jones' careless driving. The incident causes Smith to miss her flight. In the course of the flight to Smith's desired destination, the aeroplane is hit by a freak quadruple bird strike whilst over the ocean, causing it to crash, killing everyone on board. It is as certain as anything can be that Smith would have died in the crash if she had not been injured by Jones.[2]

This example is important as it illustrates in a striking way the difference between *iniuria* and *damnum*. In English we express this distinction as being that between injury and harm, a civil wrong and its consequences, rights and loss. It is central to understanding the law of torts. In English we can lose sight of the distinction because as a matter of everyday usage the words injury and harm can be used interchangeably.

There is no doubt that Smith has been the victim of a tort, a species of civil wrong. A civil wrong is committed when a duty owed to another

[2] The example, slightly amended, is from EJ Weinrib, 'Right and Advantage in Private Law' (1989) 10 *Cardozo Law Review* 1283. The amendment is to make it clear that the death that Smith has avoided was non-wrongful.

is breached. The duties in private law do not exist in the air. Duties of this kind are also not owed to society, or to ourselves, or to God, or to the state as a placeholder for all of us. Rather, *private* duties are owed to other people. I owe a duty to Tony Blair not to punch him on the nose and I owe the same, but separate, duty to David Cameron. We can emphasise the relational nature of this duty, and stress that it is not of the same kind as my duty not to drink alcohol to excess or not to be cruel to animals or not to make graven images, by talking in terms of the (claim) rights of those to whom the duty is owed.[3] Claim rights always have correlative duties, but it is a basic mistake to think that this entails the converse proposition. I could have entitled my book on the subject[4] *Torts and the Duties We Owe One to Another* but that wouldn't have been quite so snappy. The series of conferences at one of which this chapter was originally delivered are said to be devoted to the 'law of obligations', but this is a misnomer for their subject matter. The obligations imposed by the criminal law or by public law upon state bodies and officials fall outside of its purview. The label 'Private Rights' would much more accurately capture its scope.

It should be stressed that not all scholars share my view as to the nature of all of the duties in private law. So, some take the view that within negligence the duty to take care is, like our criminal law duty not to be in possession of heroin, a duty in the air which is not owed to other individuals.[5] Still others take the more extreme view that the duty to take care is, like the 'duty' to mitigate loss in quantifying damages, not a duty at all but rather a 'control device'[6] or 'incidence rule'[7] for defining when loss caused by negligence must be paid for. The way in which the law of torts is taught, at my current institution, my previous one and elsewhere in the United Kingdom, would indicate that the latter view is widely held.

If we take rights seriously however, in driving my car around Magdalen roundabout in Oxford I owe no duty to take care not to injure towards

---

[3] I do not mean to make any claim here as to whether or not animals can be the bearers of moral rights, any more than I am making any claim about the existence or non-existence of any deity. Rather I am observing that as a matter of law, animals do not have rights. Rover cannot claim in his own name, nor can claims on his behalf be brought. God(s) has/ have no legal rights either, even assuming existence. I do have a criminal law duty not to be cruel to animals (Animal Welfare Act 2006, s 4) but no longer a duty not to commit blasphemy (Criminal Justice and Immigration Act 2008, s 79).

[4] R Stevens, *Torts and Rights* (Oxford, Oxford University Press, 2007).

[5] See, eg, D Howarth, 'Many Duties of Care—Or a Duty of Care? Notes from the Underground' (2006) 26 *Oxford Journal of Legal Studies* 449.

[6] JG Fleming, 'Remoteness and Duty: The Control Devices in Liability for Negligence' (1953) 31 *Canadian Bar Review* 471; *Dorset Yacht Co Ltd v Home Office* [1969] 2 QB 412 (CA) 426 (Lord Denning MR); *D v East Berkshire Community Health NHS Trust* [2005] UKHL 23, [2005] 2 AC 373 [94] (Lord Nicholls).

[7] J Stapleton, 'Evaluating Goldberg and Zipursky's Civil Recourse Theory' (2006) 75 *Fordham Law Review* 1529, 1532–35.

those strolling down the boulevards of Paris or sitting on the beach in Sydney, as it is not reasonably foreseeable that my negligence could injure them. Conversely, I have no right that drivers in Cornwall take care not to injure me through their driving when I am lecturing in London, even though it is possible, albeit highly unlikely, that a chain of events could unfold which did result in my being hurt. That the duty to take care not to injure is not owed to the whole world is, in the United States, surprisingly controversial as a proposition of law, as is reflected in the division in the New York Court of Appeals between Cardozo CJ for the majority and Andrews J in dissent in *Palsgraf v Long Island Railroad Co.*[8] In England, and the rest of the Commonwealth, there can be no doubt that I owe a duty of care not to injure only to those persons I can foresee could be so injured, as reflected in the unanimous holding of the House of Lords in the leading case of *Bourhill v Young*[9] to this effect.

That this duty is, in law, a duty not to injure, and not a duty not to expose to the risk of injury, may be illustrated by considering the position of those whom I expose to unacceptable risk if I drive drunkenly the wrong way around my local roundabout. What is the result if my car hits another containing two children and their parents, injuring only the mother? If the mother can no longer work or care for her children, all of the occupants of the car will, in the ordinary course, be worse off and have suffered a loss. However, the children, despite having been exposed by me to an unacceptable risk of injury, and despite having suffered a loss as a result of my negligence, have no claim. It is only the injured mother who has suffered a wrong, which reflects the fact that in law it is the injuring which constitutes the wrong, the breach of the duty owed to another, not the exposure to risk. Only she can claim for her consequential loss. Law tracks morality here: a (private or personal) wrong is constituted by its impact upon another, not by the fact that it risks such impact.

Whether the violation of a right will result in loss is always contingent at the time of the wrong. Counter-intuitively, even killing someone may result in no or *de minimis* harm, so that a dependent will not necessarily have a claim under the Fatal Accidents Act 1976 or equivalent wrongful death legislation for consequential loss.[10] From the later perspective of the time of trial, no wrong *necessarily* leaves the claimant factually worse off than he or she otherwise would be absent the wrong. We can lose sight of this in many cases, and of the distinction between *iniuria* and *damnum*,

---

[8] *Palsgraf v Long Island Railroad Co* 162 NE 99 (NY 1928).
[9] *Bourhill v Young* [1943] AC 92 (HL) 98 (Lord Thankerton), 102 (Lord Russell of Killowen), 108 (Lord Wright), 116 (Lord Porter).
[10] *Kerry v England* [1898] AC 742 (PC); *Dillon v Twin State Gas & Electric Co* 163 A 111 (NH 1932). Cf M Stiggelbout, 'The Case of "Losses in Any Event": A Question of Duty, Cause or Damages?' (2010) 30 *Legal Studies* 558.

because for many wrongs it is virtually always the case that they will result in loss. This is especially true in the context of personal injury, but that the infringement of a right never necessarily results in consequential harm or loss is what I take to be the point of the example above. Even breaking someone's legs may, as things turn out, leave them no worse off, indeed better off, than they otherwise would be. Of course, someone who has had their legs broken is worse off than they were beforehand, but in determining consequential loss we take the position of hindsight at the time of trial: as things have turned out is the claimant now worse off or not? Furthermore, some wrongs, unlike breaking legs, do not even leave the claimant factually worse off compared to their starting position, such as the giving of a blood transfusion to an unconscious Jehovah's Witness contrary to their expressed wishes.[11]

A wrong, or injury, occurs in a moment of time, although some wrongs can be repeated, such as libel, or can be ongoing such as a trespass to land. D commits a civil wrong in relation to C whenever he breaches a duty to C not to do *x*. It is consequently meaningless to talk of a right not to be caused loss. If loss is suffered, it is a consequence of a breach of a duty; it cannot go to the definition of what D is under a duty to do or not do.[12] Although there are some torts which are not actionable per se, such as the general rule in slander, so that *damnum* is required in addition to *iniuria*, it is the latter which is the essential requirement. Slander is still a tort, a civil wrong, even where it is not actionable because of the absence of consequential loss. So, slander without more is sufficient to constitute 'unlawfulness' where loss is caused to a third party by unlawful means. Loss is sometimes a necessary element of actionability, but it does not go to wrongfulness. We can of course also cause loss without violating any right—*damnum sine iniuria*, or in English 'pure' loss whether economic or otherwise—but this is not without more recoverable as no tort has, as a matter of definition, been committed.

When thinking about libel, or trespass to land, or false imprisonment, or private nuisance, lawyers naturally see the essence of the claim as being the right which has been violated. In the area of liability for negligence, however, I suspect that this is no longer the way many (most?) lawyers think. It is tempting, indeed I think it is common, to see the negligent damage of another's property or the negligent injuring of another's person as a species of loss. Surely, so the thinking goes, what is important is that when these things occur the victim is, as a matter of fact, worse off as a result. What then requires explanation is why other forms of loss, 'pure' economic loss for example, are not actionable. A great deal of intellectual effort has been expended pointlessly trying to explain this apparent puz-

---

[11] *B v NHS Hospital Trust* [2002] EWHC 429 (Fam), [2002] 2 All ER 449.
[12] cf Stevens, *Torts and Rights*, above n 4, at 338.

zle.[13] One point of the initial example is to show that there is no puzzle to explain. Negligently injuring someone's person or property no more necessarily results in their being factually worse off as things turn out than does slandering their character or trespassing on their land. These are not forms of loss at all.

If I wish to claim for a tort I must show that a right I had as against the defendant has been infringed. If the wrong committed is in relation to a thing, I must show that I have a right in relation to the thing exigible against the defendant in order to have standing to bring a claim. For example, if a railway company leases the use of a bridge to enable its trains to cross, and the bridge is negligently damaged by a lorry driver causing the company loss because it is unable to operate its service, it will be able to claim because under our common law a lease of land involves the conveyance to the leaseholder of an interest in the land, a right in rem. If, by contrast, the railway company merely has a contractual licence to use the bridge, it only has a right as against the owner of the bridge, and not in relation to the bridge itself. A licence, as its name implies, involves a privilege with regard to the right-holder, not the conveyance of a right. The licensee cannot, therefore, sue the lorry driver for loss it suffers as a result of the damage. It might have a claim for breach of contract against the bridge owner, and the bridge owner will have a claim for the tort it has suffered as against the lorry driver, but the latter claim will only permit the recovery of the bridge owner's losses, not the licensee's as such.

If we allow the claimant to bring a claim for a wrong done to it for loss following from the negligent damage to the bridge we must think that the claimant has a right exigible against the defendant in relation to the bridge.[14] If we think this we must also think that it has the same right in relation to the bridge exigible against all others in the same position as the defendant. In other words the claimant *must* have some sort of property right, a right in rem. It simply cannot be that the claimant has no such right according to the law of property but does according to the law of torts. There is, and can only be, one answer to the question 'Does the claimant have a right in rem in relation to the bridge?' given by a legal system.

If we were to allow all those who suffer loss as a result of damage to any property to claim based upon a tort we would live in a legal system where all of us had rights in relation to all things. This would be a system of communal property holding. Whilst such a legal system is possible it is not, and never has been, that of the common law.

---

[13] For a thorough, scholarly but, in my view, wrong-headed example, see R Perry, 'Relational Economic Loss: An Integrated Economic Justification for the Exclusionary Rule' (2004) 56 *Rutgers Law Review* 711.

[14] But see *Canadian National Railway Co v Norsk Pacific Steamship Co* [1992] 1 SCR 1021.

By contrast, for those who conceive of property damage and injury to person as species of loss, the duty of care in the law of negligence is not really a duty at all and the above analysis will be unsatisfying. On this alternative view, the requirement of showing damage is not a requirement of showing injury but one of showing harm, so that the right disappears from the story. The slippery language of 'damage' elides the distinction between injury and consequential harm, so we find judges saying that '[d]amage in this sense is an abstract concept of being worse off, physically or economically'.[15] The duty of care becomes, on this conception, one amongst several of Holmes' bad man's conditions of liability.[16] In some areas, it is thought that as no special reasons for denying liability exist the 'control device' of the duty of care can be abandoned altogether. So, Lord Bingham in *D v East Berkshire Community Health NHS Trust*, following the urgings of a number of academics,[17] proposed abandoning the duty of care concept in the context of the liability of public bodies for negligence.[18] On Lord Bingham's conception, for a claim to succeed it would not be necessary for the claimant to establish the breach of a duty owed to him or her; rather, it would suffice that the claimant was worse off as a result of a state body acting negligently. Although the majority refused to follow this path, some academics still urge it upon the courts.

To think like this is to abandon the idea that liability for negligence arises as a result of a civil or private wrong altogether. Without the breach of a duty owed to someone else there can be no such wrong. Once that step is taken, the tie between claimant and defendant has been severed and the (moral) justification for imposing liability lost.

III. RIGHTS AND GAINS

A meme which has gained significant prominence recently within private law is the idea that damages are sometimes awarded not to compensate for losses consequential upon the suffering of a wrong, nor to strip the defendant of any gain he or she may have made as a result of a wrong, but rather because of the wrong itself. I have labelled this award substitutive

---

[15] *Rothwell v Chemical & Insulating Co Ltd* [2007] UKHL 39, [2008] 1 AC 281 (*Rothwell*) [7] (Lord Hoffmann).

[16] See generally JCP Goldberg and BC Zipursky, 'Seeing Tort Law from the Internal Point of View: Holmes and Hart on Legal Duties' (2006) 75 *Fordham Law Review* 1563.

[17] See, eg, B Markesinis, 'Plaintiff's Tort Law or Defendant's Tort Law? Is the House of Lords Moving Towards a Synthesis?' (2001) 9 *Torts Law Journal* 168, 172–73; D Fairgrieve, *State Liability in Tort: A Comparative Law Study* (Oxford, Oxford University Press, 2003) 81, 84–86, 134–35; P Craig, *Administrative Law*, 5th edn (London, Sweet & Maxwell, 2003) 902.

[18] *D v East Berkshire Community Health NHS Trust* [2005] UKHL 23, [2005] 2 AC 373 [49]. The majority fortunately rejected this change: at [94] (Lord Nicholls), [98] (Lord Rodger), [138] (Lord Brown).

damages,[19] whilst others have preferred the label vindicatory damages.[20] Although academic interest in this topic is relatively recent, the idea is firmly embedded in the case law. So, to quote from diverse judges over a considerable period of time:

'[A]n injury imports a damage, when a man is thereby hindered of his right.'[21]

'[E]very violation of a right imports damage in contemplation of law.'[22]

'[W]here you have an interference with a legal right the law presumes damage.'[23]

'[The judge] had therefore to assess the damages necessary to compensate the plaintiffs for this continuing invasion of their right.'[24]

'The claimant in such a situation ... is being compensated, not for the loss of amenity, but for the loss of the right to stop the infringement'.[25]

'[T]he purposes for which damages could have been awarded to the deceased ... are not confined to a compensatory purpose but include also, in my opinion, a vindicatory purpose.'[26]

Amongst academics the idea has been expounded by writers on breach of contract,[27] violation of intellectual property rights,[28] proprietary wrongs[29] and torts[30] more generally.

---

[19] Stevens, *Torts and Rights*, above n 4, at 59.

[20] D Pearce and R Halson, 'Damages for Breach of Contract: Compensation, Restitution and Vindication' (2008) 28 *Oxford Journal of Legal Studies* 73; N Witzleb and R Carroll, 'The Role of Vindication in Torts Damages' (2009) 17 *Tort Law Review* 16.

[21] *Ashby v White* (1703) 2 Ld Raym 398, 955; 92 ER 126, 138 (Holt CJ).

[22] *Neville v London Express Newspaper Ltd* [1919] AC 368 (HL) 392 (Viscount Haldane).

[23] *Nicholls v Ely Beet Sugar Factory Ltd* [1936] 1 Ch 343 (CA) 350 (Lord Wright MR).

[24] *Jaggard v Sawyer* [1995] 1 WLR 269 (CA) 281 (Sir Thomas Bingham MR).

[25] *Tamares (Vincent Square) Ltd v Fairpoint Properties (Vincent Square) Ltd* [2007] EWHC 212 (Ch), [2007] 1 WLR 2167 [29] (Gabriel Moss QC).

[26] *Ashley v Chief Constable of Sussex Police* [2008] UKHL 25, [2008] 1 AC 962 [22] (Lord Scott).

[27] See, eg, D Friedmann, 'The Performance Interest in Contract Damages' (1995) 111 *Law Quarterly Review* 628; B Coote, 'The Performance Interest, *Panatown*, and the Problem of Loss' (2000) 117 *Law Quarterly Review* 81; L Smith, 'Understanding Specific Performance' in N Cohen and E McKendrick (eds), *Comparative Remedies for Breach of Contract* (Oxford, Hart Publishing, 2005) 221, 228–30; E McKendrick, *Contract Law: Text, Cases, and Materials*, 3rd edn (Oxford, Oxford University Press, 2008) 860–67; F Reynolds, 'The *Golden Victory*—A Misguided Decision' (2008) 38 *Hong Kong Law Journal* 333; R Stevens, 'Damages and the Right to Performance: A *Golden Victory* or Not?' in JW Neyers, R Bronaugh and SGA Pitel (eds), *Exploring Contract Law* (Oxford, Hart Publishing, 2009) 171. *Contra* A Burrows, 'No Damages for a Third Party's Loss' (2001) 1 *Oxford University Commonwealth Law Journal* 107.

[28] M Spence, *Intellectual Property* (Oxford, Oxford University Press, 2007) 33–35.

[29] B McFarlane, *The Structure of Property Law* (Oxford, Hart Publishing, 2008) 199–200, 420–21; R Chambers, 'Trust and Theft' in E Bant and M Harding (eds), *Exploring Private Law* (Cambridge, Cambridge University Press, 2010) 223.

[30] A Tettenborn, 'What Is a Loss?' in JW Neyers, E Chamberlain and SGA Pitel (eds),

In some areas this idea is more familiar than in others, but it is a long-established feature of our law. Libel specialists, for example, would be most surprised if it were suggested to them that a claimant could only recover his or her proven consequential losses where he or she is called a paedophile in print.[31] However, nobody would be foolish enough to suggest that substantial damages are capable of being claimed for *all* wrongs regardless of consequential loss.[32] A claim for slander, unlike libel and subject to exceptions, is confined to consequential loss. *Iniuria sine damno* is not, for this wrong, sufficient. Whether a wrong is actionable per se or not depends upon the degree of seriousness with which infringement is viewed. Over time, this can change and it may be that the divisions the law has adopted need revision. That libel is more serious than slander reflected the idea that a permanent statement in print was more serious than an oral communication of the same defamatory statement. In an era of mass communication this made little sense, so broadcasts were treated as permanent by section 166(1) of the Broadcasting Act 1990. Similarly, that the imputation of unchastity to a woman is actionable per se whilst claiming that she is a habitual liar is not may be thought to reflect the mores of a bygone era.

However, some writers have sought to explain some, but not all, of the cases where damages are awarded in substitute for or vindication of the right of the claimant in terms of a gain made by the defendant. The example which has given rise to most discussion in the literature is *Wrotham Park Estate Co Ltd v Parkside Homes Ltd*.[33] Land belonging to the defendant was subject to a restrictive covenant registered as a land charge forbidding development except with approval of the owner from time to time of the Wrotham Park Estate. The defendant in breach of the covenant built 14 houses and a road on its land. The claimant warned the defendant of its right as soon as the work commenced, and sought an injunction restraining the work and seeking the demolition of the build-

---

Emerging Issues in Tort Law (Oxford, Hart Publishing, 2007) 441; Stevens, *Torts and Rights*, above n 4, at ch 4; Lord Scott, 'Damages' [2007] *Lloyd's Maritime and Commercial Law Quarterly* 465; Pearce and Halson, above n 20; Witzleb and Carroll, above n 20; J Edelman, 'Gain-Based Damages and Compensation' in A Burrows and Lord Rodger (eds), *Mapping the Law: Essays in Memory of Peter Birks* (Oxford, Oxford University Press, 2006) 141 (withdrawn J Edelman, 'The Meaning of Loss and Enrichment' in R Chambers, C Mitchell and J Penner (eds), *Philosophical Foundations of the Law of Unjust Enrichment* (Oxford, Oxford University Press, 2009) 211).

[31] *Kiam v MGN Ltd* [2002] EWCA Civ 43, [2003] QB 281; *Uren v John Fairfax & Sons Pty Ltd* (1966) 117 CLR 118, 151 (Windeyer J); *Jameel v Wall Street Journal Europe Sprl* [2006] UKHL 44, [2007] 1 AC 359.

[32] Stevens, *Torts and Rights*, above n 4, at 88–90; Stevens, 'Damages and the Right to Performance', above n 27, at 197. *Contra* T Cutts, '*Wrotham Park* Damages: Compensation, Restitution or a Substitute for the Value of the Infringement of the Right?' [2010] *Lloyd's Maritime and Commercial Law Quarterly* 215, 219.

[33] *Wrotham Park Estate Co Ltd v Parkside Homes Ltd* [1974] 1 WLR 798 (Ch) (*Wrotham Park*).

ing which had been done. The defendant was (incorrectly) advised that the covenant was unenforceable and continued work. At trial, Brightman J refused to award the injunction, but did order damages, calculated according to a reasonable price for the claimant to have released its right. This was calculated as five per cent of the £50 000 profit made by the defendant from the work: £2500.

Accepting, as almost everyone now does, that the claimant had no consequential loss, was this a claim to the gain made? The straightforward and correct answer is no, as the gain made as a matter of fact as a result of the wrong was £50 000, and this was not what was awarded. The gain made was only relevant as evidence of the value of the infringed right. Substitutive damages of this kind are assessed at the time of the wrong and are quantified objectively (save where the defendant's conduct is particularly egregious). Where the claimant suffers actual loss over and above this figure such losses are recoverable, but the damages are not reduced because no consequential loss is, as a matter of fact, suffered by the claimant.

What if the wrongdoer makes an overall loss from the use of the land? This was the question which faced the Privy Council in *Inverugie Investments Ltd v Hackett*.[34] The defendant was a landlord who had wrongfully evicted the claimant from 30 hotel apartments. The defendant made use of these over a period of 15 years. However, because of low occupancy rates in the hotel the use of these apartments over time caused the defendant to make an overall substantial loss. The defendant would, as a matter of fact, have been much better off by not making use of the apartments. Substantial damages, measured as a reasonable licence fee at market rates, were awarded (as mesne profits).

Andrew Burrows has sought to justify this result as based upon 'an objective view of compensation',[35] but as he strongly disapproves of awards to compensate which do not reflect the loss actually suffered this must mean he considers the decision to be wrongly decided.[36] More recently, he has sought to argue that the defendant is objectively benefited by the use of the land and cannot be permitted to 'subjectively devalue' (ie, prove that as a matter of fact he made no gain from the use of the land) because he was a deliberate wrongdoer.[37] Two replies are possible. First, and more importantly, this argument collapses into awarding damages because the defendant is a wrongdoer without more needing to be shown. Deeming defendants to have been saved the expense of hiring

---

[34] *Inverugie Investments Ltd v Hackett* [1995] 1 WLR 713 (PC) (*Inverugie*). See Stevens, *Torts and Rights*, above n 4, at 79–84.

[35] A Burrows, 'Are "Damages on the *Wrotham Park* Basis" Compensatory, Restitutionary or Neither?' in D Saidov and R Cunnington (eds), *Contract Damages: Domestic and International Perspectives* (Oxford, Hart Publishing, 2008) 165, 180.

[36] See generally Burrows, 'Damages on the *Wrotham Park* Basis', above n 35.

[37] A Burrows, 'Damages and Rights' ch 10 of this book.

alternative rooms, when they would not in fact have done so, and refusing to allow the offsetting of other losses suffered as a result of the wrong, is to fictionally treat them as enriched only because they are wrongdoers. Secondly, this argument is inconsistent with the facts of *Inverugie*. It was never alleged that the defendant was committing deliberate trespass, and the allowance the Privy Council made for the expenses the innocent defendant had incurred in maintaining the property shows that they were not. Where, as in *Inverugie*, a blameless wrongdoer confers a benefit upon a claimant in this way a deduction is made so that the claimant is not unjustly enriched at the defendant's expense. An innocent purchaser of stolen property may therefore be able to obtain a reduction in the damages in conversion payable where he or she has incurred expenses repairing it, whereas no such allowance is permitted for the deliberate wrongdoer.[38]

As damages do not go up where the claimant makes a greater gain than the value of the right, nor down where the defendant makes no overall gain at all, the better view of *Wrotham Park* damages is that the award is there to vindicate or to substitute for the right infringed, and is not there to strip the defendant of any gain he or she has made.

If this is accepted, then it follows that in other similar cases a gain-based analysis is only necessary where the gain made by the defendant is greater than both a quantification of the infringement of the right and any consequential loss suffered by the claimant. The number of cases where such an award has been made are, in fact, very few indeed, rendering the category of 'restitution for wrongs' almost redundant. So, within the law of torts the only examples appear to be claims for account of profits in relation to intellectual property wrongs.[39] Even here the quantification is not made according to the overall balance sheet gain made by the defendant but for the wrong, but rather according to the quantum of profit traceably attributable to the right infringed. Other opportunities foregone are ignored, and saved expenses are not recoverable.[40]

Outside of torts, we can identify claims in equity, such as the obligation of a fiduciary to account for profits made in such capacity without the beneficiary's consent in, for example, *Boardman v Phipps*,[41] and the claim against the traitor George Blake for an account of the profits made from a breach of contract.[42] The former seems justifiable. One thing the fiduciary duty to subordinate your interests to those of someone else

---

[38] *Greenwood v Bennett* [1973] QB 195 (CA) 201 (Lord Denning MR). See also Stevens, *Torts and Rights*, above n 4, at 82.

[39] *Lever v Goodwin* (1887) 36 Ch D 1 (CA) (passing off); *Slazenger & Sons v Spalding & Bros* [1910] 1 Ch 257 (Ch) (trademark infringement); Patents Act 1977, s 61(1)(d) (patents); Copyright, Designs and Patents Act 1988, s 96(2) (copyright), s 191(2) (performance right).

[40] See generally Spence, above n 28, at 33–35.

[41] *Boardman v Phipps* [1967] 2 AC 46 (HL).

[42] *A-G v Blake* [2001] 1 AC 268 (HL).

entails is that you must account for profits you make out of the relationship, unless you get the other's consent.[43] Express contractual promises to
account for profits should similarly be enforceable. The nature of the right
explains the availability of this form of relief. *A-G v Blake* by contrast
appears particularly anomalous, based as the majority's decision was upon
the 'solitary beacon'[44] of *Wrotham Park*, which, as we have seen, was
not a gain-based claim at all,[45] and the boundaries of the rule introduced
remain obscure.[46] Perhaps the result in *Blake*, if not the reasoning, can be
defended on the basis that as there is no ready market figure for releasing
traitors from their contractual obligations, the best available evidence of
the value of the Crown's right was 100 per cent of what Jonathan Cape
were prepared to pay Blake, as opposed to the five per cent of profits
awarded in *Wrotham Park*.

Unsurprisingly, those who have long subscribed to the view that a gain-
based analysis best explains those cases where the award of damages is
not made to compensate a consequential factual loss[47] have also been the
most critical of the substitutive or vindicatory analysis.[48] What are the
answers to the objections which have been raised?

James Edelman in an essay entitled 'The Meaning of Loss and Enrichment'[49] makes four arguments which require consideration.

First it is argued that if we awarded damages as a substitute for the
right infringed this would lead to the ridiculous result that a claimant
would be entitled to the full value of his or her right to a thing regardless of the seriousness of the damage inflicted.[50] If the claimant owns a
single thing, such as a car or house, why should the defendant have to
pay the full value of the thing if it is damaged in a minor way?

This objection would seem to misunderstand the basis upon which
quantification is made. If I own a chattel I own a single object save to

---

[43] PJ Millett, 'Equity's Place in the Law of Commerce' (1998) 114 *Law Quarterly Review* 214, 225–27.

[44] *A-G v Blake* [2001] AC 268 (HL) 283.

[45] See also *WWF—World Wide Fund for Nature v World Wide Wrestling Federation Entertainment Inc* [2007] EWCA Civ 286, [2008] 1 WLR 445 [56] (Chadwick LJ).

[46] The decision was also probably *per incuriam* as members of the intelligence services have no contract with the Crown: AWB Simpson, 'A Decision Per Incuriam?' (2009) 125 *Law Quarterly Review* 433. No doubt the Crown considers it preferable that the employment is not by way of contract, with the concomitant reciprocal legal obligations. It seems likely that it was for this reason that no claim for breach of contract was originally asserted, and why this way of putting the case was disowned before the Court of Appeal despite the promptings of the Court.

[47] J Edelman, *Gain-Based Damages: Contract, Tort, Equity and Intellectual Property* (Oxford, Hart Publishing, 2002); A Burrows, *The Law of Restitution*, 3rd edn (Oxford, Oxford University Press, 2011).

[48] See, eg, Burrows, 'No Damages for a Third Party's Loss', above n 27; Burrows, 'Damages on the *Wrotham Park* Basis', above n 35; Edelman, 'The Meaning of Loss and Enrichment', above n 30.

[49] Edelman, 'The Meaning of Loss and Enrichment', above n 30.

[50] ibid, at 219.

the extent that individual components are identifiable and capable of separation without damage.[51] However if I negligently scratch the paint on your Rolls Royce this does not mean that I must pay the full value of the panel, still less the full value of the car, despite the accession of the paint to the panel and the panel to the car. As I have said elsewhere,[52] what is quantified is the value of the infringement, not the full value of the indivisible right.

In the case of property rights—unlike, for example, false imprisonment or libel—this is straightforward as it is assessed by reference to the market value of the thing. So, in the case of the panel, we look to the difference between the value of the thing before and after the wrong. Unfortunately we can lose sight of the right to this award because in most, but not all, cases this difference will be the same as or less than the consequential economic loss which will actually be incurred in correcting the wrong (the cost of respraying the panel in this case).[53] This does *not* mean that we value the right itself by reference to such costs which may not be incurred as things turn out.[54]

The second example given is the well-known case of *Performance Cars v Abraham*.[55] A panel of the claimant's car is damaged by the defendant's negligence resulting in the need for a respray. Subsequently the car is hit again by another careless driver, in a way which but for the earlier accident would also have necessitated a respray. Both accidents have infringed the same right to the car, so why is it that substitutive or vindicatory damages are not available against both car drivers?

Again, as I have said elsewhere,[56] the answer is that substitutive damages are assessed at the time of the wrong, not the time of trial. What value is to be given to the infringement at the relevant moment of time? For proprietary wrongs the position is straightforward. Each driver should be liable for the diminution in the value of the panel at the point of impact. In relation to the first driver this leads to a substantial award, but no award as against the second driver. A second scratch to a panel already in need of a respray reduces its value no further. This result cannot necessarily be reached by asking simply whether, from the perspective of the time of trial, each individual defendant's actions has made the claimant's position any worse off,[57] as at that point each may be able to point to the other accident and argue that the loss would have been incurred in

---

[51] *Hendy Lennox (Industrial Engines) Ltd v Grahame Puttick Ltd* [1984] 1 WLR 485 (QB).

[52] Stevens, *Torts and Rights*, above n 4, at 85; Stevens, 'Damages and the Right to Performance', above n 27, at 195.

[53] Stevens, *Torts and Rights*, above n 4, at 61.

[54] cf Edelman, 'The Meaning of Loss and Enrichment', above n 30, at 219.

[55] *Performance Cars v Abraham* [1962] 1 QB 33 (CA) (*Performance Cars*).

[56] Stevens, *Torts and Rights*, above n 4, at 138.

[57] *contra* Edelman, 'The Meaning of Loss and Enrichment', above n 30, at 220.

any event. In fact it does not matter that the claimant has not and will not incur the cost of making good the loss; he or she is still entitled to the diminution in the value of the thing at the time of the wrong.[58]

Thirdly, it is argued that if claims assessed by reference to the value of the right were permitted in addition to claims for consequential loss this would allow the claimant to cumulate his or her claims in a way which would lead to double recovery.[59] Should the claimant in *Performance Cars* be allowed to claim both for the diminution in the value of the dented panel and the costs incurred in putting it right?

Again, as I have argued elsewhere,[60] no such cumulation is possible for precisely the same reason that no cumulation is possible if we allow claims for consequential losses suffered by the claimant and for profits made by the defendant. To the extent that the claimant recovers a penny by way of damages to reflect the decline in the value of the panel of his or her car, he or she has to that extent suffered one penny less of consequential loss. It is not possible to recover both the value of the infringement and the loss consequent upon it, because if I recover the former, to that extent, I do not suffer the latter. Recovery under one head reduces the damages recoverable under the other.

Fourthly, Edelman claims that the authorities show that before a claim on the basis asserted in *Wrotham Park* can be brought the consequences of the wrong must be subjectively undesired. Arguing, as Edelman does, that corporate litigants suffer actionable consequential misery as a result of having their property damaged is surely a step of anthropomorphism too far. Even assuming, for the sake of argument, that it is required that the wrong is subjectively undesired by the claimant this does not demonstrate that this is a claim for consequential corporate upset.

Burrows in his essay 'Are "Damages on the *Wrotham Park* Basis" Compensatory, Restitutionary or Neither?'[61] gives five further objections around the same theme as Edelman.

First, to allow a claim for substitutive or vindicatory damages would entail a right to substantial damages for every wrong. As I have said elsewhere,[62] this is not so. For some wrongs all that is actionable is consequential loss. The distinction between those wrongs which are actionable per se, such as false imprisonment, and those which are not, such as deceit, is well-established, although whether the line has been drawn in the right

---

[58] See, eg, *The Charlotte* [1908] P 206 (CA); *Obestain Inc v National Mineral Development Corp Ltd (The Sanix Ace)* [1987] 1 Lloyd's Rep 465 (QB).

[59] Burrows makes the same argument in 'Damages on the *Wrotham Park* Basis', above n 35, at 184.

[60] Stevens, *Torts and Rights*, above n 4, at 61; Stevens, 'Damages and the Right to Performance', above n 27, at 181.

[61] Burrows, 'Damages on the *Wrotham Park* Basis', above n 35, at 184.

[62] Stevens, *Torts and Rights*, above n 4, at 88–91; Stevens, 'Damages and the Right to Performance', above n 27, at 176.

place for all wrongs requires consideration. It has not been suggested by anyone that lies which are believed should be actionable without more. It is also suggested that allowing such damages 'undermin[es] the whole of our conventional understanding of damages'.[63] Here, I think I can do no more than rely upon the academic writers cited above and the judiciary quoted, not all of whom strike me as dangerous radicals.

Secondly, it is argued that to permit substitutive or vindicatory damages contradicts the law on mitigation and the duty to mitigate. If one takes the view that damages are not always compensatory for consequential loss one might object that this simply assumes what you are trying to prove. As the rules on mitigation of loss are, obviously, concerned with the quantification of consequential loss they have no application to substitutive or vindicatory damages, any more than they do to punitive damages or a claim for account of profits.

However, it may be that Burrows is here taking the view, which he adopts elsewhere, that the rules on mitigation are part of our law for instrumentalist reasons. So, he has written that 'the policy is one of encouraging the claimant, once a wrong has occurred, to be to a reasonable extent self-reliant, or, in economists' terminology, to be efficient.'[64] The proper response is that this instrumental goal is not the justification for our rules on mitigation. If it were then substitutive or vindicatory damages would indeed undermine the encouragement given, but so would *any* measure of recovery which is not quantified by reference to consequential loss suffered to which the rules on mitigation similarly do not apply. So, the action for the agreed sum where the rules on mitigation have no application would also be objectionable, and this is indeed Burrows' view as he disapproves of the leading case on the point.[65]

The leading decision of the House of Lords on our rules of mitigation is *British Westinghouse Electric and Manufacturing Co Ltd v Underground Electric Railways Co of London Ltd*[66] and provides a useful illustration of the true position. In 1902 the defendants agreed to sell eight steam turbines for electricity generation to the claimant railway company for £250 000. The turbines proved to be defective. The claimant sought damages of upwards of £280 000 for losses that they estimated would be caused by the excessive coal consumption over the life of the machines. Alternatively, they claimed the cost of installing eight new turbines, with superior kilowatt capacity, which they had purchased in 1908 when the seller's machines proved insufficient. They estimated the cost of these

---

[63] Burrows, 'Damages on the *Wrotham Park* Basis', above n 35, at 182.

[64] A Burrows, *Remedies for Torts and Breach of Contract*, 3rd edn (Oxford, Oxford University Press, 2004) 122.

[65] *White & Carter (Councils) Ltd v McGregor* [1962] AC 413 (HL); Burrows, ibid, at 440.

[66] *British Westinghouse Electric and Manufacturing Co Ltd v Underground Electric Railways Co of London Ltd* [1912] AC 673 (HL) (*British Westinghouse*).

machines to be £78 186. Even if the seller's machines had complied with the conditions of the contract, it would still have been to the advantage of the buyers (at their own cost) to have replaced the machines supplied with the new machines as soon as the latter became available on the market.

It should be apparent that the claim for damages as framed was one for *consequential loss*. These losses were not in fact suffered because 'the superiority of the [replacement] machines and of their efficiency in reducing working expenses was in point of fact such that all loss was extinguished, and that actually the respondents made a profit by the course they took.'[67] The claim was not one for the difference in market value between the machines promised and those delivered. It was not a claim based upon a valuation of the contractual right to performance at all. Indeed such a claim could not have been brought in addition to that which was asserted. The claimant had already recovered substantial damages for the losses incurred because the machines were defective during the years up until their replacement, and these damages were far in excess of the difference in value between the machines promised and those delivered. As we have seen, a claimant cannot get double recovery, here the difference in value between what it was promised and what it received, *and* the expense it in fact incurs in making good the defective performance.

It is important to contrast *Britsh Westinghouse* with the subsequent decision of the Privy Council in *Jamal v Moolla Dawood Sons & Co.*[68] The contract concerned the sale of a quantity of shares for 185 000 rupees, with delivery to take place some months later on 30 December 1911. The shares fell substantially in value and the defendant buyer refused to complete. Subsequent to the buyer's repudiation, the seller began to sell the shares elsewhere. The seller managed to sell at prices significantly higher than the market price at the time of breach, thereby avoiding the loss he would otherwise have suffered. The defendant buyer argued that this should be taken into account in quantifying damages. The Privy Council correctly rejected this contention, assessing damages by reference to the value of the right to performance at the time of breach. As principles of mitigation are concerned with the question of whether a loss is attributable to the wrong which has been suffered, it has no application to a claim for damages which is not concerned with the quantification of loss.

Thirdly, Burrows correctly states that damages are generally assessed at the time of trial, taking into account subsequent events, whereas substitutive damages would normally be assessed at the time of the wrong.

This objection is best seen as an argument in favour of substitutive

---

[67] ibid, at 688 (Viscount Haldane LC).

[68] *Jamal v Moolla Dawood Sons & Co* [1916] 1 AC 175 (PC) (*Jamal*). Viscount Haldane LC, who delivered the speech for the House in *British Westinghouse*, was a member of the panel. See also *Campbell Mostyn (Provisions) Ltd v Barnett Trading Co* [1954] 1 Lloyd's Rep 65 (CA).

damages. If Burrows were correct that damages are only ever awarded for consequential losses (or gains) then it would only ever make sense to quantify such damages at the time of trial. Why should subsequent events ever be ignored? However, it is not the case that damages are always assessed at the time of trial, as *Jamal* illustrates. Where the claim is for consequential loss the date of trial should be used, and a right should also be valued at the date of trial where damages are awarded in lieu of an injunction or specific performance under Lord Cairns' Act. Normally, however, the correct point in time for valuing the infringement of a right is the time of its infringement, save in the case of anticipatory breach of contract where the right to performance has not yet accrued.[69] One of the great advantages of the analysis suggested here is that it explains when and why damages are sometimes assessed at the time of the wrong and sometimes at the time of trial. By contrast, arguing that the approach to the timing of quantification is 'flexible'[70] fails to explain why one point or another is in principle applicable.

Fourthly, Burrows claims that no room is left for 'nominal damages' if substitutive or vindicatory damages are available. As I have said elsewhere,[71] this is not so. First, as we have seen, as we are quantifying the infringement of a right this may be notional, as where someone takes one step onto a farmer's field. Secondly, the right infringed may be valueless. If, for example, I were to be summarily sacked from my job without justification, only nominal damages would be available to me at common law. Although I have suffered a wrong, my right to contractual counter-performance from my employer is essentially valueless. My right to be paid my salary is conditional. In order to earn it, I must work. The work I provide, in terms of teaching, research, supervision and administration is objectively worth far more than the pittance I am paid. Unless I could prove consequential loss, no substantial damages would be payable as my right to be paid at the end of each month is worth less than the work I must do each month in order to get it. If in addition to breach of contract I could show that my dismissal also amounted to sexual or racial discrimination I could claim substantial damages, even though I may have no greater factual loss, because damages will be awarded to reflect the valuable but quite different right not to be so discriminated against.

Fifthly, and in agreement with Edelman, Burrows argues that it is not meaningful to assess the value of a right without considering the consequential impact of the infringement. However, as we have seen, very serious wrongs, such as deliberately breaking someone's legs, may, as

---

[69] *Golden Strait Corp v Nippon Yusen Kabishika Kaisha (The Golden Victory)* [2007] UKHL 12, [2007] 2 AC 353.
[70] Burrows, *Remedies for Torts and Breach of Contract*, above n 64, at 189.
[71] Stevens, *Torts and Rights*, above n 4, at 84; Stevens, 'Damages and the Right to Performance', above n 27, at 194–95.

things turn out, leave the claimant no worse off—indeed better off—
overall, whilst minor wrongs, such as being a day late in delivering a
boiler, may have terrible consequences. A wrong and its consequences
are not the same thing.

The dangers of conflating rights and gains are demonstrated by the
speech of Lord Nicholls in *Sempra Metals Ltd v Inland Revenue Commissioners*.[72] The case concerned the premature payment of tax due to a
mistake of law. The central issue was the extent to which the Revenue
was enriched by having had the use of the money over time. Lord Nicholls
took the view that the time value of money should be valued objectively,
and not according to the benefits a defendant actually derived from the
use of the money.[73] However all of the authorities relied upon by Lord
Nicholls for this proposition[74] concerned wrongdoing (ie, the infringement
of a right) and in only one[75] was any mention of benefit made. If the
thesis put forward here is accepted, none of them concerned recovery of
an actual gain made by the defendant. Lord Mance's view in dissent that
these cases of wrongdoing were of no relevance to the claim before the
Court,[76] that ordinary principles would require the claimant to establish
the actual gain made and that the result reached by the majority reversed
the legal onus without justification[77] is correct.

We may test *Sempra Metals* by considering an example of the use of
property where we remove the wrong from the story. Suppose I mistakenly
believe that a set of golf clubs that I own are in fact ones I borrowed
from you several months before. I have them delivered to you and you,
rather puzzled, put them in a cupboard for six months, where they remain
untouched because you have no need for them. No doubt I have a right
to the return of the clubs, but can I sue you for the gain made by your
having had their use for six months? Is it really to be presumed that you
are enriched by having had the use of my property over time, so that you
must prove that you 'changed your position' or can 'subjectively devalue'
to resist my claim? If a claim is available at all, why should it not be for
the claimant to show that the defendant would have hired another set of

---

[72] *Sempra Metals Ltd v Inland Revenue Commissioners* [2007] UKHL 34, [2008] 1 AC
561 (*Sempra Metals*) [51]–[130], especially at [116]–[117]. Lord Nicholls also gave the
speech for the majority in *A-G v Blake* [2001] AC 268 (HL).
[73] *Sempra Metals* [2007] UKHL 34, [2008] 1 AC 561 [117]. Lord Hope similarly suggested that enrichment should be presumed at [48].
[74] *Owners of the Steamship Mediana v Owners, Master and Crew of the Lightship Comet
(The Mediana)* [1900] AC 113 (HL) 117 (Earl of Halsbury LC); *Watson, Laidlaw & Co
Ltd v Pott, Cassels & Williamson* (1914) 31 RPC 104 (HL) 119 (Lord Shaw); *Whitwham
v Westminster Brymbo Coal & Coke Co* [1896] 2 Ch 538 (CA); *Penarth Dock Engineering Co v Pounds* [1963] 1 Lloyd's Rep 359 (QB) (*Penarth*).
[75] *Penarth* [1963] 1 Lloyd's Rep 359 (QB).
[76] *Sempra Metals* [2007] UKHL 34, [2008] 1 AC 561 [230].
[77] ibid, at [233].

clubs but for the mistake? Why should the defendant be put to proof of his or her dislike of golf?

Can we confine *Sempra Metals* to a claim for the use of money, as opposed to golf clubs or land? It is arguable that whilst a recipient of money *may* not make any use of it, or *may* not borrow any less as a result, he or she usually will, so that the onus of proof of enrichment shifts, in a way which it does not with the receipt of golf clubs. It could be argued that this is especially so where the defendant is a government running a deficit. However, none of the cases where support for the 'objective' measure of gain was found actually concerned the use of money, but rather land and goods. Furthermore, this argument would support the shifting of the *evidential* onus, not, as the majority found, the *legal* onus of proof.[78] Even governments which run deficits are not forever careless as to their size so that lower revenue in one year will lead to lower overall expenditure in the future, rather than necessarily higher levels of borrowing, as we in the United Kingdom are in the process of painfully discovering.

IV. RIGHTS AND INTERESTS

Another source of confusion is the modern day tendency to refer to the law of torts as protecting 'interests', as opposed to rights.

Many rights do take the reason for their existence from a particular interest in the world to which they relate. So, my interest in my reputation or my interest in my home or, even, my interest in being able to go where I choose, all provide reasons for the existence of the rights which have these interests as their subject matter.

However, not all rights relate to any identifiable separate interest. I have a right that you do not punch me on the nose. This is not the same right as the right to damages I have against you once you have delivered the blow. You are under a liability to me because I have the power to go to court and get an order made against you for the wrong I have suffered, with various remedial consequences which then arise after the order is made. Prior to the order, however, you are also under an obligation to me to pay damages. There is an obligation and a liability and whilst these two are sometimes treated as synonymous, they are not. Your obligation to pay damages, with my correlative right to recover damages, arises as soon as the blow is delivered and is not contingent upon the court declaring its existence. We can prove the existence of this obligation by virtue of the fact that if you pay me the sum owed by way of damages I am entitled to keep it, regardless of the absence of any court order in my

---

[78] ibid.

favour or any contract of settlement between us. Once the power to claim has become barred by the expiry of the applicable limitation period, the obligation, although unenforceable before a court (ie, there is no longer any liability), still persists, so that payments made after this time are also unrecoverable.[79] Further, interest on damages payable for loss of amenity will accrue at a rate of two per cent from date of injury until date of trial, even though such damages are quantified according to the going rate for a punch on the nose at the date of trial. Such interest reflects the fact that the defendant was obliged to pay as soon as the wrong occurred and the claimant has been kept out of the money which ought to have been paid to him or her at the earlier point.[80]

The right to be paid damages does not, however, relate to any interest separate from the right at all (and nor does the right arising from the court order). We could say that the relevant interest was the interest in being paid damages, but this is otiose and unhelpful.

Similar are the rights which arise because of another's unjust enrichment at our expense. If I repair your car by mistake in such a way as to give rise to a claim in unjust enrichment,[81] what interest of mine is protected by the right to restitution that I have? We cannot say that it is my interest in the work I have done, or my interest in how I spend my time, as I no longer have either of these and these formulations are both too broad, as I have no general rights in relation to my work or time, and too narrow, as they fail to cover other cases of unjust enrichment. Again, if we say that the interest protected is the interest that others are not unjustifiably enriched at our expense this is again simply a restatement of what the right is. We have not identified any independent subject matter or interest in the world to which it relates.

Clerk and Lindsell on Torts provides us with a list of the interests said to be protected by the law of torts.[82] This list includes: bodily integrity, personal liberty, physical security from injury, psychiatric harm, distress, family interests, educational neglect and mental disability, reputation, privacy, autonomy, possession of property, physical damage to property, enjoyment of property, intangible property, pure economic loss, unfair competition, loss of a chance, public rights, due process, constitutional rights and breach of statutory duty. This incoherent rag-bag of interests confuses together claim rights, liberties, types of loss and other things.

---

[79] *Moses v Macferlan* (1760) 2 Burr 1005, 97 ER 676.

[80] *Wright v British Railways Board* [1983] 2 AC 773 (HL). For an example in relation to goods see *Metal Box Ltd v Currys Ltd* [1988] 1 WLR 175 (QB). Contrast the absence of any such interest when quantifying *consequential* loss suffered after the time of the wrong: *Saunders v Edwards* [1987] 1 WLR 1116 (CA); *Giles v Thompson* [1994] 1 AC 142 (HL).

[81] cf *Greenwood v Bennett* [1973] QB 195 (CA).

[82] AM Dugdale et al (eds), *Clerk and Lindsell on Torts*, 19th edn (London, Sweet & Maxwell, 2006) paras 1-21–1-42.

Taking some examples, autonomy as such is not something which is protected directly by a right; rather it means liberty, the vast domain of freedom of choice I have where others have no rights against me. In *Rees v Darlington Memorial Hospital NHS Trust*[83] a disabled mother gave birth to a healthy but unwanted child following a failed sterilisation procedure performed at a hospital managed by the defendants. The House of Lords had previously held that damages for the consequential expense of bringing up an unwanted child could not be claimed as the presumed rewards of parenthood offset any potential harm suffered.[84] In *Rees* a majority approved an award of £15 000 which was made 'to recognise that in respect of the birth the mother had suffered a legal wrong.'[85] Seen as an award to vindicate the right rather than to compensate for consequential loss we can justify the different treatment of this head of damages as it could not be offset by the gains of parenthood, unlike, say, the cost of clothing. However some members of the House of Lords phrased recovery as being to recognise the claimant's loss of autonomy. So, Lord Bingham stated that the award was to recognise that the claimant no longer had 'the opportunity to live her life in the way she wished and planned.'[86] However, as Lord Hope stated in dissent, the consequential loss of autonomy was not the wrong itself; the conception of the child following the failed sterilisation was.[87] If loss of autonomy is a form of harm for which damages are recoverable, should it not always be recoverable? Puncturing the tyres of my bicycle reduces my autonomy as well. If the award in *Rees* is for a form of harm or loss, why can it not be offset by the immeasurable gain of the child like the other heads of damage? It would have been better to state that damages were awarded for the wrong itself, without any gloss. This would entail the award of precisely the same damages where the child is subsequently put up for adoption,[88] restoring the parent's autonomy. Whether the parents' autonomy is as a matter of fact subsequently impaired should in principle be irrelevant.

Similarly, we have no general right not to suffer distress, but when we are wronged distress consequential upon the infringement of another right may be recoverable. Again, I do not have a general right against others protecting my interest in chances, such as my chance of winning a beauty contest, but if I am wronged by, for example, being horribly

---

[83] *Rees v Darlington Memorial Hospital NHS Trust* [2003] UKHL 52, [2004] 1 AC 309 (*Rees*).

[84] *McFarlane v Tayside Health Board* [2000] 2 AC 59 (HL), noted in J Thomson, 'Abandoning the Law of Delict' 2000 SLT 43.

[85] *Rees* [2003] UKHL 52, [2004] 1 AC 309 [17] (Lord Nicholls).

[86] ibid, at [8]. Lord Millett stated that the award was to protect the parents' 'personal autonomy': at [123].

[87] ibid, at [70] (Lord Hope). See also *Cattanach v Melchior* [2003] HCA 38, (2003) 215 CLR 1 [23] (Gleeson CJ).

[88] J Thomson, 'Unplanned Conceptions from Failed Sterilisations' (2004) 72 *Scottish Law Gazette* 21.

disfigured in a car accident, if I previously had this chance I may be able to recover the value of its loss as damages. These 'interests' are forms of loss, not rights.

Eric Descheemaeker, in arguing that the law of defamation protects interests other than that of reputation, states:

> If the tort of defamation simply protects my reputation, why should it compensate me if I lose my job? There is no reason at all why it should. The fact that it does evidences in my mind that defamation *does* take an interest in more than my reputation and injuries thereto; it is also concerned with (in this example) my economic position. Wealth also comes within its scope of protection.[89]

This is to conflate the right and the consequential loss. We have an 'interest' in both, but they are not the same thing. The obligation to pay damages is imposed in order to achieve the next best position to the wrong not having been committed in the first place.[90] This does not necessarily entail making good consequential harm, as there may not be any, but where there is it is a sufficient explanation of recovery. Although the secondary right is (observably) not the same as the primary right, it is the form the primary right takes after the violation. It is the ugly butterfly to the primary right's caterpillar. If loss consequential upon the wrong were not recoverable the claimant would not be being placed in the nearest position to the wrong not having occurred. Net consequential economic losses are recoverable for *all* common law wrongs, and to say that the law of defamation, or any other wrong, 'protects' wealth is not merely surplusage, it is misleading.

Another way of showing that recovery of consequential loss is not always central may be illustrated by the wrongs which may be committed by a signatory state to the European Convention on Human Rights. Here the European Court of Human Rights has awarded adequate sums of money as damages where necessary to vindicate the violation of the relevant right. This frequently falls short of full compensation for loss suffered,[91] because that is not what is sought to be achieved. That full compensation for loss consequent upon the right violation under the Human Rights Act 1998 (HRA 1998) is not awarded does not prevent these wrongs from being torts, which are civil wrongs other than breaches of contract or equitable wrongdoing. Whether something is or is not a tort follows from the definition of what a tort is, just as whether something is or is not a mammal is determined by the definition of what constitutes a mammal. The duck-billed platypus is undoubtedly a mammal despite

---

[89] E Descheemaeker, 'Protecting Reputation: Defamation and Negligence' (2009) 29 *Oxford Journal of Legal Studies* 603, 615 (emphasis in original).

[90] *Livingstone v Rawyards Coal Co* (1880) 5 App Cas 25 (HL).

[91] See, eg, *R (Greenfield) v Secretary of State for the Home Department* [2005] UKHL 14, [2005] 1 WLR 673.

its having the unusual feature that it lays eggs. That the statutory torts under the HRA 1998 do not share all of the features of many common law torts is true, but irrelevant, just as it is with the platypus. That the claim is statutory in origin and not judge made, for example, has no significance. One thing the wrongs created by the HRA 1998 are observably not are *public* wrongs (such as crimes) as here the duty is owed to specific individuals (ie, right-holders) and not to society at large.

A related cause of the failure to think in terms of rights may be that English law has in the past been a formulary system, with the claim having to be fitted within a formula for relief, in much the same way as was the case in Roman law. The various 'interests' could be seen as parts of the incantation required for relief. On the rights-based approach, a right may be infringed in a number of different ways (scratching and kicking, on Tuesdays and Thursdays, deliberately and carelessly, directly and indirectly) but where the reason for the existence of the right is the same, the same wrong is committed. Infringements of the same right involve the same kind of wrong, although some infringements are more serious than others. Conversely where different rights are infringed, different wrongs are committed.

So, property rights in relation to things arise from possession. I have a better right to my wedding ring than you do because in a world of limited physical things I possessed it before you did. At base, this is true of all rights to things, even where my right is acquired from another in some way other than possession (eg, gift, sale, inheritance, specification). Intellectual property rights *must* arise for different, generally probably instrumental, reasons because one cannot possess something with no physical existence. A right to a trademark is not therefore a right of the same kind as my right to the clothes on my back. Copying a DVD is not therefore the same sort of wrong as stealing a car.

On this view there cannot be a tort or wrong of negligence as the rights that may be negligently infringed are different and diverse. Again, what constitutes a different tort follows inexorably from the definition of what a tort is.[92] Nothing more needs to be, or can be, said. This doesn't mean that there is no liability for negligent wrongdoing—clearly there is a great deal of that—but rather that it cannot be a single tort. My negligently smashing your car is the same sort of wrong as my deliberately doing so. Negligently locking someone in a toilet cubicle[93] is not the same sort of wrong as negligent libel.[94] Negligent breach of a voluntary assumed

---

[92] *contra* E Descheemaeker, *The Division of Wrongs: A Historical Comparative Study* (Oxford, Oxford University Press, 2009).

[93] *Sayers v Harlow Urban District Council* [1958] 1 WLR 623 (CA).

[94] *Huth v Huth* [1915] 3 KB 151 (CA).

obligation,[95] what in old money was called *assumpsit*,[96] is a quite different sort of wrong with different characteristics from negligent poisoning.[97] Liability for negligence is no different in kind from liability for wrongs generally, such as trespass to land, as the duty to take care, with its correlative right, is an essential element of the claim. However, it is not a unified wrong, nor could it be.

If, by contrast, we adopt the Roman formulary approach and don't see torts as civil wrongs involving the breach of duties owed to others, but instead see the claims as recipes for relief,[98] each individual recipe can be formulated in any way we choose. We could then group the recipes as we liked. So, we could group claims according to degrees of fault. Roman law adopted a tripartite classification—*dolus, culpa, casus*—but there seems to be no reason why this threefold classification is necessarily correct, so we could have any number of finer degrees of fault we choose. Alternatively we could classify our recipes by context (fire, products), different types of defendants (natural persons, companies), days of the week (Tuesday Torts, Sunday Torts) and so on. A 'tort of negligence' could then be made to fit, although it makes no rational sense even on this formulary approach to mix together classes of wrongs based upon degrees of fault (eg, negligence), specific rights (eg, defamation) and contexts (eg, product liability), as most torts books and courses do.

V. RIGHTS AND DEONTOLOGY

Some conduct, such as eating children, is wrongful regardless of what the law says on the matter (*malum in se*), whilst other conduct, such as not paying taxes, is only wrongful because the law says so (*malum prohibitum*). Similarly, some rights exist independently of their embodiment in the law, whilst others do not.

It is not only perfectly possible to conceive of (primary) private rights which are created by law for instrumentalist reasons, but we can probably point to examples of such rights within our law as it is now.

As anyone who has watched a Hollywood blockbuster on a DVD will tell you, before the main feature commences an anti-piracy message must be watched. Until recently this began with a leather-jacketed youth breaking into a Mercedes Benz with the caption 'you wouldn't steal a car', concluding that downloading movies was the same sort of wrong. How-

---

[95] As exemplified by *Hedley Byrne v Heller & Partners Ltd* [1964] AC 465 (HL) and *Glanzer v Shepard* 135 NE 275 (NY 1922).

[96] See the careful analysis of P Mitchell, '*Hedley Byrne & Co Ltd v Heller & Partners Ltd* (1963)' in C Mitchell and P Mitchell (eds), *Landmark Cases in the Law of Tort* (Oxford, Hart Publishing, 2010) 171.

[97] *Donoghue v Stevenson* [1932] AC 562 (HL).

[98] Descheemaeker, *The Division of Wrongs*, above n 92, at 264.

ever, reflection would tell us that the analogy is, at best, inexact. Copying information of any kind does not deprive someone else of anything they previously had. In a world which is not one of limitless abundance, we need rules for determining who is entitled to physical things, but these rules which are at base ones of first possession have little application to ideas or information which cannot be possessed.

More recently the message at the start of DVDs has changed. The current message from the United Kingdom's Industry Trust for Intellectual Property Awareness, called 'You make the movies', satirises movies such as *Reservoir Dogs* and *Toy Story* by arguing that infringing copyright will deprive the producer of important revenue and, as a result, prevent good movies from being made.

This seems, at least to me, to be a much more productive argument. It is perfectly possible to imagine a civilised society which permitted the unlimited copying of books or works of art, whereas it is not possible to imagine a civilised society which permitted the burning of a farmer's crops or one where each of us was able to take the clothes off one another's backs. Most intellectual property rights are primarily justifiable in terms of the goals they pursue. Trademarks enable purchasers of goods to make educated choices in the market and, over time, provide consumers some assurance as to quality. Patents encourage research by securing the financial reward of innovation. In my view it is no accident that rights of this kind were created by legislation, rather than being judge-made. Those intellectual property wrongs which require no instrumental justification (eg, passing off, which involves a form of lying) are those which were recognised first, and were also judge-made.[99]

This is not to say that copying DVDs is perfectly moral even though unlawful. Rights can become moral rights precisely because they are enacted within a legal system. It is immoral not to pay one's tax bill. However, one of the ways in which instrumental legal rights can achieve their goals is that they seek to piggyback upon the core case of moral rights, encouraging respect for them, as demonstrated by the first advert mentioned above. Further it is not immoral for the law to seek to pursue these instrumentalist goals in this way, so long as our (moral) rights are not infringed by so doing.

Once the possibility of legal rights being enacted for legitimate instrumentalist reasons is accepted, as I think it must be regardless of whether it is also accepted that intellectual property rights are as a matter of fact a good example, the question arises as to whether other or indeed all private rights do not similarly take their justification from the good ends they achieve. Does the recognition in law of the right not to be carelessly

---

[99] On the history of passing off see *Singer Manufacturing Co v Wilson* (1876) 2 Ch D 434 (CA) 453–57 (Mellish LJ).

run over whilst crossing the street serve the goal of reducing the number of accidents that there are, resulting in fewer broken legs?

In providing an answer to this question, my view is that it is unfortunately impossible to do so without getting down and dirty with the economists and their pragmatic fellow travellers and proving that as a matter of empirical observation the vast bulk of our rights, and the details of the rules which embody them, cannot be explained in such instrumentalist terms. No high theory can provide sufficient proof simply by looking at the structure of the law. Fortunately, this work has long since been done and we have known for many years that imposing liability for carelessly running people over is a poor and expensive way of deterring accidents, and that compensating so few people at such great expense makes little sense if what we are trying to do is give compensation to the victims of such accidents.[100] Furthermore, the details of the rules—for example, the way in which damages are quantified, discussed above—do not seem to be best explained on the basis that we are looking forward and seeking to prevent similar situations occurring again. Rather we are looking back to place the claimant in the next best position now obtainable to the wrong not having occurred.

Even if it could be shown beyond peradventure that the bulk of the common law of torts had no good side effects we should not think this a sufficient proof of the case for abolition. It is just wrong to negligently run other people over (*malum in se*) and a judge should, if he or she were at the roadside with a magic court order which could stop it, order in any individual instance for it not to be done. In a world of judges without such magical powers he or she should compel the wrongdoer to do the next best thing to not running over the victim which can now be compelled, which is to pay a sum of money which places the rightholder as close to the position of the wrong not having occurred as is now possible (which unfortunately may not be very near at all). Both the magical court order to stop the crash and the real world one to pay damages afterwards are justifiable regardless of any consequences other than promoting justice as between the parties. One fewer injustice in the world is consequence enough.

Asking what the common law of torts is for is like asking what the purpose of justice is.

For those, such as myself, who take the view that an attempt to understand all of our rights recognised by the common law and their detailed content in wholly utilitarian or other consequentialist terms is bound to fail, but who are reluctant to accept that the common law is just an incoherent mess of competing ideas, some sort of deontological approach

---

[100] P Cane, *Atiyah's Accidents, Compensation and the Law*, 7th edn (Cambridge, Cambridge University Press, 2006).

is inevitable. For good or ill, this inevitably points us towards Immanuel Kant. I am reluctant to go further as a little philosophy, like a little law, is a very dangerous thing, but it may be useful to set out my own views, if only so that others can explain where I have gone wrong. The literature here is vast, daunting and, to the untrained, such as myself, difficult. My purpose in what follows is *not* to examine Kant's ethics or his theory of law, but rather to argue that we can obtain a working understanding of our private rights in our common law without having to swallow Kant down holus-bolus.

Kant's moral philosophy is intuitively attractive to lawyers (like me) as it is a system of rules and duties: our bread and butter. I shall focus here on Kant's formulations of the categorical imperative,[101] although Kant himself did not intend that these should be applied directly to law.

Not all of the formulations of the categorical imperative seem to me to be equally helpful, or indeed acceptable. Only if they are read together as a whole do they assist. So, the first formulation is: 'Act only according to that maxim whereby you can at the same time will that it should become a universal law.'[102] On its own this formulation does not take us very far, although I suspect that Kant did not intend that it should. I only eat seafood when there is an 'r' in the month, and whilst this seems compatible with Kant's formulation I rather doubt that it tells us very much about the morality of doing so, still less about what the law should be about eating mussels in May. Worse, there seem to me to be some things that I could rationally will as a universal law which would be deeply immoral. 'Everyone except Robert Stevens should always tell the truth' could be a universal law, but not one with much appeal to anyone but me I suspect. If it is retorted that such a rule is not categorical because it is subject to an exception and therefore unacceptable, then most lawyers will rebel. No serious lawyer would be happy with trying to construct a system of conduct where no rule was subject to any exception. Kant must be construed here as setting out a *constraint* upon what can count as a moral principle, rather than a formula which itself constitutes a moral principle as a guidance norm for action. This constraint is one which a strict utilitarian would have no difficulty accepting.

The formulation, 'every rational being must so act as if he were through his maxim always a legislating member in the universal kingdom of ends',[103] whilst important in addressing the correct *perspective* to adopt in deciding how to act in goodwill, does not alone clarify the duties we owe. It does not tell us what the 'legislating member in the

---

[101] Introduced in I Kant, *Grounding for the Metaphysics of Morals: On a Supposed Right to Lie Because of Philanthropic Concerns*, 3rd edn (JW Ellington tr, Indianapolis, Hackett Publishing, 1993).

[102] ibid, at 30.

[103] ibid, at 43.

universal kingdom of ends' should do, and again, on its own, does not take us very far.

Far more hopeful, because it is the statement of a moral principle, is another formulation by Kant: 'Act in such a way that you treat humanity, whether in your own person or in the person of any other, always at the same time as an end and never simply as a means.'[104] This formulation has nothing to say about when we should eat seafood and makes it clear that it would not be OK for me to tell you lies for my own gain. However, how does this formulation differ from the ancient negative formulation of the Golden Rule: we should not do unto others what we would not want done unto ourselves?

The most obvious difference is that Kant includes within the category of persons to whom one owes a duty of action oneself. So, for him suicide would always be immoral. However, this aspect of his ethics can be put to one side (for now) as private lawyers are concerned with our rights one against another, not the duties to oneself. Personal morality and interpersonal justice are not the same.

Kant was notoriously critical of the Golden Rule and claimed that what he was postulating was not simply a version of it. However, his criticisms seem to be easily rebuttable, albeit that in doing so we help to clarify what we mean by the Golden Rule. It may be that this is what Kant intended, and that he was seeking to fill out what was, without more, incomplete but already understood.

If I am a masochist who enjoys being tortured, does the Golden Rule mean that I am free to torture others as that is what I would want if I were in their place? The answer, contrary to Kant, is no, because the Golden Rule requires that we treat others as if we were them, not as if they were us.[105]

Kant also claims that the application of the Golden Rule would entail that 'a criminal could argue against the judge punishing him', as the judge would not wish to be punished if he or she were in the criminal's place. However the judge must treat *all* others as he or she would wish to be treated.[106] The judge has taken an oath of office for the benefit of all and would be acting wrongfully with respect to all others were he or she not to sentence the criminal. The Golden Rule is not simply a bilateral norm.

Kant is correct however that the class of persons whose interests I must have regard to in determining how to act with regard to others includes myself.[107] So, if I am freezing to death on a hillside I may be justified in breaking into your log cabin in order to save myself. If I am caught

---

[104] ibid, at 36.
[105] Stevens, *Torts and Rights*, above n 4, at 332.
[106] ibid, at 333.
[107] See D Parfit, *On What Matters*, vol 1 (Oxford, Oxford University Press, 2011) 327.

in a storm whilst out sailing I may be justified in tying up to your dock to save my vessel even if you refuse me permission to do so. In both of these cases I only remain within my privilege to act as I did, and do not become a wrongdoer, if I behave in the way which entails the minimum infringement of your rights. One thing this entails is that I must subsequently make good any harm I have so caused, something a court will compel me to do.[108] Payment in such a case anticipates a wrong being committed; it is not an obligation arising because the defendant's actions constituted a wrong. Once payment is made, no wrong has ever been committed.

Derek Parfit in *On What Matters* rephrases the Golden Rule in the light of these and other considerations as follows:

> We ought to treat *everyone* as we would rationally be willing to be treated if we were going to be in all of these people's positions, and would be relevantly like them.[109]

This formulation does not entail that we should simply aggregate all of our interests together, in the way that a utilitarian would, and ask what will eventually be best for everyone overall. It is not, I think, a consequentialist principle at all. We cannot kill one person in order to save the lives of two others, because not killing someone does not offend the negative formulation of the Golden Rule as it involves no doing unto. More banally, I cannot play loud music keeping my neighbour awake all night even if the pleasure I get from so doing is far greater than the misery I inflict.

Seeking to defend our common law as based upon a proper understanding of the Golden Rule is an easier sell to lawyers than trying to argue that we all need to be disciples of an eighteenth century German philosopher, and that the judges always have been even though they did not know it. In the Commonwealth this is so not least because Lord Atkin also thought that the entire law of torts was best explained in terms of the Golden Rule,[110] and not just, as lawyers all learn before we can crawl, liability for negligence.[111] Kant himself would, I suspect, agree, as he maintained, rightly I think, that he was telling us what we knew already, rather than setting out something wholly novel as a modern day academic (like me) would usually seek to assert. Resistance comes in part, I think, from the belief that the Golden Rule is without content or childish. Such a belief is wrong.

---

[108] *Vincent v Lake Erie Transportation Co* 124 NW 221 (Minn 1910). See also R Stevens, 'The Conflict of Rights' in A Robertson and HW Tang (eds), *The Goals of Private Law* (Oxford, Hart Publishing, 2009) 139.

[109] Parfit, above n 107, at 327 (emphasis in original).

[110] Lord Atkin, 'Law as an Educational Subject' [1932] *Journal of the Society of Public Teachers of Law* 27, 30.

[111] *Donoghue v Stevenson* [1932] AC 562 (HL).

VI. RIGHTS AND CORRECTIVE JUSTICE

In the light of the above, it is possible to say something about the proper scope of the concept of 'corrective justice.' Three different approaches to the concept are discernible, here given in ascending order of significance.

The first is that legal obligations which take the form of a correction must be independently explained.[112] Corrective justice is what requires justification, it itself justifies nothing at all. In support of this view corrective justice may be contrasted with distributive justice. The different ways in which a distribution of a particular good could be justified are many and will differ in different situations. In deciding how to distribute a cake amongst a group of children a number of different rules of distribution could be formulated: equality, age, height, hunger, merit etc. Why one *pattern* of distribution was chosen rather than another (or none) would be the very thing needing to be accounted for. Similarly, within the law there are, observably, rules requiring correction which have different underlying justifications. One person who has been unjustly enriched at another's expense must make restitution. A negligent driver must pay for the lost earnings of his or her victim. Although both the obligation to make restitution and the obligation to pay damages are corrective in *pattern*, it seems unlikely that the same justification underlies them both, and why we are correcting at all is the very thing which needs to be accounted for.

On this approach, the fact that a rule is corrective in pattern does not prove that it is a good one. So, Article 1382 of the French Civil Code states:

> Every act whatever of man which causes damage to another obliges him by whose fault the damage occurred to repair it.

There is no mention of any right violation or private wrong or tort in this provision, nor is this form of liability given such a label in the Code ('*La responsabilité civile extracontractuelle*'). It is on its face simply a requirement that those who cause loss through fault must pay for it. Regardless of whether French law, when push comes to shove, actually adopts this approach, it is a principle which is corrective in pattern and the question of whether it or the rights-based approach of the common law is superior (as I confess I think the common law position clearly is) must be faced.

However, most writers on corrective justice have regarded it as having explanatory power. On a second weak formulation, which is suggested by its name, corrective justice is concerned with correcting injustice. Given

---

[112] cf J Gardner, *What Is Tort Law For? Part I: The Place of Corrective Justice* (Oxford Legal Studies Research Paper No 1/2010, University of Oxford, 18 January 2010) at ssrn.com/abstract=1538342, accessed on 28 January 2011.

the existence of primary rights, their infringement requires that this be corrected in the way which is the next best position now achievable to the wrong not having occurred. I have more than once invoked this idea above, which is given its best legal articulation in the House of Lords decision *Livingstone v Rawyards Coal Co.*[113] That we should do the next best now possible to the wrong not having occurred, and that the court should make an order to compel this where it can, is true regardless of whatever justification underpins the underlying primary right.

Some writers seem to me to be adopting this weak or thin version of corrective justice as an explanation for the imposition of some—but not all—obligations,[114] but if so it is a trite claim of little importance. My children grasped the moral sense behind this sense of justice before they could read. We all learn that we should apologise if we tread on another's foot, or care for those we injure. Courts make awards of damages, rather than orders that wrongdoers care for those they injure, because without magic that is the next best which can be compelled to be done, rather than the next best which can in fact be done. As we have seen, it is theoretically possible that all of our primary legal rights are best justified in instrumentalist terms; this cannot be disproved by the truism that the infringement of all rights require correction, and that courts will compel such correction where they can.

Can our primary rights, for example my right to bodily safety or property, be justified in terms of corrective justice? Some think they can and, despite some statements indicating the contrary, Ernest Weinrib must be such a person, as his is a theory of all of private law.[115] This third version of what is meant by corrective justice is an important claim.

Again, it is fair as between you and me that you do not take away my toy aeroplane as I had it first. As that is what is fair as between you and me it is also what is fair as between me and everyone else (save anyone who had it before me).[116] The rights to the toy aeroplane can be justified not in terms of any instrumental goal but rather by reference to what is fair as between each of us. What is true of my toy aeroplane is also true of all other things. The label 'corrective justice' is unhelpful on this broader conception as it does not necessarily involve correcting anything. The wider sense of justice this example illustrates has been called commutative justice,[117] and, more recently, interactive[118] or interpersonal

---

[113] *Livingstone v Rawyards Coal Co* (1880) 5 App Cas 25 (HL).

[114] See, eg, J Coleman, *The Practice of Principle: In Defence of a Pragmatist Approach to Legal Theory* (Oxford, Oxford University Press, 2001) 34–35.

[115] See, eg, EJ Weinrib, 'Correlativity, Personality, and the Emerging Consensus on Corrective Justice' (2001) 2 *Theoretical Inquiries in Law* 107.

[116] *Armory v Delamirie* (1722) 1 Stra 505, 93 ER 664.

[117] J Finnis, *Natural Law and Natural Rights* (Oxford, Clarendon Press, 1980) 178–79.

[118] RW Wright, 'Substantive Corrective Justice' (1992) 77 *Iowa Law Review* 625.

justice.[119] It can justify the right to the toy aeroplane, and not just the obligation to pay for negligently smashing it. This 'fat' version of corrective justice includes the 'thin' or trite conception within it.

Although this justification for allocating the (moral) right to things is distributive in *pattern* (physical things are initially allocated to those with first possession) it is not a substantive principle of distributive justice as it neither involves anybody distributing anything, nor is the allocation made in order to achieve any principle of overall distributive fairness. *All* rights have distributive effects, but it seems unhelpful to argue that they are as a result all rules of distributive justice.[120] The above argument for allocating the right to things according to prior possession does not do so on the basis that this will result in a distributively fair result overall[121] as it obviously will not by any criterion save by chance, which is why we have supplementary rules for the (re-)distribution of the rights to things (usually by taxation) which have been based upon first or prior possession. Further when a judge or legislator posits the relative legal rights to things according to the moral reasoning of prior possession, they are, in a sense, allocating or distributing rights, but this is again not being done on the basis that this will lead to the most distributively just result overall. The judge or legislator does not have a finite box of rights which is being divvied up amongst us according to what will lead to a fair distribution overall. Again, therefore, as the law-maker's justification for the legal right is not that it will achieve distributive fairness, it seems unhelpful to describe it as an example of distributive justice merely because it has distributive effects. The contrary view leads to there being two quite different senses of distributive justice: 'general' and 'local'.

However, although the 'fat' formulation of corrective justice—commutative justice—is observably different from 'general' or substantive distributive justice it is, I think, the same as the idea underlying the deontological formulations considered above. It is also *not* simply a bilateral principle, unlike the narrow or thin formulation of the obligation to correct an injustice. One determinant of the scope of the rights that you have against me is the scope of the rights others have against me, all of which must be capable of co-existing together. So, just as a judge is entitled to sentence a criminal, as a matter of private law it may be permissible to drive my car in such a way as would usually impose unacceptable risks on others, because of an emergency to save a third party's life.

---

[119] A Beever, *Rediscovering the Law of Negligence* (Oxford, Hart Publishing, 2007) 61.
[120] *contra* Gardner, above n 112.
[121] Robert Nozick in *Anarchy, State, and Utopia* (Oxford, Blackwell, 1974) 153–55 provides no reasons for thinking that allocating property rights based upon first possession and free exchange will be distributively fair by any criterion.

VII. RIGHTS AND PRIVATE LAW

When a claimant seeks judicial review, he or she is not standing upon his or her own personal or private right. The claimant is seeking to enforce a *public* duty. Just as my legal duty not to be cruel to animals is not owed to any particular person, the *public* duties of the constituent parts of the state are not owed to specific individuals. An individual may be given the standing, or the power, to enforce the public duty by judicial review, in the same way that individuals have standing to bring private prosecutions. The claimant is not however enforcing a duty owed to him or her personally but one owed to all society. We have standing requirements to ensure that only those with an interest have the power to bring the claim but, as we have seen, having an interest is not the same as having a right. Similarly, a public prosecutor may have the *power* to commence proceedings for a crime (a breach of a duty owed to society) but he or she does not stand upon his or her own (claim) *right* in doing so. So, if I am prosecuted for despoiling the environment, the public prosecutor is not asserting that the wrong has been done to him or her personally—in other words, that he or she personally had any (claim) right against me—nor that a right of the environment has been violated, but rather that a breach of a public duty has occurred and that he or she has the standing (ie, the power) to enforce it. Again, it is basic to understanding the difference between public and private law that duties do not always have correlative rights, and that when they do not we are no longer within the realm of private law. Whether we approve of them or not it is perfectly possible to contemplate crimes with no specific victim (eg, conspiracy to corrupt public morals, insider trading, possession of banned substances), which is not true of private law wrongs.

Where the claimant can in addition show that the breach of the public duty also constitutes a violation of his or her private rights he or she should be able to claim damages. There are then two wrongs in play. It would be highly inconvenient if someone seeking judicial review of the performance of a public duty were also required to institute a separate set of proceedings for damages for the violation of a private right. Fortunately, this is not the law. The Administrative Court does have power to award damages where the public body's conduct has also violated a private right of the claimant.[122] However, *damnum sine iniuria* should not be, and is not, actionable as such. The court should have no power to distribute public funds where the claimant has not had a right infringed. To confer upon the courts the discretion to distribute public funds in this way would be contrary to the rule of law. Fortunately, the Law Commission's proposals that damages should be generally available as a remedy

---

[122] Supreme Court Act 1981, s 31(4); CPR r 54.3.

for the commission of public law wrongs, which represented a confusion of the difference between private and public law, have been dropped.[123]

AV Dicey's principle of equality ('every official from the Prime Minister down to a constable or a collector of taxes, is under the same responsibility for every act done without legal justification as any other citizen'[124]) has two limbs. First, that the state and its agents should have no special privileges as such, except where exceptionally authorised by legislation. Secondly, that individuals should have no special rights against the state unless legislation stipulates to the contrary.

The first limb is the more important. Contrary to the views of the Law Commission,[125] it is impossible to justify giving police officers a special privilege to negligently run people over simply by virtue of their carrying out a public activity.

The most significant derogation from the second limb in the United Kingdom is the HRA 1998, which gives each of us rights against public bodies that they secure for us a variety of goods, such as education, freedom of expression and privacy. If we think that public and private law are mutually exclusive, and if we define public law's domain as concerned with the relationship between the state and its citizens, not all rights belong within private law.

It is at least arguable that there are certain ways in which the state can injure its citizens which persons generally cannot, which have not yet been adequately dealt with. Examples include the incorrect refusal of a licence to a taxi driver, or a mistaken restriction placed on the movement of a farmer's cattle where the outbreak of disease is suspected, and where no protection is afforded by the legislation under which the public body acted. In enacting regulatory powers it is vital that Parliament considers whether individuals adversely affected should be given personal (or private) rights in relation to their exercise, and it may be queried whether this has been carefully or consistently done in every case. If the Law Commission were to conduct the difficult task of a considered review of regulatory legislation and consider whether in specific instances new rights for those potentially adversely affected need to be introduced, this would be productive. Simply assuming that the exercise of public duties and powers should *always* give rise to private rights, or a public wrong the availability of damages, is unjustifiable.

---

[123] Law Commission, *Administrative Redress: Public Bodies and the Citizen* (Law Com No 322, 2010).

[124] AV Dicey, *Introduction to the Study of the Law of the Constitution* (London, Macmillan, 1885) 178.

[125] Law Commission, above n 123, at paras 3.15–3.23.

VIII. CONCLUSION

That we call the subject 'torts' by that name is most unfortunate ('delict' is no better). A label from archaic French gives the impression that this is a remote technical legal subject detached from any corresponding idea known to the person on the street. The claims by some textbook writers that it is a subject incapable of definition reinforce this impression for the beginner. The language of wrongs at least has the merit of reconnecting the subject to its moral basis, and the language of rights reminds us of the sort of wrongs we are concerned with.

The task above has not been the sexy one of uncovering hitherto unknown truths, but the more pedestrian one of trying to ensure that what we should already know is not forgotten or overlooked. It is to be hoped that the result has not been too bruising.

6

Beyond 'Right' and 'Duty': Lundstedt's Theory of Obligations

I. INTRODUCTION: OBLIGATIONS AS FACT

THE DEBATE OVER the law of obligations in the common law world has seen virtually every possible jurisprudential theory pressed into service to support or oppose points of view in the debate. To this, there has been one exception: Scandinavian legal realism. This omission is unfortunate, as there is a voluminous Scandinavian realist literature on the law of obligations, produced principally by Anders Vilhelm Lundstedt, arguably the most orthodox of the Scandinavian legal realists. The Scandinavian realists, even more than their American counterparts, were deeply engaged in debates concerning issues of substantive law. Alf Ross wrote widely on Danish criminal law, as did Karl Olivecrona on civil procedure in Sweden. The bulk of Lundstedt's substantive work was on the law of obligations, which he presented in seven volumes published over a 30 year period between 1920 and 1953 collectively titled *Föreläsningar över valda delar av obligationsrätten* ('Lectures on Selected Portions of the Law of Obligations') and which was still incomplete at his death. Much of the theoretical work for which Lundstedt is known was formulated and first presented in the context of the law of obligations.

Lundstedt's views on obligations have not, as far as I am aware, been discussed in English until now. Lundstedt's works were never as well-known or widely read as those of Ross and Olivecrona—he is arguably

* Email: t.t.arvind@york.ac.uk. A previous version of this chapter was presented at a meeting of the North-East Regional Obligations Group. I am grateful to participants there, and at the Obligations V Conference, for their comments. Particular thanks go to David Campbell, Richard Mullender, Mårten Schultz, Jenny Steele and Lindsay Stirton for their encouragement and comments at various stages of this chapter's preparation.

the least well-known of the three[1]—and much of his thought has therefore been interpreted in the light of their theories. Given that Lundstedt disagreed with both Ross and Olivecrona on fundamental questions, this presents what can at best be called a very distorted picture of his thought. But perhaps most importantly, major aspects of Lundstedt's and Axel Hägerström's work—in particular, their critique of legal concepts, such as rights—cannot be understood without looking at their place within Hägerström's broader philosophical project. Unfortunately, significant aspects of Hägerström's philosophy—most importantly for our purposes, his theory of knowledge and of the emotional basis of concepts—have only very recently begun to be discussed in English, and are as yet not widely known in legal circles. As a result, the Hägerström–Lundstedt critique of rights and legal concepts is frequently misunderstood—for example, it is usually discussed as if it were rooted in a theory of semantics, which it is not.[2]

Yet, as I argue in this chapter, Lundstedt's theoretical work on obligations has a significant contribution to make to the debate in common law circles about the nature, structure and purpose of the law of obligations. This relevance lies not so much in Lundstedt's views on specific rules of positive law, most of which either relate to rules that are peculiar to the Scandinavian legal systems or to laws, principles and rules that have since undergone significant change. It lies, rather, in the broader theoretical framework which he presented as a way of conceptualising and analysing the law of obligations. Lundstedt considered a wide-ranging set of issues—including the nature of an obligation, the purpose of the law of obligations, the relationship between obligations and rights, taxonomy and classificatory categories within the law, and the nature and basis of liability for breach of an obligation—many of which have obvious relevance to ongoing common law debates about the common law of obligations and represent a perspective—classical Scandinavian realism—whose voice is rarely heard in this context.

Lundstedt's theoretical discussion on obligations goes to the heart of the question: what is the thing an obligation protects? And how can we understand the structure of the law of obligations in the light of our understanding about what the thing it protects is? Lundstedt's answer to these questions was provocative. The core of his 'Lectures' are two

---

[1] The only Scandinavian realist less well-known in the English-speaking world than Lundstedt is Ingemar Hedenius, whose name and work are rarely if ever mentioned in discussions of Scandinavian legal realism, despite his importance (as discussed below).

[2] As I discuss in part III below, this misunderstanding is at least in part due to poor translations, and in Lundstedt's case the opaqueness of much of his English writing, and his use of very literal English equivalents for Swedish words and of phrases that mean rather different things in English as compared with Swedish. As I show in this chapter, read in the context of Hägerström's broader theory, Lundstedt's theory of law assumes a very different character in comparison with the way it is usually understood and interpreted by common law jurists. For reasons of space and coherence, I discuss these in footnotes inserted at relevant points, rather than in the main text of this chapter.

volumes titled *Obligationsbegreppet* ('The Concept of an Obligation').
Halfway through the early chapters of the first of these volumes, Lundstedt set out what he held to be the heart of his theory of obligations:
'There are no rights and no duties.'³ And, later, he expanded on this to
add: 'there are no such things as rules of law.'⁴

On the face of it, this is a most extraordinary claim. By saying that
we cannot conceptualise the law of obligations as being about rights or
as being about duties, or even as a set of rules of law, Lundstedt with
one stroke sweeps away just about every theory of obligations that has
been articulated in the common law discourse about the subject. What
did he mean?

To answer this question, we need to first examine a concept that was
the base—the foundation—of Scandinavian legal realism: the idea of 'law
as fact', made famous by Olivecrona who used it as the title of not one
but two different books.⁵ When the Scandinavian realists spoke of 'law
as fact', what they meant to distinguish it from was the idea of 'law as
opinion'. It was this concern that lay behind their critique of metaphysical
perspectives on law. Metaphysics, they argued, had its base in opinion, not
fact, and their project to rid legal science of metaphysical influences was
thus principally intended to place the study of law on a solid factual—and
hence more scholarly and scientific—base. This distinction between 'fact'
and 'opinion' is a subtle one which is worth spending some time on. In
order to get to grips with it, we need to understand the philosophical and
theoretical concepts that were at the core of Scandinavian legal realism.

In part II of this chapter, I discuss the the broader context of the
'Uppsala school of philosophy' (*uppsalafilosofin*) of which Scandinavian
legal realism was an outgrowth, and of Hägerström's theory of values
and ethics, on which it was founded. My reading draws heavily on new
readings of Hägerström that have been published in recent years which,
as I discuss, draw on manuscript sources and an integrated reading of
Hägerström's entire *oeuvre* to present a far more complete account of his
philosophy, which differs radically from the limited accounts presented
in the majority of works on legal theory in the common law world. In
part III, I turn to Lundstedt's specific critique of the use of the concept
of rights in law. In parts IV and V, I discuss how Lundstedt extended

---

³ AV Lundstedt, *Obligationsbegreppet I: Fakta och fiktioner* (Uppsala, L Norblads
Bokhandel, 1929) 107, 124.

⁴ Quoted in S Ljungman, 'Minnesord' in H Eek (ed), *Vilhelm Lundstedt: tänkare og
kämpe* (Stockholm, Tidens Förlag, 1956) 41, 45.

⁵ K Olivecrona, *Law as Fact*, 1st edn (London, Oxford University Press, 1939); K Olivecrona, *Law as Fact*, 2nd edn (London, Stevens & Sons, 1971). Although the second book
is styled as a new edition of the earlier book, it was in fact a substantially different book,
and the Swedish versions of the two books were published under different titles (the first
as *Om Lagen och Staten* ('On Law and the State') (Lund, Gleerup, 1940) and the second
as *Rättsordningen* ('The Legal Order') (Lund, Gleerup, 1966)).

this critique to also cover other accounts of obligations, including those based on reliance, responsibility or culpability, and taxonomic classification. In part VI, I discuss Lundstedt's attempt to present an alternate account of the law of obligations, centred around the idea of what he called *samhällsnyttan*, which roughly translates to 'usefulness to society'. I conclude by discussing what Lundstedt's account of obligations can contribute to modern efforts within common law to present theoretical accounts of the law of obligations.

II. THE PHILOSOPHICAL BASIS OF SCANDINAVIAN LEGAL REALISM

Scandinavian legal realists, unlike the American realists, did not produce a 'law and economics' or 'law and politics' movement. The Scandinavian realists did seek to define the proper limits of legal science[6] and they saw it as having a clear relationship with other disciplines even across the range of questions that were its proper province. Some—such as Ross—took narrower views as to what its proper province was than others—such as Lundstedt—but they did not go as far as the American realists. To some extent, this is attributable to their early intellectual history, which was marked by strong doctrinal influences.[7] But it also illustrates the fundamental gulf between American and Scandinavian legal realism.

An early American reviewer of one of Lundstedt's books pointed out that a critical distinction between Scandinavian and American legal realisms was that American legal realism was principally concerned with the question of what it is the courts and the legal system actually are doing, in comparison with what they claim to be doing. Scandinavian legal realism, however, was a lot more concerned with the question of what the legal system actually knows—and what it can know, what it is possible and feasible for the legal system to know—in comparison with what it claims to know or what theorists assume it knows or can know.[8]

This is an accurate summary. Unlike American legal realism, Scandinavian legal realism is rooted in a form of philosophical scepticism, and not

---

[6] In Swedish, *rättsvetenskap*. *Vetenskap* in Swedish means both 'science' and 'scholarship', much like its German cognate *Wissenschaft*. In this chapter, I mostly translate it as 'science', but I also use 'scholarship' or 'scholarly activity' where this meaning is more appropriate to the context.

[7] Lundstedt was trained in German conceptual jurisprudence (*Begriffsjurisprudenz*) and wrote several treatises based on this method, even gaining a chair in civil law at Uppsala, before his 'conversion' by Hägerström. Ross wrote a dissertation on Kelsen, and only came to study with Hägerström after it was rejected by the Faculty of Law at the University of Copenhagen.

[8] HW Jones, 'Review of *Legal Thinking Revised: My Views on Law* by A Vilhelm Lundstedt' (1958) 58 *Columbia Law Review* 755, 758.

pragmatism.[9] In consequence, whilst both varieties of realism were rule-sceptical, there were fundamental differences in the form this scepticism took. In American legal realism, it took the form of result-scepticism—of scepticism as to the extent to which the results of individual cases were actually influenced by rules, and of ascertaining the other factors that actually lay behind judicial decisions (represented in contemporary times, for example, by the judicial politics literature, or the economic literature on judicial decision-making). From a normative point of view, it led to a search for ways to remedy this, through formulating objective, pragmatically justifiable standards that could form the basis for legal decision-making.[10] Either way, it was characterised by pragmatism.[11]

The Scandinavian legal realist version of rule-scepticism, in contrast, principally took the form of idea-scepticism, or concept-scepticism. Scandinavian realists explored fundamental ideas or concepts upon which the legal system was based—causation, obligation, guilt, responsibility, culpability—and questioned legal assumptions about the scope, meaning and significance of these concepts. They did this not from the point of view of seeing whether judges actually applied them in the way the law assumed, but from the point of view of examining whether the conceptual and philosophical underpinnings of these ideas were coherent and grounded in the real world—whether the facts they assumed were real, empirically knowable facts. Pragmatism featured very little, if at all, in their jurisprudence.[12]

In its approach to analysing concepts, Scandinavian legal realism was particularly influenced by the 'Uppsala school of philosophy' (*uppsalafilosofin*), a general trend in Swedish philosophy that began at the University of Uppsala in the first decade of the twentieth century as a reaction against Swedish idealism.[13] The key elements of the Uppsala school of philosophy were a critique of subjectivism (or idealism), a critique of metaphysics, a commitment to the analysis of concepts (*begreppsanalyse*)

---

[9] cf GS Alexander, 'Comparing the Two Legal Realisms—American and Scandinavian' (2002) 50 *American Journal of Comparative Law* 131.

[10] For example, the standard of Kaldor-Hicks efficiency favoured by early adherents of law and economics, or the minimisation of transaction costs favoured by others.

[11] cf the discussion in ACS Ryssdal, *Legal Realism and Economics as Behaviour: A Scandinavian Look at Economic Analysis of Law* (Oslo, Juridisk Forlag, 1995).

[12] As Scandinavian commentators have pointed out, Scandinavia had its own pragmatic tradition, represented in the philosophy of jurists such as Fredrik Stangs, Ragnar Knophs and Gunnar Hoels. The Scandinavian realists did not see themselves as being connected with this tradition, nor did they try to build upon it. See S Blandohl, 'Rettspragmatismen i Fredrik Stangs, Ragnar Knophs og Gunnar Astrup Hoels forfatterskap' (2004) 1–2 *Tidsskrift for Rettsvitenskap* 7.

[13] S Nordin, *Från Hägerström till Hedenius: Den Moderna Svenska Filosofin* (Bodafors, Doxa, 1983) 9–59; S Källström, *Den Gode Nihilisten: Axel Hägerström och striderna kring uppsalafilosofin* (Kristianstad, Rabén and Sjögren, 1986) 9–14. A briefer account in English is provided in R Sandin, 'The Founding of the Uppsala School' (1962) 23 *Journal of the History of Ideas* 496.

and a radical theory of values,[14] which later came—incorrectly—to be called 'value-nihilism' (*värdenihilismen*).[15] The Uppsala school's technique of concept analysis was principally the work of Adolf Phalén, professor of theoretical philosophy at Uppsala. The words that describe the fundamental concepts of most philosophies, Phalén argued, have their origins in the way the relevant concept is used in everyday life. The concepts are initially absorbed into philosophical language without significant reflection on their polysemy or their lack of a single, clear connotation. In ordinary communication, this polysemy and multifarity does not pose a significant problem. As a result, followers of philosophical theories assume the fundamental concepts on which their theories are based to be far clearer and evident than they actually are. Over time, however, as they engage more deeply with the meaning of the concept in question, contradictions—and conflicts with observable reality—begin to emerge, either compounding the problem the philosophers originally sought to solve with the concept, or calling their solution into question. The result is a multiplicity of mutually contradictory philosophical systems, where none is obviously more correct than the other. Under these circumstances, a student of a philosophical system cannot claim to be engaged in scholarly work if all he or she is doing is studying the system in order to practise it. The method of constructing new philosophical systems must be abandoned as a scholarly activity. Scholarship, Phalén insisted, consisted of the analysis of the core concepts of philosophical systems from the position of standing outside them, with a clearer vision of the goals and using tools that were radically different from those that would have been adopted by those standing within the system.[16]

Phalén's method of concept analysis by itself has clear and obvious relevance to several aspects of the debate surrounding the law of obligations in common law. But Hägerström—co-founder with Phalén of the Uppsala school of philosophy, and the first Scandinavian legal realist—took the theory one step further. In his famous inaugural lecture 'On the Truth of Moral Conceptions',[17] Hägerström presented a conclusion that

---

[14] Källström, *Den Gode Nihilisten*, above n 13, at 15–31.

[15] The term was first used by John Landquist, a leading opponent of the school, as a derogatory term. Neither Hägerström nor Lundstedt used it to describe their own theories, and it was not adopted by adherents of Uppsala philosophy until after Hägerström's death, and even then only by Hedenius, who disagreed with major portions of both Hägerström's and Lundstedt's theories. See P Mindus, *A Real Mind: The Life and Work of Axel Hägerström* (Dordrecht, Springer, 2009) 81–82.

[16] See, eg, A Phalén, 'Ur erfarenhetsbegreppets historia' in *Festskrift tillägnad prof Vitalis Norström på 60-årsdagen den 29 januari 1916* (Göteborg, Elanders Boktryckeri, 1916) 52.

[17] A Hägerström, *Sosialfilosofiska Uppsatser* (M Fries ed, Stockholm, Bonniers, 1939) 35–57 ('Om moraliska föreställningars sanning'). The title is frequently erroneously translated as 'moral propositions'. Hägerström uses the Swedish phrase 'moraliska föreställningar' which, in Swedish, can mean 'moral conceptions', 'moral ideas' or 'moral representations'—all of which refer to mental, rather than verbal, processes. The use of the phrase 'moral

agreed with Phalén's, namely, that we cannot study morality or ethics—or rights—as a scientific or scholarly activity. We can simply study about them. However, Hägerström's methods, which Lundstedt adopted in toto, ran deeper than the philosophical semantic analyses Phalén used: the roots of his technique of concept analysis lay not in semantics, but in a theory of the means of knowledge acquisition. The reason we cannot study morality or ethics (or rights) as a scholarly activity, Hägerström said, is because they are not an objective truth of which we can acquire knowledge. Moral ideas (including notions of rights) are therefore inherently incapable of being true or false—they refer not to objective states, but to subjective states, in particular emotions and the expression of feelings.[18]

The acquisition of factual knowledge, Hägerström argued, involved both the gathering of empirical data and the making of a judgment on the data through rational thought—it was not simply one or the other.[19] The judgment involved in acquiring knowledge about things or facts is a two step process, where in the first step one assesses the internal consistency and freedom from contradiction of the conception that constitutes the knowledge to be acquired, and in the second step judges its consistency with the wider real-world context. One judges something to be true if there is a correspondence between what it claims or suggests should be true, and what one actually observes.[20] Hägerström gives the example of the conception 'men who breathe through gills'. In a world where men *do* breathe through gills, a reasoning subject will judge the conception

propositions' in English which—unlike the original Swedish phrase—does have a strongly semantic sense, goes back to Robert Sandin's original English translation: A Hägerström, *On the Truth of Moral Propositions* (R Sandin tr, London, Allen & Unwin, 1964). Whilst 'moral propositions' is closer to standard English philosophical usage than 'moral conceptions', it gives the erroneous impression that Hägerström's ideas were much more rooted in semantics than they actually were. Cf the points made by Mindus, above n 15, at 96 and E Pattaro, 'I Will Tell You about Axel Hägerström: His Ontology and Theory of Judgment' (2010) 23 *Ratio Juris* 123, 152.

[18] Hägerström's views on morals are succinctly summarised in his inaugural lecture, 'Om moraliska föreställningars sanning', above n 17. His views on rights are scattered across various works. Jes Bjarup presents a brief English summary in J Bjarup, 'The Philosophy of Scandinavian Legal Realism' (2005) 18 *Ratio Juris* 1, 6–10.

[19] Hägerström makes this aspect of his thought clearest in A Hägerström, *Botanisten och filosofen: Om kunskapsfilosofiens nödvändighet* (Stockholm, Bonniers, 1910), but the most detailed account is in A Hägerström, *Filosofi och vetenskap* (Stockholm, Ehlin, 1957). Cf the discussion in Mindus, above n 15, at 59–60, 63–70.

[20] A detailed analysis of Hägerström's theories in relation to the acquisition of knowledge and the judgments involved therein is found in a recent study by Enrico Pattaro. As Pattaro points out, this aspect of Hägerström's thought has been much misunderstood because the two words he uses to express the two stages of this process are both usually rendered in English as 'reality': Pattaro, above n 17, at 127. If the distinction between the two is maintained, Hägerström's theories resemble aspects of Wittgenstein's: at 133. Contrast the views of Michael Freeman who, based on existing translations that do not make this distinction, concludes that the Scandinavian realists fail to appreciate Wittgenstein's distinctions as to different types of statements: MDA Freeman, *Lloyd's Introduction to Jurisprudence*, 8th edn (London, Sweet & Maxwell, 2008).

to be true; in a world where men breathe through lungs, he or she will judge the conception to be false.[21]

Moral conceptions and conceptions of rights, in contrast, do not follow this pattern. Whereas the truth or falsity of the subject matter of a factual conception is judged with reference to objective reality, moral conceptions do not involve a *judgment* (*omdöme*), in that the subject does not attempt to verify the extent to which the conception corresponds with objective reality. The mental (or psychological) processes involved, instead, are subjective[22] and involve an emotional element. Hägerström describes these processes as 'evaluation' (*värdering*).[23] This is not to say that they are *exclusively* emotional. There is a clear rational element here, in that the formulation of a conception involves mental processes that are cognitive, and the assessment of its internal consistency involves processes of rational assessment. It is the final assessment as to the validity of a moral conception, Hägerström says, that is emotional:[24] we validate the conception by comparing it not to objective reality, but to our own subjective feelings.

The result is that morality or ethics (or rights) are not an objective truth of which we can acquire knowledge. Moral ideas (including notions of rights) are therefore inherently incapable of being true or false—they refer not to objective states, but to subjective states, in particular emotions and the expression of feelings. A statement that 'if you injure someone while driving a car you can be held liable to pay compensation by a court' is a true statement. A statement to a driver that 'you have a duty to drive carefully' is a statement that is neither true nor false—it describes your feelings, not the reality of any objectively existing duty. Because they are inherently subjective, we cannot study them. We can only study about them.

It is important to note that in Hägerström's theory, it is the absence of a genuine judgment in relation to moral conceptions or conceptions of rights—of an attempt to verify whether the conception corresponds with an objective reality external to itself and independent of the con-

---

[21] Hägerström, *Filosofi och vetenskap*, above n 19, at 117 ff.

[22] It is worth noting in this context that the Scandinavian languages distinguish between two types of opinion. If you present an opinion as to what you believe the objective state of things to be, you would say (in Swedish) *jag tror* (etymologically related to the English 'true'). If, on the other hand, you express a subjective opinion, you would say *jag tycker* (etymologically related to the English 'think'). To a speaker of a Scandinavian language, therefore, the distinction between subjective and objective opinion is linguistically clearer and more self-evident than it necessarily is to a native English speaker.

[23] Note that the link between 'value' (*värde*) and 'evaluation' (*värdering*) is much more obvious in Swedish than it is in English.

[24] Hägerström's terminology is rooted in early twentieth century German *Aktpsychologie*, and its threefold classification of mental processes as 'conceptions', 'judgments' and 'emotions': Mindus, above n 15, at 96–97. Even if one rejects the shoehorning of all non-cognitive and non-rational processes into the category of 'emotions', however, the distinction Hägerström makes between judgments and evaluations stands.

ception—that leads to the conclusion that moral conceptions cannot be said to be either true or false and that there can, in consequence, be no 'moral facts'. Does this mean that moral ideas or ideas of rights are semantically meaningless? No, because Hägerström's critique of moral conceptions or rights is not primarily semantic—it is, instead, epistemological and psychological.[25] This has important implications for how we understand Hägerström's characterisation of certain concepts as 'meaningless'. In saying that a concept that is principally a matter of opinion is meaningless because it is neither true nor false, Hägerström is not saying that the words are without semantic meaning. Rather, they are meaningless as referents to objective reality, and as sources of knowledge about the objective world. They are not necessarily meaningless as referents to the subjective emotional state of the utterer, and they can be understood in psychological terms as giving voice to inner emotions and feelings. Equally, they can have semantic meaning as attempts to convince the hearer of the subjective position of the utterer and bring the hearer around to the utterer's point of view. But they are incapable of describing any objective reality the utterer of the words may claim to describe through them.[26]

This, then, was the distinction the Scandinavian realists had in mind when they spoke of law as fact and distinguished it from law as opinion. They separated the objective reality of the law, or the fact of law, from subjective concepts based on the opinions and emotions of those who work with the law. When Lundstedt said that there are no rights, no duties and no legal rules,[27] what he meant was that rights, duties and even the common conception of legal rules belonged to the latter category, and were therefore simply expressions of the emotional state or opinion of persons

---

[25] After the deaths of Phalén and Hägerström, several of Phalén's disciples—most notably Gunnar Oxenstierna and Hedenius—made a concerted effort to defend Phalén as the true founder of the Uppsala school, and to portray Hägerström's theory as a simple application of Phalén's ideas to moral concepts. See, eg, G Oxenstierna, *Vad är uppsalafilosofien?* (Stockholm, Bonnier, 1938) 57–64; I Hedenius, *Om rätt och moral* (Stockholm, Wahlström and Widstrand, 1963) 8–34. Their interpretation, and particularly Hedenius', was influential and for a long time determined the received understanding of Hägerström, even though—as Hedenius himself admitted—his understanding of Hägerström's philosophy differed quite from Hägerström's own: J Hansson and S Nordin, *Ernst Cassirer: The Swedish Years* (Bern, Peter Lang, 2006) 161–65. This was in part because the obscurity of Hägerström's writing made him hard to read in the original, but it played a major role in the predominance of the semantic interpretation of Hägerström. Modern commentators have, however, demonstrated that this distorts Hägerström's own presentation of his theories: see, eg, Mindus, above n 15, at 77–108. Cf Bjarup's criticism of the 'received view' of Hägerström's philosophy: J Bjarup, 'Ought and Reality: Hägerström's Inaugural Lecture Reconsidered' (2000) 40 *Scandinavian Studies in Law* 11, especially at 12–15.

[26] cf the emphasis Lundstedt placed on the idea that rights were *theoretically* meaningless: AV Lundstedt, *Det Hägerström-Lundstedtska misstaget: Sju föreläsningar samt efterskrift* (Uppsala, L Norblads Bokhandel, 1942) 15.

[27] See above nn 3–4 and accompanying text.

who wrote about them—they had nothing to do with the reality of the legal system. In the next part, I discuss this conclusion in more detail.

III. THE 'MEANINGLESSNESS' OF RIGHTS

Whilst Hägerström frequently commented on legal concepts, he did not directly concern himself with questions concerning contemporary issues in substantive law. It is here that Lundstedt entered the picture. Lundstedt saw himself as picking up where Hägerström had left off (and Hägerström agreed, much to the chagrin of Uppsala theorists who thought they agreed with Hägerström but disagreed with Lundstedt), and he extended Hägerström's critique of moral concepts and the concept of rights to a broader, more jurisprudentially-focused analysis. Lundstedt applied Hägerström's theories to a wide range of issues, but the bulk of his work concerned the law of obligations. What, he asked, was an 'obligation' and what was its connection to the concept of rights?

What do we mean by the concept of a 'right'? The general social conception of a 'right', Lundstedt said, following Hägerström, is subjective. The feeling involved when an individual asserts a 'right' is an assertion or conceptualisation that he or she has power over another. Yet assertions of power are commonly made when individuals are in reality in a state of powerlessness, feeling themselves or their interests threatened by another's actions. They do not in reality have the power they claim to have—they simply voice a feeling or an opinion that they believe they ought to have the power that was the subject of their conception. Consequently, this conception of power, in much the same way as a moral conception, has its base in emotion and not reality. Rights, therefore, are matters of opinion, of the same nature as a moral conception, and hence incapable of being true or false. And, in addition, a 'right sentence'—a statement that asserts the positive existence of the power that constitutes the basis of the right—is, to the extent such a power does not actually exist, false.

Lundstedt built further upon this base by drawing a distinction between the use of the concept of a 'right' as a descriptor of legal relationships and legal consequences, and its use in what he termed the 'legal ideology' (*rättsideologien*) that provided the 'foundation of legal science' (*fundament för rättsvetenskapen*).[28] The former seeks to describe the law as it existed, and the language of rights it uses is simply a way of describing the relationships and consequences produced by the action of the legal machinery.[29] Legal ideology, in contrast, seeks—implicitly or explicitly—to

---

[28] Lundstedt, *Det Hägerström-Lundstedtska misstaget*, above n 26, at 31–34.
[29] ibid. Lundstedt's views as to the nature of positive law and legal rules were also somewhat different from the standard view, in that he believed that referring to the text of a law

define the conceptual basis of the law, not merely to describe its content. To the extent theorists claim that the conceptual basis of the law lies in legal concepts such as 'rights' or 'duties', they are claiming that these concepts have an objective existence that is independent of the legal machinery itself.[30] In legal ideology, therefore, 'rights' are not a creation of the law—they are the reason for the law. The purpose of law is the protection of these objectively existing concepts exterior to itself. They are the foundation on which it is built.[31]

Lundstedt argued that the former descriptive use of the concept of a 'right' is acceptable, but the latter, normative use is not. If rights have any real existence—by producing actual (and not merely mental) effects that can be felt and measured—it is the existence they derive from the law. In determining whether the proposition 'A has this right' is valid, the *only* real thing we can use as the object of comparison is the law. If we attempt to take the verificatory step by comparing it to morality, we are only saying 'A *ought* to have this right'—we are not saying, and we cannot say, that A *actually* has this right, in that A will be able to successfully bring about the production of the consequences that are commonly associated with the possession of the right. All we are left with is subjective opinion, or subjective morality. Rights cannot, therefore, have a real objective existence outside the law, contrary to the argument of rights theorists that the law exists for the purpose of protecting rights.

Most critics of Lundstedt fail to appreciate both the importance and the nature of this distinction. Lundstedt's contemporary, Ingemar Hedenius, in his extended critique of Hägerström's and Lundstedt's views titled *Det Hägerström-Lundstedtska misstaget* ('The Hägerström-Lundstedt Error'), argued that even if most people's personal conceptions of rights were riddled with superstitious beliefs, it did not alter the fact that when people spoke of legal rights, they were referring to something real—namely, that if certain factual criteria were satisfied, a particular reaction would follow from the state machinery whatever the philosophical problems with the underlying concept of 'rights' itself might be. To say, as Hägerström and Lundstedt did, that rights could not have any real existence because of the metaphysical nature of the concept ignored the fact that the legal terminology associated with rights was very effective at describing real facts and real relations.[32] The right to property, for example, was a con-

---

as a 'legal rule' without reference to how it was applied by courts and other institutions was erroneous. He preferred the term 'legal statements' or 'legal declarations' to describe what are conventionally called principles or rules of law. A full consideration of this view is well beyond the scope of this chapter, but an overview is contained in AV Lundstedt, *Legal Thinking Revised: My Views on Law* (Stockholm, Almqvist & Wiksell, 1956) 305–27.

[30] Lundstedt, *Det Hägerström-Lundstedtska misstaget*, above n 26, at 33–34.
[31] ibid, at 31–42.
[32] Hedenius, above n 25, at 68–75.

glomerate of hypothetical facts, whose components included restitution, compensation, punishment and so on.[33] The alleged problems pointed to by Lundstedt and Hägerström were common to the use of any conceptual language. They were no different from the conceptual problems created by a statement such as 'my, the time really flew by', and were just as capable of referring to factual realities.[34] Ross' critique was built on a similar base. Lundstedt, he argued, confused the concept of rights with the word 'rights'. Whilst the concept may well be metaphysical, that did not mean that the word could not correspond to realities, because a name was not part of the essence of a thing.[35] The term, Ross agreed, did not refer to anything real, but it nonetheless functioned as a way of connecting or tying together diverse operative facts and legal consequences.[36]

These criticisms levelled by Lundstedt's contemporaries are similar to modern critiques of Lundstedt's views,[37] but—as Lundstedt strenuously pointed out—they fail to take account of the distinction between 'ordinary legal language' on the one hand and 'legal ideology' on the other, which is fundamental to his critique of rights. The distinction Lundstedt was seeking to draw was between the *content* of the law, and the *conceptual underpinnings* of the law. 'Ordinary legal language', as he called it, related to the former. 'Legal ideology', in contrast, related to the latter. It was this latter use that Lundstedt argued was unscholarly and meaningless. Rights, he said, could be used as labels or categories to describe the content of the law. They could not be used as justificatory concepts that determined the content of the law. The first belonged to the category of 'is' and the second to the category of 'ought', which were sharply and fundamentally distinct, and should not be confused.[38]

In the law of obligations, for example, the law of conversion and nuisance cannot be 'about' protecting property rights because you do not have a property right save to the extent you stand in a legally upheld

---

[33] ibid, at 92.

[34] ibid, at 64.

[35] A Ross, *Virklighed og Gyldighed i Retslæren: En kritik af den teoretisk Retsvidenskabs Grundbegreber* (Copenhagen, Munksgaard, 1934) 227–29.

[36] A Ross, *On Law and Justice* (Berkeley, University of California Press, 1959) 172–83.

[37] See, eg, Freeman, above n 20, at 1039–40. The resemblence is not a coincidence. Modern criticisms of Lundstedt and Hägerström are largely a result of the fact that the standard interpretation of Hägerström came to be greatly influenced by the manner in which Hedenius presented his ideas. Hägerström was notoriously difficult to read; CD Broad described his style as resembling 'glue thickened with sawdust': CD Broad, 'Hägerström's Account of Sense of Duty and Certain Allied Experiences' (1951) 26 *Philosophy* 99, 99. Students were often left bewildered by the practical implications of his theories. To many students, as Gunnar Heckscher puts it, Hedenius' book helped resolve this problem: G Heckscher, 'Cambridge, Uppsala och verkligheten' (1982) 1 *Statsvetenskaplig tidskrift* 1, 5. Hedenius ultimately came to be hailed as the 'saviour of Swedish jurisprudence': S Nordin, *Ingemar Hedenius: En filosof och hans tid* (Stockholm, Natur och Kultur, 2004) 115.

[38] Hägerström, 'Om moraliska föreställningars sanning', above n 17, at 49–52. See also Mindus, above n 15, at 78–79.

relationship to others that lets you maintain actions against them under the laws of trespass, conversion, trust, nuisance, alienation and so on. It is the law of obligations that creates these relationships, and they cannot therefore be its purpose, not even if you choose to give them the label of 'rights'.[39] You cannot intelligibly say that the purpose of the law is to uphold the relationships created by the law. This is to resort either to a *petitio principii*—begging the question, as it were, through a circular argument—or to anthropomorphism—endowing the law of obligations with the imagined ability to set its own goals and define its own being, ignoring the fact that it is not sentient and is the creation of human beings.[40] This means that the law cannot be about preserving rights. Yet, Lundstedt argued, legal theorists regularly confuse the two, claiming that the law is about the preservation of rights, as opposed to simply using rights as a label to describe relationships created and upheld by the law.

The result of this, Lundstedt argued, is that judges and jurists in practice fall back on legal ideology when faced with deciding what, exactly, the law means or requires in a particular complex situation, or when critically examining a particular legal statement, even if they claim that all they are doing is interpreting the patterns of relationships that already exist in the law.[41]

Lundstedt took the example of property rights, and their use in arguments against expropriation. If rights are taken as descriptive categories, then they are whatever the law says they are. You cannot 'have' a property right which prevents the state from expropriating your property, because the property right you have was created by the law, and the law can fully well define it to exclude the ability to complain about expropriation. There may well be an argument to say that the law should give you the right to complain about expropriation, but that is an argument that must be justified on some other terms than with reference to a supposed 'right' which transcends the law.[42] This, Lundstedt argued, was a paradigmatic example of the confusion in legal scholarship about 'is' and 'ought' in relation to rights.

The same problem, Lundstedt said, affects attempts to define rights with reference to legally protected interests. This formulation, which originated with Rudolf von Jhering, had been enthusiastically adopted by Anglo-American jurists. Yet, Lundstedt argued, it could not form the justificatory

---

[39] Lundstedt, *Obligationsbegreppet I*, above n 3, at 107–08, 118–27.

[40] This last criticism applies not just to rights-based accounts of the law of obligations, but also to modern accounts which treat it as being an end in itself, whose sole goal is to be itself. See, eg, EJ Weinrib, *The Idea of Private Law* (Cambridge MA, Harvard University Press, 1995) 3–6.

[41] AV Lundstedt, *Obligationsbegreppet II: Den i förra delen hävdada åskådningen ytterligare konfronterad med jurisprudensens läror* (Uppsala, L Norblads Bokhandel, 1930) 258–59.

[42] Lundstedt, *Obligationsbegreppet I*, above n 3, at 109–18.

basis of the law. The idea of a 'legally protected interest' assumes an evaluation of the range of possible interests to determine which is worth protecting. This, again, is a value decision, rooted not in a judgment properly called, but in a mere evaluation. Consequently, there is no way of objectively identifying what interests are protected or deserve protection, save with reference to the law. Once you remove the law from the equation, therefore, you are left with nothing at all—there is nothing to indicate what the content of the right is. This is problematic even if all you are trying to do was describe the law. As the alleged justificatory basis of the law, it is so circular as to be useless.[43]

But is it possible to find some sort of objective existence for rights outside the law and thus say that the law does, in fact, exist for the purpose of protecting these rights—that, for example, decisions to legally protect a particular interest simply reflect the existence of these rights? Lundstedt likened standard attempts to do this to an entrenched superstition. The objective reality of 'rights' is usually asserted with reference either to natural law or to positive law theories of objective rights (or objective law). Natural law is rhetorically powerful. 'We hold these truths to be self-evident'; 'all men are endowed by their creator with certain rights': when we no longer believe in a right reason or in the notion of god-given rights, where then do these rights come from? Not from morality. Morality can argue that these rights ought to exist. But morality cannot give the rights an existence beyond the realm of the ought, not unless you buy into the idea of right reason or of some higher power—a magical or superstitious power—that causes some change of status when you claim a right. When early thinkers spoke of 'god-given rights', they meant, literally, that divine command had decreed that all men should have these rights. Or they believed that the existence of these rights was clearly apparent to anyone who exercised some form of universal reasoning of wisdom that transcended the individual and of which everyone was capable. In essence, therefore, these theories depended on the existence of a trans-human will whose opinions had an absolute character for humans. Yet no such trans-individual exists, nor do most modern thinkers who followed these theories believe that it exists. Modern thinkers frequently attempt to replace the traditional invocation of 'right reason' with a more modern appeal to common rationality or a shared rationality,[44] but this

---

[43] ibid. Lundstedt also gives a brief—and less clear—version of this argument in his English work: Lundstedt, *Legal Thinking Revised*, above n 29, at 78–93.

[44] cf Robert Stevens' assertion in R Stevens, *Torts and Rights* (Oxford, Oxford University Press, 2007) 330 that

the moral rights we have, and those which ought to be given the force of law, are capable of being deduced from the nature and experience of ourselves, and the world and society in which we live. Rational people can recognize such rights independently of their being given force of law.

is in substance the same thing.[45] The idea of rights as objective truths—so fundamental to most legal systems—was therefore rooted in social superstition, in ideas that could only be described as a belief in the magical properties of words, which were supported and upheld by the legal machinery and its rituals.[46]

Lundstedt then asked if a subjective conception of rights could form the basis of the law. Only, he answered, if the law had actually issued from a person or group of persons who held that subjective conception.[47] This, Lundstedt held, was impossible for several reasons. First, drawing on Hägerström's critique of the 'will theory' of positive law, he argued that in the modern constitutional state, there was no despotic sovereign whose powers made the law. Nor was there a 'collective will'—criminals, Hägerström had pointed out, were hardly likely to join with the rest of the populace in supporting a criminal law that would be enforced against them.[48] Equally, Lundstedt argued, it was incorrect to treat the law as consisting *solely* of what one found in the statute books. Even if you had a legal system all of whose laws had been promulgated at one point of time by an absolute despot, and which had then continued with these laws unchanged, the law would be affected by the manner in which it was interpreted and applied by the machinery—judicial and administrative—tasked with its enforcement. This 'collection of wills' could not be reduced to a single will and, hence, could not express a single opinion. In effect, he argued, theorists were attempting to substitute a transcendent individual will—such as the notion of a sovereign will—for the divine will, which was no more real than the divine will.[49]

Rights and interests, Lundstedt concluded, could not therefore be the ends of the law. The law does not exist for the purpose of protecting rights or interests. The creation of rights and the protection of interests may be part of the machinery or tools which the law uses to its ends, but they are not the law's principal objects nor are they its main sub-

---

[45] Lundstedt, *Obligationsbegreppet II*, above n 41, at 9–13, 292–97; Hägerström, *Sosialfilosofiska Uppsatser*, above n 17, at 77–96 ('Om sociala vidskepelser').

[46] Most accounts of Hägerström's thought presented by common law theorists place a lot of emphasis on this last aspect of Hägerström's thinking, seeming at times to treat it almost as if it was the foundation of his critique of rights, possibly because of its prominence in his relatively later and more overtly legal works, which have had larger portions translated into English. As the discussion in this part should have demonstrated, however, the idea of the 'magical' origin and 'magical' function of rights was far from central to Hägerström's critique—it formed part of his attempt to account for the role rights actually played in classical and modern legal systems, and of how the legal order developed as it did. It played little if any role in his or Lundstedt's account of why the concept itself was fundamentally flawed.

[47] Lundstedt, *Obligationsbegreppet II*, above n 41, at 39–44.

[48] A Hägerström, 'Är gällande rätt uttryck att vilja?' in *Festskrift tillägnad prof Vitalis Norström på 60-årsdagen den 29 januari 1916* (Göteborg, Elanders Boktryckeri, 1916) 171.

[49] ibid.

ject, and they cannot be because they are not objective. The failure of rights-based thinkers to identify precisely what the objective rights were which they claimed the law protected—recently re-emphasised by Steve Hedley[50]—was in Lundstedt's view not simply the result of insufficient work. The project was impossible and inherently doomed to fail, because the scope of a subjective conception could never be objectively delineated. You can never reach objective agreement on something that is inherently subjective.

Why, then, was the concept of an 'objective right' so pervasive in the legal system? One reason was that concepts, as Phalén had pointed out, tend to persist in scholarship long after their initial meaning or initial basis—in this case, the belief in a supra-individual will—is lost. Legal theory in particular, Lundstedt said, has a tendency (much like theology) to cling on to basic postulates once they are formulated, regardless of usefulness or scholarly accuracy.[51] But a second, and more understandable, reason for the entrenchment of rights, Lundstedt argued, was the fact that in the years since the Enlightenment, rights had played an important, and positive, role in achieving full political and legal equality. Hägerström had said that one of the uses of moral concepts was rhetorical, to attempt to win others over to your subjective point of view. The rhetoric of rights and the claim to have rights, Lundstedt said, had the same use and had historically been put to use in this way, despite their roots in subjective opinion and their ties to superstition. Simultaneously, they had co-evolved with society as it changed socially and economically. The capitalist revolution, with its need for economic freedom, had for example brought in its wake ideas of other types of freedoms. In effect, Lundstedt argued that the apparent past successes of the rhetorical use of rights had led to the idea of rights occupying a key place in the modern legal system, despite their shortcomings and despite the fact that they, objectively speaking, did not have an independent existence outside the machinery of the law.[52]

Lundstedt then went one step further. Although it was *valid* to use the terminology of rights descriptively, it was nonetheless *dangerous* to do so. Lundstedt advanced two reasons for this. First, there is a substantive difference between what the content of a right is commonly stated to be and what the law actually protects. The state does not protect the 'right to property'—no state has the capacity to prevent theft altogether, and the best it can do is to try to assist the victim of a theft, with no guarantee of success. Equally, the remedies granted for the violation of

[50] S Hedley, 'Looking Outward or Looking Inward? Obligations Scholarship in the Early 21st Century' in A Robertson and HW Tang (eds), *The Goals of Private Law* (Oxford, Hart Publishing, 2009) 193.

[51] AV Lundstedt, 'Kritik av nordiska skadeståndsläror' [1923] *Tidskrift for Rettsvitenskap* 55, 152.

[52] See generally AV Lundstedt, *Socialdemokratisk idépolitik* (Stockholm, Tidens Förlag, 1929).

property rights often have little connection with the right they claim to protect. The tort of conversion, for example, is commonly said to protect property rights.[53] Yet the remedy that would effectively protect the property right in the converted goods—specific delivery—is an exceptional one which is rarely awarded.[54] The general remedy at common law is payment of the value of the goods, which whilst appropriate to protect a contractual right to receive payment for goods is hardly the best way of protecting a property right.

The same holds true for contracts and personal obligations—no state guarantees the performance of such obligations, and the laws relating to them tend to be so technical and filled with so many exceptions that there are many situations where the obligation will not be fulfilled despite it involving an ostensible right.[55] This can be overcome by a careful use of the word 'right' and a careful explanation of precisely what an author means when he or she discusses 'property rights', but legal writers are for the most part not careful when they use the language of rights.

Secondly, and more fundamentally, Lundstedt said that legal writers have significant difficulties keeping the moral (subjective, ought-based) and strictly legal (labels for relationships created and upheld by the law) senses of rights apart. Because the two senses of the word are so closely intertwined in common parlance, there is a strong tendency for the one to collapse into the other in the analysis of complex situations and particularly those with tricky moral dimensions, and for legal scholars to base their ostensibly objective descriptions of the law on their own subjective moral evaluations. This is problematic, not just because of the introduction of subjectivity, but because—as Lundstedt tried to show in his analysis of rights—the *legal* conception of a right differs in so many ways from the *moral* conception of the right with which it happens to share a name. In effect, legal concepts are interpreted and applied with reference to moral standards that are *not* the source of the relevant legal concept. Ideally, it would be possible to devise a different terminology, and as an example Lundstedt attempted to find a different word for 'duty',[56] but he conceded that the task of creating a new conceptual terminology had

---

[53] Stevens, above n 44, at 342. See also S Green, 'Rights and Wrongs: An Introduction to the Wrongful Interference Actions' ch 18 of this book, which makes a rights-based argument in relation to *all* the torts that deal with wrongful interference with goods.

[54] See, eg, *Whiteley Ltd v Hilt* [1918] 2 KB 808 (CA) 819 (Swinfen Eady MR).

[55] Lundstedt uses the example, taken from Swedish law, of an onward sale to a third party where the first sale was defective to argue that the complex set of relations the law actually creates has very little connection to what we understand to be a 'property right' or a 'contractual right': Lundstedt, *Obligationsbegreppet I*, above n 3, at 43–48. The English counterpart would be the *nemo dat* rule, the identification of the principles behind which has perplexed many jurists.

[56] AV Lundstedt, 'Några anmärkningar om skadeståndsrättens systematisering och om kausalitetsfrågan i juridiken' in OA Borum and K Illum (eds), *Festskrift til Henry Ussing* (Copenhagen, Juristforbundet, 1951) 328, 328–34.

proved beyond him. He said that he, himself, was at least very careful
to use rights in only the legal sense, and argued that it was critical that
legal writers maintain this distinction—if they did not, their works must
be held to fall short of the standards of legal scholarship.[57]

IV. DUTIES, CAUSATION AND TAXONOMY

What, then, of other legal concepts? Could they, perhaps, contribute to
providing a valid conceptual basis for the law? Lundstedt took the view
that that they could not: the problems he had identified with the attempts
to use the concept of a 'right' as the foundation of the law—rather than
a mere shorthand way of representing the relations created and upheld
by the law—applied in exactly the same way to every attempt to give a
legal concept an existence independent of the law.

Consider, for example, the concept of a 'duty'. As with a 'right', a
'duty' is principally a moral concept. In Hägerström's conception, much
as a 'right' is associated with a conception of power, a duty is associated with a conception that something *ought* to be done. A 'duty' is, in
other words, closely associated with the conception of a sense of a duty
(*pliktsmedvetendet*) in the mind of the person who bears the duty. There
is, in the mind of the person experiencing the duty, a sense of reception or
acknowledgment of the fact that he or she is bound to discharge the duty.
The term 'duty' could also be used to utter or articulate moral commands
or moral imperatives, which are framed with the intention of inducing the
feeling of a sense of duty in the person to whom they are addressed.[58]

In either case, however, 'duty' becomes a subjective concept which, as
the expression of an emotion or feeling, can neither be true nor false,
and hence cannot provide an objective conceptual basis for the law. And,
Lundstedt points out, once again the 'duties' that are the subject of law
are *created* by the law. They do not depend on the subjective mental state
of the person owing the duty. Instead, the term simply describes relations
created by the law. As such, whilst it can be used descriptively, it has no
role to play in determining the conceptual basis of the law, as the duties
that are the subject of law only exist because the law creates them—they
have no existence independent of the law. Nor does it help to add the
phrase 'legal' before the term 'duty', for the same reason adding 'legally
protected' before the term 'interest' did not make Jhering's conception of
rights more useful—all it does is make it a *petitio principii*.[59] The basis of

---

[57] Lundstedt, *Det Hägerström-Lundstedtska misstaget*, above n 26, at 29–42.
[58] See Hägerström, *Sosialfilosofiska Uppsatser*, above n 17, at 58–76 ('Om Pliktmed-
vetendet'). See also the account in CD Broad, 'Hägerström's Account of Sense of Duty and
Certain Allied Experiences' (1951) 26 *Philosophy* 99.
[59] Lundstedt, *Obligationsbegreppet II*, above n 41, at 39–44.

declaring certain acts to be the breach of a legal duty cannot be simply that the acts are declared by law to be contrary to a legal duty. This tells us nothing of any use about the conceptual foundations of the law.

This argument, Lundstedt said, could be extended to the entire conceptual vocabulary of the law of obligations, including concepts used to distinguish one area of the law of obligations from another. Lundstedt took the example of the distinction between contract and tort. This distinction, he said, had been traced to two different principles both of which were advanced as representing the conceptual basis of the law of contract. The first was the 'will theory' which holds that the will of the promisor to be bound by his or her promise, as expressed through the process of contracting, is the source of the binding obligation. Seen in general terms, the 'intention to be bound' is subjective, depending as it does on the mental state of the promisor. The state of being 'bound' is a feeling, akin to the feeling of duty, and hence is also incapable of being either true or false. If, in contrast, we speak not of the intention to be morally bound but the intention to be legally bound, we arrive at the same type of circular reasoning that affects the concept of 'legal rights' or 'legal duties'—namely, that an intention to be 'legally' bound cannot have an existence independent of the law, and hence cannot constitute the conceptual basis of the law. All 'legally bound' can be is a convenient label to attach to the set of relations created by the law. Thus, Lundstedt argued, the theory as such could tell us nothing about the basis of the obligation—ie, why certain instances of possessing the feeling of being 'bound' create legal obligations while others do not, beyond that it is what the law says it is.[60] This applied just as much to the second principle, the 'reliance theory', for here, too, 'reliance' had to be treated either as a subjective mental state, or simply as what the law said it was.[61]

This point has of course been made in the common law literature about obligations—most notably by Patrick Atiyah.[62] More recently, commentators such as Steve Hedley have also pointed out that the 'many fictions of contract' have implications for how we understand the boundary between tort and contract, and between contract and restitution—and, particularly, in the case of the latter, for the very basis on which we make the classification and conceptualise a category such as 'restitution'.[63] The problems created by the orthodox test of the distinction between contract and other branches of the law of obligations is also evidenced by the

---

[60] Lundstedt, *Obligationsbegreppet I*, above n 3, at 128–31.

[61] ibid, at 131–38. See also the brief overview in AV Lundstedt, *Superstition or Rationality in Action for Peace? Arguments against Founding a World Peace on the Common Sense of Justice* (Uppsala, L Norblads Bokhandel, 1929) 96–109.

[62] PS Atiyah, *The Rise and Fall of Freedom of Contract* (Oxford, Oxford University Press, 1979).

[63] S Hedley, *Restitution: Its Divisions and Ordering* (London, Sweet & Maxwell, 2001) 34–84.

difficulty of classifying cases such as *South Australia Asset Management Corp v York Montague Ltd*,[64] which many academic commentators treat as a negligence case despite the clear view of some of the judges that it was a contract case.[65] Some commentators, such as Stephen Waddams, argue that these problems reflect a simple fact: the 'interrelation of legal concepts' involves a 'greater complexity' than taxonomic categories or explanatory principles can capture.[66]

Lundstedt, however, went one step further than the existing common law literature. Orthodox classification exercises, in Lundstedt's account, are problematic not simply because of the complexity of the law or because concepts in different areas of the law will inevitably be interrelated. They are, instead, problematic because they attempt to use concepts rooted in 'legal ideology', which are necessarily *subjective*, to classify and categorise the manner in which the legal system functions, which is necessarily *objective*. Subjective categories rooted in individual opinion—and not in facts—cannot create a system of classification or taxonomy that has objective validity. Any attempt to come up with an objectively valid classification of legal rules must ground itself in objective facts, not in subjective opinion. But orthodox theories of the classification, ordering or taxonomy of the law of obligations, including virtually every theory that has been advanced in the common law, do not do this. They always base themselves on subjective, metaphysical notions such as the 'type' of right involved, or the intention to be 'bound' or the extent of a party's 'reliance' on the other. Lundstedt's critique therefore affects not just the types of descriptive and prescriptive theories with which Waddams dealt, but also theories that attempt to abstract general philosophical or moral principles that unite and separate legal cases—such as the Kantian system advocated by Jacob Weinrib[67]—or interpretive theories of classification of the sort advanced by Allan Beever and Charles Rickett,[68] inasmuch as the latter continue to rely on non-objective criteria.[69]

In consequence, Lundstedt levelled the same critique at other criteria

---

[64] *South Australia Asset Management Corp v York Montague Ltd* [1997] AC 191 (HL).

[65] Lord Hoffmann, 'The Achilleas: Custom and Practice or Foreseeability?' (2010) 14 *Edinburgh Law Review* 47, 58–59.

[66] S Waddams, *Dimensions of Private Law: Categories and Concepts in Anglo-American Legal Reasoning* (Cambridge, Cambridge University Press, 2003) vi.

[67] J Weinrib, 'What Can Kant Teach Us about Legal Classification' (2010) 23 *Canadian Journal of Law and Jurisprudence* 203.

[68] A Beever and C Rickett, 'Interpretive Legal Theory and the Academic Lawyer' (2005) 68 *Modern Law Review* 320.

[69] In the case of Beever and Rickett, ibid, this is a specific result of the centrality of concepts such as 'consent' to their theory. In contrast, an interpretive approach to classification that based itself on genuinely objective criteria (such as the criterion of 'benefit to society' discussed in part VI) would arguably stand a chance of producing an objectively valid classification. Lundstedt himself had hoped to work on such an approach in the 'positive' component of his theory of obligations, which he never completed.

used to delineate taxonomic categories. He denied, for example, that there was any real distinction in the basis of strict liability and negligence. In both cases, Lundstedt argued, liability was in a general sense strict. The law did not look to the actual mental state of the alleged tortfeasor. The moment the law set an objective reasonable standard as its test, it was no longer looking at whether there was real negligence on the tortfeasor's part; rather, all you had was simply a different standard of strict liability.[70] Taxonomy also, therefore, does not provide a conceptual account of the law or explain the basis of the law, and is not even particularly persuasive in providing a clear basis to describe the law as it is.

For Lundstedt, the same held true of causation, a concept which has recently been advanced with some vigour as providing a justificatory basis for significant parts of private law.[71] In virtually all cases that are ostensibly about causation, Lundstedt argued, it is clear whether the defendant's act caused (in a naturalistic sense) the harm suffered by the claimant or not. To determine whether causation occured in a naturalistic sense, a jurist, as Lundstedt put it, does not need any more skill or knowledge 'than those which any sensible farmhand would have.'[72] Instead, what courts actually do is to decide whether, given the (known or easily discovered) extent to which the act has contributed to the harm, it is *appropriate* or *desirable* to hold the defendant liable to the claimant for the harm. Thus, Lundstedt argued, what passes for 'causation' in legal argumentation actually conceals beneath the surface a seething mass of subjective evaluation and conceptions rather than anything that would ordinarily be associated with the study of causation,[73] and it is to the identification and investigation of these factors that legal scholarship should direct itself. One can stick the label 'causation in law' on this inquiry, but to do so is as misleading and unhelpful as to speak of rights as 'protected interests'—it obscures the nature of what is really going on in the law.[74] Lundstedt's critique certainly does seem to fit with many cases in the common law that are ostensibly about causation, such as the mesothelioma cases. In neither *Barker v Corus UK Ltd*[75] nor *Fairchild v Glenhaven Funeral Services Ltd*[76] was there actually a question of causation—the question, instead, was whether it was appropriate to hold the defendants responsible given what was known about the degree of causation (or rather, given that it was scientifically impossible to discover the actual answer to the question

---

[70] AV Lundstedt, *Grundlinjer i skadeståndsrätten I: Culpa-regeln* (Uppsala, L Norblads Bokhandel, 1935).

[71] See, eg, MS Moore, *Causation and Responsibility: An Essay in Law, Morals, and Metaphysics* (Oxford, Oxford University Press, 2009).

[72] Lundstedt, *Grundlinjer i skadeståndsrätten I*, above n 70, at 200.

[73] Lundstedt, 'Kritik av nordiska skadeståndsläror', above n 51, at 151–52.

[74] Lundstedt, 'Kausalitetsfrågan', above n 56.

[75] *Barker v Corus UK Ltd* [2006] UKHL 20, [2006] 2 AC 572.

[76] *Fairchild v Glenhaven Funeral Services Ltd* [2002] UKHL 22, [2003] 1 AC 32.

of whether the claimant's mesothelioma was caused by the defendants). This, as Lundstedt argued, is actually an evaluation in relation to responsibility, not causation. Much the same could be said for cases such *Baker v Willoughby*[77] or *Jobling v Associated Dairies*[78] that ostensibly relate to the 'chain of causation' or the novus actus interveniens principle. In these and similar cases, the actual issue that the court determined was the extent to which, given what we know about the various factors that contributed to the harm suffered by the claimant, it was appropriate to hold the defendant liable to the claimant. The question of causation itself—whether the harm was 'caused' by the defendant—was not at issue.

Every single attempt to outline a conceptual basis for the law of obligations rooted in legal theory, Lundstedt said, had therefore failed, either because it led to a mere opinion with no basis for deciding whose opinion would be selected and why, or because it amounted to saying little more than that an obligation existed when the law said it did. None of this would be a problem if legal science did not pretend that these terms were *more* than labels to describe relations created and upheld by the law, that they in some way had an existence independent of the law and that the law was merely giving effect to and supporting this objective, independent existence, and that they constituted the real explanatory basis of the law. Yet it was precisely these explanations that were offered by legal orthodoxy, and that on the face of it informed the functioning of the law.

V. SHARED MORALITIES AND SHARED UNDERSTANDING

Can we rescue a moral basis for the law by actually identifying a shared morality in society? Are there actual moral beliefs that are shared by everybody in society? There are not, not even amongst the relatively small section of society from which the judiciary or the ruling classes are drawn, and most certainly not when you look at the polity as a whole. Lundstedt gave the example, taken from his time, of the value of class solidarity. This, he said, was much prized by the labour movement, but it stood in opposition to the value of full freedom of action, which was strongly advanced by the commercial classes as a reason to outlaw striker pickets. Morality, Lundstedt pointed out, is always contested—to speak of the law as rooted in a 'shared' morality necessarily falls back on the idea of right reason, or of some ineffable 'national character' of the sort celebrated by the German idealists such as Johann Herder which privileges one set of competing moral principles over another. None of these have a real existence.

---

[77] *Baker v Willoughby* [1970] AC 467 (HL).
[78] *Jobling v Associated Dairies* [1982] AC 794 (HL).

Lundstedt went further. Morality and ideas of moral duties, he argued, were not responsible for the shape and structure of the law. It was, if anything, the other way around. The legal machinery took moral concepts and common conceptions of justice, right and wrong and pressed them into its service to uphold and enforce the law. Lundstedt drew here on Hägerström's theory of suggestion and feedback.[79] Legal commands have a suggestive effect, whereby by their existence, by the force of their social acceptance, and the power and authority they command, they trigger a sense of moral duty in the people to whom they are addressed.[80] The result is that the legal system can by itself produce a 'sense of justice' (*rättsmedvetandet*)[81] that is influenced by and linked to the law. The law in force in a given jurisdiction, therefore, has an effect in shaping what people in that jurisdiction consider to be just, and an astute ruler can convince people to accept all manner of duties by framing them in a manner that makes them seem to conform to the popular idea of justice.[82]

If there is no shared morality in society, can we still speak of a Dworkinian contest between competing positions, through which the law will 'work itself pure' or—even if you reject the 'one right answer' thesis—ultimately arrive at an acceptable consensus? No, Lundstedt said, because it ignores the way judges actually use precedent. When a judge takes a previous statement as to the existence or scope of a 'right' and issues a decision based upon it, or incrementally advancing upon it, he or she does not always agree with the moral opinions of the previous judge, and he or she is not necessarily endorsing the moral opinions of the previous judge. The reason a judge approves of a precedent or chooses to apply a precedent is rather because he or she believes that the form of social relations created or upheld by the consistent application of that particular precedent is desirable. The contest is between the visions of society produced by competing moral principles, not the principles themselves or between different accounts of morality.[83]

VI. RECONSTRUCTING LAW: THE METHOD OF SOCIAL UTILITY

The reader may at this stage pose a fundamental question: if the attempt to articulate a conceptual basis for the law is fraught with so many problems, *need* we bother to articulate such a theory? Will it not suffice to simply say that the law is as it is, logical or illogical, and that our task as jurists is simply to describe and apply it, as Hedenius and Ross said?

[79] A Hägerström, *Till frågan om den objektiva rättens begrepp I: Viljeteorien* (Uppsala, Almqvist & Wiksell, 1917). See also Mindus, above n 15, at 142–48.
[80] There is a basic similarity here with HLA Hart's rule of recognition.
[81] This is analogous to the 'sense of duty' (*pliktmedvetandet*) discussed earlier.
[82] Lundstedt, *Obligationsbegreppet II*, above n 41, at 74–91.
[83] ibid, at 209 ff.

Can we not, in other words, retreat into a form of legal formalism and leave normative and other questions, including questions of justifying the law, to other disciplines? In Lundstedt's theory of law, the answer to this question is a clear 'no', and it will be useful at this stage to explore the reasons why he felt it was so important for legal theory to be able address questions of this type.

Although the Scandinavian legal system is not strictly speaking a branch of civil law, it has nonetheless been influenced by civil law trends, particularly in relation to legal theory. The Scandinavian realists were, therefore, embedded in a tradition which distinguished between questions *de lege lata*, *de lege ferenda*, and *de sententia ferenda*. Questions *de lege lata* deal with describing the law as it is, whereas questions *de lege ferenda* deal with normative issues, and questions of what the law ought to be. Questions *de sententia ferenda* deal with the issue of the manner in which a judge should decide a specific case—what legal declarations he or she should apply, how he or she should apply them and what the outcome should be.

This distinction had a fundamental impact on the work of both Ross and Lundstedt, but in very different ways. To Ross, questions *de lege ferenda* were political questions, and their determination was up to law-makers—as elected political officials—based on their evaluation of competing policy and social objectives and their considered opinions as to desirable outcomes. The proper role of a lawyer was that of a technician, who could tell politicians about the various legal tools at their disposal, and help them select the correct tool, and implement it properly.[84] Questions *de lege sententia* and questions *de lege lata* were very closely intertwined, in that describing the law as it stood necessarily involved advising the court as to how to decide future cases concerning that rule, and these were the proper domain of legal studies.[85] The former were conceptually and practically distinct from questions *de lege ferenda*, and were neither normative nor political in the sense the latter were.[86] This did not, of course, mean that lawyers could not participate in debates concerning questions *de lege ferenda*. Ross himself did so quite frequently—most notably in his book *Hvorfor Demokrati?*[87] (translated into English as *Why Democracy?*[88]), but also in a large number of other Danish works, including regular newspaper columns.[89] But, as he made clear in *Hvorfor Demokrati?*, he did

[84] A Ross, *Om Ret og Retfærdighed: En indførelse i den analytiske retsfilosofi* (Copenhagen, Nyt Nordisk Forlag, 1953) 472.

[85] Ross, *On Law and Justice*, above n 36, at 45–50.

[86] ibid, at 327–39.

[87] A Ross, *Hvorfor Demokrati?* (Koebenhavn, Ejnar Munksgaard, 1946).

[88] A Ross, *Why Democracy?* (D Gatley-Philip tr, Cambridge MA, Harvard University Press, 1952).

[89] A selection of Ross's newspaper columns were published in Danish as A Ross, *Demokrati, magt og ret: Indlæg i dagens debat* (Copenhagen, Lindhardt og Ringhof, 1974).

so in a non-legal capacity and with no claim to the objective, scientific validity of his position. He spoke, instead, as a politically engaged citizen seeking to persuade others of his point of view.[90]

Lundstedt's view was very different. Lundstedt took the view that lawyers could contribute to debates on questions *de lege ferenda* as lawyers. Although he did not consider the relationship between the three types of questions as expressly as Ross did, he appears to have implicitly taken the view that all three questions were within the proper domain of legal theory, and a properly framed legal theory should be capable of being applied to all questions.[91]

This difference is central to much of Lundstedt's critique of existing theories of law, and is directly responsible for his attempt to construct a positive theory of law. Lundstedt was an active member of the Swedish Social Democrats,[92] and had been since his student days, and he was deeply troubled by the way the law was being used in relation to the labour movement. Legislation was introduced to criminalise attempts to intimidate strike-breakers, at a time when attempts to commit most other criminal offences were not punishable, and to impose levels of civil liability on striking workers for loss caused to their employers which were significantly higher than those for similar levels of damage caused in ordinary circumstances.[93] Yet the incident that seemed to have sparked off his work on the law of obligations was a trial that began in 1916.

Lundstedt began his 'Lectures' with a volume on fundamental principles of criminal law. He justified this by saying that the conceptual critique he planned to advance was more evident in the context of criminal law, and that this volume therefore served as an introduction to his analysis of the law of obligations. But it is likely that he was prompted to question the basis of criminal law by the prosecution for treason in 1916 of three leading Social Democrats. There was a plan at the time by a section of the political class to bring Sweden into the First World War on the side of Germany. The three had reacted to this by saying that they would call for a general strike if this should happen. All were found guilty of treason and sentenced to lengthy terms in prison. Lundstedt played a leading role in formulating the arguments for their defence and for their—ultimately successful—appeal. The tenor of his work, as well as the specific issues he takes up, suggest strongly that he had this case in mind.

Lundstedt was equally troubled by international events, in particular the treatment of Germany by the victorious allies on the basis that they

---

[90] Ross, *Hvorfor Demokrati?*, above n 87, at 91–94.

[91] See AV Lundstedt, *Principindelning: Kritik av straffrättans grundåskådningar* (Uppsala, L Norblads Bokhandel, 1920).

[92] He represented them in the upper chamber of the Swedish Riksdag for over 20 years.

[93] See Källström, *Den Gode Nihilisten*, above n 13, at 32–35, 60–65.

had a *right* to demand punitive reparations and then a *right* to occupy German territory when Germany was unable to pay, and by Germany's eventual assertion—as a reaction—that it had a *right* to rearm and a *right* to reconquer its lost territory.[94] Rather than preventing conflict, existing legal theory was exacerbating it and creating new conflict on all levels, from the municipal to the national.

It was these concerns that led Lundstedt to develop his theory of the relationship between law and morality, and to focus on the effect that the law in force in a jurisdiction had on popular ideas of what was just. This, he argued, made the unscientific character of legal science even more troubling. In the absence of a solid, scientifically grounded account of the conceptual basis of the law of obligations, or law more generally, law-makers, jurists and decision-makers simply used their own evaluations—subjective evaluations, rather than objective judgments.[95] It was this, Lundstedt argued, that led to legal conceptions having an unproductive, destructive effect on society generally, and to these conceptions being accepted by the public as being 'true'.[96] And it was for this reason that he devoted his life to investigating legal theory, and the theory of the law of obligations, with a view to exposing the hollow basis of the legal concepts upon which so many claims were made and which were invoked to justify so many actions that, in the long run, harmed the interests of people and society. It was Hägerström, Lundstedt said, who opened his eyes to the role played by law and legal concepts in creating and sustaining this state of things, and to the possible role of legal scholarship in remedying them.[97]

To replace one set of subjective concepts with another, however, could not be a solution, and Lundstedt therefore attempted to locate the basis of the law in something objective, something that could be the subject of a genuine factual judgment and not just of an evaluation rooted in one's own prejudices, biases and preconceptions. He found this in what he called *samhällsnyttan* which, literally, means 'benefit to society' or 'utility to society'.[98]

The real basis of all obligations, Lundstedt argued, is the need to meet some form of social necessity. Legislators do so by introducing laws which create new relations or alter existing relations in a way that is of benefit

---

[94] See AV Lundstedt, *Två vårsfesttal i Uppsala vardera efter ett världskrig* (Uppsala, L Norblads Bokhandel, 1946).

[95] Lundstedt, *Obligationsbegreppet II*, above n 41, at 258–59.

[96] AV Lundstedt, 'The Responsibility of Legal Science for the Fate of Man and Nations' (1933) 10 *New York University Law Quarterly Review* 326.

[97] Lundstedt, *Det Hägerström-Lundstedtska misstaget*, above n 26, at 185–87.

[98] In his English writing, Lundstedt translated this phrase as 'social welfare'. His main concern seems to have been to avoid being associated with utilitarianism, and he seems not to have noticed the very different connotation of that phrase in English. In this chapter, I use a more accurate English rendering of the Swedish phrase.

to society and that meets the relevant social necessity. The basis of the law of contract, for example, is not an ineffable 'will' or an unidentifiable 'reliance', but the simple need to create instruments that make exchange and other business or social transactions possible. The purpose of the law of property—ranging from legal provisions on embezzlement to trespass and nuisance—is to preserve and uphold the incentive to productive work. And, similarly, for every other obligation, on a proper analysis, the underlying social benefit or social utility for the purpose of which the obligation was created can be found.

Popular theories of obligations miss this point completely, because their bases—rights, duties, rules of law—are closely connected with a particular view of law, namely, as an instrument of correcting wrongs. But for Lundstedt, this was a badly limited view. The law of obligations did not achieve its goals of social benefits just by resolving disputes and providing remedies. More fundamentally, it played a key role in preventing disputes from arising in the first place. Its dispute prevention function, in turn, was not just achieved through deterrence, as some of the Anglo-American realists would have it. As important was the role played by the legal machinery in pressing popular conceptions of justice into its service, and shaping the idea of justice in the image of the law, so that people obeyed the law not just because they feared the consequence of disobeying it, but because they believed that they were under a moral duty to do so.[99]

This makes a rights-based argument actually harmful, because more often than not, its effect would be to exacerbate disputes, not to mitigate them. Lundstedt argued that the examples he cited from international law and domestic law, including the law of obligations, showed that conceptualising the base of law as being a 'right' resulted in views and approaches that ran counter to the purposes for which the law exists as a social institution. And whilst historically, before the advent of liberal democracy, the idea of rights was useful as a rhetorical tool to push the ruling classes to take account of the goals and needs of other classes in society, and whilst rights had at that time actually played a positive role, this need had passed.[100]

Lundstedt's account of *samhällsnyttan* as the real, objective basis of the law was attacked by his contemporaries on two principal grounds. The first, advanced most strongly by Ross, was that Lundstedt's account was as subjective as the theories he opposed, and it was simply that he

---

[99] Lundstedt, *Obligationsbegreppet II*, above n 41, at 74–91; Lundstedt, *Legal Thinking Revised*, above n 29, at 93–114. Cf Jon Elster's more recent work on the role played by the emotions in guiding conduct and, in particular, the distinction he draws between the role of guilt and shame in preventing illegal action and the role of cost- or punishment-based deterrence: J Elster, 'Emotions and Economic Theory' (1998) 36 *Journal of Economic Literature* 47.

[100] See the extended discussion in Lundstedt, *Socialdemokratisk idépolitik*, above n 52.

lacked the ability to see it.[101] The second, advanced most strongly by Hedenius, was that Lundstedt's theory was simply a badly constructed cover for Lundstedt's social democratic prejudices.[102] Lundstedt strongly denied both criticisms. In a reply to Ross, he denied that his conception of the law was as subjective or metaphysical as the theories he criticised.[103] Like Hägerström, Lundstedt too used the analogy of law as a 'machine'. To Lundstedt, saying that the basis of the law lay in its role of meeting social necessity by providing a benefit to society was no more a normative statement than saying that the function of a bicycle was to transport persons from one place to another. It was a judgment, in the Hägerströmian sense, based on comparing one's initial conception against objective reality. It was, in other words, grounded in objective, empirically verifiable fact—in a factual assessment of the role the legal machinery actually plays—and not on a feeling or emotional response in relation to the role it ought to play.[104]

Lundstedt also argued that his theory was not political, contrary to Hedenius's claims, and in this Hägerström agreed with him.[105] His aim, instead, was to depoliticise law and legal discourse, by delinking debates on questions as to what the law should be from the realm of mere opinion and, instead, providing an objective, empirical basis for discussion and debate.[106] To some extent, Lundstedt's own use of the concept bears this out. Although Lundstedt was himself a Social Democrat, he was frequently at odds with them over their political programme. He supported a much higher level of protection of private property than many of them would have liked:[107] just as there was no 'right' to property, he argued, there was also no 'right' to equal distribution and the extravagent demands made by activists on the left would, if implemented, 'make the machinery of society go out of order.'[108] As early as the 1930s, he argued for the decriminalisation of homosexuality and tried to introduce

---

[101] A Ross, 'Realismen i retsvidenskaben og samfundsnyttekimæren' (1932) 4 *Svensk Juristtidning* 324.

[102] I Hedenius and A Wedberg, 'Professor Lundstedt och uppsalafilosofien: En förklaring' (1934) 5 *Fönstret* 3.

[103] AV Lundstedt, 'Är det metafysik att beakta samhällets intressen i rättsvetenskapen?' (1932) 4 *Svensk Juristtidning* 324.

[104] Lundstedt, *Obligationsbegreppet II*, above n 41, at 209 ff; Lundstedt, *Legal Thinking Revised*, above n 29, at 171–95.

[105] A Hägerström, 'Ein Stein, Ihr Herren, ist ein schlechtes Argument' (1934) 6–7 *Fönstret* 3.

[106] Lundstedt, *Obligationsbegreppet II*, above n 41, at 209 ff; Lundstedt, *Legal Thinking Revised*, above n 29, at 200–03.

[107] See S Källström, *En filosof i politiken: Vilhelm Lundstedt och äganderätten* (Stockholm, Avdelningen för idéhistoria, 1991) 21–22; N Berggren, 'Rättspositivism och Äganderätt' in N Berggren and N Karlson (eds), *Äganderättens konsekvenser och grunder* (Stockholm, Ratio, 2005) 180, 210.

[108] AV Lundstedt, 'Samhället och rättsordningen: En revolt mot rättsskolastiken' [1922] *Tiden* 150.

a Bill in the Swedish Riksdag to achieve this. After the Second World War, he was virtually the only Social Democrat in Sweden to argue for Swedish membership of NATO, on the basis that a league of democracies was necessary to bring order to international relations. The fact that Lundstedt denied the existence of objective rights does not mean that he—or, for that matter Hägerström—believed in an absolutist state or in the subordination of individual claims to social claims, as his views on the importance of protecting private property clearly indicate. The point of Lundstedt and Hägerström's critique was, instead, that arguments as to the desirable shape of the law should be constructed on a rational basis with reference to rationally verifiable circumstances. The fact that you were possessed of a particular opinion, or that you had a particular set of feelings, was no reason for the law to take your side. Indeed, in the absence of objective arguments that favour the jural relations you desired, it would be irrational for the law to do so.

VII. CONCLUSIONS

What, then, is the relevance of Lundstedt's theory for today's debate about obligations in the common law? I have discussed several in the course of this chapter, but in conclusion I would like to highlight three specific implications that are of particular importance.

In the first place, Lundstedt's perspective is one that is not much heard in the common law debate, but should be. The distinction Lundstedt makes between the descriptive and the ideological use of concepts is an important one which goes to the root of several positions that are commonly taken in the debate, and is a position we should think about more. As I have tried to demonstrate in this chapter, the resultant problems he points out with rights-based, moral, taxonomic and other theoretical approaches, and the limitations he highlights in relation to what these approaches can actually tell us about the law of obligations, deserve serious consideration.

More importantly, however, Lundstedt's theory transcends several divisions that have plagued the common law. The first of these is the notorious divide between internalists and externalists. Lundstedt's theory, in its emphasis on social benefit as the key organising principle of law, is canonically externalist. Yet, he emphasises, this externalist insight must feed into our internalist understanding and conceptualisation of the law. Rights, duties and other terms can be nothing more than labels—the law of obligations is not about them, even if it is sometimes articulated in their terms. If legal theory is to be capable of providing effective guidance on how to decide novel cases, or of what the law should say, it must be capable of relating the social benefit towards which the law strives with the terms in which it is articulated. Lundstedt, in other words, demands that internalists incorporate externalism into their theories, and that externalists consider the implications of their theories for our understanding of the structure of the law—and not merely say that they are illuminating policy choices as they are wont to do. Equally, Lundstedt's theories must lead to a rejection of the distinction between policy and principle. In a well-functioning legal system, neither principles nor policies are mere value choices. Both, instead, represent attempts to define ways to the same goal—that of ensuring that the law is implemented and enforced in a manner that promotes the social benefit that is its concern.

This leads us to what is perhaps the most provocative part of Lundstedt's theory—his argument that a consideration of 'benefit to society' is already inherent in the legal system, and that judges do this implicitly in framing moral or doctrinal arguments. Much has been written about the 'pragmatism' of English judges, particularly in the context of private law,[109] and of the extent to which they take account of 'policy';[110] and the upper judiciary, particularly in England, has repeatedly emphasised the importance of taking a pragmatic view.[111] This literature has shown just how systematic the judicial consideration of policy is, and the order that exists within judicial pragmatism. Could it be that what the courts are actually doing in their pragmatic consideration of policy factors is looking to some aspect of what Lundstedt described as 'benefit to society'? If this is true, and the literature suggests there is reason to believe that it is at least a possibility, then Lundstedt is right to ask for this process to be informed by evidence—by a real consideration of the social benefit or social need to which the relevant rule of law relates and which it seeks to advance—rather than letting it be obscured in and disguised behind the language of rights or of moral opinion.

The result is that Lundstedt presents the most compelling and complete realist account yet of obligations. His account integrates a detailed consideration of the structure of law with a study of its impact on society within one conceptual framework. He engages deeply with the concept of rights, with the role they actually have played in the law, and the reason why their use as analytical and conceptual tools is so pervasive in the law and resonates so strongly in society—and, as a result, puts himself in a position to also discuss the limits of the contribution the idea of rights can make to our understanding of the law of obligations. He discusses the relationship between law and morality, and why there does seem to

---

[109] PS Atiyah, *Pragmatism and Theory in English Law* (London, Stevens & Sons, 1987).

[110] J Bell, *Policy Arguments in Judicial Decisions* (Oxford, Clarendon Press, 1983).

[111] One of the best-known examples is the insistence of Lords Bridge, Roskill and Oliver in *Caparo Industries plc v Dickman* [1990] 2 AC 605 (HL) that the inquiry as to whether a duty of care existed is in large part a pragmatic one.

be such a relationship, which again lets him expose its limitations. At the same time, his idea of social necessity, with its strongly empirical base and its necessary link to concepts that constitute legal doctrine, provides a powerful common framework to relate functionalist and doctrinal accounts of the law of obligations. His theory therefore challenges us to abandon our preconceptions and do more to understand precisely what it is the law of obligations is about, and how its functions relate to its structure. For all the difficulties it presents, it is therefore worth taking the trouble to make sense of and engage with his views.

7

Of Rights Superstructural, Inchoate and Triangular: The Role of Rights in Blackstone's *Commentaries*

HELGE DEDEK*

I. INTRODUCTION

I N THE THIRD volume of the *Commentaries*,[1] William Blackstone, in his treatment of 'Private Wrongs', states that 'it is a general and indisputable rule, that where there is a legal right, there is also a legal remedy, by suit or action at law, whenever that right is invaded.'[2] The statement appears to establish an order—temporal and even logical—that places the right over the remedy: the remedy is the response to the invasion of a right. In other words: *ubi ius, ibi remedium*. A remarkable statement—after all, 'the' common law is said to have traditionally favoured a pragmatic approach that focuses on remedies rather than rights: *ubi remedium, ibi ius*.[3] However, academics have been known to be more

---

* Email: helge.dedek@mcgill.ca. An earlier version of this paper was presented at the conference Obligations V: Rights and Private Law, University of Oxford, 14–16 July 2010. I wish to thank Joshua Getzler, Francesco Giglio, John Goldberg, Daniel Jutras, William Lucy, Jason Neyers, Chaim Saiman, Martin Schermaier, Lionel Smith, Stephen Smith, and Stephen Waddams for their helpful comments and advice—all errors are, of course, mine. I am greatly indebted to my research assistant Andrei Molchynsky; I also to wish to thank Nicholas Melling for editing assistance. Research for this paper was supported by the Ratpan Fund.

[1] The *Commentaries* experienced many editions; the eighth edition was the last by Blackstone himself. The citations hereafter are to the first edition, published in four volumes: *Commentaries on the Law of England* (Oxford, Clarendon Press, 1765–69; reprint, Chicago, University of Chicago Press, 1979). The changes made in later editions are not material to this chapter.

[2] 3 Bl Comm 23; as exceptions Blackstone enumerates cases of self-help, retainer and remitter.

[3] See, eg, PS Atiyah, *Pragmatism and Theory in English Law* (London, Stevens & Sons, 1987) 21.

inclined to musings on the metaphysics of rights than practitioners. The learned professors of the continental civil law, in particular, elaborated on private law as a system of rights, duties and obligations, abstract from their procedural realisation.[4] It is, therefore, not entirely surprising to find the concept of right figuring prominently in the work of Blackstone, an author who, as frequent references in his text underline,[5] was well versed in civilian scholarship and the natural law theory of his day.

Yet, one cannot help being struck by the unique and pivotal importance that Blackstone assigns to right(s). The *Commentaries* are composed around the dichotomy of 'rights' and 'wrongs', and, on a theoretical level, Blackstone's idea of law and legal order seems to be constructed around the concept.[6] Being strongly influenced by the previous achievements of Matthew Hale,[7] Blackstone thus paved the way for a scholarly tradition of rights-based accounts of private law in the common law. However, Blackstone's predilection for the use of the word 'right' in and of itself does not tell us much about his vision of private law. 'Right', in Blackstone's private law cosmos, might not signify the same as it does to the modern reader.[8] The frequent use of the word 'right' in various, very different contexts makes it difficult to understand the concept—or concepts—of 'right' that Blackstone envisaged.

With a concept as 'weighty' as 'right', it is tempting to reconstruct Blackstone's ideas by situating him vis-a-vis those thinkers whose theories shaped the perception of individual or 'subjective'[9] rights in Western political philosophy. It is in this spirit that scholars such as Guy Augé claimed that Blackstone devised a catalogue of individual ('subjective')

---

[4] H Dedek, 'From Norms to Facts: The Realization of Rights in Common and Civil Private Law' (2010) 56 *McGill Law Journal* 77.

[5] Blackstone frequently cites the *Digests*, the *Institutes* and the works of Hugo Grotius and Samuel Pufendorf; see below n 12. See also, as a general introduction on the connections between continental and English legal thought, P Stein, 'Continental Influences on English Legal Thought: 1600–1900' in Società italiana di storia del diritto (ed), *La formazione storica del diritto moderno in Europa* (Florence, LS Olschki, 1977) 1105.

[6] See, eg, DJ Boorstin, *The Mysterious Science of the Law: An Essay on Blackstone's Commentaries* (Boston, Beacon Press, 1958) 162.

[7] M Hale, *The History of the Common Law of England and an Analysis of the Civil Part of the Law*, 6th edn (first published 1713, London, Butterworths, 1820). In his own *Analysis*, Blackstone acknowledges Hale's system as 'the most natural and most scientific of any, as well as the most comprehensive': W Blackstone, *An Analysis of the Laws of England* (Oxford, Clarendon Press, 1756) vii. Some scholars have treated the parallels between Hale's and Blackstone's outlines as an almost exhaustive explanation for the organisational peculiarities of the *Commentaries*: see below n 148 and accompanying text.

[8] See, eg, G Samuel, 'Epistemology, Propaganda, and Roman Law' (1989) 20 *Journal of Legal History* 164; B Tierney, 'Villey, Ockham and the Origin of Individual Rights' in J Witte and FS Alexander (eds), *The Weightier Matters of the Law: Essays on Law and Religion—A Tribute to Harold J Berman* (Atlanta, Scholars Press, 1988) 1, 5.

[9] See, eg, Tierney, 'Villey, Ockham and the Origin of Individual Rights', above n 8; AS Brett, *Liberty, Right and Nature: Individual Rights in Later Scholastic Thought* (Cambridge, Cambridge University Press, 1997).

rights 'in the best Lockean sense'.[10] Similarly, German author Richard Benser maintained that Blackstone perceived law *exclusively* as a system of 'subjective' rights based entirely on Samuel Pufendorf's ideas.[11] To be sure, Blackstone was familiar with the philosophical debate of his day, and he frequently cited the works of John Locke and Pufendorf;[12] both, as we will see, indeed significantly inspired Blackstone's theory of rights. However, both thinkers at times diverge considerably in their theories of rights.[13] Situating Blackstone readily in a 'Lockean' or 'Pufendorfian' intellectual tradition obscures rather than explicates many of the idiosyncrasies of Blackstone's particular theoretical amalgam, which he concocted from various philosophical and juridical sources.[14] Blackstone's use of legal philosophy, we have to keep in mind, reflects the concerns of the jurist and the lawyer;[15] Blackstone himself would have been 'surprised indeed had he been called a philosopher'.[16] For Blackstone holds true what Tony Honoré observed in an article on Ulpian: 'philosophically-minded lawyers are not members of this or that school of philosophy. ... The nature of the discipline requires lawyers to be eclectic, to compromise between different aims.'[17] A pragmatic and insouciant (and frequently criticised) eclecticism is indeed the very hallmark of Blackstone's forays into legal theory and philosophy.[18]

Therefore, it might do better justice to Blackstone's work as a jurist if we begin the analysis of the use of 'right' in the *Commentaries* with a 'juridical' perspective, and ask how Blackstone envisioned the conceptual

---

[10] See G Augé, 'Aspects de la philosophie juridique de Sir William Blackstone' (1970) 15 *Archives de Philosophie du Droit* 71, 84 ('Blackstone, enfin, complète son exposé par une théorie des droits individuels dans la meilleure perspective lockienne: il existe des droits subjectifs, inhérent aux personnes ou portant sur les choses, qui sont «absolus» ou «relatifs»'). See also H Rinck, 'Blackstone and the Law of Nature' (1960) 2 *Ratio* 162, 173.

[11] R Benser, *Die Systematik des Privatrechts in Blackstone's 'Commentaries on the Laws of England'* (Heide, Boyens & Co, 1938) 30.

[12] Locke is cited at 1 Bl Comm 7, 52, 56, 122, 157, 172, 206, 236, 244 and Pufendorf at 43, 236, 246, 251, 435, 438. Blackstone also frequently cites the *Digests*, the *Institutes* and the works of Grotius.

[13] See, eg, J Tully, *A Discourse on Property: John Locke and His Adversaries* (Cambridge, Cambridge University Press, 1980) 72 as to Pufendorf's and Locke's definition of the concept of property: 'The different and opposed definitions of Pufendorf and Locke embody two radically dissimilar views of the relation of man to the world.'

[14] For an introduction to Blackstone's sources, see P Lucas, 'Ex Parte Sir William Blackstone, "Plagiarist": A Note on Blackstone and the Natural Law' (1963) 7 *American Journal of Legal History* 142.

[15] On 'Blackstone the lawyer and judge' see, eg, E Kadens, 'Justice Blackstone's Common Law Orthodoxy' (2009) 103 *Northwestern University Law Review* 1553. See also the comprehensive biographical account rendered by W Prest, *William Blackstone: Life and Letters in the Eighteenth Century* (Oxford, Oxford University Press, 2008) 71 ff, 200 ff.

[16] HG Hanbury, 'Blackstone in Retrospect' (1950) 66 *Law Quarterly Review* 318, 321.

[17] T Honoré, 'Ulpian, Natural Law and Stoic Influence' (2010) 78 *Legal History Review* 199, 208.

[18] See, eg, JW McKnight, 'Blackstone, Quasi-Jurisprudent' (1959) 13 *Southwestern Law Journal* 399, 402: 'muddled, contradictory, disorderly.'

operation of his maxim *ubi ius, ibi remedium*—'where there is a legal right, there is also a legal remedy, by suit or action at law, whenever that right is invaded.'[19] Peter Birks has famously described the way in which rights operate in Blackstone's legal cosmos as 'superstructural.'[20] In order to fully understand what this assessment entails, we will have to take a closer look at how the elements of Blackstone's conceptual mechanism— right/wrong, rights, wrongs, and remedies—interact and complement each other.

This 'juridical' analysis, however, will inevitably take us back to the more foundational aspects of Blackstone's vision of private law. In a formalist jurisprudence, as Ernest Weinrib has explained,[21] conceptual constructions and philosophical foundations are closely and intrinsically linked in the sense that the former are the expression of the latter—an insight particularly helpful, I believe, in Blackstone's case, where the explicit verbalisation of philosophical underpinnings remains fragmentary and basic theoretical assumptions have to be gleaned from doctrinal construction and categorisation.

As we shall see, the rights/remedies division in Blackstone's organisational scheme is the expression of a 'dualist'[22] conception of the rights–remedies relationship: Blackstone's perception of private law is not a Weinribian vision of a coherent, transactional unit, defined by the correlativity of right and duty.[23] The 'rights' that come into existence when a 'wrong' is committed are of such a nature that they can only be perceived as a relationship that necessarily involves plaintiff, defendant *and the state*. This particular description of the *publicness of private law* (to borrow a phrase coined by Weinrib)[24] bears close resemblance to the philosophy of private law expounded by Benjamin Zipursky, which is actually inspired by a 'Locke/Blackstone synthesis'.[25] Yet before we delve into the treatment of such questions of the conceptual workings and philosophical underpinnings of private law, we have to familiarise ourselves with Blackstone's *language* of 'right'.

---

[19] See above n 2 and accompanying text.

[20] P Birks, 'Rights, Wrongs, and Remedies' (2000) 20 *Oxford Journal of Legal Studies* 1, 5, 25, 26.

[21] EJ Weinrib, *The Idea of Private Law* (Cambridge MA, Harvard University Press, 1995) 29 ff.

[22] See, eg, G Hammond, 'Rethinking Remedies: The Changing Conception of the Relationship Between Legal and Equitable Remedies' in J Berryman (ed), *Remedies: Issues and Perspectives* (Toronto, Carswell, 1991) 87, 90–91; M Tilbury, 'Remedies and the Classification of Obligations' in A Robertson (ed), *The Law of Obligations: Connections and Boundaries* (London, Cavendish, 2004) 11, 17 ff.

[23] Weinrib, *The Idea of Private Law*, above n 21, at 84 ff.

[24] ibid, at 218.

[25] BC Zipursky, 'Philosophy of Private Law' in J Coleman and S Shapiro (eds), *The Oxford Handbook of Jurisprudence and Philosophy of Law* (Oxford, Oxford University Press, 2002) 623, 642.

II. THE *COMMENTARIES* AND THE LANGUAGE OF 'RIGHT'

A. Blackstone's Use of 'Right' and the Positivist Critique

When explaining the organisation of the *Commentaries*, Blackstone famously states that 'municipal law is a rule of civil conduct, commanding what is right, and prohibiting what is wrong.' From this he deduces that the 'principal objects of the law are RIGHTS and WRONGS,' and therefore the *Commentaries* are to be organised according to a scheme that considers 'the *rights* that are commanded, and secondly the *wrongs* that are forbidden, by the laws of England.'[26] The dichotomy of 'rights' and 'wrongs' is the central organising principle of the *Commentaries*. In his explanation, Blackstone derives the noun 'right' from the adjective 'right', which indicates that something is 'straight' or conforms to a certain standard of which the speaker approves.[27] 'Rights', in the plural, as commanded by law, could describe a multitude of such states of affairs, which are commanded by the law as what is 'right'. However, with the substantivization occurs a slippage: 'right', an indication of conformity with a standard or command, now serves as a translation of *ius*. *Ius*, however, is usually understood to comprise two meanings that are expressed in the English language through two distinct terms: right and law. French and German legal languages share the Latin approach, which is at least one reason for the use of the qualifiers 'objective' (law) and 'subjective' (right).[28] Counter-intuitively, at least for the modern reader, Blackstone firstly uses 'right' to translate *ius quod ad personas/ad res pertinet*—not as the law of persons and the law of things, but as the rights of persons and the rights of things.[29] Following the translation chosen by Hale, Blackstone thus integrates Gaian/Justinian categories of systematisation[30]—*personae*, *res*—into his 'un-Roman'[31] ordering scheme by declaring them to be subcategories of the two reigning categories: rights and wrongs. He then moves on to subdivide the 'rights of persons' into two kinds. First, there are rights that are due from the citizen—these are rights in the sense of a command of 'what is right', which are in fact *duties*. Secondly, there are rights which *belong* to the citizen, 'which is the more popular acceptation

---

[26] 1 Bl Comm 118 (emphases in original).

[27] *The Oxford English Dictionary* (online, 2011) *s.v.* 'right'; WE Hearn, *The Theory of Legal Duties and Rights: An Introduction to Analytical Jurisprudence* (Melbourne, John Ferres, 1883) 142.

[28] See below n 37 and accompanying text.

[29] 1 Bl Comm 118.

[30] JW Cairns, 'Blackstone, An English Institutist: Legal Literature and the Rise of the Nation State' (1984) 4 *Oxford Journal of Legal Studies* 318, 342–43; M Lobban, 'Blackstone and the Science of Law' (1987) 30 *The Historical Journal* 311; A Watson, 'The Structure of Blackstone's *Commentaries*' (1988) 97 *Yale Law Journal* 795.

[31] P Birks and G McLeod (trs), *Justinian's Institutes* (London, Gerald Duckworth & Co, 1987) 24.

of *rights* or *jura*.[32] Only here does Blackstone finally concern himself with what rights are usually understood to mean—individual rights that (without going into the subtle details of Hohfeldian definitions) demarcate a personal sphere of entitlement. Rights, understood in this sense, establish one element of another dominant dichotomy in Blackstone's organisational scheme: that between right and remedy. If such a right is violated, a 'wrong' has occurred. A 'wrong', in turn, is rectified by a remedy, by way of orderly procedure.[33]

It is not necessary to reiterate in great detail the harsh criticism amassed through the centuries regarding this organisational scheme in general.[34] It is interesting, however, to trace how this criticism is linked to Blackstone's use of the word 'right' in particular. Without endowing 'right' with different dimensions of meaning, Blackstone could not have used it as a broad, umbrella-like category to place at the top of his taxonomic pyramid.[35] It is often said that Blackstone, following Hale, mistranslated the Latin *iura rerum*.[36] Thomas Erskine Holland makes it clear that he disapproves of Blackstone's way of using 'right' instead of 'law' as a translation of the Latin *ius (quod ad personas/res pertinet)*, thus lowering himself to the level of the unfortunate Germans who are 'obliged to resort to such phrases as "objectives" and "subjectives Recht", meaning by the former "Law" in the abstract, and by the latter a concrete right.'[37] Even harsher is his criticism of Blackstone's basic tenet that 'rights' derive from 'what is right'. Holland thinks of this first step in Blackstone's reasoning as falling victim to 'a mere similarity that has led to an endless confusion'; he calls (by inference) the making of this connection 'an absurdity.'[38] Australian legal philosopher William Hearn finds stronger words still:

> This inference [that law commands what is right and prohibits what is wrong, and the law's primary concerns therefore are rights and wrongs], which forms the basis of Blackstone's great work, rests upon a mere verbal puzzle, the confusion, namely, between moral right and legal right. ... [S]uch dicta rest on a mere equivoque, a similarity in sound between two words and a dissimilarity in their sense. They stand on the same level as the celebrated puzzle of the horse chestnut and the chestnut horse.[39]

---

[32] I Bl Comm 119 (emphases in original).

[33] See above n 2 and accompanying text.

[34] See, eg, JDW Andrews, *Jurisprudence and Legal Institutions* (Chicago, LaSalle Extension University, 1950) 120 ff.

[35] JCP Goldberg, 'The Constitutional Status of Tort Law: Due Process and the Right to a Law for the Redress of Wrongs' (2005) 115 *Yale Law Journal* 524, 546 speaks of the 'broad (and loose) use of the term "rights"' upon which Blackstone's taxonomic scheme turns.

[36] See, eg, Cairns, 'Blackstone, An English Institutist', above n 30, at 342–43.

[37] TE Holland, *The Elements of Jurisprudence*, 3rd edn (Oxford, Oxford University Press, 1888) 70.

[38] ibid.

[39] Hearn, above n 27, at 143–44.

By equating 'that what is right' with 'moral right', the latter quote reveals the reason for the stern reprimand: to nineteenth century dyed-in-the-wool positivists, such as the authors of these quotes, the progression from the adjective 'right' to 'right' in the objective and subjective senses insinuates a connection between law and morality that was perceived as utterly misguided. However, the postulate of such a connection is of course exactly what characterises natural law thought—a school of thought which plays an important role in the *Commentaries*.[40]

B. A Similar Multivalence: The Latin *Ius*

The parallel between Blackstone's use of 'right' and the way natural law thinkers connected terminology with the fundamental question of how law and individual rights relate to morality becomes more obvious when we look at Hugo Grotius' exposition of the organisation of his *De Jure Belli ac Pacis Libri Tres*.[41] Grotius explains that in order to treat the subject set out by the title, it would be necessary to define *bellum* and *ius* ('De Belli ergo jure acturi, videndum habemus, quid bellum sit, de quo quaeritur: quid jus, quod quaeritur').[42] Having defined 'war', Grotius states that since his treatise is entitled *De Jure Belli*, the inevitable question to ask is whether war can be just—*justum*. This is, he claims, because *jus* signifies here, as the first step of his definition, nothing else than what is just ('nam jus hic nihil aliud quam justum est significat').[43] Just as Blackstone does in the case of 'right', Grotius creates the connection between the adjective *iustum* and the noun *ius*. From this starting point, Grotius explicates further meanings of *ius*: it can describe a faculty that belongs to an individual—the *ius* 'strictly so called'.[44] And it can also signify *lex*, but only in its broadest possible meaning as a moral order, obligating us to do what is *rectum*, that is, 'right' ('obligans ad id quod rectum est').[45]

The multivalence of *ius* in this passage is more than a 'mere equivoque'. *Ius* is not a simple homonym with distinct meanings[46] (as, say, 'trunk'). Instead, its shades of meaning lead to a suspension of one definite meaning in a particular context (one might call this effect *différance*), thus creating

---

[40] JM Finnis, 'Blackstone's Theoretical Intentions' (1967) 12 *Natural Law Forum* 163.

[41] On Grotius' exposition, see R Tuck, *Natural Rights Theories: Their Origin and Development* (Cambridge, Cambridge University Press, 1979) 74 ff; B Tierney, *The Idea of Natural Rights* (Atlanta GA, Scholars Press, 1997) 326. See also M Gregor, 'Kant on Obligation, Rights and Virtue' (1993) 1 *Annual Review of Law and Ethics* 69, 76.

[42] H Grotius, *De Jure Belli ac Pacis Libri Tres* (Amsterdam, Joan Blaeu, 1646) book 1 ch 1 para 2.

[43] ibid, at book 1 ch 1 para 3.

[44] ibid, at book 1 ch 1 para 5.

[45] ibid, at book 1 ch 1 para 9.

[46] See, eg, P Paul, 'Homonyms, Semantic Divergence and Valency' (1982) 58 *Lingua* 291.

a sense of intrinsic connection. The effect is a sense of being three and one at the same time—a trinity with three hypostases of one underlying idea: the inextricable interconnectedness of law and morals.

C. Translating *Ius*: A 'Continental' Use of 'Right'

How can this effect be mirrored in the English language?[47] In this context, the very distinction between 'law' and 'right', praised for its accuracy by scholars such as Holland, turns out to be an obstacle. The ambivalence of *ius* survived in the German *Recht* and the French *droit*. The latter term had once been part of the terminological arsenal of the English jurist, but, as Albert Kiralfy points out, '[w]ith the decline in spoken law-French by the fourteenth century, and in written law-French by the sixteenth, English was left with no specific word which meant law and right in the same concept, only the one imperative word "law".'[48]

In Blackstone's time, three English translations of Grotius' *De Jure Belli ac Pacis Libri Tres* existed: one prepared by Clement Barksdale (1654), which was called by William Whewell, who published a translation in 1853, a 'small and worthless abridgment';[49] one by William Evats (1682);[50] and one by John Morrice (1715).[51] Barksdale translates the title of Grotius' opus as *Of the Laws of Warre and Peace*, and Grotius' question 'quid ius?' as 'What is Law'. He also reduces the original threefold discussion of *ius* to the third part of Grotius' definition: *ius* as *lex* (obliging us to what is *rectum*, which he translates as 'right').[52] This is not surprising, given that this last signification of *ius* is the only one that could properly be captured by the translation 'law'. Evats[53] and Morrice,[54] however, translate the title of the treatise as the 'Rights' of war and peace. They choose 'right' as the English word that comes closest to the multivalence of *ius*. This is the same choice that modern philosophers make when nowadays

---

[47] On this problem, see especially E Pattaro, *The Law and the Right* (Dordrecht, Springer, 2005) 6.

[48] A Kiralfy, 'Law and Right in English Legal History' (1985) 6 *Journal of Legal History* 49, 57.

[49] H Grotius, *Grotius on the Rights of War and Peace: An Abridged Translation* (W Whewell tr and ed, London, John W Parker, 1853) vol 1, xv.

[50] H Grotius, *The Three Books Treating of the Rights of War and Peace* (W Evats tr, London, Thomas Basset, 1682).

[51] H Grotius, *The Rights of War and Peace in Three Books* (J Morrice tr, London, 1738). Morrice's translation was part of the influential 1738 edition that included a translation of Jean Barbeyrac's comments. See JS Reeves, 'Grotius, *De Jure Belli ac Pacis*: A Bibliographical Account' (1925) 19 *American Journal of International Law* 251, 258, 261.

[52] H Grotius, *Of the Law of Warre and Peace: With Annotations* (C Barksdale tr, London, William Lee, 1655) 2.

[53] Grotius (Evats tr), above n 50.

[54] Grotius (Morrice tr), above n 51.

translating works by Immanuel Kant or GWF Hegel, which turn on the multivalence of the German *Recht*.[55]

The French *droit* is derived from *directum*, which in medieval Latin had come to replace *ius* in many contexts and had equally grown to contain the notions of 'law', 'right' and 'rightness'[56] (as in *directum facere*—to do justice).[57] *Ius, directum, rectus*, and 'right' all share the imagery of something that is straight (and therefore desirable), as opposed to something that is twisted, wrung (hence: wrong) or distorted (hence: tort). The Latin *rectum* reverberates in the English 'right'[58] and thus preserves, to a certain degree, its multivalence, as illustrated, for example, by Sir Edward Coke's comment on the due process clause of the Magna Carta—*nulli vendemus, nulli negabimus, aut differemus justitiam, vel rectum*:[59]

> *Rectum*, right, is taken here for law, in the same sense that *jus*, often is so called. 1. Because it is the right line, whereby justice distributive is guided, and directed ... 2. The law is called *rectum*, because it discovereth, that which is tort, crooked, or wrong, for as right signifieth law, so tort, crooked or wrong signifieth injuria, and *injuria est contra jus*, against right ... 3. It is called right, because it is the best birthright the subject hath, for thereby his goods, lands, wife, children, his body, life, honor, and estimation are protected from injury, and wrong ...[60]

In using 'right' in a very similar fashion, as an adjective, and as a noun standing for 'law' and for (individual) rights, Blackstone does not simply instrumentalize a 'verbal puzzle' to force matters that have nothing to do with each other under a random organisational scheme. Rather, and beyond just following the scheme employed by Hale, he situates himself in a tradition of using 'right' as a multivalent term that is the closest equivalent to the Latin *ius* or *rectum*. In this context, it might become doubtful whether it is accurate to claim that Blackstone just 'mistranslates' *iura rerum*—granted, as it has been pointed out, the translation 'rights of things' sounds clumsy, as if things *had* rights.[61] However, is

---

[55] See, eg, the explanation given by Mary Gregor in I Kant, *The Metaphysics of Morals* (M Gregor tr and ed, Cambridge, Cambridge University Press, 1996) xxxivf.

[56] FAC Mantello and AG Rigg, *Medieval Latin: An Introduction and Bibliographical Guide* (Washington DC, The Catholic University of America Press, 1999) 220. See also Kiralfy, above n 48, at 55 ff; JL Nelson, 'England and the Continent in the Ninth Century: III, Rights and Rituals' (2004) 14 *Transactions of the Royal Historical Society* 1, 5.

[57] A Brachet, *Etymological Dictionary of the French Language*, 3rd edn (GW Kitchen tr, Oxford, Clarendon Press, 1882) *s.v.* 'droit'.

[58] See, stemming from Blackstone's time, N Bailey, *An Universal Etymological English Dictionary* (London, 1773) *s.v.* 'right'.

[59] Blackstone cites the due process clause as well and also adopts the translation of *rectum* as 'right': 1 Bl Comm 137.

[60] 2 Co Inst 56.

[61] See, eg, Andrews, above n 34, at 128 ('The classification ostensibly made was of rights, but so artificially is it done that rights are apparently accorded to things').

not the translation 'Rights of War and Peace' prone to the same grammatical confusion?

Kiralfy wrote about the French *droit* and the German *Recht*, terms that conserve the shades of meaning contained in *ius* and *directum*: 'The survival of the idea that law and right were the same, with right also being used to refer to individual rights created by law, must have given law an assumed element of inherent rightness.'[62] Blackstone uses 'right' in an almost 'continental' way, and, in his progression from 'what is right' to individual rights, one cannot help but feel the same effect Kiralfy describes. That is not to say that this use of 'right' places Blackstone distinctly in a certain, maybe Grotian, tradition of natural rights theory. This question is, of course, a matter of great contention.[63] Some scholars have held that Blackstone just used natural law ideas instrumentally to justify the positive legal order.[64] Even if one subscribes to this point of view, it would make sense to assume that Blackstone backed his apologetic enterprise by endowing the law with 'inherent rightness'. The effect created by using the slippage in the meaning of 'right', however, is not only one of 'inherent rightness'; it also emphasises the dimension of 'right' as something that belongs to individuals. This is the signification of 'right' that Blackstone calls the more common popular 'acceptation'[65] (Grotius even writes: rights 'strictly so called'[66]). In regard to Grotius' theory, Richard Tuck has focused in particular on this effect of highlighting the function of rights as the bulwark of the individual, which, according to Tuck, expressed the non-Aristotelian character of Grotius' theory of justice.[67] However, the effect works in the opposite direction as well: it is an effect

---

[62] Kiralfy, above n 48, at 53. See also Pattaro, above n 47, at 6: 'The question is not only linguistic, but also conceptual and ontological.' Cf Wesley Hohfeld, who acknowledges the effect as a 'psychological and linguistic principle', but, in search of taxonomic clarity, dismisses it with an air of disgust as a 'principle of linguistic contamination': WN Hohfeld, 'Fundamental Legal Conceptions as Applied in Judicial Reasoning' (1917) 26 *Yale Law Journal* 710, 716.

[63] WS Holdsworth, *A History of English Law*, vol 12 (London, Methuen, 1938) 733 posits that Grotius, transmitted through Jean-Jacques Burlmaqui, was Blackstone's most important source of natural law thought. See also DJ Ibbetson, 'Natural Law and Common Law' (2001) 5 *Edinburgh Law Review* 4, 6 on a connection between Grotius and Hale (and subsequently Grotius and Blackstone) and McKnight, above n 18, at 407, calling Blackstone a 'maverick'. See also Lobban, above n 30, at 330 for the view that Blackstone derived individual rights only from positive law. See also SN Katz, 'Introduction' in W Blackstone, *Commentaries on the Laws of England* (Chicago IL, University of Chicago Press, 1979) vol 1, i, vi, who portrays Blackstone as a staunch positivist whose treatment of natural law was mainly a concession to the taste of the age ('This is an obligatory eighteenth century exercise, in which Blackstone accords to natural and revealed law about the same importance as Newton accorded to God in the operation of the physical universe').

[64] HLA Hart, 'Blackstone's Use of the Law of Nature' [1956] *Butterworths South African Law Review* 169; SI Shuman, *Legal Positivism: Its Scope and Limitations* (Detroit MI, Wayne State University Press, 1963) 185–86.

[65] See above n 32 and accompanying text.

[66] See above n 44 and accompanying text.

[67] Tuck, above n 41, at 74.

of intrinsic coherence that ties the individual right back to 'rightness' and the 'objective' order (or law or 'right'). As seen in the case of Grotius' use of *ius*, Blackstone's use of 'right' creates a sense of oneness. The different hypostases of 'right' are not only each linked to 'rightness' but they also constitute harmonious parts forming a whole. They are parts in consonance with each other. Not only are the objective order and (individual) right derived from the command of 'what is right', they also concordantly complement each other. Thus individual rights are embedded in the (objective) legal order.[68] But what exactly is the relationship between individual right and legal order against the backdrop of the dichotomy of 'rights' and 'wrongs'? In other words, in Blackstone's conceptual cosmos, how do individual rights operate in private law?

III. THE FRAMEWORK OF 'RIGHTS' AS 'SUPERSTRUCTURE'

A. Absolute and Relative Rights

The station of man, we learn from Blackstone, is entirely defined in terms of 'rights'. The 'rights of persons' are subdivided into absolute and relative rights. Absolute rights are rights that antedate society: 'By absolute rights of individuals we mean those which are so in their primary and strictest sense; such as would belong to their persons in a state of nature, and which every man is intitled to enjoy whether out of society or in it.'[69] Those 'absolute rights' are, in particular, personal security (enjoyment of life, limb, body and reputation),[70] personal liberty,[71] and private property.[72] Relative personal 'rights', on the other hand, define the status of a person as a member of society in relation to others.[73] Blackstone first treats 'public relations' between citizen and government (and, most prominently, the structure of government itself),[74] and then the 'three great relations in private life': master and servant, husband and wife, as well as parent and child (or guardian and ward, respectively).[75] Note again the ambivalence

---

[68] The relationship between individual right and objective right that this use of language hints at is mirrored in the way the relationship between individual and community is envisioned by Blackstone; on this aspect, see AW Alschuler, 'Rediscovering Blackstone' (1996) 145 *University of Pennsylvania Law Review* 1, 47. On the connection of this idea with Lockean thought see below n 165 and accompanying text.

[69] 1 Bl Comm 119.

[70] ibid, at 125 ff.

[71] ibid, at 130 ff.

[72] ibid, at 134 ff.

[73] ibid, at 119. See also D Kennedy, 'The Structure of Blackstone's *Commentaries*' (1979) 28 *Buffalo Law Review* 205, 226 ('Taken as a group, this collection of roles defined the social structure of 18th century England').

[74] 1 Bl Comm 142 ff.

[75] ibid, at 410.

of 'right'. While used in 'absolute rights' in the sense of individual spheres of liberty and security, the term 'relative rights' describes objective legal status in a relational sense, in the way the German term *Rechtsverhältnis* describes legal relations. Similarly, Blackstone, in the second volume of the *Commentaries*, elaborates on the 'right of things', again, of course, in the sense of their legal status.[76]

B. Rights, Wrongs, and the Superstructure

Having thus established a framework of 'rights', Blackstone, in the third volume of the *Commentaries*, turns to wrongs, which are 'forbidden and redressed by the laws of England.'[77] Wrongs are 'nothing else but the privation of a right.'[78] As the subject of our inquiry is the concept of right in private law, we will concern ourselves with what Blackstone calls 'private wrongs'—the 'privation of private or civil rights'.[79] At this point, we are able to put in context the quote we encountered at the very beginning of our enterprise. Since rights are commanded and wrongs are prohibited, a privation of a right will be redressed by the legal system: 'where there is a legal right, there is also a legal remedy, by suit or action at law, whenever that right is invaded.'[80]

What we witnessed up to this point is a comprehensive restatement of a legal order that was founded on procedural forms in terms of substantive 'rights'. Although this restatement might have followed Hale to a certain extent and also been part of a tradition of Institutionist writing,[81] it still was a novel and formidable reformulation that showed the English legal system to be in unison with the liberal ideas of the day.[82] Turning from 'rights' to 'wrongs', this language of 'rights' suddenly runs out. As

---

[76] 2 Bl Comm 23.

[77] 3 Bl Comm 1.

[78] ibid, at 2.

[79] ibid.

[80] ibid, at 23. Joshua Getzler has pointed out that Blackstone, as a matter of epistemology, insists that 'rights' have to be defined prior to 'wrongs', but de facto frequently uses the 'wrong' to define the shape of 'rights': 'A larger idea expressed here is that justice is defined by the sense of injustice, of wrongful disturbance; we discover distributive justice by pursuing our intuitions about corrective justice' (J Getzler, *A History of Water Rights at Common Law* (Oxford, Oxford University Press, 2004) 181).

[81] See Cairns, 'Blackstone, An English Institutist', above n 30; Watson, above n 30.

[82] J Stoner Jr, *Common Law and Liberal Theory: Coke, Hobbes and the Origins of American Constitutionalism* (Lawrence KS, University Press of Kansas, 1992) 163 ff; MP Zuckert, 'Social Compact, Common Law, and the American Amalgam: The Contribution of William Blackstone' in MP Zuckert (ed), *Launching Liberalism: On Lockean Political Philosophy* (Lawrence KS, University Press of Kansas, 2002) 235, 239; Kennedy, above n 73, at 234 ff. Duncan Kennedy's failure to elaborate in more detail on the debt to Hale and the Institutional scheme is criticised by Watson as the greatest weakness of Kennedy's text: Watson, above n 30, at 795, 801–02.

Duncan Kennedy observed: 'Blackstone was ... nothing like a 19th century analytical jurist: he refused to carry out completely the program of subordinating the forms of action to his theory of rights.'[83] Indeed, unlike later taxonomists such as John Austin,[84] Blackstone does not (at least not prima facie) seem to conceive of the response to the violation of a right as giving rise to another, *secondary* right. Instead, he views the response to the wrong as the *remedy*, and the remedy is to be sought by civil action, and finally administered by a state court.

For this particular conceptualisation of right, Birks has coined the term 'superstructural'. According to Birks, in the *Commentaries*, 'rights' provide the '[f]ramework which explained the wrongs which alone were the business of the courts. The courts did not deal in the direct enforcement of rights, they dealt in remedies for wrongs.'[85] In the Birksian terminology, 'superstructural' rights, as Birks pointed out in his introduction to the tome *English Private Law*, are *primary* rights that manifest themselves in the wrongs which infringe them, but are not, prior to the 'manifestation', realisable in court.[86] Following Austin's path,[87] Birks had expounded such a two-tiered model of primary and secondary right (or obligation) earlier: the secondary right arises in response to a violation of the primary right. Such primary rights constitute the first tier, which is called 'superstructure'.[88] If, therefore, Birks deems Blackstone's use of 'right' to be 'always superstructural', then this insinuates that in Blackstone's system, at least if one looks at the language used, rights only operate on one level—the primary tier. There seem to be primary, but no secondary, rights. Rights define, in the abstract, status, freedom and security of the individual. If a violation of a right occurs, however, the response is not conceptualised in the terminology of right, but in the terminology of 'remedy', administered by a court.

[83] Kennedy, above n 73, at 233.

[84] J Austin, *Lectures on Jurisprudence*, 5th edn (London, John Murray, 1885) lectures 45–49.

[85] Birks, 'Rights, Wrongs, and Remedies', above n 20, at 5.

[86] P Birks, 'Introduction' in P Birks (ed), *English Private Law* (Oxford, Oxford University Press, 2000) vol 1, xxxv, xxxviii n 3.

[87] See Austin, above n 84, at lectures 45–49.

[88] P Birks, 'Obligations: One Tier or Two?' in PG Stein and ADE Lewis (eds), *Studies in Justinian's Institutes in Memory of JAC Thomas* (London, Sweet & Maxwell, 1983) 18. See also M Tilbury, 'Remedy as Right' in C Rickett and R Grantham (eds), *Structure and Justification in Private Law: Essays for Peter Birks* (Oxford, Hart Publishing, 2008) 421, 422 (primary rights—those whose existence is not dependent on the breach of another right—are sometimes styled 'superstructural'). A slightly different use—superstructural rights as a residual category—is offered by E Descheemaeker, *The Division of Wrongs: A Historical Comparative Study* (Oxford, Oxford University Press, 2009) 20–21.

C. A Property Model of Superstructural Rights

The image of a superstructure of rights implies a static model of human relations. It is not concerned with change or obligation to undertake future acts, but with a preservation of a status quo. Rights are meant to protect against interference; they are thought of as the bulwark of the individual, domains whose demarcation lines must not be overstepped.[89] Property rights are often perceived as demarcating a sphere—in many cases an actual, physical sphere—that must not be infringed.[90] In a private law context, property rights thus become the metaphoric paradigm of the way rights work.

Blackstone famously defined the right of property as 'that sole and despotic dominion which one man claims and exercises over the external things of the world, in total exclusion of the right of any other individual in the universe.'[91] Much has been written about this grandiose and rather sweeping definition of property.[92] This definition, which equates property with dominion, and which seems to be strangely at odds with the actual common law of Blackstone's day,[93] bears an obvious resemblance to the rhetoric of political liberalism, and in particularly with the language used by Locke.[94] However, Blackstone's approach to property also appears to be another example of the influence of continental legal theory on his thought.[95] We find a very similar formula in Pufendorf[96] (whose exposition on property Blackstone cites[97]), who stands in a long tradition of continental scholarship that viewed exclusion as the defining characteristic of property.[98] In this tradition, *dominium* and *ius* had

[89] See Rinck, above n 10, at 173. On the history of individual rights as areas of personal autonomy, see Tierney, *The Idea of Natural Rights*, above n 41, at 117.

[90] See also RB Grantham and CEF Rickett, 'Property Rights as a Legally Significant Event' [2003] *Cambridge Law Journal* 717, 730 ('Property rights are ... in a sense inert or superstructural rights').

[91] 2 Bl Comm 2.

[92] See, eg, the recent overview rendered by DB Schorr, 'How Blackstone Became a Blackstonian' (2009) 10 *Theoretical Inquiries in Law* 103, 114 ff; D Schultz, 'Political Theory and Legal History: Conflicting Depictions of Property in the American Political Founding' (1993) 37 *American Journal of Legal History* 464, 473 ff. See also CM Rose, 'Canons of Property Talk, or Blackstone's Anxiety' (1998) 108 *Yale Law Journal* 601, 602, pointing out that although the passage is cited by numerous authors, not many seem to have actually studied Blackstone's theory of property in depth.

[93] FG Whelan, 'Property as Artifice: Hume and Blackstone' in JR Pennock and JW Chapman (eds), *Nomos XXII: Property* (New York, New York University Press, 1980) 101, 128 n 15.

[94] Schultz, above n 92, at 474. See also A Reeve, *Property* (Atlantic Highlands, Humanities Press International, 1986) 142–43.

[95] Tully, above n 13, at 73.

[96] S Pufendorf, *Of the Law of Nature and Nations*, 4th edn (B Kennett tr, London, 1729) book 4 ch 4 para 2.

[97] 2 Bl Comm 3.

[98] See Barbeyrac's comment in Pufendorf, above n 96, at 362 n 3 on Pufendorf's focus on the exclusion of others as the hallmark of property: 'So the Civil law speaks' (followed

become one: the idea of the inviolable and exclusive domain had become the model of all rights, and shaped the modern concept of the individual, the subjective right.[99]

Placing himself in this tradition, Blackstone not only perceives property as one of men's paramount 'absolute' rights, but views every individual right through the prism of property. The exclusive domain, the protected individual sphere becomes an all-encompassing metaphor.[100] Blackstone generally defines the violation of a right and subsequent redress in a language that invokes images of ownership ('the one natural remedy for every species of wrong is the being put in possession of that right, whereof the party injured is deprived'[101]), thus conjuring the image of someone being unlawfully removed from their property.

Commentators have remarked on similar tendencies in the way Locke uses the concept of property right as the model of all rights.[102] However, Blackstone, the jurist and lawyer, is confronted with different questions than the philosopher: questions of doctrinal construction. In other words: does the metaphor fit the legal materials? If we assume that Blackstone adheres to a property-inspired idea of rights as a superstructure of protected spheres, how do *relational* 'rights'—rights that are, if we stick to the imagery, 'bipolar' rather than 'spherical'—fit into this conception?

(i) Relative Personal Rights

Let us first look at what Blackstone calls 'relative personal rights'. As we have seen, Blackstone's absolute/relative dichotomy is not co-extensive with the known distinction between absolute rights in rem and relative rights in personam. When Blackstone discusses relative personal rights, he is not concerned with *obligations*, but with how the situation of a

---

by a citation to Dig 13.6.5.15). On the role of exclusion in Grotius' theory of property, see MJ Schermaier, 'Res Communes Omnium: The History of an Idea from Greek Philosophy to Grotian Jurisprudence' (2009) 30 *Grotiana* 20, 21 n 5. On exclusion as the foundational element from the perspective of property theory see, eg, T Honoré, *Making Law Bind* (Oxford, Clarendon Press, 1987) 166–68.

[99] See, eg, Brett, above n 9, at 10 ff. This development is complemented by the influence of *potestas*: individual rights as dominion and power: see, eg, Tierney, *The Idea of Natural Rights*, above n 41, at 104 ff.

[100] See LC Becker, *Property Rights: Philosophic Foundations* (London, Routledge & Kegan Paul, 1977) 120 n 11: 'Writers like Blackstone, Hobbes, and Locke occasionally used it [the term 'property rights'] to refer to all a person's legal rights'. See also J Waldron, *The Right to Private Property* (Oxford, Oxford University Press 1988) 181. On the use of Blackstone's 'exclusive domain' slogan as metaphor or trope see Rose, above n 92, at 602–03 (not touching on the use of domain as a metaphor that can be transferred to *every* individual right).

[101] 3 Bl Comm 1.

[102] See LS Underkuffler, 'On Property: An Essay' (1990) 100 *Yale Law Journal* 127, 138. On property as the right that exemplifies the 'moral space' within which the individual can thrive see Reeve, above n 94, at 142–43.

person is defined vis-a-vis the government and other members of society. However, in his treatment of wrongs, Blackstone also devises a category of 'private wrongs' constituted by the violation of one of the 'three great relations of private life'.[103] It is very interesting to see how Blackstone conceptualises the wrong in this context, given that he describes the 'relative right' not as an individual right 'strictly so called' but rather as an objective determination of legal status. Blackstone's treatment of the matter[104] shows that he envisions a 'wrong' against the relationship as the infringement of a right of ownership. The relationship as such is not protected. Rather, the asymmetrical relationships—master/servant, husband/wife, parent/child—constitute situations in which absolute rights of the weaker party are, stopping short only of slavery, defined by an absolute power of the stronger party over the life and fortune of the weaker;[105] it is as if the rights-sphere of the weaker is merged into and consumed by the sphere of the stronger. The status of the wife 'in coverture' is the most obvious illustration, where the 'very being or legal existence of the woman is suspended during the marriage, or at least is incorporated or consolidated into that of the husband.'[106] The effect is not only the loss of legal personhood towards the world, but also subordination within the relationship. Therefore, if the wife is taken away or beaten, the husband can seek redress,[107] but not the other way around:

> We may observe that, in these relative injuries, notice is only taken of the wrong done to the superior of the parties related, by the breach and dissolution of either the relation itself, or at least the advantages accruing therefrom; while the loss of the inferior by such injuries is totally unregarded. One reason for this may be this: that the inferior has no kind of property in the company, care or assistance of the superior, as the superior is held to have in those of the inferior; and therefore the inferior can suffer no loss or injury. The wife cannot recover damages for the beating of the husband, for she hath no separate interest in anything during her coverture. The child hath no property in his father or guardian as they have in him ...[108]

---

[103] 1 Bl Comm 410.

[104] 3 Bl Comm 138 ff.

[105] 1 Bl Comm 411.

[106] ibid, at 430. On the role of this fiction and its relation to the doctrine of 'coverture' see T Stretton, 'Coverture and Unity of Person in Blackstone's *Commentaries*' in W Prest (ed), *Blackstone and His Commentaries: Biography, Law, History* (Oxford, Hart Publishing, 2009) 111.

[107] 3 Bl Comm 140.

[108] ibid, at 142–43. It has to be stressed, however, that Blackstone conceptualises these relationships in terms of property because he sees all rights to be modelled after property; this is not to say that he actually, as a matter of legal doctrine, postulated that married women were actually their husbands' property or chattels: cf Stretton, above n 106, at 121. See also T Michals, '"That Sole and Despotic Dominion": Slaves, Wives, and Game in Blackstone's *Commentaries*' (1993–94) 27 *Eighteenth-Century Studies* 195, 202.

(ii) Contract

This formulation of the personal rights relation in terms of property law is in line with a more general display of disinterest in rights that cannot be captured well in the metaphor of the domain: obligations. Kennedy's 'The Structure of Blackstone's *Commentaries*' (an article that has been ridiculed for its historical inaccuracies or simply ignored[109]) provides the very valuable insight that the concept of 'obligation' had no role to play in Blackstone's taxonomic scheme.[110] Otto Kahn-Freund made the same observation.[111] The litmus test is the treatment of the law of contract, of which two of the 'civil relations'—master/servant[112] and husband/wife[113]—are just specific examples (although the development from 'status to contract' has, at this point, clearly not yet come to an end, Blackstone nevertheless applies the doctrinal categories of contract law to these relationships).[114] Relational rights arising from torts, just as those arising from a breach of contract, are, as we will see, a matter of the *response* to wrongs, not a matter of the 'superstructure' itself.[115]

If we analyse Blackstone's treatment of the law of contract, we first notice the minimal role it plays in the organisational scheme of the *Commentaries*. The law of contracts does not dwell in a category of its own; instead, it is completely subordinated to the law of property. In the second volume, dedicated to the 'rights of things', Blackstone deals with contracts as a means of acquiring title,[116] and he dedicates as much as 28 pages to this topic. In the chapter 'Of Injuries to Personal Property' in the third volume on private wrongs, he spends another 13 pages on contracts. This number already includes the category of 'implied contracts' such as quantum meruit or quantum valebat that most would nowadays understand as instances of unjust enrichment.[117]

---

[109] See, eg, Watson, above n 30, at 795 ('interesting but wrong'), 801–02.

[110] Kennedy, above n 73, at 327.

[111] See O Kahn-Freund, 'Blackstone's Neglected Child: The Contract of Employment' (1977) 93 *Law Quarterly Review* 508, 509.

[112] 1 Bl Comm 413 ff.

[113] ibid, at 422 ff.

[114] Kahn-Freund, above n 111, at 512. Cf from a comparative perspective (and critical of Kahn-Freund's argument that Blackstone's view of the master-servant relationship was particularly backwards) JW Cairns, 'Blackstone, Kahn-Freund and the Contract of Employment' (1989) 105 *Law Quarterly Review* 300.

[115] See part IV(C) below for more on this topic.

[116] 2 Bl Comm ch 30 ('Of Title by Gift, Grant and Contract'), following ch 29 ('Of Title by Succession, Marriage and Judgment').

[117] On the persistence of 'implied contract' language see P Birks, *Unjust Enrichment*, 2nd edn (Oxford, Oxford University Press, 2005) 284. In Blackstone's day, however, such situations were of course tied to contracts through the common form of assumpsit, which became available because of the implication of a promise: see D Ibbetson, *A Historical Introduction to the Law of Obligations* (Oxford, Oxford University Press, 1999) 269 ff. On Blackstone's doctrine and its historical connection with civil law scholarship on obligations *quasi ex contractu* see P Birks and G McLeod, 'The Implied Contract Theory of

Contract law thus treated amounts to nothing more than what Patrick Atiyah called an 'appendage to the law of property'.[118] Very similarly, continental scholars have characterised the role of the civil law of contracts before the nineteenth century as that of a 'footnote to the law of property'.[119] It seems to be a well-established insight of continental as well as Anglo-American legal history that only the late eighteenth century—or, on the Continent, the early nineteenth century—brought about a shift in private law from property as the reigning paradigm towards a 'Golden Age of Contract'. Usually, a connection is drawn between the heightened importance ascribed to the law of contract and the comprehensive societal change occurring at this time. While the exchange of goods was accelerated through the growth of the market economy, and the entire society was literally set in motion due to the movement from 'status to contract', private law shifted away from the 'static' paradigm of property towards the more 'dynamic' paradigm of contract as the model that implies transfer and exchange.[120] In the nineteenth century, writes Atiyah (citing Pound), a man's wealth consisted mainly of physical property; in the modern world, it consists of promises.[121]

Blackstone stood at the threshold of this development. Nevertheless, he still perceived private law through a conceptual framework of property.[122] It is important to note that the subordination of contract to property is not only a matter of believing that contract has no other significance than to explain the transfer of title. The subordination is epistemological as

---

Quasi-Contract: Civilian Opinion Current in the Century before Blackstone' (1986) 6 *Oxford Journal of Legal Studies* 46, 53 ff.

[118] PS Atiyah, *The Rise and Fall of Freedom of Contract* (Oxford, Oxford University Press, 1979) 102.

[119] E Bucher, 'Hundert Jahre schweizerisches Obligationenrecht: Wo stehen wir heute im Vertragsrecht?' (1983) 102 *Zeitschrift für schweizerisches Recht* 251, 376; E Bucher, 'Die Eigentums-Translativwirkung von Schuldverträgen: Das "Woher" und "Wohin" dieses Modells im Code Civil' (1998) 6 *Zeitschrift für Europäisches Privatrecht* 615, 624 ff; G Dilcher, 'Die janusköpfige Kodifikation. Das preußische Allgemeine Landrecht (1794) und die europäische Rechtsgeschichte' (1994) 2 *Zeitschrift für Europäisches Privatrecht* 446.

[120] See, eg, Atiyah, *Rise and Fall*, above n 118, at 103 ff; MJ Horwitz, *The Transformation of American Law 1780–1860* (Cambridge MA, Harvard University Press, 1979) 160; S Simitis, 'The Case of the Employment Relationship: Elements of a Comparison' in W Steinmetz (ed), *Private Law and Social Inequality in the Industrial Age* (Oxford, Oxford University Press 2000) 181. Cf, as a 'classic' in sociological writing, M Weber, *Wirtschaft und Gesellschaft*, 5th edn (Tübingen, Mohr Siebeck, 1972) 198, 401. See also AWB Simpson, 'Innovation in Nineteenth Century Contract Law' (1975) 91 *Law Quarterly Review* 247, 251 ff.

[121] Atiyah, *Rise and Fall*, above n 118, at 102.

[122] cf Michals, above n 108, at 200–01: at the same time, the 'primary model' of property was real property, transmitted through inheritance, rather than property as a 'marketable commodity, circulating through contractual exchange'. On this process of the 'dephysicalisation' of property—describing, in particular, the paradigm shift from Blackstone's to Bentham's concept of property—see N Graham, 'Restoring the "Real" to Real Property Law: A Return to Blackstone?' in W Prest (ed), *Blackstone and His Commentaries: Biography, Law, History* (Oxford, Hart Publishing, 2009) 151.

well; contract itself was conceptualised in terms of property law. Again, this is a hallmark of the natural law inspired contract theory of the pre-industrial age.[123] Contract was understood as 'translational' in the sense that the main effect of a contract was not to give rise to an obligation, but to immediately rearrange the demarcation lines between the two parties' domains of property or other rights that were conceptualised in a property-like manner. As a paradigmatic example, we can again refer to Grotius.[124] According to Grotius' theory of contracts, a serious contractual promise (a 'promise of the third degree') has the

> Same Effect as the Alienation of a Man's Property. For it is either an Introduction to the Alienating of a Thing, or the Alienation of some part of our Liberty. To the former belong our Promises to give, to the latter our Promises to do something.[125]

Thus, even if the promise made does not pertain to the transfer of property, but is a promise to perform an act, its *effect* is still perceived as a process of the immediate transfer. A part of the promisor's liberty is alienated and immediately accrues to the sphere of liberty of the promisee, with the borders between the two spheres newly aligned. German legal historian Malte Diesselhorst called this a '[p]eculiar, reifying notion of personal liberty: the image of a static sphere of freedom, separated from the outside world through a sharply defined border',[126] likening human agency to the ownership of things.

Likewise, Blackstone envisions the superstructure of rights as property-like domains bordering on each other, and contract as a means of rearranging their borderlines. This is made obvious by the way he treats contracts—including, for example, the contract of hire—under the heading of property; and even more tellingly, as we already observed,[127] by

---

[123] Bucher, 'Die Eigentums-Translativwirkung von Schuldverträgen', above n 119, at 624 ff. It deserves to be mentioned that Kant still perceived contract completely in the categories of 'mine' and 'thine' as well: see Kant, above n 55, at paras 6:271–6:276; MJ Schermaier, *Die Bestimmung des wesentlichen Irrtums von den Glossatoren bis zum BGB* (Cologne, Böhlau, 2000) 430.

[124] See M Diesselhorst, *Die Lehre des Hugo Grotius vom Versprechen* (Cologne, Böhlau, 1959) 30 ff. Peter Benson explicitly names Grotius's theory as one of his inspirations for his own transfer theory of contract: P Benson, 'The Unity of Contract Law' in P Benson (ed), *The Theory of Contract Law: New Essays* (Cambridge, Cambridge University Press, 2001) 118, 128 n 17.

[125] Grotius (Morrice tr), above n 51, at vol 2, 232. This is a translation of Grotius, above n 42, at book 2 ch 11 para 4, which states: 'Tertius gradus est, ubi ad determinationem talem accedit signum volendi jus proprium alteri conferre: quae perfecta promissio est, similem habens effectum qualem alientatio dominii. Est enim aut via ad alienationem rei, aut alienatio particulae cuiusdam nostrae libertatis.'

[126] Translation of Diesselhorst, above n 124, at 51:

> eine eigentümliche vergegenständlichende Auffassung von der Freiheit der Person ... das Bild eines statischen, nach außen scharf abgegrenzten ... Freiheitsbereiches.

[127] See above n 108 and accompanying text.

the way he justifies the right to redress in cases of interference with the 'civil relationships'. His 'reifying' treatment of services to be rendered in a master/servant relationship (which is, according to Blackstone, a contract of hire) is particularly interesting:[128] if someone hires or retains

> my servant, being in my service, for which the servant departeth from me and goeth to serve the other, I may have an action for damages against both the new master and the servant, or either of them ... The reason and foundation upon which all this doctrine is built, seem to be the property that every man has in the service of his domestics; acquired by the contract of hiring, and purchased by giving him wages.[129]

Another aspect of translational contract theory—particularly evident in its application to a contract of hire—that must have been attractive to Blackstone is that it resonates with Locke's treatment of *labour as property* that can be alienated in return for wages.[130] Locke referred not only to the product of the labour, but also to the labour itself, as an alienable commodity.[131]

(iii) The 'Chose in Action'

The seminal concept in which this property-centred approach crystallises is that of the 'chose in action'. In his introductory chapter on 'Property in Things Personal' ('things personal' is synonymous with 'movables'), Blackstone defines property in movables as always

> either in *possession*; which is where a man hath not only the right to enjoy, but hath the actual enjoyment of the thing: or else it is in *action*; where a man hath only a bare right, without any occupation or enjoyment.[132]

Blackstone makes it clear that the term 'chose in action' describes a form of property that comes into existence as the legal effect of debt. It can also arise as a consequence of the breach of a contract. In this instance, 'chose in action' describes the entitlement to compensation.[133] To the modern

---

[128] On this treatment of services see Kahn-Freund, above n 111, at 515–16.

[129] 1 Bl Comm 417. It is interesting to remind oneself in this context of the history of inducement to breach of contract as a tort: see, eg, GHL Fridman, '*Lumley v Gye* and the (Over?)Protection of Contracts' in JW Neyers, R Bronaugh and SGA Pitel (eds), *Exploring Contract Law* (Oxford, Hart Publishing, 2009) 224.

[130] J Locke, *Two Treatises of Government* (London, 1689) book 2 §§ 27–28. I am grateful to Joshua Getzler for bringing up this point.

[131] See, eg, CB Macpherson, *The Political Theory of Possessive Individualism* (Oxford, Oxford University Press, 1962) 214–15; JP Day, 'Locke on Property' (1966) 16 *Philosophical Quarterly* 207; EJ Hundert, 'The Making of Homo Faber: John Locke Between Ideology and History' (1972) 33 *Journal of the History of Ideas* 3, 10 ff; Waldron, above n 100, at 179 ff; G Sreenivasan, *The Limits of Lockean Rights in Property* (Oxford, Oxford University Press, 1995) 67.

[132] 2 Bl Comm 389 (emphasis in original).

[133] ibid, at 397 ff.

lawyer, what Blackstone describes sounds very much like an obligation, with the distinctive feature that the term 'chose in action' emphasises the necessity of realising this right by civil action. That seems to be the way in which more recent common law thinkers have understood the concept.[134] Around the turn of the nineteenth century, American common lawyers in particular vividly discussed the legal nature of the 'chose in action'; their debate was instigated by the question of whether a 'chose in action' was assignable or not. Among the many contributions to this discussion, an article by Walter Cook deserves to be mentioned, which used the Hohfeldian categories to analyse the concept of the 'chose in action'.[135] At this point, 'chose in action' was used as a synonym for terms such as right and claim, or, if viewed 'from the other end', duty and obligation. The fact that the concept was called 'chose'—*a thing*—in action, was understood to refer to the classification of rights as 'incorporeal things'. Accordingly, William Holdsworth traced the concept back to Henry de Bracton's classification of *actiones* as *res incorporales*.[136] Watson, analysing Hale's organisational scheme, seems to come to the conclusion that Blackstone's forerunner, when speaking of 'things in action', in truth just used a different label for 'obligation' and subsumed it under incorporeal things in true Justinian fashion.[137]

However, we must be very careful when assuming that Blackstone, as an 'Institutist writer', simply meant 'obligation' by 'chose in action', the label 'chose' here signifying the quality of the obligation being classified as an incorporeal thing. The issue is more complicated. We must not underestimate the epistemological grip of Blackstone's property-based vision of the 'superstructure'.[138] The concept of obligation does not fit well in a grid that is determined strictly by what is *owned* and not by what is *owed*. Again, we have to pay very close attention to the language Blackstone uses. Blackstone contrasts 'chose in possession' and 'chose in action'. In

---

[134] See, eg, JW Harris, *Property and Justice* (Oxford, Oxford University Press, 2001) 50–51; Honoré, *Making Law Bind*, above n 98, at 181–82 (allowing for alienability and transmissibility 'reifies' rights in a way that they can be 'owned').

[135] WW Cook, 'The Alienability of Choses in Action' (1916) 29 *Harvard Law Review* 816, 819 ff.

[136] WS Holdsworth, 'The History of the Treatment of the *Choses* in Action by the Common Law' (1920) 33 *Harvard Law Review* 997, 1000.

[137] Inst 2.2.2: *Incorporales autem sunt, quae tangi non possunt; qualia sunt ea, quae in iure consistent: sicut hereditas, usus fructus, obligationes quoquomodo contractae* ('Incorporal things cannot be touched.—They consist of legal rights—inheritance, usufruct, obligations however contracted': Birks and McLeod, above n 31, at 61).

[138] But see Watson, above n 30, at 801 n 25, where he states that 'this approach to the classification is sufficiently reasonable for it to recur elsewhere, for instance in the French Code Civil of 1804.' He does not mention this approach being a staple of natural law thought, which had repercussions in all 'natural law codes': the Austrian, Prussian, and the French. Apparently unaware of this, he makes it look as if it were a sheer matter of convenience when Hale tried to fit the underdeveloped common law of contract into the Justinian scheme.

the term 'chose in possession', the 'chose' clearly is the movable itself, the (physical) object of property right as well as the factual relation of possession; 'chose in possession' presupposes that 'a man hath both the right and the occupation of the thing.'[139]

Blackstone takes the expression 'chose in action' seriously as having a parallel syntactic structure. He does not invert its structure by defining 'chose in action' in the sense of 'action as chose' (as if the point were to categorise actions as *res* in the Institutist sense). Rather, Blackstone leaves no doubt that 'chose' refers to the object that is about to be recovered, and not to the action itself. This is underlined by the use of 'property in action' as synonymous with 'chose in action':

> We will proceed next to take a short view of the property in action, or such where a man hath not the occupation, but merely a bare right to occupy the thing in question; the possession whereof may however be recovered by a suit or action at law: from whence the *thing so recoverable* is called a thing or *chose, in action*. Thus money due on a bond is a chose in action; for a property in the debt vests at the time of forfeiture mentioned in the obligation, but there is no possession till recovered by course of law.[140]

This passage clearly shows how contracts are understood in a 'translational' sense, in categories of property law, or as AWB Simpson put it, as a 'sort of conveyance'.[141] 'Chose in action' epitomises this view by formulating the effects of contracts not in terms of the future binding effect of a promise, but in terms of transferring a 'chose'. The fact that this thing is not 'in possession' and has yet to be recovered in a lawsuit is expressed by the attribute 'in action'. As we have seen, even contractual rights to services are explained in terms of property.[142] However, explicitly saying that a service *is* a 'chose' is a different thing; this might have sounded awkward to Blackstone himself. Simpson surmises that this explains why contracts for services are 'hardly mentioned' in Blackstone's treatment of contracts.[143]

Thus is the structure of the 'superstructure'. The conceptualisation of those rights that form the superstructure is modelled after property, the paradigm of a superstructural right. The supremacy of the proprietary terminology and concepts, including the term 'chose in action' as used by Blackstone, is the doctrinal expression of a political philosophy that underlies the works of writers such as Grotius as well: this thinking understands rights first and foremost as an idea that guarantees the liberty, security and property of the individual. We will turn to this background

---

[139] 2 Bl Comm 396.

[140] ibid, at 396–97 (emphasis added).

[141] AWB Simpson, 'Introduction' in W Blackstone, *Commentaries on the Laws of England* (Chicago, University of Chicago Press, 1979) vol 2, i, xiii.

[142] See text accompanying nn 128–29 above.

[143] Simpson, 'Introduction', above n 141, at xiv.

once we have taken a closer look at the doctrinal construction of the next step in Blackstone's sequence. Having inquired into 'rights', which form the 'superstructure', we will now move on to the next phase: the infringement of a right, called a wrong, triggering the legal response, the remedy. Are we indeed completely leaving behind the conceptual world of rights when we are entering the realm of remedies? We will see that this is not entirely the case, and we will encounter again the peculiar doctrinal construct of the 'chose in action'. Most importantly, however, we will see that moving from 'rights' to 'remedies' involves an additional actor entering the stage: the state.

IV. FROM 'RIGHTS' TO 'REMEDIES'

A. From Rights to Wrongs to Remedies: What Lies beyond the Superstructure?

We have seen so far what it means to call Blackstone's vision of rights 'superstructural'. Rights are domains or spheres, bordering on each other and forming together a static protective layer that conserves the status quo. Now, let us assume a wrong is committed, actualising the very purpose of the rights that so far had been lying dormant. What happens now? Post-Austinian common law scholars have conceptualised this violation of a superstructural or primary right as giving rise to a secondary or remedial right,[144] or, as Weinrib would have it, the initial right as a 'domain of freedom' is not replaced or supplemented by a secondary right, but is instead 'transformed' into an entitlement or claim.[145] In Blackstone's legal cosmos, when making the transition from rights to remedies, we seem, at least at first glance, to leave the world of rights altogether. At the same time, we appear to proceed from substance to procedure. While Blackstone, up to this point, has expounded 'rights' as a matter of substantive law,[146] he seems to understand the response to 'wrongs' mainly as a matter of procedure. The treatment of wrongs in the third volume is a treatment of the general structure of the court system, and of the forms of actions available in a case of a 'wrong'.

Two explanations have been put forth to account for this transition. John Langbein has explained this 'mislabelling' (as he called it) as a result of substance and procedure still being inextricably entangled in

---

[144] See, eg, Birks, 'Rights, Wrongs, and Remedies', above n 20, at 12 ff; Birks, 'Obligations: One Tier or Two?', above n 88; Birks, 'Introduction', above n 86. See also Tilbury, 'Remedy as Right', above n 88; Descheemaeker, above n 88.

[145] EJ Weinrib, 'Two Conceptions of Remedies' in CEF Rickett (ed), *Justifying Private Law Remedies* (Oxford, Hart Publishing, 2008) 3, 12–13.

[146] Watson, above n 30, at 805.

Blackstone's day: the substantive content, in the words of Henry Maine, 'secreted in the interstices of procedure'.[147] Watson offers a taxonomical explanation: Blackstone was facing the problem that he *had* to deal with the law of procedure, and since he was following Hale anyway, he did so in the context of the remedial part of the law.[148] Both might be true. However, one cannot help but feel that there is more to the transition, particularly because Blackstone, by making the right/wrong dichotomy the divide that governs the structure of the entire *Commentaries*, emphasises this opposition much more fervently than Hale. There is a deeper connection, I would like to posit, between the formulation of this transition and the way that Blackstone envisions the purpose and the operation of 'rights'.

B. Rights, the State, Locke and Blackstone: The Original Contract

We have seen how aptly Blackstone plays on the shades of meaning of 'right'. While his point of departure is the command of what is (objectively) right and the second meaning he offers ('rights of persons', 'rights of things') can be best understood as signifying 'law' in the sense of 'objective right', we notice as well that Blackstone ascribes the individual a central role in this multivalent system of 'right'. Absolute rights define the spheres of bodily integrity, liberty, and private property of every individual; relative rights define his or her status, rank and place in society. If a wrong is committed, Blackstone's emphasis is clearly not on the relationship between the victim and the perpetrator—the other individual in what many scholars would think of as the 'bipolar' relation so typical of private law. What matters to Blackstone is the relationship between the victim and the state. The third volume of the *Commentaries* deals with the victim of a wrong who turns towards the state for redress. The crucial—and quite fundamental—question before us is thus: what role does the state have to play in Blackstone's vision of private law? The following key passage, taken from the first volume of the *Commentaries*, addresses the role of the state in relation to the rights of the individual:

> Human laws define and enforce as well those rights which belong to man considered as an individual, as those which belong to him considered in his relation to others. For the principal aim of society is to protect individuals in the enjoyment of those absolute rights which were vested in them by the

[147] JH Langbein, 'Introduction' in W Blackstone, *Commentaries on the Laws of England* (Chicago, University of Chicago Press, 1979) vol 3, i, iii. See also, along the same lines, JH Langbein, 'Blackstone, Litchfield, Yale: The Founding of Yale Law School' in AT Kronman (ed), *History of Yale Law School: The Tercentennial Lectures* (Harrisonburg VA, Yale University Press, 2004) 21.

[148] Watson, above n 30, at 805–06.

immutable laws of nature; but which could not be preserved in peace without that mutual assistance and intercourse which is gained by the institution of friendly and social communities. Hence, it follows that the first and primary end of human laws is to maintain and regulate these *absolute* rights of individuals. Such rights as are social and relative result from, and are posterior to, the formation of states and societies: so that to maintain and regulate these, is clearly a subsequent consideration. And therefore the principal view of human laws is, or ought to be, to explain, protect, and enforce such rights as are absolute, which in themselves are few and simple; and, then, such rights as are relative, which arising, from a variety of connexions, will be far more numerous and more complicated.[149]

A similar account is given, in particular, with respect to the protection of property:

> Necessity begat property; and, in order to insure that property, recourse was had to civil society, which brought along with it a long train of inseparable concomitants; states, government, laws, punishments, and the public exercise of religious duties.[150]

These passages explicate Blackstone's view of the state as the guardian of rights. The very purpose of forming societies and states is to safeguard those rights that antedate societies—Blackstone calls these rights 'absolute'. Similarly, those rights that spring from sociality are to be protected and maintained by the state as well. This instrumental view of the state, its principal aim and sole justification being the protection of rights, is commonly held to be a slightly modified 'retelling' of Lockean philosophy.[151] It is, obviously, closely connected with the idea of the Original Contract. John Goldberg states that '[a]lthough hardly bedfellows in the seventeenth century, common law and social contract theories would join forces by the end of the eighteenth. The chief architect of the merger was William Blackstone.'[152]

Blackstone did not believe in the empiric existence of a social contract that marked the exodus from the 'state of nature.'[153] He did believe, however, that the shared sense that the individual is in need of protection by the community was the foundation of an 'implied' social contract:

> And this is what we mean by the original contract of society; which, though perhaps in no instance it has ever been formally expressed at the first institution of a state, yet in nature and reason must always be understood and implied, in

---

[149] 1 Bl Comm 120–21.

[150] 2 Bl Comm 8. See also RP Burns, 'Blackstone's Theory of the "Absolute" Rights of Property' (1985) 54 *University of Cincinnati Law Review* 67, 76.

[151] Zuckert, above n 82, at 254, 261; Augé, above n 10, at 84; Zipursky, 'Philosophy of Private Law', above n 25, at 641–42; Goldberg, above n 35, at 545 ff.

[152] Goldberg, above n 35, at 545. See also the interesting overview by S Buckle and D Castiglione, 'Hume's Critique of the Contract Theory' (1991) 12 *History of Political Thought* 457.

[153] On this aspect see Zuckert, above n 82, at 255.

the very act of associating together: namely, that the whole should protect all its parts, and that every part should pay obedience to the will of the whole, or, in other words, that the community should guard the rights of each individual member, and that in return for this protection each individual should submit to the laws of the community ...[154]

In his *Analysis of the Laws of England*, Blackstone had reduced his version of the Original Contract to the concise statement that 'Society is formed for the Protection of Individuals; and States, or Government, for the Preservation of Society.'[155] Its dual structure reveals its roots in, as John Finnis put it, 'the orthodox contemporary theory of a double original contract.'[156] Such theories, as, for example, put forth by Pufendorf, posit that the formation of a state requires two contracts: one reciprocal agreement of all involved individuals among each other to become fellow citizens, and a second agreement by which the association vests in some the power of government to provide common security, while binding itself to obedience.[157] This second agreement affects, in particular, the administration of justice and the preservation of rights:

> Unless some superior be constituted, whose commands and decisions all the members are bound to obey, they would still remain as in a state of nature, without any judge upon earth to define their several rights, and *redress their several wrongs*.[158]

Thus, entrusting the state with the preservation and maintenance of rights (and, at the same time, giving up the possibility of self-help, some rare exceptions notwithstanding),[159] puts the state in charge of the redress of wrongs. This diagnosis is in line with our description of the 'superstructural' function of rights as safeguarding the status quo, a guardianship which is latent until a violation occurs. At this point, the state machinery takes over: if 'right' is turned to 'wrong', it is the state that must make it right again.

C. A Right to Redress?

The event of a violation of a right appears to move the playing field from the private into the public realm. While Blackstone's language shifts from 'rights' to 'remedies', the question arises which role is accorded to the

---

[154] 1 Bl Comm 47–48.

[155] Blackstone, *An Analysis of the Laws of England*, above n 7, at 2.

[156] Finnis, above n 40, at 178.

[157] See S Pufendorf, *On the Duty of Man and Citizen According to Natural Law* (M Silverthorne tr, Cambridge, Cambridge University Press, 1991) book 2 ch 6 paras 7–9.

[158] 1 Bl Comm 48 (emphasis added).

[159] 3 Bl Comm 2 ff. This aspect is highlighted by Zipursky, 'Philosophy of Private Law', above n 25, at 642.

victim of the transgression. Is the status of the person whose rights have been violated, at this stage, still defined by 'rights'?

(i) Administration of Remedies: Exclusively Determined by 'Objective Right'?

Blackstone firmly states that the administration of remedies is not to be understood as arbitrary or discretionary, but as a matter of the rule of law. The judicial response to a wrong does not depend 'on the arbitrary caprice of the judge, but on the settled and invariable principles of justice. The judgment in short is the remedy prescribed by law for the redress of injuries.'[160] It is more difficult to establish, however, that Blackstone also believed that the injured individual had a subjective right to redress. Individual entitlement to a certain remedy is by no means the *logical* consequence of the assumption that the judge is bound by law to administer a certain remedy. In Hans Kelsen's *Reine Rechtslehre* ('Pure Theory of Law'), for example, individual rights are described as mere factual side effects or 'reflexes' of the judicial maintenance of an 'objective order'. The fact that a plaintiff has to bring a civil action is seen simply as a *condition* of issuing the sanction that the legal order attaches to what is defined as an illegal act.[161]

However, as we know by now, rights were more than just 'reflexes' to Blackstone. To him, the sentence *ubi ius, ibi remedium* was not just a 'misleading formulation of a tautology':[162] rights do indeed take precedence (at least epistemologically) over the remedial system. When Blackstone maintains that the administration of remedies is a matter of 'law', he does not refer to the 'objective right' in the Kelsenian way in order to dispense with the category of individual entitlement. On the contrary, for Blackstone, the protection of individual rights and the protection of the law as 'objective right' are one and the same because the 'objective order' is built around the protection and maintenance of the pre-eminent individual rights.[163] Once again, both dimensions of 'right' turn out to be

---

[160] 3 Bl Comm 396.

[161] H Kelsen, *Reine Rechtslehre* (Tübingen, Mohr Siebeck, 1934) 47–52 (under the heading 'Die Reduktion des subjektiven Rechts auf das objective'). For the common law, a similarly radical account is given by positivist legal philosopher Hearn, above n 27, at 145, who opines that a 'right' is just the effect of a command, given for the benefit of a particular person, the 'donee'. On the idea of the 'right' as a mere reflex of the objective command, see HLA Hart, *Essays on Bentham: Studies in Jurisprudence and Political Theory* (Oxford, Oxford University Press, 1982) 180. See also Weinrib, 'Two Conceptions of Remedies', above n 145, at 5, pointing out that in Kelsen's view, the act itself that is defined as 'wrong' is merely seen as such a 'condition' of the administration of a remedy as well.

[162] Kennedy, above n 73, at 240.

[163] One might say that in this respect, Blackstone perceives the 'objective right' as a reflex of the 'subjective right'.

the same thing viewed from a slightly different angle.[164] This resonates with another tenet of Lockean philosophy: the preservation of individual rights is, at same time, a matter of the public good.[165]

Birks was convinced that when Blackstone spoke of the 'protection of the law'[166] through the administration of remedies, what he actually had in mind was a subjective 'remedial' right of the wronged to a remedy. Birks stated that if he had had a chance to ask him, Blackstone (despite his misleading omission to use the word 'right') 'would almost certainly admit, not only that the judgment generated a right, but also that the judgment was obtained as a matter of right. ... He would be appalled to be thought weak on rights.'[167] Continued Birks: 'Although [Blackstone] never says so, ... the victim has, in his view, but only in our terms, a right to the award which the judgment makes.'[168] Is there truly no textual evidence at all regarding such a 'remedial right'?

(ii) The 'Structural' Right to Civil Recourse

The purpose of the state is to protect rights. The mere declaration of rights is insufficient; the law has to provide for a 'method of recovering and asserting' rights.[169] Blackstone makes the same point again when discussing the protection of 'absolute personal rights':

> But in vain would these rights be declared, ascertained, and protected by the dead letter of the law, if the constitution had provided no other method to secure their actual enjoyment. It has therefore established certain other auxiliary subordinate rights of the subject, which serve principally as outworks or barriers, to protect and maintain inviolate the three great and primary rights ...[170]

The third of these subordinate or auxiliary rights is that of 'applying to the courts of justice for redress of injuries'.[171] This right guarantees every citizen open access to justice. This implies, however, a right to the establishment of institutions that make such access to justice possible,

---

[164] Other passages in Blackstone's *Commentaries* also emphasise that judgments in civil matters have to be rendered as a matter of *law* and are prescribed by justice, while not mentioning individual entitlement. However, in this context Blackstone's intention is to highlight that the administration of remedies is not arbitrary or discretionary, but a matter of the 'rule of law'—not depending 'on the arbitrary caprice of the judge, but on the settled and invariable principles of justice. The judgment in short is the remedy prescribed by law for the redress of injuries': 3 Bl Comm 396.

[165] See, eg, Locke, above n 130, at book 2 §§ 6, 135; Tully, above n 13, at 163. See also Alschuler, above n 68, at 47 and the text accompanying n 68 above.

[166] 1 Bl Comm 55–56.

[167] Birks, 'Rights, Wrongs and Remedies', above n 20, at 15.

[168] ibid, at 16.

[169] 1 Bl Comm 55–56.

[170] ibid, at 136.

[171] ibid, at 137.

and ensure an effective protection of rights; namely, courts and a remedial law, substantive and procedural, which regulates the vindication of rights. Goldberg, who has worked extensively on this question in the context of inquiring into a possible right to tort reform in the United States, has called this a 'fundamental right to a law for the redress of private wrongs',[172] and a 'structural right.'[173] Such a structural right to safeguard the enjoyment of the rights of the 'superstructure' is also implied in the double social contract theory that, as we have seen, Blackstone is said to have subscribed to. Rights that might even exist in a state of nature are but illusory without a state that promulgates laws and enforces them. If human beings associate to have their rights protected and realised, and subject themselves, in a second covenant, voluntarily to a government, it is the duty of this government to take the measures and create the institutional framework that guarantees the enjoyment of rights; at the same time this system justifies the requirement to abstain from self-help.[174]

This structural right to seek redress, or a right to civil recourse in general is, however, obviously not the right that Birks had in mind when claiming that Blackstone firmly believed that the victim of a wrong, from the moment the wrong was committed, had a 'remedial right' to a specific award.

(iii) After the Wrong—A 'Remedial Right'?

(1) Three Versions of Remedial Rights

'Remedial rights' could be conceptualised in different ways. We could imagine a remedial right to be a right that arises after a 'superstructural' right has been violated, and which is directed against the wrongdoer. This would be a substantive claim to reparation or compensation. Such a right could be perceived as the manifestation or actualisation of the hitherto only latent superstructural right. The existence of such a right would emphasise primarily the bipolarity of the relationship between the wronged and the wrongdoer. Weinrib has elaborated in great detail on this feature of bipolarity, which he sees as rooted in the principle of corrective justice, and which for him epitomises the hallmark of a private law relationship.[175] Weinrib insists that, on an analytical level, the conceptual coherence of the bipolar relationship dictates that the rights relationship between the wronged and wrongdoer is governed by the original right, only in a transformed state, and not by a secondary 'remedial' right.[176]

However, we have also seen that Blackstone perceives the wrong as an

---

[172] Goldberg, above n 35, at 552.
[173] ibid, at 551.
[174] See, eg, Locke, above n 130, at book 2 §§ 129–31.
[175] See Weinrib, *The Idea of Private Law*, above n 21, at 63 ff, 75 ff.
[176] Weinrib, 'Two Conceptions of Remedies', above n 145, at 12–13.

event that triggers a response from the state: the victim of the violation has to turn to the state to seek redress. Weinrib sees the infliction of a wrong as transactional, leading to a normative loss on the part of the wronged and a normative gain on the part of the wrongdoer, leading to a right/duty relationship that ties both together in a unit.[177] Blackstone's focus, however, seems to be not so much on the 'correlativity' between loss of the victim and gain of the violator but rather on the damage done to the superstructure of rights which the state is supposed to protect and preserve, and the restoration of the status quo ante through the granting of a remedy. The state has to rectify the wrong and mete out (corrective) justice. One could, therefore, imagine that if rights in Blackstone's cosmos were to operate indeed exclusively superstructurally, a violation of a right would not create a bipolar correlative relationship between wronged and wrongdoer at all. Instead, the injured citizen could be seen as holding a right against the state (the court), and only the court subsequently creates a new duty on the part of the defendant by issuing a decree to this extent. Indeed, some scholars have defined the term 'remedial right' as a right against the state and against the court[178]—the 'representatives of organized society'[179]—to be granted a specific remedy.

If we look closely, we find statements by Blackstone that indicate that he indeed thought of 'wrong' as giving rise to further rights. These statements show that he actually believed in a 'remedial right' that brought together the characteristics of *both* of the possible definitions: a right against the wrongdoer *and* a right against the court. In the third volume of the *Commentaries*, Blackstone states:

> And, such as it is, it [sc.: a clear and distinct notion of the nature of remedies] arises principally from the excellence of our English laws; which adapt their redress exactly to circumstances of the injury, and do not furnish one and the same action for different wrongs, which are impossible to be brought within one and the same description: whereby every man knows what satisfaction he is entitled to expect from the courts of justice, and as little as possible is left in the breast of the judges, whom the law appoints to administer and not to prescribe the remedy.[180]

Here, Blackstone again underlines that remedies are to be administered as a matter of law, not as a matter of judicial discretion;[181] however, he also points out that the individual is *entitled* to a specific remedial reaction of the court that suits the injury he has suffered. This, how-

---

[177] Weinrib, *The Idea of Private Law*, above n 21, at 122 ff.

[178] SA Smith, 'The Law of Damages: Rules for Citizens or Rules for Courts?' in D Saidov and R Cunnington (eds), *Contract Damages: Domestic and International Perspectives* (Oxford, Hart Publishing, 2008) 33, 38–39.

[179] CE Clark, 'The Code Cause of Action' (1924) 33 *Yale Law Journal* 817, 824. See also AL Corbin, 'Rights and Duties' (1924) 33 *Yale Law Journal* 501, 517.

[180] 3 Bl Comm 266.

[181] See above n 160 and accompanying text.

ever, does not exclude a claim to compensation against the wrongdoer, although this claim is not spelled out as a relationship of obligation. In several passages,[182] Blackstone indeed does explicitly mention that a right to compensation is vested in the victim at the moment the injury is committed; at the same time, he explains that this right remains 'incomplete or inchoate'—more of a proto-right—and is not 'fully ascertained' until it is 'assessed by the intervention of the law'.[183] Blackstone does not bother with a detailed definition of these inchoate rights: it is clear that they are in need of realisation in court. The constellation is therefore not 'bipolar', but rather 'triangular'.

Triangularity is what characterises the model of private law relations as expounded by Zipursky. As a counterpoint to Weinrib's bipolarity, Zipursky's idea of corrective justice emphasises the importance of civil recourse; the focal point of his philosophy of private law is therefore not a rights/duties relationship between wronged and wrongdoer, but the 'right of action', the right to act through the state against the defendant.[184] Zipursky's work is inspired by Blackstone's model of civil redress[185] as a way of putting to work Lockean social contract theory.[186] In Zipursky's model, corrective justice indeed unfolds as a triangular transaction, as a detour through the state without taking the shortcut between wronged and wrongdoer: an obligation on the part of the defendant is neither a necessary nor a sufficient condition of a right of action.[187]

(2) Blackstone's 'Right of Action'

Although Zipursky does not seem to derive the details of his theory from drawing on concrete Blackstonian rights doctrine, we still find a very similar structure in Blackstone's work. Evidence in the *Commentaries* is of course relatively sparse when it comes to the transition from rights to concrete remedies. In order to understand the version of 'triangularity' that Blackstone adheres to, we have to once again look at the 'chose in action'.[188] As we have seen, Blackstone depicts the legal effects of contracts as creating a 'chose in action', which puts them in terms of property

---

[182] 3 Bl Comm 116; 2 Bl Comm 396–97, 438.

[183] 3 Bl Comm 116.

[184] BC Zipursky, 'Rights, Wrongs, and Recourse in the Law of Torts' (1998) 51 *Vanderbilt Law Review* 1, 79 ff; Zipursky, 'Philosophy of Private Law', above n 25, at 632 ff; BC Zipursky, 'Civil Recourse, Not Corrective Justice' (2003) 91 *Georgetown Law Journal* 695, 733 ff. See also the critique offered by J Stapleton, 'Evaluating Goldberg and Zipursky's Civil Recourse Theory' (2006) 75 *Fordham Law Review* 1529.

[185] Zipursky, 'Philosophy of Private Law', above n 25, at 641–42. See also JCP Goldberg and BC Zipursky, 'Torts as Wrongs' (2010) 88 *Texas Law Review* 917, 982.

[186] Zipursky, 'Rights, Wrongs, and Recourse', above n 184, at 85; Zipursky, 'Civil Recourse', above n 184, at 735.

[187] Zipursky, 'Philosophy of Private Law', above n 25, at 635–36.

[188] See part III(C)(iii) above.

law. The breach of a contract can therefore be explained as the infringe-ment of a property right and be treated in the chapter on the 'rights of personal things'. We also mentioned, in passing, that the breach of the contract itself again creates a 'chose in action':

> If a man promises, or covenants with me, to do any act, and fails in it, whereby I suffer damage; the recompense for this damage is a chose in action; for though a right to some recompense vests in me, at the time the damage is done, yet what and how large such recompense shall be, can only be ascertained by verdict; and the possession can only be given me by legal judgment and execution.[189]

Blackstone concedes that the breach, the violation of the superstructural right, immediately gives rise to a secondary right. Yet Blackstone has no interest in analysing this right in more detail—without its possible reali-sation in court, it is 'incomplete and inchoate':

> [U]pon all contracts and promises ... the law gives action of some sort or other to the party injured in case of non-performance; to compel the wrongdoer to do justice to the party with whom he has contracted, and, on failure of performing the identical thing he engaged to do, to render a satisfaction equivalent to the damage sustained. But while the thing, or its equivalent, remains in suspense, and the injured party has only the right and not the occupation, it is called a chose in action; being a thing rather *in potentia* than in *esse*: though the owner may have as absolute property of such things in action, as of things in possession.[190]

It is important to emphasise again that the right that comes into existence in the moment of the breach is *not* conceptualised as an obligation. It is a property right in the promised object or its equivalent, damages. On the one hand, Blackstone describes this as a full-blown, absolute prop-erty right, to be distinguished from the 'chose in possession' only through the lack of physical occupation or possession. On the other hand, it is the very nature of this right that it can only be realised in court; or, to go even further, the 'chose' itself can only be brought into existence in court. The contract damages already *belong* to the plaintiff even before a court order to this extent is issued. Yet they exist solely *in potentia*, and only come into being through the verdict, which also entitles the plaintiff to execution and thus enables, finally, the acquisition of possession. It is only the action that is personal; and only in this context does Blackstone make fleeting mention of an obligation, as a reference to the civil law, citing from the *Institutes*.[191] As opposed to the bipolar obligation between

---

[189] 2 Bl Comm 397.

[190] ibid, at 397–98.

[191] 3 Bl Comm 117: 'Personal actions are such whereby a man claims a debt, personal duty, or damages in lieu thereof; and likewise whereby a man claims a satisfaction in dam-ages for some injury done to his person or property. The former are said to be founded in contracts, the latter upon torts or wrongs: and they are the same which the civil law calls *"actiones in personam, quae adversis eum intenduntur, qui ex contractu vel delicto obligatus*

wronged and wrongdoer, the 'chose in action' is by definition 'triangular' because it inevitably includes the court as an actor. The 'chose in action' is, in Blackstone's words, 'property' that *is* a 'right of action'.[192]

Blackstone then moves on and deals with torts: those 'wrongs' that we would see as the focal point of a scheme that is built around 'rights' and 'wrongs'.[193] He reaches the conclusion that the right to compensation that comes into existence at the moment the injury occurs is too inchoate to be put on the same level as the right to contract damages; it is too inchoate to be treated as a 'chose in action'. In the case of a 'chose in action', property is already vested in the owner but awaits its realisation in court. In the case of a tort, the property is vested in the claimant only at a later point, when the judgment is rendered:

> A judgment, in consequence of some suit or action in a court of justice, is frequently the means of vesting the right and property of chattel interests in the prevailing party. And here we must distinguish between property, the right of which is before vested in the party, and of which only possession is recovered by suit or action; and property, to which a man before had no determinate title or certain claim, but he gains as well the rights as the possession by the process and judgment of the law. Of the former sort are all debts and *choses in action*; ... But there is also a species of property to which a man has not any claim or title whatsoever, till after suit commenced and judgment obtained in a court of law; where the right and the remedy do not follow each other, as in common cases, but accrue at the same time.[194]

This passage is so particularly remarkable because of Blackstone's statement that cases where there is no determinate title (not even to a thing *in potentia*) are the only cases where the right does not antedate the remedy. Tortious injuries are of such a nature. Because Blackstone goes on to draw the arguably most startling (and explicit) conclusion on the role of the state in the administration of private law, the next passage deserves to be related in full length:

> Another species of property, that is acquired and lost by suit and judgment at law, is that of damages given to a man by a jury, as a compensation and satisfaction for some injury sustained; as for battery, for imprisonment, for slander, or for trespass. Here the plaintiff has no certain demand till after the verdict; but when the jury has assessed his damages, and judgment is given

---

est aliquid dare vel concedere".' Blackstone identifies the quote as Inst 4.6.15. However, Inst. 4.6.15 reads, in the editions available in Blackstone's time (see, eg, G Harris (tr), *D Justiani Institutionum Libri Quatuor*, 2nd edn (London, M Withers, 1761)): '... in personam vero actiones, quibus dare aut facere oportere intenditur, condictiones' ('the personal actions in the form "ought to give or do" are ... condictions': Birks and McLeod, above n 31, at 131).

[192] 2 Bl Comm 397 treats both as synonymous: 'In the former cases [of 'choses in action'], the student will observe that the *property, or right in action*, depends upon ...' (emphasis added).

[193] See Zipursky, 'Rights, Wrongs, and Recourse', above n 184; Goldberg and Zipursky, 'Torts as Wrongs', above n 185.

[194] 2 Bl Comm 437.

thereupon, whether they amount to twenty pounds or twenty shillings, he instantly acquires, and the defendant loses at the same time, a right to that specific sum. It is true, that this is not an acquisition so perfectly original as in the former instance [sc.: the application of certain specific statutory penalties]: for here the injured party has unquestionably a vague and indeterminate right to some damages or other, the instance he receives the injury; and the verdict of the jurors, and judgment of the court thereupon, do not in this case so properly vest a new title in him as fix and ascertain an old one; they do not give, but define, the right. But however, though strictly speaking the primary right to satisfaction is given by the law of nature, and the suit is only the means of ascertaining and recovering that satisfaction; yet, as the legal proceedings are the only visible means of the acquisition of property, we may fairly enough rank such damages, or satisfaction assessed, under the head of property acquired by suit and judgment at law.[195]

Now, we finally see the full picture of how we are supposed to perceive the 'triangular' rights relationship in the paradigmatic cases of breach of contract and torts. If a 'superstructural' right has been violated, the wronged has, beyond a general, structural right to institutions that allow for the rectification of 'wrongs',[196] a concrete 'remedial right' in the sense of a claim to have a remedy issued that exactly fits and as far as possible undoes the wrong. However, the violation of the 'superstructural' right also effects a substantive change vis-a-vis the wrongdoer: a 'primary right of satisfaction' arises, 'given by the law of nature'. It is 'primary' to Blackstone because it antedates the right that is subsequently created by the court order; in reference to the violation of the 'superstructural right', a modern common law scholar would think of it as a 'secondary' right. This natural right to satisfaction, however, is, in the case of breach of contract as well as in the case of torts, 'inchoate and incomplete.'[197] The court order is not a simple replication of a pre-existing right between wrong and wrongdoer (Stephen Smith calls this model of adjudication 'rubber stamping'[198]), but it is the 'intervention of the law'[199] that not only enforces, but renders complete and determinate the previously amorphous natural right. For the case of breach of contract, this thought is expressed in the doctrinal concept of the 'chose in action': the moment the breach occurs, the wronged acquires property as to the compensatory damages (Blackstone obviously did not yet think of problematic constellations such as consequential damages[200]), but the damages have to be specified by verdict. Although the wronged already held a property right,

---

[195] ibid, at 438. Note the criticism voiced by JJ Kehoe, *A Treatise on the Law of Choses in Action* (Toronto, Carswell, 1881) 19 (rights arising from torts should be included in the concept of 'chose in action').

[196] See part IV(C)(ii) above.

[197] 3 Bl Comm 116.

[198] See Smith, above n 178, at 54.

[199] 3 Bl Comm 116.

[200] See Smith, above n 178, at 61–62.

only the court order elevates it from a thing '*in potentia*' to a thing '*in esse*'.[201] In the case of a tort, the natural 'right to satisfaction' is even more amorphous and ill-defined; it does not even amount to a 'chose in action'. In both cases, the natural right can only come into its own with the help of the state.

The idea that a natural right to redress accrues to the wronged is in line with Blackstone's theoretical foundations in Lockean theory. In the *Second Treatise of Government*, Locke defines a natural right to seek reparation from the wrongdoer as a matter of 'self-preservation'.[202] When man advances from the state of nature into the civil state, this right to self-preservation, unlike the right to punish, is not 'wholly given up' but only given up 'to be regulated by the laws made by society'.[203] The individual does not renounce this right, but, as Goldberg put it, 'consents only to channel the exercise of this right through the law.'[204] According to Blackstone, however, the natural right is but a proto-right, which only through the process of 'channelling' realises its potential. This is made clear when Blackstone describes the 'chose in action' as a property right to a thing, but the thing itself is thought of as a mere thing *in potentia*. The 'chose in action' is therefore synonymous with 'property in action'. It is a property right that fully develops only in action, and therefore is, as Blackstone explicitly states, a *right of action*.[205]

At this point, Blackstone rises above his own foundations in Lockean-esque natural law thought. The natural right to redress is in need of being 'channelled' through public institutions not only because rights are de facto illusory in the state of nature, where they lack impartial judges and mechanisms of enforcement. The right to redress is too shapeless, amorphous: it can only come into a meaningful existence within a system that gives it shape, with a 'judge upon earth to *define* their several rights'.[206] In this reasoning, we might recognise proto-Kantian thought. Not unlike Kant, Blackstone here recognises a defect of the natural right itself that can accomplish its own perfection only through adjudication. Kant held that in the state of nature, private law remains necessarily imperfect; not because of the factual circumstances or for anthropological reasons (as most extremely postulated by Hobbes), but because of the inherent defects, the lack of concreteness of the regulations of natural law.[207] In the state of nature, private law faces its own imperfection and comes

---

[201] 2 Bl Comm 397.
[202] Locke, above n 130, at book 2 §§ 10–11.
[203] ibid, at book 2 §§ 129–130.
[204] Goldberg, above n 35, at 541.
[205] 2 Bl Comm 397.
[206] 1 Bl Comm 48 (emphasis added).
[207] See W Kersting, *Wohlgeordnete Freiheit*, 2nd edn (Paderborn, Mentis, 2007) 258 ff; A Ripstein, *Force and Freedom* (Cambridge MA, Harvard University Press, 2009) 145 ff.

to terms with the necessity for a transition into the civil state:[208] thus, 'from private right in the state of nature there proceeds the postulate of public right'.[209] Of course, Blackstone knows nothing of Kant's highly complex theoretical foundations;[210] yet the parallel helps us better understand Blackstone's particular notion of the *'publicness* of private law'.[211] The importance Blackstone ascribes to this aspect of publicness helps us understand why such a fundamental shift of perspective occurs when Blackstone moves from 'rights' (individual rights as 'superstructure') to 'remedies' (as avenues of civil recourse).

V. CONCLUSION

When Blackstone states his allegiance to the maxim *ubi remedium, ibi ius*, it is not just the 'misleading formulation of a tautology'.[212] The *Commentaries* create a legal cosmos where rights, understood in the terms of contemporary political theory, demarcate domains of freedom, security and property. The state protects those rights through an institutional system that provides a civil recourse for every possible violation of a right. In conformity with the Lockean theory of the Original Contract, Blackstone sees the protection of individual rights as the very reason why human beings associate and subject themselves to public authority. At the same time, the protection of individual rights is a matter of the public good as well. This utility is reflected in the multivalence of the word 'right', making the individual and objective dimensions of right both hypostases of 'what is right'.

We have seen that Birks has aptly called 'superstructural' the way that these individual rights operate juridically. The superstructure is envisioned as a system of sharply demarcated domains, an imagery that implies a tendency towards a terminology and conception that draws on property law. When Blackstone devised his organisational scheme, he was in all likelihood inspired by Hale and by the attractive prospect of subjecting the unwieldy common law under the taxonomic regime of the *Institutes*. However, the proprietary bias of Blackstone's system indicates that this explanation is not exhaustive. Blackstone presents himself as very uncivilian in devising a scheme in which 'obligation' has virtually no role to play.[213]

---

[208] Kersting, above n 207, at 259.

[209] Kant, above n 55, at para 6:307.

[210] See, eg, A Ripstein, 'Private Order and Public Justice: Kant and Rawls' (2006) 92 *Virginia Law Review* 1391, 1406 ff.

[211] Weinrib, *The Idea of Private Law*, above n 21, at 218. See also Weinrib, 'Two Conceptions of Remedies', above n 145, at 27.

[212] Kennedy, above n 73, at 240.

[213] See part III(C) above.

This finally takes us to the remedial stage of Blackstone's system. When Blackstone shifts his perspective from 'rights' to the rectification of 'wrongs', he also shifts from 'rights' to 'remedies'—that is, court orders that put the wronged 'in possession'[214] of the right of which he has been deprived. Yet we do not leave the world of rights when we enter the world of remedies. The rights that accrue to the individual after a 'superstructural' right is violated are rights of action, a notion that encapsulates the 'triangularity' of the Blackstonian private law relationship that always presupposes the inclusion of the state. Even the 'natural' right to redress (which comes into existence the moment an injury occurs) conceptually requires its own realisation through adjudication. Blackstone's vision of private law is therefore distinctly 'dualist':[215] to him, the remedy is surely not the 'the same [thing] as the right, looked at from the other end.'[216]

For Blackstone, private law ordering works on two different planes. On a deontic level, private human relationships are defined by the static system of domains of freedom, the 'superstructure' that outlines demarcation lines that must not be crossed. Once a violation of such a right has occurred, however, private law inevitably moves into the public forum; the state as main actor enters the stage. Only through the detour of public institutions can the rights relationship between the wronged and the wrongdoer be formulated in a meaningful way. Arthur Ripstein once described Lockean Original Contract theory as treating the relationship between individuals and the state as if it were merely a matter of private ordering:

> The Lockean strategy collapses public justice into private law by denying the normative significance of the most significantly obvious public aspect of private right, the resolution of disputes through public procedures for applying antecedently articulated laws governing all citizens—in short, the rule of law.[217]

Blackstone may never have concerned himself with the philosophical depths of this question; nor did he have to. Yet Blackstone, the jurist and lawyer, thoroughly understood the significance of this *publicness*; he made it the very foundation of his idea of private law.

---

[214] 3 Bl Comm 116.

[215] See above n 22 and accompanying text.

[216] P Birks, 'Definition and Division: A Meditation on *Institutes* 3.13' in P Birks (ed), *The Classification of Obligations* (Oxford, Oxford University Press, 1997) 1, 24.

[217] Ripstein, 'Private Order and Public Justice', above n 210, at 1413–14.

8

Rule-Based Rights and Court-Ordered Rights

STEPHEN A SMITH*

I. INTRODUCTION

A. The Problem

HOW DO WE know what rights we have? In particular, how do we know what rights we hold against other citizens? The usual answer in common law jurisdictions is that our rights against other citizens ('private law rights') are established by judicial decisions. The typical explanation for why a citizen has a legal duty to do X is that a case or line of cases establishes a rule requiring X. This answer raises an immediate issue. Judicial decisions are not decisions about the duties that citizens generally owe to one another or even decisions about the duties that the particular litigants owed to each other. In a typical case,[1] a judicial decision is a decision about whether to order the defendant to do or not to do something. Judicial decisions are decisions about the 'court-ordered rights' that claimants will enjoy when they leave the court, not about the 'rule-based rights' that they (or anyone else) enjoyed before the litigation. A typical tort claim, for example, is a claim for damages; the court's task is to determine whether the defendant should be ordered to pay damages and, if so, how much.

---

* I am grateful to Hanoch Dagan and Helge Dedek for comments on an earlier version.

[1] The main exceptions are cases in which courts contemplate awarding constitutive or declaratory orders. Constitutive orders are self-executing orders, for example an order that vests property in a plaintiff or that decrees a divorce. Declaratory orders are orders that declare an existing legal status or duty. I focus in what follows on orders to do or not do things ('performative' orders), but most of my arguments apply to final orders generally. Constitutive and declaratory orders are closely related to performative orders in that they either confirm that a particular performance is required by law (in the case of declarations of legal duties) or they articulate a legal status, which status then confirms, creates, or extinguishes particular duties.

Contemporary common law courts do, of course, typically discuss litigants' rule-based rights in their decisions. Courts will usually only grant an order to do something if they are satisfied that the defendant failed to comply or threatened not to comply with one of the claimant's rule-based rights.[2] To decide if this is the case, the court must determine whether the claimant possessed the relevant right. Yet, precisely because a court's primary task is to determine whether to grant an order, judicial decisions often provide limited guidance about the parties' rule-based rights. The majority of the court must agree on the order, and the order itself must be expressed clearly and briefly. The majority need not, however, agree on the reasons for making the order, much less must they state those reasons clearly or briefly. More importantly, it is generally not necessary for courts to distinguish the rule-based rights that claimants hold against defendants from the 'action rights' that claimants hold against courts to obtain particular orders.[3] To obtain a court order, the claimant must prove certain facts. These facts typically include, but are not generally limited to, facts that show the defendant failed to comply with a rule-based duty. Whether any particular fact goes towards proving the existence of a rule-based duty or is a separate part of the cause of action is generally immaterial. If the required facts are proven, the end result is the same: the order is granted.[4] Thus, a court will not order damages in respect of pain and suffering in a negligence case without proof that, in

---

[2] In cases where the only order sought is an order to perform a primary duty, for example an order to perform a contract, it is not strictly necessary for the claimant to prove a breach of the duty, but only that the duty is due and has not been fulfilled. By definition, however, if a duty is due and not fulfilled then the duty has been breached.

[3] Action rights are rights to orders. An example is the right that a contractual debtor has, on proving the debt before a court, that the court order the debtor to pay the debt. Action rights are rule-based, but they differ from the rule-based rights that are my concern in this chapter because they are rights against courts, not other citizens. The law of action rights consists of rules telling courts when and in what ways they should make court orders.

[4] There are exceptions. Conflict of law rules draw a distinction between substantive and procedural law that roughly parallels the distinction between rule-based rights and action rights. Other rules that, arguably, may require courts to distinguish rule-based rights from action rights are found in the law governing damages and interest for late payments, restitution for mistaken transfers, tenders and settlements, set-off, assignment, and limitation periods. I have argued elsewhere that these rules are of limited assistance: S Smith, 'The Law of Damages: Rules for Citizens or Rules for Courts?' in D Saidov and R Cunnington (eds), *Contract Damages: Domestic and International Perspectives* (Oxford, Hart Publishing, 2008) 33, 50–52. The evidence they provide is often inconsistent (see the rules on conflicts and those on interest for late payments), they rarely appear based on considered views about our rule-based rights (see the rules on pre-judgment interest), and they can often be explained on alternative grounds. For example, the rules that provide for the payment of pre-judgment interest on restitutionary and damage awards might be explained in three different ways: (1) as designed to translate an earlier sum due into current dollars (and thus consistent with the sum being due at an earlier time); (2) as a rough-and-ready calculation of the loss caused by failing to make the payment earlier (again consistent with the duty arising earlier); or (3) as a means of determining the extent of the loss or injury suffered up to the moment of trial (and thus consistent with the idea that duties to pay restitution and damages arise only at the moment of a court order).

addition to breaching a duty of care, the defendant's actions caused pain and suffering. The latter requirement is consistent with believing that the defendant came under a rule-based duty, at the moment the pain and suffering happened, to pay the claimant a sum of money *or* with believing that the defendant had no duty to pay until the court made an order. It is difficult to tell from what courts say about pain and suffering awards which of these propositions they believe or if they have even considered the question.[5]

Against this background, it is no surprise that lawyers often draw conclusions about rule-based rights on the basis of the one part of a judicial decision that is certain and clear, namely the order. It is the conventional view, for example, that the duty to make restitution following a defective transfer is a duty to return the monetary value of the transferred property, not the property itself. If one asks how we know the duty is monetary, most lawyers would probably point to the fact that, exceptional cases aside, the only orders courts will make in cases involving defective transfers are monetary orders. This way of thinking about substantive rights has a long pedigree. Common law lawyers call personal property 'personal' because common law courts rarely order defendants to return chattels to their owners. Like the mistaken transferee or the reneging promisor, the wrongful possessor is typically only ordered to pay a sum of money to the claimant. Indeed, if the historians who say that early English law was in large part a law about the availability of judicial remedies (ie, court orders) are correct, most of our ideas about rule-based rights first developed from thinking about the law governing court orders.[6]

Reasoning in this way clearly presumes there is a relationship between orders and rule-based rights. The problem is that we don't know what that relationship is. The restitution example just mentioned suggests a simple relationship in which court orders are assumed to direct defendants to do the very thing that the law of rule-based rights already required them to do. In other contexts, however, a different relationship is assumed. For example, judges regularly say that contracting parties have legal obligations to perform their contractual promises, yet they regularly refuse to order such promises to be specifically performed.

There is in fact no settled view, whether in the courts or academia, as

---

[5] Judges sometimes say that the duty to pay damages arises at the moment of injury: see, eg, Lord Diplock in *Moschi v Lep Air Services Ltd* [1973] AC 331 (HL) 350–51. On the other hand, the language that judges use in describing the quantification of damages rules, particularly in cases involving pain and suffering, suggests that they regard the rules as directed at courts, not citizens: see, eg, *H West & Son Ltd v Shephard* [1964] AC 326 (HL) 364 (Lord Pearce); *Heil v Rankin* [2001] QB 272 (CA) [25] (Lord Woolf MR).

[6] FW Maitland, *The Forms of Action* (Cambridge, Cambridge University Press, 1954) 4–5; SFC Milsom, *Historical Foundations of the Common Law*, 2nd edn (London, Butterworths, 1981) 243–46; JH Baker, *An Introduction to English Legal History*, 4th edn (London, Butterworths, 2002) 53.

to whether anything can be said in a general way about the relationship between rule-based rights and court orders. The question is hardly ever asked.[7] The maxims *ubi jus ibi remedium* (where there's a right there's a remedy) and *ubi remedium ibi jus* (where there's a remedy there's a right) are invoked from time to time by lawyers, but their meaning is rarely clear. 'Remedy' might refer to a court order (eg, an order to pay a sum of money), but it might also mean a remedial rule-based duty (eg, a rule-based duty to make restitution or pay damages), and many other things as well.[8] Even if one takes remedies to mean court orders, do the maxims imply that orders and rights have the same content, or merely that, if you have a right, you must get *an* order (and vice versa), though the content of the right and order may differ? And what of 'cured' rights infringements? Do the maxims imply that orders are available in cases where the defendant had been in breach of a rule-based monetary obligation but then fulfilled the obligation (along with full interest) prior to litigation?[9] Finally, if the maxims are meant to describe the law, what are we to make of judicial statements that flatly contradict them? It is orthodox law that the expiry of a limitation period extinguishes the possibility of obtaining a court order, but does not extinguish the underlying right.

B. The Task

If we want to draw inferences about rule-based rights from the orders courts make—and it is inevitable that common law lawyers will want to do this—then we need a better understanding of their relationship. In particular, we need to know if there is anything that can be said in a general way about how rule-based rights are related to court orders. Broadly speaking, this task might be pursued in two ways. The inductive

---

[7] An important counter-example is R Zakrzewski, *Remedies Reclassified* (Oxford, Oxford University Press, 2005). The question is sometimes asked with respect to specific categories of orders; for example, a great deal of ink has been spilled over whether the courts' apparent reluctance to grant specific performance orders in contract means that the duty to perform a contractual promise is in most cases a duty merely to hand over the monetary value of that promise. More recently, the question whether duties to pay damages predate damages orders has attracted attention from tort theorists: see JCP Goldberg and BC Zipursky, 'Rights and Responsibility in the Law of Torts' ch 9 of this book; see also BC Zipursky, 'Philosophy of Private Law' in J Coleman and S Shapiro (eds), *The Oxford Handbook of Jurisprudence and Philosophy of Law* (Oxford, Oxford University Press, 2002) 623.

[8] See P Birks, 'Rights, Wrongs, and Remedies' (2000) 20 *Oxford Journal of Legal Studies* 1.

[9] It is a long-standing common law rule that, unless there has been a settlement, payment of full damages by a defendant prior to litigation does not extinguish the claimant's right to an order for damages (it only extinguishes the right to enforce that order). On the other hand, the payment of a debt, even if late, extinguishes the right to an order to pay the debt: see *Edmunds v Lloyds Italico & l'Ancora Compagnia di Assicurazione e Riassicurazione SpA* [1986] 1 WLR 492 (CA) 495 (Sir John Donaldson MR).

or bottom-up method examines the orders courts award alongside the statements they make about rule-based rights, to see if any general pattern emerges. By contrast, the deductive or top-down method attempts to discern the relationship by asking how, given the general features of common law systems, one might reasonably expect orders to be related to rule-based rights. Neither approach is sufficient on its own. The main limitations of the bottom-up approach have been mentioned or alluded to: courts do not always distinguish rule-based rights from other rights, and what they say is often based on assumptions about the relationship we are trying to understand.[10] On the other hand, it cannot be assumed that the relationship is the same as what we would reasonably expect it to be. The law is a human artefact.

In previous work, I made some tentative stabs at exploring the relationship between rule-based rights and orders from a primarily bottom-up perspective.[11] This chapter adopts a primarily top-down approach. The discussion proceeds in two stages. In part II, I explore but ultimately reject a number of arguments that attempt to establish a necessary or conceptual link between rule-based rights and court orders (ie, arguments that might allow one to say, for example, that if a court makes X order, Y right must exist). In part III, I then examine various reasons, based on general features of court orders and rule-based rights, that one might expect courts to make (or not make) particular kinds of orders. The theme of part III is that there are a number of considerations that courts might be expected to take into account when they make orders. Some of these considerations support orders that replicate rule-based rights, but others argue for orders that transform or limit rule-based rights or even for orders that create entirely new rights. The final conclusion is therefore messy: there is no single or unique relationship between rights and orders.

In practice, this conclusion means that court orders tell us something, but only something, about our rule-based rights. Determining what the availability of any particular order tells us about rule-based rights is a complex process. The first step is to come up with a preliminary idea, based on the best evidence and arguments, *other than* evidence and arguments based on the availability of the order itself, of what those rights might be. With that preliminary idea in hand, the next step is to consider,

---

[10] Perhaps the most famous example is Oliver Wendell Holmes' view that a contract is merely an obligation to perform or pay damages: OW Holmes, 'The Path of the Law' (1897) 10 *Harvard Law Review* 457, 462. Holmes made this statement extra-judicially, but for a recent judicial statement to the same effect see *Greater Fredericton Airport Authority v NAV Canada* (2008) 290 DLR (4th) 405 (New Brunswick Court of Appeal) [46] (Robertson JA): 'a threatened breach of contract is not only lawful but in fact constitutes a right which can be exercised subject to the obligation to pay damages and possibly to an order for specific performance'.

[11] Smith, 'The Law of Damages', above n 4; S Smith, 'Rights and Remedies: A Complex Relationship' in RJ Sharpe and K Roach (eds), *Taking Remedies Seriously* (Ottawa, Canadian Institute for the Administration of Justice, 2010) 31.

in light of the various ways in which rule-based rights might be expected to be linked to orders, which of those ideas fits best with the orders that courts make. Court orders are thus one piece of evidence, but only one piece, that we can use to help determine our rights. In part III, I offer a few examples to suggest how this evidence might be used in specific cases, but my primary aim in this chapter is to develop the groundwork for making such inquiries in future.

The discussion throughout focuses on final or dispositive 'performatory' orders, by which I mean orders that, as part of the final disposition of a private law claim, require a defendant to do or not do something. Examples include orders that defendants perform contractual promises, vacate land, cease a particular activity, pay sums of money,[12] and so on. There are other kinds of orders that courts make in the course of, or that are related to, the adjudication of private law claims, and nearly all of them have a relationship to the parties' rule-based rights. But it is final performatory orders that are invoked most commonly in discussions of rule-based rights.

II. A NECESSARY CONNECTION?

Lawyers often assume or at least appear to assume that there is a necessary connection between rule-based rights and court orders. I already noted that such a connection is implied by the maxims 'no right without a remedy' and 'no remedy without a right'. I also noted that it is not clear how the connection is understood. Four possibilities are examined below. Although each is ultimately rejected, the effort to understand them provides important clues into the nature and role of court orders.

---

[12] In the United Kingdom, a monetary award, like an injunction or order of specific performance, is made in the form of an order directing the defendant to do something, in this case to pay a sum of money. A typical monetary award reads: 'It is ordered that the defendant pay the claimant the sum of ...' (CPR pt 40, form 45). Thus, while the methods of enforcing monetary and non-monetary orders may differ, both are orders in the ordinary meaning of the word. It might be queried whether this was the case when, in earlier times (and still today in many common law jurisdictions outside the UK), monetary awards did not literally order the defendant to do something but instead stated that the claimant 'shall recover' a certain amount from the defendant. This language might be thought to suggest the award was intended not to guide the defendant, but instead to commence the enforcement process by providing the claimant with a proof of liability that could be taken to the bailiff. This interpretation seems implausible, however, given that 'shall recover' orders invariably gave the defendant a period of time to make payment. Only after payment was not made could the claimant proceed to enforcement. If the purpose of the order was merely to authorise enforcement, there would be no reason to give the defendant time to pay voluntarily.

A. All Private Law Rights Are Court-Ordered Rights

One possible understanding of the relationship between court orders and rule-based rights is that there isn't one because rule-based rights don't exist. According to this view, all private law rights are created by court orders. If this view is correct, the only time that we could say an individual is under a legal obligation to, say, pay a sum of money to another individual is when a court has made an order requiring such payment.

Not surprisingly, it is difficult to find modern authors who explicitly adopt this view.[13] The sanction-based theories of law found in the works of John Austin, Hans Kelsen, Oliver Wendell Holmes and their followers lead, however, to something very close. For each of these writers, legal duties arise when, and only when, the legal regime prescribes that a sanction should be imposed on the occurrence of specified behaviour.[14] In Kelsen's words, 'Certain human conduct is a delict because the legal order attaches to this conduct, as a condition, a sanction as consequence.'[15] Kelsen appeared to assume that the conditions that trigger sanctions are for the most part set out in the general substantive law, that is to say, in the law that is conventionally understood to stipulate our rule-based legal duties. In the case of criminal law, from which Kelsen's examples are usually drawn, this appears to be correct. Following Kelsen, we could say that there is a duty not to commit murder because there is a rule stipulating that citizens who commit murder shall be imprisoned.

In the case of private law duties, however, this assumption seems incorrect. There is no rule requiring or authorising legal officials to sanction citizens on proof that they have broken a contract, failed to return money transferred by mistake, carelessly injured another or engaged in any other behaviour conventionally regarded as the breach of a private law rule-based duty. To be sure, courts are required to make orders on proof of a breach of duty, but these orders are performative orders (eg, damages, specific performance orders, injunctions, etc); as such, they are directed at defendants, not legal officials. Performative orders are not sanctions nor do they impose a sanction. A defendant who fails to comply with a performative order may, eventually, be subject to a sanction, typically in the form of having his or her property seized or being thrown in jail, and that sanction may itself (though need not) be initiated by a court order. But the sanction-imposing order is separate from the performative

---

[13] But see J Frank, *Law and the Modern Mind*, 2nd edn (London, Stevens, 1963) 50: 'For any particular person, the law, with respect to any particular set of facts, is a decision of a court with respect to those facts so far as that decision affects that particular person. Until a court has passed on those facts no law on that subject is yet in existence.'

[14] J Austin, *The Province of Jurisprudence Determined* (London, John Murray, 1832); H Kelsen, *General Theory of Law and State* (Anders Wedberg tr, New York, Russell & Russell, 1961) 51 ff; Holmes, above n 10, at 462.

[15] Kelsen, above n 14, at 51.

order, and it is directed—as it must be if it imposes a sanction—at a legal official, not a defendant. Further, rather than being imposed *by* performative orders, private law sanctions are imposed, and only imposed, *for failing to comply with* performative orders. If a judgment debtor pays the money he or she is required to pay within the allotted time span, no sanction will be imposed. Moreover, a failure to satisfy a performative order is the only condition that must be satisfied in order to impose a sanction.[16] A claimant who seeks a writ of execution or seeks to have a defendant punished for contempt is only required to prove that a performative order was made and not satisfied. The reasons the order was made are immaterial.

Strictly interpreted, therefore, the theories of Kelsen and other writers who define duties in terms of sanction-attracting behaviour support the idea that private law duties are exclusively court-ordered duties.[17] As I explain in a moment, this idea is vulnerable to an obvious objection, but it is important to stress that there is nothing incoherent in the idea that there could be legal rights that arise when, and only when, a court order is made, or even in the idea that a legal system's private law rights might consist entirely of court-ordered rights. It might be queried whether such a system could properly be called a 'legal' system, but it should be remembered that the early common law is often described in just this way. When it is said that the early common law was basically a law of remedies, what is meant is that the law consisted of rules about how and when citizens could obtain court orders. Indeed, for writers who believe that rule-based rights exist only insofar as citizens have a right to assert them in court, the fact that prior to the abolition of the forms of action claimants could only get before a court with the permission of the Chancellor means that the common law had no rule-based rights until at least 1832.[18]

---

[16] In cases where the contemplated sanction is imprisonment or a fine, the court will usually also want to know why the defendant failed to comply with the order.

[17] Kelsen acknowledged that court orders create legal duties, but did not consider the possibility that this is the only way legal duties could be created. Indeed, in the same discussion where he observes that orders can create duties, he assumes that sanctions can be imposed without orders. In reference to a case in which the judge orders a debtor to pay $100, Kelsen writes (above n 14, at 38):

> By expressly or tacitly threatening A with a civil sanction in case of non-payment, the judge here 'commands' A to pay $100 to B. The decision of the judge is a legal norm in the same sense and for the same reasons as the general principle that if somebody does not return a loan then a civil sanction ought to be inflicted upon him on the motion of the creditor.

So far as I am aware, the rules governing the imposition of sanctions in the civilian systems with which Kelsen was most familiar are similar to the common law rules in that they require that an order be made, and then not satisfied, before any sanction is imposed.

[18] HP Glenn, *Legal Traditions of the World* (Oxford, Oxford University Press, 2000) 223–24. Even today, some writers query whether the common law recognises rule-based rights, in part on the ground that there is no formal 'right' to a court order in the sense that

We can also easily imagine how a legal system without rule-based rights might develop. If the law's role is thought to be merely to settle disputes, rule-based rights are strictly superfluous. Courts resolve disputes by telling the disputants how to behave in future, that is, by making or not making orders. For such a process to qualify as legal it would need to be governed by rules regulating the availability of court orders, but it would not need to include rules telling citizens how to behave towards one another. In practice, it is likely that the courts or legislatures in such a system would take the next step of introducing rules that tell citizens how to behave so as to avoid disputes in future, but this is not inevitable. As any parent knows, it can be difficult to develop effective rules to guide behaviour. If one makes a mistake, one may find one's hands tied in undesirable ways. In societies where knowledge of, and obedience to, the law is less certain, the cost of developing rule-based private law rights might not be worth the effort. Even highly sophisticated organisations usually accept that some issues are better addressed by *ex post* adjudication rather than *ex ante* rules.

The idea that a legal system's private law rights might owe their existence entirely to court orders is therefore neither incoherent nor implausible. As the basis for a general description of private law rights in contemporary common law systems, however, it is a non-starter. The obvious objection is that it leaves completely unexplained nearly the entirety of what is conventionally regarded as the law of obligations. If all legal rights are court-ordered, then the rules that appear to establish private law duties to perform contracts, refrain from trespassing, avoid nuisances, and so on must be interpreted, if they are to mean anything, as rules setting out certain of the conditions that must be satisfied if courts are to make orders. This might be thought to fit neatly with Kelsen's view that all legal rules are ultimately directions to judges. Consistent with his general approach, however, Kelsen held that for directions to courts to count as law they must be directions to apply sanctions. As already noted, orders are not sanctions. It follows that private rules cannot be interpreted as conditions for sanctions. The only other possibility is that the substantive law of obligations sets out conditions for establishing the validity of an order. But this does not work either since it is not possible to challenge a private law sanction on the ground that the order was invalid. The unavoidable conclusion is that in the model now under consideration, the vast body of apparent law on rule-based rights is simply not law.

This conclusion is not surprising. The standard jurisprudential objection to sanction-based legal theories is that they fail to explain legal norma-

---

a claimant might be able to sue a court for failing to grant an order: FH Lawson, *Many Laws: Selected Essays, Volume I* (Amsterdam, North-Holland Publishing Co, 1977) ch 8; G Samuel, '"Le Droit Subjectif" and English Law' [1987] *Cambridge Law Journal* 264.

tivity.[19] It is characteristic of law that it purports to provide citizens with moral, rather than merely prudential, reasons for action; we call legal duties 'duties' because they describe actions that, from the law's perspective, ought morally to be done. Perhaps the clearest evidence of law's normativity is found in the rules that set up rule-based duties. According to the conventional view, there are legal rules specifying that contracts should be performed, that money paid by mistake should be returned, that property should not be damaged, and so on. We have just seen that these rules have no place in a legal system in which all private law rights are court-ordered rights. This is exactly what we would expect if the justification for describing private law rights in this way is that legal duties are duties not to engage in sanction-attracting behaviour.

B. Rule-Based Rights Are Defined by Court-Ordered Rights

A second suggestion is that rule-based rights mirror precisely the orders that courts are willing to make. In this view, we have rule-based duties, but they are duties to do exactly those things that courts are willing to order defendants to do, and in exactly the circumstances that courts are willing to make such orders. In this view, then, citizens have a duty to return mistaken payments because, and only because, courts are willing to order citizens who fail to return mistaken payments to do just this. It also follows from this view that, exceptional cases aside, contractual duties are always duties to pay money.

This second suggestion fits neatly with the idea that the common law was originally a law of remedies. If the law of rule-based rights developed out of the law of court orders, it might be thought natural that the former would be defined in terms of the latter. A related point is that a clear advantage of defining rule-based rights in terms of the availability of court orders is that it is then relatively easy to determine what rule-based rights we enjoy. Although it remains necessary to wade through lengthy decisions to determine on what facts a right arises, the content of our rights will be clear from the orders that courts make. If a court orders a defendant to do X, we know that the defendant was under a duty to do X. Neither of these observations, however, demonstrates that rule-based rights *must* be defined in terms of the availability of court orders. Nor is there any rule or principle to this effect in the positive law. Judges regularly distinguish the rule-based rights that claimants enjoy prior to coming to court from the court-ordered rights with which they leave. As already mentioned, judges regularly say there is a duty to per-

---

[19] HLA Hart, *The Concept of Law* (Oxford, Oxford University Press, 1961) 20–49; J Raz, *Practical Reasons and Norms*, 2nd edn (Oxford, Oxford University Press, 1990) 154–62.

form contractual promises and regularly refuse to order the performance of contractual promises.

It is sometimes thought that the sanction-based theories of law discussed above define rule-based rights in terms of the availability of court orders. Court orders are often described as 'sanctions'[20] and sanction theories define legal duties as duties to avoid behaviour to which the law attaches sanctions. Holmes' famous description of the law as 'prophecies of what the courts will do in fact'[21] appears to support this interpretation since the obvious thing that courts do 'in fact' is make orders. As we have already seen, however, to the extent that sanction theories are interested in court orders, they are (or at least should be) interested in orders to legal officials rather than performative orders. Neither Austin nor Kelsen makes this clear (perhaps because they focused primarily on criminal law examples, where court orders typically are sanction-imposing). Holmes, however, correctly noted that the prophecies that mattered in his account were prophecies about the likelihood of a court imposing 'disagreeable consequences by way of imprisonment or compulsory payment of money.'[22]

In the case of non-monetary performative orders, the distinction between the order and the sanction is clear: the standard sanction for failing to comply with an injunction or specific performance order is imprisonment, and this sanction is only imposed after a separate hearing before a court. In the case of monetary orders, the distinction is less obvious. The typical sanction for not complying with a monetary order is that the defendant's property is seized and sold to satisfy the judgment. To initiate execution, a claimant must make an application, but it is not normally necessary to go before a judge. Writs of execution are typically issued by a legal official on production of the appropriate documents; the entire process is usually very simple. In the case of monetary orders, therefore, although the order and the sanction are formally separate, it can at least be said that the sanction follows directly from, and its contents are directly defined by, the performative order. Yet, even if it were accepted for the sake of argument that monetary orders are effectively sanctions,[23] it does not follow that sanction theories regard the availability of such orders as defining the *content* of rule-based rights. Neither Austin nor Kelsen supposed that the content of legal duties is determined by the content of the sanction for breaching the duty. For both, it was sufficient for a duty to exist that there be *a* sanction, but it was not necessary that the sanction have any

[20] FH Lawson, *Remedies of English Law*, 2nd edn (London, Butterworths, 1980) 12–14.
[21] Holmes, above n 10, at 461.
[22] ibid.
[23] Which they are not: see above n 12. Nonetheless, Holmes appears to have assumed that a monetary order is a sanction.

substantive connection to the duty. In Austin's words, 'the magnitude of the evil, and the magnitude of the chance of incurring it, are foreign to the matter in question [ie, the definition of a duty]'.[24]

Holmes took a different position. For Holmes, the availability of a monetary order (but not a non-monetary order[25]) not only established that citizens were under legal duties in the circumstances that gave rise to the order, but also determined the content of those duties. This is why he described the duty to keep a contract as 'a prediction that you must pay damages if you do not keep it,—and nothing else.'[26] Hart's observation that sanction theories fail to explain how legal duties are presented, used, and understood by legal officials (namely as normative directions) applies with particular force to the Holmesian extension of Austin and Kelsen's approach. Austin and Kelsen could at least say that they focused on sanctions only in order to distinguish legal from non-legal duties. For Holmes, our duties are effectively duties to do whatever is required by the law's sanctions. It is difficult to find anyone who will defend this position today.[27] Holmes' own arguments do not support his conclusion. Holmes' justification for focusing on sanctions is that sanctions are what people care about when they think about the law.[28] An obvious objection is that sanctions in the form of the seizure of property will not matter to citizens who have no property. Do we say, then, that impecunious citizens have no private law duties save those whose breach could lead to imprisonment? A more general objection is that the theory assumes an implausible view of human nature. No doubt most people do care about sanctions and no doubt some people—Holmes' famous 'bad men'—care only about sanctions. But it is clear that some people regard the law, at least some of the time, as providing the moral reasons for action that it purports to provide.[29] Numerous empirical studies confirm the common-

---

[24] Austin, above n 14, at 23.

[25] Holmes sensibly did not attempt to argue that the defendant's duty in situations where she was liable to have a non-monetary order made against her was to imprison or fine herself: above n 10, at 461.

[26] ibid, at 462.

[27] Even writers who argue that sanctions should play a significant role in any general theory of law do not argue that legal duties are defined by the availability of sanctions: see, eg, F Schauer, 'Was Austin Right After All? On the Role of Sanctions in a Theory of Law' (2010) 23 *Ratio Juris* 1; N Stavropoulos, 'The Relevance of Coercion: Some Preliminaries' (2009) 22 *Ratio Juris* 339; G Lamond, 'Coercion and the Nature of Law' (2001) 7 *Legal Theory* 35.

[28] Holmes, above n 10, at 457:

> People want to know under what circumstances and how far they will run the risk of coming against what is so much stronger than themselves, and hence it becomes a business to find out when this danger is to be feared. The object of our study, then, is prediction, the prediction of the incidence of the public force through the instrumentality of the courts.

[29] I discuss the implications of this fact for understanding private law in more detail in SA Smith, 'The Normativity of Private Law' (2011) 31 *Oxford Journal of Legal Studies* 215.

sense observation that some people obey the law just because it is the law.[30] Thus, even if our concern is solely with how the law influences behaviour, there is no justification for defining legal duties in terms of the likelihood of sanctions.

C. All Court-Ordered Rights Replicate Rule-Based Rights

A third suggestion supposes the exact opposite relationship between rule-based rights and court orders as the previous suggestion. According to this view, court orders merely confirm or 'rubber-stamp' already-existing rule-based rights. In every case, the court's job is to determine whether the defendant was in breach of a rule-based duty owed to the claimant and, if this is the case, to order the defendant to perform that duty. Court orders, in this view, merely direct defendants to do what the general law already required them to do. It follows from this view that, while rule-based rights are not derived from court orders, the availability of a court order is proof that a rule-based right exists, and the content of the order reflects the content of the duty.

Judges clearly assume that many court orders fit the rubber-stamp model. When courts order performance of a contractual obligation, when they order trespassers to vacate land, and when they make injunctions against nuisances or torts, they assume that they are ordering defendants to do the very thing that the defendants' rule-based duties already required them to do. The rubber-stamp view is also a prima facie attractive account of the role of court orders. From the courts' perspective, rule-based duties by definition should be performed. By authoritatively ordering that they be performed, courts can eliminate any uncertainty regarding their existence or content. Court orders that replicate existing duties can also motivate defendants to comply with those duties by providing them with a clear, public, and authoritative reminder. Finally, replicative orders provide a natural basis on which enforcement may proceed. As we have noted, enforcement in practice means enforcement of court orders. On the reasonable assumption that the primary role of enforcement is to ensure that claimants receive what was due to them, it might seem to follow that the orders that the law enforces should be orders directing that this happen.

These and other arguments in support of replicative orders are exam-

---

[30] See especially TR Tyler, *Why People Obey the Law* (New Haven, Yale University Press, 1990). Tyler summarises previous studies as follows: 'Although the studies examined differ in many ways ... they all reinforce the conclusion that normative support for the system leads to compliant behaviour': at 37–38. See also PH Robinson and JM Darley, 'The Utility of Desert' (1997) 91 *Northwestern University Law Review* 453, 468–71; A Licht, 'Social Norms and the Law: Why Peoples Obey the Law' (2008) 4 *Review of Law and Economics* 3.

ined in more detail in part III. For the present, it is sufficient to note that there is no legal rule or principle in the common law that requires courts to limit themselves to making replicative orders, and that in practice courts regularly make orders that differ from their understanding of the parties' rule-based rights. Courts do this, for example, when they order damages in lieu of specific performance, make an award of punitive damages, declare a remedial constructive trust, or refuse to order the payment of a time-expired debt.

Might it be argued that judges are just confused when they say that there are duties to perform non-monetary contractual promises and so on? The argument can, of course, be made, but not without assuming what the argument is meant to prove, namely that the availability of a court order is proof of a rule-based right. Admittedly, it might be possible in a few cases to show, without saying anything about court orders, that judges are confused when they assume that a particular rule-based right exists. In the case of duties to perform non-monetary contractual promises, for example, it might be argued that such promises are in fact understood by those who make them to be disjunctive promises to perform the promised act or to pay to the promisee the value of performance. On this basis, it might be argued that, regardless of what courts say, an order to pay damages in lieu of an order to perform an outstanding non-monetary contractual obligation is a replicative order. But it is highly unlikely that it could be shown that judges are consistently confused when they say that a court order does not replicate a rule-based right without relying on an argument that assumes we already know how court orders are related to rule-based rights. On what basis—other than the fact that courts refuse to make orders once a limitation period has expired—could it be argued that courts are mistaken to believe that limitation periods do not extinguish rule-based rights? On what basis—other than the fact that courts are willing to order punitive damages—could it be argued that courts are mistaken to assume that there are no rule-based duties to pay such damages? In short, for the rubber-stamp view to be necessarily true, or even for it to be true in practice, it must be the case that our rule-based rights are determined by the availability of court orders. This possibility has already been rejected.

D. All Rule-Based Rights Are Supported by Court Orders and All Court Orders Support Rule-Based Rights

The previous two suggestions argued for a one-to-one link between rule-based rights and court orders, such that for every right an identical court order is available, and vice versa. The final suggestion, or more strictly final pair of suggestions, supposes a less direct, though still necessary, connection between rule-based rights and court orders. According to what I will call the 'weak' thesis, although the content of rule-based rights and court orders may diverge, it is necessarily the case that every time a rule-based right is infringed[31] the right-holder has a right to *a* court order and, further, every time a court makes an order *a* rule-based right held by the claimant has been infringed. If the weak thesis is true, therefore, while it would not be possible to say anything about the content of rule-based rights from the availability of court orders, we can at least say that the claimant enjoys or enjoyed[32] a rule-based right against the defendant in any case where an order is made or could have been made.

The two halves of the weak thesis are best examined separately.

(i) For Every Right, a Court Order

The idea that rights infringements always give rise to rights to court orders is the natural and easiest-to-satisfy interpretation of the maxim 'where there's a right there's a remedy'. As we have already noted, however, this interpretation is inconsistent with what courts themselves say, as, for example, when they say that limitation periods do not extinguish rule-based duties but do extinguish the possibility of obtaining a court order.[33] It is also surprisingly difficult to find anyone who has explicitly argued that rule-based rights must be supported by court orders.

It might be thought, yet again, that the ideas of the sanction theorists, in particular Kelsen and Austin, could be used to construct such an argument. Although performative orders are not sanctions, a sanction cannot be imposed unless a court has first made a performative order. It might seem to follow that insofar as legal wrongs are defined, following Kelsen and Austin, as behaviour for which legal sanctions are available, court orders must necessarily be available in respect of any legal wrong. If committing a legal wrong necessarily makes one liable to a sanction, and if a

---

[31] An 'infringement', as understood here, includes both a past wrong (eg, a battery) and an ongoing failure to perform an obligation (eg, a failure to pay a debt). The weak thesis thus allows for the possibility that the response to a rights infringement may be an order to act in compliance with the right and/or an order to do something else.

[32] 'Enjoyed' because the weak thesis allows for the possibility that an order might be made in a case where, although the defendant is not currently in breach of a duty to the claimant, the defendant previously breached such a duty. Suppose that the defendant was late delivering contractually promised goods, but the delay caused no loss or injury. On these facts, a claimant would normally be granted an order of nominal damages. If it were the case that court orders necessarily replicated rule-based rights, then to explain such orders we would need to say that the defendant was under a duty to pay nominal damages from the moment of breach. The weak thesis, by contrast, allows for the possibility that the duty to pay nominal damages was created by the order.

[33] Another example is a contractual obligation that is unenforceable (but not invalid) for want of a formality. Section 4 of the Statute of Frauds 1677, for example, states merely that 'no action shall be brought' on a contract not in writing. The Statute does not say that the contract is invalid.

sanction cannot be imposed unless a court first makes an order, it seems to follow that legal wrongs must give rise to rights to orders.

Even if one accepts the discredited idea that legal duties are defined by the availability of sanctions, this reasoning is flawed. The first objection is that it is not necessary in any conceptual sense for courts to make performative orders before they, or a legal official, impose a sanction. Although this appears to be the practice in contemporary common law systems, one could easily imagine a legal system in which courts had the authority, on proof that a defendant committed a legal wrong, to immediately order legal officials to sanction the defendant, for example by seizing the defendant's property. Criminal courts do this when they order a defendant to be imprisoned. The second, more fundamental objection is that a court order is not merely a prerequisite to the imposition of a sanction, but also specifies the behaviour that triggers the sanction's availability. As we have already noted, civil defendants are only liable to be imprisoned or to have their property seized if they have failed to comply with a performative order. This line of reasoning therefore leads straight to the argument rejected earlier that all private law rights are court-ordered rights.

Are there any other grounds on which a necessary connection, even if only a weak necessary connection, between rights and orders might be established? The only other possibility appears to be that it is just part of the concept of a legal duty that the courts are bound to recognise legal duties by making orders when they are breached. This is what is presumably meant when it is said that the defining feature of a legal, as opposed to a merely moral, duty is that it is enforced in the courts or, more weakly, that it can be 'realised' in the courts.[34] The suggestion is prima facie appealing. The only official 'act' that courts perform when they adjudicate disputes is to make or not make an order. The courts' reasons are just that—reasons. If legal duties are legal because they are recognised as such by the legal system, and if the only way that courts can provide official recognition is by making a court order, it might seem to follow that legal duties exist only if claimants can obtain court orders when they have been breached. Nonetheless, the suggestion must be rejected for the basic reason that it cannot be part of the concept of a legal duty that orders must be available for the breach of a duty if legal officials themselves deny that this is the case. Our concepts of law and of legal duties are formed by those who participate in the practice of law, in particular by legal officials. As I have noted several times, courts regularly acknowledge the existence of legal duties for which orders are unavailable. If the courts themselves say that legal rights exist that they will not enforce by

---

[34] 'Private law is above all concerned with rights which, one against another, people are able to realise in courts': P Birks, *English Private Law* (Oxford, Oxford University Press, 2000) xxxvi.

making an order, then it can hardly be said that the legal system does not recognise rights other than those enforceable by orders.

(ii) For Every Court Order, a Right

The counterpart to the idea that for every right there is a remedy (ie, an order) is the idea that for every remedy there is a right. Like the previous suggestion, this is an intuitively appealing idea. Although court orders are not sanctions, they can lead to sanctions if they are disobeyed. It follows that potential addressees of court orders have good reasons to defend themselves against legal suits initiated by the potential beneficiaries of such orders. Defending oneself in court requires time and money. Exceptional cases aside, citizens should not be required to undertake such efforts unless, at a minimum, they are alleged to have done something wrong. Law-abiding citizens should be able to determine their legal duties, and so plan their lives, without having to go to court. If court orders can be made without proof of failure to comply with a legal duty, this principle is compromised. The state, for its part, also has reasons not to give courts powers to make orders without proof of a rights infringement. Compared to rules, court orders are an inefficient way to guide behaviour, especially the behaviour of large groups.[35]

These are important considerations. Nonetheless, it is clear that there is no legal rule or principle that prevents courts from making orders in cases where there is no proof of an actual or threatened rights infringement. Most common law countries have legislation that allows courts to make orders in family law disputes involving custody, maintenance or division of property without proof or even an allegation of wrongdoing.[36] The usual justification for such authority is that it is difficult, if not impossible, to fashion a rule sufficiently flexible and fine-grained to deal with all possible contingencies.

The merits of such orders (or at least the merits of relying on courts to make them) may be questioned, but there is no basis on which it could be said that it is not possible for courts to make orders where no right was infringed or threatened. One might try to argue, following Holmes, that wherever an order is made, a duty can be inferred, but this runs into the objection that when courts are given the authority to grant orders

---

[35] Assuming that court orders are awarded only on the basis of publicly available rules, these defects are less serious in practice than might be thought because citizens can adjust their behaviour in reliance on the rules.

[36] See, eg, s 15.2(1) of the Divorce Act, RSC 1985, c 3 (2nd Supp), which states that a court may 'on application by either or both spouses, make an order requiring a spouse to secure or pay, or to secure and pay, such lump sum or periodic sums, or such lump sum and periodic sums, as the court thinks reasonable for the support of the other spouse.' See also s 16(1) of the same Act, and the Family Relations Act, RSBC 1996, c 128. Most constitutive orders can also be made without proof of wrongdoing.

without proof of wrongdoing, such authority is typically accompanied by wide discretion as to both the availability and the content of the order. Indeed, it is precisely because of the difficulty of fashioning a general rule that the courts are given such discretion. For example, a typical family law statute dealing with custody might require the courts to do no more than take into account 'the best interests of the child' in fashioning its order. Where courts are given wide discretion of this kind, it is extremely difficult to make propositions about the nature of citizens' rule-based rights by reasoning backwards from the likelihood of an order being made.

E. No Necessary Link

The conclusion to be drawn from the preceding observations is that there is no necessary connection between rule-based rights and court orders. Rule-based rights may, but need not, reflect or give rise to court orders, and court orders may, but need not, reflect or arise from rule-based rights. As a matter of positive law, we know this because courts often distinguish the orders they make from claimants' rule-based rights. As a matter of legal theory, the answer is more complex, but the general explanation (which I elaborate below) is that the rules that give rise to rule-based rights and the orders that give rise to court-ordered rights perform different roles in our legal system. The law governing the existence and content of rule-based rights is directed fundamentally at citizens; this law tells citizens how they are meant to behave in their interactions with other citizens. The law governing court-ordered rights is directed fundamentally at courts; this law tells the courts what they should do when a citizen approaches them with a complaint or other request.

III. WHY DO COURTS MAKE ORDERS (AND WHY DO THEY MAKE THE ORDERS THEY MAKE)?

The preceding discussion rejected the possibility of a necessary connection between rule-based rights and court orders, but it did not reject the possibility that we can learn something about rule-based rights by examining court orders. To the contrary, we identified a number of reasons for which a legal system that recognised rule-based rights might want to make or not make court orders. In what follows, I examine these and other reasons in a more systematic fashion. All of the reasons that I discuss are justificatory, that is to say, they are reasons a court might invoke if asked to justify why it made or did not make a particular order. This does not mean that they are persuasive justifications. My aim in this chapter is to understand what courts are doing when they make orders. This task requires that we consider the kinds of reasons that might plausibly motivate a court, regardless of their merits.

The discussion is organised around three reasons that courts might make court orders and three reasons that they might refuse to make an order, or at least refuse to make a particular kind or order. I believe that each reason has influenced the positive law, but beyond offering a few examples, I leave the task of demonstrating that influence to another time. The primary aim of the present discussion is to provide a broad overview of the kinds of considerations that might be expected to influence courts when they make orders.

(A) Three Reasons to Make Orders

(i) Support Rule-Based Rights

The rules that set out rule-based rights do not always achieve their goal of guiding citizens' behaviour. Assuming that it is still possible to perform the relevant duty, one way the state might respond to non-compliance is to threaten non-complying citizens with sanctions if they continue not to comply. But another, simpler way is just to tell them, personally, to perform their duties. At first blush, this suggestion is puzzling: why would merely *telling* someone to do something that, by definition, they were already told to do, have any effect? The explanation lies in the different ways that legal rules and legal orders provide guidance. Rules are abstract statements, addressed to the population at large, specifying how citizens should behave in such and such general circumstances. Precisely because they are general instructions, legal rules are effective tools for guiding the behaviour of large groups of people in a wide range of circumstances. But for the same reason, they often have weak motivational force on particular individuals in specific circumstances. It is relatively easy to rationalise that a rule does not apply to one's own circumstances. It is also relatively easy to ignore a rule. Orders, which are personalised directives that publicly and authoritatively remind individual citizens of their duties, are difficult to rationalise away or ignore. For citizens who are inclined to obey the law on normative grounds but who may lack the will to do so on their own, orders can act something like the voice of their conscience: orders bring home in a clear and vivid way what the law expects the defendant to do. Similarly, for citizens who care only about the law's sanctions, orders provide a vivid and clear reminder of what they must do in order to avoid those sanctions. This is why nearly all rule-issuing authorities, legal or otherwise, supplement their rules with orders. Continuing with the parenting analogy mentioned earlier, making an order is often a good way to motivate a child to do the very thing required by a previously announced rule.

This first rationale for making court orders calls for orders that confirm defendants' already-existing rule-based duties, for example, an order that requires a defendant to deliver contractually promised goods.

(ii) Specify Rule-Based Rights

Because a rule is a general direction, there will inevitably be circumstances where it is not clear if the rule applies or, if it does, what behaviour it requires. The law cannot effectively guide citizens' behaviour unless they know what the law requires them to do. Nor is it fair to impose sanctions on citizens for non-compliance in cases where the citizen could not reasonably have known what was required in advance. A second natural role for court orders is therefore to provide an authoritative specification of the meaning of rule-based rights.[37]

The obvious way for a court to specify the content of a rule-based right is to make a declaration, but it is not the only way. Performative orders can also be used to specify rights. Like a declaration, a performative order specifies what the defendant is legally required to do. Whichever form of order is used, declaratory or performative, if the order is intended to specify the content of a duty, then the order's content should be, as in the previous case, the same as the content of the duty.

(iii) Create New Rights

We saw in part II that it is possible to imagine a legal system in which all private law rights are court-ordered rights. The contemporary common law is not, for good reasons, like this, but it would not be surprising to find that courts sometimes use orders to create new rights. There appear to be two broad categories of cases in which we might expect, or at least not be surprised to find, that this happens. Each raises difficult justificatory issues.

(a) New Rights Created Because the Desired Behaviour Cannot Be Stipulated by a Rule

A legal authority that wants to enact directives for the purpose of guiding its subjects' behaviour would normally be expected to try to do this, in the first instance anyway, by passing rules rather than making individual orders. Orders may provide a useful backup where a rule fails to motivate, but rules have obvious advantages where the goal is to guide large numbers of people. There are certain situations, however, where it is not

---

[37] This is roughly Immanuel Kant's argument for adjudication: I Kant, *The Metaphysics of Morals* (M Gregor tr and ed, Cambridge, Cambridge University Press, 1996) para 6:312. Kant's position is explained and defended in A Ripstein, *Force and Freedom* (Cambridge MA, Harvard University Press, 2009) 168–76.

possible, or at least not practical, to use a rule to guide behaviour. Many of these cases will be of no interest to the law. But with respect to some of these cases it seems possible that courts might choose to use orders, standing alone, to guide behaviour.

One situation where legal rules are an impractical method for guiding behaviour is where the subjects whose behaviour the law-maker wishes to guide cannot reasonably be expected to obtain the information that, according to the rule, is meant to determine how they should act. Consider, for example, the rules that currently govern the quantification of damages for consequential losses. If these rules are meant to be directed at citizens, that is to say, if they are meant to inform citizens what they should do in the case where they have committed a legal wrong, they raise an obvious problem. Nearly all the evidence that determines whether a breach has been committed and, more importantly, that determines the existence and magnitude of the consequential losses attendant to that breach will be known only to the victim. Of course, the victim may well provide the evidence to the wrongdoer. But the victim may also want nothing further to do with the wrongdoer. And what if the wrongdoer has questions about the victim's evidence? What is the standard of proof required? Must the victim provide expert witnesses, and so on? In practice, victims and wrongdoers are often able to agree on an appropriate level of damages. But in principle it seems inappropriate, and in practice unworkable, to have a rule that requires wrongdoers to do things that can only be established on the basis of information provided by their victims. This problem does not arise, however, if the duty is created by a court order. A court is an appropriate and competent institution for gathering and assessing the kind of evidence required by the rules for quantifying consequential damages.

Clearly, there are limits to the kinds of court-ordered rights that judges might reasonably want to create on this basis. For example, in the case of rights not to be harmed (eg, a right not to be assaulted), it would be impractical to attempt to guide the relevant behaviour solely by passing orders because the harm will normally have already happened by the time the parties get to court. Standing alone, court orders are normally only appropriate for guiding behaviour that is not time-sensitive. The payment of damages for consequential losses is one example. It might be ideal that damages for consequential losses be paid immediately on injury, but it is not strictly necessary. It might also reasonably be thought inappropriate to permit courts to make onerous performative orders against defendants who have done nothing wrong. It might be thought that only wrongdoers should be liable in this way. Again, an order requiring payment of consequential damages or, indeed, damages of any kind, would pass this test.

A second, more straightforward situation where a rule may not be a practical means of guiding behaviour is where, because of the complexity of the relevant facts and/or the rarity with which they arise, the costs of framing an appropriate rule outweigh the benefits. For example, it might be very costly, if not impossible, to fashion a rule that specifies in advance the amount of maintenance appropriate between separated spouses, or to fashion a rule that specifies how separated partners should share child-rearing duties. It might be thought that every case is unique and that the best that can be done is to give courts a list of factors to take into account and then to ask them to use their judgment. Of course, if this leads to courts being besieged by parties seeking orders, it might be better to live with an imperfect rule.

In addition to the concerns already mentioned (eg, the time-sensitivity of the relevant behaviour), the possibility of employing right-creating orders in lieu of difficult-to-frame rules raises a further justificatory issue. If orders are to be used for this purpose, then by definition the courts will need to have considerable discretion over the existence and content of the relevant orders. The practice of making such orders will therefore conflict with the principle of the rule of law. At the same time, it seems inevitable that some disputes that the state will want to resolve can, practically, only be resolved by individualised directives. The real question is whether courts are the proper institutions to perform such a task. There is also the question of whether it is appropriate to cloak discretionary decision-making of this kind with the mantle of law. For the present, however, it is sufficient to note that it is possible for court orders to be used in just this way, and that it would be surprising if that opportunity was never taken up.

(b) New Rights Created to Give Effect to 'State-Based' Reasons: Vindicatory Orders

A second situation in which a court might wish to use an order to create a new right is where the court wants to give effect to what I will loosely call 'state-based reasons'. In broad terms, the possibility of using orders to give effect to state-based reasons arises because when a court orders a defendant to perform an action, the action, when performed, can carry a different meaning from where the action is required by virtue of a general rule. The clearest example, albeit from the criminal law, is an order to pay a fine or to do something else intended as a punishment. Part of the reason that the payment of a fine is regarded as a punishment is because the payment will have been required by an order, rather than a rule.[38] Where a payment to the state is required by a general rule, directed at citizens, it will be regarded as a tax or something similar. The reason fines

---

[38] The judge who imposes the fine is likely to be following a rule, but my point is that there is no rule, directed at citizens, that requires the citizen to pay the fine prior to a court making an order.

are not imposed by rules arises from an important difference in the legal meanings of rules and orders. From the law's perspective, legal rules are meant to give citizens moral guidance; they are meant to specify actions that, from the law's perspective, are morally obligatory.[39] Another way of stating this is that legal rules are meant to reflect reasons that already apply to their subjects. Thus, the legal explanation for why there is a rule requiring that contracting parties perform their contracts is that, morally, they ought to be performed. So too the legal justification for the rule prohibiting assault is that assault is wrong. This is not to deny that legal rules often are intended to make indeterminate moral duties determinate, nor does it presume that the law upholds all moral duties. The point is merely that a legal rule is presented as based on reasons, even if sometimes very general reasons, that apply already to those subject to them.

As we have seen, court orders often carry a similar meaning. The content of an order to perform a contract is justified, from the law's perspective, on the same basis as the rule that contracts should be performed, namely that the law regards it as morally obligatory to perform a contract. The court order to perform, like the anterior rule, is meant to reflect reasons that already apply to the subject. In contrast to rules, however, court orders need not carry this meaning. It is not part of the concept of a court order, as it is of a legal rule, that it is meant to reflect reasons that apply to the subject. As the example of an order to pay a fine demonstrates, an order may be based on reasons that do not apply to the subject. In particular, court orders are sometimes based on reasons that are, broadly speaking, state-based, for example an interest in ensuring that wrongdoers are punished. There may be a good reason that a defendant who breaks the law should pay a fine, but that reason is not one that already applied to the subject. A fine is not meant to confirm or make determinate an already existing moral duty, inchoate or otherwise, to pay money to the state. No theory of punishment supposes that we have moral duties to punish ourselves.

Because of this difference between rules and orders, we might expect courts to occasionally make orders so as to give effect to state-based reasons. More specifically, I suggest we might expect courts sometimes to make orders that have the aim, broadly speaking, of 'vindicating' the claimant's rights. The intentionally loose idea of vindication is meant to capture what a court is doing when its primary aim is to make clear either that a right exists, that the right is important, that the defendant's behaviour was wrongful, that the consequences of infringing the right were serious, or some or all of the above. These are state-based reasons, in the loose sense in which I am using this term, because they are not

[39] See J Raz, *Ethics in the Public Domain: Essays in the Morality of Law and Politics* (Oxford, Oxford University Press, 1994) 210–20.

based on the court's view of what the defendant has a moral obligation to do, but instead on the state's interest in things like informing citizens of their rights, deterring undesirable behaviour, assuaging frustration, avoiding vengeance, and quelling public unrest. Whether such aims justify making substantive orders is debatable. But given how frequently judges mention such aims in their judgments, it would be surprising if they were not given effect occasionally.

In most cases, whatever interest the state may have in vindicating rights will be satisfied by ordering defendants to respect the relevant rights and/or by ordering defendants to pay compensatory damages for any losses suffered from the failure to respect those rights.[40] Thus, in most cases courts that want to vindicate rights do not need to do anything they would not have done for other reasons. But there are at least two situations where it might be thought that the otherwise available orders are insufficient to vindicate the claimants' rights. The first is where a past breach caused no loss or where the loss was cured. Short of ordering the defendant to apologise,[41] there appears to be no basis, in such a case, on which a court could make a 'non-vindicatory' order.[42] Of course, a court could simply explain in its decision that the defendant's rights were infringed. But the vindicatory message will be much stronger if it is communicated by making a court order in favour of the claimant. Court orders are official legal acts. On this basis, we might expect courts to be willing to make symbolic orders in the form of declarations or orders to pay nominal damages in cases where the claimant's rights have been infringed, but no other order is available.

The other situation where it might be thought that ordinary orders are insufficient to vindicate the claimant's rights is where the actions prescribed by the order appear trivial in comparison to the callousness of the defendant's behaviour or the nature of the claimant's injury. In such cases, a court might plausibly think that the only way to make clear the importance of the right, the egregiousness of the defendant's behaviour and/or the seriousness of the claimant's injury is to make a further substantive award. Awards ordering punitive damages or damages for pain and

---

[40] To avoid complications, I am accepting without argument the conventional view that compensatory damages—by which I mean damages quantified by reference to direct or consequential pecuniary losses—are not vindicatory. Some writers, including two contributors to this volume (Benjamin Zipursky and John Goldberg), regard all damages as essentially vindicatory: see B Zipursky, 'Civil Recourse, Not Corrective Justice' (2002) 91 *Georgetown Law Journal* 695, 726–29; JCP Goldberg and BC Zipursky, 'Torts as Wrongs' (2010) 88 *Texas Law Review* 917. This view is consistent with, but not required by, the above account of vindicatory orders.

[41] An order to apologise could plausibly be interpreted as non-vindicatory because it might reasonably be assumed that the defendant in such a case had moral reasons to apologise.

[42] This problem is not solved by a rule stipulating that every rights infringement gives rise to a duty to pay nominal damages, because in this case a rights infringer can avoid official condemnation by paying the nominal sum.

suffering might be explained in this way (though alternative explanations are possible[43]). In each case, the award might plausibly be interpreted as essentially symbolic.

There are obvious objections to symbolic awards that achieve their symbolism by imposing significant burdens on a defendant. The symbolism is achieved at the defendant's expense. It may well be, as many believe, that if such orders are made at all, they should only be made following a criminal trial. Still, it would not be surprising if civil courts occasionally made such awards. A civil court that wants either to condemn a defendant's behaviour or to make clear the defendant's responsibility for the claimant's suffering has few other options.

B. Three Reasons Not to Make Orders

We have seen the main reason for courts to make court orders is that orders can do useful things that rules cannot do or cannot do as well. It should be no surprise, then, to find that orders sometimes do things that rules cannot (or do not) do that are not useful. Three examples are discussed below.

(i) Orders Are Costly

It may well be, as many writers believe, that economic considerations should play no role when courts are determining citizens' rule-based rights. But the question of what the courts should do to assist in giving effect to those rights is different. Justice is a public good, but so are roads and schools. It seems entirely legitimate and unexceptional for courts to say to claimants, 'we will help you, but not at any cost'. It is unexceptional, in other words, for courts to say that the defendant is or was in breach of a duty owed to the claimant, but then to add that in the circumstances the state is unwilling to expend resources to do anything about the breach.

It is an important fact about court orders, therefore, that they are costly. This is true not of the actual orders themselves, but of the steps that litigants and courts must go through prior to making an order. Those costs typically increase if a claimant delays before bringing a claim. Memories fade, witnesses disappear, and evidence generally goes stale. On this basis, courts might be expected to refuse to make orders—any orders—if the claimant has waited too long before asserting his or her rights. Or they might penalise a claimant by substituting a monetary order for a non-monetary order in the way described in the previous section. The costs of

---

[43] For example, it might be argued that these awards are designed to compensate for difficult-to-assess, but real, losses.

making orders might also be expected to lead courts to refuse to entertain applications for orders in respect of trivial rights infringements.

(ii) Orders Are the Basis for Enforcement

It is not necessary to define legal duties in terms of the availability of sanctions to see the practical need for sanctions in any real-life legal system. Whatever justification is given for rule-based duties (individual rights, utility, etc), the justification will be frustrated unless means exist to compel unwilling citizens to perform their duties (eg, by threat of punishment) or, in cases which allow, to allow the duty to be executed by a third party (eg, by using the defendant's assets to satisfy a monetary duty).

As we have seen, performative court orders are not enforcement orders. Enforcement, if it happens, comes later when the state seizes the defendant's property to satisfy a monetary judgment or throws the defendant in jail to compel the performance of a non-monetary duty. In contemporary common law systems, however, orders and enforcement are closely linked. The enforcement process is triggered by the breach of a court order, not the breach of a rule-based right. In addition, it is the court order, not the rule-based right, that is enforced. In the case of monetary orders, enforcement takes the form of seizing and selling the defendant's assets in order to satisfy—and only satisfy—the sum owed by virtue of the order. In the case of non-monetary orders, enforcement takes the form of imprisoning or (more rarely) fining the defendant for the primary purpose of compelling him or her to comply with the order. We could imagine a system that severed this link. For example, we could imagine a system in which court orders always replicated rule-based rights, but where enforcement proceeded on the basis of a different set of orders. Thus, a court might order a defendant to perform a contractual promise to build a house, but then, when it came time for enforcement, order an enforcement official to seize such assets as required to give the claimant funds to hire an alternative builder. This is not, however, how the common law evolved and at this point it would be costly and inconvenient to introduce a further stage in the litigation process.

Because of the structural link between orders and enforcement it is inevitable and reasonable for courts to think about enforcement when they make orders. Prima facie, this introduces no new considerations since one would expect that the rights the law wants to enforce are the same rights that it otherwise wants to confirm by orders. But in practice, the link to enforcement raises a new issue. Enforcement is costly. To proceed with enforcement, it is necessary to determine if the order has been breached and, if it has, to take steps to execute or compel performance. For this reason, courts might be expected to consider whether the orders they make give rise to significant enforcement costs and, if so, what alternatives might be available. On this basis, a court might, for example, decide to substitute a monetary order for a non-monetary order, particularly in cases where the defendant can use the money to obtain substitute performance. It is relatively simple to determine if a monetary order has been satisfied: the only issue is whether the defendant has paid over a sum of money. By contrast, to determine if a non-monetary order has been satisfied, something close to a new trial may be required, particularly if the order is to perform a service. A second advantage of monetary orders is that they are relatively easy to enforce by seizing or otherwise taking control over the defendant's assets. By contrast, the only practical way to enforce most non-monetary obligations is to imprison the defendant. Aside from the fact that this may not work (and so leave the claimant empty-handed), the legal system rightly requires a separate trial before a defendant can be imprisoned. And prisons are expensive. On the other hand, many non-monetary obligations, particularly if they involve performing a service or transferring fungible property, can easily be performed by third parties. In these cases, money is a reasonable substitute for direct performance.[44]

These brief observations have significant implications for understanding rule-based rights. Monetary orders are the norm in the common law. Moreover, they are the norm in a number of situations where, if one knew nothing of the orders available, one would assume that the defendant's rule-based duty was non-monetary. A defendant who has failed to perform a contractual promise, or failed to return mistakenly transferred property, or failed to return property that was lent to him or her is in most cases only liable to be ordered to pay a sum of money. On this basis, it is often assumed that the defendant's rule-based duty is in every case a monetary duty. An alternative explanation is that the order in such cases replaces a non-monetary rule-based duty with a monetary court-ordered duty.

(iii) Orders Are Personalised Directions from the State

Even where court orders replicate rule-based rights, their legal effect is to extinguish whatever rule-based rights the claimant brought to court and to replace them with the rights announced in the court order. Thus, while the explanation for why the defendant owes the claimant a sum of money prior to the order might be, say, that the defendant purchased goods from the claimant, the explanation after the order is made is that the defendant was ordered to pay the money. It is necessary that court orders have this effect lest the defendant be subject to conflicting duties and, more generally, to remove any debate as to the content of the defendant's future duty.

---

[44] I discuss the practice of granting monetary orders in lieu of specific relief in more detail in SA Smith, 'Substitutionary Damages' in CEF Rickett (ed), *Justifying Private Law Remedies* (Oxford, Hart Publishing, 2008) 93.

The novation of rule-based rights by court-ordered rights can, however, change the way that the right is viewed. Even where a court-ordered right exactly replicates a rule-based right, the right is different, or at least may be viewed differently, because it is court-ordered. A court order is just that—an order. In Western cultures, orders from the state carry special meanings. For historical reasons, orders to perform personal services, in particular, carry special meanings. Specifically, they are associated with ideas of servitude. Even where such orders do no more than order defendants to do what they already agreed to do, they carry a different meaning from a general rule to the effect that contractual obligations should be performed. An order is a command from the state, directed to a specific individual, the non-performance of which may lead directly to state sanctions. The rules that establish rule-based duties are abstract guidelines, communicated to the population at large, the non-performance of which is not directly sanctioned.

I have noted twice before that courts often have the option, when considering a request for a non-monetary order, to order a near-substitute monetary order. It would not be surprising if courts considered this option in cases where a non-monetary order will carry a negative symbolic message. By substituting a monetary order, the court is not denying that the underlying duty is non-monetary; it is merely limiting the ways in which it will support the duty.

IV. CONCLUSION

Lawyers in common law jurisdictions frequently make assumptions about the duties citizens owe one another on the basis of the orders that judges make when citizens go to court. These assumptions often rest on undefended ideas about the relationship between rule-based rights and court orders. In an attempt to better understand this relationship, I have advanced two main arguments in this chapter. First, there is no necessary or conceptual connection between rule-based rights and court orders. The arguments for such a connection rest, in almost every case, on two propositions: (1) legal duties exist when, and only when, the law imposes sanctions on specified behaviour; and (2) court orders are sanctions. Neither proposition is plausible, but the second, in particular, is easily disproved. The non-performance of a court order may, if further steps are taken, lead to a sanction, but the order itself does not impose a sanction. Court orders are directives, addressed to specific individuals, telling them what the law expects them to do in future.

The second main argument is that in practice the relationship between court orders and rule-based rights is likely to be complex. Like the rules that articulate rule-based rights, court orders are fundamentally instruments for guiding citizens' behaviour. In comparison to rules, however, orders have obvious practical and normative drawbacks. Indeed, it might be wondered why the law would employ orders at all. Sanctions may be practically necessary, but what is the point of ordering individual citizens to do things if there are (or could be) legal rules that require the same behaviour? The answer, in broad terms, is that rules also have limitations. Rules have weak motivational force and rules are not self-applying (ie, it is not always clear what a rule requires). Orders, by contrast, have strong motivational force and are relatively self-applying. If these were the only reasons for making court orders, we would expect that the content of court orders would always mirror the content of claimants' rule-based rights. It is of crucial importance, therefore, that some of the ways in which orders can be used to supplement rules call for orders that create new rights. Thus, court orders can be used to guide behaviour in cases where the relevant behaviour is determined by evidence that the defendant could not reasonably be expected to obtain, or where it may be too difficult or costly to specify in a rule how citizens should act. Court orders can also be used to vindicate rule-based rights, and so give effect to state-based reasons, in ways that rules cannot. Finally, courts might not want to make orders or particular kinds of orders for several reasons, for example the order may be too costly, may carry an undesirable symbolic message or would make enforcement unduly costly or difficult.

The reasons courts might want to create new rights by orders or not give effect to existing rights by orders are controversial. They contemplate that courts might use orders to change the legal relationship between litigants from what it was when they entered the court. In many cases, the change would be relatively minor, as, for example, if a court uses an order of nominal damages to vindicate a right or if it grants a monetary order in lieu of a non-monetary order to facilitate enforcement. In other cases, however, the change could be significant, as, for example, if a court decides to create a new, substantive right to send a symbolic message or to respond to the difficulty of specifying in advance the behaviour desired by the law. Whether our goal is to better understand our rule-based rights or to critically evaluate the basis on which orders are made, it is important, therefore, to determine how often courts make orders that require defendants to do things other than what they were already legally required to do. Although I have not answered the question, I have, I hope, taken some first steps towards an answer.

9

Rights and Responsibility in the Law of Torts

JOHN CP GOLDBERG AND BENJAMIN C ZIPURSKY*

I. INTRODUCTION

TORT LAW MIGHT seem to be among the least complicated areas of law.[1] Some would even say that it boils down to a single idea, such as that of the cheapest cost avoider. In fact, the analytic structure of tort law is complex. Thinking about torts in terms of rights—in particular, thinking about the several different respects in which rights figure in the law of torts—will provide a more accurate account of tort law's structure. It will also enable us to attain a greater appreciation of tort law's normative underpinnings. Relying in part on Wesley Hohfeld's famous typology,[2] we will explain that there are at least four different ways that rights figure in tort law. To understand torts, one must distinguish among the various aspects of rights in torts and one must grasp how they are linked to one another.

* For helpful comments on earlier drafts, we are grateful to the participants in the Obligations V Conference held at the University of Oxford, the Harvard Law School faculty workshop, and the Tufts University Philosophy of Tort Law seminar. Remaining errors are our own.
   [1] See RA Epstein, 'A Theory of Strict Liability' (1973) 2 *Journal of Legal Studies* 151, 151 (observing that, although tort law seems very straightforward because it concerns itself with everyday problems of responsibility, appearances are deceiving).
   [2] WN Hohfeld, 'Some Fundamental Legal Conceptions as Applied in Judicial Reasoning' (1913) 23 *Yale Law Journal* 16, 19–20 (noting the potential for confusion in oversimplification).

II. RIGHTS IN MODERN TORT THEORY:
A HURRIED OVERVIEW

A. Tort Law as Public Law

The law of the United States (US) is sometimes described as rights-centric. Most visibly, it deals with certain contentious issues (eg, the availability of abortion) as questions of constitutional *right*, whereas some other Western democracies address them through ordinary political processes. Today, this contrast is less sharp than it once was, particularly given the emergence of a robust law of European Human Rights. But regardless of how best to characterise differences between the public law of the US and that of other nations, the conception of the US system as rights-centric is off the mark when it comes to private law.

For nearly 150 years, and especially in the past 75 years, American legal scholars have overwhelmingly embraced the legal realist mantra that 'all law is public law'. This slogan is meant to emphasise that one should not think of contracts, torts, and restitution as built around correlative primary rights and duties, and matching secondary rights and duties of repair. Of course, private litigation is usually an effort by one person to hold another liable. But liability is, in the end, imposed by state actors (judges) for reasons of state; it is a state-imposed sanction for undesirable conduct, which sanction happens to take the form of an order to indemnify another for losses caused by that conduct. A civil plaintiff has a 'right' to a remedy, it is said, only in the sense that government has decided that something good will come from allowing persons such as the plaintiff, under the circumstances of the case, to be indemnified for their losses.

The academic effort to recast private law as public law has had another, related objective, which is to undermine any suggestion that the departments of private law should be regarded as connected to basic rights or principles of justice. To expose tort or contract law as a 'mere' means by which governmental officials in given historical periods have pursued certain policy objectives is to reveal that private law has no necessary linkage to such principles.

It may help to illuminate these points by focusing more specifically on the state of academic discourse about tort law. Since the late nineteenth century, the dominant tendency in the US legal academy has been to equate tort law with accident law.[3] In turn, the basic question of accident law is said to be an instrumental one: what can government accomplish by having one class of persons or another bear the losses flowing

---

[3] JCP Goldberg and BC Zipursky, 'Torts as Wrongs' (2010) 88 *Texas Law Review* 917, 920–28 (discussing the dominant academic conception of tort as law for allocating the costs of accidents).

from vehicular crashes, slips and falls, and product-related injuries? This view of tort law, its proponents insist, best accords with on-the-ground litigation realities. Ordinary tort suits are not handled by human rights advocates pursuing some exalted notion of justice, but by contingent-fee lawyers and insurance adjusters. Likewise, the judges and legislatures who have shaped the rules of tort law are practical men and women moved, in significant part, by pragmatic concerns such as: who is in a better or worse position to bear or spread a certain kind of recurring loss? Which forms of liability imposition will appropriately incentivise future actors to guard against such losses?

To treat tort law as accident law is likewise to capture its contingent and indeed parochial nature. Although some—most notably Richard Posner[4]—argue that a system of one-off lawsuits is a sensible mechanism for addressing the 'problem of accidents', most contemporary scholars believe the opposite: that reliance on torts to deal with accidents is a testament to the primitive political conditions that obtained when tort law first emerged. That tort law has persisted rather than being wholly supplanted by more 'rational' regulatory and insurance schemes is, they say, mainly a testament to unique facets of American political economy and culture, including a politically powerful plaintiff's bar, a pervasive distrust of centralised government, and a romantic attachment to vengeance-based notions of justice. Surely a body of law that is so heavily path-dependent is unlikely to have anything to do with contemporary understandings of rights or justice.

B. First-Generation Rights Theories

Starting in the mid-1960s, the above-described academic orthodoxy began to meet some resistance in legal practice and theory. This timing was not accidental, for the same period also saw the rise to public prominence of the civil rights movement. That movement primarily played itself out in national politics and in the constitutional law of equal protection and due process. But it also had implications for tort law.

Monroe v Pape re-animated a federal statute, 42 USC § 1983, by interpreting it to provide a private right of action to individuals whose constitutional rights have been violated by state governmental officials acting under a claim of authority.[5] In *Bivens v Six Unknown Named Agents of Federal Bureau of Narcotics*,[6] the Court extended this right to

---

[4] See, eg, WH Landes and RA Posner, *The Economic Structure of Tort Law* (Cambridge MA, Harvard University Press, 1987) 28 (emphasising the degree to which tort law operates to allocate efficiently resources spent on safety).

[5] *Monroe v Pape* 365 US 171 (1961) (*Monroe*).

[6] *Bivens v Six Unknown Named Agents of Federal Bureau of Narcotics* 403 US 388 (1971) (*Bivens*).

victims of unlawful searches and seizures undertaken by federal officials. Meanwhile, federal civil rights legislation empowered victims of employment discrimination to sue their employers for injunctive relief. In each of these instances, Congress and the Court drew a kind of connection between tort law—law that defines wrongs for which victims can obtain redress—and fundamental rights, including rights not to be battered, seized, or discriminated against on the basis of race and gender. Indeed, *Monroe* and *Bivens* gave rise to a distinct field of US law now known as 'constitutional torts'. In this domain, at least, tort law has nothing to do with accidents or loss-shifting, and everything to do with vindicating rights.[7]

Meanwhile, in the realm of theory, the early 1970s saw some initial efforts to reconnect tort law to rights and justice. In particular, George Fletcher and Richard Epstein attempted to harness, respectively, egalitarian and libertarian rights theory to support accounts of the nature and function of tort law that departed, at least in certain respects, from both the utilitarian orthodoxy of William Prosser and the burgeoning law-and-economics movement of Guido Calabresi, Ronald Coase and Posner.[8] Epstein envisioned tort doctrine as a scheme of corrective justice that exists to protect and reinforce each individual's rightful holdings. Far from being the happily depoliticised and decentralised regulatory scheme envisioned by Posner, tort law was for Epstein fundamentally pre-regulatory and even pre-legislative, giving force to a Lockean notion of a natural right to one's person and property.[9] An actor who harms another is held prima facie liable to the other simply because his or her volitional act caused damage to another's things. *You break it, you pay*, Epstein argued, is the default rule that flows from a proper account of natural rights.

Building on a distinct and more egalitarian strand of rights theory,[10] Fletcher argued that tort law is a system for the fair allocation of risks and losses. Each of us, he argued, has an equal right not to be exposed to an excessive risk of injury. When an actor violates that right by imposing an excessive risk on another, that actor shall, if the risk is realised, bear

---

[7] The recognition of the distinct field of constitutional torts has been a double-edged sword. It identifies a domain of tort law that vividly illustrates how torts and rights intersect, yet at the same time seals it off from the rest of tort law, permitting academics to persist in their mistaken view that 'real' tort law is accident law.

In recent years, litigation of claims brought under the Alien Tort Statute, 28 USC § 1350 (ATS) has drawn an even more explicit link between tort law and human rights law. See *Sosa v Alvarez-Machain* 542 US 692 (2004) (holding that the ATS grants jurisdiction to US courts to adjudicate claims against aliens alleged to have violated widely-adopted rules of international law prohibiting basic forms of mistreatment, such as laws prohibiting enslavement and piracy).

[8] GP Fletcher, 'Fairness and Utility in Tort Law' (1972) 85 *Harvard Law Review* 537; Epstein, above n 1. In other respects, especially their focus on tort as a law for the allocation of losses, Epstein and Fletcher bought into tort orthodoxy.

[9] Epstein, above n 1, at 203–04.

[10] Fletcher, above n 8, at 550 (invoking Rawls' theory of justice 'by analogy').

the loss.[11] According to Fletcher, the Posnerian and utilitarian emphasis on the centrality of cost–benefit analysis to tort law (and negligence law in particular) is understandable yet misguided. The application of tort law may involve balancing, but what is being balanced is not the social costs and expected benefits of precaution-taking. Instead, courts in tort cases balance the victim's right to bodily security as against the potential unfairness of holding the defendant liable.

For various reasons, neither Epstein's nor Fletcher's efforts made much of a dent in utilitarian and economic conceptions of tort law. The interpretive plausibility of Epstein's theory was substantially undermined by his broad rejection of negligence; his call for a default rule of strict liability did not and does not track existing doctrine. At the same time, the theory's prescriptive appeal was limited by tightly linking of tort to a stridently libertarian version of liberalism. For his part, Fletcher offered an intriguing explanation of certain corners of tort doctrine, particularly strict liability for abnormally dangerous activities. Nonetheless, the key notion of 'non-reciprocal' risk—the sort of risk for which one, in fairness, should be held liable for imposing—has proved difficult to pin down. This is notwithstanding the impressive efforts of subsequent scholars, particularly Gregory Keating and Arthur Ripstein (in his earlier work), to provide sophisticated Rawlsian accounts of specific tort concepts (eg, reasonableness), particular tort principles (such as 'enterprise liability' in the case of Keating) and tort law generally as instantiating and vindicating each person's right to equal liberty and security.[12]

C. Corrective Justice, Rights and Responsibility

The next counter-movement in tort theory, which has proceeded mainly under the banner of 'corrective justice theory', has also invoked conceptions of rights to counter dominant accounts of tort law. Yet the notion of rights at work is a very different one. Indeed, in contrast to Epstein and Fletcher, founders of contemporary corrective justice theory, including Ernest Weinrib and Jules Coleman, have not mainly been concerned to offer normative or prescriptive accounts of tort law. Rather, they have cast their projects as principally analytical and interpretive, emphasising the methodological and jurisprudential aspects of tort theory.

At least through the publication of *Risks and Wrongs*, the concept of

---

[11] ibid, at 554. On Fletcher's view, the imposition of excessive risk renders the actor prima facie liable. He may still be spared liability if he can establish a valid excuse.

[12] See, eg, GC Keating, 'Reasonableness and Rationality in Negligence Theory' (1996) 48 *Stanford Law Review* 311; G Keating, 'The Idea of Fairness in the Law of Enterprise Liability' (1997) 95 *Michigan Law Review* 1266; A Ripstein, *Equality, Responsibility, and the Law* (Cambridge, Cambridge University Press, 1998).

rights played a significant analytic role in Coleman's articulation of the principle of corrective justice.[13] According to his rendition of that principle, one who has caused a wrongful loss to another has a moral duty to repair that loss.[14] Coleman defines the concept of 'wrongful loss' disjunctively: it is a loss caused *either* by wrongdoing or by a wrong.[15] The question thus arises: is there really any daylight between the notion of a loss caused by wrongdoing and a loss caused by a wrong? To answer this question affirmatively, Coleman relies on an important analytic distinction in rights theory. As Joel Feinberg and Judith Thomson argued, an 'infringement' of a right (a justified rights invasion) can be distinguished from a 'violation' of a right (an unjustified rights invasion).[16] Corrective justice, Coleman argued, can intelligibly require the repair of losses caused both by rights infringements (wrongs) and rights violations (wrongdoings). For example, a person who, without permission, occupies another's land, yet does so out of necessity (and hence reasonably), can still count as having done a wrong, and as being morally obligated to make good on the loss caused by this wrong. In this respect, the idea of rights is crucial to Coleman's effort to explain how prominent instances of 'strict' liability—as is sometimes said to have been imposed in *Vincent v Lake Erie Transportation Co*[17]—can still be about wrongs, and hence can still count as instantiations of corrective justice.

In *The Idea of Private Law*, Weinrib deploys concepts of right in a rather different manner than Coleman does.[18] The most striking feature of Weinrib's analysis is its 'formalist' effort to explain tort law as an entailment of an abstract concept of human agency.[19] From the very idea of a rational agent, Weinrib derives a set of correlative rights to be free from certain injuries at the hands of others and duties not to inflict such injuries. In turn, these give rise to correlative secondary rights to repair (and duties of repair). Ultimately, Weinrib argues, it is the dyadic nature of these rights and duties that explains how and why tort law instantiates the principle of corrective justice, and explains why tort adjudication is fundamentally a matter of identifying attributes of two actors' interactions, and not a matter of shaping liability rules to achieve extrinsic consequences such as deterrence or compensation.

---

[13] JL Coleman, *Risks and Wrongs* (Cambridge, Cambridge University Press, 1992).

[14] ibid, at 325.

[15] ibid, at 330–32.

[16] J Feinberg, 'Voluntary Euthanasia and the Inalienable Right to Life' (1978) 7 *Philosophy & Public Affairs* 108; JJ Thomson, *Rights, Restitution, and Risk: Essays in Moral Theory* (W Parent ed, Cambridge MA, Harvard University Press, 1986) 51; Coleman, above n 13, at 300.

[17] *Vincent v Lake Erie Transportation Co* 124 NW 221 (Minn 1910).

[18] EJ Weinrib, *The Idea of Private Law* (Cambridge MA, Harvard University Press, 1995).

[19] ibid, at 84–113 (locating the normative root of corrective justice in a Kantian conception of self-determining agency).

The important point for now is that Coleman and Weinrib each give rights a role that, in contrast to the usage of Epstein and Fletcher, is primarily analytical and descriptive. Economists and utilitarians, they argue, can offer only ad hoc accounts of the plaintiff-versus-defendant structure of tort suits, the substance of tort doctrine, and the characteristic forms of judicial reasoning about torts. Corrective justice theory, by contrast, can offer an integrated account of these phenomena. Tort law looks and operates the way it does, they maintain, because it is built around a moral principle specifying that one person's wronging of another (or one's wrongful causing of a loss to another) generates a moral duty of repair owed by the wrongdoer to the victim. Of course, to grasp this fundamental point, one must have a suitably nuanced account of what it means for one person to 'wrong' another, or to 'wrongfully' cause a loss to another. And in different ways, Coleman and Weinrib invoke the concept of right to fill out the key notions of wrongdoing, duty, and repair. But neither connects corrective justice to a Rawlsian notion of a right to equal liberty and security, or to a Lockean or Nozickian right of ownership in one's self and one's property.[20] Indeed, both are keen to insulate corrective justice from such notions. Robert Stevens, although not a self-identified corrective justice theorist, continues this tradition in his excellent *Torts and Rights*, playing it out with expert attention to the full complexity of tort doctrine.[21] In Stevens' work too, rights are deemed critical to an explanation of both the structure of tort law and the particular terms on which it imposes liability.

Our hurried tour of the place of rights in modern tort theory is almost complete, but requires that we consider a distinct strand of corrective justice theory, one associated most strongly with Tony Honoré and Stephen Perry (and, in different ways, Peter Cane and John Gardner).[22] Perry forcefully argued that Weinrib and Coleman, in the end, fail to capture tort law's moral core. The idea that tort embodies a special kind of justice by providing for a victim's loss to be transferred to a wrongdoer, he suggests, fails to capture fully the notion of *responsibility* that stands at the centre of tort doctrine. Tort law does not simply redistribute or reallocate losses according to a principle of justice. It assigns liability as a way of holding a person responsible for certain consequences that his or

---

[20] Admittedly, in a later work with Ripstein, Coleman seemed interested in connecting corrective justice to a notion of fairness in the distribution of losses: JL Coleman and A Ripstein, 'Mischief and Misfortune' (1995) 41 *McGill Law Review* 91.

[21] R Stevens, *Torts and Rights* (Oxford, Oxford University Press, 2007).

[22] T Honoré, 'Responsibility and Luck: The Moral Basis of Strict Liability' (1988) 104 *Law Quarterly Review* 530; SR Perry, 'The Moral Foundations of Tort Law' (1992) 77 *Iowa Law Review* 449; P Cane, *Responsibility in Law and Morality* (Oxford, Hart Publishing, 2002); J Gardner, *What Is Tort Law For? Part 1: The Place of Corrective Justice* (Oxford Legal Studies Research Paper No 1/2010, University of Oxford, 18 January 2010) at ssrn. com/abstract=1538342, accessed on 28 January 2011.

her conduct has had for another. In tort, liability is a form of responsibility. Hence any tort theory that aims to take tort law seriously on its
own terms must include a robust notion of responsibility.

To meet this challenge, Perry invokes a variation on Honoré's concept
of 'outcome-responsibility'.[23] According to Perry, the duty of repair at the
centre of the principle of corrective justice is in the first instance grounded
in an agent having *caused* a loss to another under circumstances in which
the loss was foreseeable and therefore avoidable. The connection between
the exercise of a person's agency and the loss renders the loss *his or her*
responsibility, rather than someone else's; it is what generates *for that
person* a special responsibility in relation to the loss.[24]

Yet although outcome-responsibility is a necessary ground of a moral
duty of repair, and hence, on Perry's view, essential to an adequate account
of tort, it is not sufficient. This is because outcome-responsibility is, as
Perry rightly emphasises, a normatively thin concept. To identify a person
as outcome-responsible is merely to say that his or her having played a
role in causing an avoidable loss generates for him or her a reason to do
something with respect to that loss that other persons, unconnected to
the loss, do not have. In many instances, even a not-at-fault victim will
be among those whose acts contributed to his or her injury, and who is
therefore outcome-responsible. And nothing yet has been said about what,
exactly, the various persons who might be outcome-responsible for a given
loss now have reason to do. For example, they may merely have reason
to feel some regret over their connection to the loss. One must therefore
add to the idea of outcome-responsibility a distributive principle that
connects responsibility to the duty of repair or indemnification. In our
system, Perry argues, this is the work done by the fault principle.[25] An
actor who causes a foreseeable (and hence avoidable) loss to another *by
means of faulty conduct* owes a duty of repair to the victim who suffers
the loss. The actor owes the injured person a duty of repair for the loss
both because he or she is responsible for it—in the sense that the loss is
connected to the actor's agency in the right way—and because he or she
acted in violation of a norm of careful conduct, such that it is fair (at
least fair as between an at-fault actor and an innocent victim) to require
the actor to cover the loss.

Perry's emphasis on the need for a tort theory to offer an adequate
account of responsibility strikes us as sound. Tort law is a practice that
is centrally about recognising responsibilities that one owes to others—an
idea that is distinct from the notion that tort law exists to see to it that a
just allocation of resources is achieved between or among certain persons.
Yet outcome-responsibility seems a poor candidate for capturing the par-

---

[23] Honoré, above n 22, at 539–41.
[24] Perry, above n 22, at 497.
[25] ibid, at 499.

ticular sense(s) of responsibility at work in tort. The main problem with it is an interpretive one. Liability based on outcome-responsibility, even qualified by the requirement of fault, would seem to call for a regime of liability that is in important respects much broader than what one finds in any US or Commonwealth tort system. Specifically, it calls for the imposition of liability for any instance in which an actor acts in a faulty manner and in so doing causes a foreseeable loss to another. Tort liability does not reach so far and never has; there is no liability even for faulty conduct causing foreseeable losses to another if the wrongdoer did not breach a duty of care owed to the other.[26]

D. Summary

We now have some perspective on the state of contemporary academic theorising about torts and rights. As in the political and constitutional theory of the 1970s, rights discourse in tort theory initially seemed to promise foundational, normative deontological justifications for the area of law it aimed to capture. In Epstein's work, for example, tort law could be seen as a corollary to an underlying theory of natural rights. Yet these efforts made limited headway. A new generation of theorists would soon forsake the effort to supply a normative justification for tort law by using rights concepts, turning instead to the positive project of supplying an adequate analysis of the structure of tort law. The more limited aspirations of this body of work in turn has left a normative deficit or puzzle: what is the linkage between rights and responsibility? In torts scholarship, contemporary rights theory tends to do analytical work, while responsibility tends to do normative work, and the connection between the two continues to call out for explanation.

III. RIGHTS AND RESPONSIBILITY IN TORT

As we now aim to demonstrate, a more satisfactory account of tort law's linkage of rights and responsibility is available in the form of a theory of tort that we have dubbed the 'civil recourse' theory. In explicating that theory, we begin by reconsidering the place of rights in torts. To make analytic progress, however, we must first recall Hohfeld's admonition that

---

[26] JCP Goldberg and BC Zipursky, 'The *Restatement (Third)* and the Place of Duty in Negligence Law' (2001) 54 *Vanderbilt Law Review* 657, 665–72. There is also a question whether a theory of tort based on outcome-responsibility is able to account for liability for breaches of affirmative duties. In such cases, or at least some such cases, there may be liability even though the defendant has not caused the plaintiff's loss, but merely failed to intervene so as to prevent it.

the terms 'right' and 'rights', as used in Anglo-American law, have multiple meanings. With that admonition in mind, we distinguish among four different senses in which 'rights' figure in the structure of tort law. The remainder of this chapter explicates this structure and thereby sets the stage for a clearer understanding of tort law and the normative case to be made for it.

A. Legal Directives, Relational Duties and Rights Against Mistreatment

We begin our reconstruction of tort law with the idea of a 'legal directive'. That phrase, as we use it, refers to a norm that is embedded in the law of a legal system and enjoins conduct. As such, the concept is akin to HLA Hart's concept of a 'duty-imposing rule'.[27] Here are some examples of possible (or actual) legal directives:

> A person may not intentionally touch another in a manner that is harmful or offensive.

> No person may seize or take movable property owned by another, without the consent of the owner, and with the intention of depriving the owner of the property for a substantial period of time.

> No person may sell, market, or dispense [drugs of a certain description] without prior approval from the federal Food and Drug Administration.

Sometimes there is ambiguity as to whether a given law actually contains a legal directive. Consider a provision in a criminal code which reads as follows: 'Knowing possession of [narcotics of a certain description] in an amount less than 500 grams is a Class B felony.' The code in turn defines Class B felonies as punishable with one to 10 years imprisonment and a fine of up to $50 000. The provision could be construed as a power-conferring rule that merely specifies punishments that executive and judicial branch officials may impose. However, given its presence in the criminal code, the historic meaning of the term 'felony', and so on, it is better interpreted as also containing a legal directive. Persons subject to this law are instructed not to possess the relevant narcotics.

Our first claim—interpretive and definitional in nature—is that the US legal system contains legal directives, that these directives create legal duties, and that violations of legal directives—breaches of these legal duties—are *legal wrongs*.

Our next claim is analytic and taxonomic. There are at least two different types of legal directives. Some are *simple* directives, others are *relational*. Simple legal directives enjoin conduct without reference to per-

---

[27] HLA Hart, *The Concept of Law*, 2nd edn (New York, Oxford University Press, 1994) 81.

sons other than the target(s) of the directive. Relational legal directives enjoin actors not to act in certain ways toward others or upon others, or enjoin them to act in certain ways upon others or toward others. Relational directives prohibit or require acts *to or upon others*, and the structure of the norms they generate is such that the norms not only range over a class of addressees, but also over a class (or classes) of possible objects or *beneficiaries* of those addressees' enjoined acts. Here are two simple directives one might find in a given jurisdiction's law:

> Dispose of hazardous household wastes at appropriate facilities.

> Take care to dispose of hazardous household wastes at appropriate facilities.

By contrast, the following directives are relational:

> A person may not intentionally touch another in a harmful or offensive manner.

> Take care to avoid causing physical harm to anyone who might foreseeably be physically harmed by one's careless conduct.[28]

Duties generated by relational directives can be called 'relational duties'.

Duties generated by simple directives can be called 'simple duties'. Breaches of relational legal duties would accordingly be deemed 'relational legal wrongs', while breaches of simple legal duties would be deemed 'simple legal wrongs'. Analytically, the victim of a relational legal wrong— and only that victim—has suffered an invasion of a legal right not to be so wronged.

Via this route we arrive at the first of the four respects in which rights figure in tort. All torts are relational wrongs, and hence all are, by definition, rights invasions. A tort is a breach of a relational legal duty of non-injury.[29] For example, the tort law of each State in the US contains a directive stating (roughly) that a person must not, by means of a misrepresentation, intentionally induce another to part with a thing of value in reliance on that misrepresentation. This is a relational legal directive that creates a relational legal duty. A violation of this duty constitutes the relational legal wrong known as fraud or deceit. That wrong in turn constitutes a violation of the victim's right not to be deceived in a certain kind of transactional setting.

---

[28] As should be apparent from these examples, a directive can be relational even if it addresses how one must act toward a loosely defined class, as opposed to specifying how one must act toward particular persons, or toward persons with whom one maintains a pre-existing relationship. Likewise, the distinction between simple and relational directives does not concern different standards of conduct (eg, fault versus intentionality).

[29] In contrasting simple and relational directives, and in claiming that torts always rest on relational directives, we do not suggest that criminal law and regulatory law contain only simple directives. Clearly many criminal and regulatory offences consist of violations of duties owed to others. Also, we are not here taking a position on the appropriate domains of criminal, regulatory and tort law.

A different directive, also widely recognised in US law, specifies (roughly) that a commercial seller of products must not injure any person by placing into the stream of commerce a product containing a defect.[30] This directive also creates a relational legal duty, the violation of which is a relational legal wrong. In turn, this wrong, when committed, amounts to a violation of the injured person's right to be free from injury caused by the sale of a defective product by a commercial seller.

Now we can better appreciate the first of four senses in which rights figure in tort law. They figure as Hohfeldian claim rights that stand as analytic counterparts to relational duties. Because all torts are relational wrongs, by definition a tort always involves the violation of the victim's legal right not to be wronged in the manner defined by the particular tort.

At this juncture, it is worth pointing out two advantages of this way of thinking about rights in tort. First, it permits us (at least for now) to sidestep a basic philosophical question about the nature of rights—specifically, whether rights are by definition connected to certain important human interests, such as the interest in bodily integrity, dominion over property, and the like. Regardless of whether the institution of tort law has some deep connection to basic human interests, it is plain that, as a doctrinal matter, the specific duties and rights articulated by tort law do not merely enjoin and give rights against interferences with basic interests. On our account, it is the inherent relationality of tortious wrongdoing, rather than the nature of the interest being protected or vindicated, that in the first instance links torts to rights. Libel and invasion of privacy and malicious prosecution, for example, are relational wrongs: there is a right not be libelled, not to have one's privacy invaded, and not to be maliciously prosecuted. To say that a tort is a rights violation in the particular sense of being a breach of a duty owed to the victim, and hence a mistreatment of the victim, is not (yet) to make a claim about the normative significance of tort law, or its connection (if any) to natural rights or principles of justice.

A second advantage of this account—which we, following Coleman and Weinrib, regard as critical—is that it explains the sense in which tort law is not best characterised as a set of liability rules. The rights protected by tort law are, by and large, *rights against being mistreated in certain ways by others*. They are not akin to holdings, although they may correspond to holdings. They are domains of legal protection against mistreatment. Correspondingly, the duties of tort law are not disjunctive duties to forbear or pay, as a liability rule theory would suggest. They are duties of conduct—duties not to batter, not to inflict physical injury or property damage carelessly, not to defraud, not to imprison falsely, and so on.

---

[30] See *Restatement of the Law, Third: Torts — Products Liability* (St Paul MN, American Law Institute, 1998) § 2.

Almost any rights-inclusive theory of tort has the advantage of explaining the sense in which tort law is not a law of liability rules. But even within this broad class, a rights-inclusive account that is linked, as is ours, to the concept of relational wrongs offers a particularly valuable jurisprudential and phenomenological lesson. The legal duties of tort law are not just duties to act or refrain from acting, full stop. They are, for the most part, duties to refrain from 'doing unto others' in certain ways— they are duties whose structure is such as to involve aspects of others' well-being. It is not simply that the justification for the imposition of the duty relates to the protection of the welfare of others. The acts enjoined by the relational directives of tort law are acts *upon* others. To avoid being a tortfeasor is a matter of refraining from interfering with others in certain ways (or, in some cases, a matter of providing certain forms of assistance to others). Put differently, the conception of torts as breaches of relational duties and therefore as rights violations helps to capture the particular notion of obligation that is at the core of tort law. We shall return to this point below.

B. Rights and Liability: A Puzzle

Assuming that the conditions of tort liability are captured by a notion of rights correlative to relational duties, and assuming that relational duties are aptly understood as outgrowths of directives that enjoin us not to interfere with others in particular ways, there remains an important puzzle. What does *liability* have to do with rights? Why should the violation by one person of the rights of another entail a transfer of assets from the one to the other, as opposed to the punishment of the wrongdoer? Why is the provision of compensation for losses that flow from a rights violation an appropriate response?

Some contemporary tort theories offer a seemingly promising response to these inquiries. Epstein's is the prototype.[31] These theories conceive of all torts as involving interferences with 'stuff' (or 'things') that one actually owns: one's person, one's possessions, and one's reputation. Let us call these, somewhat tendentiously, 'commodification tort theories'. Ripstein's recent work arguably takes a related approach.[32] What one really owns, he says, is not merely what one is born with and what one acquires. Rather, there is a moral dimension to ownership—what one truly owns is determined in part by rights to liberty and equality. However, once this background is established, tort law really is about protection of the 'means' to which one has a right—including one's bodily integrity and

[31] See Epstein, above n 1.
[32] A Ripstein, 'As If It Never Happened' (2007) 48 *William and Mary Law Review* 1957.

one's rightfully owned things. Let us call such a theory a 'quasi-commod-ification tort theory'. Commodification and quasi-commodification tort theories suggest a particular bridge from rights to liability. The protection of the victim's right is not just a matter of enjoining others to refrain from acts that amount to rights violations; it is also a matter of restitution. Once a tort has occurred, tort actions permit the retrieval of an owned thing or its equivalent. They allow one to retain control of one's 'stuff', and empower a person to take back from the tortfeasor the stuff he or she has taken or damaged.[33]

With rights conceptualised as entitlements to 'stuff', and torts concep-tualised as interferences with those entitlements, the notion of liability for compensatory damages as an appropriate response to the commission of tort makes a lot of sense. On this view, there is an inherent element of conversion in every tort. A tort is always a taking or using of another's stuff. When the stuff cannot literally be given back, damages are provided as an equivalent. Tort liability is in this sense inherently restorative.

Unfortunately, theories such as these face two interpretive challenges, each of which is insoluble within their framework, in our view. The first is that it is implausible to depict the wide array of torts as interference with stuff—even when one's holdings are determined by reference to a conception of justice. We do not see how torts such as libel, assault, and malicious prosecution, not to mention invasion of privacy and a variety of other dignitary torts, can be plausibly accommodated in even a quasi-commodification theory. Not all the wrongs of tort are wrongs because they interfere with the means to carry out one's purposes. An undeserved reputation as a philanderer caused by a defendant's libel—and for that matter a disfigured face or painful back resulting from a carelessly caused car crash—are not captured by the idea that one's purposiveness or abil-ity to carry out one's plans has been substantially altered. The wide array of wrongs that count as torts can be captured by a relational directives theory, but not by a theory that relies on even a moralised account of what one 'owns'.

The second interpretive problem of commodification or quasi-commod-ification theories is that they rely too heavily on the notion of 'making whole' in explaining the phenomenon of liability. Imagine a plaintiff who sues her gynaecological surgeon because the surgeon negligently has removed her only healthy fallopian tube, rendering her infertile. A jury awards her $80 000 for economic damages associated with the surgery

---

[33] ibid. Ripstein, building on Kant, argues that each person enjoys an equal right to be secure against all others in her means—ie, her ability to pursue her own purposes. These 'means' consist of one's person (one's capacity to set and act in pursuit of one's purposes) and one's property (things that one has at one's disposal to use in the pursuit of one's pur-poses). Tort law enjoins each of us not to deprive others of their means, or to use their means without authorisation. When such a deprivation occurs, tort law in turn permits the victim to retrieve what has been taken from her.

and $240 000 for non-economic damages. This plaintiff cannot be 'made whole' in any meaningful sense. The commodification theorist perhaps will agree, arguing that the jury's verdict is a second-best alternative to a literal restoration of the plaintiff's 'means'. Again, we are dubious. Juries are instructed to calibrate their verdicts to the perceived seriousness of a plaintiff's injury, and undoubtedly they strive to do so, for the most part. It hardly follows that this calibration process is best captured by the idea of giving back to the plaintiff that which was taken from her. In a case like the one hypothesised above, a damage award has more in common with the practice of compensating someone with a bonus for an especially good work performance. Compensation of this sort is calibrated rather than wholly discretionary, but the criterion of calibration is not captured by the idea of a thing having been bestowed and now being returned. Instead, one is compensated for a job well-done—a 'compensation *for*' rather than a 'returning or restoring to'. Although tort damages are, of course, set by reference to distinct criteria, we will suggest that these criteria are of a similar nature to the criteria used in determining compensation for a job well-done.

C. Rights of Action

A more satisfactory solution to the puzzle of tort law's linkage of rights and liability requires appreciation of the second sense in which rights figure in tort. Torts are commonly said to create in the victim a 'cause of action' or a 'right of action'. These phrases quite evidently refer to a legal *power*—an entitlement to act against an alleged tortfeasor. Specifically, the plaintiff's right of action is a power to obtain a remedy from the defendant. Here, of course, the language of tort fits Hohfeld's correlates like a glove. As Hohfeld observed, the correlate of a legal power is a legal *liability*.[34] The imposition of liability on a tortfeasor for the commission of a tort is the counterpart to tort law's conferral on the victim of a power to proceed against the tortfeasor. Tort law thus both recognises Hohfeldian claim rights against being mistreated (as discussed above) and grants to those whose rights have been violated a Hohfeldian power. To this power there is a corresponding vulnerability—the defendant's susceptibility to a court-ordered remedy. In this latter sense, tort law is also about rights.

As we describe it, the power conferred on tort victims is a power to hold to account a person who has committed a relational legal wrong against the victim. Of course that power is initially invoked by a *putative* victim who merely alleges a wrong. Only by proving her allegations

[34] Hohfeld, above n 2, at 44.

under proper procedures does the putative victim perfect her claim to be entitled to hold the wrongdoer accountable to her. The victim's power, in other words, is always asserted provisionally or conditionally, subject to an authoritative determination by a court as to the validity of the assertion. Yet there is no reason to infer from this feature of the tort system that the power conferred by tort law is anything other than a power to hold the defendant accountable or liable. A complaint's allegations are in this respect analogous to the US Congress enacting legislation under a claim of authority to do so by virtue of the Commerce Clause of the US Constitution.[35] Given the practice of judicial review, the implicit claim behind such legislation—that it in fact falls within the ambit of Congress's constitutionally enumerated powers—is necessarily provisional. It is nonetheless an assertion by Congress of a power to legislate, not merely a power to propose legislation.

It is easy to collapse the two sense of rights we have thus far distinguished—the right against mistreatment and the power to respond to the wrongdoer—because, for reasons we elaborate below, it is in the very nature of tort law to link the recognition of primary rights and the conferral of private rights of action to victims. Historically, what it has meant for a common law court to deem a form of mistreatment such as the defrauding of another as a 'tort' is for the court to identify a wrong involving the infringement of a right that is correlative to a relational duty, which infringement generates a right of action in the victim against the breaching party. Yet it is not difficult to identify laws that decouple these two integral aspects of torts. Doing so will help give us perspective on what is distinctive about tort law.

Although tort law is still predominantly defined by common law, statutes obviously play a larger role in this domain than they once did. And there is certainly nothing inherent in the idea of tort law, as we define it, that precludes it from being a matter of legislation. However, precisely because legislatures enjoy a broader authority to regulate in the public interest than do courts, the axiomatic linkage between the identification of relational wrongs and the provision of rights of action does not hold in the legislative domain. Indeed, even statutes that identify relational wrongs and confer remedies on victims of those wrongs often do not create or recognise genuine torts.

For example, criminal prosecutions sometimes result in the sentencing judge ordering the defendant to pay restitution to his or her victims. Similarly, many State consumer protection laws permit Attorneys-General to seek restitution for fraud victims. The 'right' of these victims to receive compensation under criminal or consumer protection laws is quite differ-

---

[35] US Constitution, art I § 8.

ent from the power to demand it.[36] These sorts of statutes do not confer on the victims of wrongs a power to hold wrongdoers accountable to them, even though they do provide victims with relief for having been wrongfully injured.[37]

Whether a given statutory wrong is a tort—in the sense of linking a relational duty and a right against mistreatment to a power in the right-holder to hold the duty-bearer to account for breaching the duty—is an issue of statutory interpretation. Sometimes, the question is easily resolved, other times it is not. Consider, for example, two wrongs recognised in New York legislation. New York has enacted a privacy statute that contains a relational legal directive enjoining people from misappropriating another person's name or likeness for trade or advertising.[38] New York's statutes also contain a relational legal norm prohibiting one person from electronically eavesdropping on another.[39] As to both, one must ask whether that right corresponds to a legal power afforded to victims to obtain a remedy from a person who has violated his or her right. In the case of the first, victims clearly do enjoy such a power—it is expressly provided for in the statute. As to the second, it is not clear.

In some instances, torts emerge as judicial–legislative hybrids. Probably the most familiar example in the US of this phenomenon is the action for securities fraud recognised by the Supreme Court to be implicitly authorised by section 10(b) of the Securities Exchange Act of 1934[40] and by rule 10b-5 as promulgated by the Securities and Exchange Commission.[41] Although the Act itself is silent as to whether it was intended to create a federal securities fraud tort, the Court eventually adopted the view that the creation of a primary legal right against certain fraudulent transactions was implicitly a creation of a full-fledged individual right, including a right of redress.[42] Courts have since treated investors as holders of a power to exact a remedy upon proof of the violation of the right not to be manipulated or defrauded in connection with the purchase or sale of securities.

Unlike the Securities Exchange Act, federal employment discrimination statutes have expressly created a private right of action for discrimination

---

[36] Such a power might be conferred on these same victims by tort law, but that is a separate issue.

[37] In many other American States, there is no such legislation, but there is recognition in case law of the right against misappropriation. Even criminal statutes that *mandate* restitution for certain offences are not triggered until there is a prosecution, and the decision to prosecute is not in the victim's hands. Moreover, a prosecutor retains the power to seek a negotiated settlement of the charges against the defendant, which settlement might exclude a guilty plea to any of the offences for which restitution is mandated.

[38] NY Civil Rights Law §§ 50–51.

[39] NY Penal Law § 250.05.

[40] 15 USC § 78j(b).

[41] 17 CFR § 240.10b-5.

[42] *JI Case Co v Borak* 377 US 426 (1964).

on the basis of characteristics such as race, gender and disability.[43] By their terms these statutes provide a primary right to be free of certain kinds of workplace wrongs and a remedial right to the state's assistance in exacting a remedy for such rights violations. Here too, however, the judiciary has played a prominent role in defining the statutory wrong of discrimination. For example, the recognition of workplace sexual harassment as a form of gender discrimination has involved the judicial articulation of a relational legal directive that identifies a primary right against certain kinds of sexualised treatment at the workplace.

D. Rights of Recourse: Civil and Natural

To this point, our invocations of rights might strike readers as narrowly positivistic. After all, we have so far claimed only that there are in fact laws in the US that define certain forms of conduct as wrongs *to* particular persons and hence as violations of a corresponding right not be mistreated, and that these same laws often confer on victims of such violations a power to obtain a remedy from the rights violator. As we now aim to demonstrate, the tort victim's power as against the tortfeasor is linked to a third notion of rights.

The legal power of a tort victim to respond against the wrongdoer for having been wronged is not merely a product of tort law, though it is that. It is the recognition, through tort law, of a principle that connects the plaintiff's underlying claim right not to be mistreated to the conferral on the plaintiff of the power to obtain a remedy. We have dubbed this the 'principle of civil recourse'. It states that a person whose right not to be mistreated has been violated by a wrongdoer is *entitled* to be provided with a means by which to respond, through the legal system, to the wrongdoer. This, we believe, is precisely the principle embodied in the hoary common law maxim *ubi jus ibi remedium*—for every right a remedy. A victim who is the holder of a claim right by virtue of a relational legal directive, and who suffers a rights violation at the hands of the defendant, can demand *of the state* a means of responding to the wrongdoer for the rights violation.

The principle of civil recourse is a legal principle; it is part of our law. As such, it generates a distinct kind of legal right. Unlike the claim rights that potential victims enjoy against actors who are subject to relational legal directives, this claim right does not run against other persons. Rather, it is a right enjoyed by each citizen *against government*: the Hohfeldian duty-bearer is the state. Government, in other words, is obligated to provide a body of law that defines wrongs and empowers victims of wrongs to respond to those who have wronged them. This is obviously a right

[43] 42 USC § 2000e-5.

to redress in a very different sense than the Hohfeldian power conferred on tort victims to obtain remedies from wrongdoers. To invoke the language of an old US Supreme Court opinion, it is a 'right to *a law* for the redress of wrongs'[44]—ie, an affirmative right to be provided with a means of responding, through the legal system, to certain kinds of mistreatment at the hands of others.

What is the status of the individual's right to a law of redress? As noted above, we think it is at a minimum a right enshrined in the common law's *ubi jus* maxim. In addition, several State constitutions contain provisions recognising the right to a body of recourse law as a constitutional right. Indeed, on the basis of these provisions, some State courts have struck down legislation stripping away the remedial rights of tort victims.[45] One of us has argued that the Fourteenth Amendment to the US Constitution is properly read to confer a right to a law of recourse on all US citizens.[46] Alternatively, one might say that the right to a law of recourse is a right to which a liberal democratic government, given its other commitments, ought to adhere.

This last thought leads us to the fourth, most overtly normative, and perhaps most controversial claim about the way in which rights figure in US tort law. The claim here is that the legal right to be provided by the state with a means of recourse is linked to a pre-legal right grounded in political morality. Contrary to the arguments of Epstein, Fletcher and others, this right is *not* a right to equal liberty or to equal security against physical injury. Indeed, it is not a Hohfeldian claim right at all. Rather it is a Hohfeldian *privilege* or liberty that corresponds to what Hohfeld called a 'no-right'.[47] Specifically, it is the privilege to engage in self-preservative acts against wrongdoers. The notion is that a person's natural right not to be subjected to certain forms of aggression by others is partially forfeited by virtue of his or her wronging of another. Correlative to this Hohfeldian 'no-right' is a privilege or liberty on the part of the victim to assert him or herself against the wrongdoer by way of responding to the wrong. So long as one is willing to utilise the term 'right' to cover liberties and privileges, this too may be termed a 'right'.

Following Locke, we can explicate this privilege by invoking the fiction

---

[44] *Missouri Pacific Railway Co v Humes* 115 US 512 (1885) 521 (Field J for the Court) (emphasis added).

[45] See, eg, *Ferdon v Wisconsin Patients Compensation Fund* 701 NW 2d 440 (Wis 2005) (striking down the State's medical malpractice reform statute as violating the Wisconsin Constitution's guarantee of separation of powers). Other State courts have either declined to recognise such a right, or have opted to under-enforce it through the use of deferential rational-basis review. For citations to relevant State constitutional provisions and court decisions, see RF Williams, 'Rights' in GA Tarr and RF Williams (eds), *State Constitutions for the Twenty-First Century*, vol 3 (Albany NY, State University of New York Press, 2006) 7, 18–19.

[46] JCP Goldberg, 'The Constitutional Status of Tort Law: Due Process and the Right to a Law for the Redress of Wrongs' (2005) 115 *Yale Law Journal* 524.

[47] Hohfeld, above n 2, at 32–33.

of the state of nature.[48] In that condition, whenever an individual suffers 'injury' (ie, a wronging) at the hands of another, the victimised individual, according to Locke, has a right to obtain reparations for the injury from the injurer. This privilege, he suggests, is connected to other privileges, including the privilege of each person to punish wrongdoers for the public or criminal aspect of their wrongdoing, and the privilege of each person to take action to preserve oneself against wrongful attack.

To be sure, Locke argued that, in the transition from the state of nature to civil society, individuals lose most of these privileges. A member of a civil society cannot take it upon himself to punish a wrongdoer or to use self-help to obtain reparations from the wrongdoer, though he can still invoke the privilege of self-defence. However, Locke insisted that this 'loss' or transfer of power is *conditional*. It is only when government actually takes over the job of seeing to it that criminals are punished and that victims of wrongs are given an avenue of recourse against wrongdoers that individuals lose their natural self-protective and responsive privileges. In the name of civil peace, individuals relinquish these privileges and *entrust* them to the state. The state, in turn, holds them in trust. The state is thus obligated to see to it that an equivalent is provided in the form of criminal law and civil recourse law. If governments are going to insist—as they should—that victims of wrongs relinquish the right to respond directly to wrongdoers, then governments are required to provide some alternative avenue of response. Hence the legal right of civil recourse flows from a pre-legal privilege enjoyed by a victim to respond to a wrongdoer for having wronged him or her.

To summarise: rights figure in the law of torts in at least four senses. First, tort law contains relational norms of conduct that impose duties on defendants not to mistreat others and recognises correlative claim rights not to be mistreated. Secondly, it confers on victims a power to alter the legal rights and duties of wrongdoers—that is, to hold wrongdoers liable. Thirdly, it grants this power in accordance with the legal principle of civil recourse, which recognises the individual victim's claim right, good against the state, to a means by which to hold the wrongdoer accountable to him or her. Finally, the legal principle of civil recourse is in turn illuminated by appeal to what might be called a 'natural right'

---

[48] This discussion draws on our previous treatments of Locke on recourse. See Goldberg, above n 46; BC Zipursky, 'Philosophy of Private Law' in J Coleman and S Shapiro (eds), *The Oxford Handbook of Jurisprudence and Philosophy of Law* (Oxford, Oxford University Press, 2002) 623. Needless to say, there are many pitfalls associated with state of nature arguments, particularly insofar as they are offered as part of a foundationalist effort to derive principles of just government from a set of supposedly uncontroversial first principles. We mean to invoke the state of nature metaphor only as a means of testing our judgments about the sort of privileges to which a person can plausibly claim title given our society's relatively longstanding and deep commitments—however imperfectly realised—to ideals of equality and liberty.

of response to wrongdoing. A state's justified refusal to give legal recognition to this natural privilege—its barring of certain direct responses by victims against wrongdoers—is, in part, what grounds the legal principle of civil recourse.

E. Liability and Responsibility Revisited

Armed with this multi-level account of the place of rights in tort, we can revisit several of the puzzles identified above. To begin with, why would a legal system rely on tort liability (rather than, eg, criminal or regulatory law) to protect citizens' rights against mistreatment? One part of the answer is that many of the rights recognised by tort law—the right not to be battered or killed or the right not to have one's property converted—are in fact protected by other forms of law. For these wrongs, a choice among different forms of law need not be made. The deeper response, however, is that tort law specifically gives legal powers to the victim of a legal wrong because a central commitment from which tort law springs is that the victims of relational legal wrongs enjoy a special entitlement to respond to having been wronged. This power is a legal power and the right to have such a legal power is itself a legal entitlement. The principle that individual victims are entitled to respond to having been wronged is a principle of political morality, embedded in the law. That the plaintiff herself has been wronged provides a reason to regard the plaintiff as having a right to exact damages for having been wrongfully injured.

This is perhaps an appropriate moment to say why it is that we have resisted being classified as corrective justice theorists, notwithstanding the many respects in which our work builds on that of theorists such as Weinrib and Coleman. We reject the central metaphor of corrective justice because, in at least one respect, it partakes too much of public law conceptions of tort. Specifically, it suggests that the state, through tort law, is aiming to achieve justice by itself rectifying private wrongs. This is not our view of what is happening in a tort suit. Our view is that the state, through tort law, empowers private parties to redress wrongs done to them, if they so choose. Tort law does not aim for making whole any more than criminal law's recognition of a privilege of self-defence aims for punishment of the assailant. A person who reasonably perceives herself to be under a threat of imminent attack is not acting as an agent of the state when she assails the attacker. Rather, she is exercising a privilege of self-preservation. Similarly, a person who has been tortiously injured and sues the injurer for damages is not acting as an agent of the state when she prosecutes her tort action. Rather, she is exercising her own right, one that grows out of the privilege to respond to mistreatment.

In turn, the depiction of tort claims as a form of self-assertion by the victim against a person who has mistreated her sheds light on the nature of tort damages. To appreciate that tort law is all about a victim's right to respond, and to look to the state for an avenue of response, is to appreciate how far the notion of tort damages is from the idea of a 'restoration' of something that has been taken from the victim. A tort suit exacting a damages award is closer to an act of self-defence than it is to the indemnification of a loss. For a defendant to be subject to tort liability is for the defendant to be rendered vulnerable and answerable to a victim for what he or she has done to the victim. Tort law enables the plaintiff to seek and obtain a satisfaction for what has been done to her. To the extent the plaintiff is entitled to compensation, it is compensation akin to the sort we saw above in the medical malpractice example: compensation for *what has been done to her*, not compensation in the sense of restoring to her what has been taken from her. Of course, the ideas of recapturing things that have been taken and of enabling one's own self-repair fit comfortably within the notion of satisfaction for what has been done. But there is no reason to suppose these more specific ideas exhaust the notion of satisfaction.

Attention to the complex of rights at work in tort permits us, finally, to explain the centrality to tort of notions of responsibility and the connection between responsibility and rights. Obviously, it is perfectly cogent to depict the duties set forth by the relational directives of tort law as setting out responsibilities that actors owe to one another. Tort law articulates duties, such as the duty to take care not to cause bodily injury to others that one might foresee causing. The more fundamental point is that, in tort, 'responsible' *means* answerable or accountable.[49] It is not just that, by virtue of tort law, one is in certain circumstances legally responsible to take care, to forbear from defrauding, etc. It is that one will be held liable to another in the particular sense of being *held to account to another* for something that one has done to another (or failed to do for another).[50] For one person to mistreat another in a manner that amounts to a tort is for that person to render herself vulnerable to that other, to be the object of a power that the other can now exercise over her. In this sense, a tortfeasor is not only responsible, but *response-able*.

---

[49] It is perhaps illuminating to recall the origins of Anglo-American tort law in the medieval writ system. Royal writs initially consisted of executive orders summarily resolving disputes (*praecipe* writs). From these gradually emerged a very different kind of writ, exemplified by the writ of trespass *vi et armis*—namely, *ostensurus quare* writs. The latter were issued by the King at the behest of a complainant, and instead of peremptorily resolving a dispute, summoned an alleged wrongdoer to account for his treatment of the complainant—to appear before a judge and 'show why' he did what he was alleged to have done. See JH Langbein, RL Lerner and BP Smith, *History of the Common Law: The Development of Anglo-American Legal Institutions* (New York, Wolters Kluwer Law & Business, 2009) 88–91.

[50] See Hohfeld, above n 2, at 54 (quoting approvingly from judicial opinions asserting that liability *is* responsibility).

A basic principle of tort doctrine—perhaps the most basic principle of tort doctrine—is that one person can hold another to account for having injured him or her, but only if the other violated his or her right not to be mistreated. A tort plaintiff sues in his or her own right, not as the vicarious beneficiary of a duty owed to another.[51] Under the relational wrongs analysis we have offered, it is not enough that a defendant has acted antisocially, or that he or she has acted antisocially so as to cause harm to the plaintiff. Nor is it enough that a defendant has acted antisocially so as to cause foreseeable harm to the plaintiff. An actor is answerable in the tort sense only if he or she has violated a relational directive enjoining him or her not to subject a person such as the plaintiff to a certain kind of mistreatment—ie, only if he or she has violated the plaintiff's right. To say the same thing, a defendant is answerable to the plaintiff only if the defendant violated the plaintiff's right. Invasions of rights (in the sense of primary rights correlative to duties not to injure others) generate responsibility (the liability or answerability of one person to another). This is the linkage, in tort, of rights to responsibility.

It may be tempting to suppose that the account just provided is viciously circular. It is not. The primary claim rights enjoyed by individuals are defined by relational directives—legal norms of non-injury. Responsibility or accountability exists for those who have invaded rights because of the law's recognition of a right to a means of redressing wrongs. The state, pursuant to a duty to provide an avenue of civil recourse to those who have been wronged, confers a power to exact a remedy from a wrong-doer onto those who can establish that they have been wronged. Those subject to this power are potentially liable only if they have violated the victim's right. Liability travels with responsibility and responsibility turns on whether the defendant violated the plaintiff's right.

IV. CONCLUSION

The ambiguities of the term 'right' are more than a trap for the unwary and an opportunity for the rhetorician. The common law of torts has utilised the concept of a right in a way that self-consciously—and for good reason—merges the notion of a right as the correlative of a duty and the notion of a right as the correlative of a liability. It is a fundamental principle guiding courts in the exercise of their authority that those to whom relational legal duties have been breached are entitled to have the courts back their demands for a remedy against those who have breached those duties. More succinctly, a person whose legal right against mistreatment

---

[51] *Palsgraf v Long Island Railroad Co* 162 NE 99 (NY 1928) 101 (Cardozo CJ for Cardozo CJ, Pound, Lehman and Kellogg JJ).

has been violated by a wrongdoer enjoys a right to hold the wrongdoer responsible.

Despite the double duty being pulled by the term 'right' in the preceding statement, it should be clear by now that this usage is not tautological. The invasion of a primary right of conduct ordinarily generates a right, in the sense of a power, against the wrongdoer. It does so by virtue of a substantive principle of political morality that, depending on to whom it applies, may or may not be a legal principle. If a state's legal system includes relational directives that enjoin certain actors not to mistreat others, then for that very reason the state has a duty to empower victims of mistreatment to hold wrongdoers responsible for having wronged them. In the domain of established domestic tort law, this state duty has the status of law; it is a legal duty owed by the state to its citizens.

10

Damages and Rights

ANDREW BURROWS*

I. INTRODUCTION

I N RECENT YEARS in England, the relationship between damages
and rights has been topical in two different respects. The major division in this chapter reflects those two aspects. The first main section
(part II) looks at what rights theorists, epitomised by Robert Stevens,
have been arguing in relation to damages. That is of general wide-ranging importance whatever jurisdiction one is concerned with. The second
main section (part III) looks at an issue of more local concern which is
what the approach to damages should be for infringement of Convention
rights under the Human Rights Act 1998 and, in particular, whether the
approach of the House of Lords in *R (Greenfield) v Secretary of State
for the Home Department*[1] is correct. A final shorter section (part IV)
touches on both those two main sections by exploring what is meant by
'vindicatory damages'.

II. THE SUBSTITUTIVE DAMAGES THESIS

A. Introduction

The substitutive damages thesis has been put forward particularly clearly
and forcefully by Stevens in his superb book *Torts and Rights*.[2] One finds

---

* I am grateful to Roderick Bagshaw and James Edelman for their very helpful com-
ments on an earlier draft of this paper. I would also like to take this opportunity to thank
Donal Nolan and Andrew Robertson for inviting me to give this paper at the Obligations
V conference and for their impeccable organisation of the conference.

[1] *R (Greenfield) v Secretary of State for the Home Department* [2005] UKHL 14, [2005]
1 WLR 673 (*Greenfield*).

[2] R Stevens, *Torts and Rights* (Oxford, Oxford University Press, 2007) ch 4. See also
R Stevens, 'Damages and the Right to Performance: A *Golden Victory* or Not?' in JW Neyers,
R Bronaugh and SGA Pitel (eds), *Exploring Contract Law* (Oxford, Hart Publishing, 2009)
171.

support for it, or at least for aspects of it, in the work of other respected academics.[3]

As recently as the 1960s, the law of damages was under-theorised. The attitude of many judges was typified by statements to the effect that the quantum of damages was a question of fact and many still adhered to the view that on most issues concerning damages there were very few principles involved.[4] Two books in the early 1960s were particularly influential in inspiring a change in the approach of English lawyers to the law of damages. The first was the 12th edition in 1961 of *Mayne and McGregor on Damages*, which was the first version of that work undertaken (and indeed completely rewritten) by Harvey McGregor.[5] The second was *The Principles of the Law of Damages* by Harry Street, published in 1962.[6] Street was a remarkably gifted academic as shown not only by the range of his writing but also by his unrivalled ability to foresee trends in the law and legal scholarship.[7] So, for example, it was he who first spearheaded scholarship on rights in this country with his path-breaking book in 1963, *Freedom, the Individual and the Law*.[8] A few years later, he was one of the first English academics to advocate a no-fault state compensation scheme for road accidents.[9] The title for Street's 1962 book on damages was precisely chosen so as to make people sit up and think because to

---

[3] See, eg, A Tettenborn, 'What Is a Loss?' in JW Neyers, E Chamberlain and SGA Pitel (eds), *Emerging Issues in Tort Law* (Oxford, Hart Publishing, 2007) 441; D Pearce and R Halson, 'Damages for Breach of Contract: Compensation, Restitution and Vindication' (2008) 28 *Oxford Journal of Legal Studies* 73; F Reynolds, 'The *Golden Victory*—A Misguided Decision' (2008) 38 *Hong Kong Law Journal* 333. It was flirted with by J Edelman, 'Gain-Based Damages and Compensation' in A Burrows and Lord Rodger (eds), *Mapping the Law: Essays in Memory of Peter Birks* (Oxford, Oxford University Press, 2006) 141–60 but he has subsequently abandoned that position.

[4] See, eg, *British Westinghouse Electric and Manufacturing Co Ltd v Underground Railways Co of London Ltd* [1912] AC 673 (HL) 688–89 (Viscount Haldane LC): 'The quantum of damage is a question of fact'; *Charterhouse Credit Co Ltd v Tolly* [1963] 2 QB 683 (CA) 712 (Upjohn LJ): 'the assessment of damages has never been an exact science; it is essentially practical'.

[5] H McGregor, *Mayne and McGregor on Damages*, 12th edn (London, Sweet & Maxwell, 1961). From the 13th edition onwards, reflecting the extent of the rewriting since the 11th edition, the book has been called merely *McGregor on Damages*. The most recent edition is H McGregor, *McGregor on Damages*, 18th edn (London, Sweet & Maxwell, 2009).

[6] H Street, *The Principles of the Law of Damages* (London, Sweet & Maxwell, 1962).

[7] At my interview for a lectureship at Manchester University in 1980 he asked me whether a person who infringed another's right to light by building a hotel could be made to give up its profits to the victim. Over 25 years later, that question has just been dealt with by the courts: see *Forsyth-Grant v Allen* [2008] EWCA Civ 505, [2008] EnvLR 41. I am indebted to the late Professor Street not only for giving me the job but also for encouraging me (or, more accurately, ordering me) to start writing and publishing from my very first days in post.

[8] H Street, *Freedom, the Individual and the Law* (Harmondsworth, Penguin, 1963). Five editions of the book were written by Street before his death. The sixth and seventh editions were written by Geoffrey Robertson QC, the most recent edition being G Robertson, *Freedom, the Individual and the Law*, 7th edn (London, Penguin, 1993).

[9] DW Elliott and H Street, *Road Accidents* (London, Penguin, 1968).

many at the time the law of damages was a dull area of practice devoid of principle. As Street wrote in his Preface, 'Hitherto the law of damages has been quite remarkable for the lack of interest shown by jurists in its fundamental rules.'[10] One certainly could not say that today.

One particular feature of scholarship over the last 40 years has been the labelling given to different types of damages. As our analysis has become more sophisticated, there has been a proliferation in the labels given by commentators and judges to describe different types of damages. Indeed it may be a surprise to some to realise that even the label 'compensatory damages' is relatively new because the traditional starting assumption was that all damages, with a few minor exceptions, aim to compensate loss. So apart from compensatory damages and its subcategory of 'aggravated damages' and the long-established exceptions of 'exemplary damages' (otherwise known as 'punitive damages') and 'nominal damages', we now have references, for example, to 'reliance damages', 'restitutionary damages', 'disgorgement damages', 'restorative damages', 'negotiating damages', '*Wrotham Park* damages', 'vindicatory damages' and, the one I now want to deal with, 'substitutive damages'.

In *Torts and Rights*,[11] Stevens has argued that the basic award of damages in all cases of tort and breach of contract is non-compensatory. Rather, the basic award of damages is to provide a substitute for, and hence to vindicate, the right that has been infringed. They are substitutive damages. They are concerned to value the right infringed and will be assessed, if there is no ready market value, by the methodology of constructing a reasonable hypothetical bargain between the parties. It is irrelevant to these damages whether a claimant has suffered any loss although, where it has, consequential compensatory damages can be added. The same applies to restitutionary damages: where the defendant has made a gain by committing the wrong, these can be added as consequential damages to the claimant's basic award of substitutive damages.

Therefore, applying Stevens' approach, every infringement of a right triggers an award of damages for the value of that right and compensatory damages are merely additional consequential damages in so far as losses have been suffered. So, for example, a personal injury award in the tort of negligence is seen as awarding damages for the value of the infringed right to bodily integrity plus consequential compensatory damages for any financial or non-financial losses, such as pain and suffering. Damages for false imprisonment are awarded for the value of the infringed right to freedom plus consequential compensatory damages for any financial or non-financial loss caused. Damages for breach of contract are awarded for the value of the contractual right infringed plus consequential compensatory damages for any financial or non-financial losses caused.

---

[10] Street, *The Principles of the Law of Damages*, above n 6, at v.
[11] Stevens, *Torts and Rights*, above n 2.

Stevens' thesis cannot, and does not, stop short of seeking to alter the whole of our conventional understanding of damages which has seen compensatory damages as lying at the heart of damages. By any standards, therefore, the substitutive damages thesis constitutes a radical and novel reinterpretation of the law. It requires us to accept that McGregor, Street and countless other commentators and judges have been wrong. That is a bold claim and, with respect, I do not think it stands up to close scrutiny although it is very important to the future of the law of damages to pinpoint precisely the objections to it. I suggest that there are six such objections.

B. Six Objections

1. The Stevens thesis appears to contradict the law on the duty to mitigate, mitigation and compensating advantages. Take the leading case on mitigation in contract, *British Westinghouse Electric and Manufacturing Co Ltd v Underground Electric Railways Co of London Ltd*.[12] The defendant had delivered defective turbines which the claimant had replaced by turbines that turned out to be more efficient and profitable than the old turbines would have been even if non-defective. The principle laid down by the House of Lords was that, in assessing the purchaser's damages, one should take into account to reduce damages, the greater efficiency of the replacement turbines. In other words, one is concerned to compensate the overall loss, having deducted all mitigating gains, and it would follow that if all the losses (including those in purchasing the replacements) were outweighed by the mitigating gains, no substantial damages at all would be awarded. Yet on Stevens' approach, substantial damages should still be awarded in that situation for the infringement of the right to delivery of non-defective turbines (presumably measured by the difference in market price between the turbines delivered and those that should have been delivered). Similarly, in *Uzinterimpex JSC v Standard Bank Plc* it was accepted by the Court of Appeal that the duty to mitigate applies to the tort of conversion in the same way that it applies to other legal wrongs.[13] So if the owner unreasonably turns down an offer by the tortfeasor for the goods to be returned, or for deteriorating goods to be sold off and the

---

[12] *British Westinghouse Electric and Manufacturing Co Ltd v Underground Electric Railways Co of London Ltd* [1912] AC 673 (HL).

[13] *Uzinterimpex JSC v Standard Bank Plc* [2008] EWCA Civ 819, [2008] 2 Lloyd's Rep 456. See also Lord Nicholls' speech in *Kuwait Airways Corp v Iraqi Airways Co* [2002] UKHL 19, [2002] 2 AC 883, in which he referred to various cases in which the courts refused to award substantial damages for conversion because no loss had been suffered including, eg, *Hiort v London and North Western Railway* (1879) 4 Ex D 188 (CA), *Wickham Holdings Ltd v Brooke House Motors Ltd* [1967] 1 WLR 295 (CA) and *Brandeis Goldschmidt & Co Ltd v Western Transport Ltd* [1981] QB 864 (CA).

sale proceeds paid into a joint account pending resolution of the dispute, no damages may be recovered in the tort of conversion for subsequently being deprived of the goods or for the deterioration in the value of the goods. Yet according to Stevens' thesis, damages should be awarded for conversion assessed according to the market value of the goods converted and irrespective of a failure in the duty to mitigate.

2. The approach contradicts the standard approach to causation of loss. To use the example put forward by James Edelman,[14] say D1 negligently crashes into the claimant's car denting a panel which will therefore need replacing. The claimant is entitled to damages for the cost of that replacement. Say before that work has been carried out, D2 negligently crashes into the claimant's car and puts a second dent into the same panel. Applying the traditional law, D2 will not be liable to pay substantial damages because it has caused the claimant no loss.[15] The panel needed repairing anyway. But on Stevens' thesis, there ought to be a substantial award of damages against D2 because D2 has infringed the claimant's right not to be crashed into just as much as D1. The same basic damages ought therefore to be awarded against both.

3. Closely linked to the last two points is that the courts take account of events subsequent to the breach of contract or tort as this may increase or reduce the claimant's loss.[16] A rigid 'date of breach' or 'date of tort' rule for the date of assessment for damages has been replaced by a more flexible approach that seeks to ensure true compensation while not undermining the duty to mitigate. As Oliver J said in *Radford v De Froberville*, 'the proper approach is to assess the damages at the date of the hearing unless it can be said that the plaintiff ought reasonably to have mitigated by seeking an alternative performance at an earlier date.'[17] Yet for Stevens it would appear that there is never a good reason for assessing the value of the right infringed other than at the date of the infringement.

4. Applying the logic of Stevens' approach, it is not clear that one can avoid an unacceptable overlap between the damages for the value of the right infringed and the consequential compensatory damages. If my car is damaged beyond repair by your negligence, but the next day I spend £10 000 to replace it with a new car, one surely would not wish to award the market value of the right infringed—which is presumably the market

---

[14] J Edelman, 'The Meaning of Loss and Enrichment' in R Chambers, C Mitchell and J Penner (eds), *Philosophical Foundations of the Law of Unjust Enrichment* (Oxford, Oxford University Press, 2009) 211, 220.

[15] *Performance Cars Ltd v Abraham* [1962] 1 QB 33 (CA).

[16] Two leading decisions of the House of Lords on the date of assessment in contract are *Johnson v Agnew* [1980] AC 367 and *Golden Strait Corp v Nippon Yusen Kabishika Kaisha (The Golden Victory)* [2007] UKHL 12, [2007] 2 AC 353.

[17] *Radford v De Froberville* [1977] 1 WLR 1262 (Ch) 1286.

value of the destroyed car—plus the £10 000 replacement cost. Yet, if these are two different types of damages, then they ought to be cumulative rather than alternative and there can be no justification for requiring an election between them. The logic of Stevens' approach would allow both to be recovered.

5. It is not clear that there is any role for 'nominal damages' in Stevens' scheme. Every infringement of a right would seem to require a substantial sum of damages assessed according to the market value of the right infringed. The idea of a nominal sum[18] for wrongs actionable per se, *not reflecting any loss suffered*,[19] would appear to be redundant. This may be no bad thing because there is a strong argument that nominal damages are unnecessary given that one can always seek a declaration that one's rights have been infringed.[20] However, under the present law, for better or worse, nominal damages do exist and Stevens' thesis cannot account for them.

6. Underpinning several of the above difficulties is that the Stevens approach falls down in imagining that we sensibly can, or would want to, put a value on the right that has been infringed rather than the consequential impact of that infringement. As Edelman points out,[21] if one were truly concerned to value the right, the nature of the infringement and its consequences should be irrelevant. So, for example, the value of the right to the integrity of one's car is the same whether the right is infringed by a tiny dent or a colossal crash.[22] But it cannot be correct for the basic award of damages to be the same in both situations and that is because one is not concerned with the value of a right infringed but rather with the consequences of the infringement for the victim; and that is what the traditional compensatory approach focuses on.

---

[18] The normal sum awarded appears to range from £1 to £10.

[19] As McGregor points out the term 'nominal damages' has very occasionally been used in the different sense of a sum of compensatory damages awarded where a loss has been proved but insufficient evidence of the loss has been provided to put an accurate figure on the loss: *McGregor on Damages*, above n 5, at paras 10-004–10-005. In McGregor's words, 'the fact of a loss is shown but the necessary evidence as to its amount is not given': at para 10-004. I am grateful to James Edelman for drawing my attention to a modern example of this usage in *Greer v Alstons Engineering Sales and Services Ltd* [2003] UKPC 46, (2003) 147 SJLB 783. The criticism that Stevens' thesis cannot account for nominal damages applies only to nominal damages in the main sense, referred to in the text, in which that term is used.

[20] See, eg, Lord Millett's obiter dicta in *Cullen v Chief Constable of the Royal Ulster Constabulary* [2003] UKHL 39, [2003] 1 WLR 1763 [81].

[21] Edelman, 'The Meaning of Loss and Enrichment', above n 14, at 219.

[22] One might be able to divide up certain rights into more important and less important rights. For example, it may be realistic to divide up a right to bodily integrity so that the right to see or hear is distinguished from the right to the use of a toe. But the point remains that the same right might be infringed in a more or less serious way depending on the consequences for the claimant (eg, the right to the use of a toe may be infringed by a cut or by being cut off).

C. Some Problematic Cases

While, for the above reasons, the substitutive damages thesis appears to be flawed, one has to concede that there are decisions which, applying a conventional compensatory or restitutionary analysis, are problematic. These decisions test to the limits our belief in a compensatory or restitutionary analysis and may be thought to offer support to the substitutive damages thesis. To illustrate the point, I have chosen four such cases, two challenging the conventional compensation analysis and two challenging the conventional restitutionary analysis. The four cases are *The Mediana*,[23] *Burdis v Livsey*,[24] *Inverugie Investments Ltd v Hackett*[25] and *Pell Frischmann Engineering v Bow Valley Iran Ltd*.[26] Not surprisingly the first three of these feature heavily in Stevens' book and one would imagine that the fourth would also have done so had it been decided prior to the book's publication.

(i) The Mediana[27]

In this case the claimant harbour authority's lightship was damaged in a shipping accident caused by the negligence of the defendant's ship so that the lightship had to be withdrawn for repairs. In addition to the cost of repairs, the claimant was held entitled to damages for the loss of use of the lightship. That was so even though the lightship was not profit-earning and even though the claimant did not need to hire a replacement because it kept a spare lightship as cover in the event of damage to the first. In other words, damages were awarded for loss of use even when there seemed to be no loss flowing from the inability to use the damaged lightship. Although the House of Lords did not itself have to assess the damages, which were agreed, they were based on the cost of maintaining the spare lightship.

Seeing the problems with a compensatory analysis, Stevens treats this case as supporting his substitutive damages thesis. Damages in his view were awarded as a substitute for the infringed right to use the ship during the period of repair. They were given for the value of that right. In his words, 'Although the loss of the use of the ship had resulted in no consequential loss, damages were payable for the lost right to use the ship during the period of repair.'[28]

---

[23] *Owners of the Steamship Mediana v Owners, Master and Crew of the Lightship Comet (The Mediana)* [1900] AC 113 (HL).

[24] *Burdis v Livsey* [2002] EWCA Civ 510, [2003] QB 36.

[25] *Inverugie Investments Ltd v Hackett* [1995] 1 WLR 713 (PC) (*Inverugie*).

[26] *Pell Frischmann Engineering v Bow Valley Iran Ltd* [2009] UKPC 45, [2010] BLR 73 (*Pell Frischmann*).

[27] *The Mediana* [1900] AC 113 (HL).

[28] Stevens, *Torts and Rights*, above n 2, at 73–74.

One should note immediately, however, that on that view the damages should surely have been straightforwardly measured by the cost of hiring an equivalent ship and should not have been based on the cost of maintaining the spare ship.

I have previously expressed, and maintain, the view that there was no pecuniary loss in *The Mediana*.[29] In line with that, if we are to defend the decision in terms of compensation, it should be viewed as a decision awarding damages for non-pecuniary loss.[30] In other words, the loss suffered by the harbour authority was the upsetting of its peace of mind because in having to use the spare lightship it no longer had the security of there being a spare in the event that that lightship was also damaged. The background facts indicated that damage to lightships was not an unusual occurrence and it was precisely for that reason that a spare was maintained. Moreover, if we do think in terms of 'peace of mind' one can understand why the parties applied the cost of maintaining the spare as the way to measure the damages. That was precisely what the harbour authority was paying for its 'peace of mind'.

However, a difficulty with that analysis is that, although this has rarely been discussed by the courts, the traditional view is that a non-human person, such as a company or public authority, is incapable of suffering non-pecuniary loss. So, for example, in the libel case *Collins Stewart Ltd v The Financial Times Ltd*, it was held that aggravated damages, concerned to compensate mental distress, could not be awarded in favour of a company.[31] The logic is that non-pecuniary loss, which is not a loss of wealth, is ultimately concerned with the claimant's mental distress or loss of happiness and that is not something that a non-human person can experience. But in so far as this is a general restriction it seems unsatisfactory. Much of what a public authority and many private companies are concerned with is the pursuit of non-profit-making goals. These include,

---

[29] A Burrows, *Remedies for Torts and Breach of Contract*, 3rd edn (Oxford, Oxford University Press, 2004) 244–46. More than one participant at the conference expressed the view to me that the decision is best viewed as compensating for a pecuniary loss where the loss constitutes advance or preventive mitigation. The difficulty with this is that the wrong comes after the incurring of the expense and so it is not easy to establish the causal link.

[30] For a similar analysis—which focuses on the 'undesired' non-pecuniary consequence of the damage to the lightship—see Edelman, 'The Meaning of Loss and Enrichment', above n 14, especially at 215–18.

[31] *Collins Stewart Ltd v The Financial Times Ltd* [2005] EWHC 262 (QB), [2006] EMLR 5. But aggravated damages were awarded in favour of a company at first instance in *Messenger Newspaper Group Ltd v National Graphical Association* [1984] IRLR 397 (QB); and, as pointed out by the Law Commission, *Damages under the Human Rights Act 1998* (Law Com No 266, 2000) para 3.28, the Strasbourg Court has awarded damages for non-pecuniary loss to companies under the European Convention on Human Rights. Rather surprisingly the previous government put forward draft legislation to override the impact of the *Collins Stewart* case, so as to allow aggravated damages to be awarded in favour of companies, in the specific context of certain intellectual property torts. See the Ministry of Justice, *Civil Law Reform—A Draft Bill* (Cm 7773, 2009) 5 cl 9; Ministry of Justice, *Civil Law Reform Bill — Consultation* (Law Com CP No 53, 2009) 49–50.

for example, the protection of the environment or, as in *The Mediana*, the safety of the public. Just as a holidaymaker whose holiday is ruined is entitled to mental distress damages for breach of contract, so a public authority concerned with public safety should be entitled to damages for the disruption of its 'peace of mind' as regards the safety of the public. If necessary so to do, one might conceptualise this as reflecting the mental distress of those individuals who constitute the controlling mind and will of the public authority or company.[32]

(ii) Burdis v Livsey[33]

The question at issue in this case was whether damages for the cost of repairs to a car, damaged by the defendant's negligence, should be awarded where the claimant had not itself incurred those costs because they had been paid for under what, it transpired, was an unenforceable consumer credit agreement. In other words, could the claimant recover damages for the cost of repairs where a third party had paid for those repairs and had done so neither benevolently nor in accordance with a valid insurance contract (which are the two recognised exceptions to the general principle that compensating advantages[34] are deducted)?

The Court of Appeal decided that the claimant was entitled to damages for the cost of repairs. The earlier House of Lords decision in *Dimond v Lovell*[35]—where, in exactly the same situation, damages for *hire* costs that would not be incurred were held irrecoverable—was distinguished on the ground that that case was dealing with consequential loss whereas one was here concerned with direct loss. That is, the damage to the car, causing a diminution in value, was a direct loss which was measured by the cost of repairs.

Stevens regards both those decisions as correct. This is because for him substitutive damages were claimed and awarded in *Burdis v Livsey* whereas in *Dimond v Lovell* it was consequential compensatory damages that were in issue. He writes:

> The stark difference in result is justified by the fact that in *Burdis v Livsey* the repair costs were awarded to reflect the diminution in value of the car upon being damaged. The claimant was seeking damages ... as a substitute for his lost property right to the car. This ... crystallised as soon as the car was damaged ... That the claimant suffered no financial loss as a consequence of the infringement of this right is irrelevant to the claim for this head of damages. By contrast, in *Dimond v Lovell* the claimant was seeking to claim for her economic loss consequential upon the infringement of her right to her

---

[32] Or, in some situations, the mental distress of those who the public authority or company were concerned to benefit.
[33] *Burdis v Livsey* [2002] EWCA Civ 510, [2003] QB 36.
[34] Often referred to as 'collateral benefits'.
[35] *Dimond v Lovell* [2002] 1 AC 384 (HL).

car ... As this consequential economic loss, the hire charges, was not in fact incurred it could not be recovered.[36]

The better view is that the two cases are irreconcilable and that, applying *Dimond v Lovell*, the Court of Appeal in *Burdis v Livsey* should have held (as Gray J in an excellent judgement at first instance had decided) that damages for the costs of repair should not be awarded as these had not been, and would not be, incurred by the claimant because of the unenforceability of the consumer credit agreement; and there was no good reason to extend to this situation the exceptions to the prima facie principle that compensating advantages should be deducted in assessing compensatory damages.

Indeed, even if one were to accept the substitutive damages thesis, it seems misleading to treat it as offering a valid explanation of the difference between the two cases. If damages were being awarded in *The Mediana* for the 'lost right to use the ship during the period of repair' why were not damages available to Mrs Dimond for the loss of the right to use her car during the period of repair? In other words, why are there not two rights involved: the right to the physical integrity of the car (measured by the repair cost) and the right to the use of the car (measured by the hire cost)? It is surely not being suggested by Stevens that Mrs Dimond was denied the hire costs because her claim had been incorrectly pleaded. Nothing in the leading speech of Lord Hoffmann hinted at that and Lord Hobhouse, in examining the principles applicable to the damages, explicitly stated that Mrs Dimond 'did in fact lose the use of her car during the period of repair'[37] so that loss of use was clearly in his mind. It follows that, while the compensatory analysis does involve treating *Burdis v Livsey* as wrongly decided, the substitutive damages thesis fares no better and, even on its own terms, does not offer a convincing reconciliation of *Dimond v Lovell* and *Burdis v Livsey*.

(iii) Inverugie Investments Ltd v Hackett[38]

Until relatively recently, the idea that damages are compensatory was so dominant that the notion that they might sometimes be concerned to reverse a gain made by the defendant wrongdoer was ignored. Today this is no longer viewed as heretical and it is widely accepted by judges and commentators alike that damages for a civil wrong may be gain-based (and therefore, according to the terminology I would adopt, 'restitutionary'). However, controversy rages over the situations in which such damages are, or should be, awarded.

One of the major disputed areas is where the civil wrong has involved

---

[36] Stevens, *Torts and Rights*, above n 2, at 72–73.
[37] *Dimond v Lovell* [2002] 1 AC 384 (HL) 406.
[38] *Inverugie* [1995] 1 WLR 713 (PC).

the use of another's property, whether real or personal. Say, for example, the defendant has, without permission, borrowed the claimant's bicycle and, before the claimant has missed it, has returned it undamaged. In a claim for damages for trespass to goods, it may be difficult to say that the claimant has suffered any loss. In particular, the argument that the claimant has lost the opportunity to hire out the bike to the defendant or a third party seems unrealistic where we know that the claimant would not have hired out the bicycle even if the defendant had approached him. In contrast, it may be more straightforward to apply a restitutionary analysis which recognises that the defendant has had the benefit of using the bicycle and should therefore be required to pay damages assessed according to the value of that use. This alternative restitutionary analysis can go a long way to explaining a number of decisions but, at the margins, it too may run into difficulty and, to avoid fiction, the substitutive damages thesis might at that point be thought attractive.

So against those favouring a restitutionary analysis of many cases on the wrongful use of another's property, it will not be long before supporters of 'substitutive damages' play an apparent trump card by putting the question, 'What about *Inverugie*?' In the *Inverugie* case the defendant trespasser was a landlord who had wrongfully evicted the claimant tenant from 30 hotel apartments and had refused to give up possession of those apartments over a period of 15 years. The occupancy rate of those apartments during that period had been at about 35 per cent of full capacity so that the defendant was running the hotel at a loss. The claimant was awarded 'mesne profits' for trespass to land, measured by a reasonable fee for the use of land, even though the claimant had not suffered a loss equivalent to the reasonable fee and the trespass was non-profitable for the trespasser because its business was running at a loss.

One might argue therefore that while the decision cannot be justified as awarding compensation, nor can it be recast as restitutionary because the defendant had made no benefit from its trespass. On the contrary, it had made a loss. So in Stevens' words:

> The preferable approach is to award the claimant damages as a substitute for the value of the right infringed: even where this causes no loss to the claimant and no gain to the defendant. Lord Lloyd ... applied this approach in the decision of the Privy Council in *Inverugie* ... Only if the award is seen as substitutive for the right infringed can the refusal to allow the defendants to offset the losses made from the wrong be explained ... No factual gain was proved in *Inverugie*.[39]

However, a restitutionary analysis can be realistically applied if one treats the relevant benefit in question as being not the consequential profit but rather the initial use value of the land. In Lord Lloyd's words the defend-

---

[39] Stevens, *Torts and Rights*, above n 2, at 81–82.

ant, applying the 'user principle', should be 'obliged to pay a reasonable fee for the use which he has enjoyed'.[40] The defendant had had the use of the apartments and that use was *objectively* beneficial and appropriately measured by a reasonable fee irrespective of whether profits were made or not. The question of whether there should have been a deduction to reflect the defendant's loss from the use turns on the well-known concept within the law of restitution of 'subjective devaluation'.[41] In general, where the cause of action is a wrong, at least where the defendant has freely 'taken' the benefit, subjective devaluation should not be permitted. In other words, a conscious trespasser should not be permitted to subjectively devalue the objective use value of the land taken.[42]

(iv) Pell Frischmann Engineering Ltd v Bow Valley Iran Ltd[43]

In order to understand this case which, in my view, is the most difficult of this quartet, one first needs to recognise that in *Wrotham Park Estate Co Ltd v Parkside Homes Ltd*[44] a new way of measuring damages was articulated. The defendants in *Wrotham Park* had built a number of houses on land in breach of a restrictive covenant enforceable in equity by the claimant neighbouring landowner. Brightman J refused an injunction ordering the demolition of the houses but held that, although the claimant's land had not been diminished in value, the defendants were liable to pay substantial damages assessed by reference to a 'hypothetical release bargain'. That is, he asked what would have been a reasonable contract price for the claimant to have accepted for relaxation of the covenant. And in working out that price, the major factor taken into account was the defendants' profits from the housing development.

'*Wrotham Park* damages' or, as they have more recently been referred to in the courts, 'negotiating damages',[45] are damages assessed according to a hypothetical release bargain and, subsequent to the *Wrotham Park*

---

[40] *Inverugie* [1995] 1 WLR 713 (PC) 718.

[41] P Birks, *An Introduction to the Law of Restitution*, rev edn (Oxford, Clarendon Press, 1989) 109–10; *Cressman v Coys of Kensington (Sales) Ltd* [2004] EWCA Civ 47, [2004] 1 WLR 2775 [28] (Mance LJ); *Sempra Metals Ltd v IRC* [2007] UKHL 34, [2008] 1 AC 561 [118]–[199] (Lord Nicholls).

[42] Contrast the decision in *Ministry of Defence v Ashman* (1993) 66 P & CR 195 (CA) where the defendant had wrongly stayed on in RAF accommodation and yet in assessing restitutionary damages for that trespass the benefit to her was held to be not the market value of that accommodation but rather the rental cost of local authority housing. But in that case, in contrast to *Inverugie*, the defendant had had no real choice other than to stay on in the highly subsidised RAF accommodation because there was no available suitable local authority accommodation.

[43] *Pell Frischmann* [2009] UKPC 45, [2010] BLR 73.

[44] *Wrotham Park Estate Co Ltd v Parkside Homes Ltd* [1974] 1 WLR 798 (Ch) (*Wrotham Park*).

[45] This was the term used by Neuberger LJ in *Lunn Poly Ltd v Liverpool and Lancashire Properties Ltd* [2006] EWCA Civ 430, [2006] 2 EGLR 29 and by the Privy Council in *Pell Frischmann* [2009] UKPC 45, [2010] BLR 73.

case, they have been awarded in a range of tort and contract cases. So, for example, they have been awarded for breach of a restrictive covenant over land, as in *Wrotham Park* itself;[46] for breach of a collateral contract restricting the development of land;[47] for tortious trespass to land;[48] for the tort of nuisance by infringement of the right to light;[49] for the breach of negative contractual obligations concerned to restrict the defendants' use of master tapes[50] or of particular initials;[51] and for the breach of negative obligations, contractual and non-contractual, restricting the use of confidential information.[52]

There is an ongoing debate, which I have previously directly written on,[53] as to whether *Wrotham Park* damages are compensatory or restitutionary or, depending on the facts, both. In my view they are not 'substitutive damages', albeit that they lie at the heart of Stevens' analysis.

With that background in mind we come to *Pell Frischmann* where the question raised, which one might regard as analogous to that in *Inverugie*, was whether one can award more under *Wrotham Park* damages than the profit eventually made from the breach of contract. The Privy Council held that one could. The case concerned a failed joint venture for an offshore oilfield. Confidentiality agreements were entered into between the parties. These were subsequently broken by the defendants by going ahead with the joint venture with a different partner than the claimants. The claimants sought *Wrotham Park* damages for breach of contract. At the time prior to breach, when it was assumed the hypothetical release bargain would have taken place, the parties anticipated that the profits from the joint venture—and hence from the breach of contract by going ahead without the claimants—would be greater than the $1.8 million profit actually made. The Privy Council awarded damages of $2.5 million on the reasoning that the eventual profit was not determinative of the price that would have been reasonably negotiated. This was particularly

---

[46] *Amec Developments Ltd v Jury's Hotel Management (UK) Ltd* (2000) 82 P & CR 286 (Ch).

[47] *Lane v O'Brien Homes Ltd* [2004] EWHC 303 (QB).

[48] *Bracewell v Appleby* [1975] Ch 408 (Ch); *Jaggard v Sawyer* [1995] 1 WLR 269 (CA); *Severn Trent Water Ltd v Barnes* [2004] EWCA Civ 570, [2004] 2 EGLR 95.

[49] *Carr-Saunders v Dick McNeil Associated Ltd* [1986] 2 All ER 888 (Ch); *Tamares (Vincent Square) Ltd v Fairpoint Properties (Vincent Square) Ltd* [2007] EWHC 212 (Ch), [2007] 1 WLR 2167.

[50] *Experience Hendrix LLC v PPX Enterprises Inc* [2003] EWCA Civ 323; [2003] 1 All ER (Comm) 830.

[51] *WWF—World Wide Fund for Nature v World Wide Wrestling Federation Entertainment Inc* [2006] EWHC 184 (Ch), [2006] FSR 38, revd [2007] EWCA Civ 286, [2008] 1 WLR 445.

[52] *Vercoe v Rutland Fund Management Ltd* [2010] EWHC 424 (Ch).

[53] A Burrows, 'Are "Damages on the *Wrotham Park* Basis" Compensatory, Restitutionary or Neither?' in D Saidov and R Cunnington (eds), *Contract Damages: Domestic and International Perspectives* (Oxford, Hart Publishing, 2008) 165. See also C Rotherham, '"*Wrotham Park* Damages" and Accounts of Profits: Compensation or Restitution?' [2008] *Lloyd's Maritime and Commercial Law Quarterly* 25.

so because the claimants and defendants had almost reached a concluded 'buy-out' agreement by which the claimants would have given up its right to prevent the defendants going ahead with any other partner in return for an upfront payment of $3 million and further payments at various stages of the production of $4.5 million plus $2.5 million if the project was extended in a particular way.

How do we justify that decision? No doubt Stevens would say that it straightforwardly exemplifies substitutive damages where the value of the right, fixed as at the time of breach, might very well exceed its later valuation. However, given the objections that we have raised to his thesis, it is incumbent on us to articulate an alternative explanation. This is not easy.

One possibility is that the damages should be regarded as compensating for the lost opportunity to bargain in a situation where that may have been a realistic analysis, given that the parties were willing to enter into a release bargain. However, the main difficulty with that analysis is that we know that those negotiations had in practice broken down so that it would appear fictional to imagine that they would have struck the deal postulated by the court.

The better view is probably that the damages were restitutionary. Admittedly the damages were not designed to strip some or all of the defendant's profits because the sum awarded exceeded those profits. Nor in contrast to *Inverugie* can it be said that the amount represented the objective use value of *property taken* by the defendants because, even if confidential information is treated as property, the breach in question covered the contractual obligation not to deal with anyone else as well as the contractual obligation not to use confidential information. Nevertheless, one can draw a loose analogy to *Inverugie* by treating the benefit in question as being the value of the opportunity for gain by conducting oneself as if free of the contractual obligation in question. After all, when we talk of a wrongdoer having the use value of property we mean that the defendant has had the use of the property as if free of the claimant's proprietary right.[54] So in *Pell Frischmann* what was being valued was the opportunity for gain by holding oneself out as if free of the contractual obligation in question in a situation where it was anticipated that that freedom would be profitable. It did not matter that the objective value of that benefit outweighed the profits that the defendant ultimately made from the breach because the defendant, as a cynical contract-breaker, could not subjectively devalue that objective benefit.

---

[54] An even closer analogy, because there is no *tangible* property involved, would be with where a wrongdoer 'uses' another's intellectual property. To say that the wrongdoer has had the use value of the intellectual property—and should pay a reasonable licence fee for it—means that the defendant has conducted itself as if free of the claimant's intellectual property right.

In an excellent recent case note on *Pell Frischmann* Tatiana Cutts argues that the Privy Council explicitly rejected a restitutionary analysis; that the case is best seen as an award of substitutive damages representing the value of the *infringement* of the right; and that *Wrotham Park* damages constitute an individual pocket of damages awarded to solve an exceptional problem, namely to provide 'a deserving claimant with a remedy in circumstances in which traditional compensatory methods fail to produce the desired result.'[55]

But with respect, when Lord Walker said that the Privy Council was not here concerned with 'an account of profits *alias* restitutionary damages',[56] he was merely clarifying the point that one was not concerned with a disgorgement of all or some of the defendant's profits. The restitutionary analysis offered above is consistent with that. Moreover, while Cutts' criticisms of Stevens' analysis are in line with my own, the 'substitutive damages' thesis cannot be rescued by recasting it, as she does,[57] as if concerned to value the infringement of the right. Stevens' thesis stands or falls on the right infringed being substituted by damages. It makes no sense to talk of damages substituting the infringement of the right because an infringement of a right, in contrast to the right itself, cannot be valued, bought and sold. Furthermore, while it is possible to argue that the 'substitutive damages' thesis is best confined to exceptional circumstances, where traditional compensatory damages are inadequate, that is not how it is presented by Stevens and, while so confining it limits the inconsistencies with the present law, it does nothing to cure the central objections to it.

D. Conclusion

The emphasis on rights in recent scholarship has greatly enhanced our understanding of much of private law. In particular, Stevens has offered an illuminating new picture of the law of tort. However, overextending the use of one's favourite concepts is an ever-present danger for legal commentators and the substitutive damages thesis exhibits that tendency. Compensation and, more recently, restitution are well-established remedial goals in relation to damages and, while debate still rages as to the normative justification of restitution for wrongs, the normative justification of compensation is clear and well-understood. In contrast, the substitutive

---

[55] T Cutts, '*Wrotham Park* Damages: Compensation, Restitution or a Substitute for the Value of the Infringement of the Right?' [2010] *Lloyd's Maritime and Commercial Law Quarterly* 215, 220.

[56] *Pell Frischmann* [2009] UKPC 45, [2010] BLR 73 [48].

[57] In this she is following a suggestion made by Edelman, in exploring whether Stevens' thesis could be 'saved' (Edelman ultimately thought not), in 'The Meaning of Loss and Enrichment', above n 14, at 219.

damages thesis does not offer a convincing interpretation of the present law. While at the extremes there are some cases that cannot be straight-forwardly analysed as awarding compensatory or restitutionary damages, it would be a fundamental mistake to give up on working through these difficulties in favour of the superficially attractive, but ultimately flawed, substitutive damages analysis.

III. DAMAGES UNDER THE HUMAN RIGHTS ACT 1998

A. Introduction

I now want to shift focus to the damages that are awarded for the cause of action against public authorities created by the Human Rights Act 1998 (HRA 1998). The HRA 1998 has of course had an impact on various aspects of English law. In particular, the provisions in sections 3–5 have affected the way in which the courts interpret statutes; and the Act has affected the determination of whether public authorities have acted out-side their powers in applications for judicial review. Moreover, because the definition of a public authority includes a court, the HRA 1998 has had some limited impact 'horizontally' (that is, in actions between 'private parties') by, for example, stimulating the development of the equitable wrong of breach of confidence so as to play a more vibrant role in pro-tecting privacy.

My concern in this chapter, however, is solely with the 'vertical' cause of action created by sections 6–8 of the HRA 1998 which is triggered when a public authority contravenes a person's Convention rights. For convenience I shall refer to this throughout as the HRA 1998 cause of action. The question I am asking is, what are the principles governing the damages for that cause of action and, in particular, was the House of Lords in *R (Greenfield) v Secretary of State for the Home Department*[58] correct to reject as inapplicable the scale of compensatory damages for non-pecuniary loss in domestic tort cases?

Crucial to this is section 8 of the HRA 1998 and therefore at the outset we should remind ourselves of the central provisions of that section. Sec-tion 8(1)–(4) reads as follows:

(1) In relation to any act (or proposed act) of a public authority which the court finds is (or would be) unlawful, it may grant such relief or remedy, or make such order, within its powers as it considers just and appropriate.
(2) But damages may be awarded only by a court which has power to award damages, or to order the payment of compensation, in civil proceedings.

---

[58] *Greenfield* [2005] UKHL 14, [2005] 1 WLR 673.

(3) No award of damages is to be made unless, taking account of all the circumstances of the case, including—
 (a) any other relief or remedy granted, or order made, in relation to the act in question (by that or any other court), and
 (b) the consequences of any decision (of that or any other court) in respect of that act,
 the court is satisfied that the award is necessary to afford just satisfaction to the person in whose favour it is made.

(4) In determining—
 (a) whether to award damages, or
 (b) the amount of an award,
 the court must take into account the principles applied by the European Court of Human Rights in relation to the award of compensation under Article 41 of the Convention.

B. The Nature of the HRA 1998 Cause of Action: A Non-Tortious Public Law Wrong

In order to answer our question about damages, it is helpful initially— although ultimately this is not determinative—to clarify the precise nature of the HRA 1998 cause of action. Previously when enforcement of the European Convention on Human Rights (ECHR) required going to the European Court of Human Rights (Strasbourg Court), the question as to the nature of the cause of action being brought under the ECHR was of tangential importance for English law. The Strasbourg jurisprudence lay outside domestic law and it was only when domestic remedies had been exhausted that a remedy would be given by the Strasbourg Court. A remedy in Strasbourg was therefore a last resort which fell outside our domestic scheme. But now that 'rights have been brought home'[59] by the HRA 1998 we must answer this question if we are to understand properly this area of what is now our domestic law.

Two broad analyses of the HRA 1998 cause of action have been proposed. The first treats the HRA 1998 cause of action as a tort. This was very much the early understanding of commentators. So, for example, Anthony Lester and David Pannick referred to the cause of action as a 'new public law tort of acting in breach of the victim's Convention rights'.[60] While pointing out that there is no right to damages under the HRA 1998 cause of action, Keith Stanton, Michael Harris, Paul Skidmore and Jane Wright wrote in *Statutory Torts*, 'It has always been the case … that a right of action and remedies are different creatures and it does

---

[59] Home Office, *Rights Brought Home: The Human Rights Bill* (Cm 3782, 1997).
[60] A Lester and D Pannick, 'The Impact of the Human Rights Act on Private Law: The Knight's Move' (2000) 116 *Law Quarterly Review* 380, 382.

seem appropriate to speak of the HRA 1998 remedy as a tort, if attention is focused on the nature of the wrong rather than the remedy.'[61] Somewhat similarly, the Law Commission said in its report *Damages under the Human Rights Act 1998*, 'Sections 6 and 7 of the HRA 1998 create a new cause of action, which is in effect a form of action for breach of statutory duty, but with the difference that the remedy is discretionary, rather than as of right.'[62] And they went on to argue that the quantum of compensatory damages applicable to the HRA 1998 cause of action should be that applied to domestic torts. In the 18th edition of *Clerk and Lindsell on Torts* the HRA 1998 cause of action was referred to as a 'constitutional tort'.[63] And in my own book *Remedies for Torts and Breach of Contract* I wrote, 'This new cause of action is most conveniently viewed as a tort.'[64]

Ranged against that is an analysis which treats the HRA 1998 cause of action as a sui generis public law wrong. It is a statutory wrong but it is not a tort. On a map of the English law of obligations, it is located alongside other miscellaneous statutory wrongs triggering compensation that are not torts, such as unfair dismissal. The list of civil wrongs comprises torts, breach of contract, equitable wrongs and statutory wrongs that are not torts; and it is that last small sub-category that includes the HRA 1998 cause of action.

Ten years on from the coming into effect of the HRA 1998 it now seems clear that the English courts regard the second 'non-tortious public wrong' analysis as correct. Indeed this reflects the way in which English judges sitting in the Privy Council have for decades analysed claims for damages for breach of constitutional rights in Commonwealth countries. So, for example, in *Maharaj v A-G of Trinidad and Tobago (No 2)* Lord Diplock contrasted 'the existing law of torts' and the claim for breach of a constitutional right in issue which he said was 'concerned with public law not private law'.[65]

Six reasons can be given for why the 'non-tortious public wrong' analysis seems more accurate. The first three of these reasons are at the level of *describing* differences between tort and the HRA 1998 cause of action as laid down in the HRA 1998 or by the English courts.[66] The remaining three are at a deeper level.

---

[61] K Stanton et al, *Statutory Torts* (London, Sweet & Maxwell, 2003) 144.

[62] Law Commission, above n 31, at para 4.20.

[63] AM Dugdale et al (eds), *Clerk and Lindsell on Torts*, 18th edn (London, Sweet & Maxwell, 2000) paras 1-04, 12-75–12-79.

[64] Burrows, *Remedies for Torts and Breach of Contract*, above n 29, at 16.

[65] *Maharaj v A-G of Trinidad and Tobago (No 2)* [1979] AC 385 (PC) 396.

[66] A further difference suggested by the Law Commission is that Strasbourg damages are more generous in respect of mental distress. For example, loss of love and companionship are compensated by the Strasbourg Court, whereas they are not compensated in England: Law Commission, above n 31, at para 4.64. This is misleading. Once a tort has been established, there appears to be no bar in English law to recovering such damages consequent

1. There is no right to damages for the HRA 1998 cause of action. In other words, establishing the cause of action does not necessarily mean that an award of damages will be made. This follows not only from the wording of section 8(3)—damages may not be necessary to achieve just satisfaction—but also from the jurisprudence of the Strasbourg Court which must be taken into account under section 8(4). In contrast a characteristic of all torts is that there is a right to damages. For torts actionable only on proof of damage (eg, negligence, nuisance, deceit, misfeasance in public office[67]) the damage proved will entitle the claimant to compensatory damages; and for torts actionable per se (eg, libel, malicious prosecution, trespass to the person, goods or land) if actionable damage is proved there is an entitlement to compensatory damages but, in any event, nominal damages will be awarded even if no damage is proved.

2. Punitive damages cannot be awarded for the HRA 1998 cause of action. This is in line with the words—'just *satisfaction*' to the claimant—in section 8(3). Punitive damages do not fall happily within that phrase and in any event have never been (overtly) awarded by the Strasbourg Court.[68] That punitive damages cannot be awarded under section 8(3) has been confirmed in *Anufrijeva v Southwark London BC*[69] and *Watkins v Secretary of State for the Home Department*.[70] In contrast, one might say that it is a characteristic of all torts after *Kuddus v Chief Constable of Leicestershire Constabulary*[71] that, provided the facts fall within one of the *Rookes v Barnard*[72] categories, punitive damages may be awarded.

3. In the leading case of *Greenfield*[73] it was made clear that, contrary to the view of the Law Commission and the approach advocated in some earlier cases, the quantum of compensatory damages for non-pecuniary loss should be fixed in line with the jurisprudence of the Strasbourg Court

---

on a personal injury or even in a claim for false imprisonment. The fact that there is no free-standing claim for loss of consortium is a separate point going to liability not damages. It has also sometimes been suggested that Strasbourg has a looser approach to causation: see, eg, *Van Colle v Chief Constable of the Hertfordshire Police* [2008] UKHL 50, [2009] 1 AC 225 [138] (Lord Brown). But again this seems misleading: see McGregor, *McGregor on Damages*, above n 5, at paras 43-046–43-053. In particular, loss of a chance damages, even free-standing, are often available in English law: see, eg, *Allied Maples Group Ltd v Simmons & Simmons* [1995] 1 WLR 1602 (CA); A Burrows, 'Uncertainty about Uncertainty: Damages for Loss of a Chance' [2008] *Journal of Personal Injury Law* 31.

[67] It was recently established in *Watkins v Secretary of State for the Home Department* [2006] UKHL 17, [2006] 2 AC 395 (*Watkins*) that this tort requires proof of damage.
[68] See, eg, *BB v United Kingdom* (2004) 39 EHRR 635 [36].
[69] *Anufrijeva v Southwark London Borough Council* [2003] EWCA Civ 1406, [2004] QB 1124 [55] (Lord Woolf CJ for the Court).
[70] *Watkins* [2006] UKHL 17, [2006] 2 AC 395 [26] (Lord Bingham), [32] (Lord Hope), [64] (Lord Rodger).
[71] *Kuddus v Chief Constable of Leicestershire Constabulary* [2001] UKHL 29, [2002] 2 AC 122 (*Kuddus*).
[72] *Rookes v Barnard* [1964] AC 1129 (HL).
[73] *Greenfield* [2005] UKHL 14, [2005] 1 WLR 673.

and not in line with domestic torts. Although not an easy comparator, because the Strasbourg jurisprudence is notoriously flexible, it would seem that this will almost always mean that an award will be no higher and will commonly be lower than for a domestic tort.[74] As Lord Bingham said in *Watkins*, 'monetary compensation awarded at Strasbourg tends, in comparison with domestic levels of award, to be ungenerous'.[75]

4. At a deeper level, one can say that the rights protected are different. The HRA 1998 cause of action is concerned only with protecting rights that are rights against the state. They are not rights against any other person. They are public law rights not private law rights. While we know that private law rights can be invoked against public authorities (ie, one can use any tort, most obviously trespass to the person or negligence or nuisance, against a public authority) that is on the basis that the rule of law demands that public authorities should not be treated any more favourably than other defendants. The reverse proposition does not hold true: the HRA 1998 cause of action can only be invoked against a public authority.

5. Lord Bingham, giving the leading speech in *Greenfield*,[76] reasoned that the functions of the remedies for the HRA 1998 cause of action and tort differ. He saw the primary function of remedies in tort as being to compensate whereas the primary function of remedies for the HRA 1998 cause of action is the vindication of rights. He said:

> [T]he 1998 Act is not a tort statute. Its objects are different and broader. Even in a case where a finding of violation is not judged to afford the applicant just satisfaction, such a finding will be an important part of his remedy and an important vindication of the right he has asserted.[77]

---

[74] A possible exception to this is that the amount of bereavement damages awarded in the Strasbourg Court may be higher than under the Fatal Accidents Act 1976 which imposes a fixed sum and is recoverable only by a parent or parents: see, eg, *Van Colle v Chief Constable of the Hertfordshire Police* [2007] EWCA Civ 325, [2007] 1 WLR 1821 (overturned on liability by the House of Lords: [2008] UKHL 50, [2009] 1 AC 225). However, it is not entirely clear that such claims are permitted under the ECHR (and HRA 1998 s 7(7) relies on the ECHR for the meaning of 'victim') because the victims are indirect. This point was not taken by the defendant in *Van Colle*: see [2007] EWCA Civ 325, [2007] 1 WLR 1821 [114] (Sir Anthony Clarke MR for the Court). In *Savage v South Essex Partnership NHS Foundation Trust* [2008] UKHL 74, [2009] 1 AC 681 [5] Lord Scott, in obiter dicta, doubted whether such a claim was possible. But the contrary view was applied by Mackay J at trial in the same case: [2010] EWHC 865 (QB), [2010] HRLR 24 [69]–[73]. The issue was discussed but not decided by Simon J in *Rabone v Pennine Care NHS Trust* [2009] EWHC 1827 (QB), [2010] PIQR P2 [113]–[118].

[75] *Watkins* [2006] UKHL 17, [2006] 2 AC 395 [26].

[76] See also his comments in *Watkins* [2006] UKHL 17, [2006] 2 AC 395 [9]. See also Waller LJ, giving the judgment of the Court of Appeal, in *Dobson v Thames Water Utilities Ltd* [2009] EWCA Civ 28, [2009] 3 All ER 319 [42]: 'The Convention serves principally public law aims; the principal objective is to declare any infringement and to put a stop to it. Compensation is ancillary and discretionary. The interests of the individual are part of the equation, but so are those of the wider public.'

[77] *Greenfield* [2005] UKHL 14, [2005] 1 WLR 673 [19].

While Lord Bingham would no doubt accept that both compensation and vindication are important functions in relation to both types of action, so that this is matter of degree rather than kind, his fundamental point is that the balance between them is different in relation to tort and the HRA 1998 cause of action.

6. One might add that a further reason why one would expect the English courts to be particularly keen to treat the HRA 1998 cause of action as being different from a tort is that this more easily allows the traditions of the common law to be maintained. Had it been accepted that the HRA 1998 cause of action was a tort, this would have required accepting that the approach of the courts to the tortious liability of public authorities had been transformed by the 1998 Act. So, for example, the rejection of liability in negligence in many claims against public authorities and the non-acceptance of a tort of loss caused by an ultra vires action would have been outflanked. That would not merely be a radical change but would seem to involve accepting that the development of the common law as regards tort claims against public authorities had hitherto not been fully compliant with human rights. Not surprisingly that is not an analysis that the judges would wish to accept. Adopting the analysis that the HRA 1998 cause of action belongs outside, albeit alongside, the liability in tort of public authorities may be thought to allow the courts their traditional freedom in deciding how the tortious liability of public authorities should be developed.

Indeed, one might even say—and this has been borne out by recent cases—that, because the claimant now has the HRA 1998 cause of action to fall back on within domestic law, any previous pressure to amend the domestic tortious liability of public authorities has been removed. So, for example, in *Watkins* Lord Bingham said, in relation to the tort of misfeasance in public office: 'It may reasonably be inferred that Parliament intended infringement of the core human (and constitutional) rights protected by the Act to be remedied under it and not by the development of parallel remedies.'[78] And in Lord Rodger's words:

> Now that the Human Rights Act is in place, such heroic efforts [to deploy the concept of constitutional rights in the law of tort] are unnecessary. ... In general, at least, where the matter is not already covered by the common law but falls within the scope of a Convention right, a claimant can be expected to invoke his remedy under the 1998 Act rather than to seek to fashion a new common law right.[79]

Similarly in *Van Colle v Chief Constable of the Hertfordshire Police* Lord Hope said:

---

[78] *Watkins* [2006] UKHL 17, [2006] 2 AC 395 [26].
[79] ibid, at [64].

[T]he common law [in relation to a breach by a public authority] ... should be allowed to stand on its own feet side by side with the alternative remedy ... [Any] perceived shortfall in the way that it deals with cases ... can now be dealt with in domestic law under the 1998 Act.[80]

In the same case, Lord Brown stated:

[C]ertainly in the present context your Lordships should not feel tempted to develop the common law in harmony with Convention rights. ... Clearly, the violation of a fundamental right is a very serious thing and happily, since the 1998 Act, it gives rise to a cause of action in domestic law. I see no sound reason, however, for matching this with a common law claim also.[81]

At the very least, the judges regard themselves as free to apply and develop the domestic liability in tort of public authorities in the same way as they traditionally have done, taking into account the jurisprudence in Strasbourg as a relevant, but not decisive, factor. The main impact of the HRA 1998 on the development of the tortious liability of public authorities has been to provide an alternative fall-back position which previously would have involved the claimant going off to Strasbourg (having exhausted his domestic remedies) but can now be relied on in the English courts. Put shortly, it is not surprising that the HRA 1998 cause of action has been viewed by the judges as a non-tortious public law wrong because that view more readily allows the traditional incremental development of the tortious liability of public authorities to continue as before.

It is submitted that, for all these reasons, it would be misleading to regard the HRA 1998 cause of action as a tort. It is best viewed as a sui generis public law wrong.

B. Was the House of Lords in *Greenfield* Correct to Reject the Analogy of Damages in Tort?[82]

To accept that the HRA 1998 cause of action is not a tort does not, however, mean that the House of Lords in *Greenfield* was correct to reject the scales of quantum for compensation for non-pecuniary loss adopted in domestic tort law in favour of that applied in Strasbourg cases. Rejec-

---

[80] *Van Colle* [2008] UKHL 50, [2009] 1 AC 225 [82].

[81] ibid, at [138]–[139]. In contrast, Lord Bingham, dissenting and adopting an approach that is not easy to reconcile with his comments in *Watkins*, said at [58] that he thought that 'the common law should develop in the light of Convention rights and in harmony with a Convention right concerning the same ground.'

[82] For two very helpful articles on this issue, which arrive at a similar conclusion on *Greenfield* as this chapter, albeit by rather different reasoning, see J Steele, 'Damages in Tort and under the Human Rights Act: Remedial or Functional Separation?' [2008] *Cambridge Law Journal* 606; JNE Varuhas, 'A Tort-Based Approach to Damages under the Human Rights Act 1998' (2009) 72 *Modern Law Review* 750. See also McGregor, *McGregor on Damages*, above n 5, at ch 43.

tion of the tort analysis does not necessarily preclude applying the scales of quantum for tort compensation *by analogy* in assessing compensation under the non-tortious HRA 1998 cause of action.

In the *Greenfield* case the applicant was a prisoner who, at a hearing before the deputy Governor, had been given an additional 21 days of imprisonment for taking drugs contrary to the prison rules. By the time the case reached the House of Lords the Secretary of State accepted that the prisoner's Convention right to a fair trial under Article 6 had been infringed. This was because the proceedings involved a criminal charge and the applicant was therefore entitled to an independent tribunal— which the deputy Governor was not—and to legal representation, which had been denied to him. It was accepted that the applicant was entitled to declarations that the Secretary of State had acted unlawfully, contrary to Article 6, in those two respects. The dispute was about damages. The House of Lords decided that the applicant was not entitled to any damages because the declarations in the applicant's favour afforded just satisfaction and an award of damages was not necessary. The applicant sought damages for non-pecuniary loss on two grounds. First, that by being denied legal representation he had been deprived of the opportunity of a more favourable outcome (thereby avoiding all or some of the extra days of imprisonment). This was, in any event, held to be too speculative. Secondly, he argued that he had suffered anxiety and frustration because he did not think that he would be fairly tried given that the tribunal was not independent. There was held to be no special feature in this case warranting damages on that basis.

The importance of the case, however, is that the House of Lords used it as an opportunity to deal with the issue of whether the scale of damages for non-pecuniary loss in English tort law should apply where damages are being awarded for the HRA 1998 cause of action. In what was technically obiter dicta Lord Bingham, with whom the other Lords agreed, reasoned that that scale should not apply. He stated that English courts 'should not aim to be significantly more or less generous than the [Strasbourg] court might be expected to be, in a case where it was willing to make an award at all.'[83] The contrary approach supported by three earlier cases and the Law Commission should not be followed.[84]

Lord Bingham gave three reasons for his view. First, as we have seen, he argued that 'the 1998 Act is not a tort statute. Its objects are different and broader'.[85] Secondly, he said that:

---

[83] *Greenfield* [2005] UKHL 14, [2005] 1 WLR 673 [19].

[84] *R (Bernard) v Enfield London BC* [2002] EWHC 2282 (Admin), [2003] HRLR 4; *R (KB) v Mental Health Review Tribunal* [2003] EWHC 193 (Admin), [2003] 2 All ER 209; *Anufrijeva v Southwark London Borough Council* [2003] EWCA Civ 1406, [2004] 1 All ER 833; Law Commission, above n 31.

[85] *Greenfield* [2005] UKHL 14, [2005] 1 WLR 673 [19].

[T]he purpose of incorporating the Convention in domestic law through the 1998 Act was not to give the victims better remedies at home than they could recover in Strasbourg but to give them the same remedies without the delay and expense of resort to Strasbourg.[86]

Thirdly, he argued that section 8(4) clearly indicates that 'courts in this country should look to Strasbourg and not to domestic precedents'.[87]

However, this reasoning runs counter to a very powerful argument of principle for applying the tort scale of compensation. This can be expressed as follows. The rights protected by the HRA 1998 cause of action are fundamental rights. They are at least as important as the rights protected by the law of tort. *If a victim suffers, and is being compensated for, a loss as a result of a breach by a public authority of his or her Convention rights, he or she should receive at least the same compensation as he or she would be entitled to in tort for suffering the same loss. One is otherwise treating a breach of a Convention right less seriously than the breach of a right protected in tort.*

Do Lord Bingham's reasons sufficiently answer that argument of principle? The first of his reasons—that tort has different functions—might be elaborated on by stressing that the types of rights in issue are different. As we have seen above, the rights protected by the HRA 1998 cause of action are viewed as public law rather than private law rights. This might then lead to the view that the primary function of the remedies is different as being a vindication of those rights rather than compensation. So the argument might go, just as it is appropriate for compensation to be displaced entirely where the courts consider that a non-monetary remedy (ie, a declaration) sufficiently vindicates the right so the courts must be free to apply a different scale of quantum where compensation is being awarded.

The difficulty with this argument is its last stage. One can accept that, under the HRA 1998 cause of action, compensation is not inevitable because the rights protected differ in type from those in private law and because the primary function of the remedies, in contrast to tort, is to vindicate the right by a declaration. But what is very difficult to accept is that, having decided that compensation is appropriate, one should then abandon the scales of quantum devised in one's domestic law to effect full and proper compensation. If £x is thought the correct compensation for (the non-pecuniary aspects of) a psychiatric illness in the tort of negligence, it is hard to see why the same psychiatric illness is thought to be properly compensated by less than £x in a claim under the HRA 1998. If a broken leg is valued at £x for the tort of trespass, it is hard to see why it should be worth less than £x when it has been the result of torture in

---

[86] ibid.
[87] ibid.

a claim under the HRA 1998. If a week of lost freedom is worth £x in a tort claim for false imprisonment, it is hard to see why a week of lost freedom can be worth less than £x in a claim under the HRA 1998. To accept *Greenfield* is tantamount to saying that the courts when awarding compensation under the HRA 1998 action have discretion to award what by English standards is only partial and not full compensation for a loss suffered. That must be to treat the infringement of Convention rights less seriously than the infringement of private law rights protected in tort where full compensation for an actionable loss has always been the avowed aim.[88]

Of course, one might say that the scales of non-pecuniary loss are so indeterminate and arbitrary that it is false to say that domestic law has a clear view as to the value of certain losses. However, that would be to make a mockery of the scales of non-pecuniary loss that have been devised by the courts and which the judges have been anxious to stress must keep pace with what is regarded as fair by the standards of our society.[89] Correct and incorrect assessment in relation to non-pecuniary loss cannot be proved mathematically but it can be proved by the scales of assessment that the courts have devised. Just as one should not allow non-pecuniary loss in a false imprisonment or defamation case to be valued in a way that is inconsistent with values in a personal injury case[90] and just as damages for personal injury in a tort case must be valued in the same way as an actionable personal injury in a claim for breach of contract, so

---

[88] *Heil v Rankin* [2001] QB 272 (CA) [23] (Lord Woolf MR): '[The] principle of "full compensation" applies to pecuniary and non-pecuniary damage alike'. Similarly, there is no suggestion that the Strasbourg Court, if it decides to award damages, is concerned to effect anything other than *full* compensation for pecuniary and non-pecuniary loss caused: see Law Commission, above n 31, at paras 3.16–3.30.

[89] See, eg, *Heil v Rankin* [2001] QB 272 (CA) [27] (Lord Woolf MR): 'The compensation must remain fair, reasonable and just'.

[90] See *John v MGN Ltd* [1997] QB 586 (CA) (defamation); *Thompson v Commissioner of Police for the Metropolis* [1998] QB 498 (CA) (false imprisonment and malicious prosecution). See also *Vento v Chief Constable of West Yorkshire (No 2)* [2002] EWCA Civ 1871, [2003] IRLR 102 (consistency desirable between the level of compensation for injured feelings in sex and race discrimination cases and awards for non-pecuniary loss in personal injury cases). In *Bone v Seale* [1975] 1 WLR 797 (CA), in assessing 'loss of amenity' damages for 'inconvenience, discomfort and annoyance' for the tort of private nuisance, the Court of Appeal tentatively drew an analogy with assessing damages for loss of amenity in a personal injury action. Surprisingly, and with respect erroneously, this was rejected by Lord Hoffmann in *Hunter v Canary Wharf Ltd* [1997] AC 655 (HL) 706. In assessing contractual damages for physical inconvenience and mental distress consequent on a ruined holiday in *Milner v Carnival plc* [2010] EWCA Civ 389, [2010] 3 All ER 701 [36]–[38] Ward LJ (with whom Richards and Goldring LJJ agreed) said:

> In the area of conventional awards, comparability matters ... The search for comparability must extend beyond comparing one holiday with another. There must be some consistency with the level of damages awarded in other fields. The obvious comparison to make is the assessment of general damages in personal injury cases and the awards when psychiatric injury has been suffered.

consistency dictates that non-pecuniary loss should in principle be valued in the same way under the HRA 1998 cause of action.

Nor is it convincing to say that, within English domestic law, non-pecuniary loss is valued differently under state benefit or compensation schemes (eg, social security benefits or the Criminal Injuries Compensation Scheme) than in tort. The amounts available under those schemes are geared towards the resources which the state wishes to devote—so that there is no principle of full compensation in respect of non-pecuniary loss—and the state pays even though it has not itself committed any wrong. In contrast, the HRA 1998 cause of action attributes liability to a public authority precisely because it has committed a wrong infringing an individual's rights. It would be an obvious distortion of the true position to describe the HRA 1998 cause of action as a form of social security or a state compensation scheme.

In addition to the central argument of principle, there are three pragmatic reasons why one might consider *Greenfield* to be problematic. These are reasons challenging how workable it is in practice.

First, there is a problem about equivalence of monetary value. An award of €x to a claimant from one jurisdiction may be worth more or less to a person from another jurisdiction because of disparities in earnings and in the cost of living as between the different countries. This is not a problem for pecuniary loss which, through the loss of earnings or costs incurred, will itself reflect the wealth of the particular society. But it is a significant problem for non-pecuniary loss.[91]

Secondly, it is not entirely clear how precedent is meant to operate once one takes the view that the Strasbourg Court's approach is binding. A first instance judge faced with a decision on the quantum of non-pecuniary loss under the HRA 1998 cause of action given by the Court of Appeal may be bound to go back to the decisions of the Strasbourg Court and might not be able simply to rely on that previous English decision.[92]

Thirdly, as was stressed by the Law Commission and judges in cases prior to *Greenfield*, there is a difficulty in asking the English courts to apply the scale or quantum applied by the Strasbourg Court because this

---

[91] As Lord Woolf MR explained in *Heil v Rankin* [2001] QB 272 [38], while 'economic consequences' were irrelevant when assessing damages for pecuniary loss it is a different matter when assessing damages for non-pecuniary loss.

> [The court] is concerned with determining what is the fair, reasonable and just equivalent in monetary terms of an injury and the resultant PSLA [pain, suffering and loss of amenity]. The decision has to be taken against the background of the society in which the court makes the award. The position is well-illustrated by the decisions of the courts of Hong Kong. As the prosperity of Hong Kong expanded, the courts by stages increased their tariff for damages so that it approached the level in England.

[92] Although the position would presumably be different if the Court of Appeal was laying down what it interpreted the Strasbourg Court as requiring.

is not easy to discover.[93] The approach of the Strasbourg Court to precedent is loose and flexible. In practice, it is likely that an English court
will be presented in each case with a mass of decisions which it will be
bound to consider.[94]

The third of these difficulties is borne out by the recent first instance
decision in *R (Pennington) v Parole Board*[95] which is the most important
case on the approach to damages under the HRA 1998 since *Greenfield*.
The claimant was a prisoner. In a judicial review application he succeeded
in establishing that, contrary to Article 5(4) of the ECHR, there had been
an unlawful delay of some three months in his being informed that he
was to be released on licence. In a separate hearing on damages under
the HRA 1998, Judge Pelling QC looked at three possible approaches to
assessing damages.[96] First, the purely domestic law approach; secondly,
the purely Strasbourg Court approach; and thirdly, what he termed the
hybrid approach where one starts from domestic law but tempers that
by the 'principles' emerging from the Strasbourg Court. He held that,
as established by *Greenfield*, it was the second approach that must be
applied. The reference by counsel for the claimant to the domestic scale
of quantum for the tort of false imprisonment, shown in a case like *R v
Governor of Brockhill Prison (No 2)* in which £5000 had been awarded
for non-pecuniary loss for 59 days of false (albeit mistaken) imprisonment, was therefore irrelevant. In reaching that conclusion, Judge Pelling
QC rejected the argument that there is no difference between the first and
second approaches because the Strasbourg Court itself applies the tariff
applied by the applicant's domestic courts. Although that had arguably
been the approach of the Strasbourg Court in *Perks v United Kingdom*,[97]
it was certainly not the general approach in Strasbourg.

---

[93] In applying *Greenfield* in *Savage v South Essex Partnership NHS Foundation Trust*
[2010] EWHC 865 (QB), [2010] HRLR 24 [76] Mackay J said, 'it is far from simple to
see the principles which ECtHR applies.' There is the further problem of how, if at all, one
is to update awards for inflation. That awards for non-pecuniary loss should be so updated
is well-accepted in English domestic law and there is a clear method for doing this based
on the retail prices index. But it is not clear that that is the approach in the Strasbourg
Court and it is therefore unclear what an English judge applying *Greenfield* is meant to
do. In *R (Pennington) v Parole Board* [2010] EWHC 78 (Admin) [25] Judge Pelling QC
referred to the need to update the awards of the Strasbourg Court but did not mention
how this would be done.
[94] In *Savage v South Essex Partnership NHS Foundation Trust* [2010] EWHC 865 (QB),
[2010] HRLR 24 [97] Mackay J said that he had been referred by counsel for the claimant
to a schedule dealing with cases awarding damages for non-pecuniary loss from the beginning
of 2008. This was set out over 17 pages and showed that the range was wide and seemed
to run from about €5000 to €60 000. In the end, and without any clear explanation as
to how he arrived at this figure, he awarded £10 000 to a daughter for the non-pecuniary
loss consequent on the death, by suicide, of her mother.
[95] *R (Pennington) v Parole Board* [2010] EWHC 78 (Admin).
[96] These are the three approaches set out in McGregor, *McGregor on Damages*, above
n 5, at paras 43-032–43-040. Contrary to *Greenfield*, the hybrid approach is favoured in
that work.
[97] *Perks v United Kingdom* (1999) 30 EHRR 33.

The real point of interest, however, is how the 'purely' Strasbourg approach from *Greenfield* was applied in *R (Pennington) v Parole Board*. The defendant not surprisingly suggested that one should take analogous cases decided by the Strasbourg Court, see what awards had been made and then apply that standard to the particular facts of the case. But Judge Pelling QC found that the inconsistency of jurisprudence from the Strasbourg Court made that approach unworkable and that, in the light of Lord Bingham's speech in *Greenfield*, one needed to be more sensitive to the need to reach a fair sum on the particular facts. Judge Pelling QC said:

> It is submitted by the Defendant that the appropriate course is to attempt to extrapolate from the awards made by the ECtHR in supposedly closely analogous cases a figure that equates to a conventional award for three months extended detention. There are a number of difficulties with this essentially mathematical and mechanical approach. First, it is clear that this is not the approach adopted by the ECtHR. Time and again the court has emphasised that the figures arrived at have been arrived at equitably having regard to the particular facts of individual cases. Secondly, it is not at all clear from the reports how the ECtHR arrived at particular figures. It is clear that in some cases the sums awarded have been reduced to take account of conduct but no attempt has been made to identify the start point much less to identify the process by which the effect of reduction has been arrived at. Thirdly, none of the cases relied on by the Defendant have a common starting point for the calculation of damages. Thus, whilst I accept that the aim of this court should be to arrive at a figure that is not significantly more or less generous than would be awarded by the ECtHR, it is also the case that such damages cannot be precisely calculated but as Lord Bingham said in *Greenfield* must be a sum that is judged fair in the individual case.[98]

This clearly indicates why, in practice, the *Greenfield* approach does not work. The judge ends up essentially plucking a figure from the air. So in this case, Judge Pelling QC awarded £1750 as damages for non-pecuniary loss but we are none the wiser as to how he arrived at that figure.

One is driven to the view that *as a matter of both principle and pragmatism* the approach in *Greenfield* is unwelcome. Was that approach nevertheless dictated by the best interpretation of the HRA 1998?

As we have seen, two reasons of statutory interpretation were given by Lord Bingham in *Greenfield*. As regards the first—that the purpose of the HRA 1998 was not to give victims better remedies at home than they could recover in the Strasbourg Court—he referred for support to the White Paper which referred to people being 'able to receive compensation from a domestic court equivalent to what they would have received in Strasbourg.'[99] The second was that the wording of section 8(4) of the

---

[98] *R (Pennington) v Parole Board* [2010] EWHC 78 (Admin) [16].
[99] *Greenfield* [2005] UKHL 14, [2005] 1 WLR 673 [19], citing Home Office, above n 59, at para 2.6.

HRA 1998 requires the courts to 'take into account the principles applied by the European Court of Human Rights in relation to the award of compensation' not only in deciding whether to award damages but also in determining the amount of an award. This approach to the interpretation of the Act has been labelled the 'mirror' approach in that it sees the role of the English courts as being to mirror or match what would be awarded in the Strasbourg Court.[100]

While of course this is a possible interpretation of the HRA 1998, one might counter-argue that the question of the correct scale of damages is not directly dictated by the Act, and that the wording used, and indeed the extract from the White Paper relied on by Lord Bingham, do lend themselves to a wider interpretation which requires the courts to apply the general principles of the Strasbourg Court (eg, compensation not punishment, and compensation for both pecuniary and non-pecuniary loss) but leaves open the scales of compensation. 'To bring home' rights might be thought to require that rights are compensated in the way that home regards as appropriate.

It is submitted, therefore, that there is no necessity to interpret the HRA 1998 in the way chosen by Lord Bingham. As his interpretation conflicts with both the arguments of principle and pragmatism set out above, it is an interpretation that should be rejected.

C. Conclusion

The conclusion reached is that the approach in *Greenfield* should be departed from as soon as possible (and as we have said, it was technically only obiter dicta) and the analysis adopted by the Law Commission and by some earlier cases should instead be applied. That is, while general Strasbourg principles—such as the aim being to compensate the claimant for pecuniary and non-pecuniary loss and not awarding punitive damages—should be applied, the scale of damages for non-pecuniary loss in domestic tort cases should be used to assess damages for the HRA 1998 cause of action.

IV. WHAT ARE VINDICATORY DAMAGES?

There is a final linked puzzle that we must try to solve.[101] In several recent cases on appeal from Commonwealth courts, the Privy Council has awarded what have been termed 'vindicatory damages', in addition

---

[100] See the two articles referred to at above n 82.

[101] In considering this puzzle, I have found the following particularly helpful: J Edelman, 'In Defence of Exemplary Damages' in CEF Rickett (ed), *Justifying Private Law Remedies*

to compensatory damages, for the breach of constitutional rights.[102] The difficulty lies in understanding exactly what these damages are for. It is submitted that the key to unlocking this mystery is to recognise that the label being used to describe these damages is misleading and that true understanding is obfuscated if one treats the primary function of these damages as being to 'vindicate the right'. Indeed, we here come back to Stevens' thesis because, although he does not refer to these awards, if their role is to vindicate the right infringed, they might be regarded as very similar to his 'substitutive damages'.

The truth of the matter is that all judicial monetary and non-monetary remedies for civil wrongs can be seen as having the *subsidiary* function of vindicating the right infringed. So, for example, the primary function of compensatory damages is to compensate the claimant's loss but, in so doing, one is also inevitably vindicating the right infringed; the primary function of restitutionary damages is to reverse the gain made by the wrong but, in so doing, one is also vindicating the underlying right; and an order of specific performance, while primarily concerned to compel performance of a positive contractual obligation, is also inevitably concerned to vindicate the contractual right infringed (or about to be infringed). It is only in respect of declarations and nominal damages that, in contrast, can one come close to saying that the *primary* function is to vindicate the right.

So the question becomes, what exactly is the primary function of so-called vindicatory damages? The leading and most penetrating judicial analysis is, characteristically, that of Lord Nicholls in giving the judgment of the Privy Council in *A-G of Trinidad and Tobago v Ramanoop*.[103] He said:

> An award of compensation will go some distance towards vindicating the infringed constitutional right. How far it goes will depend on the circumstances, but in principle it may well not suffice. The fact that the right violated was a constitutional right adds an extra dimension to the wrong. An additional award, not necessarily of substantial size, may be needed to reflect the sense of public outrage, emphasise the importance of the constitutional right and the gravity of the breach, and deter further breaches. All these elements have a place in this additional award ... Although such an award, where called for, is likely in most cases to cover much the same ground in financial terms as would an award by way of punishment in the strict sense of retribution, punishment in the latter sense is not its object. Accordingly, the expressions

(Oxford, Hart Publishing, 2008) 221; N Witzleb and R Carroll, 'The Role of Vindication in Torts Damages' (2009) 17 *Tort Law Review* 16.

[102] *A-G of Trinidad and Tobago v Ramanoop* [2005] UKPC 15, [2006] 1 AC 328 (*Ramanoop*); *Inniss v A-G of Saint Christopher and Nevis* [2008] UKPC 42; *Takitota v A-G of the Bahamas* [2009] UKPC 11. Such damages were being awarded for breach of constitutional rights at common law but were not being awarded in tort.
[103] *Ramanoop* [2005] UKPC 15, [2006] 1 AC 328.

'punitive damages' or 'exemplary damages' are better avoided as descriptions of this type of additional award.[104]

Lord Nicholls is therefore saying that 'vindicatory damages' are multi-functional and are concerned, where compensatory damages are inadequate to achieve these aims, to reflect public outrage, to emphasise the importance of the right or the seriousness of its infringement, and to deter future wrongdoing.

It is immediately apparent, once one has rigorously unpacked the functions in this way, how very similar those functions are to those which are offered as justifying punitive or exemplary damages in tort. So, for example, Lord Devlin in *Rookes v Barnard* spoke of exemplary damages as serving 'a useful purpose in vindicating the strength of the law'[105] and in *Kuddus* Lord Nicholls, in explaining when exemplary damages can be awarded, referred to the 'contumelious' nature of the infringement and to the underlying rationale being 'the sense of outrage which a defendant's conduct sometimes evokes'.[106] If Lord Nicholls in *Ramanoop* had added 'retribution' or 'teaching the wrongdoer a lesson' to the functions of 'vindicatory damages', the match would have been exact.

It is therefore not at all surprising that, most recently, in *Takitota v A-G of the Bahamas*[107] the Privy Council decided that, to avoid duplication, one should not award both exemplary damages for a tort and vindicatory damages for breach of a constitutional right. Lord Carswell giving the judgment said the following:

> Their Lordships consider that it would not be appropriate to make an award both by way of exemplary damages and for breach of constitutional rights. When the vindicatory function of the latter head of damages has been discharged, with the element of deterrence that a substantial award carries with it, the purpose of exemplary damages has largely been achieved. To make a further award of exemplary damages, as the appellant's counsel sought, would be to introduce duplication.[108]

Indeed, given the close match to exemplary or punitive damages, it is not at all clear why the element of retribution was excluded from Lord Nicholls' list of the functions driving vindicatory damages. On the face of it one would have thought that that function was as relevant to the outrageous infringement of a constitutional right as to the outrageous infringement of a private law right in tort. Perhaps the best explanation is that it was simply thought inappropriate to exact retribution where the defendant is inevitably a public authority rather than an individual.

---

[104] ibid, at [19].
[105] *Rookes v Barnard* [1964] AC 1129 (HL) 1226.
[106] *Kuddus* [2001] UKHL 29, [2002] 2 AC 122 [63]–[65].
[107] *Takitota v A-G of the Bahamas* [2009] UKPC 11.
[108] ibid, at [15].

However, the crucial point that emerges is that so-called 'vindicatory damages' for the infringement of constitutional rights must be seen alongside, and as very closely linked to, exemplary or punitive damages so that, like those damages, they should only be granted in exceptional circumstances. It would appear to be the case that, if one has objections to the existence of exemplary or punitive damages one ought, if one is being consistent, to be objecting also to 'vindicatory damages'. Rationally it is hard to see how merely adding retribution to the list of functions could in itself turn the acceptable into the unacceptable.[109]

It further follows that, given the existence of punitive or exemplary damages in tort law, there would be nothing to be gained, except confusion, by introducing the idea of awarding 'vindicatory damages' into tort law.[110] Above all, one should not be fooled by the label into thinking that 'vindicatory damages' should be routinely available. When properly understood they are in truth a far cry from Stevens' substitutive damages conceived as the basic award, valuing the right, for every infringement of a right.[111] Nor is there any role for vindicatory damages as a form of discretionary emphatic declaration sitting alongside nominal damages but awarding a substantial, rather than a nominal, sum. Such a purpose would be achievable by the court's declaration (and the words of its judgement) alone and any sum of damages awarded would be entirely arbitrary. Moreover, such a development would fly in the face of calls for nominal damages to be abolished as serving no valid purpose beyond that of a declaration,[112] and would directly contradict the Strasbourg Court jurisprudence where even compensatory damages take second place to the declaration so that the declaration is commonly thought to be sufficient

---

[109] But this is the view taken by Lord Scott who does not like exemplary damages (see his speech in *Kuddus* [2001] UKHL 29, [2002] 2 AC 122) but likes vindicatory damages: see the next footnote. See also Lord Scott, 'Damages' [2007] *Lloyd's Maritime and Commercial Law Quarterly* 465, 471, arguing that vindicatory damages in tort can better serve the legitimate aim of deterrence than 'punitive damages' which he regards as 'unprincipled'.

[110] In obiter dicta in *Ashley v Chief Constable of Sussex Police* [2008] UKHL 25, [2008] 1 AC 962 [23] Lord Scott indicated that vindicatory damages might be awarded in a tort action for trespass to the person. The action was brought by relatives of the deceased Mr Ashley, who had been shot dead by a police officer. With respect, his Lordship can be criticised for not making clear that this would be a radical departure from the present law given that no such damages have ever been awarded in tort. None of the other Lords can be said to have supported this obiter dicta and Lord Rodger specifically said that, in respect of the right to bodily integrity protected by the tort actionable per se of trespass to the person, 'the law vindicates that right by awarding nominal damages': at [60].

[111] Oddly, Stevens argues that punitive damages can be justified 'as a form of substitutive damages for the right infringed': *Torts and Rights*, above n 2, at 85–88. But, with respect, he here drifts away from valuing the right infringed to an argument based on the seriousness of the infringement of the right. His argument can only be understood as directed to explaining punitive damages not as substitutive damages but as a supplement to compensatory or restitutionary damages and, in line with this, he does at one point say that the best label here might be 'retributory damages': at 85.

[112] See above n 20 and accompanying text.

'vindication of the right' without the need even to compensate the loss suffered by the claimant.

There is one final point for completeness. In contrast to the breach of constitutional rights in the Commonwealth, it would seem clear that 'vindicatory damages' cannot be awarded under the HRA 1998. This is because they do not naturally fall within the words 'just satisfaction' in section 8(3) and, like punitive damages, they have never been awarded by the Strasbourg Court. Nothing could show more clearly the inappropriateness of the label describing those damages. Although the main function of the HRA 1998 cause of action is the vindication of Convention rights, 'vindicatory damages' are not available.

V. OVERALL CONCLUSIONS

My overall conclusions are as follows:

1. The 'substitutive damages' thesis, while brilliantly presented by Stevens, should be rejected.
2. The approach of the House of Lords in the *Greenfield* case should be departed from. The scale of non-pecuniary loss awards in domestic tort law should be applied by analogy to non-pecuniary loss awards for breach of Convention rights by a public authority under the Human Rights Act 1998.
3. The inappropriately labelled 'vindicatory damages', which have been awarded for breach of Commonwealth constitutional rights, cannot be awarded under the Human Rights Act 1998 and have no place in English tort law.

11

Explaining the Inexplicable? Four Manifestations of Abuse of Rights in English Law

JW NEYERS*

I. INTRODUCTION

U NTIL FAIRLY RECENTLY, rights-based accounts of private law have, quite rightly, been focused on explaining the most fundamental divisions and principles in the law of obligations. Although plausible explanations of the central aspects of tort,[1] contract,[2] fiduciary duty,[3] and unjust enrichment[4] have been offered, doubt remains as to whether these theories can account for the many nuanced and com-

* This research was funded in part by a Standard Research Grant from the Social Sciences and Humanities Research Council of Canada. The author would like to thank Allan Beever, Peter Benson, Rick Bigwood, Andrew Botterell, Erika Chamberlain, Rande Kostal, Margaret Martin, John Murphy, Stephen Pitel, Arthur Ripstein and Ernest Weinrib for their comments on earlier drafts of this chapter. The usual disclaimer applies.

[1] See, eg, EJ Weinrib, *The Idea of Private Law* (Cambridge MA, Harvard University Press, 1995); R Stevens, *Torts and Rights* (Oxford, Oxford University Press, 2007); A Beever, *Rediscovering the Law of Negligence* (Oxford, Hart Publishing, 2007).

[2] See, eg, P Benson, 'The Idea of a Public Basis of Justification for Contract' (1995) 33 *Osgoode Hall Journal* 273; P Benson, 'The Unity of Contract Law' in P Benson (ed), *The Theory of Contract Law: New Essays* (Cambridge, Cambridge University Press, 2001) 118; EJ Weinrib, 'Punishment and Disgorgement as Contract Remedies' (2003) 78 *Chicago-Kent Law Review* 55; P Benson, 'Contract as a Transfer of Ownership' (2007) 48 *William and Mary Law Review* 1673.

[3] See, eg, EJ Weinrib, 'The Juridical Classification of Obligations' in P Birks (ed), *The Classification of Obligations* (Oxford, Oxford University Press, 1997) 37; L Smith, 'The Motive, Not the Deed' in J Getzler (ed), *Rationalizing Property, Equity and Trusts: Essays in Honour of Edward Burn* (London, Butterworths, 2003) 53; P Miller, 'Essays Toward a Theory of Fiduciary Law' (DPhil thesis, University of Toronto 2008); J Edelman, 'When Do Fiduciary Duties Arise?' (2010) 126 *Law Quarterly Review* 302.

[4] See, eg, L Smith, 'Restitution: The Heart of Corrective Justice' (2001) 79 *Texas Law Review* 2115; EJ Weinrib, 'The Normative Structure of Unjust Enrichment' in C Rickett and R Grantham (eds), *Structure and Justification in Private Law: Essays for Peter Birks* (Oxford, Hart Publishing, 2008) 21; EJ Weinrib, 'Correctively Unjust Enrichment' in R Chambers,

plex intermediate and lower-level doctrines that are found interspersed throughout the law.[5] With this in mind, the purpose of this chapter will be to suggest that a rights-based account of the law can indeed explain several doctrines (namely, marshalling, misfeasance in public office, lawful means conspiracy, and lawful act duress) which are generally regarded, even by some other rights-based theorists, as anomalous and thus incapable of fitting coherently alongside the established core of the law of obligations. It therefore hopes to expand the number, and generality, of doctrines thought explainable using a rights-based analysis.

The argument of this chapter is two-fold: first, that these four doctrines are all explainable as manifestations, in one form or another, of the common law's version of what civilians call 'abuse of rights'; and, secondly, that this prohibition on the targeted infliction of gratuitous harm is consistent with the idea of rights embodied in the established core of the law of obligations. Part II of the chapter will deal with the latter argument and part III will address the former.

II. TARGETED GRATUITOUS HARM AND ABUSE OF RIGHTS[6]

In a series of recent articles and public lectures,[7] Ernest Weinrib has sought to explain how the simple idea that our rights are protected and only fully enjoyable in a civil condition or system of rights[8] might affect the set of rights that would pertain solely as a matter of justice between individuals in a state of nature.[9] His argument is that systematic concerns

---

C Mitchell, and J Penner (eds), *Philosophical Foundations of the Law of Unjust Enrichment* (Oxford, Oxford University Press, 2009) 31.

[5] See, eg, J Murphy, 'Rights, Reductionism and Tort Law' (2008) 28 *Oxford Journal of Legal Studies* 393; P Cane, 'Rights in Private Law' ch 2 of this book.

[6] For the sake of clarity, it should be noted that the Kantian view of rights, described herein, is wider than that developed by Hohfeld. Accordingly, the following discussions of abuse of rights would include, in Hohfeldian terms, abuses of liberties, privileges, and so on: for a discussion see N Lazarev, 'Hohfeld's Analysis of Rights: An Essential Approach to a Conceptual and Practical Understanding of the Nature of Rights' (2005) 12 *Murdoch University Electronic Journal of Law* www.murdoch.edu.au/elaw/issues/v12n1_2/Lavarev12_2.html, accessed on 23 January 2011.

[7] See E Weinrib, 'Poverty and Property in Kant's System of Rights' (2003) 78 *Notre Dame Law Review* 795; EJ Weinrib, 'Two Conceptions of Remedies' in CEF Rickett (ed), *Justifying Private Law Remedies* (Oxford, Hart Publishing, 2008) 3; EJ Weinrib, 'Private Law and Public Right' (2011) 61 *University of Toronto Law Journal* 191.

[8] For a detailed discussion of this issue, see A Ripstein, *Force and Freedom: Kant's Legal and Political Philosophy* (Cambridge MA, Harvard University Press, 2009) ch 6.

[9] Such as rights to bodily integrity, to property, to contractual performance, and to reputation: see Cave J's enunciation of these rights in *Allen v Flood* [1898] AC 1 (HL) 29; Weinrib, 'Private Law and Public Right', above n 7, at 194–96. It should be noted that in Kantian terms, a state of nature is not a historical condition, nor one where rights are non-existent, but rather one that is lacking in a public authority entitled to enforce private rights and apply them in cases of dispute: see CK Allen, 'Legal Morality and the *Ius Abutendi*'

that bear 'on the relation of the norms to one another, to the institutions from which they arise, and to the legal community whose members are all subject to them'[10] may, 'relative to the rights available in the state of nature, either extend or narrow the effect of a right of the [claimant].'[11] This expansion and/or contraction, however, need not be seen as incoherent or policy-based since it is inherent in our idea of rights that there will be a system in which to enforce them. As Weinrib notes, a person claiming a right necessarily acknowledges both (1) 'that others also have rights with which the claimant's right must systematically exist' and (2) that 'rights have to be enforced by a court, that is, by a disinterested and impartial public authority'.[12]

According to Weinrib,[13] an example of the systematic nature of private law expanding a right is the tort of inducing breach of contract. Whereas in the state of nature contracts bind only those who are parties to them, in a system of rights everyone is expected to respect the contracts of others. As he explains:

> When everyone is united under a system of laws that assures the rights of all, everyone is obligated to respect everyone else's contractual rights. Because a court operates under the authority of public right, it is not merely a private arbitrator of a private arrangement between the promisor and the promisee. Rather, it has the public function of making everyone secure in her rights against everyone else. This function would be unfulfilled if parties external to the contract could procure violations of another's contractual rights at their will. Accordingly, whereas, in the state of nature, the parties to a contract are not secure even against each other, public right makes their rights secure against everyone by attaching liability not only to a breach of contract by the other contracting party but also to the procuring by third parties of such a breach. Thus, public right makes the contract a juridical object for everyone, thereby creating a system of reciprocal assurance that relates all to all.[14]

In this series of articles and lectures, Weinrib also provides an example of the systematic nature of private law contracting a right. The example that Weinrib gives is the discretion given to a court by *Shelfer v City of*

(1924) 40 *Law Quarterly Review* 164, 180–81; Ripstein, above n 8, at ch 6. All subsequent references to the 'state of nature' should be understood in these terms.

[10] Weinrib, 'Private Law and Public Right', above n 7, at 197.
[11] ibid, at 204.
[12] Weinrib, 'Two Conceptions of Remedies', above n 7, at 27.
[13] I say 'according to Weinrib', since it seems possible to explain the tort of inducing breach of contract relying only on the rights and principles available in a state of nature: see P Benson, 'The Basis for Excluding Liability for Economic Loss in Tort Law' in DG Owen (ed), *Philosophical Foundations of Tort Law* (Oxford, Oxford University Press, 1995) 427; JW Neyers, 'The Economic Torts as Corrective Justice' (2009) 17 *Torts Law Journal* 162. For a view similar to that of Weinrib (ie, that there exists a separate right not to have a breach of contract procured that exists independently of the contract) see Stevens, *Torts and Rights*, above n 1, at 275 ff.
[14] Weinrib, 'Private Law and Public Right', above n 7, at 205.

London Electric Lighting Co to refuse an injunction provided certain criteria are met.[15] Whereas in a state of nature the claimant's property right would demand an injunction since 'the wrong of nuisance is an interference with the [claimant's] use and enjoyment' of his or her land and the injunction simply 'restores to the [claimant] the very thing of which the [claimant] was wrongfully deprived,' in a system of rights he or she might be unable to receive one.[16] This is due to the fact that when there is a small injury to the claimant's rights that can adequately be compensated in money and an injunction would be oppressive to the defendant, the only point of insisting on 'an injunction would be to damage the defendant rather than to promote any legitimate interest of the [claimant].'[17] Thus, the claimant is given damages in lieu of an injunction in order to prevent the claimant from abusing the defendant's rights.

As Weinrib realises, talk about abuse of rights is often greeted with scepticism in common law and rights-based circles.[18] This is due to the fact that the modern civilian doctrine of abuse of rights is associated with the introduction of considerations of social policy and morality that are alien to the idea of rights.[19] As he argues, however, this scepticism is unwarranted if one adopts a more limited and coherent view of abuse of rights:

> The idea that the law should not legitimise the infliction on another of gratuitous harm is fully consonant with the normative presuppositions of a system of rights. ... [P]articipants in the system of rights are conceived as persons with a self-determining capacity for purposive action. Within this system each person pursues one's self-chosen purposes, subject only to the constraint that one's action be capable of coexisting with the purposiveness of others. This requires

---

[15] *Shelfer v City of London Electric Lighting Co* [1895] 1 Ch 287 (CA).

[16] Weinrib, 'Two Conceptions of Remedies', above n 7, at 28.

[17] ibid.

[18] See, eg, FH Lawson, *Negligence in the Civil Law* (Oxford, Clarendon Press, 1950) 18–19:

> [I]t is clear that as soon as the theory of abuse of rights passes the stage where subjective malice is the sole test, it is really a socialist doctrine. It implies that a man's right is no longer, as it were, a sphere within which he is sovereign, over which he may dispose according to his own view of his interest and his ideas of right and wrong; it is to be subject to the control of society in the person of the judge, who exercises a veto over his decisions in accordance with what he considers to be the purpose for which society has conferred the right.

[19] Weinrib, 'Two Conceptions of Remedies', above n 7, at 29. For discussion of abuse of rights from this social morality and policy perspective, see S Herman, 'Classical Social Theories and the Doctrine of Abuse of Right' (1976) 37 *Louisiana Law Review* 747; AN Yiannopoulos, 'Abuse of Right in Louisiana Civil Law' in AM Rabello (ed), *Aequitas and Equity: Equity in Civil Law and Mixed Jurisdictions* (Jerusalem, Hebrew University of Jerusalem, 1997) 690. For an excellent summary of both the history of abuse of rights and the modern doctrine in France, Scotland, Quebec, Louisiana, and South Africa, see E Reid, 'Abuse of Rights in Scots Law' (1998) 2 *Edinburgh Law Review* 129.

that one pursue one's purposes as ends that one is trying to achieve for oneself, not as an obstacle against what someone else is trying to achieve. Actions for the sake of creating mutual obstacles against the actions of others cannot systemically coexist.

As juridical manifestations of self-determining freedom, rights provide the space within which all right holders may pursue ends of their own. Such ends are consistent with the self-determining freedom of others only if the point of pursuing them is independent of the adverse effect on someone else. When all act to pursue ends of their own in this sense, they all rank equally as persons whose activities can coexist within the system of rights. Conversely, if the freedom to perform an act merely to frustrate the purposes of another were legitimate, rights would be transformed from markers of mutual freedom to instruments of subordination. Accordingly, it would be inconsistent with what is normatively presupposed in the system of rights to allow a right to operate in a way that would harm another without promoting (in the language of the civilians) a 'serious and legitimate interest' of the right holder.[20]

The argument of this chapter is that the doctrines of marshalling, misfeasance in public office, lawful means conspiracy and lawful act duress can be explained on the basis that what the common law is doing is preventing parties from gratuitously harming others (ie, from acting with the primary purpose of injuring them). Upon examination it will be found that the courts do this in one of two ways: they either stop claimants from asserting a right in a situation where such an assertion would be abusive (thereby contracting their rights) or they award damages to claimants for the infliction of gratuitous harm (thereby expanding the set of rights enjoyed in a state of nature). In essence, in certain circumstances the common law will recognise a claim right in an individual to be free from the targeted infliction of gratuitous harm.

III. THE VARIOUS DOCTRINES

This part will examine the doctrines of marshalling, misfeasance in public office, lawful means conspiracy and lawful act duress. Each section in this part will simultaneously do two things: first, it will outline the doctrine and the reasons by which it is generally thought to be anomalous; secondly, it will demonstrate how each of these doctrines might be explained from a rights-based perspective that incorporates the systematic concerns outlined by Weinrib in part II.

[20] Weinrib, 'Two Conceptions of Remedies', above n 7, at 30.

A. Marshalling of Securities

The equitable doctrine of marshalling of securities is the name given to the process by which the law protects junior creditors from the realisation choices of senior creditors.[21] In its most classic form, the doctrine

> applies where one secured party (the 'senior creditor') holds a first-ranking security interest (the 'senior security interest') over two or more assets of a security provider and another secured party (the 'junior creditor') holds a second-ranking security interest (the 'junior security interest') over one of those assets. In the event that the senior creditor satisfies the obligations owed to it (the 'senior secured obligations') out of the asset which is subject to the junior security interest, with the consequence that that asset is no longer sufficient to discharge the obligations owed to the junior creditor (the 'junior secured obligations'), the junior creditor may be able to rectify the deterioration in its priority position by marshalling the senior security interest.[22]

While the historical origins of the doctrine are unclear,[23] in its earliest incarnations it is clear that the doctrine operated by stopping the senior creditor from enforcing its senior security interest on the jointly charged asset. As Cotton LJ explained in *Webb v Smith*:

> [I]f A. has a charge upon Whiteacre and Blackacre, and if B. also has a charge upon Blackacre only, A. must take payment of his charge out of Whiteacre, and must leave Blackacre, so that B., the other creditor, may follow it and obtain payment of his debt out of it: in other words, if two estates, Whiteacre and Blackacre, are mortgaged to one person, and subsequently one of them, Blackacre, is mortgaged to another person, unless Blackacre is sufficient to pay both charges, *the first mortgagee will be compelled* to take satisfaction out of Whiteacre, in order to leave to the second mortgagee Blackacre, upon which alone he can go.[24]

Over time this coercive method of marshalling largely gave way to the now-dominant technique called the 'post-realisation' method.[25] This method of marshalling does not compel the senior creditor but merely subrogates the junior creditor to the senior security interest after the senior

---

[21] PAU Ali, *Marshalling of Securities: Equity and Priority-Ranking of Secured Debt* (New York, Oxford University Press, 1999) 3.

[22] PAU Ali, *The Law of Secured Finance: An International Survey of Security Interests over Personal Property* (New York, Oxford University Press, 2002) 238. See also GW Keeton and LA Sheridan, *Equity*, 3rd edn (Chichester, Barry Rose, 1987) 341: '[Marshalling] operates when two persons, A and B, are interested in the same property and A, whose interest has priority to that of B, could equally well deal with his interest in either of two ways, one of which would prejudice B and the other would not.'

[23] See Ali, *Marshalling of Securities*, above n 21, at ch 2 outlining the debate as to whether it was an indigenous common law doctrine or one imported from Roman law.

[24] *Webb v Smith* (1885) 30 Ch D 192 (CA) 200.

[25] See Ali, *Marshalling of Securities*, above n 21, at ch 3; B MacDougall, 'Marshalling and the Personal Property Security Acts: Doing unto Others ...' (1994) 28 *University of British Columbia Law Review* 91, 116–22.

creditor has satisfied its claim. This 'post-realisation' method is said to have the advantage of interfering less with the right of the senior creditor to enforce its security as it sees fit and with dealing with situations where the junior creditor could not get to court to stop the senior creditor before realisation.[26] But, in essence, it differs little from the coercive version since, as Lord Hoffmann noted in *Re Bank of Credit and Commerce International SA (No 8)*,[27] it merely treats the senior security holder as having satisfied itself out of the fund over which the junior creditor had no claim rather than forcing it to do so.[28]

What justifies this doctrine's existence? As noted in the leading text on the subject, *Marshalling of Securities* by Paul Ali, marshalling is extremely difficult to justify.[29] The doctrine cannot be explained on the basis of contract because in the typical situation there is no contractual relationship between the senior and junior creditor and the doctrine operates without the consent of the parties.[30] It also cannot be explained on a tort law basis since the senior creditor is merely exercising its undoubted right to enforce its security[31] and, moreover, is not interfering with any of the junior creditor's classically delineated rights. Although some argue that unjust enrichment is the justification,[32] such an analysis does not work since the requisite elements are missing from each of the possible claims against the senior creditor, the debtor and the unsecured creditors. The unjust enrichment claim against the senior creditor should fail on the twin bases that although the junior creditor is deprived, the senior creditor is not relevantly enriched and, even if it were, there is a juristic reason for the enrichment in the senior security interest.[33] Equally, the claim against the debtor should fail because, as marshalling 'is neutral in its impact upon the residue available to the debtor following discharge of its creditors' claims', the debtor is not enriched either.[34] That leaves the claim of the

---

[26] Ali, *Marshalling of Securities*, above n 21, at 46–50; T Cleaver, 'Marshalling' (1991) 21 *Victoria University of Wellington Law Review* 275, 277–81.

[27] *Re Bank of Credit and Commerce International SA (No 8)* [1998] AC 214 (HL) 230–31:

> [Marshalling] is a principle for doing equity between two or more creditors, each of whom are owed debts by the same debtor, but one of whom can enforce his claim against more than one security or fund and the other can resort to only one. It gives the latter an equity to require that the first creditor satisfy himself (or be treated as having satisfied himself) so far as possible out of the security or fund to which the latter has no claim.

[28] See also Ali, *Marshalling of Securities*, above n 21, at 48.

[29] ibid, at 101–102.

[30] ibid, at 40, 98; MacDougall, above n 25, at 92.

[31] Ali, *Marshalling of Securities*, above n 21, at 41.

[32] See, eg, M Evans, *Outline of Equity and Trusts*, 3rd edn (Sydney, Butterworths, 1996) para 11.9.

[33] Ali, *Marshalling of Securities*, above n 21, at 74.

[34] ibid, at 75.

unsecured creditors. Although the unsecured creditors might be enriched at the junior creditor's expense if there was not any subrogation,[35] there is seemingly no unjust factor that would justify a claim and a clear juristic reason for the enrichment in the *pari passu* rules of bankruptcy. Given these difficulties, Ali comes to the conclusion that marshalling 'is an anomalous doctrine ... that is not readily susceptible to classification'.[36] This view was shared by CC Langdell, who commented 'that the doctrine [of marshalling] ... cannot be sustained upon any principle.'[37]

Given these problems and its anomalous nature, Ali argues that the best understanding of the doctrine is not juridical but rather one based on the policy of protecting junior security interests. As he explains:

> Under the conventional theory [of security], the law accords secured creditors priority over unsecured creditors because it recognises that security allows debtors access to credit which might not otherwise have been made available ...
>
> As a corollary of the conventional theory of security, the law will do all it can to protect security and preserve the preferential status of secured claims, for by so doing it protects the supply of credit to debtors. It is this policy imperative which underpins the doctrine of marshalling securities.
>
> The law takes the position that the secured claim of a junior creditor should not arbitrarily be placed in jeopardy merely because a senior creditor has, out of the various assets available to it, chosen to enforce its security against the very asset over which the junior creditor holds security. Should that occur, marshalling will redress the loss sustained by the junior creditor by redistributing the assets of the debtor from the debtor's unsecured creditors to the junior creditor.[38]

If the argument presented in part II is sound, this recourse to policy is not necessary to explain the doctrine of marshalling. Instead, the doctrine is justified in the same way as the rules that limit the availability of an injunction for a nuisance. In a situation such as that envisaged in the classic marshalling example, the only point of the senior creditor insisting on realising its security on the shared asset can be to harm the junior creditor without any gain for itself.[39] The senior creditor is not allowed to do this when its obligations can be met perfectly through the realisation of another security. As Joseph Story noted in his *Commentaries* in relation to marshalling, 'natural justice requires that one man should not be permitted, from wantonness, or caprice, or rashness, to do an injury to another.'[40] That this abuse of rights justification is a plausible inter-

---

[35] ibid, at 75–76.

[36] ibid, at 101.

[37] CC Langdell, *A Brief Survey of Equity Jurisdiction*, 2nd edn (Cambridge MA, The Harvard Law Review Association, 1908) 16.

[38] Ali, *Marshalling of Securities*, above n 21, at 115.

[39] See the similar discussion in Weinrib, 'Two Conceptions of Remedies', above n 7, at 29 in relation to injunctions.

[40] MM Bigelow, *Story's Commentaries on Equity Jurisprudence*, 13th edn (Boston, Little, Brown & Co, 1886) § 633.

pretation of the doctrine is buttressed by the fact that the senior creditor is not required to allow the junior creditor to marshal its securities when the senior creditor has a good reason to enforce its claim on the shared asset. Thus, in *Webb v Smith* it was held that the senior creditor was entitled to exercise its security interest (a lien) over the shared fund since the senior creditor only enjoyed an unsecured set-off in relation to the non-shared fund and could not be compelled to take this lesser remedy.[41]

B. Misfeasance in Public Office

Prior to its re-emergence in *Roncarelli v Duplessis*,[42] the tort of misfeasance in public office was relatively easy to explain from a rights-based perspective.[43] The tort was generally understood to be available only to claimants who could prove that one of their pre-existing rights had been interfered with by the defendant public officer.[44] Thus, the interference by the public official would be a wrong (at least conceptually) unless the public officer had some privilege or lawful authority to act as he or she did.[45] If the public official was acting maliciously—ie, with the primary purpose of injuring the claimant or 'for a reason and purpose knowingly foreign to the administration'[46]—he or she would be acting outside the scope of his or her privilege or lawful authority (as all public law powers can only be exercised for the public good[47]) and would therefore be liable. The only independent work done by the tort of misfeasance was to act as a catch-all in situations where the right violated had not traditionally been protected by another free-standing tort.[48]

---

[41] *Webb v Smith* (1885) 30 Ch D 192 (CA). See also *The Arab* (1859) 5 Jur NS 417 (Court of Admiralty) where the Court held that senior creditors could not be forced to rely upon unsecured personal actions (as opposed to secured maritime liens) so that a junior creditor could satisfy a bond from the shared asset.

[42] *Roncarelli v Duplessis* [1959] SCR 121. See also *David v Abdul Cader* [1963] 1 WLR 834 (PC).

[43] For a similar view, see the comprehensive discussion in Erika Chamberlain, 'Misfeasance in a Public Office: A Justifiable Anomaly within the Rights-Based Approach?' ch 19 of this book.

[44] E Chamberlain, 'The Need for a "Standing" Rule in Misfeasance in a Public Office' (2008) 7 *Oxford University Commonwealth Law Journal* 215, 218–20; S Kneebone, 'Misfeasance in a Public Office after Mengel's Case: A "Special" Tort No More?' (1996) 4 *Tort Law Review* 111, 124. See, eg, *Ashby v White* (1703) 3 Ld Raym 320, 92 ER 710; *Tampion v Anderson* [1973] VR 715.

[45] See Brennan J in *Northern Territory v Mengel* (1995) 185 CLR 307 (*Mengel*) 358: 'Public officers, like all other subjects, are liable for conduct that amounts to a tort unless their conduct is authorised, justified or excused by statute.'

[46] *Roncarelli v Duplessis* [1959] SCR 121, 141 (Rand J).

[47] *Jones v Swansea City Council* [1990] 1 WLR 54 (CA); *Three Rivers District Council v Governor and Company of the Bank of England (No 3)* [2003] 2 AC 1 (HL) (*Three Rivers*) 190 (Lord Steyn).

[48] As was the case in *Harman v Tappenden* (1801) 1 East 555, 102 ER 214 (although the claim failed for lack of proof of the requisite malice).

This understanding of the tort of misfeasance in public office came to a decisive end with the House of Lords' decision in *Three Rivers District Council v Governor and Company of the Bank of England (No 3)*.[49] In that case, it was determined that the claimant need not have a pre-existing right in order to sue for misfeasance. As Lord Steyn noted (adopting the formulation of the trial judge):

> I can see no reason in principle why the [claimant] should identify a legal right which is being infringed or a particular duty owed to him, beyond the right not to be damaged or injured by a deliberate abuse of power by a public officer.[50]

Instead of focusing on a legal right, modern courts have instead focused on the requirement that the claimant suffer loss[51] and that there be a deliberate abuse of power. This abuse is said to arise in one of two ways (often called Category A and Category B).[52] In Category A, the public officer acts with the primary purpose of injuring a person or class of persons; whereas in Category B the public officer acts with knowledge both that he or she has no power to do the act complained of and that the act will likely injure the claimant.[53]

Much like the other doctrines examined in this chapter, the modern tort of misfeasance in public office is generally regarded as being special, exceptional and therefore anomalous.[54] This is so for several reasons. First, unlike almost all other torts, it does not require a pre-existing legal right in the claimant grounding his or her entitlement to sue.[55] Secondly, as Lord Steyn noted in *Three Rivers* it seemingly is in conflict with the fact that (1) 'there is no overarching principle in English law of liability in tort

---

[49] *Three Rivers* [2003] 2 AC 1 (HL).

[50] ibid, at 193. See also Lord Hobhouse at 239 where he states that the tort of misfeasance in public office 'does not, and does not need to, apply where the defendant has invaded a legally protected right of the [claimant]'. For a similar view, see the discussion of Brennan J in *Mengel* (1995) 185 CLR 307, 357 where he states: 'there is no additional element which requires the identification of the [claimant] as a member of a class to whom the public officer owes a particular duty.'

[51] See *Watkins v Home Office* [2006] UKHL 17, [2006] 2 AC 395.

[52] See *Odhavji Estate v Woodhouse* [2003] SCC 69, [2003] 3 SCR 263 [22] (Iacobucci J for the Court).

[53] *Three Rivers* [2003] 2 AC 1 (HL) 191; ibid.

[54] See Chamberlain, 'Misfeasance in a Public Office', above n 43; Kneebone, above n 44, at 112; RJ Sadler, 'Liability for Misfeasance in a Public Office' (1992) 14 *Sydney Law Review* 137.

[55] See Chamberlain, 'The Need for a "Standing" Rule', above n 44, at 215; Stevens, *Torts and Rights*, above n 1, at 242. The only other examples are conspiracy (discussed below) and the unlawful means tort (explained in Neyers, 'The Economic Torts as Corrective Justice', above n 13). Although the rights-based analysis of negligence has fallen out of favour in modern judicial thinking it is implicit in the patterns of liability found in English law: see Beever, above n 1, at ch 7; P Benson, 'The Basis for Excluding Liability for Economic Loss in Tort Law', above n 13; JW Neyers, '*Tate & Lyle Food & Distribution Ltd v Greater London Council* (1983)' in C Mitchell and P Mitchell (eds), *Landmark Cases in the Law of Tort* (Oxford, Hart Publishing, 2010) 227.

for "unlawful, intentional and positive acts",[56] and (2) that an action will not lie merely because loss is caused by an *ultra vires* act.[57] Thirdly, it is a tort that applies only to public officers and thus 'is the only exception to the principle that ... a public officer is not liable in tort unless the act complained of would, if done by a private individual, be actionable'.[58] Fourthly, it appears to be in conflict with general private law (or state of nature[59]) principles that: (1) 'if conduct is lawful apart from motive, a bad motive will not make [a defendant] liable'[60] and (2) the infliction of loss, absent a violation of right, is not actionable.[61] Given these difficulties, it is not surprising that at one time the Court of Appeal denied the tort's existence[62] and that in *Torts and Rights*, Robert Stevens concludes that a rights-based analysis of the tort is impossible because the action 'is a genuinely public wrong' which needs to find its justification in administrative and constitutional law.[63]

The argument of this chapter is that much of the modern doctrine of misfeasance in public office can be explained if one accepts, as argued above, that there exists in English law an implicit doctrine of abuse of rights that prevents persons from acting for the primary purpose of injuring others. If this is correct, then it is clear that Category A of misfeasance can be justified. When a public officer acts with the primary purpose of injuring a member of the public, they have violated a claim-right created by the system of rights even though they have not violated any of the rights that would have been enjoyed in a state of nature. On this analysis,

---

[56] *Three Rivers* [2003] 2 AC 1 (HL) 190 citing *Lonrho Ltd v Shell Petroleum Co Ltd (No 2)* [1982] AC 173 (HL). See also *Mengel* (1995) 185 CLR 307.

[57] *Three Rivers* [2003] 2 AC 1 (HL) 190 (Lord Steyn, citing *X (Minors) v Bedfordshire County Council* [1995] 2 AC 633 (HL)), 229 (Lord Hobhouse). See also *Dunlop v Woollahra Municipal Council* [1982] AC 158 (HL).

[58] Sadler, above n 54, at 138. See also Kneebone, above n 44, at 112; M Andenas and D Fairgrieve, 'Misfeasance in Public Office, Governmental Liability, and European Influences' (2002) 51 *International & Comparative Law Quarterly* 757, 761.

[59] As used in the Kantian sense, outlined above in part II and especially at above n 9.

[60] *Three Rivers* [2003] 2 AC 1 (HL) 190 (Lord Steyn) citing *Allen v Flood* [1898] AC 1 (HL) and *Bradford Corp v Pickles* [1895] AC 587 (HL). See also the judgment of Scrutton LJ in *Ware and de Freville Ltd v Motor Trade Association* [1921] 3 KB 40 (CA) 67 where he states:

> I take *Allen v Flood* and *Bradford Corporation v Pickles* to decide that an act otherwise lawful, though harmful, does not become actionable by being done maliciously in the sense of with a bad motive or with intent to injure another.

[61] Stevens, *Torts and Rights*, above n 1, at 242.

[62] *Davis v Bromley* [1908] 1 KB 170 (CA).

[63] Stevens, *Torts and Rights*, above n 1, at 242. See also Murphy, 'Rights, Reductionism and Tort Law', above n 5, at 401 (suggesting that misfeasance in public office is inexplicable from a rights-based perspective). For an argument similar to that of Stevens, namely that misfeasance belongs to public, rather than private, law, see S Dench, 'The Tort of Misfeasance in a Public Office' (1981) 4 *Auckland University Law Review* 182, 182. See also the discussion in M Aronson, 'Some Australian Reflections on *Roncarelli v Duplessis*' (2010) 55 *McGill Law Journal* 615, 629–30.

many of the anomalies mentioned above can be explained away. Since the claimant in a Category A misfeasance action is in fact suing on the basis of a right, his or her loss is not therefore *damnum absque injuria*, and although motive is generally not relevant to liability in a state of nature, it becomes limitedly relevant in a civil condition. The abuse of rights analysis also makes it clear that the wrong of misfeasance is not unique to public officers since private individuals can also be civilly liable for the targeted infliction of gratuitous harm (at least when there is a conspiracy to do so).[64] The only difficult issue, one that will be addressed below,[65] is why there is an apparent immunity should only one person act with the predominant purpose of injuring another. In addition, the fact that, in reality, the tort of misfeasance is a manifestation of a wider abuse of rights principle may also help to explain why the courts have defined the tort's limiting concepts (such as 'public officer'[66] and the requirement of 'exercising power as a public officer'[67]) liberally to catch more and more conduct by more and more people.

It is probably impossible to explain all the Category B misfeasance cases from a rights-based perspective even if one accepts the addition of systematic rights to those more conventionally defined. With that said, however, many of the cases can be explained in one of two ways. The first explanation is that some of the cases are merely examples of the traditional 'pre-existing right/lack of a privilege' analysis of misfeasance offered at the outset of this section.[68] The second explanation is that some of the cases are really abuse of rights cases but the abuse has to be proven through a series of derivations. The classic example would be a situation where what the public officer offers as his or her primary purpose is not one that officer, to his or her knowledge, is in fact entitled to have; and therefore all that the court is left with is the secondary purpose to injure which then predominates. An example of a case that might be explained

---

[64] Mason J noted this similarity in *Mengel* (1995) 185 CLR 307, 347: 'And principle suggests that misfeasance in public office is a counterpart to, and should be confined in the same way as, those torts which impose liability on private individuals for the intentional infliction of harm.' See also *McGillivray v Kimber* (1915) 52 SCR 146, 163–64 (Duff J) and *Gerrard v Manitoba* (1992) 98 DLR (4th) 167 (Manitoba Court of Appeal) 172 (Scott CJM) where it is argued that the liability of public officers and private individuals for malicious acts is based on essentially similar principles. Conspiracy is discussed in the next section.

[65] See part IV below.

[66] See *Three Rivers* [2003] 2 AC 1 (HL) 191 (public office to be defined in 'a relatively wide sense'); *Freeman-Maloy v York University* (2006) 267 DLR (4th) 37 (Ontario Court of Appeal) (it is arguable that a University President is a public officer despite not being considered under government control for constitutional purposes).

[67] See *Jones v Swansea City Council* [1990] 1 WLR 54 (CA) (local authority exercising rights created by private lease caught by the tort).

[68] See, eg, *Ontario Racing Commission v O'Dwyer* [2008] ONCA 446, (2008) 293 DLR (4th) 559 (allowing a claim for misfeasance in public office for denying a claimant his statutory right to a hearing under the Racing Commission Act 2000, SO 2000, c 20).

on this basis is *Bourgoin v Ministry of Agriculture, Fisheries and Food*.[69] In that case, the Minister of Agriculture banned the import of turkeys from France, supposedly in order to stop the spread of Newcastle disease in the United Kingdom. It was later found by the European Court of Justice that the ban was unlawful because the real aim of the action was to protect domestic producers from foreign competition. The claimants sued for their loss of profits on the basis that the Minister had committed the tort of misfeasance in public office. The defendant moved to have the claim dismissed as disclosing no cause of action. For the purposes of the preliminary issue, the Minister accepted: (1) that the purpose of the ban was to protect English turkey producers; (2) that he knew at the time he instituted the ban that this was not a purpose he was entitled to have under either Community rules or domestic legislation; and (3) that he knew that the ban would cause damage to the claimants.[70] The Minister argued, however, that he could not be liable because the claimants could not show 'targeted malice', since his primary purpose was to further the interests of the domestic producers. Speaking for the Court on this issue, Oliver LJ found for the claimants. As he stated:

> If it be shown that the minister's motive was to further the interests of English turkey producers by keeping out the produce of French turkey producers — an act which must necessarily injure them — it seems to me entirely immaterial that the one purpose was dominant and the second merely a subsidiary purpose for giving effect to the dominant purpose. If an act is done deliberately and with knowledge of its consequences, I do not think that the actor can sensibly say that he did not 'intend' the consequences or that the act was not 'aimed' at the person who, it is known, will suffer them.[71]

Although subsequent cases have used this reasoning as a justification for the existence of Category B misfeasance,[72] it is equally consistent with the view that what appears to be a secondary purpose can be elevated to a predominant purpose given the right conglomeration of facts. Thus, although not every case of Category B misfeasance can be explained from a rights-based perspective, most can be justified as either a 'pre-existing right/lack of a privilege' type of case[73] or as a 'predominant purpose through derivation' type of case.

[69] *Bourgoin v Ministry of Agriculture, Fisheries and Food* [1986] QB 716 (CA).
[70] ibid, at 775–76 (Oliver LJ).
[71] ibid, at 777.
[72] See *Three Rivers* [2003] 2 AC 1 (HL) 191.
[73] Discussed at the beginning of this section.

C. Lawful Means Conspiracy[74]

The modern tort of conspiracy emerged from the crime of the same name and developed into two branches, one dealing with the use of unlawful means and the other dealing with the use of means otherwise lawful.[75] For a period of time, it appeared that the two branches had merged,[76] but the traditional bipartite approach was reasserted by subsequent decisions of the House of Lords[77] and other Commonwealth appellate courts.[78] Thus, in modern times, the law allows a claim in conspiracy:

> (1) whether the means used by the defendants are lawful or unlawful, [where] the predominant purpose of the defendants' conduct is to cause injury to the [claimant]; or
>
> (2) where the conduct of the defendants is unlawful, the conduct is directed towards the [claimant] (alone or together with others), and the defendants should know in the circumstances that injury to the [claimant] is likely to and does result.[79]

While it seems clear that the unlawful means version of conspiracy can be explained as a manifestation of the rules relating to joint tortfeasance supplemented by the tort of unlawful interference with economic relations where necessary,[80] the current orthodox understanding of the tort of

[74] The doctrine is also sometimes known as simple conspiracy (see H Carty, *An Analysis of the Economic Torts* (Oxford, Oxford University Press, 2001) 26), though as will become clear on the orthodox view there is little that is simple about it. The analysis in this section relies upon JW Neyers, 'The Economic Torts as Corrective Justice', above n 13.

[75] For the history of the tort, see Carty, above n 74, at ch 2; *Crofter Hand Woven Harris Tweed Co Ltd v Veitch* [1942] AC 435 (HL).

[76] See the laconic judgment of Lord Diplock in *Lonrho Ltd v Shell Petroleum Co Ltd (No 2)* [1982] AC 173 (HL), which was criticised by Lord Wedderburn, 'Rocking the Torts' (1983) 46 *Modern Law Review* 224, 227 as follows: 'the Law Lords purported to restate the entire English law on "innominate torts" and on the tort of conspiracy in a mere nine pages; referring to 13 authorities and having had only nine others cited'. See also *Metall und Rohstoff AG v Donaldson Lufkin & Jenrette Inc* [1990] 1 QB 391 (CA), which considered that the two conspiracies were fused.

[77] *Lonrho plc v Fayed* [1992] 1 AC 448 (HL).

[78] See, eg, *Canada Cement LaFarge Ltd v British Columbia Lightweight Aggregate Ltd* [1983] 1 SCR 452.

[79] ibid, at 471–72 (Estey J for the Court). See *Lonrho plc v Fayed* [1992] 1 AC 448 (HL) 465–66 (Lord Bridge):

> Where conspirators act with the predominant purpose of injuring the [claimant] and in fact inflict damage on him, but do nothing which would have been actionable if done by an individual acting alone, it is in the fact of their concerted action for that illegitimate purpose that the law, however anomalous it may now seem, finds a sufficient ground to condemn their action as illegal and tortious. But when conspirators intentionally injure the [claimant] and use unlawful means to do so, it is no defence for them to show that their primary purpose was to further or protect their own interests; it is sufficient to make their action tortious that the means used were unlawful.

[80] See Carty, above n 74, at 24–26; Stevens, *Torts and Rights*, above n 1, at 248–51; Neyers, 'The Economic Torts as Corrective Justice', above n 13, at 196–201. Although their Lordships' decision in *Revenue and Customs Commissioners v Total Network SL* [2008]

lawful means conspiracy is that it is genuinely 'anomalous'[81] and therefore unable to be explained from a rights-based perspective.

The reasons for this view are essentially twofold. First, lawful means conspiracy allows a claimant to sue if two (or more) people combine with the predominant purpose of causing economic loss to the claimant even if this loss is accomplished using otherwise *lawful* means which *do not* violate any public or private law prohibition (other than that posited by the law of conspiracy itself).[82] The tort thus presents itself to be an instance of the generally prohibited *damnum absque injuria*, since no primary right of the claimant has been violated. As Stevens notes:

> Unless a right of the claimant is infringed, it is difficult to see why, consistently with the principle that the intentional infliction of economic harm is not per se actionable, the mere fact that the loss is inflicted because of a combination of persons should make any difference.[83]

Secondly, much like misfeasance in public office, lawful means conspiracy is in violation of the well-accepted common law principle that 'an act that is legal in itself will not be made illegal because the motive of the act may be bad.'[84] As a result of these deficiencies, the 'modern tort of conspiracy stands condemned, almost universally, as the vehicle of judicial anti-unionism' and therefore a manifestation of a policy long since abandoned.[85]

Given these difficulties, how can lawful means conspiracy be explained from a rights-based perspective? While it is true that in a state of nature and deploying only the rights contained therein, it would be impossible to account for the doctrine, once one accepts that in a system of rights it is impermissible to act with the primary purpose of inflicting harm on another, the doctrine is easily explainable. Lawful means conspiracy is a classic example of an abuse of rights,[86] and claimants are therefore liable

---

UKHL 19, [2008] 1 AC 1174 is seemingly at odds with this understanding of the law, given the reasoning deployed in the case it need not be seen to be so: see Neyers, 'The Economic Torts as Corrective Justice', above n 13, at 198–99; J Lee and P Morgan, 'The Province of *OBG v Allan* Determined: The Economic Torts Return to the House of Lords' (2009) 20 *King's Law Journal* 338, 343–44.

[81] See *Lonrho Ltd v Shell Petroleum Co Ltd (No 2)* [1982] AC 173 (HL) 188 (Lord Diplock): 'Regarded as a civil tort ... conspiracy is a highly anomalous cause of action'. See also *Lonrho plc v Fayed* [1992] 1 AC 448 (HL) 463 (Lord Bridge); *OBG Ltd v Allan* [2007] UKHL 21, [2008] 1 AC 1 [15] (Lord Hoffmann); Carty, above n 74, at 26; J Murphy, *Street on Torts*, 12th edn (Oxford, Oxford University Press, 2007) 359; K Oliphant (ed), *The Law of Tort*, 2nd edn (London, LexisNexis Butterworths, 2007) para 29.8.

[82] *Quinn v Leathem* [1901] AC 495 (HL); *Crofter Hand Woven Harris Tweed Co Ltd v Veitch* [1942] AC 435 (HL).

[83] Stevens, *Torts and Rights*, above n 1, at 251.

[84] *Sorrell v Smith* [1925] AC 700 (HL) 718–19 (Lord Dunedin).

[85] HW Arthurs, 'Tort Liability for Strikes in Canada: Some Problems of Judicial Workmanship' (1960) 38 *Canadian Bar Review* 346, 362.

[86] See Reid, above n 19, at 142. See also B Napier, 'Abuse of Rights in British Law' in M Rotondi (ed), *L'Abus de Droit* (Padova, CEDAM, 1979) 265, 280–81.

because they are using their own rights and liberties to inflict 'gratuitous harm' in order to 'frustrate the purposes' of others rather than to further any 'legitimate interest' of their own.[87] As with misfeasance in public office, once it is recognised that conspirators are violating a claim-right created by the system of rights, the liability is no longer *damnum absque injuria*. Similarly, judicial statements as to the irrelevance of motive can be explained as being concerned with rights in a state of nature, not with their systematic enjoyment in a civil condition.[88] Thus, if the analysis presented in part II is correct, the current anomaly in English law is not the recognition of lawful means conspiracy or misfeasance in public office but rather its refusal to recognise the actionability of targeted gratuitous harm when it is committed by a single private individual.[89] The concerns that might explain this anomaly are addressed in part IV below.

D. Lawful Act Duress[90]

Under the modern law, a successful restitutionary action for duress requires two elements to be proven: (1) 'pressure amounting to compulsion of the will of the victim'; and (2) 'the illegitimacy of the pressure exerted'.[91] In a well-known passage, Lord Scarman explained the concept of illegitimacy as follows:

> In determining what is legitimate two matters may have to be considered. The first is as to the nature of the pressure. In many cases this will be decisive,

[87] Using the language of Weinrib, 'Two Conceptions of Remedies', above n 7, at 29–30.

[88] For an example of a classic case which takes this form, see *Rogers v Dutt* (1860) 8 Moo PC 209, 240–41; 15 ER 78, 90 where Dr Lushington explains that 'it is essential to an action in tort that the act complained of ... must prejudicially affect [the claimant] in some legal right; merely that it will ... do him harm in his interests, is not enough', but qualifies this by stating that if malice was alleged 'the decision of such a case would turn on totally different principles'.

[89] That is, in a situation of '*Quinn v Leathem* without the conspiracy': *Rookes v Barnard* [1964] AC 1129 (HL) 1215–16 (Lord Devlin). For recognition of such liability, see the famous American case of *Tuttle v Buck* 119 NW 946 (Minn 1909) where a rich banker was held liable for spitefully driving a barber out of business. But as Lord Nicholls forcefully stated in *OBG Ltd v Allan* [2007] UKHL 21, [2008] 1 AC 1 [145]: '*Tuttle v Buck* ... is not the law in England.'

[90] In this chapter, I have used the term 'lawful act duress' to refer to a group of cases that sometimes go by other names such as actual undue influence, equitable pressure or undue pressure. As Birks noted, however, 'nowadays actual undue influence and duress seem to be one and the same phenomenon': P Birks, *An Introduction to the Law of Restitution* (Oxford, Clarendon Press, 1985) 184. See also MH Ogilvie, 'Economic Duress in Contract: Departure, Detour or Dead-End' (2001) 34 *Canadian Business Law Journal* 194, 227–29; R Bigwood, *Exploitative Contracts* (Oxford, Oxford University Press, 2003) 371 ('all cases of actual undue influence ... are cases of duress as well, namely lawful act duress').

[91] *Universe Tankships Inc of Monrovia v International Transport Workers Federation (The Universe Sentinel)* [1983] 1 AC 366 (HL) 400 (Lord Scarman).

though not in every case. And so the second question may have to be considered, namely, the nature of the demand which the pressure is applied to support.

The origin of the doctrine of duress in threats to life or limb, or to property, suggests strongly that the law regards the threat of unlawful action as illegitimate, whatever the demand. Duress can, of course, exist even if the threat is one of lawful action: whether it does so depends upon the nature of the demand. Blackmail is often a demand supported by a threat to do what is lawful, e.g. to report criminal conduct to the police. In many cases, therefore, 'What [one] has to justify is not the threat, but the demand ...'[92]

The picture that therefore emerges is that threats to do something independently unlawful (such as to assault, falsely imprison or destroy property) are invariably illegitimate and that threats to do things that are not independently unlawful might be illegitimate depending on the circumstances.[93]

A classic example of the type of situation that raises concerns of lawful act duress was given by Lord Wright in *Thorne v Motor Trade Association*: X is possessed of knowledge of discreditable incidents in Y's life and threatens Y that he will disclose this information to Y's spouse, Y's employer or to the local media unless Y pays X a sum of money.[94] Assuming that the sum of money demanded is a reasonable one all things considered (such that the agreement would not be unconscionable on that basis[95]), how are courts to determine if such activity is illegitimate? The dominant view is that the answer is not to be found in the law but instead is to be found in conventional morality and policy.[96] This is due to the fact that the law cannot but give the (possibly counter-intuitive)

---

[92] ibid, at 401, citing *Thorne v Motor Trade Association* [1937] AC 797 (HL) (*Thorne*) 806 (Lord Atkin).

[93] See *"R" v A-G for England and Wales* [2003] UKPC 22, [2003] EMLR 24 [16]; R Bigwood, 'Throwing the Baby Out with the Bathwater? Four Questions on the Demise of Lawful-Act Duress in New South Wales' (2008) 27 *University of Queensland Law Journal* 41, 58. Cf A Stewart, 'Economic Duress—Legal Regulation of Commercial Pressure' (1984) 14 *Melbourne University Law Review* 410, 428–29.

[94] *Thorne* [1937] AC 797 (HL) 822.

[95] As to how this type of unconscionability might be explained on rights-based grounds, see P Benson, 'Abstract Right and the Possibility of a Nondistributive Conception of Contract: Hegel and Contemporary Contract Theory' (1989) 10 *Cardozo Law Review* 1077 and P Benson, 'The Unity of Contract Law', above n 2.

[96] It should be noted that relying on the mere existence of the crime of blackmail is not of much assistance in determining the issue of illegitimacy for otherwise lawful acts in duress since the criminal law has always required that the demand be 'without any reasonable or probable cause' (Larceny Act 1916, s 29(1)(i)) or 'unwarranted' and not 'proper' (Theft Act 1968, s 21(1)). In other words, the criminal law wrestles with the same problems of defining illegitimacy as does the private law: see A Ashworth, *Principles of Criminal Law*, 6th edn (Oxford, Oxford University Press, 2009) 385–86. As Rick Bigwood forcefully notes, 'it cannot be argued that because blackmail is ... a crime, it therefore constitutes illegitimate pressure ... blackmail is not duress because it involves a crime or threatened crime; it is, presumably, a crime *because* it is regarded by the state as illegitimately coercive (hence involving duress)': Bigwood, 'Throwing the Baby Out with the Bathwater', above n 93, at 60 n 85.

answer that the pressure is legitimate. Given that X is lawfully entitled to publicly disclose the (non-defamatory) information and that X is lawfully entitled to the sell the information to Y, how can the combination of two lawful acts ever become illegitimate?[97]

In the leading case of *CTN Cash and Carry Ltd v Gallaher Ltd*[98] the Court relied on the following excerpt from Peter Birks' *An Introduction to the Law of Restitution*[99] to justify its conclusion that a restitutionary action for lawful act duress, although possible in the English law, raised extra-legal concerns:

> Can lawful pressures also count? This is a difficult question, because, if the answer is that they can, the only viable basis for discriminating between acceptable and unacceptable pressures is not positive law but social morality. In other words, the judges must say what pressures (though lawful outside the restitutionary context) are improper as contrary to prevailing standards. That makes the judges, not the law or the legislature, the arbiters of social evaluation. On the other hand, if the answer is that lawful pressures are always exempt, those who devise outrageous but technically lawful means of compulsion must always escape restitution until the legislature declares the abuse unlawful. It is tolerably clear that, at least where they can be confident of a general consensus in favour of their evaluation, the courts are willing to apply a standard of impropriety rather than technical unlawfulness.[100]

The Court of Appeal concluded, however, that although resort could be had to social morality, for reasons of commercial certainty and policy, successful assertions of lawful act duress should be rare in commercial contexts. As Steyn LJ noted:

> The aim of our commercial law ought to be to encourage fair dealing between parties. But it is a mistake for the law to set its sights too highly when the critical enquiry is not whether the conduct is lawful but whether it is morally or socially unacceptable.[101]

A view similar to that of Birks and the Court of Appeal has been offered by Rick Bigwood in his leading text, *Exploitative Contracts*. While offering a rights-based justification for duress in general, in relation to lawful

---

[97] See the forceful judgment of Scrutton LJ to this effect in *Hardie & Lane Ltd v Chilton* [1928] 2 KB 306 (CA). In the context of the criminal law, this is known as the paradox of blackmail. For discussion, see, eg, J Lindgren, 'Unravelling the Paradox of Blackmail' (1984) 84 *Columbia Law Review* 670; W Gordon, 'Truth and Consequences: The Force of Blackmail's Central Case' (1993) 141 *University of Pennsylvania Law Review* 1741; G Lamond, 'Coercion, Threats, and the Puzzle of Blackmail' in A Simester and ATH Smith (eds), *Harm and Culpability* (Oxford, Oxford University Press, 1996) 215. See also the other contributions to the 'Blackmail Symposium' in (1993) 141 *University of Pennsylvania Law Review* 1565.

[98] *CTN Cash and Carry Ltd v Gallaher Ltd* [1994] 4 All ER 714 (CA).

[99] Birks, above n 90, at 177.

[100] *CTN Cash and Carry v Gallaher Ltd* [1994] 4 All ER 714 (CA) 718 (Steyn LJ).

[101] ibid, at 719.

act duress cases he argues that a claimant's baseline is no longer 'primarily determined by strict legal rights and technical legal standards, such as those applying to crimes and torts; it has been extended to consult the standards of decency that stem from the "moral sense of the community" more generally'.[102] Thus, the orthodox view is that lawful act duress is anomalous and therefore seemingly inexplicable from a rights-based perspective.[103]

The argument of this chapter is that this escape to morality and policy is not necessary to justify the existence of lawful act duress in English law. If, as has been argued above, there exists a claim-right to be free from targeted gratuitous harm, then the doctrine can largely be accounted for on an abuse of rights analysis.[104] In the cases where the courts have allowed recovery of money paid under lawful act duress, the threat of the defendant is basically: 'I will harm you for no (independent) reason[105] unless you give me money'. Thus, in the classic case of *Williams v Bayley*,[106] the House of Lords set aside an equitable mortgage procured by the defendant bank from the claimant father. The mortgage was given after the bank impliedly threatened that it would prosecute the claimant's adult son for forgery (a crime that at the time would have resulted in a punishment of transportation for life) unless the father somehow covered the bank's losses on the forgeries.[107] In cases, however, where defendants can prove that they had an independent reason to do the threatened action or to demand payment—such as to settle a bona fide claim,[108] enforce a retail policy that was believed to protect both suppliers and consumers,[109] or

---

[102] Bigwood, *Exploitative Contracts*, above n 90, at 325. See also Bigwood, 'Throwing the Baby Out with the Bathwater', above n 93, at 67.

[103] See also Stewart, 'Economic Duress', above n 93, at 429, 441; R O'Dair, 'Restitution on the Grounds of Duress—Handle with Care: The Evia Luck' [1992] *Lloyd's Maritime and Commercial Law Quarterly* 145, 146; TK Leng, 'Lawful Act Duress' (1995) 7 *Singapore Academy of Law Journal* 208.

[104] For a similar view, although one based primarily on the presuppositions inherent in freedom of contract, see H Stewart, 'A Formal Approach to Contractual Duress' (1997) 47 *University of Toronto Law Journal* 175. See also the analysis given in N Enonchong, *Duress, Undue Influence and Unconscionable Dealings* (London, Sweet & Maxwell, 2006) para 3-013 ff where an abuse of rights (in the sense of using a right for a purpose other than the purpose intended by the law) view of lawful act duress is offered. The difficulty with Enonchong's analysis is that he offers no way to determine a right's true purpose.

[105] ie, some reason unrelated to the receipt of the money requested: see *Thorne* [1937] AC 797 (HL) 807 (Lord Atkin). As Grant Lamond notes, in the typical case 'the maker of the threat proposes to bring about the unwelcome consequence *because* the consequence is unwelcome to the recipient': above n 97, at 225.

[106] *Williams v Bayley* (1866) LR 1 HL 200 (HL).

[107] See also *Kaufman v Gerson* [1904] 1 KB 591 (CA); *Mutual Finance Ltd v John Wetton & Sons Ltd* [1937] 2 KB 389 (KB); *Borelli v Ting* [2010] UKPC 21.

[108] As in *CTN Cash and Carry v Gallaher Ltd* [1994] 4 All ER 714 (CA).

[109] As in *Ware and de Freville Ltd v Motor Trade Association* [1921] 3 KB 40 (CA), approved in *Sorrell v Smith* [1925] AC 700 (HL) and *Thorne* [1937] AC 797 (HL). For a discussion, see W Friedmann, 'The Harris Tweed Case and Freedom of Trade' (1942) 6 *Modern Law Review* 1, 18–19.

safeguard the operational effectiveness of the special forces[110]—claims of lawful act duress fail.[111] Thus, the abuse of rights analysis offers a reasonable explanation for the existence and scope of the lawful act duress doctrine, one that also explains marshalling, misfeasance in public office and conspiracy.

In fact, the only difference between the liability in conspiracy and that in lawful act duress is that the courts do not seem as willing to accept that self-interest—ie, the pursuit of payment from the claimant—can count as a good reason for the threat in lawful act duress as they are to recognise that self-interest can count as a good reason to justify harm in a conspiracy. As Lord Atkin noted in *Thorne*, in order for the defendant's threat to be justified, he or she 'must no doubt be acting ... for some legitimate purpose other than the mere acquisition of the money'.[112] Although it is not exactly clear why this is the case, and it is possible that the two sets of views might in fact be reconciled,[113] the apparent difference is likely influenced by the fact that in the central example of lawful act duress (as outlined above) Y invariably suffers a detriment: if Y pays he loses; but if Y does not pay and the information is disclosed, he also loses.[114] In any event, given the relative obscurity and anomalous nature of the various doctrines under consideration it would be unrealistic that they would perfectly cohere prior to explicit recognition of the theoretical basis that unites them.

IV. CONCLUSION

This chapter has sought to demonstrate two things. First, that the otherwise anomalous doctrines of marshalling, misfeasance in public office, lawful means conspiracy, and lawful act duress are all (more or less) explicable from a rights-based perspective if one accepts that there exists in English law a principle that prohibits the infliction of targeted gratuitous harm. Secondly, relying on the work of noted rights-based theorist Ernest Weinrib, that the existence of such a principle is consistent with recognising that the law of obligations is concerned solely with the realisation of rights and not with public policy and social morality.

As was noted above, the analysis presented in this chapter raises an obvious question: why is the infliction of gratuitous harm only actionable

---

[110] See *"R" v A-G for England and Wales* [2003] UKPC 22, [2003] EMLR 24.

[111] See also the discussion, in relation to blackmail, in Lamond, above n 97, at 236.

[112] *Thorne* [1937] AC 797 (HL) 807.

[113] For example, Carty comments that if someone was induced to enter into a lawful act conspiracy for payment (without any other interest in the matter) it would be unlikely that they would be protected by the law or by claims of 'self-interest': above n 74, at 31.

[114] See Stewart, 'A Formal Approach to Contractual Duress', above n 104, at 196.

in damages when done by a public officer or in combination with others? Beyond the obvious historical reasons—such as the laissez-faire attitudes of the nineteenth-century judges[115] and the strict rules of stare decisis that forced courts to reconcile inconsistent decisions (viz, *Allen v Flood* and *Quinn v Leathem*) on fairly insubstantial grounds[116]—I would suggest that misguided legal pragmatism played and continues to play a role. It is not surprising that a case-based system of justice that was concerned both with individual freedom and justice, but also about rights becoming tools of oppression, would focus first on the most serious abuses: those done by government officials[117] and those done in combination.[118] Only after satisfying itself that a coherent and workable system of liability had been created in relation to these areas would one expect liability to be extended to cover other factual situations. The difficulty has been that English law has never satisfied itself that it has created a coherent and workable system for either tort.

The reasons for this dissatisfaction are twofold. First, English law has not dealt with the theoretical underpinnings of the doctrines discussed in this chapter but has instead 'swept them under the rug' by continuously describing them as anomalous or special. Without a clear justification for why it does what it does, English law has been unable and unwilling to develop by analogy.[119] To paraphrase Lord Wedderburn: the gratuitous

---

[115] See M Taggart, *Private Property and Abuse of Rights in Victorian England: The Story of Edward Pickles and the Bradford Water Supply* (Oxford, Oxford University Press, 2002) 158, citing HC Gutteridge, 'Abuse of Rights' (1933) 5 *Cambridge Law Journal* 22, 43–44:

> At the time *Pickles* was decided the suspicion [of abuse of rights] took several forms— suspicion of novelty, of 'rights' talk, of things foreign, of social purpose tempering proprietary interests, and possibly even 'socialism'. Writing in the 1930s, a Professor of Comparative Law in the University of Cambridge harboured the 'grave' objection to the abuse of rights doctrine that 'it may get out of hand and result in serious inroad on individual rights, thus becoming an instrument of dangerous potency in the hands of the demagogue and the revolutionary'.

For other historical explanations, such as judicial distrust of the civil jury, see J Getzler, 'The Fate of the Civil Jury in Late Victorian England: Malicious Prosecution as a Test Case' in JW Cairns and G McLeod (eds), *'The Dearest Birth Right of the People of England': The Jury in the History of the Common Law* (Oxford, Hart Publishing, 2002) 217, 236–37.

[116] See Carty, above n 74, at 28–29.

[117] As Sadler, above n 54, at 139 notes:

> The significance of the exceptional nature of the tort of misfeasance in a public office should not be understated. Malicious or willful abuse of official power is socially intolerable. This social intolerability is compounded if the person injured as a result of the abuse is denied compensation.

See also Aronson, above n 63, at 628.

[118] See *Mogul Steamship Co Ltd v McGregor, Gow & Co* [1892] AC 25 (HL) 45 (Lord Bramwell).

[119] As Stevens notes in *Torts and Rights*, above n 1, at 252 the next logical move is to impose liability on corporations for abuses of rights:

> It may be thought that two persons acting together in order to inflict loss on another is a more serious act of bullying than one person acting alone. However, within a

harm or abuse of rights doctrines are 'still awaiting their Atkin'.[120] The second reason for this dissatisfaction is that when English law looks for guidance and examines modern civil law and American law on the subject of abuse of rights and prima facie torts[121] it is confronted with issues of public policy, conventional morality, and economics that seem ill-suited to judicial determination and anathema to the system's concerns with individual rights and freedoms. Thus, it is not surprising to find Lord Hoffmann state in *OBG Ltd v Allan*:

> Some writers regret the failure of English law to accept bad motive as a ground for liability, as it is in the United States and Germany ... But I agree with Tony Weir's opinion ... that we are better off without it. It seems to have created a good deal of uncertainty in the countries which have adopted such a principle. Furthermore, the rarity of actions for conspiracy (in which a bad motive can, exceptionally, found liability) suggests that it would not have made much practical difference.[122]

Hopefully, this chapter has demonstrated that there is a unifying theme to the doctrines of marshalling, misfeasance in public office, lawful means conspiracy and lawful act duress—namely that one is prohibited from acting for the predominant purpose of harming another—and that this prohibition is not anathema to the idea of rights but is arguably necessitated by their systematic realisation.

---

legal system which allows incorporation, this is an impossible distinction to defend. Microsoft is a single legal person able to bully more effectively than any two natural persons acting in concert.

See also Aronson, above n 63, at 631 n 81.

[120] Wedderburn, above n 76, at 229.

[121] The prima facie tort doctrine posits that the intentional infliction of damage or injury without justification or excuse is tortious: see KJ Vandevelde, 'The Modern Prima Facie Tort Doctrine' (1990–91) 79 *Kentucky Law Journal* 519; C Witting, 'Of Principle and Prima Facie Tort' (1999) 25 *Monash University Law Review* 295; K Oliphant, 'The Structure of the Intentional Torts' in JW Neyers, E Chamberlain and SGA Pitel (eds), *Emerging Issues in Tort Law* (Oxford, Hart Publishing, 2007) 509. See also the classic decisions of Holmes J in *Aikens v Wisconsin* 195 US 194 (1904) and *Vegelahn v Gunter* 167 Mass 92 (1896).

[122] *OBG Ltd v Allan* [2007] UKHL 21, [2008] 1 AC 1 [14], citing T Weir, *Economic Torts* (Oxford, Oxford University Press, 1997).

12

Rights and the Basis of Tort Law

NICHOLAS J McBRIDE*

I. A DISQUIETING SUGGESTION

T HE HEADING IS borrowed from the title of the first chapter of Alasdair MacIntyre's book *After Virtue*.[1] In that chapter, MacIntyre paints a picture of a world where:

[T]he natural sciences ... suffer the effects of a catastrophe. A series of environmental disasters are blamed by the general public on the scientists. Widespread riots occur, laboratories are burnt down, physicists are lynched, books and instruments are destroyed. Finally, a Know-Nothing political movement takes power and successfully abolishes science teaching in schools and universities, imprisoning and executing the remaining scientists.[2]

Generations later, an attempt is made to revive scientific teaching and learning using the remaining fragments of scientific activity that have managed to survive the catastrophe: 'parts of theories ... instruments whose use has been forgotten; half-chapters from books, single pages from articles.'[3] Such an attempt is doomed to failure. Too much knowledge has been lost. As a result, scientific language and scientific argument after the catastrophe becomes arbitrary and inconclusive in a way that it never was before the catastrophe.

MacIntyre's disquieting suggestion is that moral philosophy has undergone such a catastrophe over the last few centuries, with the result that we do not really understand either what we are talking about when we

* I am very grateful to Roderick Bagshaw, Jason Neyers, Donal Nolan, Amanda Perreau-Saussine, Nigel Simmonds, Sandy Steel, and Rob Stevens for saving me from many errors with their comments on earlier drafts of this chapter. All remaining errors are, of course, my responsibility.
[1] A MacIntyre, *After Virtue*, 3rd edn (London, Duckworth, 2007).
[2] ibid, at 1.
[3] ibid.

discuss what is right and wrong, or how we can tell what is right and wrong. *My* disquieting suggestion is that the study of tort law has undergone a MacIntyrean catastrophe at some point in the twentieth century, with the result that we no longer really understand what we are talking about when we talk about tort law. The signs that such a catastrophe has occurred are all around us, if we have eyes to see:[4]

1. Reputable textbooks on tort law, written by very intelligent authors, make statements in their opening pages such as: 'Numerous attempts have been made to define "a tort" or "tortious liability", with varying degrees of lack of success. ... It is not possible to assign any one aim to the law of tort'[5] and '[t]o provide a definition which encompasses the whole of this area of law is impossible ... [T]he law of tort is ... concerned with behaviour which is legally classified as 'wrong' or 'tortious', so as to entitle the claimant to a remedy. It must be conceded that this definition is somewhat circular, but it is the only one that will suffice.'[6]

2. Just as the distant descendants of the survivors of a nuclear apocalypse might come across a compass amid the burned out remains of their ancestors' civilisation and wonder 'what is this?' and throw it aside as 'useless' or suggest 'maybe it's a toy?', tort lawyers who consider the duty of care requirement in negligence routinely propose that we should abolish it as 'redundant'[7] or suggest 'maybe it's a control device?'[8]

---

[4] One of the marks of a MacIntyrean catastrophe is that it works to conceal the fact that there has been a catastrophe because the catastrophe redefines what is 'normal'. So, in the scenario depicted by MacIntyre, after a few years of attempting to get scientific teaching and learning back on track, people may well say, 'Nothing has changed—everything is back to normal.' In fact everything has changed, and by the standards of the pre-catastrophe community, nothing is back to normal. But the catastrophe is so serious in its effects, people find it hard to realise that this is the case.

[5] WVH Rogers, *Winfield and Jolowicz on Tort*, 18th edn (London, Sweet & Maxwell, 2010) paras 1-1-1-2.

[6] P Giliker and S Beckwith, *Tort*, 3rd edn (London, Sweet & Maxwell, 2008) 1.

[7] See *D v East Berkshire Community Health NHS Trust* [2005] UKHL 23, [2005] AC 373 [92]–[93], where Lord Nicholls suggested with breathtaking casualness that the 'radical suggestion' of 'jettison[ing] the concept of duty of care as a universal prerequisite to liability in negligence ... is not without attraction'. See also J O'Sullivan, 'Liability for Criminal Acts of Third Parties in Negligence' [2009] *Cambridge Law Journal* 270, 272, arguing that because in *one* particular case a defendant was held not liable on the ground of 'no duty of care' when they could also have been held not liable on the ground of 'no fault', 'maybe Lord Nicholls' radical suggestion of jettisoning the duty of care concept should be reconsidered'.

[8] See JG Fleming, *The Law of Torts*, 8th edn (Sydney, Lawbook, 1992) 135–36:

> The basic problem in the 'tort' of negligence is that of limitation of liability. One or more control devices were required to prevent the incidence of liability from getting out of hand. Among these, 'duty of care' occupies today a paramount position.

Note the use of scare quotes around 'tort' and 'duty of care'. Such thinking still flourishes today: see I Gilead, 'Harm Screening under Negligence Law' in JW Neyers, E Chamberlain and SGA Pitel (eds), *Emerging Issues in Tort Law* (Oxford, Hart Publishing, 2007) 251, characterising the duty of care requirement in negligence as a 'screening device' on liability in negligence.

3. Many tort academics experience the same uncomprehending reaction when they contemplate the law of tort as a whole, and propose that we should throw it aside in favour of loss compensation schemes of one kind or another that seem on the surface to do something similar to what we think, so far as we can tell, tort law may be doing.[9]

4. The vast amount of academic writing on the nature and basis of tort law that has been produced in the last few decades[10] is not—as some might see it—a sign of health, but rather a sign of sickness within the study of tort law.[11] If the community of academic tort lawyers was capable of understanding tort law, don't you think we would have understood it by now, with the result that the wellspring of academic articles on the nature and basis of tort law would have dried up long before now? It is, when you think about it, truly astonishing that in 2011, with all the intellectual and material resources available to us, we are still discussing these kinds of issues and have not settled them long ago.

If the study of tort law has undergone a MacIntyrean catastrophe, we can only—at the moment—speculate as to what caused it.[12] But one thing is for sure: the catastrophe happened long before I was a law student at Oxford between 1988 and 1992. By then, the community of tort academics was stuck firmly in the wilderness, unable to make any kind of sense of their subject. They were huddled together under the banner 'Tort Law = Compensation for Loss', having arrived at the consensus that the function of tort law was to determine when a plaintiff would be able to claim compensation for a loss that the defendant had caused the plaintiff to suffer.[13] At the same time, tort academics were intelligent enough to

---

[9] The most vocal proponent of this view in the past few decades has been Patrick Atiyah: see his *Accidents, Compensation and the Law* (now edited by Peter Cane: 7th edn (Cambridge, Cambridge University Press, 2006)) and PS Atiyah, *The Damages Lottery* (Oxford, Hart Publishing, 1997).

[10] For a survey, see P Cane, 'The Anatomy of Private Law Theory: A 25th Anniversary Essay' (2005) 25 *Oxford Journal of Legal Studies* 203.

[11] In the same way, MacIntyre, above n 1, at 6 argues that the best evidence that the study of moral philosophy has undergone a catastrophe similar to the imaginary catastrophe that he depicts the natural sciences as undergoing in the first chapter of *After Virtue* is that

> the debates in which ... disagreements [over moral questions] are expressed [are] interminable [in] character. I do not mean by this just that such debates go on and on and on—although they do—but also that they apparently can find no terminus.

[12] My own speculation is that the catastrophe was triggered by the growing interest in, and affinity for, left-wing politics among Britain's intelligentsia from the 1920s onwards. This meant that legal academic energies were almost exclusively focused on determining how great the powers of the state should be, and what form the relations between the state and its citizens should take. As a result, very little interest was paid to tort law—which was very much concerned with relations between citizens—and inherited understandings of what tort law was all about were as a result allowed to wither on the vine.

[13] The result, of course, of this emphasis on compensation as the key to understanding tort law is that other remedies that are available to tort plaintiffs have been almost com-

realise that such a view of tort law made a complete nonsense of their subject. If this view of tort law were correct, in a case where a defendant has carelessly caused a plaintiff loss, why would tort law *ever* deny the plaintiff's claim for compensation from the defendant, as it threatens to do when it requires the plaintiff to show that the defendant owed him or her a duty of care before it will allow the plaintiff's claim? Surely, in such a case, tort law would *always* make the defendant bear the plaintiff's loss? And why—if tort law is all about providing people with a way of suing others for compensation for losses that they have suffered—does tort law exist at all? It is a notoriously expensive, inefficient and unjust system for getting money to people who deserve to be compensated for losses that they have suffered. Tort academics had no good answers to these questions, and were as a result condemned to spend their careers criticising their subject for being a 'mess' or for being 'incoherent'.[14]

However, things are beginning to look different nowadays. Some tort law academics have now broken away from the pack, and think they have found a way out of the wilderness.

II. A NEW, BUT FRAGILE, HOPE

An increasing number of tort academics would like to burn the banner 'Tort Law = Compensation for Loss'. They think that such a view of tort law is not only misconceived, but also dangerous. It creates the impression that judges in tort cases are simply concerned to determine whether it would be 'fair, just and reasonable' to allow the plaintiff to sue the defendant for compensation for a loss that the plaintiff has suffered. They point out that this picture of what happens in tort cases is not only completely untrue, but also creates a danger that judges will begin to buy into this myth of what happens in tort law cases and start arrogating to themselves powers to redistribute losses as they see fit, according to their own private notions of what is 'fair, just and reasonable'.

pletely neglected by tort scholars. See, eg, J Murphy, 'Rethinking Injunctions in Tort Law' (2007) 27 *Oxford Journal of Legal Studies* 509, 509:

> In this jurisdiction, surprisingly little academic attention has been devoted to the availability and role of injunctions in tort law. Certainly, most of the established textbooks afford very little space to injunctions; while detailed analysis within the leading law periodicals is also largely conspicuous by its absence. Discussion, where it does exist, tends to be part of, or tangential to, some other central theme or issue. Yet why this should be the case is perplexing.

There is nothing surprising or perplexing about this—the tort academics' neglect of injunctions is an inevitable consequence of the way they have been thinking about tort law for the last 30 years or so.

[14] See D Ibbetson, 'How the Romans Did For Us: Ancient Roots of the Tort of Negligence' (2003) 26 *University of New South Wales Law Review* 475; B Hepple, 'Negligence: The Search for Coherence' [1997] *Current Legal Problems* 69.

Academics who reject this picture of what happens in tort cases argue that the function of tort law is: (1) to determine what legal rights people will automatically enjoy under the law, free of charge and without having to contract for them; and (2) to provide people with remedies when those rights[15] are violated, or threatened with violation.

On this *rights-based* view of tort law, tort law does not grant judges a general jurisdiction to reallocate losses from plaintiffs to defendants if they think that it would be 'fair, just and reasonable' to make those defendants bear those losses. The task of a judge in a tort case is much more modest. It is to determine whether the plaintiff's rights have been violated, or threatened with violation, and if they have, to provide the plaintiff with an appropriate remedy to protect those rights. In a case where the plaintiff's rights are threatened with violation by the defendant, the appropriate remedy will be an injunction, requiring the defendant not to violate the plaintiff's rights. In a case where the plaintiff's rights have already been violated, the appropriate response is compensation, to put the plaintiff in the position he or she would have been in had his or her rights not been violated.

If a plaintiff has suffered loss at a defendant's hands, but the defendant has not violated the plaintiff's rights in causing the plaintiff loss, then—on this rights-based view of tort law—the plaintiff has no case, and *cannot* have a case, for suing the defendant in tort for compensation for that loss. It does not matter how 'fair, just and reasonable' it might be to make the defendant compensate the plaintiff. The case is dead, so far as tort law is concerned. Where there is a right, there is a remedy. But where there is no right, there is no remedy (in tort).

This rights-based view of tort law would have seemed commonplace at the start of the twentieth century. But nowadays—after the MacIntyrean catastrophe that devastated the study of tort law at some point in the twentieth century—it seems strange and unfamiliar. The strangeness and unfamiliarity of such rights-based accounts of tort law is compounded by the fact that rights-based theorists of tort law have had to engage in a huge intellectual struggle to overcome the after-effects of the catastrophe they are trying to reverse. The extent of that struggle shows up all too painfully in the available rights-based accounts of tort law that can be found in the academic literature. Such accounts of tort law are invariably flawed in three principal ways:

1. *Mixing Up Different Kinds of Rights*
Robert Stevens' book *Torts and Rights*[16] represents the most sophisticated rights-based account of tort law yet published. However, his explanation

---

[15] From now on, whenever I use the word 'right' it should be understood that I mean by that word 'legal right' and not 'moral right' or any other kind of right.

[16] R Stevens, *Torts and Rights* (Oxford, Oxford University Press, 2007).

of tort law is flawed by the fact that, right at the start of his book, he mixes up different kinds of rights, leaving it unclear what kind of rights he thinks form the basis of tort law.

On page four of his book, at the start of his chapter on 'Rights', Stevens refers to rights

> that you will not defame me, hit me, or tear my clothes … that my neighbour will not create a nuisance by playing loud music all night long …

and rights

> not to be punched … not to be kicked … not to be carelessly slandered … not to be deliberately slandered …

These are very specific rights, requiring someone else not to act in a particular way.

On page five of his book, Stevens quotes a passage from Cave J's opinion in *Allen v Flood*: 'The personal rights with which we are most familiar are: 1. Rights of reputation; 2. Rights of bodily safety and freedom; 3. Rights of property.'[17] Stevens goes on to discuss these rights for the next few pages of his book, without seeming to notice that (as we will see) *these* rights are very different from the rights with which he started his chapter. These rights are very general, and do not—of and in themselves—require anyone else to do anything in particular.

The fact that Stevens mixes up these different types of rights—the ones he talks about on page four, and the ones he talks about on page five—makes it very hard to know what he actually thinks when he says that '[t]he law of torts is concerned with the secondary obligations generated by the infringement of primary rights. The infringement of rights, not the infliction of loss, is the gist of the law of torts.'[18] What *sort* of rights is Stevens talking about?[19]

2. Reductionism about Rights

Suppose that Fred carelessly crashes his lorry into a power station, with the result that there is a power cut in the surrounding area for a few hours. Wendy's factory is affected by the power cut, and she loses £10 000 in lost profits as a result.[20] It is clear that, in England at least, Wendy will not be able to sue Fred in tort for her lost profits.[21] Rights-based theor-

---

[17] *Allen v Flood* [1898] 1 AC 1 (HL) 29.

[18] Stevens, *Torts and Rights*, above n 16, at 2.

[19] Stevens would probably reply 'both'. In his view, 'rights that …' are merely special instances of more general 'rights to …' and 'rights to …', in their turn, are made up of bundles of specific 'rights that …': see ibid, at 4. However, as we will see in part III(A) below, 'rights that …' do not exist in the same relation to 'rights to …' as, say, 'greyhound' does to 'dog'. They are very different beasts; different in almost every imaginable respect.

[20] This example is discussed further in NJ McBride and R Bagshaw, *Tort Law*, 3rd edn (Harlow, Pearson Education, 2008) 200–02, 209–10.

[21] *Spartan Steel & Alloys Ltd v Martin & Co (Contractors) Ltd* [1973] 1 QB 27 (CA).

ists of tort law agree that Wendy cannot sue here because Fred did not violate any of Wendy's rights in crashing into the power station.

Peter Benson is one such theorist. He argues that Fred did not violate Wendy's rights in carelessly crashing into the power station because Wendy did not have a *proprietary interest* in the power station: the power station did not belong to her, nor is it in her possession. His argument goes as follows:

> At common law, a proprietary or possessory right is something that entitles a person to exclude anyone else from using it without his consent, so long as the first person has, relative to the others, a better claim to it in ownership or possession. If a plaintiff lacks a proprietary or possessory right in something, he has no legal standing to constrain a defendant from intentionally using it as the defendant sees fit, even if this impairs or interferes with the plaintiff's interests.[22]

We can immediately note something a little bit fishy about this argument: Wendy is not claiming that she had a right to prevent Fred *using* the power station as he saw fit. This is *not* a case where two people are fighting over the same thing—where the winner is, and can only be, the person with a better title to the thing. Wendy is claiming that she had a right that Fred not *carelessly crash* into the power station so as to cause a power cut. Now—if Wendy *had* had a proprietary interest in the power station, she would have no problem establishing that she had a right that Fred not carelessly crash into the power station. But she did not. For Benson, that ends the matter. For him, the *only* way Wendy could establish that she had a right that Fred not crash into the power station is by showing that she had a proprietary interest in the power station. But there seems no logical reason why the law should take such a stand. While Wendy did *not* have a *proprietary interest* in the power station, she *did* have an *interest in the power station not being crashed into* which *could* form the basis for the law granting her a right that Fred take care not to crash into the power station.[23]

---

[22] P Benson, 'The Basis for Excluding Liability for Economic Loss in Tort Law' in DG Owen (ed), *Philosophical Foundations of Tort Law* (Oxford, Oxford University Press, 1995) 427, 435 (footnote omitted).

[23] In P Benson, 'The Problem with Pure Economic Loss' (2009) 60 *South Carolina Law Review* 823, 865, Benson argues that

> the significance of a requirement of a possessory or proprietary interest is that, in virtue of this, the plaintiff can assert a right, exclusive as against the defendant, to having or using an item free from interference by the defendant. In the absence of a contract or some other basis of personal right against the defendant, the plaintiff cannot have an exclusive right in any other way.

What I am suggesting is that Wendy's interest in the power station not being crashed into could form 'some other basis of personal right against' Fred that he take care not to crash into the power station. However, Benson seems not to advert to this possibility at all: it seems that Wendy can only establish a right against Fred that he take care not to crash into the power station based on her having an interest in the power station, or a contract with

Benson's argument suffers from a very common vice that afflicts many rights-based accounts of tort law. This is the vice of *reductionism about rights*: in other words, placing *artificial* limits on what sort of rights under-lie tort law. We see the same vice in another paper of Benson's, where he asserts that in order to establish that a defendant owes a plaintiff a duty of care in negligence, it has to be shown that the defendant's conduct threatens 'an *existing* legally protected interest which rightfully belongs to the plaintiff as against the defendant.'[24] So if we are to protect a given interest of the plaintiff's by requiring a defendant to take care not to damage that interest, we have to show that that interest is *already* pro-tected under the law. This seems illogical. If the plaintiff's interest (in the context of Benson's paper, a beneficiary's interest in receiving a legacy that a testator wants her to receive) is worthy of being protected by the law of negligence, shouldn't we get on with protecting it, and not refuse to protect it merely because it isn't protected by any other area of the law? In fact, if an interest is worthy of protection by the law of negligence, but is not protected by any other area of the law, doesn't that make that interest *especially* worthy of protection by the law of negligence?

The same vice of reductionism can be found in Allan Beever's book, *Rediscovering the Law of Negligence*, when he asserts that 'the law of negligence protects primary rights that arise in the law of property and primary rights that arise in the law of persons'[25]—with the result that the law of negligence cannot assist Wendy in her claim against Fred because she cannot establish that Fred's actions violated her personality rights, or her proprietary rights. But why is the law of negligence just confined to protecting personality rights and proprietary rights? Why *can't* it protect other kinds of rights—such as a right that other people take care not to cut off the power supply to your business?

Jason Neyers falls into the same vice of reductionism, but in a slightly different way, when he considers a variation on Wendy's case. In this case, Fred—angered by Wendy's refusal to go out with him—*deliberately* crashes his lorry into a power station, with the *intention* of cutting off the power to Wendy's factory, so that she will suffer a loss of profits. In such a case, it is clearly established that Wendy *will* be entitled to sue Fred in tort for compensation for her loss of profits: Fred will have com-mitted the tort of intentional infliction of harm using unlawful means in relation to Wendy by acting as he did. In two papers, Neyers worries

Fred. The possibility of Wendy's establishing 'some other basis of personal right against' Fred disappears entirely.

[24] P Benson, 'Should *White v Jones* Represent Canadian Law: A Return to First Principles' in JW Neyers, E Chamberlain and SGA Pitel (eds), *Emerging Issues in Tort Law* (Oxford, Hart Publishing, 2007) 141, 149 (emphasis altered).

[25] A Beever, *Rediscovering the Law of Negligence* (Oxford, Hart Publishing, 2007) 214.

whether we can say that in this case, Fred violated Wendy's rights.[26] To see whether he did or not, Neyers canvasses a wide range of possible rights of Wendy's that Fred might have violated in this case: a right to trade, a right that Fred not abuse his rights, and a right that Fred not violate the criminal law. As Roderick Bagshaw has already pointed out, at no point does Neyers consider whether Wendy simply has a right that Fred not intentionally cause her harm using unlawful means to do so.[27] It seems that, for Neyers, it is just not possible that the law might give Wendy (and everyone else) such a *measured* or *limited* right against Fred. For Neyers, it seems, rights are all or nothing. Either Wendy has a general right to trade, with the result that everyone else has a duty not to get in the way of her trading; or she has nothing. There is no 'in between' right allowed—but why not?

3. The Relevance of Public Policy

One possible explanation[28] of why Neyers is not willing to accept the existence of such a *measured* or *limited* right is that for him—and for other rights-based theorists of tort law—a rights-based account of tort law should provide us with an account of tort law *that makes no reference to the public interest*, and should certainly not see tort law as existing to serve the public interest.

For such theorists, the idea that Wendy might have a right that Fred not intentionally cause her harm using unlawful means to do so must be anathema. We can only explain why Wendy might have such a *measured* or *limited* right by reference to considerations of the public interest: 'In principle, the courts would like to say that if you take two given individuals, A and B, A will have a right against B that B not intentionally harm A for no good reason. But such a right is too vague to be effectively enforced or observed, so instead of giving A a right against B that B not intentionally harm A for no good reason, the courts instead give A a right against B that B not intentionally harm A using unlawful means to do so—it being assumed that if B uses unlawful means in order to harm A, he will be up to no good.'

I think this demand that a rights-based theory of tort law abjure any reference to the public interest all the way down—not only in its account of why and when tort remedies will be available, but also in its account of what rights we have and what rights we don't have—is a big mistake.

---

[26] See JW Neyers, 'Rights-Based Justifications for the Tort of Unlawful Interference with Economic Relations' (2008) 28 *Legal Studies* 215; JW Neyers, 'The Economic Torts as Corrective Justice' (2009) 17 *Torts Law Journal* 1.

[27] See R Bagshaw, 'Tort Law, Concepts and What Really Matters' in A Robertson and HW Tang (eds), *The Goals of Private Law* (Oxford, Hart Publishing, 2009) 239, 252.

[28] I offer another possible explanation of the source of the kind of reductionism about rights evidenced by Benson, Neyers and Beever in part III(C) below. However, to be fair to them, I think they would probably reject this explanation.

Rights-based theorists of tort law are right to be suspicious of those who claim that all tort cases ultimately come down to questions of 'public policy' — but they throw the baby out with the bathwater when they claim that considerations of what is in the public interest are *never* relevant to claims in tort. Plainly they are, and plainly they should be. As Bagshaw observes, the function of tort law — like any other area of law — is ultimately to make the world a better place.[29] I would expand this slightly by saying: 'The function of tort law is to make the world a better place by granting people rights that they can assert against other people, and by providing them with remedies designed to uphold those rights.' If granting a plaintiff a particular right — for example, a right not to be offended, or a right not to be unjustly defamed on any occasion, even in a newspaper story that is on a matter of the public interest and was responsibly prepared — would make the world a worse place, it seems to me that it would be irresponsible for the courts to disregard that fact in determining what rights the plaintiff should have.

Stevens would agree with this point in that he argues that the courts should not give effect to rights that would work contrary to the public interest, such as a 'general right not to be caused economic loss' which would have the effect of making 'all commercial competition or industrial action ... actionable.'[30] However, he would go further and say that not only should the courts not give effect to such a right, they should *also* not seek to give effect to a more limited form of that right that would *not* work contrary to the public interest, as they are not equipped to determine which more limited forms of that right would still be objectionable on public policy grounds, and which more limited forms of that right would not. It seems to me there are three problems with this.

First, this is not what happens in practice. For example, giving people a general right that other people not damage their reputation would be contrary to the public interest, and the courts rightly refuse to recognise that people have such a general right. But they see nothing wrong with giving people more restricted rights that have the effect of protecting people's reputations. Secondly, if Stevens' theory were applied properly, the courts would not give anyone any rights. For example, in relation to rights not to be killed or injured, the courts would say, 'If we gave people a general right not to be killed or injured, that would be contrary to the public interest — for a start, all deaths and injuries on the roads, however caused, would be actionable, which would hugely increase drivers' insurance premiums and force many drivers off the roads. So we are not going to give people a general right not to be killed or injured — but then neither can we give them any more limited rights, such as a right that other people take care not to kill or injure them, as we are ill-equipped to decide whether

---

[29] Bagshaw, above n 27, at 249.
[30] Stevens, *Torts and Rights*, above n 16, at 338.

those more limited rights are compatible with the public interest.' The same objection could be made in relation to any other conceivable right that the courts might consider giving us. Thirdly, the fact that the courts are ill-equipped in some difficult cases to decide what is, and what is not, in the public interest does not mean that they are always incapable of reaching accurate conclusions on such issues. In a case where it is *very clear*—even to a judge—that it would be contrary to the public interest, or that it would not be contrary to the public interest, to grant someone a particular right, why should the courts not take that into account in deciding whether or not to recognise that right?

Wrong turns like these are inevitable. Rights-based theorists of tort law are attempting to recover a way of thinking about tort law that was abandoned decades ago, and was not systematically articulated even then. It would be nothing short of a miracle if they were able to come up with a perfectly clear, coherent and accurate rights-based account of tort law at the first attempt. However, such wrong turns are extremely dangerous for the future of right-based accounts of tort law. They create a risk that such accounts of tort law will fail to gain the widespread acceptance among the academic community that they need to gain if they are to survive, and flourish. Mainstream tort academics—who still stick firmly to the belief that 'Tort Law = Compensation for Loss'—can focus on these wrong turns as an excuse for thinking that rights-based accounts of tort law have nothing worthwhile to say.

My aim in this chapter is to try and provide a systematic rights-based account of tort law that will be free of such wrong turns, and will come closer to the truth of what tort law is all about than any previous rights-based account of tort law. If I achieve my ambition, my hope is that tort academics who adhere to the old ways of thinking about tort law will finally be compelled to make a choice: *either* adopt the rights-based account of tort law offered in this chapter and stop making the sort of post-catastrophe statements about tort law set out at the start of this chapter, *or* explain why exactly it makes more sense to think of tort law as concerned to determine when we can sue other people for compensation for losses than it does to think of tort law as concerned to provide us with a range of rights against other people, and help us vindicate those rights when they are violated or threatened with violation.

III. RIGHTS

Anyone attempting to provide a rights-based account of tort law has to deal with the difficulty that lawyers use the terms 'right' and 'rights' in different ways on different occasions. As a result, if someone says something like 'liability in tort arises out of the violation of a legal right', it is *immediately* unclear what exactly is being said. I will therefore begin my rights-based account of tort law by distinguishing *three* different ways in which lawyers use the term 'right':

1. Lawyers use the term 'right', first of all, to describe what A has when A has a power to perform some kind of legal act,[31] such as suing someone for damages, or terminating a contract. So lawyers will say that A has a 'right' to sue B for damages, or to terminate his or her contract with B. We can call this kind of right a *legal power right*.

2. Lawyers use the term 'right', secondly, to describe what A has when the law imposes a legal duty[32] on B to act in a particular way, and the law imposes that duty on B for A's benefit. In such a situation, lawyers will say that A has a 'right' that B do *x*. This right is correlative to the duty that (lawyers say) B *owes* A to do *x*. The right and the duty are two sides of the same coin. The right does not arise out of the duty. The duty does not arise out of the right. They are the same thing, just viewed through different ends of the telescope. We can call this kind of right a *coercive right* because if A has this kind of right, someone else is always legally required to act in a particular way.[33]

3. Lawyers use the word 'right', thirdly, to describe what A has when the law takes steps to protect some freedom or interest of A's from being interfered with by other people.

The law has two principal techniques for doing this. First, the law may

---

[31] There seems no pressing need to extend the first sense in which the word 'right' is used to cases where someone has the power to perform a *natural act*, and the freedom to perform that natural act is given no special protection by the law that would bring it within the third sense in which the word 'right' is used. So, for example, we *could* say that I have a 'right' to scratch my nose right now—because I am free to scratch my nose—but there seems no good reason why we *should* say this. It is enough to say that I am *free* to scratch my nose, without bringing the language of rights into the matter. To talk about rights in this kind of situation can create serious confusion. For example, if two people, A and B, see an abandoned newspaper on a train, each of them is free to pick it up. If we say that each of them has a 'right' to pick the newspaper up, that might be taken to suggest that if either of them picks it up, they will violate the other's rights and do something wrong. It is better—because less confusing—just to say that each of them is free to pick the newspaper up, and leave it at that. So the House of Lords was probably wrong in *Bradford Corp v Pickles* [1895] AC 587 (HL) to say that Pickles had a 'right' to extract the water from under his land. As the act of extracting water flowing under his land was a natural act that he was free to perform, and that freedom was given no special protection by the law, all the House of Lords had to say in that case was that Pickles was 'free' to extract the water from under his land, and this was so whatever his motives were for extracting the water. There was no need to bring the language of rights into the matter.

[32] Again, as with the term 'right' (see above n 15), whenever I use the word 'duty' from now on, it should be understood that I mean by that word 'legal duty' and not 'moral duty' or any other kind of duty.

[33] Some people follow Wesley Hohfeld in calling this second kind of right a 'claim right' (see WN Hohfeld, *Fundamental Legal Conceptions* (New Haven CT, Yale University Press, 1923) 38) but it seems to me this terminology has the potential to confuse this second kind of right with the first kind of right (which covers, among other things, rights to sue people).

impose duties on other people requiring them not to act in ways that will interfere, or are liable to interfere, with that freedom or interest of A's. Secondly, the law may exempt A (or grant A an 'immunity' from) certain legal rules that would otherwise have the effect of enabling other people to interfere with that freedom or interest of A's.

The law may use either or both of these techniques to offer a given freedom or interest of A's some degree of protection from being interfered with by other people. Whenever it does so, and to whatever extent, we lawyers say that A has a 'right' to use, enjoy or otherwise exploit that freedom or interest.

For example, it is normal to say that a given individual, A, has a 'right to freedom of expression'. What we mean by that is that the law takes some steps to protect A against other people interfering with his or her freedom of speech. The law does this by, first of all, imposing a duty on the government not to do something that will have the effect of interfering with A's freedom of expression if doing so would not serve a legitimate purpose or would have a disproportionately adverse effect on A's freedom of expression.[34] The law also protects A's freedom of expression from being interfered with by other people by allowing A to defame B if he or she does so in a privileged publication—for example, in a newspaper story that is on a matter of the public interest and has been prepared in a responsible way.[35]

We can call this third kind of right a *liberty/interest right* because A will only have such a right if the law intervenes in some way to protect some freedom or interest of A's from being interfered with by other people.

A. Differences Between Coercive Rights and Liberty/Interest Rights

There are a number of fundamental differences between coercive rights and liberty/interest rights that make it vital that we always keep them separate in our heads:

1. Coercive rights are *outward-looking*. They *always* take the form of a right that *someone else* act in a particular way. In contrast, liberty/interest rights are *backward-looking*. They look back at the right-holder and reflect the fact that the law gives the right-holder some protection against some freedom or interest of his or hers being interfered with by other people.[36]

[34] Human Rights Act 1998, s 6 and sch 1 pt 1 art 10.
[35] *Reynolds v Times Newspapers Ltd* [2001] 2 AC 127 (HL).
[36] See MH Kramer, 'Rights without Trimmings' in MH Kramer, NE Simmonds and H Steiner, *A Debate over Rights: Philosophical Enquiries* (Oxford, Oxford University Press, 2000) 7, 13–14.

2. Coercive rights are *fundamental*, while liberty/interest rights are *secondary*. What this means is that we can only know what liberty/interest rights we enjoy, and how far they go, once we know what coercive rights we have. This is because one of the principal ways in which the law protects our freedoms and interests from being interfered with by other people is by giving us coercive rights that other people not act in ways that interfere (or are liable to interfere) with those freedoms or interests.[37] So we can only know what freedoms or interests of ours are protected by the law after we have found out what coercive rights we enjoy under the law. For example, you cannot say that you have a 'right to bodily integrity' unless you *first* know that the law protects your bodily integrity from being interfered with by other people by giving you coercive rights against other people that they not hit you unjustifiably, and that they take care not to run you over, and so on.[38] If the law did not do any of these things, then your 'right to bodily integrity' would be a thing written on water—you would not *really* have a 'right to bodily integrity'.[39]

---

[37] This follows from what has already been said about the first technique that the law employs to protect a particular freedom or interest that someone has from being interfered with by other people—imposing duties on other people not to act in ways that will (or are liable to) interfere with that freedom or interest. For example, suppose the law imposes such a duty on B, requiring B not to do *x* because doing *x* will interfere (or is liable to interfere) with a particular freedom or interest of A's. As that duty is imposed on B for A's benefit, we can say that B owes A a duty not to do *x* and that A has a correlative coercive right that B not do *x*. So this first technique for protecting a particular freedom or interest that someone has from being interfered with by other people can be redescribed as granting that person coercive rights that other people not act in ways that will interfere (or are liable to interfere) with that freedom or interest.

[38] There are other rights of which this is not true. For example, you could say that you had a 'right to freedom of expression' even if your freedom of speech was not protected through your being given coercive rights against other people requiring them not to interfere with your freedom of speech. You could still say that you had a 'right to freedom of expression' if the law sought to protect your freedom of speech by exempting you from certain legal rules that would otherwise allow other people to interfere with your freedom of speech.

[39] Here is a practical demonstration of this point. After the French Revolution, the French Assembly adopted The Declaration of the Rights of Man and Citizen, the articles of which provided, among other things:

> 13. Every man being presumed innocent until he has been pronounced guilty, if it is thought indispensable to arrest him, all severity that may not be necessary to secure his person ought to be strictly repressed by law.

> 14. No one ought to be tried and punished except after having been heard or legally summoned, and except in virtue of a law promulgated prior to the offence. The law which would punish offences committed before it existed would be a tyranny: the retroactive effect given to the law would be a crime.

But these statements were meaningless because they were not backed up through the French courts granting accused people effective coercive rights backed by remedies that could be sought if those rights were violated, or threatened by violation. So, for example, in 1794— only one year after the final adoption of this Declaration—leading revolutionary figures such as Georges Danton and Maximilien Robespierre were each in their turn executed without any proper trial. The same point could be made about the Constitution of the former Soviet

3. Coercive rights are *practical*, while liberty/interest rights are *expressive*. What this means is that coercive rights *do* things: they compel people to act in certain ways. If the law gives me a coercive right that you do *x*, then you are required to do *x*. In contrast, liberty/interest rights don't *do* anything. When we say that I have a 'right to freedom of expression', that right does not do any work, or have any effect on the real world. All we are saying, when we say that I have a 'right to freedom of expression', is that the law takes some steps to protect my freedom of speech from being interfered with by other people by, for example, granting me coercive rights requiring other people not to interfere with my freedom of speech, or by granting me exemptions from certain legal rules that would otherwise allow other people to interfere with my freedom of speech.[40] It is by doing *those* things that the law protects my freedom of speech. My freedom of speech is not protected because I have a 'right to freedom of expression'. Rather, I have a 'right to freedom of expression' because my freedom of speech is protected.[41]

4. Coercive rights are *specific in their effects*, while liberty/interest rights are *indeterminate in their implications*. You know where you are with coercive rights. If I have a coercive right that you do *x*, that means you owe me a duty to do *x*. Liberty/interest rights are far more uncertain in their implications. If someone tells me that I have a 'right to freedom of expression', that does not tell me anything other than that the law does, *to some extent*, protect my freedom of speech from being interfered with by other people. I cannot know any more than that from the bare information that I have a 'right to freedom of expression'. I certainly cannot tell whether or not that means you have a duty not to shout me down when I am delivering a lecture on tort law. To know

Union, in which one can find admirable—but in practice utterly meaningless—statements such as: 'the State pursues the aim of giving citizens more and more real opportunities to apply their creative energies, abilities, and talents, and to develop their personalities in every way' (art 20).

[40] It may be that this is what HLA Hart meant when he said that '"right" is a term used in discourse *about* the law, used for making statements *about* individual's positions as seen in terms of the law, rather than a term used *in* the law itself' (as described in DN MacCormick, 'Rights in Legislation' in PMS Hacker and J Raz (eds), *Law, Morality and Society: Essays in Honour of HLA Hart* (Oxford, Clarendon Press, 1977) 189, 190 (emphasis in original)).

[41] It's important to remember that I am always talking about *legal* rights here. The law may well protect my freedom of speech because I have a *moral* right that people not interfere with my freedom of speech, which is based on my dignity as a human being, and my equal moral status with everyone else. (Though I doubt it: I think it is more likely that the law protects my freedom of speech because it is good for society that it does so.) But to say that I have a *legal* right to freedom of expression is merely to sum up what the facts are on the ground so far as what the law does already to protect my freedom of speech. If it does nothing to protect my freedom of speech, we cannot say I have a legal right to freedom of expression.

that, I have to be given some more information about *how far* the law protects my freedom of speech—and in particular, what coercive rights it gives me against other people that require them not to interfere with my freedom of speech.

5. Coercive rights *do not necessarily protect specific freedoms or interests*; liberty/interest rights *always relate to specific freedoms or interests*. If you have a coercive right that I pay you £1000, that right does not protect a specific freedom or interest of yours. It just exists generally for your benefit. Similarly, if you have a coercive right that I not induce you to act in a particular way by lying to you, that right does not protect a specific freedom or interest of yours. It just exists generally for your benefit. So while—as we have seen—many coercive rights exist to protect specific freedoms or interests from being interfered with, this is not true of all coercive rights. In contrast, the idea of a liberty/interest right that does not relate to a specific freedom or interest of the right-holder is a contradiction in terms. Whenever someone enjoys a liberty/interest right, it is always in relation to a particular freedom or interest of theirs that the law protects—to some extent—against being interfered with by other people.

B. Rights In Rem

There is one further feature of coercive rights that I have not mentioned so far: they always operate against a *specific individual*. If A has a coercive right of some kind, it always takes the form of a right that a *particular individual* act in a particular way. In lawyers' terminology, coercive rights are always rights in personam. It might be thought that this shows my threefold classification of the different ways in which lawyers use the term 'right' is inadequate, because it makes no room for rights in rem, which are traditionally understood to be distinct from rights in personam because they do not operate against *particular individuals*. The objection does not stand up: my threefold classification of rights is perfectly capable of accommodating the existence of whatever it is lawyers are talking about when they talk about rights in rem.

It seems to me that lawyers use the phrase 'right in rem' in three different ways:

1. Lawyers first of all use the term 'right in rem' as a convenient short-hand for saying 'A has a right in relation to a particular item of property that is exigible against everyone, or—in other words—good against the world.' What A has here is not actually a single right but billions of different coercive rights, each operating against a particular individual. So, for example, if I buy a cow called Daisy and take

her home with me, lawyers will say that I have a 'right in rem' that no one steal Daisy from me. By using this terminology, they are actually saying that I have a coercive right against you that *you* not steal Daisy from me, a coercive right against Tom that *he* not steal Daisy from me, and similar coercive rights against Dick and Harry and everyone else in the world. It is this complex reality that lawyers attempt to describe by simply saying that I have a 'right in rem' that no one steal the cow from me.

2. The first use of the term 'right in rem' confines its application to situations where someone has a right in relation to *a particular item of property* that is good against the world. But lawyers sometimes use the term 'right in rem' to describe what someone has when they have the same right against everyone in the world. For example, James Penner suggests that our rights 'not to be killed and ... to bodily security' can be characterised as 'rights in rem'.[42] So we could talk about my having a 'right in rem not to be killed'. However, the same point made in relation to proprietary rights in rem also applies to this kind of non-proprietary right in rem. What I have here is not just a single right, but a bundle of billions of coercive rights, each applying to a particular individual, and each requiring *that* individual not to kill me.[43]

3. Finally, lawyers use the term 'right in rem' as a highfalutin way of describing a *proprietary interest* in a thing that the law recognises and protects in some way against being interfered with by other people. The use of the word 'right' in this context is inexcusable: the range of proprietary interests that someone may have in a thing (ownership, charge, beneficial interest, lease) are not in and of themselves rights, and should therefore never be described as 'rights in rem'. Proprietary interests give rise to coercive rights, as the law seeks to protect those interests from being interfered with by other people, and this protection allows us to say that the interest holder has a 'right' (a liberty/interest right) to enjoy that interest. But proprietary interests do not amount to rights in and of themselves.[44]

---

[42] JE Penner, *The Idea of Property in Law* (Oxford, Clarendon Press, 1997) 27–28.

[43] See NE Simmonds, 'Rights at the Cutting Edge' in MH Kramer, NE Simmonds and H Steiner, *A Debate over Rights: Philosophical Enquiries* (Oxford, Oxford University Press, 2000) 113, 151–52 (emphasis in original): 'There is nothing ... that ... prevent[s] us from talking about a general right not to be assaulted, *provided* that such claims are understood only as summary statements about the existence of various more specific rights obtaining against particular individuals.'

[44] The fact that our first kind of rights—legal power rights—can amount to property (all forms of intangible property take the form of a power to sue someone if they act in a particular way, which is why another name for a piece of intangible property is a 'chose in action') does not affect this point. Rights can amount to property. But interests in property cannot amount to rights.

C. Reductionism Revisited

Although my threefold classification of the way lawyers use the term 'right' can easily accommodate references to 'rights in rem', I think we should be very careful in using such language when talking about English law. Sloppy or loose use of the phrase 'right in rem' can easily result in one falling into the vice of reductionism about rights that I highlighted earlier. Let me explain. Many people believe:

1.   All rights that are 'good against the world' are 'rights in rem'.

Other people believe that:

2.   All 'rights in rem' are based on the right-holder having a proprietary interest in some thing.

I think it is perfectly legitimate to believe that *either* 1. *or* 2. is true. If you want to define a 'right in rem' as a right that is 'good against the world', then go ahead. And if, alternatively, you want to define a 'right in rem' as a right that arises out of the right-holder having a proprietary interest in some thing, then feel free. But what you cannot—must not—do is believe that *both* 1. *and* 2. are true. If you do, you will end up believing:

3.   All rights that are 'good against the world' are based on the right-holder having a proprietary interest in some thing.

Assuming that the only rights that one stranger can have against another stranger are rights that are 'good against the world',[45] if you believe 3. you will also believe that:

4.   If you take two strangers, A and B, the only rights that A can have against B will arise out of A's having a proprietary interest in some thing.

Both 3. and—consequently—4. are incorrect. Let's leave aside rights not to be beaten up or to be falsely imprisoned, both of which are 'good against the world' but both of which could be said by those who believe 3. to be true to arise out of the fact that a person 'owns' him or herself. One of the rights mentioned in Stevens' catalogue of rights that are 'good against the world' is a 'right not to be lied to.'[46] That is a right that is not based on the right-holder having a proprietary interest in anything. The existence of that right shows that 3. and—consequently—4. are incorrect.

---

[45] I am happy to make this assumption *at this point* because it is an assumption that the rights-based theorists of tort law I am about to discuss in this section seem to make. They seem to assume that, as between two strangers A and B, A cannot have any *special* rights against B that are based on B's status or position. So the only rights A can assert against B are rights that A can assert against everyone, including B. It seems to me that this assumption is highly questionable, and may be another example of the vice of reductionism about rights that I discussed earlier: see text accompanying nn 23–27 above.

[46] Stevens, *Torts and Rights*, above n 16, at 8.

Those who believe—or assume—that 3. is true do so because the ambiguity in meaning attached to the term 'right in rem' tempts people to think that because some people think that 1. is true and because other people think that 2. is true, *both* 1. *and* 2. are true. This is a mistake. Either you can believe that 1. is true, and consequently reject 2. because of the existence of rights such as the right not to be lied to. Or you can believe that 2. is true, and consequently reject 1. because of the existence of rights such as the right not to be lied to. What you cannot do is believe that both 1. and 2. are true. Doing so makes you fall into the trap of thinking that 3. and—consequently—4. are true.

This is a trap that I fear many rights-based theorists of tort law have fallen into in the past. Go back to the case where Fred carelessly crashes his lorry into the power station, causing a power cut to Wendy's factory and a consequential loss of profits on Wendy's part. Unless at some deep level, Benson believes—or assumes—that 4. is true, it is hard to understand why he thinks the issue of whether Fred violated Wendy's rights can be resolved by asking whether Wendy had a proprietary interest in the power station.[47] A similar point can be made about Beever's discussion of the same issue, where he ends up arguing that Wendy would only be able to bring a claim in tort against Fred if she could show that, at the time of Fred's accident, she had a proprietary interest in the bank notes that her customers would have paid her for the goods that she never got to produce because of the power cut.[48] And again the same point can be made in relation to the case where Fred *intentionally* crashes into the power station in order to disrupt Wendy's business. The fact that Neyers never considers whether Wendy has a right 'good against the world' that other people not intentionally cause her economic loss using unlawful means to do so[49] may possibly be accounted for by a deep-lying and unspoken assumption that a right that is 'good against the world' must exist

[47] See text accompanying n 22 above.
[48] Beever, above n 25, at 241. To be fair to Beever, I think he would reject 1. and therefore 3. and 4.. But his discussion of the equivalent of Wendy and Fred's case does seem to assume that the only rights that Wendy could have against Fred are: (i) rights that are based on Wendy and Fred having a 'special relationship' or (ii) rights that are 'good against the world'. And the only rights that Wendy could have against Fred that are 'good against the world' are rights: (iia) not to have her person or reputation interfered with; and (iib) rights based on her having a proprietary interest in some thing. But it is never explained why these are the *only* rights 'good against the world' that we can have. The only expressed basis for this view seems to be that all rights that are 'good against the world' are either in rem or in personam, where rights in rem are defined as rights arising out of someone having a proprietary interest in some thing and rights in personam are assumed to be rights relating to someone's person or personality (see at 240: 'Was there a [good against the world] right in personam violated by the defendant? ... [T]here was not. Causing someone economic loss could not plausibly be regarded as a violation of her bodily integrity, freedom of movement, reputation, etc.'). This is a wholly novel use of the phrase 'right in personam', which is more usually used to describe a right that a particular person act in a particular way.
[49] See text accompanying n 27 above.

to protect some specific proprietary interest of the plaintiff's, and not a generalised interest that he or she has in not being made worse off.[50]

So the ambiguities in meaning attached to the phrase 'right in rem' can have disastrous consequences intellectually; and anyone seeking to produce a rights-based theory of tort law has to be on guard against those disasters.

IV. TORT LAW, IN A NUTSHELL

Going back to Stevens' book *Torts and Rights*, it should be clear now that the rights that Stevens talks about on page four (rights 'that you will not defame me, hit me, or tear my clothes' and so on) are examples of coercive rights. In contrast, the rights that Stevens talks about on page five (rights 'of reputation … of bodily safety and freedom … of property') are examples of liberty/interest rights.

It is equally clear that many rights-based theorists of tort law think that tort law exists to protect liberty/interest rights, and that it does this by imposing duties on us not to do things that will infringe those rights, and by providing us with remedies when those duties are breached. So, for example, Ernest Weinrib includes in his catalogue of liberty/interest rights that are protected by tort law, 'the right to the integrity of one's body … [and] the right to property in things appropriately connected to an external manifestation of the proprietor's volition'.[51] Tort law protects rights like these by imposing duties on us not to do things that will infringe on these rights: 'the plaintiff's right is the basis of the defendant's duty'.[52] '[T]he concepts and principles of tort liability set out the conditions under which the defendant's conduct counts as a wrongful infringement of the plaintiff's right.'[53]

I think this view[54] of tort law is totally upside down. (This does not

---

[50] See also Neyers' assertion that McLachlin J's judgment in *Canadian National Railway Co v Norsk Pacific Steamship Co* [1992] 1 SCR 1021, which found that the plaintiff in that case had a right that the defendant take care not to damage a bridge that the plaintiff railway company ran trains over, 'in essence argued that the [plaintiff] should be treated as a joint *owner* of the bridge'—as though ownership of the bridge was the *only* possible basis for finding that the plaintiff had a right against the defendant that the defendant not damage the bridge: JW Neyers, '*Tate & Lyle Food & Distribution Co Ltd v Greater London Council* (1983)' in C Mitchell and P Mitchell (eds), *Landmark Cases in the Law of Tort* (Oxford, Hart Publishing, 2010) 227, 242 (emphasis added).

[51] EJ Weinrib, 'Corrective Justice in a Nutshell' (2002) 52 *University of Toronto Law Journal* 349, 354.

[52] ibid, at 352.

[53] ibid, at 353.

[54] It should be noted that Weinrib's account of tort law is not touched by the points made in this paragraph if we interpret him as saying that tort law imposes on us legal duties not to infringe on people's *moral* rights to bodily integrity and property and so on. (For such a reading of Weinrib and other rights-based theories of law, see D Nolan and A Robertson,

mean that it is without merit. Quite the contrary: it is of huge merit. In order to understand the truth about tort law, all we have to do is turn this view of tort law the right way up.) The function of tort law *cannot* be to protect liberty/interest rights because—as I have said already—the law does not protect liberty/interest rights. Liberty/interest rights exist because the freedoms and interests to which they refer are *already* protected under the law, through the law—among other things—granting us coercive rights that we can assert against other people. So tort law does not do what it does because we have rights to bodily integrity, and to our reputations, and to our property, and tort law seeks to protect those rights. The truth is completely the other way round. We have rights to bodily integrity, and to our reputations, and to our property, because tort law does what it does.

So what *does* tort law do? This:

> Tort law grants us coercive rights that we can assert against other people, free of charge and without us having to contract for them, and it provides us with remedies to assist us when those rights are violated, or threatened with violation, by other people.

Tort law is not the only source of such rights,[55] but it is by far the most important. Once we understand and accept this, the effects of the catastrophe that has afflicted tort law studies in the twentieth century will be fully reversed.[56] Instead of making post-catastrophe statements of the kind listed at the start of this chapter, we will be able to say things like:

> The function of tort law is to determine—in conjunction with the law of equity and the law of restitution—what coercive rights we can assert against other people, free of charge and without us having to contract for them, and to determine what remedies will be available when those rights are violated, or threatened with violation, by other people.

'Rights and Private Law' ch 1 of this book, text accompanying n 10.) However, such an account of tort law is flawed by the fact that while it is possible to make sense of the concept of a *legal* 'right to ...' (as I have in part III above), it is hard to understand what is meant by saying that someone has a *moral* 'right to ...'. We could say that someone has a *moral* right to bodily integrity if their interest in bodily integrity is so important that other people should respect it. If that is correct, then Weinrib's account of tort law simply ends up saying that tort law imposes legal duties on us not to interfere with other people's interests when those interests are so important that we are morally bound to respect them. This may be correct, but it is also so obviously correct that it is hardly worth saying.

[55] Equity and the law of restitution are other sources of coercive rights that we may assert against other people, free of charge and without us having to contract for them.

[56] If tort law is indeed what I say it is, we can see the plausibility of the twin suggestions made at the start of this chapter: (1) that tort law studies in the twentieth century underwent a MacIntyrean catastrophe; and (2) that this catastrophe has its roots in the growth of interest in left-wing politics among the British intelligentsia from the 1920s onwards. Left-wing academics—utilitarian in outlook, and preoccupied with delineating the powers of the state over the individual—could not be expected to have any interest in any area of law that was concerned with allowing individuals to assert rights against each other.

A tort is committed if someone violates a coercive right that someone else enjoys under the law, when that right does not arise under the law of contract, or the law of equity, or the law of restitution. To put it another (identical) way: someone will commit a tort if they breach a duty owed to another under the law, when that duty does not arise under the law of contract, or the law of equity, or the law of restitution.

The duty of care requirement in negligence exists because carelessness in the abstract does not give rise to liability in tort, even where that carelessness results in the plaintiff suffering some kind of loss. Liability in tort only arises when a plaintiff is able to establish that he or she had a right that the defendant not act in the way they did. To put it another (identical) way, liability in tort only arises when a plaintiff is able to establish that the defendant owed him or her a duty not to act in the way they did. So, if a plaintiff wants to sue a defendant in negligence, the plaintiff always has to show that the defendant owed him or her, and breached, a duty to take care not to act in the way they did.

V. RECOGNITION OF COERCIVE RIGHTS

What has been said so far provides the skeleton outline of a rights-based account of tort law. But to put some flesh on the bones, we need to provide an account of when the courts should recognise that A has a coercive right that B act in a particular way. If the courts regularly find liability in tort in situations where we would expect them to find that no coercive right has been violated, and no liability in tort in situations where we would expect them to find that a coercive right has been violated, then that fundamentally weakens the contention that tort law is rights-based in nature. If, on the other hand, the courts regularly find liability in tort in situations where we would expect them to find that a coercive right has been violated, and no liability in tort in situations where we would expect them to find that no coercive right has been violated, then that—I contend—would be clinching evidence that tort law is rights-based in nature.[57]

A. The Right Conditions

So when should the courts find that A has a coercive right that B do x? In approaching this issue, it's helpful to remind ourselves of what the law does when it grants A a coercive right that B do x. When the law does this, it imposes a duty on B to do x, and it does so for A's benefit—no one else's. This suggests two conditions that should be satisfied before the courts find that A has a coercive right that B do x.

---

[57] See McBride and Bagshaw, above n 20, at Preface ('The Tort Wars') and Appendix ('Professor Stapleton's Criticisms of the Traditional View of Tort Law') for other evidence that tort law is rights-based in nature.

The first condition is this:

> The *Benefit Condition.* A should have an interest in B doing *x*. If we are going to impose a duty on B to do *x*, *for A's benefit*, then it should *actually* be of benefit to A that B do *x*.

It might be thought that in any conceivable case where A might sue B in tort, the *Benefit Condition* will always be satisfied. This is not so.

For example, if A sues his doctors, claiming that he has a right that they not use cancerous tissue that they took from his body for research,[58] A's claim should be rejected on the basis that it fails the *Benefit Condition*. A does not have a genuine interest in his doctors not using the cancerous tissue for research. He is trying it on.

Again, if A is in a permanent vegetative state, and his family attempt to argue that A has a right that his doctors continue treating him, A's family's claim should (probably)[59] be rejected on the basis that it fails the *Benefit Condition*.[60] Given A's state, A does not have a genuine interest in continuing to be treated by his doctors.

The second condition is this:

> The *Burden Condition.* Other things being equal, A's interest in B's doing *x* should be of sufficient importance that it justifies our imposing a duty on B to do *x*.

When we grant A a coercive right that B do *x*, we are saying that A's interest in B's doing *x* is so weighty that it would be right to burden B with a duty to do *x*. So it should be established that this is the case.

In determining whether the *Burden Condition* is satisfied, we are acting just like moral philosophers, who seek to determine what obligations individuals will owe each other, given their respective needs and situations.[61] So it would not be surprising if applying the *Burden Condition* yielded the following list of duties that it would be right to burden B with, for the benefit of A. The list of duties (which is not intended to be exhaustive) should be familiar because any moral code worthy of the name would recognise these duties: (1) don't murder, deliberately maim or rape A; (2) don't steal or intentionally damage A's property; (3) don't take unnecessary chances with A's life or person or property; (4) look after A if he can't look after himself, and you are in a good position to help him; (5) don't make A's life a misery for no good reason; (6) don't tell lies to A, and don't tell lies about A to other people; (7) do your best to keep any

---

[58] See *Moore v Regents of the University of California* 793 P 2d 479 (Cal 1990).

[59] The doubt arises out of the fact that the 'permanent' in 'permanent vegetative state' may be a misnomer: people who have been diagnosed as being in a permanent vegetative state have been known to recover.

[60] See *Airedale NHS Trust v Bland* [1993] AC 789 (HL).

[61] For a very illuminating discussion of how one should go about determining what we are morally required to do for each other, see D Parfit, *On What Matters* (Oxford, Oxford University Press, 2011) chs 14–17.

legitimate promises you made to A; (8) don't manipulate A into acting contrary to his own self-interest; (9) don't exploit any disability or weakness on A's part for your own, or someone else's, advantage; (10) don't betray any legitimate trust that A has placed in you, at your invitation.

The nature of coercive rights suggests that we should require that the *Benefit Condition* and the *Burden Condition* be satisfied before we grant A a coercive right that B do *x*. However, in determining whether the *Burden Condition* is satisfied, we have to ask ourselves whether, *assuming that other things are equal*, A's interest in B doing *x* is of sufficient importance that it justifies our imposing a duty on B to do *x*. In the real world, other things are rarely equal. Even if the *Burden Condition* is satisfied, granting A a coercive right that B do *x* may have knock-on effects that make it, on balance, undesirable to grant A such a right. Given this, there is a further condition that we should require to be satisfied before we find that A has a coercive right that B do *x*:

> The *Desirability Condition*. The side effects of granting A a coercive right that B do *x* should not be such that, all things considered, it would be undesirable to grant A such a right against B.

So suppose someone proposes that the law should say that if you take any two individuals A and B, A will have a coercive right against B that B help A out if A is unable to help himself and B is in good position to help A. Such a proposal would fail the *Desirability Condition*. Recognising the existence of such a right would have major adverse knock-on effects: (i) the law would become very uncertain; (ii) the courts would be flooded with litigation designed to take advantage of, and test the limits of, this right to be helped; (iii) people's incentives to put themselves in a position where they could look after themselves would be reduced; (iv) people's incentives to put themselves in a position where they could not help someone in need would be hugely increased; and (v) people would be robbed of any credit for helping someone else in need as giving such help would be a matter of legal obligation, rather than a matter of individual choice. Given the severity of these side effects, it would be—all things considered—undesirable for the courts to recognise that if you take any two individuals A and B, A will have a general right to be helped by B if A is in need of such help and B can easily provide it.

But that is not the end of the matter.[62] Even if the proposal that each of us should be given a *general* right to be helped fails the *Desirability Condition*, more limited forms and instances of that right may not. And so it proves. The law is unable responsibly to give *full* effect to the moral command that we should help other people if they are incapable of helping themselves, and we are in a good position to help them. But it

---

[62] Though it is for some rights-based theorists. See text accompanying n 30 above for a discussion of Stevens' views on this matter.

is able to give—and *does* give—*partial* effect to that moral command by giving us a set of tightly-drawn coercive rights which, because they are so tightly-drawn, do not fail the *Desirability Condition*. These coercive rights include: (i) the right a visitor to premises has that the occupier of those premises protect him or her from dangers arising due to the state of the premises; (ii) the right an employee has that his or her employer protect him or her from dangers arising out of the work the employee does; (iii) the right that a child has to be looked after properly by his or her parents, or those who have taken parental responsibility for him or her.

So far we have been assuming that we can tell for certain whether or not the above conditions are satisfied. But this will often not be the case. For example, it will often be uncertain whether it would be undesirable—all things considered—to grant A a right that B do *x*. In such cases of uncertainty, we should also require that the following condition be satisfied before finding that A has a coercive right that B do *x*:

> The *Uncertainty Condition*. We should only find that A has a coercive right that B do *x* if it is *very clear* that the *Benefit Condition*, and the *Burden Condition*, and the *Desirability Condition* are satisfied with respect to that right.

By seeing what set of rights satisfy the above conditions, we should be able to produce for any given pair of individuals A and B, a template of coercive rights that they should enjoy against each other. But respect for individual liberty suggests that A and B should be given the final word on what coercive rights they have against each other. This suggests that the coercive rights A and B enjoy against each other should be subject to one final condition:

> The *Voluntarist Condition*. If you take any two individuals A and B, A and B should be free to vary by agreement (whether adding to, or subtracting from) the coercive rights they would otherwise enjoy against each other so long as: (i) the agreement is free and fair; (ii) it is not contrary to public policy; and (iii) both A and B are of sufficient capacity to enter into such an agreement.

It is the *Voluntarist Condition* that accounts for coercive rights arising under contracts and as a result of other 'assumptions of responsibility' akin to contracts.

B. Applications

It is beyond the scope of this chapter to apply what we can call the *Right Conditions* to generate a list of coercive rights that the courts should recognise and then compare this list with a list of situations where there is either liability in tort, or no liability in tort, so as to see: (i) whether the courts are finding liability in tort in situations where we would expect the courts to find that the defendant's conduct violated a coercive right of the plaintiff's; and (ii) whether the courts are finding that there is no liability in tort in situations where we would expect the courts to find that the defendant's conduct did not violate a coercive right of the plaintiff's.[63] However, I would be surprised if we did not find a close correspondence between the courts' decisions on liability and no liability in tort, and our list of coercive rights. To illustrate the point, and the method for determining whether or not the courts should recognise that someone has a coercive right in a given situation, we will consider the two variations on Wendy's case discussed above.

(i) First Variation

In this case, Fred *carelessly* crashes his lorry into a power station, causing a power cut that puts Wendy's factory out of action, as a result of which Wendy loses money. The courts—at least in England—will not find Fred liable in tort to compensate Wendy for her loss of profits. If tort law is rights-based, does this make sense? I submit that it does.

Let's address this issue by asking whether the law should say that if you take any two given individuals, A and B, A will have a coercive right that B take care not to damage or destroy a given item of property if it is reasonably foreseeable that doing so will result in A suffering some kind of economic loss. (It is assumed that neither A nor B are owners of the item of property in question.[64]) I don't think it should.[65]

Obviously, it would be in A's interest that B take care not to damage or destroy the item of property in question—thus satisfying the *Benefit Condition*—but I don't think the *Burden Condition* is satisfied in this case. A's interest will—in the average of cases covered by this right—simply not be weighty enough to justify imposing a duty on B to look out for A's interests here. The fact that A will often be able to take steps to guard him or herself against suffering a loss in the event of B damaging or destroying the property in question further weakens the case for saying the *Burden Condition* is satisfied. And even if the *Burden Condition* were satisfied, it is very clear the *Desirability Condition* is not. Recognising

---

[63] A small-scale version of this project is undertaken in McBride and Bagshaw, above n 20, at ch 9 where we take 10 situations where the courts refuse to find liability in negligence on the ground that the plaintiff did not owe the defendant a duty of care, and test to see whether such a refusal to find that a duty of care was owed can be rationally defended. We employ a procedure for determining whether the courts should recognise that a duty of care is owed in a given situation that is very similar to the procedure outlined above for determining whether the courts should recognise that someone has a coercive right. We score the courts 10/10: in each case where they refuse to find liability on the basis that no duty of care was owed, such a finding can be rationally defended.

[64] If A were the owner, it would be obvious that he or she had such a right against B; if B were the owner, it would be obvious that A could not have such a right against B unless B had contractually, or otherwise, assumed a responsibility to A not to destroy or damage the property.

[65] McBride and Bagshaw, above n 20, at 209–10.

the existence of the kind of right contended for here would have seriously adverse effects on individual freedom, as people in all walks of life would come under a huge tranche of duties to look after other people's economic interests, and would have seriously adverse effects on the court system as it struggled to cope with the flood of claims resulting from the recognition of these rights.

Should the law recognise a narrower right that would cover Wendy's case? Should the law say that a factory owner will have a coercive right that a lorry driver driving in the vicinity of the factory take care not to crash into a power station supplying power to the factory? Again, the *Benefit Condition* would be satisfied, but it is still hard to see that this narrower right satisfies the *Burden Condition*. The type of economic loss factory owners like Wendy are liable to suffer in the event of a power cut—a loss of profits—must rank very low on a scale of economic losses that we should take care not to cause other people to suffer. It hardly compares with losing a job, or losing one's house, and—moreover—factory owners like Wendy are in an especially good position to protect themselves against the losses that they stand to suffer in a power cut. Nor is the *Desirability Condition* satisfied. If factory owners like Wendy were granted this coercive right against lorry drivers, other people who stood to suffer economic loss as a result of property belonging to third parties being damaged would demand to be granted similar coercive rights, asking: if factory owners, why not us? And once these demands were granted—as they would have to be in a legal system committed to the principle that like cases should be decided alike—all the undesirable consequences of recognising the general right discussed above would ensue.

So there is no conceivable right that Wendy could be granted in this case that would satisfy the *Right Conditions* set out above.

(ii) Second Variation

In this situation, Fred is aggrieved with Wendy and as a result he *deliberately* crashes his lorry into a power station, with the *intention* of triggering a power cut that will disrupt Wendy's business. In this case, Fred will be held liable to compensate Wendy for her loss of profits. Again, we ask the question: if tort law is rights-based, does this make sense? I submit that it should.

We can address the issue by asking whether the law should say that if you take two given individuals A and B, A will have a coercive right against B that B not intentionally cause A harm using unlawful means to do so. I think it is very clear that it should. Such a right satisfies the *Benefit Condition*—A will plainly have an interest in B not intentionally causing A harm using unlawful means to do so. The right will also plainly satisfy the *Burden Condition*. While—in the average of cases covered by this right—the harm suffered by A may not be that serious, the fact that B is actively trying to cause A to suffer that harm means that the law is justified in imposing a duty on B, for A's benefit, that B not intentionally cause A harm using unlawful means to do so. People should not have to put up with the malicious or vindictive attentions of others. Finally, the right is so tightly-drawn that it is also clear that the *Desirability Condition* will be satisfied. For example, giving A such a right would not create any uncertainty in the law; so long as 'intentionally causing harm' is defined in its normal sense of 'acting with the aim or purpose of causing harm' and 'unlawful means' is defined as 'doing that which you are not at liberty to do under the law',[66] no debilitating uncertainty could attach to the existence of this right.[67]

Given this, it seems *very clear* that the *Right Conditions* are satisfied with respect to this proposed coercive right, and that the law *should* recognise that in the case we are considering, Wendy had a right that Fred not intentionally cause her harm using unlawful means to do so. In fact, the case for recognising the existence of such a right is so clear that the courts would be brought into disrepute if they *failed* to recognise that, as between two individuals A and B, A will have a right that B not intentionally cause A harm using unlawful means to do so. In a case where B deliberately set out to cause A harm, and used unlawful means to do so, A would be astonished to be told by the courts, 'The law gives you no right that B not do this sort of thing to you.'[68]

VI. RESPONSES

Weinrib once famously compared tort law to love, arguing that it existed to serve no purpose except to be itself.[69] I think a more apt comparison is with Cinderella. Like Cinderella, tort law is—at the moment—disin-

---

[66] See P Sales and D Stilitz, 'Intentional Infliction of Harm by Unlawful Means' (1999) 115 *Law Quarterly Review* 411.

[67] Sadly, the decision of the House of Lords in *OBG Ltd v Allan* [2007] UKHL 21, [2008] 1 AC 1 has created a lot of uncertainty in this area of the law through a failure to define 'intentionally causing harm' and 'unlawful means' in such a straightforward fashion.

[68] The refusal of the courts to extend the right not to be intentionally caused harm using unlawful means to cases of intentionally inflicted emotional distress (see *Mbasogo v Logo Ltd* [2006] EWCA Civ 1370, [2007] QB 846) means that at the moment: (1) bank robbers will not violate the rights of a bank manager if they kidnap the manager's family and threaten to kill them as a means of inducing the manager to withdraw money from the bank; and (2) the father and brothers of a teenager will not violate her rights if they execute her boyfriend, with whom she has been sleeping, and show her a video of her boyfriend being executed as a warning to her not to engage in premarital sex. I think ordinary people would be rightly astonished if they were told that English law currently provides no right not to be subjected to such horrendous treatment.

[69] EJ Weinrib, *The Idea of Private Law* (Cambridge MA, Harvard University Press, 1995) 6.

herited, unloved, misused, abused, and thought to be fit only to clean up messes.[70] I hope I have said enough by now to raise the prospect that, like Cinderella, one day tort law's fortunes will change, and that people generally will come to recognise its huge importance as a legal subject in determining what coercive rights we enjoy against each other, free of charge and without having to contract for them, and in providing us with remedies where those rights are violated or threatened with violation. In a last attempt to ensure a happy ending to tort law's current tale of woe, I would like to finish by responding to some comments that I have received about earlier drafts of this chapter, in the expectation that readers generally may share some of the commentators' views.

A. The Catastrophe Thesis

The catastrophe thesis posits that: (1) there was a time when it was reasonably well understood what tort law was all about; (2) something happened to disrupt that understanding; (3) with the result that we nowadays have no real idea what tort law is all about.

A few commentators questioned whether (1) could be true, with one pointing out that as no one used to ask what tort law was all about, it would be surprising if anyone ever had the answer to that question; while another commentator pointed out that the historical record shows that our puzzlement about the basis of liability in tort law goes back at least as far as the nineteenth century—long before my suggested catastrophe occurred.

Well, it's only a thesis, but one I am still inclined to cling to as the best (and perhaps only) explanation of why we no longer understand why tort law exists, when we know for certain that tort law must exist for some purpose, as everything created by human beings always and everywhere serves some purpose or other. As for whether (1) could be true, three points can be made. First, unspoken understandings are still understandings even though they are unspoken; and indeed the things we understand best are the things we are least likely to speak about and ask questions about because we see no need to. Secondly, if there has been a catastrophe affecting our understanding of tort law, that catastrophe would contaminate legal historical researches as much as anything else and prevent us seeing what was actually going in the nineteenth century and encourage us to think that they then were in just as much of a mess about the basis of tort liability as we suppose we are in now. Thirdly, if (1) is not true,

---

[70] See JL Coleman, 'Second Thoughts and Other First Impressions' in B Bix (ed), *Analyzing Law: New Essays in Legal Theory* (Oxford, Clarendon Press, 1988) 257, 302: 'Tort law is about messes. A mess has been made, and the only question before the court is, who is to clean it up?'

where does the idea—which all tort textbooks pay lip-service to (but only lip-service)[71] and even the most diehard opponent of rights-based theories of law has been known to invoke[72]—that tort law is part of the law of wrongs come from? This idea is absolutely central to rights-based theories of tort law (as 'wrong' is just a synonym for 'violation of a right'), but it is not an invention of the recent crop of rights-based theories of tort law. Where does it come from, if not a time when people had a much clearer understanding of what tort law is all about than we do?

B. Are Rights-Based Theories of Tort Law Right-Wing?

One commentator on this chapter reproved me for suggesting that the catastrophe in our understanding of tort law was triggered by the growing popularity of left-wing political theories from the 1920s onwards, and the accompanying obsession with discussing and defining what goals the state should pursue, and what it should and should not do to the citizens under its control; all of which left tort law—which (as rights-based theorists of tort law contend) is very much concerned with the *horizontal* relationships between citizens, rather than the *vertical* relationship between citizen and state—out in the cold. The commentator suggested that this view would give comfort to those who accuse rights-based theorists of tort law of being right-wing in their political orientation. Well, maybe it will—but it shouldn't. There is nothing distinctively left-wing or right-wing about being obsessed with what powers the state should have, and what goals it should pursue, and what the relationship should be between the state and the citizens under its control. In fact, politicians on the right have been obsessed with nothing else for the last 40 years or so. So there is no significance in the fact that the growing interest in the 1920s in defining the powers of the state came from the left; ten years after that, the interest was all on the right-hand side of politics.

All of which is incidental to the main issue, which is: *are* rights-based theories of tort law right-wing?[73] There is no doubt that thinkers on the

[71] Almost all tort textbooks open by saying that a tort is a form of legal wrong, and then forget all about that by the second page and identify tort law not with an event (a wrong) but with a response (compensation for loss). I think the tort textbook I co-author with Bagshaw was the first ever to take seriously the idea of a tort being a form of legal wrong, and expel from tort law (though not from the book) liability rules that could not be seriously said to arise out of a wrong, such as the rule in *Rylands v Fletcher* and the liability rules contained in the Consumer Protection Act 1987.

[72] J Stapleton, 'The Golden Thread at the Heart of Tort Law: Protection of the Vulnerable' (2003) 24 *Australian Bar Review* 135, 149.

[73] It is a quite different question whether rights-based *theorists* of tort law are right-wing. As Neyers has pointed out to me, it is quite clear that at least some of them are not, and that those theorists argue that it is precisely because tort law is so limited in what it does that other areas of law need to be expanded or strengthened to achieve desirable social goals.

right would find the rights-based theories of tort law that we have been presented with so far much more congenial than thinkers on the left would. This is because such theories have tended to argue that the courts should only recognise and uphold very basic rights to one's person, one's property and one's reputation. Such arguments would find favour with those on the right who think that the state should play nothing more than a nightwatchman role in society, stopping people harming others. But those on the left who think that the state should take a more active role in promoting people's welfare cannot be expected to be happy at the prospect of the courts recognising and upholding such a limited range of rights. As Bagshaw has observed:

> [I]t is not realistic to suppose that people in a society such as that in England will have sufficient freedom to choose a pattern of life and flourish if private law limits itself to granting them some security for their persons, possessions and promises. Moreover protecting property ahead of less tangible economic interests tends to perpetuate inequalities with regard to the protection of welfare. Few would deny that the welfare of *many* people in England is far more closely tied to their future economic prospects than to their present property.[74]

However, I would also argue that a properly worked out rights-based theory of tort law—of the kind I have tried to set out in this chapter—will be neither right-wing nor left-wing in orientation. Of course, like any other rights-based theory of tort law, it will be strongly resistant to attempts to twist and distort tort law's basic rules and doctrines in an attempt to achieve collective goals[75] (other than the collective goal of ensuring that people are able to assert against each other the coercive rights that the *Right Conditions* tell us they should enjoy). But there is nothing distinctively left-wing or right-wing in recognising that there are limits to what we should be allowed to do to each other, and allowed to refuse to do for each other, and that the law should be involved in policing those limits, where it can do so without unacceptable side effects.

---

[74] Bagshaw, above n 27, at 254 (emphasis in original).

[75] Against E Chamberlain, 'Negligent Investigation: Tort Law as Police Ombudsman' in A Robertson and HW Tang (eds), *The Goals of Private Law* (Oxford, Hart Publishing, 2009) 283, 284, arguing that the police should be held liable in negligence for harm resulting from their failure to investigate crime properly as doing so will 'encourage greater care by [the] police and an improvement in standard investigatory techniques'. For another example of attempts to twist and distort tort law to help achieve collective goals, see the claims brought in the United States against companies for property damage caused by climate change allegedly contributed to by those companies' activities. (I am indebted to Jolene Lin for pointing this out to me.)

C. Freedom and Rights

A couple of commentators objected to my saying[76] that if there is an abandoned newspaper on a train and two passengers on the train, we should
simply say that each passenger is 'free' to pick up the newspaper and we
should not say that either passenger has a 'right' to pick up the paper.

One commentator argued that in this case, each passenger has a *legal
power right* to make the newspaper 'his'. I'm not sure we can say that
either passenger would be performing a distinctively legal act in picking
up the newspaper, which would entitle us to say that each passenger has
a legal power right in this case. I think it's more accurate to say that
each passenger is free to perform a natural act—take possession of the
newspaper—and if and when that act is performed, certain legal consequences will follow.[77]

The other commentator argued that in this case, each passenger has a
liberty/interest right to pick up the newspaper because the law protects
each passenger's freedom to pick up the newspaper through granting each
passenger coercive rights that the other passenger not hit or assault him
when he is attempting to pick up the paper. I don't think this is right.
The coercive rights that each passenger enjoys that the other passenger
not hit or assault him are not specifically intended to protect the passenger's freedom to pick up abandoned newspapers; they are intended to
protect the passenger's interest in not being hit or assaulted. Given this,
I don't think it is possible to say that the law gives either passenger's
freedom to pick up the newspaper any kind of special protection which
would allow us to say that each passenger has a liberty/interest right to
pick up the paper.

For the same reason, I don't think it's right to say that any of us has
a 'right' to walk down the street,[78] even though the law imposes on each
of us a duty not to obstruct the public highway unreasonably. That duty
is not intended to protect any particular individual's freedom to walk
down the street—for the obvious reason that a single individual's interest in being able to walk down the street unhindered is not sufficiently
strong to justify anyone else having a duty not to obstruct the highway
unreasonably. So as the law does not go out of its way specifically to
protect your or my freedom to walk down the street unhindered, neither
you nor I can say that we have a liberty/interest right to walk down the
street unhindered. Nor can anyone say that they have a coercive right
that I not obstruct the highway unreasonably as my duty not to obstruct

---

[76] See above n 31.

[77] An analogy: when a woman gives birth, she alters the legal position of the father of
the child. But I don't think the fact that her giving birth will have that effect would cause
many people to say that she has a legal power right to give birth.

[78] Against Stevens, *Torts and Rights*, above n 16, at 8.

the highway unreasonably is not imposed on me for the benefit of any particular individual, but for the good of society as a whole. So if I do obstruct the highway unreasonably, I will commit a crime (the crime of public nuisance), but not a tort. The fact that I will be liable to compensate those who suffer 'special damage' as a result of my crime does not bring my conduct within the realms of tort law. In fact, the fact that I will *only* be held liable to compensate those who suffer 'special damage' as a result of my crime shows that my conduct does not amount to a tort; if it did, a plaintiff would not need to show that he or she had suffered 'special damage' as a result of my conduct in order to bring a claim against me.

D. Conceptually Impossible Rights

In the chapter that Stevens has contributed to this book he argues that:

> A wrong ... occurs in a moment of time, although some wrongs can be repeated, such as libel, or can be ongoing such as a trespass to land. D commits a civil wrong in relation to C whenever he breaches a duty to C not to do *x*. It is consequently meaningless to talk of a right not to be caused loss. If loss is suffered, it is a consequence of a breach of duty; it cannot go to the definition of what D is under a duty to do or not do.[79]

If this argument were correct, it would be conceptually impossible for one person to owe another a duty not to cause them loss intentionally, using unlawful means to do so. If this is right, then in the *Second Variation* considered above,[80] Fred *could not* (contrary to my view) have violated Wendy's rights in intentionally crashing into the power station with the intention of disrupting her business.

Stevens' argument does not work. It does not follow from the fact that a 'wrong ... occurs in a moment of time' that it 'is meaningless to talk of a right not to be caused loss.' If A had a duty not to cause B loss, that duty would be breached exactly at the moment in time when A's actions first made B worse off. Stevens' denial that it is possible for duties not to cause others loss to exist is also hard to reconcile with his insistence, earlier in his chapter, that the duty a driver owes nearby drivers and pedestrians is 'a duty not to injure, and not a duty not to expose to the risk of injury'.[81] While 'loss' and 'injury' clearly have different meanings for Stevens,[82] the important point for our purposes here is that a duty

---

[79] R Stevens, 'Rights and Other Things' ch 5 of this book, text accompanying n 12.

[80] See part V(B)(ii) above.

[81] Stevens, 'Rights and Other Things', above n 79, text accompanying n 9.

[82] For Stevens, 'loss' equates to being made worse off, and—in this context—'injury' equates to suffering damage to one's body. Elsewhere, Stevens uses the word 'injury' as a synonym for 'wrong' but—in this context—he cannot be taken to suggest that the duty of

not to cause someone injury and a duty not to cause someone loss have exactly the same structure. Given this, it is hard to see why Stevens is happy to accept that we owe other people the first kind of duty, while condemning the second type of duty as 'meaningless'.

E. A Merely Semantic Difference?

A couple of people with whom I have discussed this chapter have argued that if the rights-based theory of tort law I advance in this chapter is correct, there is then no *essential* difference between the approach that I think the courts should (and do) adopt in deciding tort cases (ask yourself whether the defendant violated a coercive right that we should recognise the plaintiff had against the defendant) and the approach to deciding tort cases that I criticised at the start of this chapter (ask yourself whether it would be 'fair, just and reasonable', all things considered, to make the defendant compensate the plaintiff for some loss that the defendant has caused the plaintiff to suffer). The difference between the approaches, it was said, just comes down to semantics—all the things we might consider in determining whether it would be 'fair, just and reasonable' to make the defendant compensate the plaintiff for some loss that he or she has caused the plaintiff are, under my theory, simply repackaged as factors that we should consider in determining whether we should find that the defendant violated the plaintiff's rights in acting as he or she did.

I don't think the criticism is justified—even in relation to earlier drafts of this chapter, where the *Right Conditions* were, admittedly, sketched out in a much rougher form than they are now. Let's call the approach I want the courts to adopt (and which I claim they do adopt) in deciding tort cases the 'rights-based approach'. Let's call the approach that I don't want the courts to adopt (and which I claim they don't adopt) the 'loss-based approach'. The rights-based approach and the loss-based approach to deciding tort cases *are* different, both in terms of the factors they take into account, and in terms of the results they come up with.

Let's look at factors first. Both of the people to whom I talked thought that if you take into account the public interest in determining what rights we enjoy against each other, the distinction between the rights-based approach to deciding tort cases and the loss-based approach to deciding tort cases weakens considerably. I don't think this is true. The role the public interest plays in deciding tort cases is very different under each approach. Under the rights-based approach to deciding tort cases, the public interest only ever comes in as a reason for *denying* a claim

---

a driver to nearby drivers and pedestrians is a duty not to wrong them, as such a duty would be completely redundant: it would equate to a duty not to breach some further duty that the driver owes nearby drivers and pedestrians.

(on the ground that it would be contrary to the public interest to find that the plaintiff had a right that the defendant violated).[83] Under the loss-based approach to deciding tort cases, the public interest can come in as a reason for *granting* a claim (on the ground that society would be better off if the sort of conduct the defendant engaged in incurred some kind of sanction through the tort system).

Let's look at results next. Suppose that A, a driver, runs down B, a pedestrian. A was not at fault in any way for the accident, in which B is badly injured. B sues A in tort for compensation for his injuries. If we adopted a loss-based approach to deciding this case, we might well find that it is 'fair, just and reasonable' to hold A liable here. Doing so will not inconvenience A too much as she will be carrying liability insurance; and in any case, it would probably be a good idea to make drivers internalise all the costs resulting from cars being on the road so as to ensure that in time no more than an optimal number of cars will be on the road. (The optimal number being the number where the marginal costs resulting from adding one more car to the road will outweigh the marginal benefits.) But if we adopt a rights-based approach to deciding this case, we won't hesitate to dismiss B's claim. In order for B's claim to succeed, B would have to show that he had a coercive right that A *ensure* when she was driving that she not knock B down. While B would have an interest in A ensuring that she did not knock B down—thus satisfying the *Benefit Condition*—that interest could not ever be weighty enough to justify imposing on A a duty that would be so onerous to discharge. So the *Burden Condition* would not be satisfied in B's case, with the result that B would not be able to establish that A violated B's rights in running him down.

VII. CONCLUSION

I believe that the best hope of understanding tort law as an intelligible body of law lies in adopting a rights-based theory of tort law. However, those who agree with me on this point are, I fear, in danger of snatching intellectual defeat from the jaws of victory by advancing rights-based theories of tort law that are fundamentally flawed in the ways I have described in this chapter. However, my primary aim in writing this chapter has been constructive, not destructive. In setting out a rights-based theory of tort law that transcends the limitations of its predecessors, I hope to provide tort scholars with a proper basis both for determining whether or not tort law is genuinely rights-based, and—if it is—for determining what rights tort law should recognise us as having against other people.

[83] See, to the same effect, the 'pluralist approach to duty' set out in A Robertson, 'Rights, Pluralism and the Duty of Care' ch 15 of this book, part II.

13

Is the Role of Tort to Repair Wrongful Losses?

GREGORY C KEATING*

I. INTRODUCTION

O VER THE PAST 30 years, philosophers of tort law have performed invaluable work in restoring the concept of a 'wrong'
to prominence in tort scholarship, and in building a persuasive
case that no adequate account of tort can replace the idea of a 'wrong'
with the idea of a 'cost'. The backward-looking, bilateral structure of
ordinary tort adjudication—which pits an injured victim against the party
allegedly responsible for injuring that victim—is powerfully explained and
justified by the thesis that the plaintiff has a claim for redress against the
defendant when and *because* the defendant has wronged the plaintiff.
The competing thesis that tort is a regulatory mechanism designed to
minimise the combined costs of accidents and their prevention, by contrast, offers a forced and implausible account of the formal structure of
a normal tort lawsuit.

Economic analysis explains tort's preoccupation with the past as an
oblique way of shaping the future. Past wrongdoers and the sunk costs
for which they are responsible are false targets for cheapest cost-avoiders and avoidable future costs. Rational actors recognise that the past is
beyond their control. They ignore sunk costs and focus on minimising
expected costs—costs which have yet to materialise and which might still
be avoided.[1] The only reason to hold people responsible for past harm

* This chapter is part of a larger project on the role of rights and rectification in tort
law. I am grateful to participants in the Obligations V Conference as well as Scott Altman,
Kim Buchanan, Eric Claeys, Jules Coleman, Stephen Gardbaum, John Gardner, Mark Geist-
feld, Mark Greenberg, Barbara Herman, Ehud Kamar, Dan Klerman, Jennifer Mnookin, Bob
Rabin, Anthony Sebok, Cathy Sharkey, Ken Simons, Martin Stone, Gary Watson and Gideon
Yaffe for instruction and advice. I am indebted to Aness Webster, Nataline Viray-Fung and
Judy Choi for invaluable research assistance, including sound editorial advice.
[1] '[C]ost to an economist is a forward-looking concept. "Sunk" (incurred) costs do not

is to induce people to avoid future harm, insofar as it is worth avoiding. And the right people to hold responsible are not those who have done past harm wrongly, but those who are in the best position to avoid future harm efficiently. Wrongdoers are false target defendants, and they are false targets for cheapest cost-avoiders. Properly understood, then, tort adjudication is not about responsibility for past harm, wrongly inflicted. Tort adjudication is about providing proper incentives to minimise the combined costs of paying for and preventing *future* accidents.[2]

In the same vein, the only reason to recognise *plaintiffs'* claims to redress for past harm wrongly inflicted is to enlist plaintiffs' participation in minimising the combined costs of harm and its avoidance going forward. Tort plaintiffs should prevail not when they show that defendants are responsible for having done them wrongful harm, but when they show that honouring their claims will promote the social interest in minimising the combined costs of accidents and their prevention, going forward. Properly understood, then, plaintiffs are private Attorneys-General. They sue to vindicate the general good, not their own individual rights.

Philosophers of tort have been quite right to criticise this account of tort adjudication as strained and unconvincing. They have been far less persuasive, however, when they have elaborated their general claim that tort is a law of wrongs through the more particular thesis that tort is about the *rectification* of wrongs. Influential legal philosophers have argued, for example, that 'tort law is best explained by corrective justice' because 'at its core tort law seeks to repair wrongful losses'.[3] Corrective justice theory, robustly conceived, insists that the obligation to repair wrongful loss is the paramount or sovereign principle of tort, the cornerstone on which the institution is constructed. Tort law's primary norms—its articulation of those wrongs whose commission gives rise to responsibilities of repair—must fit a mould imposed by its remedial norms. Because tort is an institution of corrective justice—an institution for the repair of wrongful losses—tort wrongs must be the kinds of things that issue

---

affect a rational actor's decisions ... Rational people base their decisions on expectations of the future rather than on regrets about the past. They treat bygones as bygones': RA Posner, *Economic Analysis of Law*, 7th edn (New York, Aspen Publishers, 2007) 7.

    [2] 'I take it as axiomatic that the principal function of accident law is to reduce the sum of the costs of accidents and the costs of avoiding accidents': G Calabresi, *The Costs of Accidents* (New Haven, Yale University Press, 1970) 26.

    [3] J Coleman, *The Practice of Principle: In Defence of a Pragmatist Approach to Legal Theory* (Oxford, Oxford University Press, 2001) 9, 36. The first passage continues: 'The central concepts of tort law—harm, cause, repair, fault, and the like—hang together in a set of inferential relations that reflect a principle of corrective justice.' The principle of corrective justice 'states that individuals who are responsible for the wrongful losses of others have a duty to repair th[os]e losses': at 15 (emphasis altered). Ernest Weinrib has done as much as Jules Coleman to place the concept of corrective justice at the centre of tort scholarship. For Weinrib, tort is about 'wrongs' and although these usually result in wrongful losses, tort is not about wrongful losses. See the text accompanying n 4 below.

in wrongful loss. This requires, in turn, that tort be a realm of conduct-based wrongs.[4]

This account of tort law as an institution concerned at bottom with repairing wrongful losses is unconvincing. It suffers from two deep flaws. First, it puts the cart before the horse: primary tort obligations not to inflict wrongful harm are antecedent to and grounding of tort law's remedial responsibilities of repair. Those primary norms are not obligations to avoid committing corrective injustices. Primary tort norms articulate obligations to avoid harming people in various ways, and to respect their authority over their persons and their property in various ways. These wrongs are grounded not in a norm of corrective justice, but in rights people have as persons, such as the right to physical and psychological integrity.

Secondly, corrective justice theory itself offers an implausible account of the structure of tort law. Primary obligations in tort are neither all conduct-based nor all bilateral in their structure, and their violation does not always result in wrongful losses. Primary obligations are typically omnilateral—owed by everyone to everyone else. Some primary obligations protect rights whose violation need not result in harm, and other primary obligations are not conduct-based. Strict liabilities in tort characteristically criticise not the primary conduct responsible for harm, but secondary failures to repair harm justifiably inflicted. Strict liabilities are usually 'conditional wrongs'.

My argument will proceed in three parts. The first part explicates the robust conception of corrective justice summarised above, with particular attention to its powerful critique of the economic analysis of tort law. The second part develops the distinction between substantive or primary rights and responsibilities in tort and remedial or secondary ones. The third part explains why tort's obligation of reparation is essential to tort law, but not the master principle of tort.

Corrective justice theory, in short, faces problems both with fitting and with justifying basic features of tort. The overarching argument of this chapter, linking its various parts, is that tortfeasors are called to account for and because of their failures to discharge primary obligations, obligations either to avoid inflicting certain harms or to avoid harmlessly violating certain rights. Remedial responsibilities in tort are subordinate, not fundamental. They are conditioned on and arise out of failures to discharge antecedent primary obligations. Those primary obligations are the ground of tortfeasors' secondary responsibilities to repair the harms wrought by their torts. Repairing harm wrongly done is a next- or sec-

---

[4] The claim that tort is a law of 'conduct-based wrongful losses' is distinctive to Coleman, but related ideas such as the idea that tort is a realm of conduct-based wrongs have widespread currency: see, eg, JCP Goldberg and BC Zipursky, 'Rights and Responsibility in the Law of Torts' ch 9 of this book.

ond-best way of discharging an obligation not to do harm wrongly in the first place. Rights and remedies form a unity: the role of remedies is to enforce and restore rights. Corrective justice theories reverse this relation by putting remedy before right.

II. TORT LAW AS CORRECTIVE JUSTICE

A. Conceptions of Corrective Justice

Corrective justice is an ancient concept, and it has spawned a family of distinct modern conceptions. At its most general, corrective justice is defined in contradistinction to distributive justice and in terms of a relationship between the parties. Distributive justice, in the pertinent sense, has to do with the justice of holdings, with the distribution of wealth, income and property for example. Persons who participate in the same institutions of distributive justice have their claims against one another mediated by those institutions. Claims in distributive justice are not direct claims on other persons. We may have a claim in distributive justice to a certain share of society's wealth and income, but we do not have a claim in distributive justice against another person for that share.

Corrective justice, by contrast, involves the relationship between the parties to a claim. It requires a 'wrong' or a 'rights violation'. That wrong or rights violation must relate the parties directly to one another, and it must give rise to an obligation of reparation on the part of the defendant. Corrective justice has to do with claims that one person has against another, to repair a loss to the former for which the latter is accountable. 'Corrective justice', Ernest Weinrib tells us, 'treats the wrong, and the transfer of resources that undoes it, as a single nexus of activity and passivity where actor and victim are defined in relation to each other'.[5] Corrective justice 'joins the parties directly, through the harm that one of them inflicts on the other'.[6] It involves 'the correlativity of doing and suffering harm'.[7]

[5] EJ Weinrib, *The Idea of Private Law* (Cambridge MA, Harvard University Press, 1995) 56.
[6] ibid, at 71.
[7] ibid, at 77, 142. See also Weinrib's statement that '[c]orrective justice represents the integrated unity of doer and sufferer': at 213. Martin Stone places 'the unity of doing and suffering' at the heart of Weinrib's corrective justice theory: M Stone, 'The Significance of Doing and Suffering' in GJ Postema (ed), *Philosophy and the Law of Torts* (Cambridge, Cambridge University Press, 2001) 131, 131 ('Modern tort law looks out on a situation which is ubiquitous in human affairs and inherent, as a possibility, in the fact of human action: a situation where the actions of one person are connected to the misfortunes of another'). See also M Stone, 'On the Idea of Private Law' (1996) 9 *Canadian Journal of Law and Jurisprudence* 235. The font of this is Aristotle, *Nichomachean Ethics* (M Ostwald tr, Indianapolis, Bobbs-Merrill, 1962) paras 1132a2–1132a6:

By the time we reach Weinrib's emphasis on the 'unity of doing and suffering'[8]—with the 'doing' being the infliction of the suffering by violating the 'abstract equality of free purposive beings under the Kantian conception of right'[9]—we have left the common ground of corrective justice theories. Richard Epstein's theory of tort flies under the banner of corrective justice, but it applies the concept to an essentially causal form of liability. The concept of a wrong that is so central to Weinrib's account is attenuated in Epstein's.[10] George Fletcher, for his part, applies the term to a theory of liability for non-reciprocal risk imposition.[11] Jules Coleman asserts that the principle of corrective justice 'states that individuals who are responsible for the wrongful losses of others have a duty to repair th[os]e losses.'[12] Other conceptions can also be found in the literature.[13]

These diverse conceptions vary in a number of different ways. For our purposes, however, the important division among theories is the division between those that take corrective justice to be a subordinate principle or aspect of tort law and those that take it to be the paramount or sovereign principle of tort law. Endorsements of corrective justice as a subordinate principle of tort law are widespread. On a subordinate account, corrective justice is an aspect of tort—perhaps even a necessary and defining feature of the institution—but it does not play a fundamental role in explaining or justifying tort law. Instead, the justifications for tort law—inducing optimal accident prevention, say—call for corrective justice as an aspect of tort law.[14] Accounts which treat corrective justice as the sovereign principle of tort—a principle which grounds and explains the law of torts—work the other way around. Rather than being required by other, more basic, justifications for tort, corrective justice justifies tort law as an institution and governs its design.

> Whether a worthy person has taken something from an unworthy person or vice versa, makes no difference ... the law looks to the difference in harm alone, and it treats them as equals, if the one commits and the other suffers injustice and if the one has inflicted and the other has suffered harm.

[8] Weinrib, *The Idea of Private Law*, above n 5, at 145.

[9] ibid, at 58.

[10] RA Epstein, 'A Theory of Strict Liability' (1973) 2 *Journal of Legal Studies* 151.

[11] GP Fletcher, 'Fairness and Utility in Tort Theory' (1972) 85 *Harvard Law Review* 537.

[12] Coleman, *The Practice of Principle*, above n 3, at 15. See also above n 3 and accompanying text. For Coleman, 'wrongful losses' need not always arise from 'wrongs': J Coleman, *Risks and Wrongs* (Oxford, Oxford University Press, 2002) ch 17.

[13] See generally SR Perry, 'The Moral Foundations of Tort Law' (1992) 77 *Iowa Law Review* 449, 506–507 (taking the task of corrective justice theory to specify when the law may legitimately shift losses from one citizen to another); P Benson, 'The Basis of Corrective Justice and its Relation to Distributive Justice' (1992) 77 *Iowa Law Review* 515; RW Wright, 'Substantive Corrective Justice' (1992) 77 *Iowa Law Review* 625; A Ripstein, *Equality, Responsibility, and the Law* (Cambridge, Cambridge University Press, 1999) (taking the principle of corrective justice to specify when the state may justifiably force the transfer of one person's loss to another by means of compensatory payment).

[14] See the text accompanying nn 17–19 below for an argument of this kind.

If corrective justice is the fundamental principle on which tort law rests and if it asserts that justice requires repairing wrongful losses, then tort law must be concerned with the repair of *losses*, and those losses must be *wrongful*. More particularly, corrective justice theorists of the sovereign stripe insist that tort liability must attach to losses generated by *wrongful conduct*. On this account, corrective justice is an *independent* principle to which the law of torts answers. The proposition that wrongful losses should be repaired by those responsible for them is a free-standing principle of political morality, and it governs and justifies the law of torts. Corrective justice is also an *important* principle because it places a significant constraint on the character of tort's primary norms. For tort to be an institution of corrective justice, the primary norms of tort law must consist of conduct-based wrongs whose commission results in the infliction of loss. Wrongful losses are losses that issue from wrongful conduct.

B. Corrective Justice as the Sovereign Principle of Tort Justice

Theorists like Coleman and Weinrib take corrective justice to be the paramount principle of tort law. Recall Coleman's claim that 'tort law is best explained by corrective justice' because 'at its core tort law seeks to repair wrongful losses'.[15] For this claim to be credible, 'wrongful losses' must be a concept which does some work and which has some constraining content. It must identify a class of phenomena to which a duty of repair properly attaches. Coleman's robust conception of corrective justice thus holds that it involves responsibility for *wrongful losses, harms or rights violations*, meaning losses that result from *wrongful conduct*.[16] Such conduct disrupts the pre-existing distribution of entitlements—it violates rights, inflicts injury, or does harm—but it gives rise to liability in *corrective justice* because it is *wrongful*, not just because it is disruptive of a pre-existing pattern of entitlement. Innocent disruptions—disruptions which are not wrongful—do not give rise to claims of corrective justice. Corrective justice is thus distinguished from distributive justice, and the criteria of wrongfulness that corrective justice places at the centre of tort law do the work of determining when liability in tort is justified.

---

[15] Coleman, *The Practice of Principle*, above n 3, at 9, 36. See also Weinrib, *The Idea of Private Law*, above n 5, at 133–34 (arguing that corrective justice is 'immanent' not just in tort, but in contract and restitution as well). Corrective justice is thus characteristic of private law in general, not of tort law in particular.

[16] See, eg, JL Coleman, 'The Practice of Corrective Justice' in DG Owen (ed), *Philosophical Foundations of Tort Law* (Oxford, Oxford University Press, 1995) 53, 56–57 (explaining that corrective justice imposes a duty on an injurer to repair the loss of a victim when the injurer is responsible for having brought the loss about by virtue of the injurer's wrongful conduct). Wrongdoing understood as wrongful conduct is also essential to Weinrib's theory of corrective justice in tort. For Weinrib, however, while liability for restitution is a species of corrective justice, it is a species of corrective justice which does not require wrongful conduct: see *The Idea of Private Law*, above n 5, at 140–42, 197–98.

The proposition that corrective justice involves both the infliction of harm or the violation of a right *and conduct that is in some way wrongful* establishes the *independence* of corrective justice from distributive justice, but it does not establish the *importance* of corrective justice, or show that it explains the law of torts. Richard Posner drove these points home in an important paper. Posner distinguished between what I have called subordinate and sovereign conceptions of corrective justice in tort, and went on to argue that '[o]nce the concept of corrective justice is given its correct Aristotlelian meaning, it becomes possible to show that it is not only compatible with, but required by, the economic theory of law'.[17] Starting from the premise that corrective justice in its robust sense requires wrongful conduct, Posner argued first that economics could supply the requisite standard of conduct, and second that an economic conception of tort *required* corrective justice:

> [For an economic theory,] law is a means of bringing about an efficient (in the sense of wealth-maximizing) allocation of resources by correcting externalities and other distortions in the market's allocation of resources. The idea of rectification in the Aristotelian sense is implicit in this theory. If A fails to take precautions that would cost less than their expected benefits in accident avoidance, thus causing an accident in which B is injured, and nothing is done to rectify this wrong, the concept of efficiency as justice will be violated. ... Since A does not bear the cost (or the full cost) of his careless behavior, he will have no incentive to take precautions in the future, and there will be more accidents than is optimal. Since B receives no compensation for his injury, he may be induced to adopt in the future precautions which by hypothesis ... are more costly than the precautions that A failed to take.[18]

Corrective justice can, in short, take a standard of efficient precaution as the criterion of wrongful conduct that it requires. For its part, economics requires that corrective justice be done if tort is to induce efficient precautions.

When corrective justice is conceived of as compatible with economics in this way, however, it is neither sovereign nor justificatory. Corrective justice is a feature of tort law—a constitutive element of the legal subject. As such, it is not a justification but an aspect of the institution, which *requires* justification. For Posner, economics supplies the justification. When tort law is a society's principal mechanism for addressing accidents—and is otherwise efficient[19]—corrective justice is necessary to ensure

---

[17] RA Posner, 'The Concept of Corrective Justice in Recent Theories of Tort Law' (1981) 10 *Journal of Legal Studies* 187, 201.

[18] ibid.

[19] Posner's argument isolates reparation for harm wrongly done and assumes that tort law is otherwise efficient, in order to determine whether reparation for harm wrongly done is efficient. Without the assumption that tort law is otherwise efficient the argument does not go through. See J Gardner, 'Backward and Forward with Tort Law' in JK Campbell, M O'Rourke and D Shier (eds), *Law and Social Justice* (Cambridge MA, MIT Press, 2005) 255, 269–70.

that the law of torts as a whole induces efficient precaution. Corrective justice, in other words, is an instrument of wealth-maximisation.

Posner's account makes corrective justice a subordinate principle of tort liability even though it incorporates the idea that corrective justice involves liability for wrongful conduct. The reasons that we have for doing corrective justice are simply the reasons that we have for deploying tort law in the first place and, for Posner, those are reasons of efficiency. Tort law exists to induce efficient precaution, and corrective justice serves this end. Wrongful losses—meaning losses inflicted by inefficient and therefore wrongful conduct—must be shifted back onto the parties responsible for them, or else neither injurers nor victims will have the right incentives. Posner's theory pours the substance of efficiency into the form of corrective justice.

This union of efficiency and corrective justice is surprising. Corrective justice and the economic theory of tort appear to be rival conceptions. The economic conception of tort law is forward-looking, and it takes as its touchstone the attainment of a state of the world where value of a certain sort (wealth and, indirectly, welfare) is maximised.[20] The rights and duties of plaintiffs and defendants with respect to one another matter only insofar as they may be deployed as instruments towards the realisation of this end. Corrective justice theory, by contrast, is backward-looking. It aims to repair past wrongs. Corrective justice theory focuses on who has done what to whom, and on the immediate normative implications of that doing and suffering. It places the rights and wrongs of plaintiffs and defendants at the very centre of its account. Tort is about the obligations of wrongdoers to repair the wrongful losses that they have inflicted on their victims. The total amount of value in various states of the world is utterly beside the point.[21]

C. Corrective Justice as a Practice of Principle

The leading proponents of corrective justice theory in our time—Coleman and Weinrib—reject Posner's conclusion that corrective justice is merely a feature of tort law to be explained, or even a subordinate principle of tort law. For Coleman and Weinrib, corrective justice is tort law's sovereign principle. 'Corrective justice', Coleman writes, 'expresses the principle that

---

[20] The standard criterion is the one stated by Guido Calabresi as quoted in above n 2. This simple formulation is usually refined to incorporate administrative costs as well: see R Cooter and T Ulen, *Law and Economics*, 5th edn (Upper Saddle River NJ, Prentice Hall, 2007) 359.

[21] To invoke a distinction made famous by Robert Nozick, the economic theory of tort is an 'end-state' theory whereas corrective justice is a 'historical' theory of tort justice: R Nozick, *Anarchy, State, and Utopia* (New York, Basic Books, 1974) 153–60.

holds together and makes sense of tort law'.[22] The principle that wrongful losses should be repaired is a *morally* authoritative norm in its own right—it is sovereign, not subordinate. Tort, in a word, is a body of law grounded on the principle that wrongful losses should be repaired.

The corrective justice theories of Coleman and Weinrib are the most important, influential, and ambitious views of their kind. We must, therefore, get as clear an understanding as we can of their claims and their conception. The first step towards that understanding is to grasp their criticisms of the economic theory of tort. That theory is both their target and their foil. Powerfully and persuasively, Coleman and Weinrib argue that the economic theory of tort offers an inadequate account of tort adjudication. The economic theory of tort is instrumental, and instrumentalism does and must look forward. Tort adjudication, however, does and must look backward. Because this is so, instrumentalism cannot adequately explain and justify the law of torts.

Coleman and Weinrib's own theories spring, in turn, from their critiques of economics. Tort adjudication, they argue, must be understood to be the instantiation of a *principle* of corrective justice. For Weinrib, tort adjudication appears to be an entirely autonomous institution. Its principles are given by the *form* of tort law—especially the form of tort adjudication—and they neither need nor have any further justification.[23] For Coleman, the principle of corrective justice and the practice it sustains can be explained and justified by reference to more abstract and fundamental principles, such as the principle that the costs of life's misfortunes should be allocated fairly.[24] Tort adjudication cannot, however, be conceived of as a means to an independently valuable end. Instead, it must be understood to enforce claims that persons have the standing to

---

[22] Coleman, *The Practice of Principle*, above n 3, at 62. Coleman appears to have been more sympathetic to the idea that tort law might effect the union of efficiency and corrective justice earlier in his career. Compare JL Coleman, 'Mental Abnormality, Personal Responsibility, and Tort Liability' in BA Brody and HT Engelhardt Jr (eds), *Mental Illness: Law and Public Policy* (Boston, Springer, 1980) 107, 123 (stating 'that a duty of corrective justice is compatible with a substantive concept of unjust conduct based on economics or utilitarianism') with JL Coleman, 'The Structure of Tort Law' (1988) 97 *Yale Law Journal* 1233 (arguing that economics cannot account for the normative structure of tort law).

[23] This is epitomised by Weinrib's oft-cited remark that 'private law is just like love': Weinrib, *The Idea of Private Law*, above n 5, at 6. Weinrib writes (at 6):

> Explaining love in terms of extrinsic ends is necessarily a mistake, because love does not shine in our lives with the borrowed light of an extrinsic end. Love is its own end. My contention is that, in this respect, private law is just like love.

Cf Weinrib's discussion of formalism, immanence and the autonomy of private law at 22–24, 206–08.

[24] See, eg, Coleman, *The Practice of Principle*, above n 3, at xiii, 4, 5, 8, 9–10, 43, 55, 58. Coleman writes (at 28 n 8): 'Anglo-American tort law *expresses*, *embodies*, or *articulates* corrective justice. Tort law is an institutional realization of principle, not an instrument in the pursuit of an external and hidden goal' (emphasis in original).

assert against one another in their own names and not, say, on behalf of an independently valuable end.

The divergence between Coleman and Weinrib over the autonomy of tort law signals a divergence between their views. To get a well-defined conception on the table, I shall therefore take Coleman's writings as my canonical example of a theory which takes corrective justice to be the sovereign principle of tort. On Coleman's account, because corrective justice rests on a genuine moral *principle*—the principle that wrongful losses should be repaired—corrective justice is not the goal of tort law. It is instead a justification for holding someone accountable for harm wrongly done. As a legal practice, corrective justice is not an instrument for the realisation of an end, but the instantiation and further specification of a morally authoritative principle of responsibility. It is *fair* to hold people responsible for repairing the wrongful losses that they inflict on others. This gives corrective justice a dual relation to tort practice. On the one hand, the principle of corrective justice grounds the practice. On the other hand, the practice puts flesh on the bare bones of the principle.[25]

Wrongful human agency, *correlativity*, and *repair* lie at the core of both tort law and corrective justice.[26] That tort law is about *agency* is evident enough to the pre-theoretic eye, but obscured by the theoretical apparatus of economics with its emphasis on achieving states of the world where value is maximised. The thesis that losses are more easily borne when they are widely dispersed, for example, gives us reason to be as concerned with concentrated losses caused by natural disasters as with concentrated losses caused by human malfeasance. Yet tort law denies this equivalence: it is about malfeasance, not misfortune.[27] In this respect, the law of tort taps into deep moral sentiments, sentiments constitutive of the sense of justice itself. We have reason to resent mistreatment by others, but it is anthropomorphic nonsense to complain of mistreatment by Mother Nature.[28]

---

[25] ibid, at 62.

[26] ibid, at 58: 'corrective justice requires that the costs of misfortune owing to human agency be imposed on the person (if any) whose wrongful conduct is responsible for those costs. The losses are made his by imposing on him an enforceable duty of repair.' See also Coleman, 'The Practice of Corrective Justice', above n 16, at 56–57, 66–67.

[27] 'There is a basic pretheoretical distinction between misfortunes owing to human agency and those that are attributable to no one's agency. The traditional philosophical distinction between corrective and distributive justice reflects, among other things, this pretheoretical distinction among kinds of misfortune': Coleman, *The Practice of Principle*, above n 3, at 44 (footnote omitted).

[28] In *Two Concepts of Liberty*, Isaiah Berlin quotes Jean-Jacques Rousseau's remark that '[t]he nature of things does not madden us, only ill-will does': I Berlin, *Two Concepts of Liberty* (Oxford, Clarendon Press, 1958) 2, reprinted in I Berlin, *Four Essays on Liberty* (Oxford, Oxford University Press, 1969). The remark is not attributed and appears to be Berlin's own translation of a passage in Rousseau's *Émile*: see J Rousseau, *Oeuvres complètes*, vol 4 (B Gagnebin and M Raymond eds, Paris, Éditions Gallimard, 1959) 320. John Rawls follows Rousseau's lead here in explicating what he calls 'the sense of justice':

That the pertinent agency must be and is *wrongful* is a proposition that looks to be at once self-evident and over-determined. Wrongfulness explains why the distinction between malfeasance and misfortune is intuitively basic. By themselves, natural events are just facts. Moral appraisal applies only to our *response* to natural facts. Human agency, by contrast, is immediately and directly subject to moral appraisal, and to negative moral appraisal if it is wrong. Wrongfulness gives us a reason to hold people responsible for the losses that they inflict on others. Last, but surely not least, wrongful conduct figures very prominently in the law of torts itself. Both intentional and negligent torts involve wrongful conduct. Perhaps for these reasons, robust conceptions of corrective justice take wrongfulness to be an indispensable element of tort liability.[29]

Correlativity is central to tort because

> [t]he claims of corrective justice are limited ... to parties who bear some normatively important relationship to one another. A person does not ... have a claim in corrective justice to repair in the air, against no one in particular. It is a claim against someone in particular.[30]

Correlativity thus refers to the bilateral (or bipolar) structure of tort adjudication, which itself mirrors the underlying interaction of a tortious wrong. Weinrib explains that '[c]orrective justice joins the parties directly, through the harm that one of them inflicts on the other.'[31] It involves 'the correlativity of doing and suffering harm'.[32] '[T]he direct connection between the particular plaintiff and the particular defendant' is 'the master feature characterizing private law'.[33] Coleman concurs, saying that '[t]ort law's core is represented by case-by-case adjudication in which particular

---

see J Rawls, *Collected Papers* (S Freeman ed, Cambridge MA, Harvard University Press, 1999) ch 5, which begins with a reference to Rousseau and *Émile* (at 96) and goes on to observe (at 111) that '[r]esentment and indignation are moral feelings. Resentment is our reaction to the injuries and harms which the wrongs of others inflict upon us, and indignation is our reaction to the injuries which the wrongs of others inflict on others.' See also PF Strawson, 'Freedom and Resentment' in PF Strawson (ed), *Studies in the Philosophy of Thought and Action* (Oxford, Oxford University Press, 1968) 71 (showing that 'reactive attitudes' such as resentment are fundamental to our sensibilities and cannot be accounted for by instrumentalism).

[29] Coleman speaks of duties as specifying norms of *conduct*: 'the duties articulated in the law of torts purport to express genuine reasons for acting, or standards with which one ought to comply' (*The Practice of Principle*, above n 3, at 35 n 19). In contrast, 'economic analysis eliminates the concept of duty in tort law—that is, it eliminates the concept of something that can be defended as a *standard of conduct* and not merely as a condition of liability': at 35 n 19 (emphasis added). Recall, too, that the principle of corrective justice 'states that individuals who are responsible for the wrongful losses of others have a duty to repair the losses': at 15 (emphasis altered).

[30] Coleman, 'The Practice of Corrective Justice', above n 16, at 66–67.

[31] Weinrib, *The Idea of Private Law*, above n 5, at 71.

[32] ibid, at 73, 78. See also above n 7, including the quotes from Stone and Aristotle in that footnote.

[33] Weinrib, *The Idea of Private Law*, above n 5, at 10.

victims seek redress for certain losses from those whom they claim are responsible'.[34]

The structure of tort adjudication coheres smoothly with the basic principle of corrective justice. Having a wronged plaintiff seek reparation from the wrongdoer who has injured him or her is the most natural way to give institutional expression to the principle that persons who are responsible for wrongly injuring others ought to repair the harm they have done.[35] Economic analysis, moreover, cannot offer an equally elegant and persuasive explanation of tort's adjudicative structure. On its face, tort law is a backward-looking practice concerned with repairing harm wrongly done, but economics takes it to be a forward-looking regulatory mechanism, designed to minimise the combined costs of accidents and their prevention. Generally speaking, this requires pinning accident costs on the 'cheapest cost-avoider'—on the party in the best position to minimise the combined costs of accidents and their prevention going forward.

Because it is only contingently the case that the particular injurers responsible for particular injuries are the cheapest cost-avoiders with respect to the general classes into which those injuries fall, economic theory is hard-pressed to explain why plaintiffs always have rights against and only against those who have wronged them.[36] To induce efficient precaution going forward, we ought to pin liability on cheapest cost-avoiders going forward. The economic theory of tort can explain tort law's backward-looking focus on past wrongdoers only by saying that we have good reason to think that past wrongdoers probably are the cheapest cost-avoiders going forward.

This argument fits tort practice poorly and justifies it only very weakly. Tort law's penchant for holding wrongdoers responsible for the wrongs that they commit is deep-seated. You might, indeed, reasonably regard this feature as one of tort law's constitutive characteristics. Yet the logic of the economic theory of tort holds that wrongdoers are merely false targets for cheapest cost-avoiders. The theory's logic requires pinning lia-

[34] Coleman, *The Practice of Principle*, above n 3, at 16.

[35] For Weinrib, this relationship expresses the 'unity of doing and suffering', the intrinsic moral salience of the doer of harm as someone specially responsible for the harm that he or she has wrongly done. '[T]he private law relationship forms a normative unit that integrates the doing and suffering of harm and that dovetails with the bipolar litigation between plaintiff and defendant. ... Correlativity locks the plaintiff and defendant into a reciprocal normative embrace': Weinrib, *The Idea of Private Law*, above n 5, at 142. Weinrib's view appears more metaphysical than Coleman's in that it appears to take the structure of tort law to reflect an essential and eternal form of human interaction. Recall Stone, 'The Significance of Doing and Suffering', above n 7, at 131: 'Modern tort law looks out on a situation which is ubiquitous in human affairs and inherent, as a possibility, in the fact of human action: a situation where the actions of one person are connected to the misfortunes of another.'

[36] Hard-pressed, but not without resources. It may be, as Coleman recognises, that administrative costs (eg, search costs) make tort litigation as it now exists a far more competitive institutional mechanism for inducing optimal accident precaution than it appears to be at first glance. See, eg, Coleman, *The Practice of Principle*, above n 3, at 18–20.

bility on cheapest cost-avoiders—and not wrongdoers—whenever the two diverge and whenever we can find the cheapest cost-avoiders. Tort law shows no such tendency.

The justificatory force of the economic theory is weak because it makes tort's practice of holding wrongdoers accountable a mere rule of thumb whose rationale is epistemic. It does not capture the *normative* force of tort practice. Tort practice looks backward towards breach of pre-existing obligations and asks tortfeasors to make right the harms they have wrongly done by breaching those obligations. The proposition that society would be better off in the future if some party were held accountable for the costs of accidents which they are in the best position to minimise going forward is a reason which can contingently call for holding that party liable for harm done in the past, but it does not capture the obligatory character of defendants' duties of repair.[37]

The implausibility of the economic account of tort adjudication is thus entangled with and compounded by the weakness of its explanation of the central substantive concepts of tort law—concepts such as duty, 'harm, cause, repair, fault and the like'.[38] The failure is a failure to do justice

---

[37] ibid, at 14–21, especially at 21. Weinrib likewise argues that extrinsic goals cannot make sense of the bipolar relationship between plaintiff and defendant, and that the relationship must be understood in terms of an immanent juridical relationship: EJ Weinrib, 'Understanding Tort Law' (1989) 23 *Valparaiso University Law Review* 485; Weinrib, *The Idea of Private Law*, above n 5, at 37–38, 142, 212–13. Weinrib's argument has a more metaphysical aspect: the bipolar structure of tort adjudication is indispensable to tort law because it corresponds to the underlying structure of the interaction between persons that characterises all torts. See, eg, Weinrib, *The Idea of Private Law*, above n 5, at 215:

> The formalism of corrective justice therefore lies not in its existing somewhere apart from the social world, but in its representing the unifying structure of the doer-sufferer relationship. Because it renders the interaction of doer and sufferer intelligible from within, corrective justice takes the doing and suffering of harm—as well as the conditions under which such interaction occurs—for granted. Accordingly, corrective justice both draws on a social and empirical reality and impresses that reality with the stamp of its regulating form.

Cf Stone, above n 7 (describing the unity of doing and suffering as a possibility inherent in human action). Coleman's position is simply that the practice embodies and is grounded by a principle of corrective justice that cannot be explained instrumentally.

[38] Coleman, *The Practice of Principle*, above n 3, at 9–10. See also Coleman, 'The Structure of Tort Law', above n 22. In conjunction with the basic structural features of tort adjudication, these concepts form what Coleman calls the pre-theoretic core of tort law: Coleman, *The Practice of Principle*, above n 3, at 15 n 2. As a pragmatic conceptualist, Coleman believes that tort theory must explain how the central concepts of tort law hang together. Coleman is concerned with whether views can explain the conceptual structure that forms the heart of tort law. Weinrib similarly believes that economic instrumentalism cannot explain the structure of tort law, but as a committed legal formalist, he believes that private law must be understood on its own terms and that 'an immanent moral rationality' is latent in the form of tort law: Weinrib, *The Idea of Private Law*, above n 5, at 24–25. Legal theory elicits that logic and makes it explicit. For Weinrib, corrective justice is a distinctively juridical concept: at 210–14. Coleman and Weinrib agree that tort law is an institutional expression of corrective justice, but Weinrib thinks that concept arises within tort law itself, whereas Coleman does not. Moreover, for Coleman, corrective justice is distinctive to tort law, whereas Weinrib believes that it is characteristic of private law in general.

to the way that these concepts operate as *reasons* for the imposition of liability in tort. For the law of negligence, breach of duty is a *reason* for the imposition of liability. Duty specifies an obligatory standard of conduct. In conjunction with the other elements of a negligence claim, failure to conform to that standard is *the* reason why tort holds a defendant responsible for harm done to a victim by the breach of that duty. Tort law looks backward at the past interactions of the parties in order to determine if the defendant should be held responsible for the plaintiff's injury. Defendants are liable to plaintiffs *because* they breach duties they owe to the plaintiffs and because those breaches are the actual and proximate causes of the harms that the plaintiffs suffer.

For the economic analysis of negligence, however, breach of duty is not a premise, but a conclusion:

> [S]tandard economic account[s] ... do not use efficiency to discover an independent class of duties that are analytically prior to our liability practices. ... What counts as a 'duty' or a 'wrong' in a standard economic account depends on an assessment of what the consequences are of imposing liability in a given case.[39]

Economic analysis looks forward to the reduction of future accident costs. Legal decisions must therefore be justified by good future consequences. They cannot be vindicated (at least not directly) by the correction of past injustices. Past accident costs are sunk; rationality requires that we disregard them and assign liability to whoever is in the best position to prevent *future* accidents at the lowest cost.

For orthodox economic analysis, liability does not follow from breach of duty when breach of duty is the actual and proximate cause of harm done. Liability follows from and because of a conclusion that the imposition of liability for past harm will induce optimal prevention of accidental harm going forward. On this view, the central concepts of tort law— duty, breach, actual and proximate cause, and harm—do no real work.[40] Judges say that they are imposing liability in negligence because duty, breach, actual and proximate cause, and injury are present, but standard economic analysis takes them to be justified in what they are doing only if they are engaged in a transaction cost minimising search for cheapest cost-avoiders. On the standard economic analysis view, duty, breach,

---

[39] Coleman, *The Practice of Principle*, above n 3, at 35. Coleman casts this argument as the incarnation of a general critique of policy argument in legal reasoning, understanding policy to be concerned with achieving consequences which are desirable overall. Even sharper objections to the use of policy arguments in tort appear in Weinrib's work: see, eg, *The Idea of Private Law*, above n 5, at 210–14, 218–22 (arguing that policy arguments are impermissible because they introduce ends extrinsic to the interaction between the parties to a tortious wrong, violate the equality of the parties and are therefore incompatible with doing justice between them, and let loose objectives which must cover every case within their purview, thereby consuming the law).

[40] Coleman, *The Practice of Principle*, above n 3, at 34–36.

actual and proximate cause, and injury are not *reasons for* the imposition of liability. They are evidentiary markers which do a respectable job of identifying cheapest cost-avoiders going forward.

The separate weaknesses of the economic theory of tort compound into a larger whole because the structural and substantive elements of tort law themselves form a unified whole. 'The relations among the central concepts of tort law—wrong, duty, responsibility, and repair—are best understood as expressing the fundamental normative significance of the victim-injurer relationship as it is expressed in the principle of corrective justice.'[41] Because economic analysis fails to explain both the structural and the substantive cores of tort, it cannot do justice to the larger whole that they form.

The success of corrective justice as a theory of tort is the flip side of the failure of economic analysis. The basic structural features and main concepts of tort law embody the principle of corrective justice. The bilateral form of the lawsuit tracks the substantive responsibility of a wrongdoer for the wrongful losses that he or she has inflicted. The retrospective character of tort adjudication reflects the fact that tort law is corrective—the fact that its sovereign principle requires wrongdoers to repair the wrongful losses that they have inflicted. Duty and breach articulate criteria of *wrongfulness* and thereby ensure that the law of tort honours the principle of corrective justice in its robust form. If tort regularly enjoined repair of losses that stemmed from *innocent* conduct, it could not be said that the law of tort institutes the principle 'that individuals who are responsible for the *wrongful* losses of others have a duty to repair them.'[42] Causation connects the wrongdoer to the loss wrongfully suffered by the victim and so plays an essential role in establishing the special responsibility of the wrongdoer for that loss.

Corrective justice thus gives each of the elements of a typical tort suit an unforced, intuitive interpretation and justification. The institutional practice of tort law instantiates and fleshes out the abstract moral principle of corrective justice.

III. RIGHTS AND RESPONSIBILITIES IN TORT

In thinking about the law of torts, it is natural to distinguish between primary (or substantive) responsibilities and secondary (or remedial) ones. Primary responsibilities in tort are responsibilities to avoid harming others in various ways, to avoid violating certain of their rights even when no harm is thereby done, or to avoid unreasonably failing to repair harm

---

[41] ibid, at 23.
[42] See, eg, ibid at 15, 36 (emphasis added).

reasonably inflicted.[43] Remedial responsibilities are responsibilities of repair, responsibilities triggered by the breach of various primary obligations.

When the distinction between these two kinds of responsibilities is noted, it is natural to think that primary responsibilities are, well, primary—that is, antecedent to and more important than secondary ones. Primary responsibilities in tort are omnilateral and standing.[44] We are all obligated, for example, not to defame or defraud one another. Omnilateral obligations, moreover, are not the same as indefinitely extensible bilateral ones. When obligations are omnilateral, what we owe to one person may be affected by what we owe to other people. The incorporation of the traffic code rule 'speed limit 25 [in the vicinity of primary and secondary schools] when children are present' into Californian tort law is a mundane case in point.[45] That norm makes the care owed to any one child depend in part on whether that child is in the company of other children. Whereas primary responsibilities in tort are omnilateral and standing, tort's remedial responsibilities are bilateral and conditional. If I defame or defraud you, you may require me to repair the harm that I have done. That obligation, however, is particular to me, owed to you, and conditioned on my breach of my primary obligation of harm avoid-

---

[43] The second clause of this sentence refers to circumstances where tort law protects autonomy rights. Some batteries, trespasses, and conversions are cases in point: see text accompanying n 93 below. The last clause of the sentence describes the general character of strict liability in tort. The duty here has the structure of eminent domain doctrine, transposed to the realm of private law. Just as eminent domain makes the payment of just compensation a condition for the legitimate taking of private property for a public purpose, so too strict liability doctrines in tort make reparation for harm done a condition for the legitimate infliction of certain reasonable risks (eg, the risks of blasting) or harms (eg, the harm reasonably inflicted on the plaintiff's dock when you lash your ship to the dock in a hurricane to avoid the ship's destruction). I shall have more to say about strict liability in part IV(D)(ii) below.

The distinction between primary or substantive obligations and remedial ones in tort is a familiar one: see, eg, TC Grey, 'Accidental Torts' (2001) 54 *Vanderbilt Law Review* 1225, 1242–44. The distinction is naturally salient when corrective justice conceptions of tort are under consideration: see, eg, KW Simons, 'Jules Coleman and Corrective Justice in Tort Law: A Critique and Reformulation' (1992) 15 *Harvard Journal of Law and Public Policy* 849, 867–68; H Sheinman, 'Tort Law and Corrective Justice' (2003) 22 *Law and Philosophy* 21, 32–34. For the sake of convenience, I will refer to primary duties as 'duties of harm avoidance', even though duties of harm avoidance are only the most common kind of primary duty in tort.

[44] There are exceptions to this rule, but they all appear to involve affirmative obligations. These exceptional obligations are bilateral, affirmative, and have a quasi-contractual quality in that they arise out of assumptions of responsibility on the part of one person toward another: see R Stevens, *Torts and Rights* (Oxford, Oxford University Press, 2007) 9–14, 114–24; A Beever, *Rediscovering the Law of Negligence* (Oxford, Hart Publishing, 2007) ch 8.

[45] Cal Veh Code § 22352(a)(2). Not all tort duties are sensitive to the numbers. While greater precautions may be necessary to make a skyscraper safe, the fact that skyscrapers house more people than single family homes do is not a reason to make the homes less safe.

ance. Secondary, remedial responsibilities thus come into play only when primary, substantive responsibilities are not discharged.

The fact that primary obligations are omnilateral, not bilateral is of immense importance. Primary obligations in tort are owed by everyone, and primary rights in tort are good against everyone. This fact must play a decisive role in determining the character and content of tort obligations. To put the matter in a Kantian idiom, primary responsibilities must be articulated by asking if they could be willed generally—as binding law for a plurality of persons, with distinct ends and aspirations, concerned to interact with each other on mutually acceptable terms—not whether they could be willed bilaterally, between one particular plaintiff and one particular defendant.[46] The facts that tort rights and obligations attach to persons simply *as* persons residing within some jurisdiction, and run from every person in the jurisdiction to every other person, need to be front and centre in our thinking about the character and content of primary obligations. It is therefore unhelpful simply to relax, or broaden, our conception of corrective justice so that it encompasses primary obligations as well as secondary ones. Importing the bilateral logic of remedial rights into our understanding of primary rights only serves to distort our understanding of primary rights and responsibilities.[47]

The priority of primary responsibilities is in part a logical or conceptual one. Remedial responsibilities arise out of the breach of antecedent primary duties.[48] But the priority of primary responsibilities is not just conceptual, it is also normative.[49] Remedial responsibilities are second-best ways of complying with obligations that are best honoured by discharging primary responsibilities. Remedial responsibilities draw their obligatory force from the persisting normative pull of the primary obligation that has not been discharged. Suppose, for example, that Arthur punches Jules in the nose without provocation, excuse, or justification. Arthur has battered Jules, breaching his obligation not to do so and violating Jules' right

---

[46] Here, I think that I am in substantial agreement with a sentiment expressed by Stevens, above n 44, at 328 ('the scope of our rights is not solely determined by considerations of what is fair as between claimant and defendant, ignoring all others').

[47] For an example of such an approach see Wright, above n 13. The substantive basis of corrective justice is distinct from corrective justice itself.

[48] See, eg, Coleman, *The Practice of Principle*, above n 3, at 32 ('Someone does not incur a second-order duty of repair unless he has failed to discharge some first-order duty'); Sheinman, above n 43, at 30–31 (explaining the conceptual or functional priority of primary obligations in tort law).

[49] For observations along these lines, see N MacCormick, *Legal Right and Social Democracy: Essays in Legal and Political Philosophy* (Oxford, Oxford University Press, 1982) ch 11; J Raz, 'Personal Practical Conflicts' in P Baumann and M Betzler (eds), *Practical Conflicts: New Philosophical Essays* (Cambridge, Cambridge University Press, 2004) 172, 182. This line of argument is developed powerfully by John Gardner and is dubbed 'the continuity thesis': J Gardner, *What Is Tort Law For? Part I: The Place of Corrective Justice* (Oxford Legal Studies Research Paper No 1/2010, University of Oxford, 18 January 2010) at ssrn.com/abstract=1538342, accessed on 28 January 2011.

that he not do so. By battering Jules, Arthur has neither discharged his obligation *not* to batter Jules nor relieved himself of the responsibility to comply with that obligation. Arthur is still bound by the obligation that he has breached, but he has placed himself in a position where he cannot comply fully with its commands. Now, the best that Arthur can do is to repair the harm that he has wrongly done. His duty to repair that harm arises out of his failure to discharge his duty not to harm Jules wrongly in the first place.

What this example shows is that primary responsibilities ground remedial ones. The first-best way of complying with tort obligations is not to harm anyone, or violate their rights in ways that tort law proscribes. Repairing the harm you have done by violating someone's right is the next-best way of respecting that right. It would have been better not to violate their right in the first instance. The flip side of this coin is that primary rights—to reasonable care, not to be battered, and so on—are more important than remedial ones. My right to reasonable care is best respected when others take care not to injure me, not when they repair the harm that they have done by carelessly injuring me. Given the choice between a law of torts which effects perfect compliance with its obligations of repair and one that effects perfect compliance with primary responsibilities of harm avoidance, we should not hesitate a moment before choosing perfect compliance with primary responsibilities of harm avoidance. When the primary norms of the law of torts are perfectly complied with, there is no work left for its remedial norms.

The general point here is that in tort law, as elsewhere, remedies exist to enforce and to restore rights.[50] The *prospect* of a remedy helps to assure a right-holder that they can enforce their right if necessary and by so doing, gives others reason to respect their right. The *enforcement* of a remedy when a right has been violated serves to restore the right. To be sure, rights and remedies are reciprocal: we look to a right to determine what a remedy should be, and we look to a remedy to determine what a right is. The two go hand in hand and must be understood in relation to one another. Even so—and even though remedies are partially

---

[50] See, eg, *Smothers v Gresham Transfer Inc* 23 P 3d 333 (Or 1999) 348, 356 (Leeson J). HM Hart Jr and AM Sacks, *The Legal Process: Basic Problems in the Making and Application of Law* (WN Eskridge Jr and PP Frickey eds, New York, Foundation Press, 1994) 122 (emphases in original) give a classic formulation of this point:

> Every general directive arrangement contemplates something which it expects or hopes to happen when the arrangement works successfully. This is the primary purpose of the arrangement, and the provisions which describe what this purpose is are the *primary provisions*.

> Every arrangement, however, must contemplate also the possibility that on occasion its directions will not be complied with. ... The provisions of an arrangement which tell what happens in the event of noncompliance or other deviation may be called the *remedial provisions*.

constitutive of rights—remedies are also properly the servants of rights. Remedies are governed by and subordinate to rights because the content and the contours of a remedy ought to be fixed by determining what the enforcement or the restoration of the right requires.

In tort, the remedy fixed upon by corrective justice theorists—the duty to repair a loss—is pre-eminent because tort is preoccupied with harm in general and physical harm in particular. Harms—broken arms or legs, for example—leave their victims with injuries to be repaired (if the underlying right not to be harmed is to be restored). When this is not the case— when the underlying right is, say, to exclusive control or dominion over real property and the violation of that right does not inflict an injury to be repaired—the appropriate remedy is different, and it is quite wrong to say that the tort instantiates the corrective justice principle that wrongful losses should be repaired. For example, injunctive relief is available as a matter of right in trespass cases because injunctive relief normally restores the right to control who or what enters one's real property.[51] Remedying harmless trespasses by requiring merely that the wrongdoer repair the harm that he or she has wrongly done would not vindicate the right. The violation of the right need not result in harm. Making reparation for harm done the standard remedy for trespass would, indeed, enable those whose trespasses inflict no injury to continue trespassing as long as they were prepared to pay nominal damages.[52] In both the trespass case and the wrongful physical injury case, the remedy is governed by the right. The duty to repair wrongful loss figures prominently in tort only because most torts involve harms, and harms leave their victims worse off—in need of repair.

The lesson of these examples is that remedies are prominent in tort, but their prominence is not the consequence of tort law's adherence to a free-standing principle of corrective justice. Remedies are prominent in tort because rights are fundamental to tort and there is a unity of right

[51] 'Generally an injunction will lie to restrain repeated trespasses': *Planned Parenthood of Mid-Iowa v Maki* 478 NW 2d 637 (Iowa 1991) 639 (Larson, Carter, Lavorato and Snell JJ). See generally DB Dobbs, *Dobbs' Law of Remedies: Damages, Equity, Restitution*, 2nd edn (St Paul MN, West Publishing, 1993). The point here is not that injunctive relief is the appropriate remedy for harmless torts and only for harmless torts, but that right determines remedy in the sense that the proper remedy is the remedy that enforces, restores, or vindicates the right. Trespass is an instance of an important category of torts which protect 'autonomy rights'—powers of control or zones of discretionary choice. Following Arthur Ripstein I call torts of this kind 'sovereignty-based' torts: see below n 65 and accompanying text.

[52] In *Jacque v Steenberg Homes Inc* 563 NW 2d 154 (Wis 1997), punitive damages were awarded against a defendant who had dragged a trailer home across the plaintiff's snow-covered property without the plaintiff's permission. Because its trespass did no harm, the defendant was otherwise liable only for nominal damages. The award of punitive damages both punished a deliberate, harmless trespass and enforced the plaintiff's right to exclusive control by stripping that one-shot trespass of the economic advantage that made its commission rational.

and remedy. You do not have a legal right unless you have some remedy for its violation.[53] When Arthur punches Jules in the nose, he violates Jules' right to the physical integrity of his person. If Jules has no legal remedy for that violation of his right, his right is legally meaningless. Absent some special institutional arrangement, Jules' claim for redress is naturally directed against Arthur. After all, Arthur is the person who has violated Jules' right. By so doing, he has opened himself up to responsibility for restoring Jules' right. He stands in a special and unique relation of responsibility to Jules.

Putting remedial responsibility at the centre of tort distorts our understanding of the subject in subtler ways as well. By mistakenly identifying tort and tort alone with responsibilities of repair, remedial theories misconceive tort law's relation to the rest of private law. Rightly, remedial theories recognise that tort law enforces and restores rights in a particular way, namely, by enabling the victims of tortious wrongdoing to obtain redress for the wrongs done to them from those who have done them wrong. This, however, is a distinctive feature of private law in general, not a distinctive feature of the law of torts in particular. Contract, property, and restitution also enforce rights by empowering those whose rights have been violated to seek redress from those who have done the violating. If a duty of *repair* is more characteristic of tort than it is of contract or restitution, that is because primary tort rights differ from primary contract or restitutionary rights, and those differences are reflected in the corresponding remedies. We lose sight of the fact that private law in general has a distinctive relation to rights when we identify responsibility to restore a right wrongly violated with tort and tort alone. And we fail entirely to see that tort is distinguished from other private law subjects by the character of the primary rights and obligations it enforces.

Putting responsibilities of repair at the centre of tort law also obscures tort law's relation to administrative alternatives to tort, such as workers' compensation. When we take the common law of tort to be defined by duties of repair owed to named victims by named tortfeasors, we must regard workers' compensation and similar administrative schemes as radically discontinuous with the law of torts. After all, these schemes abolish private law duties of repair and private law mechanisms for the enforcement of rights and replace them with public law systems and mechanisms.

---

[53] *Marbury v Madison* 5 US 137 (1803) 163 famously holds that 'the very essence of civil liberty ... consists in the right of every individual to claim the protection of the laws, whenever he receives an injury'. That holding invoked William Blackstone's claims that 'it is a general and indisputable rule, that where there is a legal right, there is also a legal remedy by suit or action at law, whenever that right is invaded' and that 'every right, when withheld, must have a remedy, and every injury its proper redress': at 163, quoting 3 Bl Comm 23, 109. Blackstone himself was following Coke: see, eg, 1 Bl Comm 55–56; 2 Co Inst 55–56, citing Magna Carta cls 39–40. The remedies clauses found in many American State Constitutions are a direct expression of the maxim that 'for every right there must be a remedy'.

While it is surely correct to say that workers' compensation is 'public law' and tort is 'private law', it is misleading to insist that the two legal regimes are radically discontinuous. Workers' compensation and the common law of torts are both continuous and discontinuous, connected and competitive.[54] They are continuous because they are both legal regimes which aim to institute the right to the physical integrity of one's person.[55] They are competitive because they are alternative legal mechanisms for instituting the same right with respect to various kinds of accidental injuries,[56] and they battle for dominion over various legal domains. Workers' compensation schemes, for example, displace the common law of negligence from the domain of workplace injuries. Administrative schemes for nuclear accidents, or health injuries incident to mining coal, displace tort from other domains.[57]

The proposition that administrative schemes such as workers' compensation and the common law of torts are alternative ways of instituting the right to the physical integrity of one's person seems obvious, but it bears on our understanding of tort only if we recognise that within the law of torts itself, remedial rights and responsibilities are derivative of primary—or substantive—ones. Only then can we conceive of these regimes as both competitive and continuous. If we identify tort with bilateral duties to repair wrongful losses, the two regimes will be radically discontinuous. One of the costs of taking them to be discontinuous is that we will forgo a first principle by reference to which we might choose intelligently between them. The question 'which legal regime gives better institutional expression to the right to physical safety?' will have been swept out of sight. Our law, however, regards tort and its administrative alternatives

---

[54] See, eg, J Smith, 'Sequel to Workmen's Compensation Acts' (1914) 27 *Harvard Law Review* 235, 344 (arguing that the workmen's compensation acts were organised on a principle of strict liability which could not be reconciled with the fault liability of the common law of torts and prophesying that the common law of torts would be reconstructed to be more compatible with the normative logic of workers' compensation). For further discussion see GC Keating, 'The Theory of Enterprise Liability and Common Law Strict Liability' (2001) 54 *Vanderbilt Law Review* 1285.

[55] Historically, the law of torts has been preoccupied with physical harm, and thus with the right to physical security. Over time, however, the law of torts has come to grant more protection against psychological harm. Thus, the right that the text is referring to has been transformed from a right to physical integrity into a right to physical and psychological integrity. For simplicity, I will generally speak of this right as a right to physical or bodily integrity or security.

[56] Or even all accidental injuries, as with the New Zealand Accident Compensation Scheme.

[57] In addition to workers' compensation, these schemes include automobile no-fault plans; the Black Lung Benefits Act of 1972, 30 USC §§ 901–945; the Price-Anderson Act, 42 USC § 2210 governing nuclear accidents; the National Childhood Vaccine Injury Act of 1986, 42 USC §§ 300aa-1 to 300aa-34; and the Accident Compensation Act 2001 (NZ). This last scheme, of course, takes all accidental injuries away from tort.

as members of the same family of institutions. And it should: these institutional arrangements are alternative ways of instituting the same right.[58]

This view of the matter should not be surprising. To see why, bear in mind, first, that it is a feature of rights that they justify 'successive waves of duty'.[59] The right to reasonable care for protection against physical harm is backed by ancillary procedural and remedial rights. The same right to the physical security of one's person which justifies imposing the primary duty of reasonable care to avoid causing foreseeable physical harm to others also justifies the duty to repair harm negligently inflicted, and for that remedial right to be effective, the state must be under a duty to provide some avenue of 'civil recourse' through which rights or repair can be enforced.[60] Next, observe that the right to the physical and psychological security of one's person not only generates waves of duty, it also generates diverse primary duties. Within the law of tort itself, for example, that right justifies duties of reasonable care in negligence law, duties not to assault or batter other people, and duties to conduct abnormally dangerous activities only on condition that one repair the unavoidable harm that one does. The extension of the point that the right to the security of one's person—an abstract and protean right if ever there was one—justifies diverse primary obligations within tort is that this right may also justify displacing tort and adopting an administrative scheme, on the straightforward supposition that the administrative scheme does a

---

[58] This is most evident in litigation under State 'remedy clauses', but it is also evident in litigation under other legal doctrines over such matters as the adequacy of workers' compensation schemes or the nuclear power accident scheme. For remedy clause adjudication, see *Smothers v Gresham Transfer Inc* 23 P 3d 333 (Or 1999) 348, 356 (Leeson J); JH Bauman, 'Remedies Provisions in State Constitutions and the Proper Role of the State Courts' (1991) 26 *Wake Forest Law Review* 237; D Schuman, 'The Right to a Remedy' (1992) 65 *Temple Law Review* 1197. For other doctrines, see RE Keeton, LD Sargentich and GC Keating, *Tort and Accident Law*, 4th edn (St Paul MN, West Publishing, 2004) ch 22.

[59] J Waldron, *Liberal Rights: Collected Papers 1981–1991* (Cambridge, Cambridge University Press, 1993) 212:

> Even a particular duty, thought of as associated with a right, itself generates waves of duties that back it up and root it in the complex, messy reality of political life. The right not to be tortured, for example, clearly generates the duty not to torture. But, in various circumstances, that simple duty will be backed up by others: a duty to instruct people about the wrongness of torture; a duty to be vigilant about the danger of, and temptation to, torture; a duty to ameliorate situations in which torture might be thought likely to occur; and so on. Once it is discovered that people have been tortured, the right generates remedial duties such as the duty to rescue people from torture, the duty on governments to find out who is doing and authorizing the torture, remove them from office, and bring them to justice, the duty to set up safeguards to prevent recurrence of the abuses, and so on.

[60] This last point is emphasised by the 'civil recourse theory' of John Goldberg and Ben Zipursky: see Goldberg and Zipursky, above n 4. On the view of 'civil recourse' presented in the text it is essentially complementary to, not competitive with, corrective justice. Both involve secondary responsibilities necessary to institute effectively the primary duties of tort law.

better job of securing the right. When a common law remedy is set aside and replaced by an administrative scheme, the question that courts most commonly ask is whether the administrative scheme provides an adequate alternative remedy for the underlying right.[61] Workers' compensation and tort, for instance, are understood and assessed as alternative ways of instituting the same right to the safety of one's person.

From the vantage point of a view which takes primary rights and responsibilities to form the heart of the law of torts, these decisions ask the right question. Taking our cue from the remark in the *Second Restatement of Torts* that the interest in bodily security is 'protected against not only intentional invasion but [also] against negligent invasion or invasion by the mischances inseparable from an abnormally dangerous activity',[62] we might frame the choice between tort and various administrative alternatives as a matter of which institutional arrangement gives more satisfactory expression to the right that they share in common. The private law of tort *is the natural default* legal institution for the enforcement of the right to the physical integrity of one's person because when one person violates another person's right to the physical integrity of his or her person, responsibility to repair the harm wrongly done naturally falls on the wrongdoer. But it is *only* the natural default. The private law of tort can be displaced by administrative alternatives so long as those alternatives are defensible ways of instituting the underlying right to the security of one's person.

IV. THE STRUCTURE AND CONTENT OF PRIMARY NORMS

Corrective justice theory is right to place wrongs at the centre of tort, but wrong to call the repair of wrongful losses the 'overarching ambition or purpose' of tort law.[63] Torts are indeed wrongs—violations of rights which protect interests important enough to be made coercively enforceable by law—but it is better for wrongs not to be done in the first place than it is to erase their untoward effects once they have been committed. The corrective justice principle that wrongful losses should be repaired is indeed prominent in the law of torts, but it is not prominent because it is the fundamental principle on which the law of torts is built. It is prominent because most—though not *all*—tortious wrongs involve harms and therefore leave their victims in conditions requiring repair. Or so I have argued.[64]

---

[61] See above n 58 and accompanying text.

[62] *Restatement of the Law, Second: Torts* (St Paul MN, American Law Institute, 1965) (*Second Restatement*) § 1 comment d. The right to bodily security thus grounds diverse tort obligations. I am grateful to Mark Geistfeld for calling my attention to this comment.

[63] Coleman, *Risks and Wrongs*, above n 12, at 395.

[64] This statement may need to be qualified in the case of strict liability. Because we believe harm may be done justifiably in cases of strict liability and because the basic reason

A. Why Primary Norms Explain the Prominence of Corrective Justice in Tort

The argument that the prominent place of corrective justice in tort is accounted for by the character of tortious wrongs warrants further discussion. Most torts protect against harm in one of its manifestations. An important minority of intentional torts, however, guard aspects of our 'sovereignty'.[65] Sovereignty-based torts proscribe various interferences with zones of control or powers of discretion—control, for example, over one's physical person or one's real property. These torts protect important boundaries against unauthorised crossings. Sovereignty-based torts can be committed without doing harm, and indeed, while benefiting their victims. If I operate on your ear without your permission and succeed in curing your earache, I have not harmed you. You are better off, not worse off. Nonetheless, I have violated your rights and committed the tort of battery because I have operated on you without your consent.[66] In the same vein, I may not enter your real property without your permission, even if I thereby improve that property.[67]

For our purposes, the first lesson taught by these torts is that when primary rights do not protect against harms, the proper remedy for their violation is not repair of wrongful loss. These torts are thus clear counter-examples to the thesis that tort law instantiates the corrective justice principle that wrongful losses should be repaired. The tort of trespass pro-

for imposing such liability is to prevent the defendant from loading the cost of its justified conduct off on the plaintiff who does not benefit proportionately from that conduct, there is a question whether damages serve a corrective or commutative role. They serve a corrective role if they rectify a wrong; a commutative one if they align burden and benefit. We cannot pursue this question here.

[65] I borrow the term 'sovereignty-based' from A Ripstein, 'Beyond the Harm Principle' (2006) 34 *Philosophy and Public Affairs* 215. He is not responsible for my usage. 'Sovereignty-based' torts protect the exercise of powers whereas 'harm-based' torts ground duties whose protections are enjoyed. This distinction is drawn nicely in L Wenar, 'The Nature of Rights' (2005) 33 *Philosophy and Public Affairs* 223, 233. The shorthand distinction between 'harm-based' and 'sovereignty-based' torts is not meant to imply that the former do not involve rights whereas the latter do. The point, rather, is that some tort rights are grounded in harm whereas others are grounded in autonomy. More cumbersomely, we might call these torts 'autonomy rights-based torts' and distinguish them from 'harm rights-based torts'.

[66] See, eg, *Mohr v Williams* 104 NW 12 (Minn 1905); *Kennedy v Parrott* 90 SE 2d 754 (NC 1956). This prohibition against invasive medical procedures conducted without consent reveals a face of battery different from its usual preoccupation with physical harm. This aspect of battery protects persons' *authority* over their physical bodies. A medical procedure conducted without the consent of the subject is an affront to the subject's authority over his or her person, but does not *impair* the subject's bodily integrity in the way that physical harm does. It is one thing to impair agency and another to deny it.

[67] See, eg, *Longenecker v Zimmerman* 267 P 2d 543 (Kan 1954). Believing that cedar trees near the boundary of her property were on her side of the line, the defendant had them topped, trimmed, and cleaned of bagworms. In fact, they were on plaintiff's property. The defendant had trespassed and was liable for nominal damages, despite the plaintiff having benefited from her acts.

tects the interest in dominion over real property and the right to exclusive control that interest grounds. Put differently, the tort of trespass protects the exercise of a power, namely, the power to determine who and what will enter your property. When that right is violated and that power is denied the proper remedy is one that restores the power. That restoration is normally accomplished by injunctive relief.[68] Remedies are the servants of rights. The repair of wrongful losses—corrective justice as Coleman conceives it—is only appropriate when that is what is required to restore the relevant right. In tort, it is often but not always the case that restoration of the right requires reparation. The connection of tort to corrective justice is thus a consequence of the fact that most torts involve harms.

B. The Principle of Corrective Justice is Formal, and Not Confined to Tort

To see the dependence of tort's distinctive remedial norms on the characteristic content of its primary norms, consider the natural extension of the principle that wrongful losses ought to be repaired by those responsible for their infliction. That principle is *formal*: it does not contain within itself any criterion of wrongfulness. It latches onto many torts because we have independent reasons for thinking of torts as wrongs, and many tortious wrongs cause losses. We subconsciously supply the content that the principle requires. This is perfectly natural. We already know that tort is the canonical law of wrongs, and that harm is its principal preoccupation. Without that subconscious sleight of hand, however, the principle of corrective justice would wander the law looking for wrongful losses to repair.

The wrongs that we find, moreover, depend on the content that we supply. The domain of corrective justice is heavily shaped by how broadly or narrowly we state the principle of corrective justice. When we interpret corrective justice as having to do with the repair of wrongful *loss*, restitution does not do corrective justice because it undoes wrongful *gain*. On a broader interpretation of corrective justice, the undoing of wrongful gain might be as much a matter of corrective justice as the repair of wrongful loss.[69] And if we adopt a conception which does not insist on

---

[68] See above n 51 and accompanying text.

[69] Weinrib takes this broader view of the matter, because he thinks of correlativity of right and duty as the essence of corrective justice: *The Idea of Private Law*, above n 5, at 122–26. Restitution does corrective justice even though it involves wrongful gain not wrongful loss because it involves a breach of duty correlative to the plaintiff's right: at 140–41, 197–98. Weinrib's broad conception of corrective justice also encompasses contract damages: at 136–40.

bilaterality, we are likely to find some wrongful losses in various pockets of public law.[70]

Similar issues arise with respect to contract law. If contract is really about reliance—as Lon Fuller thought—then breach of contract results in wrongful loss and contract damages do corrective justice, even on a narrow interpretation of the principle. If, however, contract is about expectation then contract damages are about being put in the position that one would have occupied had the contract been performed.[71] That counts as corrective justice only if corrective justice is broadly construed.[72] When corrective justice is construed that broadly, however, it can no longer be presented as the paramount principle of liability in tort. It is now at least a principle of private law in general, and it may well be a general principle of law.

Just how broadly to state the principle of corrective justice is not, however, our concern. For our purposes, the point is that wrongful loss is neither unique to tort nor characteristic of all torts. Corrective justice is therefore not distinctive to tort. It is common for tort law to do corrective justice, but only because most torts involve harms and therefore result in wrongful losses. For example, unlike the tort of battery, the general duty of due care does not protect a boundary against an impermissible crossing. That duty guards the right to 'bodily security'[73] by requiring everyone to take appropriate precautions to avoid physically harming others. Breaches of the duty which violate a correlative right to 'bodily security' leave their victims in conditions where repair is required. Because most torts are like negligence in that they protect against harms, most torts bring to bear the corrective justice principle that wrongful losses should be repaired. They do so, however, not because corrective justice is the paramount principle of tort, but because this remedy restores the primary right.[74]

C. Justice and Rights in Tort

The corrective justice theory of tort goes wrong in the way that retributivism goes wrong as a theory of criminal law. Just as we do not have the criminal law in order to punish the wicked, so too we do not have

---

[70] See generally L Smith, 'Corrective Justice and Public Law' (Paper presented at the Obligations V Conference: Rights and Private Law, University of Oxford, 14–16 July 2010).

[71] See, eg, LL Fuller and WR Perdue Jr, 'The Reliance Interest in Contract Damages I' (1936) 46 *Yale Law Journal* 52, and compare D Friedmann, 'The Performance Interest in Contract Damages' (1995) 111 *Law Quarterly Review* 628 with Sheinman, above n 43, at 61–62.

[72] See above n 69.

[73] See above n 62 and accompanying text.

[74] This statement may need to be qualified in the case of strict liability. See above n 64.

the law of torts in order to repair wrongful losses.[75] The 'overarching aim or purpose' of the law of torts is not to repair harm wrongly done, but to articulate certain obligations to others, obligations grounded in interests of persons urgent enough to count as rights and ground duties. The wrongs that tort law recognises spell out an important part of what we owe to each other in the way of coercively enforceable responsibilities, by virtue of our essential interests as persons.[76] The rights that those responsibilities respect have to do, for the most part, with liberty and security, broadly construed. Primary obligations in tort are obligations not to harm other people in various ways, and to respect powers which confer on them authority over their persons and possessions. To be sure, tort guards these rights with remedial responsibilities of repair, but repair is a second-best form of protection. Tort obligations are discharged most fully when harm is not done and rights are respected in the first instance, not when harm wrongly done is repaired after the fact.

Because tort law is fundamentally concerned with the question of what we may reasonably demand from each other as a matter of right with respect to the liberty and security of our persons and property, tort is basically concerned with *justice,* but the justice that lies at the base of tort law is *not corrective.* Analytically, corrective justice is parasitic on primary obligations and those primary obligations are not obligations of corrective justice. Coleman himself observes:

> [C]orrective justice is an account of the second-order duty of repair. Someone does not incur a second-order duty of repair unless he has failed to discharge some first-order duty. However, the relevant first-order duties are not themselves duties of corrective justice.[77]

Corrective justice does not come into play until an antecedent wrong exists. With the possible exception of strict liability wrongs—where the primary duty is not to harm without repairing and where the primary wrong thus consists in harming without repairing[78]—tortious wrongs themselves are

---

[75] Coleman anticipates this criticism and argues that retributivism is a defensible explanatory and justificatory theory of punishment: *The Practice of Principle,* above n 3, at 32–33. He is quite right about this, but the observation is beside the point. Coleman claims not that corrective justice is a defensible theory of *tort remedies,* but that 'tort law is best explained by corrective justice' because 'at its core tort law seeks to repair wrongful losses': at 9, 36. See also above n 3 and accompanying text. Just as retributivism is only plausible as a theory of criminal punishment, so too corrective justice is only plausible as a theory of tort remedies. Cf Sheinman, above n 43, at 46–47.

[76] The exact content of what we owe to each other in the way of tort obligations depends on the jurisdiction in which we find ourselves, but the basis of our varying obligations is the same, namely, our equal personhood.

[77] Coleman, *The Practice of Principle,* above n 3, at 32 (emphasis altered).

[78] Under the 'private eminent domain' model of strict liability, it is permissible to undertake certain actions and activities only when two conditions are met. First, the acts and activities must be conducted reasonably. Secondly, those who undertake those acts and activities must repair any physical harm done by their conduct. Whereas negligence liabil-

not corrective injustices. It is wrong to punch someone else in the face absent justification or excuse, but it is not a corrective injustice.

Committing battery is wrong not because it fails to correct a prior wrongful interaction, but because it violates a primary obligation to avoid either (a) physically harming another person or (b) making contact with them in a way which is offensive because it denies their sovereignty over their own person. That primary obligation is, in turn, grounded in the victim's right to the integrity of his or her person.[79] More generally, torts—fraud, battery, intentional infliction of emotional distress, negligent infliction of physical injury, and the like—are wrongs which presuppose rights, not antecedent corrective injustices.[80] People have rights, for example, not to be defrauded. Deception destroys freedom every bit as much as coercion does. Autonomy is the power to set and act on one's own ends and reasons, on one's own plans and purposes. Deception manipulates people's minds and thereby robs them of their autonomous agency. Fraud's victims are no longer the authors of their own actions; they are the unwitting instruments of the wills of those who have deceived them. We have compelling reasons to object to such treatment, and even more so when our cooperation is unwittingly enlisted in economic transactions that are injurious to us.

Primary obligations in tort are thus grounded in people's rights. It is wrong to batter someone because it violates their right to physical integrity; it is wrong to imprison someone falsely because it violates their right to liberty; it is wrong to injure someone negligently because it violates their right to reasonable security; and so on. The question of what rights people have is not a question of corrective justice. If anything, it is a question of distributive justice.[81] Taxonomy aside, the substantive

---

ity is predicated on *primary* criticism of conduct, strict liability is predicated on *secondary* criticism of conduct. Negligence faults the doing of harm in the first instance; strict liability faults the failure to make reparation for harm reasonably done. Negligence liability is liability for harm done by *unreasonable* conduct whereas strict liability is liability for harm done by *reasonable* conduct. Its fundamental justification is that the costs of necessary or justified harms should be borne by those who benefit from their infliction. See, eg, Grey, above n 43, at 1275–81; FH Bohlen, 'Incomplete Privilege to Inflict Intentional Invasions of Interests of Property and Personality' (1926) 39 *Harvard Law Review* 307; RE Keeton, 'Conditional Fault in the Law of Torts' (1959) 72 *Harvard Law Review* 401.

[79] As the *Second Restatement* recognises: see above n 62.

[80] Weinrib appears to deny this. He writes, 'Corrective justice serves a normative function: a transaction is required, on pain of rectification, to conform to its contours': *The Idea of Private Law*, above n 5, at 76. Corrective justice is thus about the righting of corrective injustices (actions which, say, disturb 'the equality between the parties': at 76). This is, as Gardner says, a 'non-starter': see Gardner, above n 49, at 28. See also Sheinman, above n 43, at 34–36. With the possible exception of strict liability wrongs, where the wrong consists in harming without repairing, torts are wrongs—not corrective injustices.

[81] Theorists are split on this point. Stephen Perry, for one, thinks that rights to the liberty and integrity of our person precede questions of distributive justice: see SR Perry, 'On the Relationship Between Corrective Justice and Distributive Justice' in J Horder (ed) *Oxford Essays in Jurisprudence: Fourth Series* (Oxford, Oxford University Press, 2000) 237, 239:

point is this: tort law is not fundamentally about corrective justice, it is fundamentally about wrongs, and wrongs are grounded in rights. Corrective justice broadly construed is *an* essential aspect of tort because rights require remedies, and remedies require making right one's wrongs.[82] This truth does not, however, make the obligation to repair wrongful losses the sovereign principle of tort.

D. The Structure of Tort Law

Corrective justice theory identifies tort law with its adjudicative incarnation and its remedial phase. The structural features of tort that it counts as core—tort's bilateral marrying of a single plaintiff to a single defendant, with strictly correlative rights and duties; its backward-looking focus on whether the defendant complied with a binding standard of conduct; its concern with repairing wrongful losses—are all aspects of tort law in its remedial phase. Because the first question of tort law is just what it is that we owe to others in the way of respect for their persons, their property, and a diverse set of their 'intangible interests', it is a mistake to identify tort law with tort adjudication. The first task of tort is the articulation of primary obligations. The structure of primary obligations therefore has a better claim to be the core of tort than the structure of remedial responsibilities does. And that structure is quite different from the structure emphasised by corrective justice theories.

If corrective justice theory misconceives the content of tort law by insisting that it must involve wrongful loss, it also misconceives the structure of tort law in three distinct ways. First, by emphasising the bilateral struc-

---

At least within non-consequentialist moral theory, it makes sense to think of this [security] interest as morally fundamental, and hence as falling outside the purview of distributive justice; our physical persons belong to us from the outset, and are accordingly not subject to a social distribution of any kind.

On this conception, the question of what rights people have is a question of justice, but not a question of distributive justice. Other usages of the term distributive justice appear to include within its domain the question of what rights people have on the ground that this is one kind of question about the distribution of entitlements. HLA Hart's references to rights as concerned with the distribution of freedom in HLA Hart, 'Are There Any Natural Rights?' (1955) 64 *Philosophical Review* 175, 178 fits this description, as does Rawls' usage. See, eg, J Rawls, *A Theory of Justice*, rev edn (Cambridge MA, Harvard University Press, 1999) 54 (emphasis added): 'the basic structure of society distributes certain primary goods ... the chief primary goods *at the disposition of society* are rights, liberties, and opportunities, and income and wealth.' For an example of distributive justice being used in this broader sense in connection with private law, see P Cane, 'Corrective Justice and Correlativity in Private Law' (1996) 16 *Oxford Journal of Legal Studies* 471, 481.

[82] This broad conception of corrective justice is similar to the view taken by Tony Honoré, but it may be even broader. See T Honoré, *Responsibility and Fault* (Oxford, Hart Publishing, 1999) 73: 'On a wide view, [corrective justice] requires those who have without justification harmed others by their conduct to put the matter right.'

ture of tort lawsuits, corrective justice theory gets the formal character of primary tort norms wrong, and gives them a curiously personal cast. For the most part, primary obligations in tort are omnilateral not bilateral; they are owed by everyone and to everyone else.[83] And characteristically modern tortious wrongs have an abstract and general quality, not a personal, particular one. The negligent infliction of accidental physical harm, for example, is usually an abstract and general wrong: a failure to exercise care in order to protect an indefinite plurality of potential victims whose persons and property we might otherwise unreasonably endanger. Because primary tort norms are articulated though private lawsuits, the structure of the typical tort lawsuit conceals this truth instead of making it manifest. The bilateral and personal form of the lawsuit does not mirror the omnilateral obligations and impersonal norms that tort adjudication generates.

Secondly, not all primary obligations are properly expressed as standards of conduct and not all tort liability attaches to wrongful conduct. If corrective justice requires wrongful losses issuing from wrongful conduct, then significant chunks of tort law are not compatible with corrective justice. Strict liability in tort exists, and it attaches to conduct that is justified or innocent, not wrongful. When strict liability is the prevailing liability rule, the primary obligation is to make reparation for harm fairly attributed to one's *justified or faultless* conduct. Strict liability wrongs are wrongs, but they are not conduct-based wrongs. The wrong lies in not repairing harm faultlessly inflicted, but rightly attributed to the tortfeasor's agency, in circumstance where it is reasonable to inflict harm, but unreasonable to ask that the victim of that harm bear its financial cost.

Thirdly and lastly, even tort's remedial responsibilities have a forward-looking role to play. Remedial responsibilities enforce rights, in addition to restoring them. The prospect of remedial responsibility serves to assure compliance with primary responsibilities not to inflict harm requiring repair. Paradoxically, then, remedial responsibilities uphold the rights they guard most fully when they diminish the number of occasions on which a remedy is required.

(i) The Properties of Primary Obligations

Tort law, to be sure, is not regulation. Tort is a common law legal institution, and it develops law through adjudication. But it does apply and articulate *law*, not just settle disputes. Legal decisions are decisions in accordance with pre-existing norms, and tort rulings do not bind only the parties to the case at hand. Nor do common law legal decisions bind only retrospectively. Common law legal decisions have precedential force. Rulings in individual cases bind prospectively all who fall within their

---

[83] See above n 44.

scope. In their prospective aspect, tort rulings bind very generally. They govern indefinite classes of potential wrongdoers going forward indefinitely, and they protect indefinite classes of potential victims going forward indefinitely.[84]

In the general law of negligence, for example, duties are owed by classes of prospective injurers and to classes of potential victims. There are, indeed, few legal duties as general and few legal norms as abstract as the general obligation of reasonable care. That obligation is both owed by everyone and to everyone else and presumptively applies to all actions that create significant risks of physical harm. When corrective justice theories insist that duty and right in tort have a bilateral, one-on-one structure, they simply overlook this basic feature of the structure of rights and duties in tort. The result of this oversight is an oddly—and mistakenly—personal conception of tortious wrongs. Torts are presented as wrongs done to one named person by another.

Corrective justice gets its peculiarly personal conception of tortious wrongs from its preoccupation with the remedial dimension of tort. Tort law's remedial responsibilities *are* correlative to in personam rights. Duties of reparation in tort *are* owed to named plaintiffs and are owed by named defendants. Remedial rights are held by and against particular persons. Corrective justice theory is quite right about all of this, quite right to insist on the bilaterality of remedial rights and duties and on 'the unity of doing and suffering'.[85] Primary rights and obligations, however, are not personal in this way. Primary rights and obligations are omnilateral. Unlike contractual obligations, tort obligations do not arise between named persons. They are grounded in fundamental interests of persons qua persons and are owed by each of us to everyone else.

Again, the general law of negligence is a case in point. The obligation of reasonable care—the standing requirement that one conform one's conduct to the dictates of whatever it is that due care demands in the circumstances at hand—binds omnilaterally and prospectively, not bilaterally and retrospectively. Indeed, tort law's omnilateral and prospective primary obligations are the source of and *reason for* its bilateral remedial responsibilities. Because primary obligations are owed by each of us to all the rest of us, the responsibility to repair tortiously inflicted injury falls, in the first instance, on the person who has inflicted that injury and is owed to the person who has suffered that injury. When my doing is the source of your suffering—and tortiously so—I stand in a special relation of responsibility to you. My failure to honour my primary obligation not to tortiously injure you naturally gives rise to a special obligation to erase the effect of my wrong.

---

[84] cf Sheinman, above n 43, at 50–51 (discussing the doctrine of precedent in tort).
[85] As described by Weinrib, *The Idea of Private Law*, above n 5, at 145.

Because primary obligations and primary rights are antecedent to and grounding of remedial ones, the structure of primary rights and obligations has a better claim than the structure of remedial rights and obligations does to being an essential, structural feature of tort law.

(ii) Strict Liability Wrongs

Corrective justice theory's insistence on wrongful *conduct* as essential to tort law prevents it from giving an adequate account of strict liability in tort.[86] Negligence liability is predicated on wrongful conduct—on conduct that is unreasonable or unjustified. The competing principle of strict liability predicates responsibility not on unreasonable *conduct* in the natural and primary sense of that term, but on an unreasonable failure to repair harm reasonably inflicted. In *Vincent v Lake Erie Transportation Co*,[87] for instance, it is right and reasonable for the owner of the ship to lash the ship to the dock during the storm, even though he does not have permission to do so, but it is unreasonable and wrong for the shipowner to foist the cost of saving his ship off onto the owner of the dock. When docking results in harming, a duty to make reparation arises. That duty is breached when the dock owner doesn't volunteer, in a timely fashion, to pay for the harm he has inflicted. The lawsuit is brought to repair the wrong of failing to comply with that duty. That wrongful conduct is *secondary*, not *primary*.[88] The primary conduct—lashing the ship to the dock and damaging the dock—is not wrongful. The wrong lies in failing to step forward and repair the damage, even though that damage is justifiably done. Strict liability thus involves a wrong, but that wrong is not conduct-based in Coleman's sense of the term. Liability is not predicated on the assertion that the defendant should have behaved differently and not harmed the plaintiff.[89]

To be sure, strict liability is the exception and negligence the general rule. Strict liability is common enough, however, that we can reasonably insist that an adequate theory of tort be able to explain and justify its

---

[86] This is ironic because strict liability 'duties' are the only primary duties that might be plausibly described as corrective; they involve obligations not to harm without repairing.

[87] *Vincent v Lake Erie Transportation Co* 124 NW 221 (Minn 1910) (*Vincent*).

[88] See above n 78.

[89] The identification of tort with conduct-based wrongs is not particular to Coleman. Weinrib holds the same kind of view, a fact vividly illustrated by his criticisms of strict liability as a norm of conduct which condemns 'any penetration of the plaintiff's space': *The Idea of Private Law*, above n 5, at 177. For their part, Goldberg and Zipursky write that '[a]lthough by convention, strict liability for abnormally dangerous activities clearly is part of what lawyers define as "tort law", strictly speaking it does not belong in this department': JCP Goldberg and BC Zipursky, *The Oxford Introductions to US Law: Torts* (New York, Oxford University Press, 2010) 267. Any account of tort law which specifies the constitutive features of tortious wrongs in such a way that the account cannot acknowledge, or properly characterise, the existence of strict liability in tort is, for that reason alone, seriously defective and in need of revision.

existence as an alternative to negligence. Corrective justice theory flunks this test. In Coleman's case, corrective justice theory flunks the test in part because it conceives of much of strict liability as lying outside the core of tort that it succeeds in explaining,[90] and in part because it models strict liability on negligence. Whereas negligence liability imposes a duty to exercise reasonable care to avoid inflicting physical harm on others, strict liability, Coleman claims, imposes a duty not to harm others, full stop.

This misconceives strict liability. Structurally speaking, most strict liability in tort resembles the public law of eminent domain, not fault liability in tort. Indeed, strict liability *competes* with fault liability because it imposes liability on *reasonable* conduct. Eminent domain law holds that it is permissible for the government to take property for public use only if the government pays just compensation to those whose property it takes. This is a two part criterion. First, the taking must be justified; that is, it must be for a public use. Secondly, compensation must be paid for the property taken. In parallel fashion, strict liability in tort holds that it is permissible to undertake certain actions and activities only when two conditions are met. First, the acts and activities must be conducted reasonably. Secondly, those who undertake the acts and activities must repair any physical harm done by their conduct.[91] Whereas negligence liability criticises primary conduct, strict liability criticises a secondary failure to make reparation for harm done. Negligence liability is liability for harm done by *unreasonable* conduct whereas strict liability is liability for harm done by *reasonable* conduct. Its fundamental justification is that the costs of necessary or justified harms should be borne by those who benefit from their infliction.

This form of strict liability is embodied by a diverse set of doctrines: by private necessity cases such as *Vincent*;[92] by liability for abnormally dangerous activities; by some liability for intentional nuisance; by liability for manufacturing defects in product liability law; and by the liability

---

[90] Coleman notes in *The Practice of Principle*, above n 3, at 36 that corrective justice theory 'does not explain' various features of tort law, 'for example, vicarious liability or perhaps product liability'. In Coleman, *Risks and Wrongs*, above n 12, at 417–29 he excludes product liability from the core of tort and tentatively suggests that it should be understood not in terms of corrective justice but in terms of rational bargaining. The issues here are too complicated to be discussed adequately in this chapter. For now we must settle for noting two points. First, a theory of tort which can explain its domains of strict liability is interpretively superior to a theory which cannot. Secondly, the emergence of product liability law is the most important development in twentieth century tort law. An adequate theory of tort ought to be able to account for it.

[91] This 'private eminent domain' conception of strict liability may make its first appearance in American tort theory in the writings (some famous and some obscure) of Oliver Wendell Holmes. These writings are cited and discussed in Grey, above n 43, at 1275–81 and at greater length in TC Grey, *Holmes on Torts* (unpublished). Two other classic statements are Bohlen, above n 78 and Keeton, above n 78. See also Stevens, above n 44, at 104–05 (endorsing an account of *Vincent* along these lines).

[92] *Vincent* 124 NW 221 (Minn 1910).

of masters for the torts of their servants committed within the scope of their employment. The obligation imposed by these doctrines is an obligation to undertake an action (eg, saving your ship from destruction at the hands of a hurricane by bashing the dock to which it is moored) or conduct an activity (eg, operating a business firm) *only on the condition* that you will repair any physical harm for which your action or activity is responsible. The reciprocal right is a right to have any physical harm done to you undone by the party responsible for its doing.

There is also a second, less common form of strict liability epitomised in the torts of conversion and trespass and in some batteries.[93] Here the wrong is the violation of a right which assigns a power of control over some physical object or, in the case of battery, control over some subject. The law's specification of various powers of control over one's person and physical objects gives rise to a form of strict liability predicated on the voluntary but impermissible crossing of a boundary. If you enter my land, or appropriate my pen, without my permission, you have violated my right of exclusive control over these objects, even if your entry or appropriation is entirely reasonable and justified. The wrong consists in the failure to respect the right. Fault is simply irrelevant. Put otherwise, liability for violation of a right of exclusive control is strict for the simple reason that the right itself would be fatally compromised by tolerating all reasonable (or justified) boundary crossings, without regard to whether consent was given to those crossings. Rights of control are a species of autonomy rights. Those who hold such rights are entitled to forbid even reasonable boundary crossings, and they are presumptively wronged whenever their boundaries are crossed without permission. Their rights thus give rise to stringent 'duties to succeed' on the part of others.[94] In this class of cases, the strictness of liability in tort is a consequence of the right being protected.

The wrong committed in a sovereignty-based tort is conduct-based *in only the most attenuated sense of the term*. In negligence—the canonical example of a conduct-based wrong—liability is predicated on the wrongfulness of the defendant's *conduct*; it is that wrongfulness which does the work and triggers liability. In 'sovereignty torts' it is the violation of the plaintiff's right which does the work and triggers the liability. The duty is a duty not to violate the right, and conduct that violates the right is wrongful only because it violates the right. Viewed in isolation from the right, the conduct may be innocent and even justified. The defendant doctor in *Mohr v Williams*, for example, benefited the plaintiff by

---

[93] See above n 65 and accompanying text (discussing sovereignty-based torts).

[94] The concept of 'duties to succeed' is developed in J Gardner, 'Obligations and Outcomes in the Law of Torts' in P Cane and J Gardner (eds), *Relating to Responsibility: Essays in Honour of Tony Honoré on His 80th Birthday* (Oxford, Hart Publishing, 2001) 111.

curing her disease.[95] Moreover, sovereignty-based torts are clear counter-examples to the thesis that tort is a law of wrongful losses. These may be committed without inflicting wrongful loss because the rights at issue are powers of control not protections against harm. The essential, distinguishing features of strict liability are thus obscured and distorted by calling strict liability torts 'conduct-based wrongs'. Strict liability wrongs are based not on wrongful conduct in the normal sense of that term, but on violations of autonomy rights or on secondary failings of conduct—on conditional, not primary fault.[96]

Coleman's views on the nature of strict liability have changed over time, but he has lately taken the view that strict liability involves a duty not to harm. In contradistinction to what he calls 'the standard view', Coleman's view models strict liability on negligence liability. On the standard view, negligence liability is—and strict liability is not—based on a failure to conform one's conduct to a norm of obligatory conduct. On Coleman's contrary view, both strict liability and negligence are conduct-based norms: both involve breaches of duty. The only difference is the content of the duty:

> Strict and fault liability are different ways of articulating the content of one's duty to others. ...
>
> In torts, blasting is governed by strict liability and motoring by fault liability. The way to understand the difference is as follows. In the case of motoring, my duty of care is a duty to exercise reasonable care; it is a duty not-to-harm-you through carelessness, recklessness or intention. The law demands that I take reasonable precautions not to harm you ... In the case of blasting, however, the law imposes on me the duty-not-to-harm-you. The way I am to take your interests into account is to make sure that I don't harm you by blasting.
>
> The difference between fault and strict liability is a difference in the content of the duty of care I owe to you. ... If my duty to you is a duty-not-to-harm-you, then the only way that I can discharge that duty is by not harming you.
>
> If my duty to you is a duty-not-to-harm-you-faultily ... then I can discharge that duty either by not harming you or by not being at fault—whether or not I harm you.[97]

When strict liability is conceived of as a 'duty-not-to-harm', it conforms to the demands of corrective justice theory because, so conceived, strict liability is a conduct-based wrong.

---

[95] *Mohr v Williams* 104 NW 12 (Minn 1905). See the discussion in above n 66.

[96] This is Robert Keeton's vocabulary: see Keeton, above n 78.

[97] JL Coleman, 'Facts, Fictions, and the Grounds of Law' in JK Campbell, M O'Rourke and D Shier (eds), *Law and Social Justice* (Cambridge MA, MIT Press, 2005) 327, 329. See also Coleman, *The Practice of Principle*, above n 3, at 35:

> The concept of a duty in tort law is central both to strict and fault liability. In strict liability, the generic form of the duty is a 'duty not to harm someone', while in fault, the generic form of a duty is a 'duty not to harm someone negligently or carelessly'.

This conformance to the demands of corrective justice theory comes, however, at the cost of offering an inaccurate account of strict liability in tort. *Vincent*-type cases are clear counter-examples to Coleman's claim. When your ship is going to be destroyed by a storm if you unmoor it from the dock, lashing the ship to the dock and pounding the dock with your ship is the right—not the wrong—course of conduct. The doctrine concedes this; it does not impose a duty not to harm. Harm to the dock is to be regretted and repaired but—far from imposing an obligation not to do such harm—the law expressly permits, and indeed invites, its infliction. Better to bash the dock and save the ship than to leave the dock undamaged and let the ship be destroyed.

In *Vincent*[98] and under the doctrine of private necessity the ship owner's plight justifies their use of the dock and trumps the dock owner's right to exclude. But that trumping extends only as far as its rationale requires. It is reasonable for the owner of the ship to inflict the harm, but it is unreasonable for the ship owner not to repair the harm that it inflicts. The exigencies of the situation justify overriding the dock owner's right to exclude, but they do not justify shifting the cost of the ship owner's salvation onto the dock owner. That would both be unfair and disregard the dock owner's rights unjustifiably. The dock owner's right to exclude the ship is overridden because lashing the ship to the dock is necessary to save the ship. But it is neither necessary nor fair to shift the cost of the ship's salvation onto the dock owner's shoulders.[99] It is therefore unreasonable for the ship owner to refuse to repair the harm that he or she does in the course of saving his or her ship. The ship owner's wrong consists *not* in breaching a primary duty not to harm the dock, but in breaching a secondary duty to make reparation for harm reasonably done.[100]

---

[98] *Vincent* 124 NW 221 (Minn 1910).

[99] 'It might be said, and it has been held, when it is a question of paying damages, that a man cannot shift his misfortunes to his neighbor's shoulders': *Spade v Lynn* 52 NE 747 (Mass 1899) 747 (Holmes J for the Court). Holmes is speaking here of *Gilbert v Stone* (1647) Sty 72, 82 ER 539; he thought that the principle applied more broadly. See also the cases cited in GC Keating, 'Property Right and Tortious Wrong in *Vincent v Lake Erie*' in J Gordley (ed), *Issues in Legal Scholarship—Symposium: Vincent v Lake Erie Transportation Co and the Doctrine of Necessity* (Berkeley Electronic Press, 2005) n 53.

[100] Weinrib treats *Vincent* as an unjust enrichment case: *The Idea of Private Law*, above n 5, at 196–203. Because *Vincent* is a clear case of strict liability, moving it out of tort law furthers Weinrib's identification of tort with fault liability. The argument is unconvincing, however. The liability in *Vincent* is for harm done, and the measure of damages is injury inflicted, not benefit received. The benefit received by the defendant—saving its ship from near certain destruction—vastly exceeds the harm inflicted on the plaintiff's dock. That is why it is both rational and reasonable to authorise the trespass and the ensuing damage to the dock, after all. Liability for benefit unjustly received requires a different damage measure and much greater damages. Moreover, because the privilege authorises the trespass, the saving of the ship is an enrichment but not an unjust one. What would be unjust is for the defendant to shift the cost of its plight onto the shoulders of the plaintiff by failing to make reparation for harm done. In short: *Vincent* is not an unjust enrichment case, but unjust enrichment ideas play a role in justifying the imposition of strict liability in tort.

When we turn to cases where reasonable harm is inflicted accidentally (as it is in the blasting cases to which Coleman alludes[101]), positing a duty not to harm is equally unpersuasive. Negligence duties always backstop strict liabilities in tort, negligence liability is always available as an alternative to strict liability, and the stringency of negligence obligations of care increase with and are calibrated to the seriousness of the risk at issue. Courts often decline to impose strict liability precisely because they perceive the law's default norm of negligence liability as an adequate alternative.[102] The standing availability of negligence liability, and its capacity for calibration to the seriousness of the harm threatened, makes an *independent strict duty not to harm* superfluous. The ground of strict liability is simply different from the ground of fault liability. Strict liability asserts that when harm is done, even though all reasonable precautions have been taken, it is unfair to leave the cost of that harm on the plaintiff. The injurer ought to take the bitter with the sweet.

(iii) The Forward-Looking Role of Remedial Responsibility

Last, but surely not least, corrective justice theory takes reparation to be tort's fundamental purpose, but tort puts the *prospect* of reparation to use to *enforce* primary rights and responsibilities, not just to restore them. Tort damages perform, in part, a forward-looking role. Primary tort duties enjoin respect for the rights of others, thereby constraining our freedom and checking the pursuit of our self-interest. It is natural to chafe at these obligations and tempting to disregard them. We may, moreover, justifiably be wary of discharging our obligations to others if we are not assured that they will discharge their reciprocal responsibilities to us. The prospect of liability in tort serves as a counterweight to our self-interest, as an incentive to discharge our obligations, and as an assurance that others will comply as well. The remedial powers that tort law places in the hands of injured plaintiffs, and the correlative duties that it imposes on defendants, put teeth in its primary obligations. Damages may do their most important and effective work when they diminish the number of occasions on which they must be awarded. Insofar as reparation is a second- or next-best way of honouring primary rights and responsibilities, this forward-looking, rights-enforcing aspect of damages should not be dismissed lightly.[103]

---

[101] Coleman, 'Facts, Fictions, and the Grounds of Law', above n 97, at 329.

[102] See, eg, *Foster v City of Keyser* 501 SE 2d 165 (W Va 1997). In *Foster*, the West Virginia Supreme Court of Appeals reversed the Circuit Court's imposition of strict liability on a natural gas company for an explosion caused by the escape of gas from one of its transmission lines because 'other principles of law—a high standard of care and *res ipsa loquitur*—can sufficiently address the concerns that argue for strict liability in gas transmission line leak/explosion cases': at 175 (Starcher J for the Court).

[103] Doctrinally, this concern manifests itself most vividly in damages and proximate cause.

V. CONCLUSION

To summarise: corrective justice theory is right on two fundamental matters. First, that the economic theory of tort cannot adequately justify the normative structure of tort adjudication. Secondly, that the obligation of reparation is central to tort law. Tort obligations are owed by persons and to persons. When they are breached, responsibility for repairing their untoward effects and restoring the relationship between the breaching and injured parties naturally falls on the breaching party. But corrective justice overstates its case when it insists that the essence of tort law lies in this salient duty to repair wrongful losses. That duty is neither constitutive of—nor distinctive to—tort law. It is a contingent remedy, applicable to harm wrongly inflicted and common in tort only because most of tort law's primary norms impose duties of harm avoidance. Duties to repair are parasitic on primary duties not to harm. The principle of corrective justice, moreover, is purely formal: it cannot be brought to bear without specifying what counts, substantively, as a wrong. A theory of tort that has no account of tort wrongs is radically incomplete.

By focusing so intently on obligations of repair, corrective justice theory also misunderstands the logical structure and normative order of tort norms. Tort consists both of primary obligations of harm avoidance and secondary, remedial responsibilities of repair. Tort's primary norms are anterior to and grounding of its remedial responsibilities. Remedial responsibilities of repair arise out of breaches of primary obligations to respect certain rights and avoid certain harms and are next-best ways of discharging those obligations. Lastly, tort's primary norms of harm avoidance do not have the properties that corrective justice theory thinks are essential to tort. Tort's primary norms are omnilateral, not bilateral, they do not proscribe only conduct-based wrongs, and their commission does not always result in wrongful loss.

To both incorporate the insights of corrective justice theory and overcome its blind spots, we need to recover a deeper insight of corrective justice theory, namely, the insight that tort is a law of wrongs. To grasp that insight correctly, however, we need to place wrongs and the rights that ground them—not reparation—at the centre of our understanding of tort. Tort is a body of law concerned with the rights that persons have against each other qua persons—with rights not to be physically harmed,

Punitive damages are sometimes imposed in order to deprive certain kinds of tortious acts of their economic advantage, thereby attempting to ensure that the relevant rights will be respected and not priced out by economically rational tortfeasors: see above n 52 and accompanying text. Proximate cause cases fixing the outer perimeter of responsibility for harm tortiously done often take explicit account of whether the scope of liability is sufficient to enforce the rights at stake. This is especially evident in negligence cases involving pure economic loss and pure emotional harm: see, eg, *Barber Lines A/S v M/V Donau Maru* 764 F 2d 50 (1st Cir 1985); *Thing v La Chusa* 771 P 2d 814 (Cal 1989).

denied our authority over our persons and our property, deceived as we go about our economic lives, and so on. Tort obligations are grounded in the fundamental interests of persons as persons. They are owed by each of us to everyone else, and they are not fundamentally obligations of reparation. Fundamentally, tort obligations are obligations to avoid harming others in various ways, and to respect certain rights which safeguard and institute their autonomy.

14

The Edges of Tort Law's Rights

RODERICK BAGSHAW*

I. INTRODUCTION

O NE OF THE claims often made by proponents of a 'rights-focused account'[1] (RFA) of the law of torts is that such an account can provide a policy-free explanation for the non-existence of general non-contractual liability for harming purely economic interests in the light of the existence of general non-contractual liability for damaging or interfering with property: general rights to property exist, whilst general common law rights to pure economic benefits do not.[2] One reason why this claim is important is that if it succeeds then it helps proponents to establish that there is no need to invoke policy concerns, or instrumental reasoning, in order to explain the shape of the English common law of negligence, a shape which is similar to that found in the common law of other Commonwealth jurisdictions, because the shape is fully determined

---

* Email: roderick.bagshaw@law.ox.ac.uk.

[1] What I mean by a 'rights-focused account' (RFA) is a view that tort liability is explained, at least primarily, by the scope and shape of 'rights' which have roles *other than* to be part of tort law. In terms of central concepts such an account might be contrasted with a 'duty-focused account', which explains tort liability primarily in terms of duties that are only significant within tort law, and a 'liability-focused account', which treats the primary question as being 'should there be tort liability in circumstances such as these?' To a large extent, however, differences as to central concepts reflect a more significant division: generally speaking proponents of duty-focused and liability-focused accounts are far more willing than proponents of a RFA to allow policy concerns to determine the shape of their central concepts.

[2] Examples of RFA proponents offering explanations similar to this include: P Benson, 'The Basis for Excluding Liability for Economic Loss in Tort Law' in DG Owen (ed), *Philosophical Foundations of Tort Law* (Oxford, Oxford University Press, 1995) 427; EJ Weinrib, 'The Disintegration of Duty' in MS Madden (ed), *Exploring Tort Law* (Cambridge, Cambridge University Press, 2005) 143, 158–60; R Stevens, *Torts and Rights* (Oxford, Oxford University Press, 2007) 20–43; A Beever, *Rediscovering the Law of Negligence* (Oxford, Hart Publishing, 2007) ch 7.

by the pattern of general rights. But the significance of such a success would be substantially diminished if the current pattern of general rights is merely a temporary phenomenon, and can be revised by any judge or legislator. So most proponents of a RFA argue that not only are there *currently* no general common law rights to pure economic benefits but there are *also* good reasons *why* general common law rights to purely economic benefits should not exist whilst general common law rights to property do, or good reasons why legislators or judges should not in future create or recognise general common law rights to purely economic benefits. There is some division, however, between proponents as to what these good reasons are.

The main purpose of this chapter is to evaluate these 'good reasons' using three perspectives provided by the 'edges' of currently recognised legal rights. In the remainder of this part I will introduce these perspectives, clarify the sort of 'general common law right to a pure economic benefit' that it is most plausible to contemplate English law recognising, and, as a first step, I will catalogue a range of the 'good reasons' which are most commonly found in the writings of RFA proponents.

A. The Catalogue

This catalogue of 'good reasons' why general common law rights to purely economic benefits do not exist is organised under four headings.

(i) 'Rights' as an Explanation for Real Duties or Substitutionary Remedies

Some RFA proponents insist that it is a mistake to assume that a failure to defend some ideal pattern of general common law rights undermines the plausibility of their account. They point out, perfectly fairly, that faith in the primacy of rights does not require faith in any particular view as to what ought to be, and what ought not to be, recognised as a general common law right.[3] But if a RFA is compatible with *any* pattern of substantive rights, and policy concerns merely move to play a role in a phase of argument about what rights should be legally recognised, then it is hard to see why RFA proponents devote so much energy to proselytising.

Some RFA proponents assert that their account is superior to its rivals even if the pattern of substantive rights is impermanent because it makes it easier to explain the *reality* of duties,[4] or the *substitutionary* nature of

---

[3] Beever, above n 2, at 61–62.

[4] 'Real' duties are to be distinguished from use of the language of 'duty' as a 'control device', where what is being controlled is liability for loss. For further discussion of how we can determine whether duties are real, see NJ McBride, 'Duties of Care: Do They Really Exist?' (2004) 24 *Oxford Journal of Legal Studies* 417.

some non-specific remedies.[5] *These advantages* do not depend directly on the defensibility of any particular pattern of substantive rights: all that matters is that each 'right' explains the existence of a *real* duty, or explains the form of some supposedly basic tort remedy. There may, however, be an indirect link between these reasons for proposing a RFA and what rights such a proponent is willing to contemplate, since a scholar who advocates a RFA because of its power to explain the reality of duties, or the substitutionary nature of some non-specific remedies, will probably think that there is a good reason for refusing to recognise a legal right to a particular interest *if* that right would be unsuitable for use as the foundation for a *real* duty, or a *substitutionary* remedy.

What does 'unsuitable' mean here? Focusing on the *reality* of duties, it might be said that *real* duties must be capable of guiding *real people* in *real practical settings*, and that consequently a right would be an 'unsuitable' foundation for such a duty if a duty based on it would be useless for *real people* in *real practical settings*. This might, for example, provide an argument against recognition of a 'right to be free from unwanted attention' because a legal duty not to pay any attention to passing celebrities or people in embarrassing public situations would be incapable of eliminating instinctive curiosity. Similarly, a right would be an 'unsuitable' foundation for a substitutionary remedy if an attempt to put an objective value on the right would be absurd. Thus, as an example, there might be little difficulty in formulating a real duty founded on a right 'not to be unexpectedly told key elements in the plot of a play, book, film or television broadcast', but it would be extraordinary to treat this right as having an 'objective' value which could be awarded to each right-holder[6] in the event of a breach.

(ii) Constitutional Limits on 'Rights'

Some RFA proponents regard constitutional factors as providing the best reasons *why* general common law rights to purely economic interests do not, and should not, exist. These factors can be divided in two, according to whether they explain why it would be constitutionally illegitimate for *judges* to develop such general common law rights or, more ambitiously, explain why it would be constitutionally improper for such rights to be incorporated into a legal system by any legislator.

Claims that it would be constitutionally improper for particular rights to exist regardless of their origin usually invoke the rule of law, and two

---

[5] The claim that the basic measure of damages in the law of torts is 'substitutive', and not primarily calculated in terms of the claimant's loss, has been prominently defended by Robert Stevens, for instance, in Stevens, above n 2, at ch 4. The plausibility of this claim is the subject of debate elsewhere in this book.

[6] Perhaps in addition to damages to compensate for particular types of *individual* consequential loss.

versions of the claim are common: one emphasises a demand for predictability and the other a demand that judges should not be required to
perform constitutionally inappropriate tasks when *applying* rights. Thus
the 'predictability' objection to general rights to purely economic interests
might be that the law should only contain general rights which are capable
of yielding clear guidance as to how people ought to behave in advance,
and general rights to purely economic interests would inevitably fall short
of this requirement.[7] And the 'inappropriate task' objection might be that
the law ought not to contain general rights which could only be applied
by judges making decisions of sorts which it is not legitimate for them
to make, and general rights to purely economic interests could only be
applied if judges undertook such tasks.[8] Clearly these rule of law arguments can be presented in a strong form, which insists that legislation
(including 'judicial legislation' if this is permissible) violating the rule of
law is legally invalid; a weak form, which claims only that such legislation can be criticised; and an intermediate form, which demands that so
far as possible legislation should be interpreted so as to prevent it from
violating the rule of law.

Turning to the limits on legitimate *judicial* law-making, here we find
support for both the negative argument that judges cannot *legitimately*
make the sorts of choices that would be necessary to define tolerable general rights to purely economic interests,[9] and positive variations that insist
that judges can only *legitimately* recognise 'rights' as general common law
rights if they comply with certain conditions (for example, conditions
echoing the rule of law objections outlined above) and it is not possible
to identify any general rights to purely economic interests which comply
with these conditions.

(iii) Limits Derived from the Concept of 'Private Rights'

Some RFA proponents argue that a general right to a purely economic
benefit cannot exist because such a right would be incompatible with some

---

[7] See, eg, Stevens, above n 2, at 339:

> [T]he rule of law places limitations upon the sort of rights which can, or at least should,
> be recognized. ... It is part of the rule of law that the rights others have against us
> are capable of being determined in advance.

[8] See, eg, ibid, at 340:

> If a court is required to determine the scope of parties' rights and duties according
> to the weighing of a disparate range of open-ended policy concerns, the law itself is
> compromised. ... It is one thing for the law to be settled for the future by a legislature
> creating rights determined by the weighing of policy concerns. It is quite another for
> such policy concerns to be incorporated into the law itself, so that parties in deciding
> how to act are required to guess in advance how they will be resolved by a judge.

[9] See, eg, ibid, at 338: 'broad rights, such as a right not to be caused economic loss, are
not rights which can be judicially created.'

necessary formal feature of the concept of a 'private right'. For example, Ernest Weinrib has suggested that a person cannot have a *general* right to a prospective economic gain because one can only have a general right to an external thing that one has *acquired* and there is no mode of acquisition for a prospective economic gain.[10]

But why would anyone claim that private rights over external things require there to be a 'mode of acquisition' for the external thing? One possibility is that the underlying demand is for a test to determine whether a particular person has a general right to a particular external thing at a particular time as opposed to no one having such a right to the thing, someone else having such a right, or everyone having such a right. If this is correct then perhaps the catalogued reason for not recognising any general right to a purely economic benefit would have to be the *impossibility* of designing any test for determining whether a particular person has a general right to a particular prospective gain at a particular time as opposed to no one having such a right to it, someone else having such a right, or everyone having such a right. If the demand is understood in this way, however, it may be fair to treat it as no more than a variant of the 'rule of law' objections catalogued under the constitutional subheading. Moreover, there is room to doubt whether it would actually be impossible to design a test for identifying, for example, when a potential claimant 'acquires' the right to a prospective gain under an intended will that can form the foundation for a claim against, for example, a professional who carelessly fails to ensure that an effective will is produced.[11] Why could we not say that a potential claimant 'acquired' the necessary economic interest in the intended bequest when the testator instructed the defendant to perform the tasks necessary to achieve his intention? Perhaps one concern might be that such a 'right' would always be vulnerable to the testator changing his mind. But would the testator's superior 'right' *preclude* the law from treating the potential claimant as having a 'right' to the prospective gain against the rest of the world?[12]

This suggests a second possibility, which is that the catalogued objection ought instead to be that legal systems cannot treat one person as having a general right to some external thing if some other person has a superior right to it, and 'purely economic interests' inevitably depend on

---

[10] Weinrib, 'The Disintegration of Duty', above n 2, at 159 n 38. Weinrib presents the point as only explaining why there can be no general right to a prospective economic gain from use of some facility, such as a bridge, pipeline or cable. But if the point is valid then it may be able to explain the absence of a general right in a far wider range of situations.

[11] See, eg, *White v Jones* [1995] 2 AC 207 (HL).

[12] Special difficulties would arise if the testator asked a solicitor to prepare a will bequeathing something that he hoped to acquire in the future. For convenience I ignore such cases and concentrate on the position where if an effective will had been produced it would have conferred the benefit on the claimant in the event of the testator's immediate death.

the property or person of others or public interests.[13] For example, the objection would assert that a claimant cannot have a general common law right to the purely economic benefits from being able to continue using a facility owned by another, such as a bridge, pipeline or cable, because the facility owner has a superior right. If this is the appropriate formulation of the objection then it does not depend directly on the reality of duties, substitutionary remedies, constitutional factors or a moral vision,[14] and can be catalogued separately as a 'reason' based on the *necessary* form of 'general rights'.[15]

In truth, the two explanations suggested above do not fully capture why Weinrib regards identification of a mode of acquisition as essential to the existence of a right to an external thing. For him this demand is necessitated by a particular moral vision, where all private law rights protect a person's 'purposive capacity'.[16] An external thing cannot be used in the exercise of someone's purposive capacity if it has not yet been 'acquired', and thus there can be no right to a prospective gain: the *prospective* element of the interest means that it is not currently available as a means that can be used for pursuing chosen purposes. Given that Weinrib's conceptual demand is derived wholly from his moral vision for tort law his objection need not be treated as independent from those catalogued under the next sub-heading.

(iv) 'Rights' Compatible with a Particular Moral Vision

Under this fourth catalogue heading I group answers which claim that there is some reason why general rights to purely economic interests ought

[13] Illustrations may be helpful: purely economic interests based on the person of another include the profits a star footballer's club, team mates (who are entitled to success-based bonus payments) and various souvenir manufacturers expect to obtain as a result of the continued health of the footballer; purely economic interests based on the property of another include the expected gains that will be lost by nearby pub landlords and their suppliers if the football club's stadium is damaged and matches are played elsewhere while it is repaired; purely economic interests based on public interests include the profits that will be lost by sea fishermen if they are prevented from going to sea and acquiring property in fish.

[14] There is probably a strong link between the *formal* demand and a particular 'moral vision': the demand that a 'general right' cannot exist consistently with another person having a superior right is consistent with the 'moral vision' that 'private rights' exist to secure *independent* freedom.

[15] There are reasons to doubt whether English tort law is consistent with the formal objection to recognising X as having a legal right to some thing against everyone except Y when Y has a superior right to it. For example, the tort of 'causing loss by unlawful means' that was illuminated by the House of Lords in *OBG Ltd v Allan* [2007] UKHL 21, [2008] 1 AC 1 seems to be based on X having a legal right to Y's liberty being left free from certain types of interference. Some RFA proponents have sought to neutralise such awkward phenomena by inventing new concepts, such as 'parasitic claims', which avoid the need to treat X as having a 'right': see, eg, Stevens, above n 2, at 188–89.

[16] This point is presented most clearly in EJ Weinrib, 'Correlativity, Personality, and the Emerging Consensus on Corrective Justice' (2001) 2 *Theoretical Inquiries in Law* 107, 122.

not to be recognised other than their unsuitability for relevant *legal* functions (eg, underpinning *real* duties), constitutional objections and limits derived from the form of the concept. Such answers tend to be premised on a demand that all recognised rights must be compatible with some moral vision.[17]

Clearly one moral vision which is particularly popular amongst RFA proponents is that which insists that rights can only be recognised so far as they provide everyone with equal freedom[18] to pursue their chosen ends. Many RFA proponents argue that this vision underpins the relevant pattern of general rights:[19] your property is a means you can use in setting and pursuing your purposes, and your rights so to use it can be defined in such a way as to leave all other people equally free to set and pursue their own conception of the good, whilst 'expected economic gains' are clearly not a means which is immediately available, and no 'right' to such gains could be concocted without imposing an objectionable duty of one person 'to tailor his or her use of his or her means to the specific purposes of another'.[20]

B. Purely Economic Interests

The main task of this chapter is to evaluate the arguments which have just been catalogued in the light of three perspectives provided by the 'edges' of currently recognised legal rights. But before introducing these perspectives I must clarify the idea of 'purely economic interests'.

For clarification, it is not my intention to discuss whether there are good reasons for the non-existence of a single general general right to purely economic interests—that is some right against all the world (first 'general') to the enjoyment of *all* (second 'general') purely economic interests. The

---

[17] See, eg, J Finnis, 'Natural Law: The Classical Tradition' in J Coleman and S Shapiro (eds), *The Oxford Handbook of Jurisprudence and Philosophy of Law* (Oxford, Oxford University Press, 2002) 1, 57: 'tort law's foundations are judgments about what kinds of relationship between people are fair and reasonable, both generically and in particular kinds of context. These judgments are the main basis for recognizing primary rights and duties.'

[18] In this context 'equal freedom' does not require 'equal resources' but something like 'equal independence from the dominance of others in setting and pursuing purposes using the means that you have'.

[19] In A Ripstein, 'Tort Law in a Liberal State' (2007) 1(2) *Journal of Tort Law* art 3 www. bepress.com/jtl/vol1/iss2/art3/, accessed on 4 March 2011, at 10, Arthur Ripstein argues that the entitlements protected by tort law 'are not justified by showing that they are the most likely to enable choice or autonomy overall' but as 'the only way in which a plurality of separate persons can each set and pursue their own purposes, consistent with the others doing the same.'

[20] This formulation is also from Ripstein: ibid, at 15–16. My understanding of the moral account of the reasons for drawing a line between property and pure economic losses is largely derived from the outstandingly clear discussions of the topic provided by Ripstein in this article and also in A Ripstein, 'Private Order and Public Justice: Kant and Rawls' (2006) 92 *Virginia Law Review* 1391 and A Ripstein, 'Beyond the Harm Principle' (2006) 34 *Philosophy and Public Affairs* 215.

second 'general' invokes a category—all purely economic interests—which is far too large to be manageable. It is almost impossible to *imagine* a world in which every person must moderate his or her behaviour in order to avoid harming (or using) any of the economic prospects of others. Indeed there must be doubt as to whether the category 'all purely economic interests' could be useful in *any* analysis: it is a residue defined largely by exclusions (of interests in human physical integrity and property, and economic loss consequential on them) with only a fuzzy outer boundary. (What could be *of value*, fall outside the exclusions, and not be 'purely economic'?[21]) Rather I want to evaluate the catalogued reasons in relation to a range of more modest proposals for more narrowly defined rights against all the world (first 'general') to the enjoyment of some purely economic interest.

For example, consider the proposal that English law should recognise a general right to the non-destruction of a particular type of document that a person does not own but needs in order to secure a particular economic benefit.[22] Whether there *would be* tort liability in any situation where such a document had been destroyed might, of course, turn on further specification, such as whether the right was only that potential defendants should not *carelessly, recklessly or intentionally* cause such documents to be destroyed. But such a proposal would potentially benefit claimants who claimed, for example, that some defendant had carelessly destroyed the form (belonging to a third party) that the defendant had to lodge by a certain date if the claimant was to obtain a share of a particular fund.

As a second example, consider the proposal that English law should recognise a general right not to be prohibited[23] from undertaking activity that one reasonably expected to be able to undertake. Again, this proposal might mean that there *could be* tort liability if a defendant caused a potential claimant to be *prohibited* from undertaking a particular activity, at least where the prohibition was carelessly, recklessly or intentionally caused. Such a proposal would potentially benefit claimants who claimed,

---

[21] It is important to note that the 'excluded categories' often involve an actionable element and a non-actionable 'shadow'. For example, 'actionable psychiatric injuries' are excluded from the category 'purely economic interests', and 'non-actionable psychiatric effects', containing such things as *ordinary* grief and distress, are also excluded.

[22] *Ministry of Housing v Sharp* [1970] 2 QB 223 (CA) is not an example of such a case, but raises similar issues. Here a prospective purchaser of land obtained a certificate which did not record a planning charge (an obligation if the land was developed to repay a sum of money which had previously been paid as compensation following a refusal to allow it to be developed), and because statute made the certificate conclusive the Ministry lost its ability to claim the benefit of the charge. The Court of Appeal held that the clerk who produced the certificate which prevented the Ministry from claiming the benefit of the charge owed a duty of care to the Ministry.

[23] I intend 'prohibited' to cover only cases where the claimant is made subject to an official regulation or order underpinned by the threat of coercive sanctions. I do not intend it to cover situations where a claimant is prevented from undertaking the activity by lack of resources or other similar circumstances.

for example, that some defendant had carelessly caused them to be prohibited from running a nursing home business,[24] or from taking a job in
the insurance industry,[25] or from bidding to buy shares in a particular
company.[26]

As a third example, consider the proposal that English law should recognise a general right in C to a particular economic benefit when someone
with the power immediately to confer that benefit on C has committed
himself or herself to doing so at some later time. Clearly, supporters of
this proposal would have to specify carefully what forms of commitment
might be sufficient, but such a proposal might benefit claimants such as
those in *White v Jones*[27] and those who have entered various sorts of
'joint ventures' with property owners.[28]

It would not be difficult to add to these three examples. But the purpose of this chapter is not to establish that *these* three limited general
rights, or any others, *should* be recognised. Instead the chapter considers
whether the catalogued 'good reasons' for not recognising such limited
rights are convincing when they are evaluated from the three perspectives
introduced in the next section.

C. The Three Perspectives

The first perspective is provided by checking that the reasons for not
recognising such limited general common law rights to purely economic
interests do not grate against the sorts of choices and decision-making that
judges must undertake when dealing with the edges of well-established
rights, for example when considering what counts as 'damage to property'
and 'interference with property'.[29]

The foundation for the second perspective is provided by two facets

[24] See, eg, *Jain v Trent Strategic Health Authority* [2009] UKHL 4, [2009] 1 AC 853.

[25] See, eg, *Spring v Guardian Assurance plc* [1995] 2 AC 296 (HL). It may be that in
this case the claimant was not 'prohibited' from working as a 'company representative' since
the Lautro (Life Assurance and Unit Trust Regulatory Organisation) rules only required the
insurance company to take 'reasonable steps to satisfy itself that [a company representa-
tive] is of good character and of the requisite aptitude and competence': at 321. But clearly
examples involving prohibition can be easily imagined.

[26] See, eg, *Lonrho plc v Tebbit* [1992] 4 All ER 280 (CA).

[27] *White v Jones* [1995] 2 AC 207 (HL). This case involved a claim by the two daughters of a testator against a legal executive employed by a firm of solicitors who had failed
to act promptly when instructed by the testator to prepare a new will including substantial
gifts to them. As a result the testator had died before the new will was executed and the
majority of the testator's estate had passed to the ex-husband of one of the daughters and
the two children of that former marriage. The two daughters sought damages reflecting the
substantial gifts they would have received if the new will had been executed.

[28] See, eg, *Canadian National Railway Co v Norsk Pacific Steamship Co* [1992] 1 SCR
1021 (*Canadian National Railway*).

[29] There are many other interesting 'edges' to recognised private law rights, such as what
counts as 'imprisonment', but I cannot discuss them all.

of public law. Thus it is well-known that the European Convention on Human Rights (ECHR) protects some interests as 'possessions' which the common law of tort would not regard as 'property', and that English administrative law regards public officials as obliged to take account of a range of interests well beyond 'property'. Does the legal recognition in public law of these interests *beyond* personal safety and property challenge the catalogued 'good reasons' for the non-recognition of any general right to a purely economic benefit?

The third perspective is provided by considering two common law tort cases which have recognised general rights to purely economic benefits.[30] The question here is whether these judicial innovations confirm that there were 'good reasons' for not straying incrementally beyond the edge of the general rights to the protection of person and property.

II. THE EDGES OF PROPERTY DAMAGE AND INTERFERENCE WITH ENJOYMENT OF LAND

Am I liable if I carelessly knock your shockproof camera out of the window of a moving train, with the result that it is lost forever? Or if I carelessly mix the contents of my can of Coca-Cola into your vat of valuable claret? Or if I open a business selling pornographic DVDs in the shop next to the one where you run a successful toy shop? Or if I carelessly block the channel tunnel so that you are compelled to spend six hours sitting in a train 75 metres below the sea bed?

This part does not provide definitive answers to such questions. Rather it aims to consider whether the distinctions between actionable and non-actionable effects at the 'edges' of recognised private law rights require decisions of a different sort from those 'unconstitutional' judgments which might be required if any general right to a purely economic interest was recognised. Unless the decisions are of a different sort then there may be a problem with the catalogued constitutional 'good reasons' against extending tort law's protection to any purely economic interest.

How could we prove that the distinctions involve a different sort of decision? One possibility would be to demonstrate that decisions about the 'edges' of recognised rights are more predictable and can be drawn without undertaking any 'inappropriate task', like the trading off of a 'disparate range of open-ended policy concerns',[31] whilst decisions about the 'edges' of any general right to a purely economic interest would necessitate such tasks and be relatively unpredictable. But how could this be done? A first step might be to demonstrate that the current law has found

---

[30] *Canadian National Railway* [1992] 1 SCR 1021; *Perre v Apand Pty Ltd* (1999) 198 CLR 180 (*Perre*).

[31] Stevens, above n 2, at 340.

some factor, or combination of factors, which can be assessed without reference to 'policy', and define the necessary borderline between action-able and non-actionable effects.

But one obstacle immediately facing any attempt to identify such a factor in the current law is that the distinction between actionable and non-actionable effects does not appear to be drawn in the same place for real property and personal property. Thus since I own my house I can claim against my neighbour for the unreasonable noise which he makes at night which prevents me from sleeping, but despite the fact that my mother-in-law purchased a very expensive bed for her room in the house she cannot claim against the noise-maker for the interference with her freedom to use *it* for getting a comfortable night's sleep.[32] Similarly, I may have an action against my neighbour for his unreasonable blocking of my driveway, but my mother-in-law cannot, it seems, claim for the losses she suffers because *her* car is stuck in my garage by the blockage.[33] Whilst this does not *establish* that the relevant distinctions depend on 'policies' it at least suggests that a different factor, or combination of factors, will be required to explain the relevant distinction between actionable and non-actionable effects in cases of real and personal property. Moreover, the fact that real and personal property are treated differently will be a matter which requires attention when evaluating the claim that the distinction between general rights to property and a lack of general rights to purely economic interests is compatible with a particular moral vision.

A. Actionable Interferences with Use and Enjoyment of Land

The tort of private nuisance makes defendants liable for *some* forms of interference with a claimant's use and enjoyment of his or her land. It is important to note, however, that the tort does not extend to cover all forms of behaviour which lead to a claimant being unable to use and enjoy his or her land. For example, no authority on the tort suggests that a defendant can commit private nuisance by injuring or imprisoning the

---

[32] Perhaps someone objects that noise emanates into the airspace, which belongs to me, not the bed which belongs to my mother-in-law. But the example can easily be changed so that my neighbour's bass is of a perfect wavelength to make my mother-in-law's bed vibrate. Perhaps this raises the difficult question whether the neighbour might hereby commit the tort of 'trespass to goods'. My view, however, is that the claimant could not have succeeded in *Network Rail Infrastructure Ltd v Morris* [2004] EWCA Civ 172, [2004] Env LR 41 (*Network Rail*), discussed in text accompanying nn 41–43 below, by re-describing the claim as one of 'trespass to electric guitars'.

[33] Those who are convinced that the solution may depend on a desire to channel claims that depend on the *use* of real property through those with legal interests in that property may want to consider hypotheticals involving public spaces, for example a defendant's unreasonable emission of smoke which prevents safe air travel: again, the owner of an aircraft which cannot be used will not be entitled to a remedy for this interference.

claimant, snapping her front door key or taking steps that simply lead to certain uses of the land being prohibited,[34] despite these situations being capable of preventing the claimant from using and enjoying her land. So how does English law draw a line between unreasonably filling a claimant's nursing home with smoke so that it has to be evacuated and unreasonably obtaining an order that the claimant must cease using the premises as a nursing home? The factor that seems the prime candidate to provide a 'policy-free' distinction might be 'physical emanation', which clearly covers transfers of tangible things (smoke, dust, tree roots, etc) across the boundary. Where the defendant is responsible for some tangible thing moving across the boundary onto the claimant's land it might be argued that there is something similar to the direct *use* of the claimant's land by the defendant which the tort of trespass can redress, and this *use* is distinctly different from situations where the claimant is imprisoned or her key is broken.

The current law, however, extends liability beyond situations where *tangible things* move across the boundary line: liability in private nuisance has also been imposed in situations where there has been no intrusion of a *tangible thing*, but only a transfer of energy (noise, heat, light, vibration, etc). Moreover, any full description of the distinction between cases of liability and situations of non-liability may also have to allow the tort to cover *some*[35] negative emanations, for example the creation of conditions which unreasonably remove oxygen, or air pressure, or heat, from a claimant's land. These refinements suggest that the prime candidate may not be 'physical emanation' but 'behaviour having an effect that alters the physical condition of the claimant's premises', where physical condition includes both tangible emanations and matters such as temperature, pressure, etc. Such a factor would clearly be absent in situations where the claimant was prevented from using the land because of an effect on her person (personal injury or imprisonment), on personal property (the door key), or on legal entitlements (orders, etc).

Even this reformulated factor is not, however, sufficient to distinguish between cases where the claimant can complain and when she cannot because 'behaviour having an effect that alters the physical condition of the claimant's premises' will not give rise to liability where the effect is a

---

[34] In *D Pride & Partners v Institute for Animal Health* [2009] EWHC 685 (QB), [2009] NPC 56 (*D Pride*) the claimants argued that a defendant responsible for the release of a virus might be liable in private nuisance to farmers whose land was not contaminated but who were ordered not to move livestock present on their land in particular ways. Tugendhat J ruled that there was no prospect of such a claim succeeding: at [131]–[136].

[35] This point is not straightforward. It appears to be orthodox that a defendant can extract percolating groundwater from beneath his own land even if the consequence is to drain water from under the claimant's land and cause damage: *Langbrook Properties Ltd v Surrey County Council* [1970] 1 WLR 161 (Ch).

result of the claimant's hypersensitivity,[36] or when it is less than a claimant ought to tolerate in a particular locality.[37] Thus it seems that whether an alteration in the physical condition of premises is potentially actionable will depend on something far more complicated than the simple boundary crossing on which a claim for trespass to land can be based.

Indeed the notion of private nuisance by affront casts doubt on whether the tort requires any alteration in the physical condition of premises at all, since in affront cases the interference seems to be caused by the mental disturbance that comes from knowledge that nearby land is being used for a particular purpose, such as for prostitution[38] or the sale of hard-core pornography.[39] No doubt such a private nuisance requires there to be a special link (perhaps one of physical proximity) between the source of the claimant's disquiet and the particular premises: I cannot claim that my students are committing private nuisance by affront merely because my worrying about their unreasonable indolence disturbs my sleep (in the bedroom that I own): it might be different if it is the knowledge that a student is being mindlessly wasteful in the adjoining house which shatters my peace of mind. But a private nuisance by affront does not require any alteration in the physical condition of the claimant's premises.[40]

On the basis of this brief survey can we say that the decisions made by lawyers and judges in determining whether a defendant has committed private nuisance involve more predictability and fewer inappropriate tasks than the decisions they would have to make in order to *design* or *apply* a right not to have a vital document destroyed or a right not to have a profitable activity prohibited?

In *Network Rail Infrastructure Ltd v Morris*[41] the Court of Appeal considered whether a railway track operator could be liable for committing private nuisance by installing a signalling system which emitted electromagnetic radiation and thereby interfered with electric guitars in a nearby recording studio. Eventually the Court reached a conclusion in favour of the defendant by overturning the trial judge's finding on the issue of foreseeability. But Lord Phillips MR's brief discussion of the question whether and how 'to apply principles of the law of nuisance to the competing claims of those who wish to use equipment capable of giving rise to interference and those wishing to use equipment susceptible to interference'[42] suggests that he did not think the matter could be solved merely by asking if the situation involved an 'alteration in the physical condition' of the claimant's premises. Indeed his cautious opinion that 'it

---

[36] *Robinson v Kilvert* (1889) 41 Ch D 88 (CA).
[37] *St Helen's Smelting Co v Tipping* (1865) 11 HLC 642, 11 ER 1483.
[38] See, eg, *Thompson-Schwab v Costaki* [1956] 1 WLR 335 (CA).
[39] See, eg, *Laws v Florinplace Ltd* [1981] 1 All ER 659 (Ch).
[40] Similar points might be made about the notion of private nuisance by besetting.
[41] *Network Rail* [2004] EWCA Civ 172, [2004] Env LR 41.
[42] ibid, at [17].

may be more satisfactory that the potential problem of one neighbour causing electronic interference to another should be addressed by regulation than that it should be left to be resolved by the law of private nuisance'[43] tends to suggest that decisions about the edge of property torts involve very similar sorts of tasks to those likely to be raised by limited general rights to purely economic interests.

Perhaps it is appropriate to consider a second example in order to demonstrate that the *Network Rail* decision did not raise a peculiarly rare sort of problem. In *Birmingham Development Co Ltd v Tyler*[44] the Court of Appeal was confronted with a different difficult issue about the edge of 'actionable interference'. The claimant, in the course of developing a site next to the defendant's factory, exposed part of one of the defendant's walls which appeared to be in a dangerous condition. The development was then delayed, at an alleged cost to the claimant of £45 000 per week, whilst he tried to persuade the defendant to repair the wall. Eventually a judge granted an interim injunction and the defendant made the wall safe. At trial, however, the defendant was held not to be liable for the claimant's losses because the part of the wall which the claimant had *feared* was dangerous was *not actually* dangerous, and the only part of the wall that ever became dangerous did so because of the claimant's defective guttering. As a result the claimant's appeal raised the question[45] whether a defendant can be liable in private nuisance when he has (unreasonably) allowed his property to remain in such a state that it causes *genuine* fear to a *reasonable* neighbour, but is not actually dangerous. The Court of Appeal held that such a defendant cannot be liable, and it had to be shown, on the balance of probabilities, that there was *actual* danger.

In reaching this conclusion the Court of Appeal relied largely on precedent.[46] It did not, however, identify the possibility of a distinction between the conditions under which courts have held that an injunction can be sought *quia timet* and the circumstances in which the unreasonable creation of predictable fear may be actionable: what if, for example, a defendant's conduct led to a physical emanation which triggered fear, such as by allowing a tiny amount of a harmless white powder to drift onto the claimant's premises at a time of heightened concern about chemical attack by terrorists?[47] Certainly neither the Court of Appeal, nor

---

[43] ibid, at [19].

[44] *Birmingham Development Co Ltd v Tyler* [2008] EWCA Civ 859, [2008] BLR 445 (*Birmingham Development*).

[45] The claimant also attempted, unsuccessfully, to challenge the trial judge's approach to the pleadings and some of his findings of fact.

[46] In particular, passages from *R v Lister* (1857) Dears & B 209, 169 ER 979 and *A-G v Nottingham Corp* [1904] 1 Ch 673 (Ch) 677.

[47] Cases of private nuisance by besetting (eg, gathering outside the claimant's property and staring at it 'in a menacing manner') also look like cases where defendants can be liable for creating *fear* even if it cannot be shown that they *are* an actual risk to the claimant.

the courts responsible for the precedents it drew on, offered any simple explanation for a distinction between activities which cause affront or offence, which *can* it seems be actionable in the absence of danger, and activities that merely cause fear: surely many parents would be *offended* by a neighbour's refusal to investigate or assuage a reasonably perceived risk to the safety of their children but would tend to emphasise their *fear* ahead of that *offence*.[48]

For the purposes of this chapter, however, the primary question is not whether the decision in the *Birmingham Development* case is defensible but whether it suggests that the 'edge' between actionable and non-actionable interferences with the use and enjoyment of land is likely to be easier for courts to draw than the lines that might be required to be identified if any general right to a purely economic interest was recognised. My claim is that the case offers no support to the contention that the 'edge' of the recognised right is somehow more predictable, or can be discerned using some distinct technique.

B. Damage to Property

Perhaps someone may argue that the tort of private nuisance does not rest on a general right at all, but on the peculiar 'mutual duties of adjoining land owners'.[49] If so it is appropriate to investigate whether similar difficulties arise at the edge between cases of 'property damage' and 'loss of value of property without damage'. Here the prime candidate for a predictable and 'policy-free' edge to the protected property right might be something like 'change in physical structure'. It seems likely, however, that *some* changes in physical structure do not amount to 'property damage',

---

[48] For example, suppose that my neighbour refuses to take any steps to prevent his guests throwing hypodermic needles into the garden where my children occasionally play. Is it appropriate for the law to insist that any claim I make based on fear would have to demonstrate an *actual* danger, so that it might fail if my neighbour demonstrated that the only needles that crossed the boundary were sterile ones in sealed containers (so the prospect of them injuring my children was negligible), and to treat any *offence* I might feel at nearby intravenous drug-taking as a better foundation for liability? (Note that the guests could be liable for trespass without me having to demonstrate danger.) A further worry might be that reactions of 'offence' are so often associated with *ungrounded* fears about the effects of an activity (eg, that a sex cinema will attract criminals into a locality).

[49] Lord Macmillan famously stated in *Read v J Lyons & Co Ltd* [1947] AC 156 (HL) 173 that the rule in *Rylands v Fletcher* 'derives from a conception of mutual duties of adjoining or neighbouring landowners and its congeners are trespass and nuisance', and this statement has nudged other courts into deciding, for instance, that only an occupier of land can *commit* a private nuisance: see, eg, *Hussain v Lancaster City Council* [2000] QB 1 (CA) 23. I have argued elsewhere that such decisions mistake 'superficial symmetry for real coherence': see R Bagshaw, 'Private Nuisance by Third Parties' (2000) 8 *Tort Law Review* 165; R Bagshaw, '*Rylands* Confined' (2004) 120 *Law Quarterly Review* 388, 392; and others agree that *Hussain* is incorrect on this point: see, eg, K Oliphant (ed), *The Law of Tort*, 2nd edn (London, LexisNexis Butterworths, 2007) para 22.11.

and the capacity of personal property to be 'mixed' and 'lost' raises distinct difficulties. I will briefly survey the edge of 'property damage' before assessing the sorts of decisions being made.

(i) Changes in Physical Structure that Are Not Damage

In the pleural plaques litigation[50] the House of Lords held that physical changes to a person's body were not necessarily 'damage' for the purposes of a personal injury claim. Thus Lord Hoffmann stated that 'damage' is

> an abstract concept of being worse off, physically or economically, so that compensation is an appropriate remedy. It does not mean simply a physical change, which is consistent with making one better, as in the case of a successful operation, or with being neutral, having no perceptible effect upon one's health or capability.[51]

Thus a physical change to a human body which is painful, disabling or disfiguring *may* amount to actionable damage, provided that it is more than minimal, but a change which can only be detected by an X-ray or scan, causes no discomfort and does not *itself* carry the risk of more serious disease *will not* amount to actionable damage.

With regard to land and personal property the parallel question seems to be whether a physical change to the thing reduces its usefulness or value.[52] Thus if a defendant prevents a claimant from sending a pig to be slaughtered with the result that it grows fatter than it ought to have been in order to fetch the best price he will have 'damaged' the pig, and if a defendant prevents a claimant from picking apples so that they ripen for longer than they ought to have done in order to fetch the best price he will have 'damaged' those apples.[53]

These propositions certainly suggest that the edge of the protected right may *in fact* have been defined without attention being paid to the instru-

---

[50] *Rothwell v Chemical & Insulating Co Ltd* [2007] UKHL 39, [2008] 1 AC 281.

[51] ibid, at [7].

[52] *Hunter v Canary Wharf Ltd* [1997] AC 655 (CA) 676 (Pill LJ; Waite and Neill LJJ agreeing) (a point not addressed in the subsequent appeal to the House of Lords).

[53] *D Pride* [2009] EWHC 685 (QB), [2009] NPC 56 [74] (Tugendhat J). Elsewhere in this book Sarah Green argues that the claims in this case would have been more successful if they had been pleaded as claims for wrongful interference with an interest in goods, on the basis of an interference with the claimants' right to 'use the subject matter of their property rights as they see fit': S Green, 'Rights and Wrongs: An Introduction to the Wrongful Interference Actions' ch 18 of this book, text accompanying nn 27–42. My argument proceeds on the assumption that the English law of torts does not protect any such right against negligent interference: it is not the case that if I negligently cause an accident which blocks a motorway then all those vehicle-owners who are stuck in tail backs have a prima facie claim against me for not being able to *use* their vehicles 'as they see fit' (Green offers a different explanation for the same result in the text accompanying n 66); and it is not the case that the claimants in *Spartan Steel & Alloys Ltd v Martin & Co (Contractors) Ltd* [1973] QB 27 (CA) could have succeeded by repleading their claim as one for negligent interference with their 'right' to *use* their tools and raw materials.

mental effects of the chosen boundary. Thus the effect of *this* boundary is that an owner of property that will deteriorate physically with the passage of time will be able to claim against a defendant who delays a use which would have destroyed (or disposed of) the property but not against a defendant who temporarily prevents some other profitable use of the property (not involving destruction or disposal).[54] And it is hard to see why anyone focusing on instrumental effects would regard this difference in outcome as satisfactory: to spell the point out, why would we want to say that someone whose activities could lead to a restriction of animal movements would owe a duty to the owner of steers destined to be slaughtered but not to the owner of bulls destined to perform stud duties?

Further and different difficult questions arise, however, where items of property are closely related: for example, where one of a pair of matching vases is physically smashed it is necessary to ask whether the claimant can recover for the difference between the value of the pair and the value of the remaining vase, or must allow that part of the loss is a fall in value of the remaining vase and is consequently purely economic (since the remaining vase is undamaged). Similarly, where the wing of a classic car is damaged and must be replaced it is necessary to determine whether the claimant can recover for the fall in value which results from the car no longer being a composite of purely original parts.

Awkwardly, claimants may have an interest in treating parts of property as a unity when one part is smashed and the remainder loses value but in treating them as separable when an inherent defect in one part leads to the destruction of the other.[55] Cases considering whether property is separable or a unity for the purposes of applying the rule that a builder can be liable if his or her sub-standard work damages *other* property offer little evidence for the claim that the edge of 'property damage' is relatively predictable, and can be drawn without the inappropriate tasks that would be required in order to define and apply any limited general right to a purely economic interest.[56] Thus there are indications in *Murphy v*

---

[54] An illustration may help: suppose a farmer, C, owns sheep and a sheepdog, and D brings about circumstances which prevent C from sending the sheep to slaughter and buying extra sheep that he might use the sheepdog to manage profitably for six months. In these circumstances C will be able to claim for any loss of value of the sheep through the physical effects of ageing but not for the loss of value of the sheepdog through the physical effects of ageing (or for the cost of feeding it during the six months when it was doing little profitable work). Why? Because the use which D prevented would have stopped the sheep from ageing (they would have been slaughtered) but would only have allowed the sheepdog to earn profits *while it aged*.

[55] The claimant has an interest in treating the parts as separable in a case involving an inherent defect because damage done to a thing itself by an inherent defect is classed as pure economic loss: see, eg, *D & F Estates v Church Commissioners* [1989] AC 177 (HL).

[56] Discussion of the question whether property is separable or a unity is usually conducted under the label 'complex structure theory': see, eg, *Murphy v Brentwood District Council* [1991] 1 AC 398 (HL) (*Murphy*) 476 (Lord Bridge).

Brentwood District Council that the question whether a situation involves separable property or a unity turns on such factors as whether the same person was responsible for providing both the defective element and the other elements which were damaged, whether the elements were provided simultaneously, and whether the defective element fails to support the other element or does positive harm to it.[57] In *Payne v John Setchell Ltd* Judge Humphrey Lloyd QC decided that the 'complex structure exception' was 'no longer tenable',[58] at least in a simple case where a defective foundation has led to other damage in a house, but reached this conclusion partly by adverting to the importance of not circumventing the 'policy' conclusion reached by the House of Lords in *Murphy*.[59]

(ii) Mixtures

If a defendant mixes something with the claimant's property then does he or she 'damage' that property even if the mixing does not involve any physical change to the claimant's property? Some cases suggest that the answer is 'yes', at least where the mixing reduces the utility or value of the claimant's property. Thus in *The Orjula*[60] Mance J held that the defendants had caused physical damage to a ship where their negligence had led to hydrochloric acid leaking on to the deck, which had to be neutralised and washed off by specialist contractors. Similarly, the Court of Appeal in *Blue Circle Industries plc v Ministry of Defence*[61] held that allowing plutonium to intermingle with the topsoil of land involved causing 'physical damage' to that land.[62] But in *Barclays Bank plc v Fairclough Building Ltd*[63] it seems to have been regarded as arguable that only pure economic loss was caused to a claimant when a high pressure hose was used in such a way as to lead to asbestos fibres entering the claimant's premises, even though remedial works cost nearly £4 million. It is not clear from the report how counsel for the claimant argued that the asbes-

---

[57] ibid, at 470 (Lord Keith), 478 (Lord Bridge), 496 (Lord Jauncey). Others have proposed considering whether the defective element could have been removed without damaging the other elements: see, eg, Oliphant, above n 49, at para 19-12, referring to A Tettenborn, 'Components and Product Liability: Damage to "Other Property"' [2000] *Lloyd's Maritime and Commercial Law Quarterly* 338.

[58] *Payne v John Setchell Ltd* [2002] PNLR 7 (QB) [40].

[59] ibid, at [37].

[60] *Losinjska Plovidba v Transco Overseas Ltd (The Orjula)* [1995] 2 Lloyd's Rep 395 (Com Ct) 399.

[61] *Blue Circle Industries plc v Ministry of Defence* [1999] Ch 289 (CA).

[62] Whether the case involved a simple 'mixture' is unclear. Aldous LJ stated that he had 'no doubt that the addition of plutonium to the topsoil rendered the characteristics of the marshland different' (ibid, at 300), and used this as a basis for distinguishing *Merlin v British Nuclear Fuels plc* [1990] 2 QB 557 (QB), in which Gatehouse J had held that causing radioactive dust to be present in the claimants' house was *not* 'physical damage' to the house.

[63] *Barclays Bank plc v Fairclough Building Ltd* [1995] QB 214 (CA).

tos fibres did not cause physical damage:[64] one possible approach might have been to assert that the real problem was airborne asbestos fibres and the hazard they posed to human health, rather than any alteration to the physical structure of the building. The nature of this argument might be illuminated by drawing an analogy with the situation where a defendant causes poisonous spiders to infest the claimant's premises: would this be an instance of 'physical damage' to property?

Might a claimant want damages in any situations where 'mixing' did not lead to a reduction in the value or utility of property? Cases where the effect of the mixture is to lead to the claimant *losing* his or her property would probably be treated in accordance with the principles presented in the next section. What about cases where the claimant *acquires* additional property through the mixing, and the addition triggers some new liability? For example, consider the case where a tax is charged if more than a certain quantity of some substance is imported into the United Kingdom in a single batch, the claimant intends to import an amount just less than the threshold, and the defendant carelessly mixes a small but indistinguishable amount into the claimant's batch so that the amount actually imported is above the threshold: is this a case of *damage* to the claimant's property?[65] As before, my purpose in raising such a hypothetical is not to defend any particular answer to it but rather to ask whether such cases grate against the claim that the edge of the recognised right can be dealt with predictably and without a judge performing the sort of inappropriate tasks that would allegedly be required in order to define and apply any limited general right to a purely economic interest.

(iii) Loss

It seems likely that English law would treat negligence leading to loss of personal property as equivalent to negligence leading to physical destruction of property. In *Bailey v HSS Alarms Ltd*[66] the Court of Appeal considered a claim by the victims of a burglary who lost tools and stock against the company to which the installers of their alarm system had subcontracted the task of monitoring the system. Despite the lack of contractual privity between the claimants and the defendants, and the presence of a limitation clause in the contract between the defendants and the installers, the Court concluded that the defendants owed the claimants a duty of care, and in reaching this decision Turner J attached

---

[64] It was thought to be in the *claimant's* interest to establish that there was no tortious duty of care since this would diminish the prospect of the claimant's contractual claim being reduced for contributory negligence.

[65] Another example might involve a defendant negligently allowing his or her male animal to impregnate the claimant's female animal thereby exposing the claimant to the costs of bringing up the offspring.

[66] *Bailey v HSS Alarms Ltd* The Times, 20 June 2000 (CA) (*Bailey*).

particular importance to his categorisation of the case as one involving 'physical damage' rather than *pure* economic loss.[67] Moreover, in other cases where a defendant has been held liable to the victim of a theft of property there has been no hint of an objection that the loss was 'purely economic'.[68]

But how can a defendant's loss of property as a result of theft be distinguished from a defendant's loss of the ability to use property as a result of an official prohibition on its use in a particular way? One possible distinction might be that theft is assumed to involve a *permanent* deprivation. But this seems unsatisfactory since it must be doubtful whether the claimants in *Bailey* would have lost their right to sue if the police had recovered the stolen property after a few months, and, equally, it is doubtful if a property owner can sue for the effects of a prohibition which is effectively permanent because it lasts for the entire life span of some item of property. A second possibility might be that theft undoubtedly involves a wrong to property by the thief and the claim that the defendant has caused 'damage to property' (rather than pure economic loss) is in some way parasitic on the undoubted property wrong: by contrast there is no 'undoubted property wrong' when the deprivation is a result of an official prohibition. This explanation, however, would have the awkward consequence of distinguishing between defendants whose behaviour leads to theft of property and defendants whose behaviour leads to property being lost in other ways, such as where the shockproof camera falls from the moving train.

(iv) The Nature of the Decisions at the Edge of Damage to Property

It seems that decisions about what counts as 'property damage' are not simply decisions about what counts as a *physical* change. This is clear from the fact that physical change is insufficient unless it is associated with a reduction in utility or value, and the fact that sometimes a claimant seems to be able to claim for a loss of utility as a result of mixing even in the absence of physical change. When courts make decisions like whether to treat a claimant who has suffered a theft or loss of property as equivalent to a claimant who has suffered physical damage to personal property, and how to respond to mixtures, it is strongly arguable that the tasks that they undertake and the predictability of the outcomes which they reach are indistinguishable from those likely to be required in order to design and apply limited rights to purely economic benefits. If so, the

---

[67] ibid, at [42]. The Court of Appeal reported (at [14]) that the trial judge had also held the losses to be physical: 'the principle [*sic*] losses which occurred here, and which were foreseeable as occurring here, namely physical loss of property and damage to the plaintiff's property, are not pure economic losses. They are more direct and physical than that.'

[68] See, eg, *Stansbie v Troman* [1948] 2 KB 48 (CA).

catalogued constitutional objections to the recognition of limited rights to purely economic benefits are difficult to sustain.

C. Real Property, Personal Property and Moral Visions

The fourth heading in the catalogue (part I(A)(iv)) noted that some RFA proponents insist that private rights can only be recognised if they allow all others equal freedom to pursue their chosen ends, and whilst property rights are important to ensuring freedom, rights to purely economic interests could not be consistent with *equal* freedom. At this point I want to consider whether the equal freedom moral vision is compatible with the differences between the extent to which interests in real and personal property are protected, in particular the relative lack of protection for interference with the *use* of personal property (in the absence of physical damage, trespassory contact or conversion).

Arthur Ripstein, an ardent proponent of a RFA founded on 'equal freedom', has written that

> private law limits the means that citizens can use in setting and pursuing their private purposes. You can use your means, but not mine, and each of us can only use our means in ways that do not interfere with the entitlement of others to use theirs.[69]

From this perspective the challenge is to explain why 'equal freedom' leads to a protected entitlement with regard to personal property which is narrower than the protected entitlement with regard to real property.

One strategy for identifying an explanation that might appear promising would be to probe the significance of the fact that real property cannot be moved out of the way of something that might physically interfere with its use (such as a smell or noise) whilst personal property *often* can be. In the real world, however, it is hard to endorse the claim that my mother-in-law remains sufficiently free from my noisy neighbour's domination because she can always move her expensive bed from my house and pursue her purpose of sleeping in it elsewhere.

Perhaps an alternative key to an explanation is that there can only be a physical interference with the use of personal property when that property is located in space, and it is the right of the owner of the real property with regard to the use of the space that makes it impossible to allocate a use right to the owner of the personal property. Using the example of the expensive bed that my mother-in-law has installed in my house, the argument would be that giving her a right to use the bed for sleeping free from unreasonable noise is impossible because of my right to permit

---

[69] Ripstein, 'Tort Law in a Liberal State', above n 19, at 10–11.

a higher noise level in my house.[70] But would granting my mother-in-law a right to use her bed for sleeping in free from unreasonable noise *unless and until* the owner of the land where the bed is located permits such a level of noise be incompatible with 'equal freedom'? I believe that the answer should be 'no'. Because of the 'unless and until' qualification such a right would not restrict the freedom of the owner of the land to pursue his purposes. Moreover, if the duty of others to moderate their noise-making so as to permit the owner of the land to use his property for sleeping is consistent with equal freedom it is hard to see why demanding the same moderation for the benefit of the bed owner would leave prospective noise-makers insufficiently free.[71] No doubt there may be good and prudential reasons why tort law offers less protection to personal property than real property, but there are good reasons for doubting that the moral vision of 'equal freedom' demands the current differences between the edges of the rights concerned.

III. INTERESTS PROTECTED BY PUBLIC LAW

It will be recalled that some RFA proponents maintain that general rights to purely economic interests may be unconstitutional or inconsistent with some legally validated moral vision. This part considers whether these arguments can be reconciled with the fact that European human rights law protects a wider class of 'possessions' than the common law of torts and with English administrative law's protection of a still broader class of purely economic interests.

A. 'Possessions' in European Human Rights Law

There is scope to debate the breadth of the concept of 'possessions' in the guarantee in Article 1 of the First Protocol of the ECHR that '[e]very natural and legal person is entitled to the peaceful enjoyment of his possessions. No one shall be deprived of his possessions except in the public interest and subject to the conditions provided for by law and by the general principles of international law.' But the concept clearly extends to cover some forms of interest which the English law of torts would

---

[70] This clearly echoes the reason catalogued in part I(A)(iii) above.

[71] This is not, of course, to claim that the reason why the neighbour must moderate his noise-making is the landowner's freedom: such a claim would contravene the 'equal freedom' moral vision's essential condition that the reason why the defendant's behaviour is wrong must be the *same* reason that the claimant has a right. Instead the claim is that the neighbour's residual freedom to pursue his purposes would still be sufficient even if the bed owner was granted a right (subject to the 'unless and until' qualification) to complain about an unreasonable interference with its use.

regard as 'purely economic'. For example, present holdings of money are a 'possession', with the result that 'taxation is in principle an interference with the right guaranteed by the first paragraph of Article 1 of Protocol No 1, since it deprives the person concerned of a possession, namely the amount of money which must be paid.'[72] Further, entitlements to social security payments and pensions under statutory welfare schemes are 'possessions'.[73] Some assets of a business beyond its physical property are also protected, for example its goodwill and clientele,[74] and certain licences.[75] Does the application by the courts of the broad concept of 'possessions' in human rights cases cast doubt on the catalogued 'good reasons' for not recognising general rights to purely economic interests?

One possible answer might be that the broad concept does not challenge the 'good reasons' because the ECHR only defines what rights signatory states must respect, not what duties private individuals and companies are subject to. (Similarly, municipal administrative law defines the obligations of governmental bodies and officials, not private individuals and companies.) But this answer needs elaboration before it can explain how, for instance, tasks which it is allegedly unconstitutional for judges to undertake in cases between private parties (such as defining the scope of protected purely economic interests) are nonetheless legitimate in cases between a private individual and a state. If it is *unconstitutional* for a judge to balance and accommodate a 'disparate range of open-ended policy concerns'[76] in a private law case then how does the task become legitimate when the same judge is asked to perform it in order to settle the scope of the concept of 'possessions' in a human rights claim? Perhaps it can be argued that predictability is less of a concern where the party on which obligations are imposed is a state. But it is hard to argue that predictability is of *no concern* in such cases, since private individuals have an important interest in being able to predict how a state can act towards them, and some may also have an interest in being able to predict what a state is capable of doing to other private individuals.

Does the broad concept of 'possessions' also challenge the claim that there is some formal, conceptual reason why one person cannot have a

---

[72] *Burden v United Kingdom* (2008) 47 EHRR 38 [59].

[73] In *Carson v United Kingdom* (2009) 48 EHRR 41 [64] the Grand Chamber agreed that

> although there was no obligation on a State under Article 1 of Protocol No 1 to create a welfare or pension scheme, if a State did decide to enact legislation providing for the payment as of right of a welfare benefit or pension—whether conditional or not on the prior payment of contributions—that legislation had to be regarded as generating a proprietary interest falling within the ambit of Article 1 of Protocol No 1 for persons satisfying its requirements.

[74] *Van Marle v Netherlands* (1986) 8 EHRR 483.

[75] *Tre Traktörer Aktiebolag v Sweden* (1991) 13 EHRR 309 [53].

[76] Stevens, above n 2, at 340.

legal right to some thing if some other person has a superior right to it? It certainly suggests that there are contexts where a legal system can make use of a concept which takes this form, so that, for instance, in the context of human rights law a firm of accountants can be treated as having an interest in their 'goodwill' and 'clientele' even though their clients still retain full freedom to take their custom elsewhere.[77]

The perspective provided by the protection of a broad concept of 'possessions' in human rights law sheds no light, however, on the claim that the distinction in private law between property rights and purely economic interests reflects a particular moral vision: it can clearly be argued that it is acceptable to put more burdensome limits on the freedom of the state than on private individuals because there is no need to treat the state as having equal freedom to pursue its chosen ends.

B. Purely Economic Interests Protected by English Administrative Law

In order to discuss which interests are protected by English administrative law it is necessary to establish two useful distinctions. First, a distinction can be drawn between interests which are vested in particular individuals,[78] for instance A's interest in his or her freedom of movement or B's interest in the integrity of his or her property, and interests which are not vested in particular individuals, such as an interest in maintaining biodiversity or cultural heritage. In the discussion that follows I want to focus on the interests vested in particular individuals. A second useful distinction is between three ways in which English administrative law might protect interests:

1. some interests are sufficient to enable a claimant to seek judicial review, that is, those interests which can provide a basis for a claimant to have *standing to challenge* an administrative decision;
2. some interests are sufficient to establish that a claimant is entitled to some form of participation in the process by which an administrative decision will be made, for example a 'fair hearing'; and
3. some interests must be taken into account by an administrative decision-maker when making a decision, so that the decision will potentially be void if it is reached without taking them into account, or after attaching only an unreasonably small significance to them.

A catalogue of interests in accordance with each of the three limbs of this distinction would include many which tort lawyers would regard as 'purely economic'. Here, however, a sufficiently useful perspective is

---

[77] *Van Marle v Netherlands* (1986) 8 EHRR 483.
[78] Intended to include companies and other artificial entities with legal personality.

provided by briefly considering only the second limb.[79] There can be little doubt that an administrative decision-maker can be obliged to grant someone a fair opportunity to participate in the making of the decision even when what that person has at stake in the decision is far less than the prospect of an interference with a private law right that would be actionable in the absence of statutory authority. In particular, people with purely economic interests at stake are regularly entitled to claim an opportunity to participate in the making of a decision which will impinge on that interest.

The significance of this parallels that of the use of the broad concept of 'possessions' in human rights law. In public law fair procedure cases the judiciary do not seem to recognise that they are acting unconstitutionally when they decide what forms of purely economic interest might be sufficient to found an entitlement to fair participation, nor do they find it impossible to design concepts which identify one person as having a legally relevant interest in some thing simultaneously with others having superior interests in the same thing. Again, however, the perspective does not challenge the claim that the distinction in private law between property rights and purely economic interests reflects a particular moral vision.

IV. INNOVATIONS IN COMMONWEALTH TORT LAW

The third perspective is provided by considering two common law tort cases where courts can be treated as having recognised limited *general* rights to purely economic benefits.[80] This perspective allows us to ask whether these judicial innovations confirm that the catalogued 'good reasons' for not straying beyond the edge of the general rights to the protection of person and property are convincing.

The two cases are the Supreme Court of Canada's decision in *Canadian National Railway Co v Norsk Pacific Steamship Co*[81] and the High Court of Australia's decision in *Perre v Apand Pty Ltd*.[82] In the first the Court

---

[79] It is arguable that a catalogue in accordance with the third limb would be impossible to compile since it would be hard to identify any individual interest that no decision-maker would ever be under a duty to take into account. Moreover, a catalogue in accordance with the first limb, that is of those interests which are sufficient to enable a claimant to invoke administrative law, might be misleading, because the fact that some interest is sufficient to allow a claimant to gain standing does not mean that administrative decision-makers are subject to any duty to protect that interest. Instead, the interest may simply establish that the claimant has identified a sufficiently significant reason for the court to investigate whether the administrative decision is in compliance with law which primarily imposes obligations to advance general public interests.

[80] Cases where it can be argued that any right to protection of economic interests that the court recognised was based on the defendant's consent, or the reasonableness of treating the particular defendant *as if* he or she consented, provide a less useful perspective.

[81] *Canadian National Railway* [1992] 1 SCR 1021.

[82] *Perre* (1999) 198 CLR 180.

held, by a majority, that a party which damaged a railway bridge had owed a duty not just to the owner of that bridge but also to a railway company that was a major user of the bridge. In the second the Court held that a party which was responsible for a potato disease being brought into a particular location owed a duty to owners of property situated close to that location who were prohibited or prevented from dealing with their property in certain profitable ways. For convenience, *Perre* can be treated as if the only two successful claimants were an owner of potatoes who was prohibited from exporting them to Western Australia and the owner of a purpose-built potato packing shed who was unable to obtain business because of the prohibition on export: this simplification highlights that it would have been possible, and might have been appropriate, for the Court to have reached a conclusion which distinguished between the claimants in *Perre*.

I do not intend to show that the published judgments in the two cases offer no support to RFA proponents. On the contrary, both sets of judgments contain judicial statements which could not be applied with any predictability and cannot be reconciled with the moral vision of 'equal freedom'. But what if the cases are treated as involving the recognition of a right—in *Canadian National Railway*, a right similar to that of a property owner in those who are in a particular form of 'joint venture' with the property owner, and in *Perre*, a right of a property owner to complain about behaviour bringing about a prohibition of use of property?[83] Would these limited general rights demonstrate the validity of the catalogued reasons why tort law should not stray beyond protecting personal and property rights?

Focusing first on the 'joint venture' extension, there is no reason to think that such a right could not ground a real duty or would be too nebulous to permit a 'substitutionary' remedy. Further, there is no reason to anticipate that designing the 'edge' of 'joint venture', or applying the concept, would involve tasks more obviously unconstitutional than those involved at the edge of property rights (or at the edge of personal or contractual rights). Such a right would, however, clearly violate the formal demand that one person cannot have a right to an external thing if some other person has a superior right to it.

Would such a right also be incompatible with the moral vision of 'equal freedom'? If co-ownership is compatible with 'equal freedom' then this suggests that more than one person may be able to use an external thing simultaneously for pursuing their purposes. Moreover, the different degrees of protection for real and personal property suggest that 'equal

---

[83] The claim of the owner of a purpose-built potato packing shed in *Perre* might be thought to depend on a combination of *both* extensions: in other words, perhaps this claimant had to establish that the potato owners *could* claim *and* it was in a 'joint venture' with the owners.

freedom' does not demand a single universal degree of opportunity to use all external things to pursue purposes free from the interference of others; use of personal property can be subject to greater interference than use of real property. Combining these insights it is not clear that the sort of 'unequal joint ownership'[84] created by certain types of 'joint venture' should be immediately treated as being incapable of conferring a limited sort of private law right on the secondary party.

Turning to the extension of protection of property rights from 'damage' to 'official prohibition', here it seems even clearer that the design and application of the new 'edge' is likely to be no less predictable and no more unconstitutional than the issues at the existing 'edge' of damage. Moreover, here there is no conceptual problem with someone having a superior right to the thing (the potatoes[85]). This extension also looks more defensible with regard to compatibility with 'equal freedom' since bringing about a restriction on how property is dealt with by means of threats of criminal sanctions seems easy to classify as a serious interference with the owner's opportunity to pursue his or her purposes using his or her external thing.

V. CONCLUSION

The goal of this chapter was to evaluate the 'good reasons' that some RFA proponents have identified to explain *why* general common law rights to purely economic benefits should not exist whilst general common law rights to property do. I suggest that the perspectives provided by the 'edge' of property rights, the broader interests protected by public law and the innovations in Commonwealth tort law all suggest that these reasons are insufficient to justify any 'bright line' between property and purely economic interests. Instrumentalists and RFA proponents who are committed to 'equal freedom' will, of course, want to adopt very different strategies when assessing the merits of any proposal that the 'edge' of tort law's protected interests should be redrawn. But a preference for a RFA of the law of torts should not be treated as a licence to reject all proposals to protect limited purely economic interests out of hand.

---

[84] The 'inequality' may be such that other areas of the law, for example the law of succession, the law of compulsory purchase or the law of taxation, treat the secondary party as a non-owner. But tort law has no reason to treat these classifications as decisive because these areas of the law may not be derived wholly from the moral vision of 'equal freedom'.

[85] The state may, of course, have a power to prohibit the export of the potatoes. But *this* is not inconsistent with the defendant being under a duty not to bring about such a prohibition and the claimant having a right that no one should bring this about, because there is no need to demand that the state has only the 'equal freedom' enjoyed by private individuals.

15

Rights, Pluralism and the Duty of Care

ANDREW ROBERTSON*

I. INTRODUCTION

T HE RIGHTS-BASED MOVEMENT in private law is engaged in the task of seeking the simplest, most coherent explanation of the law. Rights-based scholars of a purist bent, most notably Allan Beever and Robert Stevens,[1] have pursued this agenda in two principal ways. First, they have sought to explain why relevant doctrines can be understood by reference to a concern for protecting primary rights. Secondly, they have strongly criticised judicial reasoning by reference to 'policy', which at its core refers to community welfare concerns, but at its broadest extends to everything that is not consistent with a theory of corrective justice based on Kantian right.[2] Primary targets of this attack include the *Anns v Merton London Borough Council*[3] and *Caparo Industries plc v Dickman*[4] approaches to the duty of care in the law of negligence, and variants of those approaches, all of which explicitly take account of community welfare concerns. While the goal of making the law of negligence simpler and more coherent is a worthy one, this chapter takes issue with the idea that community welfare considerations need to be jettisoned from the determination of duty of care issues.

The current approaches to the duty of care in England, Canada and

---

* This chapter is part of a broader project on policy-based reasoning in private law supported by the Australian Research Council under its Discovery Projects scheme. I am grateful to Allan Beever, Donal Nolan and Robert Stevens for helpful comments on an earlier draft and to Ian Malkin and participants at the Obligations V conference for helpful discussions of the topic.

[1] R Stevens, *Torts and Rights* (Oxford, Oxford University Press, 2007); A Beever, *Rediscovering the Law of Negligence* (Oxford, Hart Publishing, 2007).

[2] Beever, above n 1, at 51.

[3] *Anns v Merton London Borough Council* [1978] AC 728 (HL) (*Anns*).

[4] *Caparo Industries plc v Dickman* [1990] 2 AC 605 (HL).

Australia are pluralist approaches, which are informed by both considerations of justice between the parties and community welfare considerations.
A principal aim of this chapter is to show that a pluralist approach to the
duty of care does not, or need not, involve the kind of 'wholly undifferentiated mish-mash'[5] or 'policy-based free-for-all'[6] to which rights purists
object. This chapter is part of a broader project that is concerned with
understanding the constraints on policy-based reasoning in private law,
and with identifying the structured *via media* that exists between uncon-
strained instrumentalism and entirely policy-free rights-based or corrective
justice approaches to private law.[7]

A. Purist and Pluralist Approaches

There seem to be two distinct strands of thinking about the nature of a
'rights-based' approach to the law of negligence. One strand is founded
on the view that the law of negligence, or at least what we currently
understand as the law of negligence, is concerned with the protection
of specific primary rights, which are identifiable in the abstract.[8] These
include, for example, the right to bodily integrity, rights to property in
land and goods and, less obviously and more controversially, rights arising from undertakings. Stevens and Beever argue that what we understand
as the law of negligence should more explicitly be organised around the
identification and protection of these rights.[9] A second rights-based understanding of the law of negligence is based on the idea that the law of
negligence is concerned with identifying the circumstances in which one
person has a right against another that the second person be mindful of
the first person's legitimate interests.[10] On this view, it is obligations (and
correlative rights) arising out of the relationship between the two parties
that provide the foundation of the duty of care analysis. The approach to
the duty of care that is informed by this second rights-based understanding is sometimes described as a 'relational' approach.

The crucial distinction in rights-based thinking about the law of negligence for present purposes is between those who believe that rights

---

[5] SR Perry, 'Professor Weinrib's Formalism: The Not-So-Empty Sepulchre' (1993) 16 *Harvard Journal of Law and Public Policy* 597, 619 ('institutional pluralism need not be the
kind of undifferentiated mish-mash to which Weinrib objects').

[6] Beever, above n 1, at 142, citing EJ Weinrib, *The Idea of Private Law* (Cambridge MA,
Harvard University Press, 1995) 165–67.

[7] A Robertson, 'Constraints on Policy-Based Reasoning in Private Law' in A Robertson
and HW Tang (eds), *The Goals of Private Law* (Oxford, Hart Publishing, 2009) 261.

[8] The leading exponents of this view are Stevens, above n 1 and Beever, above n 1.

[9] Stevens, above n 1 and Beever, above n 1.

[10] S Perry, 'The Role of Duty of Care in a Rights-Based Theory of Negligence Law' in
A Robertson and HW Tang (eds), *The Goals of Private Law* (Oxford, Hart Publishing,
2009) 79, 91.

analysis does or should provide the exclusive basis on which the law of negligence develops and on which cases are decided, and those who accept that other values can legitimately inform decision-making and doctrinal development in the law of negligence. Rights purists insist that what we understand as the law of negligence is concerned only with the recognition and enforcement of primary legal rights arising from moral duties. Considerations of community welfare do not and must not come into the equation. Indeed, Beever says that the object of his book on the law of negligence is to show that the law of negligence can and should be understood in a principled way 'without appeal to policy.'[11] A pluralist rights-based approach, on the other hand, recognises that the law of negligence is primarily, but not exclusively, concerned with relational considerations.[12] On this view, while the law of negligence is concerned primarily with considerations of interpersonal justice, community welfare considerations still have a legitimate role to play in determining whether a duty of care is owed.

B. The Interpretive Claim

The first part of Beever's argument is the positive claim that a neglected but central question within the law of negligence, which is capable of resolving many problems, is whether the defendant has infringed a primary right of the claimant. A rights-based understanding of the law of negligence would, Beever says, be simpler and more coherent than the present law and would require the abandonment of only a small number of cases which are inconsistent with the theory.[13] Beever defends this argument by reference to the four limbs of the methodology of interpretive legal theory advanced by Stephen Smith.[14] Those four limbs are: *fit* (the extent to which the theory is consistent with the outcomes of cases and possibly also the accepted rules of the given body of law), *coherence* (the extent to which the theory reveals an intelligible order in the given body of law and allows it and related bodies of law to be understood as a unified system), *transparency* (the extent to which the theory is consistent with the explanations given by law-makers, which in the case of interpreting the common law means the explanations given by judges in

---

[11] Beever, above n 1, at 71.

[12] See, eg, Perry, 'Professor Weinrib's Formalism', above n 5, at 618–19; Perry, 'The Role of Duty of Care', above n 10; NJ McBride, 'Rights and the Basis of Tort Law' ch 12 of this book.

[13] Beever, above n 1, at 32.

[14] Stevens also notes that the argument he presents in the first 13 chapters of his book is 'an interpretive one: the rights-based model of the law of torts gives a better account of the common law as we find it': above n 1, at 306.

the cases), and *morality* ('how the law might be thought to be justified even if it is not justified').[15]

Although 'interpretivism' is sometimes treated as a particular camp within private law scholarship,[16] Smith's statement of interpretive legal theory describes what is really an orthodox and widely followed approach to legal analysis. The two most significant points of difference between scholars in the application of the interpretive method relate to the weight to be attributed to each of the four elements and the kinds of normative criteria that occupy the place of 'morality' in the framework. Typically, the reason the interpretive method is applied to a particular problem is that there is no explanation of the legal phenomenon under consideration which strongly satisfies all of the criteria. Different explanations will score better on different elements. A scholar must therefore make a choice as to which of the criteria should be weighted more heavily. The purist, rights-based explanation of the law of negligence clearly scores very highly on coherence (since it is far simpler and internally more coherent than a pluralist view) and poorly on transparency, since judges do not usually justify decisions in negligence cases on the basis of the identification of primary rights.

Beever argues that the law of negligence is in such a mess that we must give relatively little weight to the transparency criterion, at least in relation to cases that constitute 'the modern law of negligence'.[17] There is no doubt that if a new, simpler and more powerful explanation for a legal phenomenon is to be accepted, then transparency must inevitably be traded away in return for coherence. If one were to accept Beever's starting point, then the rights-based understanding would merit close consideration.[18] Much would depend, however, on an evaluation of its fit with the outcomes of the case law, and thus with the existing law as to whether duties of care are or are not generally owed in particular situations. This could only be done against the background of a complete understanding of the 'rights base' of the law of negligence. A significant question is whether inconsistency between certain cases and the rights-based approach demonstrates the incorrectness of those cases or the incorrectness of the rights-based approach. An obvious example of this is provided by the cases that recognise that a solicitor who is instructed to prepare a will owes a duty

[15] SA Smith, *Contract Theory* (Oxford, Oxford University Press, 2004) 18, quoted in Beever, above n 1, at 21.

[16] See, eg, S Hedley, 'The Shock of the Old: Interpretivism in Obligations' in C Rickett and R Grantham (eds), *Structure and Justification in Private Law: Essays for Peter Birks* (Oxford, Hart Publishing, 2009) 205.

[17] Beever, above n 1, at 28.

[18] I have argued elsewhere that, while there are significant problems with the current approaches to determining novel or contentious duty of care issues articulated by the ultimate appellate courts in England, Canada and Australia, those problems can be resolved through a tightening of the current framework: A Robertson, 'Justice, Community Welfare and the Duty of Care' (2011) 127 *Law Quarterly Review* 370.

of care to beneficiaries who stand to benefit under the proposed will.[19] These cases are inconsistent with the rights-based approach because, it is said, the beneficiaries have no primary right against the solicitor which could justify the recognition of a duty to them.[20] But does this lack of fit with a now well-established duty category demonstrate a problem with the cases or suggest a problem with the rights-based approach?[21]

A thorough evaluation of the rights-based approach would also require considerable attention to be paid to the fourth element of the interpretive method. Beever treats the fourth element as concerned only with 'morality' in the form of corrective justice based on Kantian right. But a broader understanding of interpretive methodology sees the fourth element as a space for analysing the extent to which the theory in question fits with whatever normative influences we think there are or should be on the law. On this view, the fourth element in the interpretive method accommodates any argument about 'what ought to happen, or about what is good or bad.'[22] 'Morality' for this purpose could, for example, take the form of economic efficiency or commercial convenience. If, therefore, we believe that the law of negligence serves important functions in protecting certain community welfare interests, or guarding against certain adverse community welfare consequences, then we would need to be satisfied that the rights-based approach adequately protects those interests and guards against those consequences. There are some obvious ways in which the rights-based approach does protect community welfare interests. The restrictions it would impose on liability for pure economic loss, for example, would have the effect of guarding against indeterminate liability, and would therefore make it unnecessary to incorporate this community welfare concern directly into the duty of care inquiry.

---

[19] *White v Jones* [1995] 2 AC 207 (HL); *Hill v Van Erp* (1997) 188 CLR 159.

[20] Beever, above n 1, at 260–69. Stevens, above n 1, at 181–82 suggests that *White v Jones* is best understood as an attempt to vindicate the testator's contractual right against the solicitor to performance. It is difficult to see this as a satisfactory explanation of the case since it is a core characteristic of a private law right that only the holder of the right may enforce it, and in this case the holder of the right had not done so. The circumstances may be seen to create some kind of injustice because the contractual right relates to the conferral of a benefit on a person who does not hold the contractual right, the holder of the right is now dead and his estate has no interest in enforcing it. The proposed beneficiaries are therefore left disappointed if they are unable to establish a non-contractual cause of action. But this is a familiar problem in contract law and the solution has not been for judges to grant to the third party an entitlement to 'vindicate' a right that he or she does not hold. It was of course the inability of judges satisfactorily to address similar injustices that led to the introduction of the Contracts (Rights of Third Parties) Act 1999.

[21] Beever, above n 1, at 32–33 argues the former on the basis that these are not 'central' cases.

[22] Smith, above n 15, at 22.

C. Criticism of Policy-Based Reasoning

This chapter is not, however, concerned with the positive claim that a rights-based understanding of the law of negligence offers a superior explanation as a matter of interpretive legal theory, but with the second limb of the argument for a rights-based understanding in so far as it applies to the duty of care. Stevens characterises the current approach as 'loss-based',[23] while Beever characterises it as 'policy-driven'.[24] The idea that the duty of care is policy-driven is supported by reference to a small number of cases, and commonly only by way of obiter dicta in those cases.[25] Close examination of a broader selection of cases shows that the contemporary approach to the duty of care is not policy-driven but is in fact dominated by relational considerations. This chapter defends a pluralist approach which takes account of both relational and community welfare concerns, considers them separately and sequentially in a two-stage test, and is dominated by the former. This approach depends on the drawing of a clear distinction between considerations of justice between the parties and considerations of community welfare.[26]

II. THE PLURALIST APPROACH TO DUTY

The pluralist approach to duty recognises that whether one person owes another a duty of care depends on both considerations of justice between the parties and community welfare considerations. This may be considered a rights-based approach in the sense that it recognises that the duty stage in the law of negligence is primarily concerned with identifying the circumstances in which one person has a right against another that the second person be mindful of the first person's legitimate interests.[27]

---

[23] Stevens, above n 1, at, eg, 20.

[24] Beever, above n 1, at 174. In Beever's account, the 'policy-driven' approach is pursued by 'policy-driven lawyers' who often fail to understand the issues ('The issues here are much more complex than policy-driven lawyers usually realise': at 258), and who tend to 'invent' policy justifications for outcomes already determined through intuition ('Of course, it is possible for those who support the negligence model to invent yet more policies to reach the appropriate result': at 292).

[25] See ibid, at 168–81.

[26] The discussion that follows draws on the explanation of the two-stage test and the distinction between justice and welfare factors in Robertson, 'Justice, Community Welfare and the Duty of Care', above n 18.

[27] Perry, 'The Role of Duty of Care', above n 10, who characterises it as a 'moral right'. Of course it is not enough that it is morally wrong for the second person to ignore the first person's interests. Rather, we are concerned with 'moral wrongdoing for which the offender must pay': *Donoghue v Stevenson* [1932] AC 562 (HL) 580 (Lord Atkin). Recognition of a duty is therefore dependent on a finding that the defendant is 'in justice obliged to make good his moral wrongdoing by compensating the victims of his negligence': *Caltex Oil Australia Pty Ltd v The Dredge 'Willemstad'* (1976) 136 CLR 529, 575 (Stephen J).

This approach recognises that relational considerations, or questions of interpersonal justice, are the principal determinants of the duty of care question. It is pluralist, however, in the sense that it recognises that community welfare considerations can come into play in a secondary way to negate the duty of care in certain limited circumstances.[28]

A. Justice between the Parties

Most of the factors taken into account in duty of care cases fall into one of two categories: they are either concerned with what is just as between the parties or what is necessary in the interests of community welfare.[29] The first question is whether it is just as between the parties that a duty be owed. This depends on three sets of considerations. The first is reasonable foreseeability (whether a reasonable person in the position of the defendant would have foreseen the risk of harm of the given type to the claimant or a class of persons including the claimant). Secondly, the courts consider a collection of factors traditionally addressed under the heading of proximity (whether the claimant was so closely and directly affected by the defendant's actions that the defendant ought to have had the claimant's interests in mind in deciding whether and how to act), including the extent of the defendant's control over the risk, the extent of the defendant's knowledge of the risk, the extent of the claimant's vulnerability to the type of harm in question, the extent to which the claimant relied on the defendant and whether the defendant assumed responsibility towards the claimant. Thirdly, the courts take into account other considerations of justice between the parties which do not appear to fall within foreseeability or proximity, such as whether a duty of care would be inconsistent with the contractual context in which the interaction between the claimant and the defendant took place and whether the duty would impose an unreasonable burden on the defendant.

B. Second Stage Considerations

The considerations taken into account at the second stage fall into two main categories: *justiciability considerations* (most commonly a concern that a court cannot or should not adjudicate on the question whether a public authority has exercised reasonable care in making a policy decision

---

[28] Stephen Perry has suggested that the pluralist approach is consistent with the two-stage *Anns* test, which 'allows policy considerations in the broader sense to come into play in a secondary or ancillary manner': 'The Role of Duty of Care', above n 10, at 91.

[29] The two principal exceptions are justiciability and deontological concerns, which are discussed below.

involving the allocation of resources)[30] and considerations of *community welfare*. Community welfare considerations themselves fall into four different categories: *first*, concerns about the effect of recognising a duty of care on other legal obligations or on the legal system (such as concern about creating a conflict of duties or a multiplicity of suits);[31] *secondly*, concerns about the effect of recognising a duty on a particular class of defendants (such as concerns about indeterminate liability or the strain on the public purse);[32] *thirdly*, concerns about creating an inefficient allocation of risk (such as by moving the burden from a party who is better placed to predict and prevent the harm or insure against it);[33] and *fourthly*, concerns about adverse behavioural effects (such as encouraging defensive practices, excessive record keeping or the diversion of public resources towards these activities).[34] There are, however, some considerations taken into account in the determination of duty questions that cannot be characterised as either justiciability or community welfare considerations, such as the notion that it might simply be wrong, regardless of the consequences, to recognise a duty in certain circumstances. An example of this is the idea that it would be wrong to recognise a duty of care owed between parties to joint criminal activity.[35]

(i) Trumping and Non-Trumping Factors

Justiciability concerns clearly operate to trump the duty of care in all circumstances in which they arise: the courts cannot and do not weigh justiciability problems against the desirability of recognising a duty.[36] One would expect that deontological concerns would similarly have an all-or-nothing effect, although it is difficult to find examples of cases in which it is clear that a duty of care has been denied on the basis that it would be wrong to recognise a duty. Some community welfare concerns also

---

[30] See, eg, *Brown v British Columbia* [1994] 1 SCR 420.

[31] See, eg, *Cooper v Hobart* [2001] SCC 79, [2001] 3 SCR 537 [37] (McLachlin CJ and Major J for the Court); *Sullivan v Moody* [2001] HCA 59, (2001) 207 CLR 562; *D v East Berkshire Community Health NHS Trust* [2005] UKHL 23, [2005] 2 AC 373.

[32] See, eg, *Cooper v Hobart* [2001] SCC 79, [2001] 3 SCR 537; *Robertson v Swincer* (1989) 52 SASR 356.

[33] See, eg, *Canadian National Railway Co v Norsk Pacific Steamship Co* [1992] 1 SCR 1021, 1122 (La Forest J, dissenting); *Marc Rich & Co v Bishop Rock Marine Co Ltd* [1996] 1 AC 211 (HL) 241 (Lord Steyn).

[34] See, eg, *Stovin v Wise* [1996] AC 923 (HL) 958 (Lord Hoffmann); *Hill v Chief Constable of West Yorkshire* [1989] 1 AC 53 (HL) 63 (Lord Keith); *D'Amato v Badger* [1996] 2 SCR 1071, 1088 (Major J for the Court); *Winnipeg Child and Family Services (Northwest Area) v G* [1997] 3 SCR 925; *Mitchell v Glasgow City Council* [2009] UKHL 11, [2009] 1 AC 874 [28] (Lord Hope).

[35] Another example is the idea expressed in *White v Chief Constable of South Yorkshire* [1999] 2 AC 455 (HL) 510 (Lord Hoffmann) that people would regard it as wrong for police to recover compensation for psychiatric injury suffered in crowd control operations when bereaved relatives receive nothing.

[36] See, eg, *Talarico v Fort Nelson* [2008] BCSC 861 [83]–[84] (Smith J).

operate as trumps in cases in which they are found to arise. It seems that a duty will always be denied when it has a sufficiently serious adverse effect on other obligations or the legal system or would give rise to indeterminate liability.[37] Other community welfare considerations require the court to engage in a balancing exercise. Concerns about the burden the duty would have on a class of potential defendants, the creation of an inefficient allocation of risk or potential adverse behavioural effects do not necessarily require the denial of a duty of care, but may provide grounds for the denial of a duty in combination with other factors or if sufficiently strong.[38]

Where community welfare concerns necessarily require the denial of a duty (ie, in cases involving trumping factors), there is no consideration of pro-duty community welfare considerations. The courts do not, for example, normally say that the recognition of the claimed duty of care would create a conflict of duties or indeterminate liability, but might nevertheless have beneficial effects.[39] The trump always decides the outcome. But where non-trumping community welfare factors arise, the courts may need to weigh the detrimental effects on the community welfare of the recognition of a duty against the community welfare benefits of recognising a duty.[40]

(ii) Pro-Duty Welfare Factors

Because some anti-duty factors do not necessarily require denial of a duty, in some circumstances it is necessary to determine whether, on balance, the community interest requires the denial of the duty. This requires the court to consider whether recognising the duty is likely to bring community welfare benefits. The most important pro-duty welfare factors are as follows. First, recognition of the duty may deter harmful conduct, provide an incentive to take care or raise standards amongst those by whom the duty would be owed.[41] Secondly, recognition of the duty may serve an ombudsman function by assisting in the identification and public exposure of systemic failures in public bodies.[42] Thirdly, the recognition of a

---

[37] See, eg, *Design Services Ltd v Canada* [2008] SCC 22, [2008] 1 SCR 737 [59]–[66] (Rothstein J for the Court); but cf *Bow Valley Husky (Bermuda) Ltd v St John Shipbuilding Ltd* [1997] 3 SCR 1210, 1251 (McLachlin and La Forest JJ).

[38] See, eg, *Marc Rich & Co AG v Bishop Rock Marine Co Ltd* [1996] 1 AC 211 (HL) 241 (Lord Steyn); *Hill v Hamilton-Wentworth Regional Police Services Board* [2007] SCC 41, [2007] 3 SCR 129 (*Hamilton-Wentworth*) [43] (McLachlin CJ for McLachlin CJ, Binnie, LeBel, Deschamps, Fish and Abella JJ).

[39] cf *Bow Valley Husky (Bermuda) Ltd v St John Shipbuilding Ltd* [1997] 3 SCR 1210, 1251 (McLachlin J for La Forest and McLachlin JJ).

[40] See, eg, *Waters v Commissioner of Police* [2000] 1 WLR 1607 (HL) 1619–20 (Lord Hutton).

[41] See, eg, *Barrett v Enfield London Borough Council* [2001] 2 AC 550 (HL) 568 (Lord Slynn); *Arthur JS Hall & Co v Simons* [2002] 1 AC 615 (HL) 681 (Lord Steyn).

[42] See, eg, *Waters v Commissioner of Police* [2000] 1 WLR 1607 (HL) 1619 (Lord Hutton); *Hamilton-Wentworth* [2007] SCC 41, [2007] 3 SCR 129.

duty may encourage socially desirable behaviour, such as the repair of dangerous buildings.[43] Fourthly, the duty may result in the efficient allocation of particular losses by shifting the burden to the party who is best placed to prevent the harm or insure against it.[44] Fifthly, recognition of the duty may serve an important vindicatory function in circumstances such as negligent police investigation.[45]

C. Can Justice and Welfare Be Separated?

Considerations of justice between the parties and considerations of community welfare are commonly grouped together under the label 'policy'. Although both require the court to make normative judgments, the normative judgments the courts are required to make at the first stage are fundamentally different from those the court is required to make at the second stage. Whether couched in the language of proximity or not, the first stage inquiry requires the court to determine whether the relationship between the parties was such that the defendant ought at the relevant time to have had the claimant's interests in contemplation when considering whether and how to act. This is a relational question, or what is sometimes described as a matter of interpersonal justice. It is not a question whether, all things considered, a duty ought to be recognised, but a question of what the claimant can reasonably expect of the defendant having regard to the relationship between them. In difficult cases, this involves an assessment of the proper scope and limits of the claimant's personal responsibility and, particularly in a case involving a positive duty to act, the proper scope and limits of the defendant's autonomy. These are questions of what, as a matter of interpersonal justice, the parties owe one another, rather than questions about broader community interests.

The second stage, on the other hand, is not concerned with what is just as between the parties, but only with the interests of the broader community. The facts of *Lowns v Woods* provide a useful illustration of the distinction.[46] This example is a useful one because it is a fact situation in which considerations of justice and welfare might be considered difficult to distinguish. Only the basic facts of the case will be used here to illustrate the issues that arise. A child was having an epileptic seizure in a flat in Sydney. His sister was sent to fetch the defendant, a local medical practi-

---

[43] See, eg, *Winnipeg Condominium Corporation No 36 v Bird Construction Co Ltd* [1995] 1 SCR 85.

[44] See, eg, *Edgeworth Contruction Ltd v ND Lea & Associates Ltd* [1993] 3 SCR 206, 221–22 (McLachlin J for Sopinka, Gonthier, Cory, McLachlin, Iacobucci and Major JJ).

[45] See, eg, *Hamilton-Wentworth* [2007] SCC 41, [2007] 3 SCR 129 [35] (McLachlin CJ for McLachlin CJ, Binnie, LeBel, Deschamps, Fish and Abella JJ).

[46] *Lowns v Woods* (1996) Aust Torts Rep 81-376 (New South Wales Court of Appeal).

tioner, who had no professional relationship with the child but was in his
surgery some 300 metres away. The doctor was told the child was having
a 'bad fit', but refused to leave his surgery and insisted that the child be
brought to him. The child suffered serious brain damage which would
probably have been prevented had the doctor provided prompt medical
attention. Whether the doctor owed the child a duty of care depended
on whether there was a relationship of sufficient proximity between the
doctor and the child. This is a question of interpersonal justice, which
requires an assessment of the proper scope of the doctor's autonomy, and
the question of what might reasonably be expected of a qualified medical
practitioner in a professional setting who is asked to provide emergency
medical assistance to a child who is a short distance away.

That relational question is quite different from the community welfare
issues raised by these facts, which might include whether recognising a
duty might deter some people from entering the medical profession, and
whether the consequent harm to the community welfare might be outweighed by the community welfare benefits of compelling or encouraging
those with medical training, when they are in their professional setting,
to provide emergency assistance to persons nearby. The question of what
the child was entitled to expect of the doctor as a matter of interpersonal
justice is distinguishable from the question whether the duty might have
community welfare benefits. Moreover, the doctor can be found to have
committed a legal wrong in failing to assist the child only if the doctor
infringed a norm of conduct existing at the time of the alleged breach.[47]
Whether there might be community welfare harm or benefits arising in
the future if the duty is recognised cannot be relevant to that question.
While community welfare considerations can be forward-looking, interpersonal justice considerations logically cannot.

There is at least one point at which there is such a strong overlap
between justice considerations and community welfare considerations that
they might be regarded as indistinguishable. That is in relation to the
burden of imposing a duty on the defendant. While the burden of the
duty is principally a question considered at the breach stage, the courts
do in some instances take it into account at the duty stage, particularly in
omissions cases where the duty is framed narrowly as a duty to avoid a
particular type of harm through particular identified means.[48] This question will overlap factually with a second stage concern about the effect
of recognising the duty on a particular class of defendants. In *Robertson
v Swincer*, for example, one of the reasons for denying a general duty on

---

[47] See JCP Goldberg and BC Zipursky, 'Torts as Wrongs' (2010) 88 *Texas Law Review* 917.
[48] See, eg, *Stovin v Wise* [1996] AC 923 (HL) 930–31 (Lord Nicholls); *Smith v Littlewoods Organisation Ltd* [1987] AC 241 (HL) 280 (Lord Goff); *Ramias v Johnson* [2009]
ABQB 386 [42] (Martin J); *Blue v Ontario* (Unreported, Ontario Superior Court of Justice,
Roberts J, 26 April 2009) [19].

the part of parents to protect their children from harm through adequate supervision was that the existence of such a duty would pose a considerable threat to the financial well-being of parents and 'might be difficult to insure against'.[49]

The first and second stage versions of this consideration do, however, involve different questions. At the first stage the question is whether, given the burden that would be imposed on the defendant, it would be unjust as between the parties for the duty to be recognised. The second stage question is whether the burden (of performance, liability, or both) on the class of persons by whom the duty would be owed would have such adverse effects on the welfare of the community that, in the interests of the community, it ought not to be recognised. An example of this is the idea that if auditors were found to owe a duty to future investors in the company, this would impose such a heavy burden on them that it would be likely to reduce the supply of auditing services, and this 'would be detrimental to the interests of creditors, investors and business generally.'[50] This is perhaps the point at which the distinction between justice and welfare considerations is at its finest and it must be conceded that when the courts are concerned about the adverse effects of a duty on the relevant class of defendants they often fail to make clear whether their ultimate concern is with considerations of justice between the parties or considerations of community welfare.

D. Should Justice and Welfare Be Treated Separately?

If it is possible to separate justice considerations from welfare considerations in the manner just suggested, then there are distinct advantages in considering them separately through a sequential two-stage test such as the modified version of the *Anns* test applied in Canada. Novel or contentious duty of care questions are then approached by asking first whether a duty of care is justified by considerations of justice between the parties. If it is just as between the parties to recognise a duty, then a prima facie duty is established. At the second stage the court asks whether considerations of community welfare require the denial of the duty, notwithstanding the fact that justice requires it. There are at least two advantages in approaching the duty question in this way, with separate and sequential treatment of justice and welfare considerations.

First, under this approach community welfare considerations are not taken into account unless and until a prima facie duty has been established on the basis of considerations of justice between the parties. If the

---

[49] *Robertson v Swincer* (1989) 52 SASR 356, 361 (King CJ).
[50] *Esanda Finance Corporation Ltd v Peat Marwick Hungerfords* (1997) 188 CLR 241, 283 (McHugh J).

community welfare is taken into account alongside proximity and fore-seeability as part of a single test or inquiry, this would raise the question of who should bear the burden of persuasion in relation to community welfare: is it for the claimant to show that there is a community welfare benefit in imposing the duty, or for the defendant to show that the public interest requires the denial of the duty?[51] The two-stage approach clearly places the burden of persuasion on the defendant.[52] Where it is just as between the parties to recognise a duty, there is a prima facie community interest in recognising it. This idea underlies the observation that the most important policy consideration is that wrongs must be remedied.[53] The idea that the burden of persuasion in relation to community welfare rests on the defendant is significant because it is consistent with the idea that private law obligations are not imposed for community welfare reasons (other than the community interest in ensuring that wrongs are remedied), but may be denied for community welfare reasons.

The second and more significant advantage of the two-stage approach is that it avoids the need for courts to weigh justice considerations against welfare considerations. Under the two-stage approach these incommensurable sets of considerations are dealt with entirely separately, with each being reduced to a yes or no question. If considerations of justice between the parties justify the recognition of a particular duty, then such a duty will be recognised unless considerations of community welfare require otherwise. The court is not required to weigh the two sets of considerations against one another because the second stage of the inquiry takes as a given the fact that, as between the parties, the duty is justified. Thus, properly understood, the two-stage approach to duty cannot be criticised on the basis that it 'calls for a balancing of incommensurables'.[54] Indeed, the defining feature of the two-stage test is its avoidance of the need for judgment as to the relative strength of justice and welfare factors through its separate and sequential treatment of those two sets of considerations.[55]

Jane Stapleton has argued that the sequential approach to the duty question 'is productive of confusing and unnecessary line-drawing' and risks

---

[51] This question is raised by D Howarth, *Textbook on Tort* (London, Butterworths, 1995) 195.

[52] cf C Booth and D Squires, *The Negligence Liability of Public Authorities* (Oxford, Oxford University Press, 2006) 86 ('Post-*Caparo*, the starting presumption is that a new category of duty will be recognised only when policy factors militate in favour of its recognition').

[53] *Waters v Commissioner of Police* [2000] 1 WLR 1607 (HL) 1618–19 (Lord Hutton, quoting *X (Minors) v Bedfordshire County Council* [1995] 2 AC 633 (HL)), 749 (Lord Browne-Wilkinson, who was in turn approving an observation made by Sir Thomas Bingham MR in *M (A Minor) v Newham London Borough Council* [1995] 2 AC 633 (CA) 663).

[54] Beever, above n 1, at 173.

[55] See further Robertson, 'Justice, Community Welfare and the Duty of Care', above n 18, esp at 293–95.

sending lower courts on the 'fruitless errand' of allocating different factors to different stages.[56] I have already suggested above that, although there is factual overlap between justice and welfare factors, close scrutiny shows that they are ultimately concerned with different questions. Separating justice and welfare therefore sheds considerable light on the issues raised by particular factors, and helps us to analyse and evaluate the role they should play. The vexed question of insurance provides an example of this. If the question is whether A owes a duty to B to take reasonable care to prevent a particular type of harm, should it be relevant to that issue to consider: (i) whether A is insured against that particular liability to B; (ii) whether people in A's position commonly do insure against such risks; or (iii) whether such insurance is available, so that a person in A's position could insure against such liability? Assume, for example, that the issue is whether a parent owes a duty to a young child to take reasonable precautions, including positive steps, to ensure the child's safety when both parent and child are in the vicinity of a road.[57] Should it be relevant to ask whether the defendant parent is insured against such liability, or whether parents can and routinely do insure themselves against risks arising from the care and control of their children?

It is much easier to analyse the relevance of insurance if these 'policy' questions are considered through the more specific lenses of justice and welfare. The question whether A *is* insured could only potentially be relevant as a question of justice between the parties, not as a question of welfare. The only way that might be considered relevant to the issue of justice between the parties is on the basis that the duty would be less burdensome to A if A were insured. But to the extent that the burden on the defendant is relevant to the justice dimension of the duty question, it is the burden of fulfilling the duty that is pertinent, not the burden of liability.[58] Whether A is insured is irrelevant to the burden of fulfilling the duty. Moreover, if the burden of liability were relevant to the justice question, then whether A has reduced that burden through insurance might properly be considered as a matter of choice for A which does not affect A's legal relationship with B.[59] Insurance must therefore be considered irrelevant to the issue of justice between the parties.

---

[56] J Stapleton, 'Duty of Care Factors: A Selection from the Judicial Menus' in P Cane and J Stapleton (eds), *The Law of Obligations: Essays in Celebration of John Fleming* (Oxford, Oxford University Press, 1998) 59, 90 n 116.

[57] This example draws on the facts and some of the reasoning in *Robertson v Swincer* (1989) 52 SASR 356.

[58] See Robertson, 'Justice, Community Welfare and the Duty of Care', above n 18, 383–84, discussing *Smith v Littlewoods Organisation Ltd* [1987] AC 241 (HL) 280 (Lord Goff), *Ramias v Johnson* [2009] ABQB 386 and *Blue v Ontario* (Unreported, Ontario Superior Court of Justice, Roberts J, 26 April 2009), all of which clearly support the point made in the text.

[59] cf J Stapleton, 'Tort, Insurance and Ideology' (1995) 58 *Modern Law Review* 820, 825–26.

The second issue is whether the availability and widespread use of insurance is a relevant consideration of community welfare. If the two-stage approach is followed, the question of insurance will only become relevant if a prima facie duty is established on the basis of relational considerations of justice between the parties. Even then, the availability of insurance as a pro-duty factor only arises for consideration if there is some anti-duty factor that calls for a balancing exercise to be carried out. The fact that a particular class of defendants is likely to be insured simply does not arise for consideration as an independent reason for imposing a duty: it is not 'a generally valid factor in the resolution of duty of care issues'.[60] But it becomes a highly relevant consideration if a concern is raised to the effect that recognition of the duty would impose an onerous and socially undesirable financial burden on the relevant class of potential defendants. The availability and use of insurance might then legitimately be taken into account to counterbalance that concern. If the court ultimately concludes that a duty ought to be recognised, it could not be said that the duty has been imposed *because* the risk is insurable by people in A's position. Rather, the duty has been imposed for reasons of justice between the parties. The availability of insurance is, however, properly taken into account for the very limited purpose of negating the anti-duty concern about the burden of liability on the particular class of defendants.

E. Constraints on the Use of Policy

The above discussion of insurance provided an illustration of the way in which the two-stage approach to duty constrains the use of community welfare considerations. In its constraining effect, the two-stage framework stands in contrast to an approach in which 'all factors for and against are balanced against one another and not evaluated separately and in sequence'.[61] The two-stage approach constrains the use of community welfare considerations in the following ways. First, the two-stage test renders community welfare considerations entirely irrelevant unless and until a prima facie duty has been established on the basis of relational considerations. Secondly, the two-stage approach limits the role of community welfare considerations by preventing them from playing a minor contributing role to a decision taken 'in the round'.[62] Because the two-stage test avoids the need for an 'in the round' evaluation of factors,

[60] Stapleton, 'Duty of Care Factors', above n 56, at 64.

[61] ibid, at 90.

[62] Decision-making in proprietary estoppel is sometimes said to require the assessment of a broad range of factors 'in the round': see A Robertson, 'Unconscionability and Proprietary Estoppel' in E Bant and M Harding (eds), *Exploring Private Law* (Cambridge, Cambridge University Press, 2010) 402, 415–21.

community welfare considerations are either determinative or dismissed. They are determinative only if, taken by themselves, they are sufficiently strong to require the denial of the duty.

Thirdly, and most significantly, the two-stage approach renders pro-duty welfare considerations irrelevant in all but very limited circumstances. Pro-duty community welfare considerations are relevant only where three requirements are satisfied. First, a prima facie duty must be established on the basis of considerations of justice between the parties. Secondly, there must be no overwhelming community welfare considerations (such as a conflict of duties, a policy decision by a government agency being called into question or indeterminate liability) which operate to trump the prima facie duty regardless of any welfare benefits. Thirdly, there must be some anti-duty welfare considerations that call for the court to engage in a balancing exercise. On this view the absence of welfare justifications for recognition of the duty, such as the idea that the duty would have no deterrent effect,[63] does not itself provide a basis for denial of the duty.[64] It is clear from the above discussion that, if a two-stage approach is followed, the question whether the duty is desirable from a community welfare point of view will only be relevant in limited circumstances and for a limited purpose.

III. CRITICISM OF THE PLURALIST APPROACH

A. Criticism of Proximity

At times both Beever and Stevens ignore the element of proximity and treat the question whether the recognition of a duty of care in a particular situation can be justified on the basis of 'policy' as the only alternative to a rights-based explanation. For example, Stevens discusses '[t]he weakness of seeking to explain *White v Jones* by appeals to policy without reference to the testator's contractual right'.[65] This is to some extent understandable since the speeches in the House of Lords in that case were focused on resolving the conceptual and practical difficulties arising from recognition of a duty that was for the most part assumed to be justified as a matter of justice between the parties. But it would indeed be misguided to attempt to explain *White v Jones* simply by reference to 'policy'. The

---

[63] See, eg, *Winnipeg Child and Family Services (Northwest Area) v G* [1997] 3 SCR 925, 951 (McLachlin J for Lamer CJ, La Forest, L'Heureux-Dube, Gonthier, Cory, McLachlin and Iacobucci JJ); *Dobson v Dobson* [1999] 2 SCR 753, 772 (Cory J for Lamer CJ, L'Heureux-Dubé, Gonthier, Iacobucci and Binnie JJ).

[64] Where a court is satisfied that there are negative community welfare effects of recognition of a duty, however, it may be relevant to note that there are no pro-duty welfare benefits sufficient to outweigh those negative effects.

[65] Stevens, above n 1, at 181.

basis for the duty of care recognised in *White v Jones* was, and could only be, grounded in considerations of justice between the parties. Cast in terms of proximity, this required a finding that the intended beneficiaries were persons so closely and directly affected by the solicitor's actions that the solicitor ought to have had them in contemplation when carrying out the testator's instructions.[66] Whether or not the proximity label is used is not of great consequence because, as Stephen Perry has pointed out, the factors that are taken into account in determining whether there was a relationship of proximity between the parties are 'among the most important considerations that bear on the question of whether one person has, as a moral matter, a *right* as against another person that the latter be mindful of the former's legitimate interests.'[67] This is borne out by the fact that the Australian courts take into account the same factors that inform the 'proximity' inquiry in England and Canada, despite the High Court of Australia's rejection of the proximity label.[68]

There is no doubt that some novel and contentious fact situations require difficult judgments to be made as to whether the defendant 'ought' to have had the claimant in contemplation. As noted above, this requires, inter alia, consideration of the proper scope and limits of the defendant's autonomy and the proper scope and limits of the claimant's personal responsibility. In some cases these are, as Beever has said, deeply political and highly controversial questions.[69] But this does not mean that proximity 'has come to mean anything and nothing', that it is 'a *tabula rasa* and is incapable of directing judicial decision making' or that it is 'meaningless'.[70] It means that difficult cases call for the exercise of judgment according to certain specified criteria, which focus the court's attention on the particular elements involved in determining this question of interpersonal justice.

---

[66] Thus Steyn LJ stated in the Court of Appeal in *White v Jones* [1995] 2 AC 207 (CA) 238 that 'The element of a close and direct relationship is present and satisfies the requirement of "proximity" or "neighbourhood" as explained in *Murphy v Brentwood District Council* [1991] 1 AC 398 and *Caparo Industries Plc v Dickman* [1990] 2 AC 605. The real question is whether it is fair, just and reasonable that the law should impose a duty.' For an explanation of reasons for this conclusion which do not rely on an assumption of responsibility, see *Hill v Van Erp* (1997) 188 CLR 159, 234 (Gummow J): the engagement of the solicitor was designed to enhance the economic position of the intended beneficiary, the solicitor exercised control over the realisation of the testator's intentions and there was a close connection between the solicitor's conduct and its effect on the intended beneficiary.

[67] Perry, 'The Role of Duty of Care', above n 10, at 91.

[68] See, eg, D Tan, 'The Salient Features of Proximity: Examining the *Spandeck* Formulation for Establishing a Duty of Care' [2010] *Singapore Journal of Legal Studies* 459, 469–81.

[69] Beever, above n 1, at 7.

[70] ibid, at 178, 184.

B. Corrective Justice, Distributive Justice and Community Welfare

Beever accepts that a two-stage approach to duty (determined primarily by relational considerations but denying duty where public interest requires it) seems sensible and consistent with the approach the courts take, but rejects it as incoherent because it amounts to the idea that the law should do corrective justice unless to do so would be distributively unjust, in which case it should do distributive justice.[71] There are two important points to be made in response to this. The first is that, at the second stage of the two-stage test for duty the courts can be said to be doing distributive justice only in the very broadest sense. Beever characterises distributive justice as a concern with the fair distribution of benefits and burdens within a society.[72] Although 'distributive justice' is an expression that has a fairly imprecise meaning, for present purposes the heart of the idea would seem to be that it refers to a scheme of distribution based on some principle or criterion such as fairness, equality or desert.[73] In the exceptional duty cases in which community welfare dictates the outcome, the courts are not refusing corrective justice because liability would be distributively unjust as between the parties. They are acting on the conclusion that, whatever might otherwise have been required by considerations of justice between the parties, for reasons of community welfare unrelated to the parties before the court the law cannot recognise a legal duty to take reasonable care in this situation. The claimant's individual interest in compensation for injury must in these circumstances yield to the greater public good. If there is a scheme operating at the second stage of the test for duty, it is a very loose one that is concerned broadly with welfare, utility or efficiency in the community as a whole, rather than one that has any concern with distribution between individuals on the basis of a principle such as fairness, equality or desert.

It may be accepted that the reasons for denying a duty of care at the second stage do not together constitute a coherent distributive scheme, and that the second stage welfare considerations do not cohere with the justice considerations taken into account at the first stage. The two-stage approach to duty is, however, perfectly coherent in a normative sense. Throughout private law there are situations in which the dictates of justice between individuals yield to overwhelming community welfare needs, and rights that might otherwise be recognised are denied.[74] Beever claims that his argument that the law of negligence can and should 'be understood in such a way that policy plays no role' cannot be defeated by showing

---

[71] ibid, at 66.

[72] ibid, at 64.

[73] This seems to be the way in which Beever uses the expression elsewhere: see, eg, ibid, at 69, 265.

[74] Robertson, 'Constraints on Policy-Based Reasoning', above n 7, at 261, 278–79.

that policy analysis plays a role outside the law of negligence.[75] But as I have argued previously, the fact that private law rights (eg, in the law of contract and confidential information) are routinely denied on the basis of community welfare considerations is relevant to our understanding of the legitimacy of legal principles that have that effect within the law of negligence.[76] While the movement between justice and welfare does make the law of negligence more complicated and less coherent than it would be if it could all be explained by reference to a single underlying idea, a consideration of other parts of private law shows us that there is a normative coherence to the idea that private law rights are denied where community welfare requires it. That does not ipso facto justify the denial of rights for welfare reasons in the law of negligence, but it does establish a baseline eligibility for such principles within the law of negligence.[77] Indeed, since considerations of justice yield to considerations of overwhelming welfare considerations elsewhere in private law, it would be odd if they did not also do so in the law of negligence.

C. Judicial Competence

Perhaps the strongest argument made by rights purists against taking community welfare considerations into account in private law in general, and in the determination of duty of care questions in particular, is that the assessment of questions of community welfare is beyond the technical competence of the courts because judges lack the necessary information and training.[78] There is no single, comprehensive answer to this concern, and perhaps we should not expect a simple answer. The community welfare considerations that inform duty questions are not homogenous in nature and the role they play in the determination of duty questions is not straightforward. There are, however, several factors that might ameliorate concerns about judicial competence. The starting point is that the assessment of community welfare considerations plays a minor role in judicial reasoning in relation to the duty of care. The number of cases actually decided on the basis of community welfare considerations alone is small. Pro-liability community welfare considerations do not decide the outcome of duty cases, but operate only to neutralise anti-duty considerations and allow cases to be decided on the basis of considerations of justice between the parties. Anti-duty welfare considerations do occasionally decide cases,

---

[75] Beever, above n 1, at 171.

[76] Robertson, 'Constraints on Policy-Based Reasoning', above n 7, at 277–79.

[77] ibid, at 272, citing N MacCormick, 'Coherence in Legal Justification' in A Peczenik, L Lindahl and B van Roermund (eds), *Theory of Legal Science* (Dordrecht, D Reidel Publishing, 1984) 235, 244.

[78] See, eg, Beever, above n 1, at 172; Stevens, above n 1, at 309–12.

but in most cases in which they are mentioned, this is done by way of obiter dicta to support a no-duty decision that has already been made on the basis of insufficient proximity. Where community welfare considerations are operative, they commonly concern issues that judges are undoubtedly qualified to decide, such as the question whether the recognition of the duty in question would place the defendant in a position where he or she would owe conflicting duties, or whether the recognition of a duty would require the court to adjudicate on an issue that is outside the court's competence, such as a policy decision by a public authority involving the allocation of resources.

The two most controversial sets of community welfare considerations are, first, those based on ideas about community values and, secondly, those based on speculation about the effects of a particular rule or decision on people's behaviour. In the assessment of community values, Beever might be thought to have some basis for claiming that '"policy" in practice reflects little more than someone's intuitions and prejudices in particular circumstances.'[79] Considerations of this kind, however, arise only in exceptional cases at the appellate level. More significantly, community values are not free-floating notions to be applied wherever the judge thinks appropriate: they operate only in limited circumstances, and the development of new categories appears to be almost exclusively the province of appellate courts. In the exceptional cases in which novel decisions need to be made in relation to community values, the court's assessment of those values can also be informed by material such as the reports of the Law Commission and the Royal Commission on New Reproductive Technologies which were relied upon in *Dobson v Dobson*.[80]

Observations about the likely effect of a duty on people's behaviour are very often mentioned in passing in judgments without directly influencing the decision. They are understood to be weak justifications and therefore tend to be treated with caution.[81] It is also, of course, open to courts to rely on published empirical studies about the effect of particular rules on people's behaviour where they are available, as the majority of the Supreme Court of Canada did in *Hill v Hamilton-Wentworth Regional Police Services Board*.[82] In that case McLachlin CJ cited and relied upon academic literature, which revealed a lack of convincing evidence to support the claim that tort liability has a detrimental effect on the investigation of crime, and indeed included evidence that contradicted that claim. This provided the basis for the conclusion that a duty of care,

---

[79] Beever, above n 1, at 54.
[80] *Dobson v Dobson* [1999] 2 SCR 753, 770–75 (Cory J for Lamer CJ, L'Heureux-Dubé, Gonthier, Cory, Iacobucci and Binnie JJ).
[81] *Barrett v Enfield London Borough Council* [1998] QB 367 (CA) 380 (Evans LJ), approved on appeal [2001] 2 AC 550 (HL) 568 (Lord Slynn), 589 (Lord Hutton).
[82] *Hamilton-Wentworth* [2007] SCC 41, [2007] 3 SCR 129 [57]–[58] (McLachlin CJ for McLachlin CJ, Binnie, LeBel, Deschamps, Fish and Abella JJ).

which had been established on justice grounds, should not be denied on the ground that it would have an adverse impact on community welfare by way of a 'chilling effect' on the investigation of crime.[83]

Beever has claimed that 'the appeal to policy in fact requires judges to make decisions of a kind that cannot be made in a public and open manner but must be made in an intuitive and private one.'[84] The basis on which this claim is made is not clear. The denial of a duty of care on community welfare grounds tends to be fairly clearly explained in judgments, and those explanations create the possibility of public scrutiny. Community welfare considerations that are articulated in judgments can be challenged, for example, by lawyers and by the organisations of lawyers that represent the interests of claimants and defendants. The legal academy, with its increasingly interdisciplinary training, has a particularly important role to play in scrutinising and challenging assumptions about the likely effect of particular rules on people's behaviour. This process is made possible by the fact that the community welfare factors that are taken into account in duty cases are rarely ad hoc or confined to the circumstances of a particular case. The factors that are taken into account are developed over time and applied with some consistency, even across jurisdictions, although of course there are important issues on which ultimate appellate courts in different jurisdictions take different approaches.

Beever raises three potential problems with the idea of judges relying on published studies. The first is that 'policy advice is often conflicting and judges are generally not in a position to decide on the merits of such advice.'[85] This ignores the narrow scope of the decision to be made on community welfare in a duty of care case, which is *not* a broad question as to whether the recognition of a duty of care would represent a good policy choice. The only decision to be made is whether recognition of the claimed duty would have sufficiently serious adverse community welfare consequences that it ought not to be recognised. If the court is not satisfied that the recognition of a duty of care would have significant adverse community welfare consequences then the duty is recognised according to considerations of interpersonal justice. Secondly, Beever argues, 'the interpretation and application of policy advice often calls for expertise in the subject matter of the advice.'[86] But in the executive branch of government policy decisions are routinely made on the advice of, rather than by, experts in the subject matter of the advice. Thirdly, Beever suggests, if judges are to rely on reports prepared by those with greater expertise then, 'at least in final appellate courts', 'we should replace those currently

---

[83] ibid.
[84] Beever, above n 1, at 175.
[85] ibid, at 173.
[86] ibid.

on the bench with the experts who write the reports.'[87] This assumes not only that policy decisions should be made by experts, rather than on the basis of expert advice, but also that the determination of policy questions is all that is involved in duty of care cases. It ignores the fact that community welfare issues in duty of care cases are, at the very most, secondary considerations nested within a decision-making framework that is primarily concerned with issues of justice between the parties.

In cases in which the facts require it, judicial speculation about consequences may be better than the alternative, which is for the courts to be blind to those consequences. The idea that the courts should be blind to consequences ignores the fundamental pragmatism of the common law. Just as contract law needs to provide 'a reasonable and fair framework for contracting',[88] 'facilitate commercial dealings'[89] and 'make commercial sense',[90] the law of negligence cannot do justice between the parties in a way that has significant adverse consequences for the rest of the community. In the law of contract there are pockets of intense debate as to which of two or more possible solutions to a particular problem is the most commercially sensible.[91] Similarly, there is scope for legitimate debate in the law of negligence as to whether a duty of care in a given situation (such as a duty owed by investigating police to a suspect) would be likely to have sufficiently serious adverse consequences for the community welfare (eg, by way of excessive record keeping, defensive policing or the diversion of resources) that it ought not to be recognised. There is also scope for legitimate debate as to whether those adverse consequences are likely to be offset by the community welfare benefits that are likely to flow from acceptance of the duty (such as the ombudsman effect).

It is now well-accepted that ultimate courts of appeal exercise significant law-making power, and no less so in relation to duty of care issues than elsewhere.[92] A quotidian first instance decision on the duty of care, however, involves nothing like a legislative choice. Under a properly structured approach to the duty of care, judges are significantly constrained as to the circumstances in which community welfare factors may be brought into account. The second stage of a two-stage test is not, as Beever has claimed, 'a license for judges to consider *anything* they believe important'[93]

---

[87] ibid.

[88] J Steyn, 'Contract Law: Fulfilling the Reasonable Expectations of Honest Men' (1997) 113 *Law Quarterly Review* 433, 442.

[89] ibid, at 436.

[90] See Lord Hoffmann, 'The Achilleas: Custom and Practice or Foreseeability?' (2010) 14 *Edinburgh Law Review* 47, 59.

[91] A good example of this is the issue discussed by Lord Hoffmann, ibid; namely, whether the remoteness rule should limit recovery where the late re-delivery of a vessel on expiration of a time charter results in the loss of a lucrative subsequent fixture in a falling market.

[92] See, eg, J Stapleton, 'The Golden Thread at the Heart of Tort Law: Protection of the Vulnerable' (2003) 24 *Australian Bar Review* 135, 137–40.

[93] Beever, above n 1, at 171 n 15 (emphasis in original).

or 'a *tabula rasa* that judges are called on to fill in however they see fit in individual cases.'[94] Nor is it accurate to say that the *Anns* test 'invites and requires judges to make open-ended political decisions' or invites them to 'pursue their personal visions of the good society.'[95] The first point is that the judgment to be made at the second stage of the *Anns* test is limited to the question whether the existence of a duty of care in the given circumstances constitutes such a threat to the community welfare that it ought not to be recognised. Neither the acceptance of a duty of care on the basis that it does not significantly threaten community welfare, nor the denial of a duty of care on the basis that it does constitute such a threat, involves an open-ended political decision. It is difficult to see how one can pursue one's vision of the good society by *denying* the existence of a duty of care. There would be far greater scope for this if a judge were free to *impose* a duty of care on the basis that this would advance community welfare, but the law clearly does not allow this. The second point relates to the kinds of considerations that can be and are taken into account. While the categories of community welfare falling within the second stage are not closed, they are well-defined and applied with remarkable consistency. Judges who might be inclined to take novel considerations into account are significantly constrained in a number of ways, both institutional and methodological, in doing so.[96]

IV. CONCLUSION

A pluralist approach to the duty of care is one that accords adequate weight to considerations of both justice and welfare. Such an approach is workable and defensible only if it is properly structured, with a well-defined role for community welfare considerations. The genius of the pluralist approach laid down by Lord Wilberforce in *Anns* is that it provides an effective mechanism for mediating between the interests of justice and welfare. It does so by prioritising relational considerations, or questions of interpersonal justice, and looking beyond the interests of the parties only where the recognition of the duty poses a threat to community welfare. The courts do not in these exceptional cases '[treat] the dispute as an occasion on which to engage in social policy debate ... ignoring one or both parties',[97] but recognise, as they do in other areas of private law, that in certain circumstances the concern to do justice between the parties must bow to overwhelming community concerns. The pluralist approach does

---

[94] ibid, at 171. 'Hence, the content of the second stage is entirely indeterminate and is, therefore, empty': at 171 n 15.

[95] ibid, at 171–72.

[96] See Robertson, 'Constraints on Policy-Based Reasoning', above n 7, at 268–70.

[97] Beever, above n 1, at 176.

take seriously the interests of the parties before the court, but also takes seriously the interests of the broader community.[98] If the two-stage test is properly applied, community welfare considerations cannot function as makeweight reasons either in favour of or against the recognition of duty. They either decide the case or are rejected and play no role. This provides a clear, manageable framework for determining duty questions and for mediating between justice and welfare in the rare circumstances in which they conflict. As a matter of form, a highly structured approach such as this stands in contrast to a pluralist, all-things-considered approach, and in stark contrast to any approach that might accurately be characterised as 'policy-driven'.

[98] cf ibid, at 204.

16

'A Tort Against Land': Private Nuisance as a Property Tort

DONAL NOLAN*

I. INTRODUCTION

T HE THESIS OF this chapter is that private nuisance can only
properly be understood as a tort which protects rights in land,
and that, understood in this way, it is a thoroughly coherent cause
of action. I will term this the 'property tort analysis' of private nuisance.
The chapter fits with the theme of this collection because the property
tort analysis of private nuisance is consistent with the argument of Robert
Stevens in his important book *Torts and Rights* that '[t]he infringement of
rights, not the infliction of loss, is the gist of the law of torts'.[1] I begin
by introducing the property tort analysis and by providing a definition
of private nuisance. The bulk of the chapter is then devoted to showing that the central doctrines of private nuisance law are consistent with
the property tort analysis. In the remainder of the chapter, I look at the
relationship between private nuisance and trespass to land, identify some
sources of confusion which have served to obscure the underlying coherence of private nuisance and consider the implications of the property tort
analysis for the traditional distinction between property and obligations.
I finish off by making some more general observations about the value
of a rights-based analysis of private law.

Three preliminary points should be made. The first is that there is not
the space to discuss every aspect of the tort of private nuisance, so I have
limited my analysis to those aspects of the cause of action which seem to
me to be most relevant to the property tort analysis. The second point is

* I am grateful to the participants in the discussion of an earlier version of this chapter
at the Obligations V conference for their comments, and also to Jason Neyers and Robert
Stevens for their helpful comments on an earlier draft. The usual caveat applies.
[1] R Stevens, *Torts and Rights* (Oxford, Oxford University Press, 2007) 2.

that my primary focus is on English law. The basic structure of the private nuisance tort and the substance of private nuisance law are similar throughout the common law world, but there are significant differences in some areas, for example when it comes to the rules on standing and the circumstances in which it is appropriate for a court to award damages in lieu of an injunction. On these, and other, questions, it will be seen that the modern English law is particularly conducive to the property tort analysis, but I hope it will be concluded that despite some inconsistencies such an analysis also provides the best interpretation of the cause of action as it has developed in other common law jurisdictions. That brings me to my final preliminary point, which is that my aim is an interpretive one: to provide the best account of private nuisance law *as it stands*.[2] My claim is not therefore that the tort of private nuisance as it has developed provides the best possible means of protecting interests in the use and enjoyment of land. It may be that if we started from scratch we could devise a cause of action (or causes of action) which would do a better job at protecting these interests than private nuisance does. However, in a common law system, there are few opportunities to start from scratch, and in the case of private nuisance doing so would mean turning our back on over 800 years of legal history,[3] and potentially creating significant incoherence within the wider law of real property. It is unlikely that such an enterprise would be worth the candle.

II. 'A TORT AGAINST LAND'

In the leading modern English authority on private nuisance, *Hunter v Canary Wharf Ltd*, Lord Hoffmann described the cause of action as 'a tort against land'.[4] His Lordship obviously did not mean this literally—torts are always against *persons*—but it was a neat way of expressing the idea that a private nuisance is a violation of real property rights, or (as Dyson LJ put it in a recent public nuisance case) that '[t]he essence of the right that is protected by the tort of private nuisance is the right to enjoy one's property'.[5] Similarly, Lord Hope said in the *Hunter* case that '[t]he tort of nuisance is an invasion of the plaintiff's interest in the possession

---

[2] On interpretive accounts or theories of law, see SA Smith, *Contract Theory* (Oxford, Oxford University Press, 2004) ch 1.

[3] John Baker traces the likely origins of private nuisance to the lost legislation which established the assize of novel disseisin in the reign of Henry II (1154–1189): JH Baker, *An Introduction to English Legal History*, 4th edn (London, LexisNexis Butterworths, 2002) 423.

[4] *Hunter v Canary Wharf Ltd* [1997] AC 655 (HL) (*Hunter*) 702. See also *Restatement of the Law, Second: Torts* (St Paul MN, American Law Institute, 1977) (*Second Restatement*) ch 40 introductory note (private nuisance is 'always a tort against land').

[5] *Corby Group Litigation Claimants v Corby Borough Council* [2008] EWCA Civ 463, [2009] QB 335 (*Corby*) [29].

and enjoyment of land',[6] and in his influential article 'The Boundaries of Nuisance', FH Newark said that private nuisance was 'a tort directed against the plaintiff's enjoyment of rights over land'.[7] As Lord Hoffmann went on to point out in *Hunter*, the fact that private nuisance is a violation of real property rights is obvious in cases of physical damage to the claimant's land, but less so when the interference is with the comfort and convenience of those occupying the land.[8] However, the property tort analysis holds with equal force for all types of private nuisance, once it is appreciated that in cases involving noise, smells and so on the gist of the action is not the discomfort of those affected, but the diminished utility of the land on which they live[9]—hence '[a] sulphurous chimney in a residential area is not a nuisance because it makes householders cough and splutter but because it prevents them taking their ease in their gardens'.[10] As we shall see, taking this idea seriously is critical to understanding the explanatory power of the property tort analysis.

Superficially, the assertion that private nuisance protects real property rights might seem uncontroversial, but there are a number of reasons why it is important that the property tort analysis be explored and defended. First, I hope to show that this analysis explains more aspects of the cause of action than is generally recognised, as well as reducing the room for manoeuvre when it comes to issues like the standing rules. Secondly, there are commentators who have expressly challenged the property tort analysis. Peter Cane has argued, for example, that unlike trespass to land, which is 'unequivocally a property tort',[11] private nuisance is 'an amalgam of property-based and obligation-based ideas', and that 'undue concentration on its property aspects is bound to produce doctrinal complications'.[12] In particular, there is a reluctance to accept that in cases of interference with comfort and convenience the gist of the action is the diminished utility of the land, with this analysis being variously described as 'odd',[13]

---

[6] *Hunter* [1997] AC 655 (HL) 723. See also at 696 (Lord Lloyd): 'the essence of private nuisance is easy enough to identify ... namely interference with land or the enjoyment of land'.

[7] FH Newark, 'The Boundaries of Nuisance' (1949) 65 *Law Quarterly Review* 480, 482. See also *Cunard v Antifyre Ltd* [1933] 1 KB 551 (KB) 556 (Talbot J) (private nuisance 'is correctly confined to injuries to property'); *Bone v Seale* [1975] 1 WLR 797 (CA) 804 (Scarman LJ) ('Nuisance is a wrong to property').

[8] *Hunter* [1997] AC 655 (HL) 706.

[9] ibid:

> In the case of nuisances 'productive of sensible personal discomfort', the action is not for causing discomfort to the person but ... for causing injury to the land. True it is that the land has not suffered 'sensible' injury, but its utility has been diminished by the existence of the nuisance.

[10] Newark, above n 7, at 489.

[11] P Cane, 'What a Nuisance!' (1997) 113 *Law Quarterly Review* 515, 515.

[12] ibid, at 517–18.

[13] T Weir, *An Introduction to Tort Law*, 2nd edn (Oxford, Oxford University Press,

'artificial'[14] and 'strained',[15] and with one textbook writer going so far as to say that it is based upon 'fictions' and barely stands up to scrutiny.[16] Academic criticism of the requirement that a claimant in private nuisance must have an interest in the affected land is also indicative of resistance to the property tort analysis.[17] Finally, the property tort analysis gives the lie to the apparently widely held conviction that private nuisance is incoherent. To some extent, this perception seems to be based on a misreading of critical remarks directed not at private nuisance, but at an unholy combination of private and public nuisance loosely termed 'nuisance' or 'the law of nuisance'. Examples of such remarks are William Prosser's famous jibe that '[t]here is perhaps no more impenetrable jungle in the entire law than that which surrounds the word "nuisance"',[18] and Newark's remark that 'the tort of nuisance' is 'the least satisfactory department' of the law of tort.[19] However, even if we set aside remarks of this kind, we find that there is plenty of criticism of private nuisance in isolation as well. In his article on the place of private nuisance in the modern law of torts, for example, Conor Gearty pulled no punches, saying variously that the tort was 'confused and confusing', suffered from a 'poverty of principle', had lost 'all sense of that for which it stands', and lacked definition, any sense of direction and 'any coherent goals or purpose'.[20] Similarly, the authors of one tort textbook say that 'even considered on its own, in isolation from public nuisance, private nuisance suffers from a lack of doctrinal clarity' and that the tort 'has yet to be united under a coherent thread of general principle'.[21] On the contrary, the property tort analysis reveals that private nuisance suffers from no such lack of doctrinal clarity, and that properly understood it is characterised by a high level of internal coherence.

2006) 159 ('It is odd, however, to say that noises and smells affect the land itself, which has neither ears nor nose'). Try telling that to an estate agent tasked with selling a house next to a busy road or a sewage works.

[14] J O'Sullivan, 'Nuisance in the House of Lords: Normal Service Resumed' [1997] *Cambridge Law Journal* 483, 485.

[15] MA Jones, *Textbook on Torts*, 8th edn (Oxford, Oxford University Press, 2002) 338.

[16] ibid, at 337–38.

[17] See part VI below.

[18] WL Prosser, *Handbook of the Law of Torts* (St Paul MN, West Publishing, 1941) 549.

[19] Newark, above n 7, at 480. See also JG Fleming, *The Law of Torts*, 9th edn (Sydney, Lawbook, 1998) 457 ('Few words in the legal vocabulary are bedevilled with so much obscurity and confusion as "nuisance"').

[20] C Gearty, 'The Place of Private Nuisance in a Modern Law of Torts' [1989] *Cambridge Law Journal* 214, 214–16.

[21] A Mullis and K Oliphant, *Torts*, 4th edn (Basingstoke, Palgrave Macmillan, 2011) 247. See also M Lee, 'What Is Private Nuisance?' (2003) 119 *Law Quarterly Review* 298, 298 (the 'difficulty, if not impossibility, of reconciling the decisions on private nuisance need not be emphasised').

III. DEFINING PRIVATE NUISANCE

Although it has been said that the word 'nuisance' is difficult to define,[22] no such difficulty attaches to the tort of private nuisance, which can be defined as an *unlawful non-trespassory interference with the private use and enjoyment of land*. It is worth taking a closer look at the elements of this definition. Some can be explained briefly. The word 'private', for example, excludes interference with a right over land which is held by members of the public generally, such as obstruction of a highway, which is not a private nuisance, but may be a public nuisance. As for the word 'unlawful', it encapsulates two important limits on the operation of the tort, both of which are explored below. One is that not all types of interference with the private use and enjoyment of land are actionable in private nuisance, but only interferences with 'natural' and 'acquired' rights. The other is that even in the case of natural or acquired rights, only a substantial interference with the right amounts to a private nuisance. Finally, the cumbersome word 'non-trespassory' expresses the fact that the torts of trespass to land and private nuisance are mutually exclusive; the precise dividing line between the two is explored below.[23]

More complexity attaches to the phrase 'interference with ... use and enjoyment' and the word 'land'. Taking the latter first, many definitions of private nuisance refer to an interference with a person's use and enjoyment of land 'or some right over, or in connection with [land]'.[24] This qualification helpfully serves to emphasise that private nuisance encompasses interferences with acquired rights or servitudes[25]—easements and profits à prendre—but is strictly unnecessary, since the word 'land' in the definition of private nuisance refers to the legal conception of land, which is usually taken to include 'incorporeal hereditaments' of this kind. According to section 205(1)(ix) of the Law of Property Act 1925, for example, 'land' includes

> land of any tenure ... buildings or parts of buildings ... and other corporeal hereditaments; also a manor, an advowson, and a rent and other incorporeal hereditaments, and an easement, right, privilege, or benefit in, over, or derived from land ...[26]

---

[22] See, eg, *Hunter* [1997] AC 655 (HL) 723 (Lord Hope); PH Winfield, 'Nuisance as a Tort' (1931) 4 *Cambridge Law Journal* 189, 189.

[23] See part IX below.

[24] See, eg, WVH Rogers, *Winfield and Jolowicz on Tort*, 18th edn (London, Sweet & Maxwell, 2010) para 14-4.

[25] Gearty, above n 20, at 216 claims that private nuisance has a definitional problem which can be solved only by recognising that it 'must be seen as distinct ... from interference with servitudes' but as we shall see there is no such distinction, and it is hard to see why the use of private nuisance to protect acquired rights in land should be considered problematic.

[26] See also *Willies-Williams v National Trust* (1993) 65 P & CR 359 (CA) 361 (Hoffmann LJ): 'An easement is ... itself "land" vested in the proprietor of the dominant tenement'.

Furthermore, since the legal conception of land encompasses not only the surface layer of the land, but also physical things attached to it, such as buildings, other structures, trees, shrubs and crops,[27] all these things rightly fall under the protection of the tort of private nuisance. By contrast, damage to personal property and personal injury are excluded by this definition from the ambit of private nuisance, with the important caveat (explored below[28]) that they could conceivably be recoverable for as consequential loss if they result from an unlawful interference with the claimant's land.

'Interference with ... use and enjoyment' of land is a broad concept: it includes, for example, causing an alteration of the physical condition of land that reduces its utility value, which explains why physical damage to the land falls within the scope of private nuisance. On the other hand, the use of this phrase excludes from the tort certain conduct which in a broad sense 'harms' the claimant's property. Opening a shop next door to a competitor may deprive the latter of much of their custom, for example, but it does not interfere with their use and enjoyment of their land.[29] And while diminution in market value may be evidence of substantial interference with the claimant's use and enjoyment of his or her land, it does not itself amount to such an interference[30]—a company which triggers a collapse in house prices in an area by closing down the main source of local employment does not thereby create a nuisance. These examples are illustrative of Allan Beever's statement that tort law 'is not interested in loss per se, but only in losses that flow from a violation of the claimant's primary legal rights',[31] in this case the right to the use and enjoyment of land. In two cases involving interlocutory relief, the English courts sailed rather close to the wind in this respect. By holding in *Laws v Florinplace*[32] that the mere presence of a sex shop in the locality could potentially amount to a nuisance, Vinelott J came close to imposing liability for diminution in value alone, and the same is true of the Court of Appeal's decision to grant an interlocutory injunction in *Thompson-Schwab v Costaki*,[33] which concerned a brothel. These two cases have been subjected to telling criticism by Richard Kidner, who argues that the fact that your neighbours are 'undesirable' and lower the tone of the area

[27] See also K Gray and SF Gray, *Elements of Land Law*, 5th edn (Oxford, Oxford University Press, 2009) ch 1.2.

[28] See part VIII.

[29] *Victoria Park Racing and Recreation Grounds Co Ltd v Taylor* (1937) 58 CLR 479, 508 (Dixon J).

[30] *Harrison v Good* (1871) LR 11 Eq 338 (Ch) 351 (Sir James Bacon V-C); *Moy v Stoop* (1909) 25 TLR 262 (KB) 263 (Channell J).

[31] A Beever, *Rediscovering the Tort of Negligence* (Oxford, Hart Publishing, 2007) 218. See also EJ Weinrib, *The Idea of Private Law* (Cambridge MA, Harvard University Press, 1995) 132, 134.

[32] *Laws v Florinplace Ltd* [1981] 1 All ER 659 (Ch).

[33] *Thompson-Schwab v Costaki* [1956] 1 WLR 335 (CA).

should not in itself give you a right of action, even if their mere presence affects the value of your property.[34]

IV. NATURAL RIGHTS, ACQUIRED RIGHTS AND 'NO RIGHTS'

The presence of the word 'unlawful' in the definition of private nuisance reminds us that not every interference with the private use and enjoyment of land is actionable, but it also conceals an important distinction which is frequently overlooked or underplayed. This is the distinction between the *types* of interference with the use and enjoyment of land which are potentially actionable in private nuisance and the question of whether the *particular* interference in question is a substantial one, and so in fact actionable.[35] In this part of the chapter I want to consider the first of these two issues.

The definition of private nuisance tells us that in general terms the right which the tort protects is the right to the private use and enjoyment of land. However, closer inspection of private nuisance law reveals that in fact this umbrella 'right' encompasses a complex substructure of more specific natural rights and acquired rights, and that the tort does not protect against certain kinds of interference with the private use and enjoyment of land at all. This threefold classification of *natural rights* (which attach automatically to the land), *acquired rights* (which the law recognises, but which must be acquired by grant or prescription) and *'no rights'* (which the law does not recognise at all) acts as a preliminary filter in private nuisance cases, which operates independently of, and anterior to, the question of whether on the facts the interference is substantial.

One of the reasons why this threefold distinction is often overlooked is that most private nuisance cases concern natural rights where the existence of protection against the type of interference in question is a given. It would be impossible to list all of these natural rights, but examples are riparian rights, the right not to have your land subjected to intolerable noise and smells, and the right to have the surface of your land supported by neighbouring land.[36] Since these rights are automatic incidents of the ownership or occupation of land, a substantial interference with such a right is actionable in private nuisance without the claimant needing to plead the existence of a servitude. In the case of acquired rights, by contrast, the existence of a servitude (an easement or a profit) must be established

---

[34] R Kidner, 'Nuisance and Rights of Property' [1998] *Conveyancer and Property Lawyer* 267.

[35] A (perhaps crude) analogy might be drawn between this distinction and the duty/breach distinction in negligence.

[36] For a fuller list, see K Oliphant (ed), *The Law of Tort*, 2nd edn (London, LexisNexis Butterworths, 2007) paras 22.30–22.38.

before the court turns to consider whether or not the interference is substantial. Examples of such rights are rights of way, rights to light, rights to take wood or turf from another's land and rights to have buildings on your land supported. Finally, 'no rights' are types of interference with the private use and enjoyment of land which are not actionable in private nuisance in any circumstances—as a nineteenth century judge put it, 'of this species of injury the law takes no cognizance'.[37] There is no natural right to be free from these kinds of interference, and such a right cannot be acquired as an easement. In such cases, the substantial interference issue never arises, with the result that, for example, even malicious interference is lawful.[38] Unlike the almost limitless variety of natural rights, the established list of 'no rights' in English law is short: there is no right to the free and uninterrupted passage of air over neighbouring land,[39] to receive percolating water from a neighbour's property,[40] not to have the view from your land obstructed,[41] not to have your land overlooked,[42] or not to have the television reception on your land interfered with by a nearby building.[43]

A number of further points can be made about this threefold classification. The first is that private nuisance affords precisely the same level of protection to acquired rights as it does to natural rights, no more and no less. Hence the requirement that the interference be substantial applies in cases on rights of way and rights to light, just as it does in cases on interference by noise or smell,[44] and once substantial interference has been established the usual nuisance remedies are available.[45] The second point is that the rules which give effect to this threefold distinction are complex and resistant to attempts at simplification.[46] It is sometimes said, for example, that the list of 'no rights' reflects a wider principle that a private nuisance either always or generally requires some sort of physical intrusion or emanation, and that therefore no action lies where the defendant simply prevents something (such as percolating water or air) from reach-

---

[37] *Tapling v Jones* (1865) 11 HL Cas 290, 317; 11 ER 1344, 1355 (Lord Chelmsford).

[38] See, eg, *Bradford Corp v Pickles* [1895] AC 587 (HL) (malicious appropriation of percolating water not actionable).

[39] *Webb v Bird* (1862) 13 CBNS 841, 143 ER 332.

[40] *Chasemore v Richards* (1859) 7 HL Cas 349, 11 ER 140; *Bradford Corp v Pickles* [1895] AC 587 (HL).

[41] See, eg, *Aldred's Case* (1610) 9 Co Rep 57b, 58b; 77 ER 816, 821 (Wray CJ). In the United States, it has also been held that no action lies in respect of the unsightly appearance of neighbouring property: see Oliphant, above n 36, at para 22.20.

[42] *Tapling v Jones* (1865) 11 HL Cas 290, 11 ER 1344; *Victoria Park Racing and Recreation Grounds Co Ltd v Taylor* (1937) 58 CLR 479.

[43] *Hunter* [1997] AC 655 (HL). See also *The People ex rel Hoogasian v Sears, Roebuck & Co* 287 NE 2d 677 (Ill 1972).

[44] See Oliphant, above n 36, at paras 22.53–22.55.

[45] *Saint v Jenner* [1973] Ch 275 (CA) 280 (Stamp LJ).

[46] See also R Bagshaw, 'The Edges of Tort Law's Rights' ch 14 of this book, part II(A).

ing the claimant's property.[47] While superficially neat, this attempt to force private nuisance into a trespass-type straightjacket fails to reflect the complex reality of private nuisance law, which gives an action, inter alia, for the withdrawal of lateral support from the claimant's land, diverting a stream or river away from the claimant's land, obstructing access to the claimant's land,[48] and for interference with acquired rights of way, rights to receive light and rights to receive air through a defined aperture or channel.[49] Similarly, although it is tempting to discern in the 'no rights' in respect of views and television reception a positive common law liberty (in Hohfeldian terms a 'privilege'[50]) to build whatever one likes on one's own land,[51] in English law this liberty may in fact be constrained by acquired rights to light and to the passage of air.

The final point concerns the rationale of the threefold scheme, and the considerations which the courts bring to bear when deciding how to classify a particular type of interference. Perhaps the best that can be said here is that in determining the rights we have against each other, an appropriate balance needs to be struck between our interest in security from harm and our interest in freedom of action,[52] and that in nuisance cases achieving the right balance between the security interests of potential claimants and the liberty interests of potential defendants cannot always be done by determining whether the particular interference is or is not substantial, but requires some form of a priori ranking of interference types. In carrying out that ranking, the courts consider both the gravity of the threat which the type of interference in question poses to potential claimants' security interests, and the extent to which granting protection against this type of interference would threaten the freedom of action of potential defendants, so that for example the 'no right to a view' rule has been justified both by denigrating the threatened security interest as a 'matter only of delight, and not of necessity'[53] and by pointing to the potentially signifi-

---

[47] See, eg, *Hunter* [1997] AC 655 (HL) 685 (Lord Goff); *Anglian Water Services Ltd v Crawshaw Robbins & Co Ltd* [2001] BLR 173 (QB) 197 (Burnton J); M Taggart, *Private Property and Abuse of Rights in Victorian England* (Oxford, Oxford University Press, 2002) 189; RW Wright, 'Private Nuisance Law: A Window on Substantive Justice' ch 17 of this book, text accompanying n 96 ff. For a more sophisticated analysis which merely places some weight on the distinction between emanation and obstruction/withdrawal, see N McBride and R Bagshaw, *Tort Law*, 3rd edn (Harlow, Pearson Longman, 2008) 371–72.

[48] *J Lyons & Sons v Wilkins* [1899] 1 Ch 255 (CA); *Hubbard v Pitt* [1976] QB 142 (CA).

[49] See also the cases involving persistent phone calls to the claimant's home: *Motherwell v Motherwell* (1976) 73 DLR (3d) 62 (Alberta Supreme Court Appellate Division); *Khorasandjian v Bush* [1993] QB 727 (CA). Is a phone call an 'emanation'?

[50] WN Hohfeld, 'Some Fundamental Legal Conceptions as Applied in Judicial Reasoning' (1913) 23 *Yale Law Journal* 16, 33.

[51] See, eg, 3 Bl Comm 217 ('every man may do what he pleases upon the upright or perpendicular of his own soil'). Less forthright (and more accurate): *Hunter* [1997] AC 655 (HL) 685 (Lord Goff), 709 (Lord Hoffmann).

[52] Stevens, *Torts and Rights*, above n 1, at 107. See further A Ripstein, *Equality, Responsibility, and the Law* (Cambridge, Cambridge University Press, 1999) ch 3.

[53] *Aldred's Case* (1610) 9 Co Rep 57b, 58b; 77 ER 816, 821 (Wray CJ).

cant impact such a right would have on the freedom to build on land over a 'very large and indefinite area'.[54] Needless to say, precisely where the lines are drawn will vary according to place and time, so that, for example, in the United States there is no acquired right to light,[55] and the existence of a right not to have television reception interfered with by an activity of the defendant was doubted in England in the 1960s,[56] accepted in Canada in the 1970s,[57] and countenanced (if not confirmed) in England in the 1990s.[58] It should of course also be borne in mind that the practical significance of some of the common law rules governing the actionability of different interference types has now been diminished by legislative interventions, such as planning controls and licensing schemes governing the abstraction of water.[59]

V. THE SUBSTANTIAL INTERFERENCE REQUIREMENT

Even where a natural or acquired right is in play, so that the interference type is potentially actionable, it must also be shown that on the facts the particular interference is substantial and therefore unlawful. In the words of a leading comparative tort lawyer, 'substantial interference represents a breach of a proprietary right which, in the absence of a specific justification, amounts to a wrongful act.'[60] Again, this requirement is necessary in order to achieve an appropriate balance between the claimant's security interests and the legitimate liberty interests of those in the vicinity of the claimant's property. In common law systems, this substantial interference requirement is often referred to as a requirement that there be an 'unreasonable user' of the defendant's land, but this language is

---

[54] *Dalton v Henry Angus & Co* (1881) 6 App Cas 740 (HL) 824 (Lord Blackburn). On the threats to freedom posed by a right to the general flow of air, a right to receive percolating water and a general right to television reception, see respectively *Webb v Bird* (1861) 10 CBNS 268, 284; 142 ER 455, 461 (Erle CJ); Taggart, above n 47, at 65–66; *Hunter* [1997] AC 655 (HL) 727 (Lord Hope).

[55] *Fontainebleau Hotel Corp v Forty-Five Twenty-Five Inc* 114 So 2d 357 (Fla Ct App 1959) 359 ('the English doctrine of "ancient lights" has been unanimously repudiated in this country').

[56] *Bridlington Relay Ltd v Yorkshire Electricity Board* [1965] Ch 436 (Ch) 447 (Buckley J).

[57] *Nor-Video Services Ltd v Ontario Hydro* (1978) 84 DLR (3d) 221 (Ontario High Court of Justice).

[58] *Hunter* [1997] AC 655 (HL) 684–85 (Lord Goff), 708 (Lord Hoffmann). Lord Cooke clearly favoured recognition of such a right (at 719).

[59] For an example of the latter, see the Water Resources Act 1991, pt II. In *Hunter* [1997] AC 655 (HL) 710, Lord Hoffmann described the planning system as 'a far more appropriate form of control ... than enlarging the right to bring actions for nuisance at common law'.

[60] C von Bar, *The Common European Law of Torts*, vol 1 (Oxford, Oxford University Press, 1998) 552–53. See also *Bürgerliches Gesetzbuch* (German Civil Code) § 906 (referring to a 'substantial impairment' of the use of the affected property).

best avoided, for two reasons. The first is that it serves to reinforce the common misconception that only the occupier of the land from which the nuisance emanates can be liable for it.[61] And the other reason is that the use of the word 'unreasonable' in this context is apt to be understood as signifying that the *conduct of the defendant* must be unreasonable, when in fact it is the *interference with the claimant's property* which must be unreasonable.[62]

Further confusion over the import of the substantial interference requirement has been generated by commentaries on private nuisance law—most famously the *Second Restatement of Torts*—which imply that this question of substantial interference is to be answered (at least in part) by some kind of cost-benefit analysis, in which the harm the interference causes the claimant is weighed against the utility of the activity of the defendant generating the interference.[63] If this were true, then it would call into question the idea that the tort protects the claimant's real property rights, since determining the question of actionability in such a way would not give property owners and occupiers an objective 'right' at all, just as I would not have a meaningful right to bodily integrity if someone who punched me on the nose were liable in battery only if I could show that the harm thereby caused to me outweighed any gratification or other benefit they received from doing the act. In fact, however, when we look at the authorities (certainly in English law) we find no evidence that this kind of cost–benefit analysis is employed in determining liability. On the contrary, ever since *Bamford v Turnley*[64] was decided in the 1860s the courts have consistently held that no matter how beneficial the defendant's activity is, if the interference it produces is intolerable, then a private

---

[61] See part VII below.

[62] R Epstein, 'Nuisance Law: Corrective Justice and Its Utilitarian Constraints' (1979) 8 *Journal of Legal Studies* 49, 85 ('"reasonableness" in nuisance cases should be ... understood as a synonym for the word "substantial" that directs judicial inquiry into the *level* of the defendant's invasion'). See also Wright, above n 47, text accompanying n 72 ('In sum, "unreasonable" refers to the impact on the plaintiff's use and enjoyment of his or her land, rather than to the defendant's conduct'). On the confusion caused by the use of the word 'unreasonable' in this context, see also part X below.

[63] See *Second Restatement*, above n 4, at § 826: 'An intentional invasion of another's interest in the use and enjoyment of land is unreasonable if (a) the gravity of the harm outweighs the utility of the actor's conduct, or (b) the harm caused by the conduct is serious and the financial burden of compensating for this and similar harm to others would not make the continuation of the conduct not feasible'. See also TW Merrill, 'Trespass, Nuisance and the Costs of Determining Property Rights' (1985) 14 *Journal of Legal Studies* 13, 13 ('as a rule the landholder must show that the costs of the intrusion outweigh its benefits'). Note, however, that in 1990 an American commentator claimed that only seven States 'can be said to employ the balance of utilities test as the primary criterion for the determination of nuisance liability': JL Lewin, '*Boomer* and the American Law of Nuisance: Past, Present, and Future' (1990) 54 *Albany Law Review* 189, 234. For a thorough critique of this aspect of the *Second Restatement* from an American perspective, see Wright, above n 47.

[64] *Bamford v Turnley* (1862) 3 B & S 66, 122 ER 27.

nuisance action will lie.[65] As that word 'intolerable' makes clear, the true determinant of whether an interference with the use and enjoyment of land is substantial, and so actionable, is whether in all the circumstances the claimant can reasonably be expected to put up with it.[66]

Three further points can be made about this claimant-sided test of substantial interference. The first is that when assessing what the claimant can reasonably be expected to tolerate, account is taken of the force of the defendant's countervailing liberty interest. Where that liberty interest is strong, the claimant can reasonably be expected to put up with a higher level of interference, as Goddard LJ explained in *Metropolitan Properties Ltd v Jones*:

> If my neighbour is going to put up some bookcases in his house, or put in a new fireplace, for a day or two I shall be exposed, no doubt, to a considerable disturbance ... but the law does not regard that as a nuisance. A man may be doing that which is necessary for his house, or his own comfort, just as I may do the same thing in my own house the following month. It is one of those things which one has to put up with.[67]

Conversely, where the defendant's liberty interest is weak or non-existent, the *less* the claimant can be expected to put up with it, so that for example where the defendant's activity has no legitimate purpose, but is motivated solely by a desire to injure the claimant, a finding of substantial interference can be expected even if the level of the interference is relatively low.[68] Similarly, the defendant's failure to take reasonable precautions to reduce or eliminate the interference caused by his or her activity will usually lead to the conclusion that it is actionable.[69]

The second point relates to the important observation made earlier that the property tort analysis of private nuisance entails that the gist of

---

[65] See, eg, *Miller v Jackson* [1977] QB 966 (CA); *Kennaway v Thompson* [1981] QB 88 (CA); *Dennis v Ministry of Defence* [2003] EWHC 793 (QB), [2003] Env LR 34. Lord Denning MR dissented on the liability issue in *Miller v Jackson* but his reasoning has not been followed and is now generally disregarded.

[66] Baker, above n 3, at 430. See also *Kennaway v Thompson* [1981] QB 88 (CA) 94 (Lawton LJ); Weir, above n 13, at 160; P Cane, *The Anatomy of Tort Law* (Oxford, Hart Publishing, 1997) 142. In Scots law, the standard is aptly described as one of 'reasonable tolerability': see, eg, *The Laws of Scotland: Stair Memorial Encyclopaedia* (Edinburgh, Butterworths, 1988) vol 14, para 2037 ff; GDL Cameron, 'Neighbourhood Liability in Scotland 1850–2000' in J Gordley (ed), *The Development of Liability Between Neighbours* (Cambridge, Cambridge University Press, 2010) 132, 139–40.

[67] *Metropolitan Properties Ltd v Jones* [1939] 2 All ER 202 (KB) 205. This also explains the rule in *Harrison v Southwark and Vauxhall Water Co* [1891] 2 Ch 409 (Ch) that temporary construction work is not actionable in nuisance if all reasonable precautions are taken to minimise the disturbance caused.

[68] See, eg, *Christie v Davey* [1893] 1 Ch 316 (Ch); *Hollywood Silver Fox Farm Ltd v Emmett* [1936] 2 KB 468 (KB).

[69] See, eg, *Moy v Stoop* (1909) 25 TLR 262 (KB); *Russell Transport Ltd v Ontario Malleable Iron Co Ltd* [1952] 4 DLR 719 (Ontario High Court).

the wrong in cases of interferences with comfort and convenience (as by noise or smell) is the reduction in the utility of the land, rather than the discomfort of the people occupying it. It follows from this that when a court considers whether a particular interference is substantial, the gravity of the interference must be assessed objectively, in terms of its impact on the land itself. Hence the question at the substantial interference stage is not whether the claimant personally considers the discomfort or inconvenience to be intolerable, but whether a reasonable person in the claimant's shoes would see it that way. Famously, this principle extends to the uses to which the claimant puts his or her land,[70] but it is less often pointed out that it also extends to the physical make-up of buildings and other fixtures on the claimant's land, so that for example there is no claim if a factory emits vibrations which cause the collapse of the claimant's house only because it is abnormally decrepit,[71] or produces smoke which kills flowers growing in the claimant's garden only because they are unusually delicate.[72] This explains why private nuisance actions in respect of noises or smells have failed where the problem is attributable to the absence of adequate sound insulation[73] or the permeability of a party wall.[74]

The objective approach to the gravity of the interference is often referred to as the 'abnormal sensitivity' rule, but this is potentially misleading, since the principle should apply with equal force where the claimant or his or her use of land is abnormally *in*sensitive, as where a deaf person is in occupation of land affected by a noise nuisance.[75] Moreover, the fact that even scholars who appear to share the rights-based view of private nuisance have put forward ingenious alternative explanations for this principle of objective assessment suggests that the full ramifications

[70] See, eg, *Robinson v Kilvert* (1889) 41 Ch D 88 (CA); *Amphitheaters Inc v Portland Meadows* 198 P 2d 847 (Or 1948). See also the rule in right-to-light cases that the extent of the right 'is neither increased nor diminished by the actual use to which the dominant owner has chosen to put his premises or any of the rooms in them': *Carr-Saunders v Dick McNeil Associates Ltd* [1986] 1 WLR 922 (Ch) 928 (Millett J).

[71] See, eg, *Cremidas v Fenton* 111 NE 855 (Mass 1916) (vibration damage to old, weak house not actionable).

[72] In *McKinnon Industries Ltd v Walker* [1951] 3 DLR 577, the Privy Council seemed to assume that damage to sensitive orchids came within the scope of the 'abnormal sensitivity' rule (which did not, however, apply on the facts).

[73] *Southwark London Borough Council v Tanner* [2001] 1 AC 1 (HL) (noise). In dismissing the claim on the grounds that the ordinary use of residential premises was not actionable in nuisance, the House of Lords arrived at the right result for the wrong reason.

[74] *Hirose Electrical UK Ltd v Peak Ingredients Ltd* [2011] EWCA Civ 987 (smell).

[75] Although there appears to be no direct authority on the point, the application of an objective approach in these circumstances is approved in the *Second Restatement*, above n 4, at § 821F comment d. See also WP Keeton et al (eds), *Prosser and Keeton on Torts*, 5th edn (St Paul MN, West Publishing, 1984) 628–29; McBride and Bagshaw, above n 47, at 369. Cf J Murphy, *Street on Torts*, 12th edn (Oxford, Oxford University Press, 2007) 431–33 (interference actionable only if the claimant is subjectively affected). Whether, as the *Second Restatement* suggests, the claimant's deafness should affect the damages recoverable is considered in part VIII below.

of the property tort analysis have not always been understood.[76] This is not to deny that a subjective approach would have unfortunate consequences—such as imposing an undue burden on potential defendants and 'paralysing industrial enterprises'[77]—but rather to emphasise that the courts have not simply chosen to adopt an objective standard because it leads to fairer or more efficient outcomes. On the contrary, the objective approach is an inevitable corollary of the fact that private nuisance is a tort against land.

This brings me to the final point I wish to make about the test of substantial interference, which concerns the 'locality principle', according to which the character of the neighbourhood is a relevant consideration in determining the actionability of the interference.[78] Again, ingenious explanations of this principle have been put forward—some commentators have argued, for example, that it amounts to a common law zoning regime,[79] while critical legal scholars have discerned in it a judicial conspiracy to keep the poor and downtrodden in their place.[80] A more plausible, if prosaic, explanation is that the locality principle is simply a logical concomitant of the reasonable tolerability test of substantial interference. The claimant's reasonable expectations cannot be assessed in the abstract, but must reflect the nature of the area in which he or she has chosen to buy or rent property; as a judge in a nuisance case once sardonically observed, '[T]his is an industrial area. The local inhabitants are not entitled to expect to sit in a sweet-smelling orchard'.[81] Viewing the locality principle through the prism of the reasonable tolerability test in this way explains why it is only one of the factors in the substantial interference inquiry, so that, for example, in *Rushmer v Polsue & Alfieri Ltd*[82] the *only* resident of an area devoted to printing and other noisy trades was granted an injunction where the night noise from printing presses next door represented a substantial addition to the pre-existing noise in the locality. As James Penner observes, cases such as this give the lie to the

---

[76] See, eg, Weinrib, above n 31, at 192–94 ('nuisance law disallows claims based on the plaintiff's hypersensitivity because they reflect the less ordinary of the parties' competing uses' and hence would allow 'the particular condition of one party ... to be decisive for the bipolar relationship of equals'). See also Epstein, above n 62, at 90–94.

[77] *Rogers v Elliott* 15 NE 768 (Mass 1888) 772 (Knowlton J).

[78] See, eg, *St Helen's Smelting Co v Tipping* (1865) 11 HL Cas 642, 11 ER 1483.

[79] See, eg, RC Ellickson, 'Alternatives to Zoning: Covenants, Nuisance Rules, and Fines as Land Use Controls' (1973) 40 *University of Chicago Law Review* 681; JF Brenner, 'Nuisance Law and the Industrial Revolution' (1974) 3 *Journal of Legal Studies* 403.

[80] See, eg, J Conaghan and W Mansell, *The Wrongs of Tort*, 2nd edn (London, Pluto Press, 1999) 137 ('an excellent vehicle for judicial prejudices ... disguising the essentially class-based nature of the exercise being carried out').

[81] *Shoreham-by-Sea Urban District Council v Dolphin Canadian Proteins Ltd* (1972) 71 LGR 261 (QB) 266 (May J). See similarly *Colls v Home and Colonial Stores Ltd* [1904] AC 179 (HL) 185 (Earl of Halsbury LC).

[82] *Rushmer v Polsue & Alfieri Ltd* [1906] 1 Ch 234 (CA), affd [1907] AC 121 (HL).

claim that private nuisance law is the judicial equivalent of zoning rules designed to prevent conflicts in land use. Rather:

> The character of the neighbourhood is invoked in the most general way as a recognition of the obvious fact that town, suburban and country life differ in the level of the sorts of noise and smells, and the proximity of commercial activity to one's residence, or other commercial activity to one's business, that one ought to expect.[83]

VI. TITLE TO SUE

The most controversial consequence of the fact that private nuisance is a property tort is the rule that the claimant in a nuisance action must have a proprietary interest in the land affected, a rule which was strongly reiterated by the House of Lords in *Hunter* following a period of uncertainty.[84] Lord Cooke, who dissented in *Hunter*, argued that the standing rule in nuisance was a question of 'policy';[85] however, if private nuisance is a tort protecting land rights, then there was no policy choice, and the majority's reasoning was self-evidently correct. Just as in other property torts, such as trespass to land and conversion—and indeed property damage claims in negligence[86]—it seems axiomatic that only someone with a right in the affected property should have standing to sue. In the words of Lord Hoffmann:

> Once it is understood that nuisances 'productive of sensible personal discomfort' do not constitute a separate tort of causing discomfort to people but are merely part of a single tort of causing injury to land, the rule that the plaintiff must have an interest in the land falls into place as logical and, indeed, inevitable ...[87]

Furthermore, when we look at the detail of the standing rules in private nuisance, we can see that there is a clear equivalence with the rules governing who can sue in trespass to land, and also with the rules governing standing in wrongful interference with goods cases. As Lord Goff explained in *Hunter*, a claim in private nuisance is usually brought by the person in actual possession of the affected land, either as freeholder or tenant of the land, or exceptionally as a licensee with exclusive posses-

---

[83] JE Penner, 'Nuisance and the Character of the Neighbourhood' (1993) 5 *Journal of Environmental Law* 1, 11.

[84] The interest in land requirement was abandoned by the Court of Appeal in *Khorasandjian v Bush* [1993] QB 727 (CA), a decision followed by the same court in *Hunter* [1997] AC 655 (CA).

[85] *Hunter* [1997] AC 655 (HL) 717.

[86] *Leigh & Sillivan Ltd v Aliakmon Shipping Co Ltd (The Aliakmon)* [1986] AC 785 (HL).

[87] *Hunter* [1997] AC 655 (HL) 707.

sion.[88] In addition, a reversioner can bring an action where the nuisance threatens their reversionary interest.[89] Precisely the same rules determine standing to sue in trespass to land,[90] and the right to sue in conversion is also based on possession, with an action available to reversioners when their interests in goods are under threat.[91]

The extent of academic criticism of the standing rules of private nuisance,[92] and the watering down of those rules in at least one common law jurisdiction,[93] show that there is considerable resistance to a thoroughgoing property tort analysis of the cause of action. It seems to me, however, that the standing issue demonstrates the desirability of the property tort analysis, as becomes clear if we consider the implications of abandoning the requirement that the claimant have an interest in the affected land. First, the courts would have to fashion an entirely new standing rule, and it is difficult to see what it would be. *Some* link with the land would obviously be required, but the test formulated by the Court of Appeal in *Hunter*—that the claimant must have a 'substantial link' with the property[94]—was so vague as to be almost useless.[95] Secondly, since presumably even the critics of the interest in land requirement would retain it for cases of encroachment or physical damage to the land, abandoning the requirement in cases of interference with comfort and convenience would effectively split the tort down the middle, with two different versions of the cause of action emerging, each with its own standing rules. Quite apart from anything else, this would clearly complicate matters in cases straddling the divide.[96] Thirdly, it is difficult to see how the objective approach to the assessment of damages for private nuisance (which focuses on the impact of the interference on the utility of the land[97]) could survive a relaxation in the standing rules, and unclear what principles would emerge in its place. And finally, it is hard to see how the line could be held at private nuisance. A trespasser may well cause distress or inconvenience to licensees such as lodgers or children living in the family home, so there would be little logic in jettisoning the

---

[88] ibid, at 688. See also at 724 (Lord Hope).

[89] See also the *Second Restatement*, above n 4, at § 821E.

[90] See Oliphant, above n 36, at para 10.13 ff.

[91] See S Green and J Randall, *The Tort of Conversion* (Oxford, Hart Publishing, 2009) ch 4.

[92] See the citations by Lord Cooke in *Hunter* [1997] AC 655 (HL) 717.

[93] In Canada, family members living in the owner's house have successfully brought nuisance actions: see *Motherwell v Motherwell* (1976) 73 DLR (3d) 62 (Alberta Supreme Court Appellate Division); *Devon Lumber Co Ltd v MacNeill* (1987) 45 DLR (4th) 300 (New Brunswick Court of Appeal).

[94] *Hunter* [1997] AC 655 (CA) 675 (Pill LJ).

[95] ibid, at 693 (Lord Goff).

[96] Such as *St Helen's Smelting Co v Tipping* (1865) 11 HLC 642, 11 ER 1483.

[97] See part VIII below.

interest in land requirement in private nuisance but maintaining it in the tort of trespass to land.

Tying the right to sue in private nuisance to 'a right to possession' or 'de facto occupation'[98] is nothing new—according to William Blackstone, for example, the action on the case for nuisance 'is maintainable by one that hath possession only'.[99] This reflects the fact that, as Lord Hoffmann said in the *Hunter* case, 'Exclusive possession de jure or de facto, now or in the future, is the bedrock of English land law',[100] and that more generally (as Stevens points out in his chapter in this book) 'property rights in relation to things arise from possession'.[101] The suggestion that the long-standing requirement of an interest in the land affected be abandoned therefore represents not only a threat to the coherence of the private nuisance action itself, but also to the very foundations of land law and property law more generally. This danger arises because critics of the standing rules have lost sight of the fact that property torts like trespass to land, private nuisance and conversion are not free-standing causes of action but are merely constituent elements of the wider law of property.[102] It follows that these torts are not free to establish their own standing rules, but that they presuppose 'some prior, independent method for defining and recognizing' the property rights which they protect.[103] Hence, the *Second Restatement of Torts* quite rightly defers to the *Restatement of Property* when it comes to the 'rules applicable in determining when a person's rights and privileges in respect to land constitute property rights and privileges' and so give title to sue in nuisance.[104] More than any other aspect of the cause of action, the rules on standing point ineluctably to the fundamental nature of private nuisance as a property tort.

VII. WHO CAN BE LIABLE

If private nuisance is a property tort, then since property rights are good against the whole world, it would follow that the creator of a nuisance should always be liable for it. This is indeed the case, and in particular there is no requirement that the defendant must be the owner or the occupier of the land from which the interference emanates, so that a trespasser[105] or licensee[106] on another's land can be sued if they create a

---

[98] *Hunter* [1997] AC 655 (HL) 703 (Lord Hoffmann).

[99] 3 Bl Comm 222.

[100] *Hunter* [1997] AC 655 (HL) 703.

[101] R Stevens, 'Rights and Other Things' ch 5 of this book, text following n 91.

[102] See part XI below.

[103] Epstein, above n 62, at 52.

[104] *Second Restatement*, above n 4, at § 821E comment b.

[105] *Kraemers v A-G of Tasmania* [1966] Tas SR 113.

[106] *Thompson v Gibson* (1841) 7 M & W 456, 151 ER 845; *Fennell v Robson Excavations Pty Ltd* [1977] 2 NSWLR 486 (New South Wales Court of Appeal).

nuisance there, and a nuisance may originate on the public highway.[107] Limiting liability to the owner or occupier of the land which is the source of the interference would of course be highly illogical, as Henry LJ has observed:

> There would be no sense in a law which prevented you from playing your music at maximum volume in the middle of the night from your home but permitted you to walk around your neighbourhood with your 'ghetto-blaster' at full pitch.[108]

Surprisingly, however, the misconception that such a limitation exists is widespread,[109] and it was one of two reasons the Court of Appeal gave in *Hussain v Lancaster City Council*[110] for dismissing a private nuisance claim brought by shopkeepers on a council estate in respect of a campaign of harassment conducted by the defendant's tenants (the other, sound, reason being that a landlord's failure to evict a tenant he or she knows is creating a nuisance does not amount to an authorisation of that nuisance).

The origins of this misconception would seem to be threefold. First, it was true that the *assize* of nuisance lay only between freeholders,[111] although this was not true of the action on the case out of which the modern tort developed.[112] Secondly, the confusion may in part be attributable to loose definitions of private nuisance, which refer to 'neighbouring occupiers' and so forth.[113] And finally, the error may be connected to the necessity of distinguishing private nuisance from trespass. This was sometimes done by asking whether the act took place on or off the claimant's land, and since in the majority of cases, off the claimant's land meant on the defendant's land, the distinction was sometimes said to rest on whether the source of the interference was the claimant's or the defendant's land, a slip that may have contributed to the misapprehension in question.

---

[107] *Halsey v Esso Petroleum Co Ltd* [1961] 1 WLR 683 (QB); *Hubbard v Pitt* [1976] QB 142 (CA). See also *Hall v Beckenham Corp* [1949] 1 KB 716 (KB), where it was assumed that persons flying model planes in a public park could be liable in nuisance.

[108] *Northampton Borough Council v Lovatt* (1997) 96 LGR 548 (CA) 556. See also *Southport Corp v Esso Petroleum Co Ltd* [1953] 2 All ER 1204 (Liverpool Assizes) 1207–1208 (Devlin J); *Lippiatt v South Gloucestershire Council* [2000] QB 51 (CA) 65 (Sir Christopher Staughton).

[109] Fleming, above n 19, at 476 describes this misconception as the 'traditional view', but there is nothing 'traditional' about it.

[110] *Hussain v Lancaster City Council* [2000] QB 1 (CA).

[111] On the likely origins of this limitation, see D Ibbetson, *A Historical Introduction to the Law of Obligations* (Oxford, Oxford University Press, 1999) 99.

[112] AK Kiralfy, *The Action on the Case* (London, Sweet & Maxwell, 1951) 55–56.

[113] See, eg, *Sedleigh-Denfield v O'Callaghan* [1940] AC 880 (HL) 896–97 (Lord Atkin); *Miller v Jackson* [1977] QB 966 (CA) 980 (Lord Denning MR); *Hunter* [1997] AC 655 (HL) 723 (Lord Hope); *Transco plc v Stockport Metropolitan Borough Council* [2003] UKHL 61, [2004] 2 AC 1 [9] (Lord Bingham). See also Weinrib, above n 31, at 191.

VIII. DAMAGES AND CONSEQUENTIAL LOSS

According to Stevens, when it comes to the assessment of damages for the commission of a tort, 'it is necessary to distinguish between damages awarded as a substitute for the right infringed and consequential damages as compensation for loss to the claimant ... consequent upon this infringement'.[114] The core 'substitutive' award is generally assessed objectively, so whether or not there is a loss to the claimant is irrelevant. Damages for consequential loss are subjective and require proof of loss having been suffered.[115] This analysis is broadly consistent with the approach of the courts to the assessment of damages in private nuisance cases, but there are a number of complications. As regards the core 'substitutive' award, it remains unclear precisely how this is to be calculated in cases where the nuisance has not diminished the capital value of the affected land. Furthermore, there is clearly some reluctance on the part of the courts to accept the full ramifications of the objective approach to the assessment of this award. As for damages for consequential loss, there is a lack of clarity about what types of consequential losses are recoverable, and why.

The House of Lords made clear in the *Hunter* case that the measure of the substitutive award is the reduction in the value of the affected land. In cases of physical damage to the land, this equates to the diminution in capital or resale value,[116] which is often (though not invariably) the same as the cost of reinstatement. In cases of interference with comfort and convenience, it equates to what the House of Lords in *Hunter* termed the diminution in the 'amenity value'[117] of the land during the period when the nuisance took place. This concept of amenity value encapsulates the fact that, as Lord Hoffmann pointed out with reference to a smell nuisance caused by a pig farm, 'the value of the right to occupy a house which smells of pigs must be less than the value of the occupation of an equivalent house which does not'.[118] But how is the diminution in amenity value to be assessed? According to the European Commission on Human Rights' interpretation of the reasoning in *Hunter*, the answer is by 'assessing a notional market rental value for [the] property without the presence of the environmental nuisance, assessing the reduction in such rental value caused by the presence of the nuisance and multiplying this reduction by the duration of the nuisance'.[119] This seems to be a sensible approach which should work in most cases, but it is unlikely that the reduction in

---

[114] Stevens, *Torts and Rights*, above n 1, at 60.
[115] ibid.
[116] *Hunter* [1997] AC 655 (HL) 695 (Lord Lloyd).
[117] ibid, at 696 (Lord Lloyd), 706 (Lord Hoffmann).
[118] ibid, at 706.
[119] *Khatun v United Kingdom* (1998) 26 EHRR CD 212, 214. See also *Dobson v Thames Water Utilities Ltd* [2009] EWCA Civ 28, [2009] 3 All ER 319 (*Dobson*) [32] (Waller LJ),

amenity value will always be captured by the market in this way,[120] and so it is desirable that a degree of flexibility should be maintained when it comes to the fixing of the substitutive award.

This focus on the impact of the nuisance on the land, as opposed to its occupiers, means that the objective approach taken to the assessment of the gravity of the interference is mirrored in the approach taken to the assessment of substitutive damages. Hence the quantum of damages is not affected by the number of people occupying the land in question—the 'reduction in amenity value is the same whether the land is occupied by the family man or the bachelor'[121]—but instead by the objective qualities of the land, such as its size, commodiousness and value.[122] It follows that if three identical flats are similarly affected by the same noise nuisance, the substitutive awards made to the occupiers should be exactly the same, even if one lives in his flat with his family, one lives in her flat alone and is stone deaf, and one uses her flat as a *pied-à-terre* and stays there only once a fortnight.

Unfortunately, however, the Court of Appeal seemed to baulk at the full rigour of the objective approach to damages in its recent decision in *Dobson v Thames Water Utilities Ltd.*[123] In the course of a discussion of the impact (if any) of an award of private nuisance damages to someone with a legal interest in the affected land on a claim under the Human Rights Act 1998 in respect of the same interference by a person resident in the property, but lacking standing in nuisance,[124] Waller LJ suggested that 'a claimant must show that he has in truth suffered a loss of amenity before substantial damages can be awarded', with the result that where a house 'is unoccupied throughout the time of the (transitory) nuisance, has suffered no physical injury, loss of value or other pecuniary damage, and would not in any event have been rented out, we are unable to see how there can be any damages beyond perhaps the nominal'.[125] With respect, this statement appears to confuse the award of substitutive damages with recovery for consequential loss, and is difficult to square with the fact that (as Waller LJ himself acknowledged) following *Hunter*

---

referring specifically to the opinion of Lord Hoffmann ('loss of (notional) rental value'); *Lawrence v Fen Tigers Ltd* [2011] EWHC 360 (QB) [314] (Judge Richard Seymour QC).

[120] This seems to have been the assumption of Lord Hope in *Hunter*, who spoke of the diminution in the 'capital or letting value' of the land as a 'relevant head of damages', but then referred to 'the measure of damages' in cases where the nuisance 'has resulted only in loss of amenity': *Hunter* [1997] AC 655 (HL) 724.

[121] ibid, at 696 (Lord Lloyd). See also at 706–07 (Lord Hoffmann), 724–25 (Lord Hope).

[122] ibid, at 706 (Lord Hoffmann).

[123] *Dobson* [2009] EWCA Civ 28, [2009] 3 All ER 319.

[124] On this issue, and the relationship between the Human Rights Act 1998 and private nuisance more generally, see D Nolan, 'Nuisance and Human Rights' in D Hoffman (ed), *The Impact of the Human Rights Act on Private Law in England and Wales* (Cambridge, Cambridge University Press, 2011) (forthcoming).

[125] *Dobson* [2009] EWCA Civ 28, [2009] 3 All ER 319 [33]–[34].

nuisance damages 'are for injury to the property and not to the sensibilities of the occupier(s)'.[126] On the other hand, his Lordship's observation that when assessing damages for loss of amenity, account should be taken of 'the actual experience of the persons in occupation of the property during the relevant period'[127] is unproblematic, since although the subjective impact of the interference on the occupiers is not the measure of damages, it will usually be good evidence of the objective impact on the land. In any case, it is to be hoped that in future judges who are actually fixing damages awards in private nuisance cases will follow the clear guidance given by the House of Lords.

In *Hunter*, Lord Hoffmann said that the claimant in a private nuisance action may also be entitled to damages for losses consequential on the violation of his or her property rights:

> There may of course be cases in which, in addition to damages for injury to his land, the owner or occupier is able to recover damages for consequential loss. He will, for example, be entitled to loss of profits which are the result of inability to use the land for the purposes of his business. Or if the land is flooded, he may also be able to recover damages for chattels or livestock lost as a result.[128]

As this statement makes clear, foreseeable economic losses which flow from an unlawful interference with the claimant's land are therefore recoverable in a private nuisance action,[129] as where rental income is lost due to the flooding of the claimant's houses,[130] or expense incurred in investigating the extent of the damage done to the land.[131] Where the consequential economic loss exceeds the diminution in the capital or amenity value of the affected land, the claimant is entitled to the higher amount. In *Andreae v Selfridge & Co Ltd*,[132] for example, the owner of a hotel was compensated for a drop in takings attributable to the noise and dust from nearby building works, regardless of whether this exceeded the reduction in the notional rental value of the property attributable to the interference. (Conversely, it of course follows from the objective assessment of the substitutive award that if in this case the drop in takings had been *less* than the diminution in amenity value, the claimant could instead have asked for the latter.)

---

[126] ibid, at [31]. '[I]t is a mistake to think that where no loss is suffered no claim for damages is available' (Stevens, *Torts and Rights*, above n 1, at 61).

[127] *Dobson* [2009] EWCA Civ 28, [2009] 3 All ER 319 [33].

[128] *Hunter* [1997] AC 655 (HL) 706.

[129] Since such loss results from the injury to the claimant's land, it is misleading to describe it as 'pure economic loss', as does Fleming, above n 19, at 493.

[130] *Rust v Victoria Graving Dock Co* (1887) 36 Ch D 113 (CA) (loss too remote on the facts).

[131] *Jan de Nul (UK) Ltd v Axa Royale Belge SA* [2002] EWCA Civ 209, [2002] 1 Lloyd's Rep 583 [80] (Schiemann LJ).

[132] *Andreae v Selfridge & Co Ltd* [1938] Ch 1 (CA).

Lord Hoffmann's statement also makes it clear that damages will be awarded for harm to the claimant's chattels which is consequential on an actionable interference with the claimant's land.[133] Such damages are not limited to cases in which the harm to the chattel results from physical damage to the claimant's land, as where stock was damaged when the claimant's shop was flooded,[134] but are also recoverable where they result from less tangible forms of interference, as where acid smuts from the defendant's oil refinery damaged washing hanging on the claimant's clothes line.[135] The principle in play here is that forms of injury which would not in themselves ground an action in private nuisance—such as economic loss and damage to personal property—may nevertheless be recoverable for when they result from the wrongful interference with the claimant's real property rights. (Another example of the operation of this principle is the rule that the damages awarded for a violation of the natural right to support of one's land may include compensation for damage to buildings affected by the loss of support, even where the right to have the buildings themselves supported has not yet been acquired.[136]) It is therefore surprising that in *Hunter* the House of Lords seemed to rule out recovery of damages for personal injury in private nuisance, even in cases where the injury is suffered by the right-holder and results from the nuisance.[137] After all, there would appear to be no logical distinction between consequential personal injury and consequential damage to personal property, and in the old case of *Malone v Laskey*[138] the Court of Appeal seem to have assumed that damages would be recoverable for the former if suffered by the owner or occupier.[139]

---

[133] See also *Hunter* [1997] AC 655 (HL) 719 (Lord Cooke). The same is perhaps implied by Blackstone in 3 Bl Comm 217: 'if one erects a smelting house for lead so near the land of another, that the vapor and smoke kills his corn and grass, *and damages his cattle therein*, this is held to be a nuisance' (emphasis added).

[134] *Howard Electric Ltd v AJ Mooney Ltd* [1974] 2 NZLR 762 (Supreme Court of New Zealand).

[135] *Halsey v Esso Petroleum Ltd* [1961] 1 WLR 683 (QB). £5 was awarded for the damaged linen. The claimant was also compensated for damage to his car caused by the acid smuts, but since his car was parked on the public highway the basis of this award was not private nuisance but public nuisance and the rule in *Rylands v Fletcher*.

[136] See Gray and Gray, above n 27, at 21.

[137] *Hunter* [1997] AC 655 (HL) 676 (Lord Lloyd), 707 (Lord Hoffmann). Cf at 719 (Lord Cooke). See also *Corby* [2008] EWCA Civ 463, [2009] QB 335 [13] (Dyson LJ).

[138] *Malone v Laskey* [1907] 2 KB 141 (CA).

[139] See also Newark, above n 7, at 490 n 55:

> It may well be that where an actionable nuisance is committed which in addition to interfering with the plaintiff's enjoyment of rights in land also damages his person or chattels, he can recover in respect of the damage to his person or chattels as consequential damages.

IX. PRIVATE NUISANCE AND TRESPASS TO LAND

Commentators who are not persuaded by the property tort analysis of private nuisance typically distinguish it in this regard from the tort of trespass to land.[140] By contrast, I want to argue that in fact there is no fundamental distinction between the two torts, and indeed that certain issues in the law of private nuisance can be illuminated by considering trespass as an analogy. The inclusion of the word 'non-trespassory' in the definition of private nuisance makes it clear that the two torts are mutually exclusive, and the dividing line between them is the ancient distinction between a trespass action and an action on the case—whether the interference was direct or indirect.[141] Two principles determine that question: (1) if no person or physical object crosses the boundary of the claimant's land, then the interference is indirect;[142] and (2) where there is a projection of a physical object onto the claimant's land, the interference is direct if the act of the defendant was unlawful from the beginning, but indirect if the act of the defendant was initially lawful, but led afterwards to an invasion of the claimant's rights.[143] Hence a sign which when erected projects into the airspace over the claimant's shop is a trespass,[144] while a fence initially flush with the boundary line which subsequently comes to lean over adjoining land is a nuisance.[145]

Although it is also said (again reflecting the trespass/case distinction) that while trespass to land is actionable per se, private nuisance requires proof of damage, in practice this notional requirement of damage is synonymous with—and so adds nothing to—the requirement of substantial interference, which is where the real significance of the distinction between the two torts lies (there being no equivalent to this requirement in trespass). This distinction is, however, easily explained. As we have seen, in

---

[140] See, eg, Cane, above n 11, at 515 (trespass to land 'is unequivocally a property tort').

[141] *Southport Corp v Esso Petroleum Co Ltd* [1953] 2 All ER 1204 (Liverpool Assizes) 1208 (Devlin J).

[142] McBride and Bagshaw, above n 47, at 367.

[143] *Reynolds v Clarke* (1725) 1 Str 634, 635; 93 ER 747, 748. Cf McBride and Bagshaw, above n 47, at 368, arguing that what matters is the degree of control which the defendant has over the thing which causes the interference. In practice, this will usually (but not invariably) track the distinction drawn in the authorities between acts which are and are not initially lawful. Richard Wright, above n 47, text accompanying n 85, distinguishes trespass to land and private nuisance by saying that while the former requires a physical invasion of the claimant's land by a tangible entity, a nuisance is always a physical invasion by an intangible entity. There are two errors here. The first is that Wright assumes that a nuisance must amount to a physical invasion, which we have seen is not the case (see part IV above). The second is Wright's assumption that physical invasion by a tangible entity cannot be a nuisance, when in fact encroachment, as by tree roots or branches, is a well-established form of private nuisance involving a tangible entity: see further Oliphant, above n 36, at para 22.34.

[144] *Kelsen v Imperial Tobacco Co* [1957] 2 QB 334 (QB).

[145] *Mann v Saulnier* (1959) 19 DLR (2d) 130 (New Brunswick Court of Appeal).

private nuisance the substantial interference requirement is necessary to achieve an appropriate balance between the competing liberty and security interests in play; in cases of direct interference, by contrast, the threat posed to the claimant's security interests is usually greater, and the legitimate liberty interests of the defendant are less likely to be engaged, so a requirement of this kind is not appropriate (although where exceptionally an important liberty interest is engaged, a defence of necessity may be available[146]).

On a purely doctrinal level, therefore, it is difficult to see any fundamental distinction between the two principal causes of action protecting land rights. Two more theoretical distinctions are nevertheless sometimes drawn.[147] The first is that in the absence of a *vindicatio*-type action, trespass to land performs an important vindicatory function in common law systems, in the sense that it is used to *establish* as well as to *protect* rights in land. However, precisely the same is true of private nuisance. If I have a private right of way over your land, and you block the path, denying my right, then I must bring an action in private nuisance in order to establish that the right exists, and the same is true where you deny my acquired right to support, light and so on. Similarly, in cases concerning natural rights I must use private nuisance to establish my property right to be free, for example, from the intolerable stench of your pig farm, or the excessive noise of your factory. It follows that only on a reductionist view of land rights as limited to the core right to possession can a distinction be drawn in this respect between trespass and private nuisance.

The second more theoretical distinction which is sometimes drawn between the two torts is that while trespass lays down 'property rules', private nuisance lays down 'liability rules',[148] an argument which rests on the assumption that whereas injunctions are available as of right in trespass cases, generally in nuisance 'an injunction will not be granted ... unless the costs of the damage exceed the costs of abating the damage'.[149] Now we should note that, even if this assumption were sound, it would establish only that nuisance law lays down a *combination* of property rules and liability rules, since injunctive relief is available—and so a property rule laid down—where this is the efficient outcome. But the real difficulty with this argument is that, whether or not a cost–benefit analysis of this kind determines the availability of specific relief in nuisance cases in the United

---

[146] See, eg, *Rigby v Chief Constable of Northamptonshire* [1985] 1 WLR 1242 (QB).

[147] For rejection of a third suggested distinction—that 'trespasses somehow involve misappropriations in a way that nuisances do not'—see C Rotherham, 'Gain-Based Relief in Tort after *Attorney General v Blake*' (2010) 126 *Law Quarterly Review* 102, 123–25.

[148] See, eg, WM Landes and RA Posner, *The Economic Structure of Tort Law* (Cambridge MA, Harvard University Press, 1987) 42–48. On the distinction between these two types of rule, see G Calabresi and AD Melamed, 'Property Rules, Liability Rules and Inalienability: One View of the Cathedral' (1972) 85 *Harvard Law Review* 1089.

[149] Landes and Posner, above n 148, at 43.

States,[150] it has certainly never done so in England, as is demonstrated by a host of authorities, ancient and modern.[151] The right-to-light cases are particularly instructive in this regard, since in some of these injunctions have been issued despite evidence that the economic cost to the defendant of compliance with the order would clearly exceed the economic benefit such compliance would bring to the claimant, in one case by a factor of up to 38 to one.[152] Nor is this refusal to take into account economic considerations at the remedy stage a peculiarity of English law: the Irish Supreme Court, for example, once issued an injunction in a nuisance case even though it was told that doing so would cause a critical shortage of cement throughout the whole country,[153] and in both Israel and Scotland the granting of damages in lieu of an injunction in such circumstances is regarded as an illegitimate expropriation of the claimant's rights.[154]

The conclusion must be, therefore, that there is in fact no fundamental distinction between trespass and private nuisance, and since it seems generally to be accepted that the former is a property tort, this is consistent with the property tort analysis of the latter. It also suggests that questions arising in private nuisance may be illuminated by considering trespass to land as an analogy. In addition to the rules on standing discussed above, there are at least two other issues where the analogy is instructive. The first is whether the fact that the claimant moved into his or her property knowing that it was subject to a nuisance should be a defence (the 'coming to the nuisance' idea).[155] The rule that it is not seems to me to be bolstered by the fact that it would surely be very odd to argue that if a person moved into a property knowing that someone else regularly trespassed on it, then for that reason he or she should be barred from

---

[150] *Boomer v Atlantic Cement Co* 257 NE 2d 870 (NY 1970) is a famous example of an American court refusing an injunction for public interest reasons. See further Wright, above n 47, text accompanying nn 120–32.

[151] See, eg, *A-G v Birmingham Borough Council* (1858) 4 K & J 528, 70 ER 220 (*Birmingham*); *Shelfer v City of London Electric Lighting Co* [1895] 1 Ch 287 (CA); *Kennaway v Thompson* [1981] QB 88 (CA); *Watson v Croft Promosport Ltd* [2009] EWCA Civ 15, [2009] 3 All ER 249. Cf *Miller v Jackson* [1977] QB 966 (CA); *Dennis v Ministry of Defence* [2003] EWHC 793 (QB), [2003] Env LR 34.

[152] *Regan v Paul Properties Ltd* [2006] EWCA Civ 1319, [2007] Ch 135 (reduction in value of claimant's land attributable to loss of light no more than £5500, but estimated cost to defendant of compliance with injunction up to £210 000). As Anthony Ogus and Genevra Richardson say in their study of the economics of private nuisance, the case law on injunctive relief 'manifestly demonstrates that ... the judiciary have little regard for economic considerations': AI Ogus and GM Richardson, 'Economics and the Environment: A Study of Private Nuisance' [1977] *Cambridge Law Journal* 284, 309.

[153] *Bellew v Cement Ltd* [1948] IR 61 (Supreme Court of Ireland).

[154] See respectively *Ata Textile Co v Schwartz* (1976) 30(3) PD 785 (Supreme Court of Israel) and *Ben Nevis Distillery (Fort William) Ltd v North British Aluminium Co Ltd* 1948 SC 592 (IH). Scottish courts do not even have the power to refuse interdict and award damages in lieu: *The Laws of Scotland: Stair Memorial Encyclopaedia*, above n 66, at para 2150.

[155] As to which, see Oliphant, above n 36, at para 22.99.

seeking an injunction to prevent further trespassing by that person, thereby short-circuiting (as would a coming to the nuisance defence) established principles governing the acquisition of land rights by prescription. And the second issue is the misguided notion that where the public benefit of the defendant's activity outweighs the harm it causes to the claimant, it should not be actionable in nuisance for that reason.[156] If the trespass analogy holds, then this is not altogether dissimilar to arguing that the owner of a factory should be able to extend it onto neighbouring land without the property owner's permission because doing so would create lots of new jobs, and the land in question is derelict and socially useless.[157]

X. THREE SOURCES OF CONFUSION

I hope to have shown thus far that private nuisance is a thoroughly coherent cause of action, once it is properly understood as a tort protecting rights in land. There are, however, a number of sources of confusion which have served to obscure the doctrinal clarity of the tort. In this part of the chapter I will advert briefly to what I perceive to be the most important of these.[158]

First and foremost is the much misunderstood relationship between the tort of private nuisance and the crime of public nuisance. The truth is that the origins of the two types of nuisance are entirely separate,[159] and although there are some overlaps between the operation of private nuisance and the action that lies where a public nuisance has caused the claimant particular damage—in particular, if its consequences are sufficiently widespread, an activity such as the generation of noxious fumes may be both a public nuisance and a private nuisance to neighbouring properties—the two forms of nuisance have very little in common. In the words of Hayne J in a decision of the High Court of Australia:

> It is ... important to recall that the crime of common or public nuisance and the tort of [private] nuisance were and are distinct. There can be no automatic transposition of the learning in one area to the other.[160]

Unfortunately, however, the terminological resemblance has caused con-

---

[156] See part V above.

[157] See also McBride and Bagshaw, above n 47, at 376–77.

[158] Other sources of confusion include the laboured (and it seems to me rather pointless) debates about the relationship between private nuisance and negligence, and the misconception that the rule in *Rylands v Fletcher* is an offshoot of private nuisance (a thesis criticised by J Murphy, 'The Merits of *Rylands v Fletcher*' (2004) 24 *Oxford Journal of Legal Studies* 643 and D Nolan, 'The Distinctiveness of *Rylands v Fletcher*' (2005) 120 *Law Quarterly Review* 421).

[159] See Kiralfy, above n 112, at 70; Ibbetson, above n 111, at 106 ('very different antecedents').

[160] *Brodie v Singleton Shire Council* [2001] HCA 29, (2001) 206 CLR 512 [257].

siderable confusion, which many who should have known better have compounded by failing adequately to differentiate the two.[161] A good recent example of this confusion was the deeply misguided argument of the defendant in *Corby Group Litigation Claimants v Corby Borough Council*[162] that because the House of Lords had said in the *Hunter* case that personal injury was not actionable in *private* nuisance it was not actionable in *public* nuisance either, despite a multiplicity of cases to the contrary, some going back 400 years.[163] Thankfully, the Court of Appeal was having none of it: the two causes of action were distinct and the rights protected by them were different.[164] One simple way of reducing the impact of this particular source of confusion would be for judges and commentators to be meticulous about referring to either 'private' or 'public' nuisance, rather than 'nuisance' in general.

A second terminological source of confusion is the use of the phrase 'unreasonable user' to describe the requirement of substantial interference.[165] So long as it is understood that it is the *interference* which must be unreasonable, and not the *defendant's conduct*, no harm is done, but inevitably this distinction is frequently lost, so that we end up with a reference to 'the centrality to the tort of nuisance of the fault-based concept of unreasonableness'[166] and the claim that no clear distinction can be drawn between negligence and nuisance, since in both 'the question is whether the defendant has acted reasonably'.[167] A recent example of the doctrinal chaos that can result is provided by the decision of the Court of Appeal in *Network Rail Infrastructure Ltd v Morris*, where Buxton LJ sought to abandon well-established principles of private nuisance law and to replace them with an 'analysis of the demands of reasonableness' in the particular case.[168] It is difficult to imagine a better recipe for uncertainty and incoherence.

Finally, confusion has arisen from the mistaken idea that 'a private nuisance always involves some degree of repetition or continuance',[169] a

---

[161] Newark, above n 7, is a serial offender, who single-handedly caused great confusion in this regard. See also the *Second Restatement*, above n 4, at ch 40 (where unhelpfully the two are dealt with in the same chapter); G Williams and BA Hepple, *Foundations of the Law of Tort* (London, Butterworths, 1976) 104–08; Murphy, *Street on Torts*, above n 75, at 423 (failing to make clear that *Bolton v Stone* [1951] AC 850 (HL) was a public nuisance case).

[162] *Corby* [2008] EWCA Civ 463, [2009] QB 335.

[163] See, eg, *Fowler v Sanders* (1617) Cro Jac 446, 79 ER 382.

[164] *Corby* [2008] EWCA Civ 463, [2009] QB 335 [30] (Dyson LJ).

[165] See also Wright, above n 47, text following n 73 (arguing that the use of the word 'unreasonable' in this context is 'likely to mislead' and therefore best avoided).

[166] Cane, above n 11, at 520.

[167] Williams and Hepple, above n 161, at 107.

[168] *Network Rail Infrastructure Ltd v Morris* [2004] EWCA Civ 172, [2004] Env LR 41 [36].

[169] *A-G v PYA Quarries Ltd* [1957] 2 QB 169 (CA) 192 (Denning LJ). See also Newark, above n 7, at 489.

claim which seems to have fed into the suggestion that cases of physical damage to land should be hived off into negligence, leaving private nuisance as a tort concerned only with amenity damage.[170] In fact, cases of physical damage caused by one-off floods, landslips and the like have long fallen within the scope of the cause of action. It would seem that the idea that some degree of continuity is required arises out of a failure to differentiate the action on the case for nuisance from the assize, a form of novel disseisin for which the primary remedy was specific relief, and which would not therefore have been appropriate once the nuisance had terminated.[171]

XI. PROPERTY AND OBLIGATIONS

Like the existence of other property torts such as trespass to land and conversion, acceptance of the property tort analysis of private nuisance calls into question the distinction commonly drawn between the 'law of property' on the one hand and the 'law of obligations' on the other. At the very least, it requires us to accept that the law of private nuisance is as much part of land law as the law of breach of contract is part of contract law (as Lord Hope said in the *Hunter* case, 'we are concerned here essentially with the law of property'[172]). It is noteworthy in this regard that the issues dealt with in common law systems by the tort of private nuisance are generally classified by civil law systems as falling within the law of property, not obligations.[173] Hence, for example, it is within the title of the Italian Civil Code dealing with property rights that we find Article 844, which refers to the obligation to tolerate 'emissions of smoke or heat, smells, noises, vibrations [and similar effects] where they do not exceed the customary measure of what is tolerable, with due consideration to the conditions prevailing within the locality'.[174] Similarly, in the German Civil Code, the provisions governing neighbour law are to be found in the sections on ownership, as elaborations of that right.[175] At the

---

[170] Gearty, above n 20.

[171] Kiralfy, above n 112, at 56. See also Ibbetson, above n 111, at 99.

[172] *Hunter* [1997] AC 655 (HL) 723.

[173] von Bar, above n 60, at 551: 'For the majority of European countries with civil codes, the law governing relationships between neighbours has traditionally been a part of property law'.

[174] Cited in ibid, at 559.

[175] *Bürgerliches Gesetzbuch* § 906 ff. See further A Their, 'Disturbances Between Neighbours in Germany 1850–2000' in J Gordley (ed), *The Development of Liability Between Neighbours* (Cambridge, Cambridge University Press, 2010) 87. In Scots law, the main role of nuisance has been described as 'a doctrine of *property law* or neighbourhood protecting interests in the use and enjoyment of land or public places from present and future interference': *The Laws of Scotland: Stair Memorial Encyclopaedia*, above n 66, at para 2017 (emphasis added).

same time, in civilian systems nuisance-type cases cannot straightforwardly be classified as falling within the law of property because the availability of damages may give them a decidedly delictual flavour.[176] In both the common law and civilian legal traditions, therefore, 'the proper location of reparable wrongs against property ... is inherently ambivalent'.[177]

The taxonomic challenges posed by property torts like private nuisance are not without their practical implications. A good example is provided by the case of *Bradburn v Lindsay*,[178] where one of the issues was whether the owner of a semi-detached house could be liable for loss of support of a neighbouring house caused by his failure to keep his own house in good repair. The claim was in nuisance, for interference with an easement of support. Since an easement can be a right to do something, or a right not to have something done, but not a right to have something done, the authorities were clear: the easement of support does not impose a duty of positive action on the servient owner. His obligation is not to do anything to remove the support, and that is all.[179] However, Judge Blackett-Ord V-C held that the defendant *was* liable for his non-feasance. The learned judge pointed to private nuisance cases which imposed positive duties on occupiers, in particular *Leakey v National Trust*,[180] and distinguished the easement cases on the ground that they dealt with 'the nature of the right of support', while the claimants had put their case on the 'wider ground' of nuisance.[181] With respect, this purported distinction between the 'right of support' and 'nuisance' simply does not exist, for the two are mutually constitutive, in the sense that the rules of private nuisance law in part determine the content of the right of support, and vice versa. The same is true of the distinction drawn by another judge between the 'law of easements' and the 'modern law of nuisance'.[182] Only the failure to appreciate that private nuisance is part and parcel of the law of real property could have brought about such profound analytical errors.

---

[176] See Their, above n 175, at 103–04 (German law); AJ Verheij, 'Fault Liability Between Neighbours in the Netherlands 1850–2000' in J Gordley (ed), *The Development of Liability Between Neighbours* (Cambridge, Cambridge University Press, 2010) 107, 110–15 (Dutch law); A Masferrer, 'Relations Between Neighbours in Spanish Law 1850–2000' in J Gordley (ed), *The Development of Liability Between Neighbours* (Cambridge, Cambridge University Press, 2010) 173, 181–83 (Spanish law). On the taxonomical difficulties to which nuisance has given rise in Scots law, see Cameron, above n 66, at 156–61.

[177] Cameron, above n 66, at 159.

[178] *Bradburn v Lindsay* [1983] 2 All ER 408 (Ch).

[179] *Sack v Jones* [1925] Ch 235 (Ch) 240 (Astbury J); *Bond v Norman* [1940] 2 All ER 12 (CA) 18 (Sir Wilfred Greene MR).

[180] *Leakey v National Trust* [1980] QB 485 (CA).

[181] *Bradburn v Lindsay* [1983] 2 All ER 408 (Ch) 413.

[182] *Abbahall Ltd v Smee* [2002] EWCA Civ 1831, [2003] 1 WLR 1472 [10] (Munby J).

488 *Donal Nolan*

XII. CONCLUSION

There is a danger that rights analysis will be misinterpreted as a high-level unitary theory of private law along the lines of those put forward by corrective justice theorists. On the contrary, while acceptance of the rights model does have obvious implications for high-level theory of this type, and while the connections between rights analysis and corrective justice theory are strong,[183] works like Stevens' *Torts and Rights*[184] are far more engaged with the detail of private law doctrine than the more abstract analysis which can be found in, for example, Ernest Weinrib's *The Idea of Private Law*[185] or Arthur Ripstein's *Equality, Responsibility, and the Law*.[186] This difference of emphasis reflects the fact that rights analysis is less concerned with identifying the philosophical foundations of private law at a general level than with understanding the internal structures and rules of private law in common law systems. It follows that to a large extent the merits of rights analysis stand to be assessed by its *analytical* force, in other words its ability to explain and rationalise not only 'the idea' of private law at a general level, but also particular private law doctrines, at a relatively high level of specificity. And in this chapter I hope to have shown that in the area of private nuisance law, at least, there is a marked degree of consistency between rights analysis and the principles and rules which emerge from the authorities.

Having said that, it would be a mistake to dismiss rights analysis as a purely analytical exercise devoid of normative significance. As James Penner has pointed out in the context of private nuisance:

When there is no judicial recognition of the distinction between rights and mere interests judges may decide that the law of nuisance turns on balancing interests. At this point the law of nuisance changes from one in which tortfeasors are restrained from violating the rights of land occupiers to one where the law is called upon to resolve conflicting land uses by sanctioning some interests over others: on the economic view the resolution is made by determining which interests have the higher social value.[187]

The normative power of rights analysis is well illustrated by the nineteenth century nuisance case of *A-G v Birmingham Borough Council*,[188] where an injunction was issued to prevent the defendant local authority from discharging raw sewage into the River Tame, even though its counsel told the court that the effect of the injunction would be to turn the

---

[183] See D Nolan and A Robertson, 'Rights and Private Law' ch 1 of this book, part IX.

[184] Above n 1.

[185] Above n 31.

[186] Above n 52.

[187] Penner, above n 83, at 21.

[188] *Birmingham* (1858) 4 K & J 528, 70 ER 220.

city of Birmingham into 'one vast cesspool' and to bring about 'a plague, which will not be confined to the 250,000 inhabitants of Birmingham, but will spread over the entire valley and become a national calamity'.[189] Sir William Page Wood V-C was unimpressed:

> There are cases at law in which it has been held, that where the question arises between two portions of the community, the convenience of one may be counterbalanced by the inconvenience to the other, where the latter are far more numerous. But in the case of an individual claiming certain private rights, and seeking to have those rights protected against an infraction of the law, the question is simply whether he has those rights, and, if so, whether the Court, looking to the precedents by which it must be governed in the exercise of its judicial discretion, can interfere to protect them.[190]

Statements like this are apt to produce two slightly different varieties of negative response. The first such response is that they are symptomatic of an individualistic common law ethos which puts private property rights above the interests of the masses—in the *Birmingham* case, the riparian rights of an aristocratic landowner above the health of those living in one of England's biggest cities.[191] And the other response is that such statements reflect a failure on the part of some common law judges to recognise that private law rules exist not to protect private rights but to maximise overall social welfare.[192]

Although those who respond in these two different ways may not always share the same political outlook, they are guilty of the same two mistakes. The first mistake is the failure to appreciate that the appropriate forum for arguments regarding social welfare is not the private law court but the legislature. Only the most diehard libertarian would deny that sometimes private rights must give way to the public interest, but one of the strengths of the rights analysis of private law is that it reserves the power to make such decisions to legislators who are democratically accountable for their actions. The second mistake is the erroneous assumption that the judiciary are in a position to assess where the interests of the masses lie, or which outcome will maximise overall welfare. Indeed, the critics are wrong to assume that *they themselves* know the answers to these questions, as recent research on the aftermath of the *Birmingham* litigation demonstrates. For an illuminating article by Ben Pontin reveals that, far from bringing about the calamity predicted by counsel for the defendant, the decision in *Birmingham* to award an injunction trig-

---

[189] ibid, at 536; 224.

[190] ibid, at 539; 225.

[191] This is the clear implication of WR Cornish and G de N Clark, *Law and Society in England 1750–1950* (London, Sweet & Maxwell, 1989) 157.

[192] L Rosenthal, 'Economic Efficiency, Nuisance and Sewage: New Lessons from *Attorney General v Council of the Borough of Birmingham*' (2007) 36 *Journal of Legal Studies* 27.

gered a spate of similar actions against other local authorities, which had the effect of bringing about desperately needed municipal investment in modern systems of sewage purification.[193] Although the normative appeal of rights analysis would in no way be diluted if the practical effects of the injunction had been less positive, there is nevertheless a rich irony in the fact that a ruling founded on the force of private rights which was long lambasted as 'inefficient' and 'regressive' turns out to have had such beneficial long-term consequences.

[193] B Pontin, 'The Secret Achievements of Nineteenth Century Nuisance Law: *Attorney General v Birmingham Corporation* (1858–95) in Context' (2007) 19 *Environmental Law and Management* 271.

17

Private Nuisance Law:
A Window on Substantive Justice

RICHARD W WRIGHT*

I. INTRODUCTION

MORE THAN ANY other tort action, the private nuisance action reveals the proper nature and full scope of tort law as an implementation of the classical principles of justice and their underlying moral norm of equal freedom.

The private wrong addressed by the private nuisance action is one of the few wrongs that it is feasible to prevent ex ante, and which often is prevented ex ante through the granting of an injunction, rather than being merely remedied ex post through monetary damages. As such, the private nuisance action clearly demonstrates the error of those, including many efficiency theorists, who describe tort law as merely setting prices, in the form of damages, for permitted invasions of others' interests, rather than, correctly, as the area of law that most fully addresses, articulates, and implements the basic principles of justice and right.

The equal freedom norm that underlies, connects, and co-ordinates these basic principles can be seen most clearly through an examination of the requirements for a successful private nuisance action. The nature of and relationship between the principles is illustrated most clearly through an examination of the remedies that are available for a successful nuisance action. The criteria for granting an injunction rather than limiting the plaintiff to a remedy in damages draw on the principle of distributive justice as well as the principle of interactive ('corrective') justice, in an integrated manner that some justice theorists have erroneously declared cannot coherently be done.[1]

---

[1] See, eg, EJ Weinrib, 'Legal Formalism: On the Immanent Rationality of Law' (1988)

Elaboration of these claims requires a substantial amount of preliminary ground clearing, since there is widespread confusion and misunderstanding regarding the principles of justice—especially the principle of interactive justice—and the nature and proper scope of the private nuisance action. In part II, I attempt to clear up the confusions and misunderstandings regarding the principles of justice. In part III, I attempt to clarify the nature and proper scope of the private nuisance action as a distinct (intentional) tort, which is explicitly grounded on the equal freedom norm. Finally, in part IV, I affirm the status of the private nuisance action as a strict liability tort by clarifying the criteria for the granting of an injunction, and I explain and justify those criteria as a co-ordinated implementation of the principles of distributive and interactive justice.

II. EQUAL FREEDOM, JUSTICE, AND RIGHTS

Over the ages, beginning with Aristotle, it has generally been assumed that the proper purpose of law is the implementation of justice: the creation and maintenance of the conditions necessary for the flourishing and fulfilment of each person in the community as a free and equal human being. One's freedom as a rational, human being has an internal aspect and an external aspect. The internal aspect, which law cannot and should not attempt to control, is a matter of personal virtue—one's shaping and living one's life by choosing and acting in accordance with the morally proper ends for a human being. The external aspect, which is the proper concern of justice and law, is one's practical exercise of one's freedom in the external world, which must be consistent with the equal external freedom of every other person.[2] As Immanuel Kant put it in his supreme principle of right: 'so act externally that the free use of your choice can coexist with the freedom of everyone in accordance with a universal law'.[3]

The external exercise of equal freedom depends on sufficient access to the instrumental goods—material resources, political powers, and civil liberties—necessary for pursuing a meaningful human life ('positive freedom') and sufficient security against interferences by others with one's person and whatever instrumental goods one happens to possess ('negative freedom'). Distributive justice defines the scope of persons' positive freedom. Interactive justice, which traditionally but misleadingly has been referenced by using the Aristotelian terms 'corrective justice' or 'rectifi-

---

97 *Yale Law Journal* 949, 973–74, 979, 981, 984–85, 987–88, criticised in RW Wright, 'Substantive Corrective Justice' (1992) 77 *Iowa Law Review* 625, 632, 707–08.

[2] RW Wright, 'The Principles of Justice' (2000) 75 *Notre Dame Law Review* 1859, 1871–83.

[3] I Kant, *The Metaphysics of Morals* (M Gregor tr and ed, Cambridge, Cambridge University Press, 1996) para 6:231.

catory justice', defines the scope of persons' negative freedom. Together, distributive justice and interactive justice seek to assure the attainment of the common good (the realisation, to the extent practicable, of each person's humanity) by providing each person with his or her equal or fair share of the social stock of instrumental goods (distributive justice) and by securing his or her person and existing stock of instrumental goods from interactions with others that are inconsistent with his or her right to equal external freedom (interactive justice).[4]

The term 'interactive justice' conveys the true nature and focus of Aristotelian 'corrective justice' and should be used instead of the latter term, which unfortunately nowadays is commonly interpreted literally and then dismissed, without investigation of Aristotle's actual philosophy. Read literally, the terms 'corrective justice' and 'rectificatory justice', which are the usual English translations of Aristotle's Greek terms, imply that this type of justice is only concerned with correcting or rectifying wrongs after they have occurred, and not with preventing them beforehand or with defining the nature of the wrong being corrected, or, as prominent scholars have erroneously assumed, that this type of justice is not distinct from but rather is merely a corollary of distributive justice—that corrective justice merely corrects deviations from the entitlements mandated by distributive justice.[5]

Neither of these assumptions is a correct interpretation of the use of these terms by Aristotle or others in the natural law/rights tradition. Aristotle clearly conceived of 'corrective justice' as being distinct and independent from distributive justice, with a different criterion of equality. He described the equality mandated by distributive justice as proportional or 'geometric': a person's just share of the resources of a society is determined by his or her relative ranking on some distributive criterion such as virtue, merit, or need. He explicitly distinguished this proportional equality from the absolute or 'arithmetic' equality demanded by 'corrective justice', which requires that, in 'transactions' (interactions) with others, the absolute equality and dignity of those others as human beings be respected regardless of their relative virtue, merit, or need. Furthermore, Aristotle discussed many of the factors that are relevant to just interactions, including intent, mistake, foreseeability, and consent.[6]

---

[4] Wright, 'The Principles of Justice', above n 2, at 1883–87.

[5] See, eg, J Rawls, *A Theory of Justice* (Cambridge MA, Harvard University Press, 1971) 10–11; R Dworkin, *Law's Empire* (Cambridge MA, Harvard University Press, 1986) 297–309; J Waldron, 'Criticizing the Economic Analysis of Law' (1990) 99 *Yale Law Journal* 1441, 1450–53 (reviewing JL Coleman, *Markets, Morals, and the Law* (Cambridge, Cambridge University Press, 1988)); J Gordley, 'Tort Law in the Aristotelian Tradition' in DG Owen (ed), *Philosophical Foundations of Tort Law* (Oxford, Oxford University Press, 1995) 131, 132–33, 135–36, 157.

[6] See, eg, Aristotle, 'Nicomachean Ethics' (WD Ross and JO Urmson trs) in J Barnes (ed), *The Complete Works of Aristotle* (Princeton NJ, Princeton University Press, 1984) vol 2, at

Compensatory damages are the most common remedy in tort law and contract law. However, although this is sometimes forgotten by those who view tort law and contract law as merely setting prices for (allegedly efficient) non-consensual interactions, they are not the only remedy available in these areas of the law. Courts provide equitable, non-monetary relief much more often than is usually understood. For example, in tort law, a plaintiff may obtain repossession of property of which he or she has been wrongfully dispossessed, and, with sufficient advance notice of imminent or ongoing tortious injury, he or she may obtain an injunction to avert such injury.[7]

All of these remedies are part of the remedial component of interactive justice. They are all concerned with preventing and, if that should fail, to the extent possible rectifying unjust interactions — interactions that are inconsistent with and adversely affect others' equal external freedom. This is the purpose of tort law and contract law. It is also the purpose of criminal law.[8] Tort law and contract law deal with 'private wrongs', unjust discrete injuries to the persons or property of specific individuals. Criminal law deals with 'public wrongs', unjust non-discrete injuries to the dignity and security of each member of society that result from (or are constituted by) criminals' acting in disregard of the society's norms of public peace and order, thereby declaring themselves to be outside the law ('outlaws').[9]

Properly understood and administered, punitive damages in tort law also compensate for discrete private injuries. When a person harms another through a deliberate disregard of the other's rights, then in addition to any non-dignitary harm that was inflicted on the victim, the victim has also suffered a discrete dignitary injury, which can be rectified through the imposition of private retribution in the form of punitive damages in tort law. These punitive damages, being private retribution for a discrete private dignitary injury, are distinct and separate from any criminal punishment that may be imposed for any non-discrete 'public wrong' that was caused to each member of the community as a result of the same conduct. This is how punitive damages once were understood in the United States[10] and are now being limited (although still without recognition of

---

paras 1131a10–1132b21, 1135a16–1136b10, discussed in Wright, 'Substantive Corrective Justice', above n 1, at 691–702.

[7] DB Dobbs, *The Law of Torts* (St Paul MN, West Publishing, 2000) 112–13, 153, 1047, 1338–39.

[8] It is also the purpose of the law of restitution and many other areas of the law. See Wright, 'Substantive Corrective Justice', above n 1, at 708–10.

[9] See RW Wright, 'Principled Adjudication: Tort Law and Beyond' (1999) 7 *Canterbury Law Review* 265, 291–92.

[10] See TB Colby, 'Beyond the Multiple Punishment Problem: Punitive Damages as Punishment for Individual, Private Wrongs' (2003) 87 *Minnesota Law Review* 583, 613–36; AJ Sebok, 'What Did Punitive Damages Do? Why Misunderstanding the History of Punitive Damages Matters Today' (2003) 78 *Chicago-Kent Law Review* 163, 180–204. Unfortu-

the private rather than public nature of the wrong being remedied) by the United States Supreme Court.[11] It is how they generally continue to be understood in common law and civil law jurisdictions outside the United States—for example, as 'aggravated damages' in England, Australia, and New Zealand and as 'satisfaction damages' in a number of countries in continental Europe.[12]

III. PRIVATE NUISANCE AS A DISTINCT TORT

In order to understand the moral foundations of the private nuisance action, we first need to identify its proper content and contours as a distinct legal action. This turns out not to be a simple task. In the cases and the secondary literature, situations properly addressed under other tort actions are often treated as private nuisance actions, which has caused unnecessary complexity and confusion. In the following text, I focus primarily on the discussion of the private nuisance action in the *Restatements of Torts* and case law in the United States. However, I also refer to discussions in leading British Commonwealth texts,[13] which indicate that an even greater failure to clarify and distinguish the private nuisance action as a distinct tort exists in the Commonwealth.

A. Distinguishing the Public Nuisance Action

The *First Restatement of Torts* emphasised the distinct natures of the private nuisance action and the public nuisance action and did not merge

---

nately, in the United States the private wrong conception of punitive damages in tort law generally has given way to a public wrong conception, which views such damages solely as a backstop to criminal law: see Colby at 584–613, 637–78; Wright, 'Principled Adjudication', above n 9, at 293.

[11] See *Philip Morris USA v Williams* 549 US 346 (2007); *State Farm Mutual Auto Insurance Co v Campbell* 538 US 408 (2003) 416–17, 422–23 (Kennedy J for Rehnquist CJ, Kennedy, Stevens, O'Connor, Souter and Breyer JJ).

[12] See JG Fleming, *The Law of Torts*, 9th edn (Sydney, Lawbook, 1998) 271–74; W van Gerven, J Lever and P Larouche, *Common Law of Europe Casebooks: Tort Law* (Oxford, Hart Publishing, 2000) para 8.1. As these sources note, distinct 'exemplary' damages are also awarded in Great Britain and the British Commonwealth in limited types of situations.

[13] See, eg, AM Dugdale et al (eds), *Clerk and Lindsell on Torts*, 19th edn (London, Sweet & Maxwell, 2006) (*Clerk and Lindsell on Torts*) ch 20; S Todd et al (eds), *The Law of Torts in New Zealand*, 2nd edn (Wellington, Brooker's, 1997) (*The Law of Torts in NZ*) ch 9; P Giliker, 'Relationships Between Neighbours: England and Wales 1850–2000' in J Gordley (ed), *The Development of Liability Between Neighbours* (Cambridge, Cambridge University Press, 2010) 29; LN Klar, *Tort Law*, 4th edn (Toronto, Thomson, 2008) ch 18; M Lunney and K Oliphant, *Tort Law: Text and Materials*, 4th edn (Oxford, Oxford University Press, 2010) ch 12; NJ McBride and R Bagshaw, *Tort Law*, 3rd edn (Harlow, Pearson Education, 2008) ch 19; K Oliphant (ed), *The Law of Tort*, 2nd edn (London, LexisNexis Butterworths, 2007) (*The Law of Tort*) ch 22; RM Solomon et al, *Cases and Materials on the Law of Torts*, 7th edn (Toronto, Thomson, 2007) ch 24.

their treatment.[14] The *Second Restatement of Torts*, although continuing to state that the two actions are 'quite different' and 'quite unrelated', unfortunately also inconsistently states that they are, with minor differences, subject to the same rules and merges their treatment.[15] It then proceeds to state different rules for each with a disjointed and confusing elaboration of the rules governing private nuisance actions due to the merged treatment of the two actions.[16]

The required legal injury for the tort of private nuisance is a significant interference, through a non-trespassory invasion, with the plaintiff's use and enjoyment of an interest in land.[17] A public nuisance is an unreasonable interference with the common interests or rights of the general public, such as the blocking of a highway or the maintenance of an illegal house of prostitution, which need not involve an interference with the use or enjoyment of an interest in land. It is a wrong to each and every member of the general public, which initially was always prosecuted as a criminal action and still is prosecuted, with respect to the interests of the general public, by the public prosecutor as a public wrong. However, an individual who suffers a discrete injury different in kind and not merely in degree from the injury suffered by the general public is granted standing to maintain a public nuisance action, in tort, for such discrete injury.[18]

Although the individual's public nuisance action is a private one encompassing only that individual and the defendant, seeking recourse only for the distinct wrong that the individual has suffered rather than also or instead for the shared non-discrete wrong to the general public, Nicholas McBride and Roderick Bagshaw deny that it is properly classified as a tort action or involves a civil wrong, since the duty that was breached was one owed to the general public rather than to the plaintiff.[19] However, the public is not an independent organic entity but a collection of individuals. The duty owed to the public is a duty owed to each of its

---

[14] *Restatement of the Law: Torts* (St Paul MN, American Law Institute, 1939) (*First Restatement*) ch 40 scope note and introductory note at 216–18. See also *The Law of Torts in NZ*, above n 13, at 519–20.

[15] *Restatement of the Law, Second: Torts* (St Paul MN, American Law Institute, 1979) (*Second Restatement*) ch 40 introductory note at 84–85.

[16] Compare *First Restatement*, above n 14, at § 822 with *Second Restatement*, above n 15, at §§ 821D, 821F, 822.

[17] *Second Restatement*, above n 15, at §§ 821D, 821F; *First Restatement*, above n 14, at § 822.

[18] *First Restatement*, above n 14, at ch 40 scope note and introductory note at 216–18; *Second Restatement*, above n 15, at §§ 821B, 821C, 826(a), 821F comment c; Dobbs, above n 7, at 1334–35; Klar, above n 13, at 715–16, 721–23; *The Law of Tort*, above n 13, at paras 22-69-22-70, 22-74-22-77; *The Law of Torts in NZ*, above n 13, at 519–21 (suggesting a plausible explanation for confusion of the two quite different actions); McBride and Bagshaw, above n 13, at 400–401; WP Keeton et al (eds), *Prosser and Keeton on Torts*, 5th edn (St Paul MN, West Publishing, 1984) 617–18, 643–52.

[19] McBride and Bagshaw, above n 13, at 28, 791.

members, each of whom suffers a shared non-discrete wrong when there is a public nuisance. Although in earlier times any member of the public could initiate a criminal action on behalf of the general public to obtain redress for the non-discrete wrong suffered by him or her and everyone else, now generally only the public prosecutor, who is best situated to act on behalf of all the public, is authorised to do so. However, for any discrete injury suffered by an individual as a result of the breach of the 'public' duty, that individual is the only one with standing to seek redress.

B. Distinguishing the Negligence and Ultrahazardous Liability Actions

In both the United States and the British Commonwealth, the private nuisance action is often described as a field of tort liability, defined by the type of injury suffered regardless of the type of tortious conduct involved.[20] Section 822 of the American Law Institute's *Second Restatement of Torts* states:

> One is subject to liability for a private nuisance if, but only if, his conduct is a legal cause of [a significant non-trespassory] invasion of another's interest in the private use and enjoyment of land, and the invasion is either
> (a) intentional and unreasonable, or
> (b) unintentional and otherwise actionable under the rules governing liability for negligent or reckless conduct, or for abnormally dangerous conditions or activities.[21]

The inclusion of sub-section (b) is puzzling. If the injury suffered is already actionable through some other tort action, there would seem to be no benefit gained, but rather only unnecessary additional analysis and confusion generated, by making available a redundant private nuisance action that requires proof of all the same elements as in the other action, plus more. If, contrary to the 'otherwise actionable' language, the other action does not currently encompass the interest in the use and enjoyment of one's land, the issue should be squarely faced as to whether that interest should be protected against the type of conduct or activity addressed by the other action. If so, it should be included as one of the interests protected by that other action; if not, it should not be snuck in through the back door through the private nuisance action under sub-section (b). For

---

[20] See, eg, *Overseas Tankship (UK) Ltd v The Miller Steamship Co Pty (The Wagon Mound)* [1967] AC 617 (PC) 639; *First Restatement*, above n 14, at ch 40 scope note and introductory note at 220–22; *Second Restatement*, above n 15, at § 822 comment a; Dobbs, above n 7, at 1321, 1324; Lunney and Oliphant, above n 13, at 653.

[21] *Second Restatement*, above n 15, at § 822; see also at §§ 821D (non-trespassory invasion required), 821F (significant harm required, 'of a kind that would be suffered by a normal person in the community or by property in normal condition and used for a normal purpose').

example, although the negligence action applies most broadly to physical harms to person or property, in many jurisdictions it also applies to certain instances of pure emotional distress and pure economic loss.[22] The policy issues involved in imposing liability for negligent interference with another's interest in the use and enjoyment of land should similarly be addressed through the doctrinal and analytical tools developed in the negligence action to address the proper breadth and scope of liability for harms caused by negligent conduct, rather than confusingly and redundantly (and perhaps inconsistently) in a private nuisance action.[23]

The same reasoning applies to harms caused by ultrahazardous[24] conditions or activities, for which a distinct strict liability action, or group of actions, is available in almost every country, by statute or court decision.[25] The seminal source in the common law is Blackburn J's opinion for the Court of Exchequer Chamber in *Fletcher v Rylands*, in which he stated:

> We think that the true rule of law is, that the person who for his own purposes brings on his lands and collects and keeps there anything likely to do mischief if it escapes, must keep it in at his peril, and, if he does not do so, is primâ facie answerable for all the damage which is the natural consequence of its escape.[26]

Unfortunately, the opinions in the House of Lords on appeal, while claiming to accept and agree with Blackburn J's true rule, restated it as a seemingly very broadly applicable rule of absolute liability for the escape of anything that merely *might* (rather than being likely to) cause harm if it escaped,[27] or that actually causes harm as a result of any 'non-natural' use of the defendant's land.[28] Subsequent judicial decisions in the British Commonwealth, in an attempt to avoid such extremely broad liability, have interpreted *Rylands v Fletcher* liability increasingly narrowly (or have even completely eliminated it), on the ground that it supposedly redundantly addresses situations already addressed by the negligence or private nuisance action.[29] Focusing solely on Blackburn J's discussion of

---

[22] See Dobbs, above n 7, at 258, 835–52, 1349–54, 1385–87; C van Dam, *European Tort Law* (Oxford, Oxford University Press, 2006) 146–49, 169–79.

[23] Keeton et al, above n 18, at 69–70; cf Dobbs, above n 7, at 1320. For discussion of cases treating negligent interferences with the use and enjoyment of land as negligence actions, see *The Law of Torts in NZ*, above n 13, at 542; Lunney and Oliphant, above n 13, at 660–61.

[24] 'Ultrahazardous' is the term used in the *First Restatement*, above n 14, at § 822. For reasons discussed in the text accompanying nn 34–41 below, the *First Restatement*'s elaboration of liability for ultrahazardous conditions or activities is highly superior to the *Second Restatement*'s elaboration of liability for abnormally dangerous conditions or activities.

[25] See, eg, van Dam, above n 22, at 353–67, 396–407.

[26] *Fletcher v Rylands* (1866) LR 1 Ex 265 (Exch Cham) 279. See also Giliker, above n 13, at 37.

[27] *Rylands v Fletcher* (1868) LR 3 HL 330 (HL) 340 (Lord Cranworth).

[28] ibid, at 339–40 (Lord Cairns).

[29] See, eg, *Transco plc v Stockport Metropolitan Borough Council* [2003] UKHL 61, [2004] 2 AC 1; *Cambridge Water Co v Eastern Counties Leathers plc* [1994] 2 AC 264 (HL) (*Cambridge Water*); *Burnie Port Authority v General Jones Pty Ltd* (1994) 179 CLR

nuisance cases, the British decisions ignore his discussion of, and reliance on, precedents involving trespassing cattle and dangerous animals when fashioning and elaborating his true rule.[30] As the following discussion explains, these precedents and the language of Blackburn's true rule point to a basis of strict liability that is distinct from the one underlying the sometimes overlapping private nuisance action.[31]

Although *Rylands v Fletcher* strict liability initially was rejected in the United States, due in large part to the mangling of Blackburn J's true rule by the House of Lords on appeal,[32] the great majority of jurisdictions in the United States now accept it.[33] The basic principle embodied in Blackburn J's true rule was incorporated and clarified in sections 519 and 520 of the *First Restatement of Torts*:

> § 519. ... [O]ne who carries on an ultrahazardous activity is liable to another whose person, land, or chattels the actor should recognize as likely to be harmed by the unpreventable miscarriage of the activity for harm resulting thereto from that which makes the activity ultrahazardous, although the utmost care is exercised to prevent the harm.

520; *Tock v St John's Metropolitan Area Board* [1989] 2 SCR 1181; *Read v J Lyons & Co Ltd* [1947] AC 156 (HL); *Rickards v Lothian* [1913] AC 263 (PC). See also *Clerk and Lindsell on Torts*, above n 13, at ch 21; *The Law of Tort*, above n 13, at paras 23-2, 23-4–23-6, 23-8–23-10; Giliker, above n 13, at 37–38, 44; Klar, above n 13, at 620 n 9, 621–24, 626–27, 629–30; Lunney and Oliphant, above n 13, at 686–703; McBride and Bagshaw, above n 13, at 401, 754–69; *The Law of Torts in NZ*, above n 13, at ch 10. But see *A-G v Geothermal Produce NZ Ltd* [1987] 2 NZLR 348 (New Zealand Court of Appeal) 354, in which Cook J noted that Blackburn J's judgment 'has hardly been taken seriously by modern English courts', which instead have focused on Lord Cairns' non-natural use requirement. McBride and Bagshaw, like other rights theorists who (incorrectly) believe that wrongs exist only when there was a duty to behave differently, treat *Rylands v Fletcher* liability as not being part of tort law since it is a strict liability rule, which holds the defendant liable despite the lack of breach of a duty to behave differently: McBride and Bagshaw, above n 13, at 25–27, 756–57. They inconsistently vacillate on whether strict liability for a harmful trespass to land in cases of necessity should be treated as part of tort law, and they employ a more capacious equal freedom conception of wrongs in order to treat strict liability for a private nuisance as part of tort law: at 366, 376–77.

[30] Dan Dobbs similarly focuses on the House of Lords' opinions in *Rylands v Fletcher* rather than Blackburn J's true rule and views *Rylands v Fletcher* as having 'anchored strict liability in the law of nuisance or competing land uses': above n 7, at 951, 954. He treats the strict liability actions for trespassing cattle, dangerous animals, abnormally dangerous activities, and private nuisances as distinct even though he assumes that they all are based on the same rationale: the fact that the defendant has engaged in an activity that is uncommon or inappropriate in the particular area or creates a non-reciprocal risk: at 941–59, 964–68.

[31] See Klar, above n 13, at 621; R Bagshaw, '*Rylands* Confined' (2004) 120 *Law Quarterly Review* 388; J Murphy, 'The Merits of *Rylands v Fletcher*' (2004) 24 *Oxford Journal of Legal Studies* 643; D Nolan, 'The Distinctiveness of *Rylands v Fletcher*' (2005) 121 *Law Quarterly Review* 421. Donal Nolan nevertheless agrees with abolition of *Rylands*-based strict liability: at 449.

[32] See, eg, *Brown v Collins* 53 NH 442 (1873).

[33] See FV Harper, F James Jr and OS Gray, *The Law of Torts*, 2nd edn (Boston MA, Little, Brown & Co, 1986) vol 3, 193–95; Dobbs, above n 7, at 958–59; Keeton et al, above n 18, at 548–53.

§ 520. An activity is ultrahazardous if it (a) necessarily involves a risk of serious harm to the person, land or chattels of others which cannot be eliminated by the exercise of the utmost care, and (b) is not a matter of common usage.[34]

When these sections are read carefully and together, they state that there is strict liability for harms (to persons or property) caused by the ultrahazardous aspect of an ultrahazardous activity, wherever it may be located, and define an activity as ultrahazardous if the defendant should know that it is *likely* to cause *serious* injury to others *if* it should 'miscarry' (escape from the defendant's control), no matter how much care the defendant exercises to prevent such miscarriage and no matter how unlikely such miscarriage may be, unless the activity is a 'common usage'. That is, the activity is ultrahazardous if the foreseeable risk of physical harm to others' person or property is qualitatively significant, given the high magnitude of both P2 (the conditional probability of injury *if* there is a loss of control) and L (the seriousness of the likely injury), even if, due to a very low P1 (the probability of escape or loss of control), the overall risk (P1 × P2 × L) is not quantitatively significant and thus not negligent. The 'common usage' exception is applied in an ad hoc, inconsistent manner in different States in the United States to prevent strict liability for some types of ultrahazardous activities, primarily the driving of automobiles[35] (which is subject to strict liability in many civil law jurisdictions[36]). A more principled and consistently applied exception, which is often described as the defence of assumption of risk and would justify many of the English decisions holding that *Rylands v Fletcher* liability is inapplicable, applies to those plaintiffs who were seeking to benefit from the ultrahazardous activity as participants, spectators, employees, etc.[37]

Setting aside the inconsistently applied 'common usage' exception, the *First Restatement*'s criteria for an ultrahazardous activity generally support the instances of strict liability for such activities that have been recognised in the United States.[38] I would like to be able to state that the *First Restatement*'s criteria are widely understood, taught, and accepted in the United States. However, this is not true. The *First Restatement*'s elaboration and clarification of Blackburn J's true rule was replaced in the *Second Restatement* by a mélange of flawed factors, none of which is necessary or sufficient for identifying 'abnormally dangerous' conditions or activities.[39] Although the *Second Restatement*'s formulation has been frequently

[34] *First Restatement*, above n 14, at §§ 519–20.

[35] See, eg, *Koos v Roth* 652 P 2d 1255 (Or 1982); *Second Restatement*, above n 15, at § 520 comment i.

[36] van Dam, above n 22, at 353–54, 359–70.

[37] Gordley, above n 5, at 156–57.

[38] K Kress, 'The Seriousness of Harm Thesis for Abnormally Dangerous Activities' in DG Owen (ed), *Philosophical Foundations of Tort Law* (Oxford, Oxford University Press, 1995) 277, 282–85.

[39] *Second Restatement*, above n 15, at §§ 519–20. Section 520 states:

and soundly criticised,[40] the criticism has not resulted in significant support for the *First Restatement*'s formulation, which continues to be misunderstood and misstated even by its proponents.[41]

In any event, there is no good reason to go through the extra analysis required to establish a private nuisance action when, as in sub-section 822(b) of the *Second Restatement*, the private nuisance liability is piggybacked and dependent on satisfaction of the requirements for some other tort.[42] Sub-section 822(b) of the *Second Restatement* (and its prior incarnation in the *First Restatement*) should be ignored, just as courts and academics in the United States[43] (but not in the British Commonwealth[44]) have ignored—indeed, generally are unaware of—the *Second Restatement*'s similar description of the trespass to land action as a field of tort liability that encompasses unintentional (negligent, reckless, or

In determining whether an activity is abnormally dangerous, the following factors are to be considered:
(a) existence of a high degree of risk of some harm to the person, land or chattels of others;
(b) likelihood that the harm that results from it will be great;
(c) inability to eliminate the risk by the exercise of reasonable care;
(d) extent to which the activity is not a matter of common usage;
(e) inappropriateness of the activity to the place where it is carried on; and
(f) extent to which its value to the community is outweighed by its dangerous attributes.

Item (a) refers to the overall risk ($P_1 \times P_2 \times L$), which is emphasised along with the equally non-explanatory criterion of non-reciprocal risk in Gordley, above n 5, at 153–55, or at least to $P_1 \times P_2$. Each of these mathematical products usually will be low rather than high due to a low P_1. Item (c) is almost always true, for any condition or activity. Item (e) is almost never true. Item (f) may be appropriate for a negligence analysis but not a strict liability analysis.

[40] See, eg, *Koos v Roth* 652 P 2d 1255 (Or 1982); Dobbs, above n 7, at 952–54; Keeton et al, above n 18, at 554–56.

[41] See, eg, Keeton et al, above n 18, at 555–56. In addition to its much better elaboration of the criteria for identifying an ultrahazardous activity, the *First Restatement* correctly insists, consistent with the cases and Blackburn J himself, that the harm for which recovery is sought must be caused by the ultrahazardous aspect of the defendant's activity, while the *Second Restatement* merely requires that the harm be caused by the activity per se. See *Second Restatement*, above n 15, at § 519; RW Wright, 'Causation in Tort Law' (1985) 73 *California Law Review* 1735, 1769–70.

[42] See Dobbs, above n 7, at 1324–25.

[43] See, eg, ibid, at 95–102; Keeton et al, above n 18, at 69–70, 73.

[44] In England, the issue seems to relate to terminology rather than substance. The courts have made it clear that, while it may (or may not) still be proper to refer to a negligent but unintentional unpermitted contact with the person of the plaintiff as a 'trespass to person' but not as a 'battery' (which requires intent), a negligently caused contact will be actionable only if it results in actual harm to the plaintiff: Lunney and Oliphant, above n 13, at 43–51. Similarly, although actions for trespass to land apparently may be based on negligence as well as intent, there is an actual harm requirement only for negligent trespasses to land: *The Law of Torts in NZ*, above n 13, at 461; *Clerk and Lindsell on Torts*, above n 13, at para 19-06. Klar states that trespass actions in Canada, for trespass to person as well as property, can still be based on negligence as well as intent, with no actual harm requirement in either case: above n 13, at 32–34, 46, 56–58, 65, 91, 106, 115. Other Canadian authors agree with respect to trespass to persons, but treat the other trespass actions as requiring intent: see, eg, Solomon et al, above n 13, at 56–58, 61, 66, 111, 145.

ultrahazardous) as well as intentional invasions of another's interest in the exclusive possession of land, with, however, a physical harm requirement for unintentional invasions.[45]

Elimination of sub-section 822(b) of the *Second Restatement* leaves sub-section 822(a), which provides liability for an *intentional* significant interference, through a non-trespassory invasion, with the plaintiff's interest in the use and enjoyment of land.[46] Private nuisance is a distinct tort only as a member of the common law's catalogue of discrete intentional torts, which are distinguished from one another primarily by the type of injury that must be intentionally caused. If the required intent does not exist, liability should depend on satisfaction of the requirements for some other recognised tort, such as negligence or ultrahazardous activity, rather than treating the situation as a private nuisance.[47]

As with the other intentional torts, the intent required for a private nuisance action may be either the defendant's *purpose* to cause the required legal injury or his or her *knowledge* that it is occurring or is substantially certain to occur as a result of his or her conduct or activity.[48] The intent in the private nuisance action is almost always the second (knowledge rather than purpose) type.[49] The knowledge type of intent will almost always exist in repetitive or continuing nuisance situations, through either direct knowledge of the legal injury's almost certain occurrence or knowledge acquired as a result of complaints by the plaintiff. It may also exist, and if so will (or should) be sufficient to establish liability, in single occurrence situations.[50]

Unfortunately, the *Second Restatement* further obscures the distinct nature of the private nuisance action as an intentional tort by adding 'and unreasonable' to 'intentional' in sub-section 822(a).[51] 'Unreasonable' implies 'negligent', especially to anyone trained in the law. However, if 'unreasonable' in this context means 'negligent', the private nuisance action is a very odd and useless intentional tort: one that requires not only intent but also satisfaction of the requirements for a negligence action. Interpreting 'unreasonable' as 'negligent' is even odder given the structure of section 822. Since negligent invasions are already included in sub-section 822(b), why mention them again in sub-section 822(a) and, moreover, add an intention requirement? What plaintiff would ever want to rely upon

---

[45] *Second Restatement*, above n 15, at §§ 165, 821D comment d.

[46] See text accompanying n 21 above.

[47] *Copart Industries Inc v Consolidated Edison* 362 NE 2d 968 (NY 1977); Keeton et al, above n 18, at 69–70, 622–26, 652–54. Unfortunately, this does not seem to be the practice in the British Commonwealth. See text accompanying nn 77–83 below.

[48] *Second Restatement*, above n 15, at § 825.

[49] ibid, at § 825 comment d; *First Restatement*, above n 14, at ch 40 scope note and introductory note at 221–23, § 825 comment b; Keeton et al, above n 18, at 624–25.

[50] *Second Restatement*, above n 15, at § 825 comment d and illustrations 1 and 2.

[51] See text accompanying n 21 above.

sub-section 822(a), which as so interpreted requires intent as well as negligence, rather than sub-section 822(b), which only requires negligence?

A reasonable assumption would be that the drafters of section 822 meant something other than 'negligent' and exhibited poor drafting skills by referring to an 'intentional and unreasonable' invasion. However, this assumption seems to be negated by the *Restatement*'s primary definition of an 'unreasonable' invasion. Section 826 of the first and second *Restatements* states that whether an intentional invasion is unreasonable depends on whether the gravity of the harm outweighs the utility of the actor's conduct,[52] which sounds very much like the definition of negligence in section 291 of the *Restatements*, which equates 'unreasonable' and 'negligent':

> Where an act is one which a reasonable man would recognise as involving risk of harm to another, the risk is unreasonable and the act is negligent if the risk is of such magnitude as to outweigh what the law regards as the utility of the act or of the particular manner in which it is done.[53]

Indeed, the *Second Restatement* explicitly analogises the definition of 'unreasonable' in section 826 for a private nuisance to the definition of 'unreasonableness' and 'negligence' in section 291. It states that the two definitions are 'very similar' and differ merely in the fact that the risk (probability times seriousness) of harm is balanced against utility in the negligence action, while only the gravity (seriousness) of harm is balanced against utility in determining the reasonableness of an intentional private nuisance, since the intent in a private nuisance action is almost always the 'knowledge of a near certainty' type and the probability of harm is therefore close to one.[54]

The implicit normative foundation is utilitarianism, or its modern elaboration, Kaldor-Hicks economic efficiency, which judge reasonableness in terms of aggregate utility or wealth maximisation, regardless of who is putting whom at risk for whose benefit. When discussing what is 'unreasonable' in the context of the private nuisance action, the *Second Restatement* states:

> The question is not whether the plaintiff or the defendant would regard the invasion as unreasonable, but whether reasonable persons generally, looking at the whole situation impartially and objectively, would consider it unreasonable. Consideration must be given not only to the interests of the person harmed but also for the interests of the actor and to the interests of the community as a whole. Determining unreasonableness is essentially a weighing process,

---

[52] *First Restatement*, above n 14, at § 826; *Second Restatement*, above n 15, at § 826(a).

[53] *First Restatement*, above n 14, at § 291(1); *Second Restatement*, above n 15, at § 291.

[54] *Second Restatement*, above n 15, at § 822 comment k; see also *First Restatement*, above n 14, at § 828 comment b.

involving a comparative evaluation of conflicting interests in various situations according to objective legal standards.[55]

An identical explanation of what makes conduct unreasonable appears in the *Second Restatement*'s discussion of the negligence action:

> *Weighing interests.* The judgment which is necessary to decide whether the risk so realized is unreasonable, is that which is necessary to determine whether the magnitude of the risk outweighs the value which the law attaches to the conduct which involves it. This requires ... that [the actor] give an impartial consideration to the harm likely to be done the interests of the other as compared with the advantages likely to accrue to his own interests, free from the natural tendency of the actor, as a party concerned, to prefer his own interests to those of others.[56]

However, despite the obvious utilitarian influences, the authors of the first and second *Restatements* did not intend to adopt utilitarian or economic efficiency interpretations of reasonableness in either the negligence or private nuisance actions. They instead wanted to avoid the supposed danger that juries would find that a defendant's creation of any risk to others was unreasonable regardless of its contribution to the common good, understood in an equal freedom rather than aggregate utility sense. The best formulations they could come up with to counteract this supposed danger at the time the *First Restatement* was drafted adopted utilitarian language, but also contained significant qualifications and exceptions.[57] I have written extensively on this with respect to the negligence action, with detailed analysis of negligence cases in the United States and the United Kingdom.[58] Common sense, as well as analysis of the cases, clearly demonstrates the fallacy of a utilitarian or economic efficiency interpretation of reasonableness or negligence. Instead, in negligence cases different standards, consistent with interactive justice's equal freedom norm, apply in different types of situations depending on who is putting whom at risk for whose benefit. In the most common situation — defendants putting others at risk — no competent defence lawyer would argue that what the defend-

---

[55] *Second Restatement*, above n 15, at § 826 comment c; similarly *First Restatement*, above n 14, at § 826 comment b.

[56] *Second Restatement*, above n 15, at § 283 comment e; similarly *First Restatement*, above n 14, at § 283 comment c.

[57] RW Wright, 'Justice and Reasonable Care in Negligence Law' (2002) 47 *American Journal of Jurisprudence* 143, 146–58. Unfortunately, these qualifications have been eliminated by the reporters for the *Third Restatement*, who instead for the first time adopt, contrary to the cases and common sense, an explicit aggregate cost-benefit balancing interpretation of reasonableness and negligence and erroneously claim that such an interpretation is just as well as efficient. See *Restatement of the Law, Third: Torts: Liability for Physical and Emotional Harm* (St Paul MN, American Law Institute, 2010) § 3 comment e and reporters' note to comment d, criticised in Wright at 159–63, 170–94.

[58] RW Wright, 'Negligence in the Courts: Introduction and Commentary' (2002) 77 *Chicago-Kent Law Review* 425; RW Wright, 'Hand, Posner, and the Myth of the "Hand Formula"' (2003) 4 *Theoretical Inquiries in Law* 145.

ant did was reasonable because the defendant's expected gains outweighed the expected losses to those put at risk. That argument is much more likely to lead to a punitive damage award than a finding of reasonableness. Unless the person(s) put at risk by the defendant's conduct or activities are trespassers on the defendant's land, in which case the defendant's rights are paramount, the defendant's creation of significant foreseeable risks to others' persons or property is unreasonable unless the risks are necessary in order for those others to obtain, directly or indirectly, desired benefits that substantially outweigh the risks, are not too serious, and are risks about which they have been warned if it was feasible to do so.[59]

The equal freedom, rights-respecting (rather than utilitarian efficiency) nature of the references to reasonableness in private nuisance doctrine is elaborated, albeit with considerable obfuscation, in the first and second *Restatements*. The gravity–utility balancing test in section 826 of each *Restatement* is a misleading charade, although one must wade through a number of other sections and comments before this becomes clear. The introductory note to the discussion of private nuisance in the *First Restatement* states: 'For the purpose of determining liability for damages for private nuisance, conduct may be regarded as unreasonable even though its utility is great and the amount of harm is relatively small.'[60] Both the first and second *Restatements* list three factors as important in determining the utility of the defendant's conduct:

(a) the social value that the law attaches to the primary purpose of the conduct;
(b) the suitability of the conduct to the character of the locality; and
(c) the impracticability of preventing or avoiding the invasion.[61]

Social value depends on whether the 'general public good' is advanced. While the general public good may be advanced by purely private enterprises, 'activities that are customary and usual in the community have relatively greater social value than those that are not, and those that produce a direct public benefit have more than those carried on primarily for the benefit of the individual.'[62] Moreover,

---

[59] Wright, 'Myth of the "Hand Formula"', above n 58, at 180–223.

[60] *First Restatement*, above n 14, at ch 40 scope note and introductory note at 223–24; similarly *Second Restatement*, above n 15, at § 822 comment d.

[61] *Second Restatement*, above n 15, at § 828; similarly *First Restatement*, above n 14, at § 828.

[62] *Second Restatement*, above n 15, at § 828 comment f; see also at § 828 comments e and g; *First Restatement*, above n 14, at § 828 comments d and e. If the defendant's conduct was malicious—done for the sole purpose of injuring the plaintiff's person or property—it is unreasonable 'as a matter of law': *Second Restatement*, above n 15, at § 829 and comment b; *The Law of Torts in NZ*, above n 13, at 559–60; McBride and Bagshaw, above n 13, at 382–83. No one even thinks of comparing the utility the defendant gains from his or her malicious conduct with the disutility suffered by the plaintiff.

It is only when the conduct has utility from the standpoint of all the factors that its merit is ever sufficient to outweigh the gravity of the harm it causes. If the conduct lacks utility from the standpoint of any one of the factors, the fact that it has utility from the standpoint of other factors is immaterial.[63]

Thus, '[i]f the particular activity or inactivity is not suited to the character of the locality, the conduct generally lacks utility and the invasion it causes is generally unreasonable as a matter of law if the harm involved is at all serious.'[64] Moreover,

When a person knows that his conduct will interfere with another's use or enjoyment of land and it would be practicable for him to prevent or avoid part or all of the interference and still achieve his purpose, his conduct lacks utility if he fails to take the necessary measures to avoid it. It is only when an intentional invasion is practically unavoidable that one can be justified in causing it; and even then, he is not justified if the gravity of the harm is too great. An invasion is practically avoidable if the actor by some means can substantially reduce the harm without incurring prohibitive expense or hardship.[65]

An invasion is deemed to be practically avoidable even if it would be less expensive or difficult for the plaintiff to take steps to avoid the harm, if those steps would impose a significant burden on the plaintiff.[66] This principle is given independent black letter treatment in sub-section 826(b) of the *Second Restatement*, as a definition of unreasonableness that is paired with, but distinct from, the gravity–utility definition in sub-section 826(a).[67]

Even when the defendant's conduct has sufficient utility from the standpoint of all three of the listed factors, an intentional invasion is declared to be unreasonable, regardless of the utility of the defendant's conduct, 'if the harm resulting from the invasion is severe and greater than the other should be required to bear without compensation'.[68] How much harm should the other be required to bear? In the main comment on 'unreasonableness' of intentional invasions,[69] the answer is given in terms of

---

[63] *First Restatement*, above n 14, at § 828 comment b; see also *Second Restatement*, above n 15, at § 828 comment c.

[64] *Second Restatement*, above n 15, at § 828 comment g; see also at § 831; *First Restatement*, above n 14, at §§ 828 comment f, 831.

[65] *Second Restatement*, above n 15, at § 828 comment h; see also at § 830; *First Restatement*, above n 14, at §§ 828 comment g, 830.

[66] *Second Restatement*, above n 15, at § 827 comment i; *First Restatement*, above n 14, at § 827 comment g.

[67] *Second Restatement*, above n 15, at § 826(b). But see *Carpenter v The Double R Cattle Co* 701 P 2d 222 (Idaho 1985) (rejecting sub-section (b) by a 3-2 vote).

[68] *Second Restatement*, above n 15, at § 829A; see also at § 827 comment b. The same point is expressed differently at § 826 comment e: 'the legal utility of the activity may also be greatly reduced by the fact the actor is operating the factory and producing the noise and smoke without compensating his neighbors for the harm done to them'.

[69] *Second Restatement*, above n 15, at § 822 comment g; *First Restatement*, above n 14, at § 822 comment j.

the equal freedom based 'give and take, live and let live' principle that Bramwell B set forth in *Bamford v Turnley*,[70] which is also reflected in the definition of a significant harm or interference in section 821F of the *Second Restatement*: 'There is liability for a nuisance only to those to whom it causes significant harm, of a kind that would be suffered by a normal person in the community or by property in normal condition and used for a normal purpose.'[71]

In sum, 'unreasonable' refers to the impact on the plaintiff's use and enjoyment of his or her land, rather than to the defendant's conduct.[72] 'Unreasonable' ends up having the same meaning as, and is used interchangeably and redundantly with, 'significant', which is interpreted objectively in accord with Bramwell B's 'give and take, live and let live' principle.[73] Even when 'unreasonable' is properly interpreted as applying to the evaluation of the plaintiff's injury rather than the defendant's conduct, its use is likely to mislead given its strong association with the negligence concept. It therefore is best to avoid any use of the word 'unreasonable' and instead to focus clearly on the nature of the legal injury that must be intentionally caused by the defendant: a significant

---

[70] *Bamford v Turnley* (1862) 3 B & S 66, 82–84; 122 ER 27, 33–34. Bramwell B's 'give and take, live and let live' principle, which is based on equal freedom, is inconsistently followed by a utilitarian argument. At 3 B & S 83–85; 122 ER 34 he states:

> It seems to me that that principle may be deduced from the character of these cases, and is this, viz,. that those acts necessary for the common and ordinary use and occupation of land and houses may be done, if conveniently done, without subjecting those who do them to an action. ... There is an obvious necessity for such a principle as I have mentioned. It is as much for the advantage of one owner as of another; for the very nuisance the one complains of, as the result of the ordinary use of his neighbour's land, he himself will create in the ordinary use of his own, and the reciprocal nuisances are of a comparatively trifling character. The convenience of such a rule may be indicated by calling it a rule of give and take, live and let live.

But later, he states (at 3 B & S 84–85; 122 ER 34):

> The public consists of all the individuals in it, and a thing is only for the public benefit when it is productive of good to those individuals on the balance of loss and gain to all. So that if all the loss and all the gain were borne and received by one individual he on the whole would be a gainer. But whenever this is the case,—whenever a thing is for the public benefit, properly understood,—the loss to the individuals of the public who lose will bear compensation out of the gains of those who gain.

Lunney and Oliphant focus on the second paragraph above, which contains the utilitarian argument, rather than the usual citation to the morally and legally relevant first paragraph, which is based on the equal freedom principle: above n 13, at 645. Their discussions of negligence and private nuisance employ utilitarian conceptions of public benefit, the common good and reasonableness, rather than equal freedom conceptions: at 166, 172–75, 640–41, 644–46.

[71] *Second Restatement*, above n 15, at § 821F; see also *First Restatement*, above n 14, at § 822 comment g (similar definition of a 'substantial invasion').

[72] See, eg, *Morgan v High Penn Oil Co* 77 SE 2d 682 (NC 1953); *Jost v Dairyland Power Cooperative* 172 NW 2d 647 (Wis 1969); Dobbs, above n 7, at 1325–26; Keeton et al, above n 18, at 623, 625, 626–29.

[73] See, eg, *Estancias Dallas Corp v Schultz* 500 SW 2d 217 (Tex Ct Civ App 1973) (*Estancias Dallas*) 221; Keeton et al, above n 18, at 627–29.

interference, through a non-trespassory invasion, with the plaintiff's use and enjoyment of his or her land, with 'significant' being evaluated from the perspective of persons of ordinary sensibilities living in the locality.

This prescription applies as well in the British Commonwealth, in which discussions of the private nuisance action by courts and secondary sources generally state that there must be an 'unreasonable user', 'unreasonable invasion', or 'unreasonable interference' by the defendant with the plaintiff's use and enjoyment of his or her land.[74] Although, as in the United States, the Commonwealth courts often state that proof of negligence is not required for a private nuisance action, and that 'unreasonable invasion', 'unreasonable user', and 'unreasonable interference' do not refer to negligent conduct by the defendant but rather to the impact on the plaintiff assessed in terms of Bramwell B's 'live and let live' principle',[75] references to 'fault' as well as unreasonable conduct by the defendant still occur and create confusion.[76]

Further confusion has been generated in the British Commonwealth by the failure to recognise intentional conduct, usually in the sense of knowing rather than purposeful causation of the required legal injury, as the typical and, preferably, only type of conduct giving rise to liability for a private nuisance.[77] There is no clear specification of the type of conduct or activity that must exist in the absence of conduct that is the basis for some other recognised tort, such as negligence or *Rylands v Fletcher* strict liability. This seems to be due in part to the severe restriction or even elimination of *Rylands v Fletcher* strict liability. Cases in which liability could and should have been imposed under a proper interpretation of Blackburn J's true rule have instead been allowed as private nuisance

[74] See, eg, McBride and Bagshaw, above n 13, at 367, 374; Lunney and Oliphant, above n 13, at 644; Solomon et al, above n 13, at 796.

[75] See, eg, *The Wagon Mound* [1967] AC 617 (PC) 639; *Cambridge Water* [1994] 2 AC 264 (HL); *The Law of Tort*, above n 13, at paras 22-17, 22-34; *The Law of Torts in NZ*, above n 13, at 532–34, 538, 540, 556–59; Giliker, above n 13, at 33–34; Klar, above n 13, at 726–30; Lunney and Oliphant, above n 13, at 653–56; McBride and Bagshaw, above n 13, at 374–81; Solomon et al, above n 13, at 795–800.

[76] See, eg, Giliker, above n 13, at 38–46; Lunney and Oliphant, above n 13, at 653–56; *The Law of Torts in NZ*, above n 13, at 538–40, each of which, in order to explain private nuisance liability, treat mere foreseeability of a significant interference with the plaintiff's use and enjoyment of an interest in land as faulty and/or unreasonable.

[77] Although appearing to discuss private nuisance as an intentional tort, Klar apparently construes 'deliberate conduct' as referring merely to the conduct itself, not to its consequences (which is the proper focus for the intent requirement in any intentional tort), and criticises Canadian decisions denying nuisance liability when the defendants did not know that their conduct would have an adverse impact on their neighbour: see Klar, above n 13, at 726, 733. The cases discussed by Klar and others (eg, *The Law of Torts in NZ*, above n 13, at 532, 539–40; Giliker, above n 13, at 39–43) that employ the *Sedleigh-Denfield* distinction between conditions created by the defendant and pre-existing conditions not created by the defendant and use negligence analysis with respect to the latter would be resolved much more simply and consistently, without the need for any such distinction, if private nuisance were always treated as an intentional tort, so that *Sedleigh-Denfield* type of situations could only be litigated as negligence actions.

actions in the absence of intentional or negligent conduct and with little or no articulation of the grounds for or limits on such strict liability.[78] In *Cambridge Water Co v Eastern Counties Leather plc*, the House of Lords stated that there must be foreseeability of the significant interference with the plaintiff's use and enjoyment of an interest in land, and it noted that actual knowledge of such interference will always exist when the remedy sought is an injunction against future interference, but it did not elaborate on the degree of foreseeability, or any other criterion, that is required in the absence of negligence when damages are sought for a past interference.[79] Mere foreseeability surely is insufficient, especially given the extremely low threshold set for foreseeability in *Bolton v Stone*[80] and *Overseas Tankship (UK) Ltd v The Miller Steamship Co Pty (The Wagon Mound)*,[81] which held that a risk is foreseeable even if it is 'remote', 'infinitesimal', 'insubstantial', 'very rare', or 'improbable', rather than 'fantastic'.[82] Contrary to the holding of the House in *Cambridge Water*, the risk of the underground flow of pollution to the plaintiff's borehole in that case likely had the minimal level of foreseeability required in *Bolton v Stone* and *The Wagon Mound*, although (supporting the rejection of liability for a private nuisance) the defendant did not have the knowledge of a near certainty required for a finding of intent.[83]

C. Distinguishing the Trespass to Land Action

Although the private nuisance action is usually defined in contrast to the trespass to land action, as a 'non-trespassory' tort,[84] the two actions are closely related and thus sometimes confused. Both actions, properly construed, require (or should require) an intentional interference with the plaintiff's legally recognised interest in land as a result of a physical invasion of something onto the land.[85] However, they protect different aspects of the plaintiff's interest in land. The trespass to land action protects a plaintiff's interest in the *possession and occupancy* of the land, regardless of whether there is any physical, economic, or emotional harm or interference with the plaintiff's use and enjoyment of the land, while the private

---

[78] See *The Law of Torts in NZ*, above n 13, at 532; Klar, above n 13, at 734–36.

[79] *Cambridge Water* [1994] 2 AC 264 (HL). See also McBride and Bagshaw, above n 13, at 374–82; *Clerk and Lindsell on Torts*, above n 13, at paras 20-35–20-38.

[80] *Bolton v Stone* [1951] AC 850 (HL).

[81] *The Wagon Mound* [1967] AC 617 (PC).

[82] See RW Wright, 'The Grounds and Extent of Legal Responsibility' (2003) 40 *San Diego Law Review* 1425, 1515–17.

[83] The *Second Restatement* presciently employs a hypothetical with facts essentially the same as those in the *Cambridge Water* case to illustrate the importance of this distinction: *Second Restatement*, above n 15, at § 825 illustration 3.

[84] See, eg, *The Law of Tort*, above n 13, at para 22-8; text accompanying n 21 above.

[85] See text accompanying nn 96–108 below.

nuisance action protects a plaintiff's interest in the *use and enjoyment* of the land, but only if there has been a significant interference from the perspective of a person with ordinary sensitivities in the locale.[86]

The traditional common law distinction between trespass and nuisance, which has its roots in the old forms of action and turns on whether the interference was 'direct' or 'indirect', bears little or no relation to the basic issue of whether there has been an actionable interference with possession or occupancy or an actionable interference with use and enjoyment. Yet, despite its unclear and unsettled meaning and lack of a principled basis, the distinction between 'direct' and 'indirect' interferences still has some support, at least in the doctrine, in the British Commonwealth.[87] It has generally been rejected in the United States and replaced by a distinction between tangible and intangible physical invasions.[88] Although the distinction between tangible and intangible physical invasions blurs at the microscopic level, there are significantly different impacts on a person's autonomy and equal freedom at the macroscopic level. Tangible physical invasions, by animate or inanimate entities, are more likely than intangible physical invasions to cause or be a significant interference with a person's occupancy, control, and use of his or her land. Moreover, it generally is much easier to avoid purposely or knowingly causing such invasions, while many intangible physical invasions—by, for example, odours, fumes, smoke, dust, or sounds—are extremely difficult if not impossible to avoid knowingly causing as a result of normal and basic everyday activities. Thus, everyone's equal freedom is promoted by making intentional tan-

---

[86] See, eg, Dobbs, above n 7, at 95–96, 104–107, 1321–23; Keeton et al, above n 18, at 70–71, 622–23.

[87] See, eg, McBride and Bagshaw, above n 13, at 368, suggesting that 'the most important factor in drawing the distinction [between direct and indirect interference] seems to be the defendant's degree of control over the thing which caused the interference', but acknowledging that 'difficulties arise' in trying to fit this interpretation with the cases. *The Law of Tort*, above n 13, at para 22-16 states that the distinction turns on whether the 'the defendant's act from the beginning is unlawful' or is 'initially lawful, but leads thereafter to an invasion of the claimant's rights'. The purported distinction is highly questionable, since both trespass and private nuisance liability exist only when the invasion of the claimant's interest in land is desired, known, or at least foreseeable at the time of the act, which makes the act 'unlawful' from the beginning. Any attempted distinction along these lines would lack a principled foundation and be subject to numerous counter-examples. Klar, above n 13, at 724 fn 65 rejects the distinction between direct and indirect interferences as applied to the private nuisance action. He states that the Canadian courts still sometimes refer to the distinction, albeit inconsistently, to distinguish the trespass and negligence actions, but argues that '[a]s a matter of contemporary policy, there are no reasons why courts should continue to distinguish between direct and indirect injuries': at 31; see also at 29–31, 47–48. Other texts pay little or no attention to the purported distinction between direct and indirect interferences. See, eg, *The Law of Torts in NZ*, above n 13, at 460–61, 521–22; Solomon et al, above n 13, at 156–59, 795.

[88] *First Restatement*, above n 14, at ch 40 scope note and introductory note at 224–25; *Second Restatement*, above n 15, at § 821D and comment e; Dobbs, above n 7, at 95–96, 104–07, 1321–23; Keeton et al, above n 18, at 70–71, 622–23.

gible invasions generally actionable,[89] while making intentional (known but not purposeful) intangible invasions actionable only if they constitute a significant interference with the plaintiff's use and enjoyment of his or her land, as judged from the perspective of a person with ordinary sensitivities in the particular community.

The *First Restatement* clearly distinguished these two torts, while noting that a plaintiff in a trespass action can recover not only for the interference with his or her possessory rights caused by the tangible invasion but also for any incidental interference with his or her use and enjoyment of the land.[90] The *Second Restatement*, while still stating that a private nuisance is 'a nontrespassory invasion of another's interest in the private use and enjoyment of land', blurs the distinction between the two actions by allowing recovery for significant interferences with the use and enjoyment of land caused by a tangible, trespassory invasion through overlapping trespass and private nuisance actions.[91]

A few courts in the United States have gone in the other direction by allowing claims involving intangible invasions to be brought as a trespass action. For example, in *Martin v Reynolds Metals Co*[92] the Supreme Court of Oregon stated that modern scientific knowledge, which has revealed the molecular and atomic structure of the physical world and the equivalence of matter and energy, has undermined the traditional distinction between tangible and intangible invasions. Relying on *Martin*, the Supreme Court of Washington held, in *Bradley v American Smelting and Refining Co*,[93] that airborne microscopic particles or substances that do not dissipate, but rather accumulate on the plaintiff's land, can constitute a trespass as well as a private nuisance. However, neither Court would allow the trespass action unless there was a substantial interference with the plaintiff's possessory interest or substantial damage, respectively, thereby reintroducing under the guise of the trespass action the more restrictive requirement for a private nuisance action.[94] In each case, what actually constituted a private nuisance was allowed to be brought as a nominal trespass action

---

[89] The equal freedom principle can also explain the somewhat different rules applied to tangible physical invasions by tree roots or branches and overflying aircraft, which are practically unavoidable and allowed unless they significantly interfere with the plaintiff's occupancy, possession, or use of the land, regardless of whether the applicable action is described as a trespass action or a private nuisance action.

[90] *First Restatement*, above n 14, at ch 40 scope note and introductory note at 215, 224–25, § 822 comment c.

[91] *Second Restatement*, above n 15, at § 821D. The same situation seems to exist in England and Wales: see Giliker, above n 13, at 31 (stating that private nuisances may involve tangible as well as intangible invasions).

[92] *Martin v Reynolds Metals Co* 342 P 2d 790 (Or 1959) (*Martin*).

[93] *Bradley v American Smelting and Refining Co* 709 P 2d 782 (Wash 1985).

[94] For other examples, see Dobbs, above n 7, at 1322 n 19; Keeton et al, above n 18, at 71 n 38.

to enable the plaintiff to take advantage of the longer limitation period for trespass actions.[95]

As with the trespass action, the significant interference with the plaintiff's interest in the use and enjoyment of land that is required for a private nuisance action must result from an (intentionally caused) physical invasion of some entity (for a nuisance, an intangible entity) across the borders of the plaintiff's land. Otherwise a property owner would be able to acquire easements for unobstructed views or the flow of (light, radio, television, telephone, internet, etc) waves across others' property without the consent of the owners of the other property and without paying for the easements.[96] An often cited case is *Fontainebleau Hotel Corp v Forty-Five Twenty-Five Inc*,[97] in which the Eden Roc Hotel unsuccessfully sought to hold the adjoining Fontainebleau Hotel liable for a private nuisance for building an addition to its hotel that 'cast a shadow on' (blocked the direct transmission of sunlight to) the Eden Roc Hotel's swimming pool. The Supreme Court of Florida summarily dismissed the suit, noting that, in the absence of contract or statute, a property owner does not have a presumptive or implied right to the free flow of light and air across adjoining land.[98] The same result, on the same grounds, was reached by

[95] See Keeton et al, above n 18, at 71–72.

[96] *Second Restatement*, above n 15, at § 821D; see Dobbs, above n 7, at 1330–33. But see Klar, above n 13, at 726 n 73 (discussing an apparently unique Canadian case that found the blocking of a view to be a nuisance). For similar reasons, the argument that the plaintiff moved to the nuisance generally is not recognised as a valid defence. Allowing such a defence would permit a defendant to acquire property rights in another's land—an easement or servitude for purposes of dumping noises, smells, fumes, etc onto the plaintiff's land—without the consent of the plaintiff or any prior owner of the land and without paying for the property right, even if the plaintiff or the prior owners had previously been unable to prevent the dumping because it had not caused a significant interference with their actual use and enjoyment of the land (most commonly, because the land previously was undeveloped and vacant): Dobbs, above n 7, at 1328; Klar, above n 13, at 727. A defence based on the plaintiff's having moved to the nuisance is equitable, and has been allowed, when (1) the plaintiff moved to the nuisance solely for the purpose of obtaining money by suing the defendant, or (2) the plaintiff moved into an area that is generally dedicated to uses such as the defendant's and is not, due to general social and economic forces, shifting away from such uses to ones more compatible with the plaintiff's use. In most instances of the second type a defence of plaintiff's having moved to the nuisance will not be necessary, since the effects of the defendant's activity on the plaintiff's use and enjoyment of his or her land would not be considered significant by a person of ordinary sensitivity in the locality: Dobbs, above n 7, at 1327–28; Klar, above n 13, at 729.

[97] *Fontainebleau Hotel Corp v Forty-Five Twenty-Five Inc* 114 So 2d 357 (Fla Ct App 1959), certiorari denied 117 So 2d 842 (Fla 1960).

[98] In *Prah v Maretti* 321 NW 2d 182 (Wis 1982), decided during the glory days of the environmental movement, the Court (over a vigorous dissent) supposedly applying the *Second Restatement*'s definition of a private nuisance, but ignoring its 'non-trespassory *invasion*' requirement, reversed a summary judgment for the defendant and remanded to allow the plaintiff to try to prove that the defendant's building of a house that allegedly interfered with solar collectors on the plaintiff's house on an adjacent lot in a new sub-division constituted an 'unreasonable' interference. On remand, the defendant's house was moved at the plaintiff's expense. However, it was not a good location for solar energy. The plaintiff's solar collectors did not work and were abandoned.

the Supreme Court of Illinois and the German *Bundesgerichtshof* in cases in which the plaintiffs sought to hold the owners of buildings liable for interfering, by the mere presence of the building, with the transmission of television and radio signals.[99]

Interference with the transmission of television signals by the construction of a building was also at issue in *Hunter v Canary Wharf Ltd*,[100] in which the House of Lords reached the same result as the *Bundesgerichtshof* and the Supreme Court of Illinois on very similar grounds. Lord Goff noted that 'for an action in private nuisance to lie in respect of interference with the plaintiff's enjoyment of his land, it will generally arise from something emanating from the defendant's land' (which thus physically invades the plaintiff's land),[101] and Lord Lloyd agreed.[102] Although Lord Goff and Lord Hoffmann relied on a person's right to build whatever he wants on his land,[103] this right is not absolute. As Lord Goff noted, a private nuisance action should be available if the defendant's building does not merely, by its presence, *block the flow* of light or other waves *across the defendant's land*, but rather *projects or reflects onto the plaintiff's land* light, noise, electromagnetic waves, or other intangible entities that significantly interfere with the plaintiffs' use and enjoyment of their property.[104] Unfortunately, explicit reliance on the physical invasion requirement seems to have been impeded in England by the anachronistic 'ancient lights' doctrine, codified in the Prescription Act of 1832, which, as Lord Hoffman noted,[105] created an anomalous conclusive presumption of a prescriptive negative easement for continuation of the flow of air and light across the defendant's land after a certain period of years. While the 'ancient lights' doctrine may have made sense as an implementation of an equal-freedom based principle of mutual necessity and advantage at a time when there were minimal means of indoor illumination or ventilation, it no longer has such a justification. It should be understood and (perhaps) preserved only as a statutorily created 'acquired right', interference with which is treated similarly to expressly granted easements for light, air and view across others' property.

Other commonly discussed cases that might be thought to be inconsist-

---

[99] *The People ex rel Hoogasian v Sears, Roebuck & Co* 287 NE 2d 677 (Ill 1972); Bundesgerichtshof [German Federal Court of Justice], V ZR 166/82, 21 October 1983 reported in (1984) 88 BGHZ 344.

[100] *Hunter v Canary Wharf Ltd* [1997] AC 655 (HL) (*Hunter*).

[101] ibid, at 685 (Lord Goff). See McBride and Bagshaw, above n 13, at 371.

[102] *Hunter* [1997] AC 655 (HL) 700 (Lord Lloyd).

[103] ibid, at 685 (Lord Goff), 709 (Lord Hoffmann).

[104] ibid, at 684–87 (Lord Goff), citing and discussing *Bridlington Relay Ltd v Yorkshire Electricity Board* [1965] Ch 436 (Ch); *Bank of New Zealand v Greenwood* [1984] 1 NZLR 525 (High Court of New Zealand); *Nor-Video Services Ltd v Ontario Hydro* (1978) 84 DLR (3d) 221 (Ontario High Court of Justice) 231 (Robins J). See also ibid, at 708–09 (Lord Hoffmann).

[105] *Hunter* [1997] AC 655 (HL) 709 (Lord Hoffmann).

ent with the physical invasion requirement, such as cases involving angst over nearby houses of prostitution or blockage of access to land,[106] would be better handled under more relevant actions (eg, as private actions for discrete harm caused by a public nuisance, or as negligence actions) rather than as private nuisance actions.

As with requirements in other torts that are sometimes ignored or relaxed to allow recovery for malicious causation of the legal injury that is addressed by those torts, the physical invasion requirement that exists for both trespass and private nuisance should be and generally is set aside (at least in North America) if the defendant acted with the sole purpose of causing the relevant legal injury—for example, if the defendant maintained a 'spite fence', a junk heap, or an atrociously painted house on his or her property for the sole purpose of interfering with the plaintiff's use and enjoyment of his or her property.[107] A better approach would be to recognise a generally applicable tort of deliberate, maliciously caused injury.[108]

IV. PRIVATE NUISANCE AS A STRICT LIABILITY TORT

If, as argued above, the private nuisance action is a distinct tort only as an intentional tort, its usual classification as a strict liability tort would be improper from the viewpoint of those who define strict liability as liability in the absence of intentional or negligent causation of the injury at issue.[109] Under the more common definition of strict liability as liability in the absence of unreasonable[110] or faulty conduct (in the objective sense of conduct or activities in which people should not engage given a particular understanding of the common good), the strict liability nature of the private nuisance action is questionable only if it gives rise to liability solely in situations in which such conduct is deemed unreasonable or faulty (in the sense indicated above). Since it is generally agreed that

---

[106] See *The Law of Torts in NZ*, above n 13, at 530–31; McBride and Bagshaw, above n 13, at 371–74, 384.

[107] Dobbs, above n 7, at 1331; Klar, above n 13, at 730. Cf *Hollywood Silver Fox Farm Ltd v Emmett* [1936] 2 KB 468 (KB), in which the Court held the defendant liable, despite the extra-sensitive nature of the plaintiff's silver foxes, when the defendant maliciously fired shots on his own property (the noise from which invaded the plaintiff's property) for the sole purpose of adversely affecting the plaintiff's foxes. English jurisprudence on this issue was thrown partially off track by the House of Lords' decision in *Bradford Corp v Pickles* [1895] AC 587 (HL), which held that the defendant was not liable for obstructing the flow of groundwater to the plaintiff's land even if he had acted solely for the purpose of extorting money from the plaintiff. See McBride and Bagshaw, above n 13, at 382–83.

[108] See, eg, *Second Restatement*, above n 15, at § 870; *Bürgerliches Gesetzbuch* (German Civil Code) § 226; JW Neyers, 'Explaining the Inexplicable? Four Manifestations of Abuse of Rights in English Law', ch 11 of this book.

[109] See, eg, Keeton et al, above n 18, at 554.

[110] See, eg, Klar, above n 13, at 619.

negligent conduct, which clearly is faulty, is not required for a private nuisance action, the issue turns on whether intentional causation of the legally cognisable injury is always faulty, at least in the context of the private nuisance action. A clear example of liability for intentional conduct that is not faulty is the liability that exists, for actual damages only, for intentional trespasses to property when there is a valid defence of private necessity.[111] If we focus specifically on the private nuisance action, the issue narrows to the question of whether imminent or continuing private nuisances are always enjoinable, as well as being subject to payment of damages.

Courts in some jurisdictions in the United States have held that any plaintiff subjected to a continuing or imminent private nuisance is automatically entitled to an injunction, as well as damages for any legally cognisable injury that has already been incurred. However, most courts have treated the issuance of an injunction as being a distinct equitable issue, which should be resolved through a 'balancing of the equities' involved in the case.[112] Contrary to the attempts of the drafters of the *Second Restatement*[113] and similarly minded academics to interpret 'balancing of the equities' in a utilitarian or aggregate cost–benefit sense, in this context as in others equity generally has been viewed in its Aristotelian sense[114] as what is just, and equitable principles are invoked (at times through distinct courts of equity) to attain such justice when it would not be obtained by the mere award of damages.

Although, as far as I am aware, no court in the Unites States has explicitly articulated all of the following criteria, an analysis of the cases makes it fairly clear that, in most jurisdictions, an injunction will be granted to halt an ongoing or imminent significant interference with the plaintiff's use and enjoyment of his or her property unless all of the following conditions are satisfied:

1. there is an important public benefit from the defendant's activity rather than a merely private benefit to the defendant;[115]

---

[111] See, eg, *Vincent v Lake Erie Transportation Co* 124 NW 221 (Minn 1910). Robert Keeton insists on describing such conduct, as well as private nuisances in which the plaintiff is limited to a damages remedy, as being faulty, not in terms of the conduct per se, but conditionally if one engages in such conduct without paying compensation for the intentionally caused injury: RE Keeton, 'Conditional Fault in the Law of Torts' (1959) 72 *Harvard Law Review* 401; Keeton et al, above n 18, at 554, 635–36, 629–30.

[112] See, eg, *Estancias Dallas* 500 SW 2d 217 (Tex Ct Civ App 1973).

[113] In its only discussion of the criteria for granting an injunction, the *Second Restatement*, above n 15, at § 941 states: 'The relative hardship likely to result to the defendant if an injunction is granted and to the plaintiff if it is denied, is one of the factors to be considered in determining the appropriateness of an injunction against tort'. See also at § 826 comment f.

[114] Wright, 'Substantive Corrective Justice', above n 1, at 686–87.

[115] See, eg, *Estancias Dallas* 500 SW 2d 217 (Tex Ct Civ App 1973); see also text accompanying nn 124–27 below.

2. granting the injunction would result in a loss of or substantial reduction in the public benefit because it is not technologically or economically feasible for the defendant to avoid causing the significant interference with the plaintiff's use and enjoyment of his or her property;[116]
3. the continuation of the nuisance would not constitute a significant threat to the plaintiff's life or health;[117]
4. the public benefit substantially outweighs the burden on the plaintiff;[118] and
5. the plaintiff is fully compensated.[119]

The most frequently cited and discussed case on this question in the United States is *Boomer v Atlantic Cement Co.*[120] Prior to *Boomer*, the rule in the State of New York had been that, once a continuing nuisance was established, the plaintiff was automatically entitled to an injunction to prevent its continuance, even if the impact on the defendant of granting the injunction greatly outweighed the impact of the nuisance on the plaintiff. *Boomer* was a widely noted departure from this rule, which is frequently described as having made the granting of the injunction turn on a utilitarian cost–benefit analysis. However, although some language in the New York Court of Appeals' opinion might seem to support this interpretation, the reality is different.

The Court claimed to focus solely on the rights and interests of the plaintiffs and the defendant, to the exclusion of the rights and interests of the public.[121] It stated that '[t]he ground for the denial of injunction, notwithstanding the finding both that there is a nuisance and that plaintiffs have been damaged substantially, is the large disparity in economic consequences of the nuisance and of the injunction'.[122] The defendant had invested more than $45 million in its new facility, while the aggregate diminution in value of the plaintiffs' land was found by the trial Court to be only $185 000.[123]

However, this was not the basis for the trial Court's or the Court of Appeals' refusal to grant an injunction against continuation of the nuisance. The trial Court emphasised the major public benefits to the local economy and schools in terms of jobs, taxes, and other indirect benefits.[124] In a footnote, the Court of Appeals referred indirectly to the public benefits, instancing not only the defendant's investment in excess of $45 million, but also the fact that over 300 jobs had been created

---

[116] See text accompanying nn 128–31 below.
[117] See text accompanying and following n 126 below.
[118] See text accompanying nn 122–25 below.
[119] See below n 132 and accompanying text.
[120] *Boomer v Atlantic Cement Co* 257 NE 2d 870 (NY 1970) (*Boomer*).
[121] ibid, at 871.
[122] ibid, at 872.
[123] ibid, at 873.
[124] *Boomer v Atlantic Cement Co* 287 NYS 2d 112 (NY Sup Ct 1967) 114 (Herzberg J).

directly through employment at the plant.[125] If the activity causing the nuisance (which reduced the value of the plaintiffs' properties by 50 to 60 per cent) had been of purely private benefit to the defendant without any major benefits to the public, surely an injunction would have been granted.

Why, then, did the Court of Appeals frame the issue as one involving only the private interests of the plaintiffs and the defendant, to the exclusion of the interests of the public in general? The answer seems to be that the plaintiffs raised the issue of the newly energised public concern over the non-discrete risks to the general public due to air pollution in general and particulate emissions from concrete plants in particular, an issue that was being vigorously debated at the time in the State and federal legislatures, leading to the enactment of the initial federal Clean Air Act in the same year, 1970. The Court of Appeals noted that courts are not institutionally competent to resolve the scientifically and geographically complex issues related to the general risks to the public created by air pollution, and there apparently were no allegations of significant imminent health risks to the plaintiffs in particular.[126] If the plaintiffs had alleged and proven significant concrete adverse health effects, a different result no doubt would have been reached.

In order to justify not taking into account the non-discrete yet substantial health risks to the public in general posed by the defendant's activity, the Court of Appeals thought it needed to appear to be framing the issue as one not involving the interests of the public, which disenabled it from relying straightforwardly on the real reason for the denial of the injunction: the major benefits to the public that were relied upon by the trial Court, which the majority referenced only incompletely, indirectly, and discreetly in a footnote. Continuing the charade, the dissenting opinion took the majority to task for authorising the forced sale to the defendant of a permanent easement for dumping pollution on the plaintiffs' lands for the defendant's private purpose, rather than any public purpose or use, contrary to the takings clauses in the State and federal constitutions.[127]

Consistently with the criteria for not granting an injunction that I listed above, the New York Court of Appeals in *Boomer* also noted that the defendant was employing the best currently available pollution control equipment, so that requiring any further reduction in the pollution would require the defendant to close down (thereby eliminating the public

---

[125] *Boomer* 257 NE 2d 870 (NY 1970) 873 n * (Bergan J for Fuld CJ, Bergan, Burke and Scileppi JJ); see also Dobbs, above n 7, at 1339, referring to the social value of the defendant's activity in *Boomer* as the explanation for the Court of Appeals' refusal to grant an injunction, and citing other similar cases in which substantial public benefits in terms of jobs and tax revenues were relied upon to justify refusal of an injunction.

[126] *Boomer* 257 NE 2d 870 (NY 1970) 871 (Bergan J for Fuld CJ, Bergan, Burke and Scileppi JJ).

[127] ibid, at 876 (Jasen J).

benefits).[128] If it had thought that further reduction in the pollution were possible without eliminating or substantially reducing the desired public benefits, it seems likely from the overall thrust of the opinion that such reduction would have been ordered.

In *Renken v Harvey Aluminum Co*,[129] the plaintiffs each suffered less than $10 000 in damage to their fruit orchards and crops as a result of periodic emissions of particulates and gases, including fluorides, from the defendant's aluminium reduction plant, which during non-windy conditions caused a smoky cloud of such emissions to cover the plaintiffs' lands and orchards. The plant was constructed at a cost in excess of $40 million, employed 550 persons who lived in the area, had a gross annual payroll of $3.5 million, and produced aluminium for industrial and national defence purposes. The Court ordered the defendant to install available hoods and electrostatic precipitators within one year to reduce the fluoride emissions to 'inconsequential' amounts, or else be enjoined from continuing operations, although it might cost over $2 million to install such devices:

> While the cost of the installations of these additional controls will be a substantial sum, the fact remains that effective controls must be exercised over the escape of these noxious fumes. Such expenditures would not be so great as to substantially deprive defendant of the use of its property. While we are not dealing with the public as such, we must recognise that air pollution is one of the great problems now facing the American public. If necessary, the cost of installing adequate controls must be passed on to the ultimate consumer. The heavy cost of corrective devices is no reason why plaintiffs should stand by and suffer substantial damage.[130]

The *Renken* Court stated that the defendant could avoid the injunction only if it

> show[ed] that the use of its property, which caused the injury, was unavoidable or that it could not be prevented except by the expenditure of such vast sums of money as would substantially deprive it of the use of its property. This seems to be the general rule.[131]

Finally, as the *Boomer* Court held, the denial of an injunction is conditioned on the plaintiff's being fully compensated for the reduced value of its land. Since an injunction will (or should) not be granted if continuation of the nuisance would result in the plaintiff's suffering any significant

---

[128] *Boomer* 257 NE 2d 870 (NY 1970) 873 (Bergan J for Fuld CJ, Bergan, Burke and Scileppi JJ).

[129] *Renken v Harvey Aluminum Co* 226 F Supp 169 (D Or 1963) (*Renken*).

[130] ibid, at 172 (Kilkenny J).

[131] ibid, at 174 (citation omitted) (Kilkenny J). See also Keeton et al, above n 18, at 630–31 (noting the likelihood of an injunction if 'there was a feasible way, economically and scientifically, to avoid a substantial amount of the harm without material impairment to the benefits').

adverse health effects, such compensation should ensure that the plaintiff is no worse off physically or economically. To make sure that this occurred in *Boomer* itself, the Court remanded with instructions to the trial Court to reconsider its prior determination of the reduced values of the plaintiffs' properties.[132]

Courts in the British Commonwealth also may refuse to enjoin a continuing or imminent private nuisance, but this apparently occurs less often than in the United States, with Canadian courts being more willing than English courts to do so.[133] Courts and academics frequently cite the criteria stated in *Shelfer v City of London Electric Lighting Co*,[134] according to which an injunction to prevent an imminent or continuing nuisance will be granted unless the injury to the plaintiff's legal rights is small, capable of being estimated in money, and can be adequately compensated by a small money payment, and it would be oppressive to the defendant to grant an injunction.[135] Note that the last factor comes into play only if all of the other factors are satisfied. An apparently rare exception[136] occurred in *Miller v Jackson*,[137] in which Lord Denning MR—a dedicated utilitarian who (alone on this point) would have refused to hold the defendant cricket club liable even for damages—and Cumming-Bruce LJ relied upon the social value to the community of the long-standing cricket club as well as the fact that the plaintiffs had come to the nuisance to refuse an injunction, despite a fairly serious diminution of the plaintiffs' use and enjoyment of their property, including a significant risk of personal injury from the cricket balls frequently landing on and damaging their property.[138]

Although the *Shelfer* criteria do not mention public benefit, the effects on the general public of granting an injunction can be and are taken into account in appropriate cases by British Commonwealth courts, more so in some countries than others, and more often when fashioning injunctive

---

[132] *Boomer* 257 NE 2d 870 (NY 1970) 873–75 (Bergan J for Fuld CJ, Bergan, Burke and Scileppi JJ). Since property valuations usually are based on objective market value, at times there may be a substantial undervaluation of the plaintiff's interest, especially for properties with significant non-pecuniary value, such as a long-occupied home or family farm. There was one such property in the *Boomer* case, and the trial Court on remand, noting the Court of Appeals' emphasis on providing 'full compensation', took into account more subjective standards: a 'special' market value rule based on inflated prices paid by the defendant for other properties in the neighbourhood, and a 'contract price' theory reflecting the amount that a private corporation would have to pay where it needs such a servitude to continue in operation as against a seller who is unwilling to sell his or her land. See *Kinley v Atlantic Cement Co* 349 NYS 2d 199 (NY Sup Ct App Div 1973) 202 (Herlihy P).

[133] Solomon et al, above n 13, at 822–23.

[134] *Shelfer v City of London Electric Lighting Co* [1895] 1 Ch 287 (CA) (*Shelfer*).

[135] *The Law of Torts in NZ*, above n 13, at 570; Klar, above n 13, at 743; Solomon et al, above n 13, at 821–23.

[136] *The Law of Torts in NZ*, above n 13, at 570.

[137] *Miller v Jackson* [1977] QB 966 (CA).

[138] Solomon et al, above n 13, at 823–27.

remedies rather than as a basis for refusing an injunction.[139] As is indicated by the *Shelfer* criteria, an injunction is likely to be granted, despite a significant public benefit from the defendant's activity, if there would be significant uncompensated harm to the plaintiffs, or if it is possible to reduce the impact on the plaintiffs' use and enjoyment of their land without significantly impairing the public benefit.[140]

The criteria for refusing to enjoin a private nuisance are inconsistent in many respects with the principles of utilitarianism and economic efficiency. Most notably, for the defendant to avoid an injunction despite a significant adverse impact on the plaintiffs' use and enjoyment of their land, the criteria require that the continuation of the nuisance be necessary for the realisation of some important public benefit, understood in the sense that it enhances the equal freedom of the members of the community, rather than some merely private benefit to the defendant or third parties. The utilitarians and efficiency theorists have no such conception of public benefit, or indeed of any distinction between public and private. For them, the public good is simply the sum of all individuals' utility or wealth, and all that matters is the sum, not how it is distributed among the members of the community. The sole test of the 'public good' is whether, in the aggregate, the nuisance increases the defendant's (and other benefited persons') private utility or wealth more than it decreases the plaintiff's (and other adversely affected persons') private utility or wealth.

The efficiency theorists state that the decision whether or not to grant an injunction should turn on whether or not the situation is one involving low or high transaction costs. If transactions costs are low, the injunction should be granted in order to force the defendant to bargain with those who are being or will be affected by the nuisance, which will better ensure that the affected parties' actual subjective valuations are taken into account and that, as a result, there will be an efficient outcome. However, if transactions costs are high, courts should not employ an injunction to force the defendant into the market, since the transaction costs may prevent an efficient result from being reached. Instead, the court should either make its own determination of the efficient outcome and impose liability for damages only if continuation of the defendant's activity would be inefficient (if not, it would be deemed reasonable and not to be a nuisance, contrary to the law as discussed in part III above) or hold the defendant strictly liable for the adverse impacts on the plaintiffs (whether or not those impacts would be deemed significant under the 'live and let live' rule, again contrary to the law as discussed in part III above) and

---

[139] *The Law of Torts in NZ*, above n 13, at 570–72; Solomon et al, above n 13, at 822–23; Klar, above n 13, at 743–44; *The Law of Tort*, above n 13, at paras 22-94–22-95.

[140] See, eg, *340909 Ontario Ltd v Huron Steel Products (Windsor) Ltd* (1990) 73 OR 2d 641 (Ontario High Court of Justice), discussed in Solomon et al, above n 13, at 796–800.

have the defendant decide whether it would be worthwhile to continue his or her activity.[141]

Transaction costs are assumed to vary depending on the number of adversely affected parties. If there are many, transaction costs are likely to be high, not only due to the sheer number of parties but also due to the increased risk of strategic bargaining as each adversely affected party tries to obtain as much as he or she can of the defendant's expected gain. If there are only a few adversely affected parties, transaction costs may be low enough to enable bargaining to an efficient result. However, even if there are only a few adversely affected parties, or even only one, transaction costs often will still be high due to strategic bargaining, since in the private nuisance context each adversely affected party is in a 'bilateral monopoly' situation with respect to the defendant, who is not able to avoid having to make a deal with the adversely affected party by instead making a deal with someone else (as would be the case with, eg, a supplier of parts for a machine).[142] It thus seems that under a utilitarian or economic efficiency approach, injunctions should rarely, if ever, be granted, contrary to the actual practice.

In any event, the courts do not base decisions on granting an injunction on whether the situation involves low or high transaction costs. Injunctions are often granted in situations involving a high number of adversely affected parties[143] and refused in situations involving only a few adversely affected parties, as was the case in *Boomer*. Not only were there only a few adversely affected parties in *Boomer*, the bargaining range presumably was huge. To justify an investment of over $45 million, the defendant must have expected a very high flow of income, while the trial court's initial assessment of the aggregate reduced value of the plaintiffs' land was only $185,000. As the New York Court of Appeals noted, '[t]he parties could settle this private litigation at any time if defendant paid enough money and the imminent threat of closing the plant would build up the pressure on defendant'.[144]

The criteria actually employed by the courts in deciding whether to grant an injunction to prevent or halt a private nuisance are consistent with the principles of justice. As the judges in *Boomer* stated, refusing to grant an injunction and instead allowing the defendant to continue to maintain the nuisance in effect is to authorise a forced sale to the defendant, at a price set by the court, of an easement on the plaintiff's lands for the continued invasion of the intangible entities generated by the defend-

---

[141] See, eg, RA Posner, *Economic Analysis of Law*, 8th edn (Boston, Wolters Kluwer, 2011) 86–88.

[142] ibid, at 89.

[143] See, eg, *Morgan v High Penn Oil Co* 77 SE 2d 682 (NC 1953); *Estancias Dallas* 500 SW 2d 217 (Text Ct Civ App 1973).

[144] *Boomer* 257 NE 2d 870 (NY 1970) 873 (Bergan J for Fuld CJ, Bergan, Burke and Scileppi JJ).

ant's activity.[145] In the absence of a proper justification, such a forced sale would be a denial of the plaintiff's equal external freedom and thus a violation of interactive justice. The justification begins, consistent with the criteria employed by the courts, with the fact that the continuation of the defendant's activity is necessary to obtain an important public benefit that enhances the equal freedom of every member of the community. This fact brings into play the principle of distributive justice. All property is held subject to the requirements of distributive justice, and is subject to being redistributed to promote the equal external freedom of all in accordance with that principle.[146]

However, in the private nuisance context, as with takings in general, the distributive justice claim is not that the person whose property is being taken has more than his or her just share of the resources needed to pursue a meaningful life, or, even if this is the case, that he or she is the only person who has more than a just share. Rather, the distributive justice claim is that the person's property is needed to accomplish some distributive objective—either redistribution of goods to those who have too little, or increasing the total amount of goods in society so that everyone's distributive share can be increased. But this satisfies only the 'output' side of the distributive justice claim, not the 'input' side. Rather than the distributive justice objective being implemented, as in the case of proper taxation, by assessing all those who have too much (the input side) and distributing the proceeds to all those who have too little (the output side), or assessing all equally who are initially distributively equal and will benefit equally from the project, the person whose property is being taken would be singled out, with no justification, to shoulder involuntarily the costs involved in achieving the distributive objective.

To have a complete, properly implemented distributive justice claim, none of the costs of the redistribution, which is intended to benefit the entire community, should fall solely on the plaintiff, who simply happens to own the property that is needed to achieve the distributive objective, but instead they should be borne by the entire community. This is a principle of justice that is firmly embedded in the jurisprudence of the United States.[147] Thus, the criteria for allowing a taking, by not granting

[145] ibid, at 875.

[146] See J Finnis, *Natural Law and Natural Rights* (Oxford, Oxford University Press, 1980) 169–73; R Nozick, *Anarchy, State, and Utopia* (New York, Basic Books, 1974) 174–82.

[147] See, eg, *First English Evangelical Lutheran Church of Glendale v County of Los Angeles* 482 US 304 (1987) 318–19 (Rehnquist CJ for Rehnquist CJ, Brennan, White, Marshall, Powell and Scalia JJ): 'It is axiomatic that the Fifth Amendment's just compensation provision is "designed to bar Government from forcing some people alone to bear public burdens which, in all fairness and justice, should be borne by the public as a whole"' (quoting *Armstrong v United States* 364 US 40 (1960) 49). Dobbs, above n 7, at 1329 n 25 cites *Armory Park Neighborhood Association v Episcopal Community Services in Arizona* 712 P 2d 914 (Ariz 1985), in which the defendant's actions in serving free meals to indigents had significant adverse effects on the plaintiffs' use and enjoyment of their lands;

an injunction, include a requirement that there be no significant adverse health effect on the plaintiff (which mere payment of money cannot prevent or undo) and that the plaintiff receive full compensation for his or her economic losses. When there is a taking by the government, the required just compensation will be paid by the government and shifted, through taxation or other means, to the members of the community. When the taking occurs through the failure to grant an injunction in a private nuisance action, the required just compensation will be paid as damages by the defendant, whose earnings will be reduced, which will result in lesser tax revenues and perhaps jobs and other benefits being generated for the surrounding community.

The last point explains why, in takings cases, including private nuisance cases in which an injunction is not granted because doing so would eliminate or substantially reduce an important public benefit being generated by the activity, the plaintiff is limited to full compensation through a forced sale, rather than being allowed to seek as much as possible of the gain generated by the taking. While, to avoid an interactive justice violation, the plaintiff must receive full compensation for the taking of his or her property, to allow the plaintiff to take advantage of the bilateral monopoly situation to attempt to obtain more than full compensation would lower and perhaps eliminate the public benefit that is being pursued as a matter of distributive justice, by increasing the government's costs when the government is acquiring the property or by lowering the defendant's gain in a private nuisance action. When no distributive justice objective is being pursued, there is no reason or justification for intruding on an interactively just bargaining situation.

V. CONCLUSION

This analysis of the private nuisance action confirms, once more, what has been shown by my analyses of other major areas and doctrines of tort law. Tort law, which has been held up by efficiency theorists as the prime example of the supposed efficiency basis of the law, is instead based on and implements the principles of justice. More than any other action, the private nuisance action, with its use of injunctions as well as damages and its reliance on the principle of distributive justice as well as interactive justice, demonstrates the full scope of tort law as an elaboration and implementation of the principles of justice and right.

---

the Court stated that the law does not allow 'the costs of a charitable enterprise to be visited in their entirety upon the residents of a single neighborhood. The problems of dealing with the unemployed, the homeless and the mentally ill are also matters of community or governmental responsibility.'

18

Rights and Wrongs: An Introduction to the Wrongful Interference Actions

SARAH GREEN*

I. INTRODUCTION

T HE COMMON LAW actions for wrongful interference with assets[1] are the most maligned of torts.[2] There would appear to be two explanations for this. One is that they are generally looked at in isolation, and are therefore incompletely analysed.[3] The other is that, looked at from a traditional, loss-based approach to the law of torts, they appear to be, at best, eccentric and, at worst, incoherent. This latter point no doubt stems from the traditional perception of the common law as having a basic dichotomy in form, with its property sphere being regarded as a law of rights, and its tort sphere seen as a law of wrongs. There is, however, nothing intrinsic in the law of wrongs which precludes

---

* I am indebted to several participants at Obligations V for their input into this chapter. I would like to express particular thanks to Simon Douglas, Donal Nolan, Roderick Bagshaw, William Swadling, Jason Neyers, Ken Oliphant, Philip Morgan, James Lee and Duncan Sheehan. All errors and misjudgements remain my own.

[1] Whilst the usual term here is 'goods', the use of such traditional legal terms to refer to the subject matter which is protected by the wrongful interference actions risks stifling or prejudging an open-minded inquiry as to what forms of property, including intangible or quasi-intangible property, are equally appropriate subjects of this area of the law. The term 'assets', on the other hand, is broader, and so more easily encompasses all forms of personal property. For a more detailed discussion of the point, see S Green, 'The Subject Matter of Conversion' [2010] *Journal of Business Law* 218.

[2] See, eg, AKR Kiralfy, 'The Problem of a Law of Property in Goods' (1949) 12 *Modern Law Review* 424; T Weir, *A Casebook on Tort*, 10th edn (London, Sweet & Maxwell, 2004) 483–87; N Curwen, 'The Remedy in Conversion: Confusing Property and Obligation' (2006) 26 *Legal Studies* 570, 570.

[3] I have extensively examined this aspect elsewhere: S Green, 'Understanding the Wrongful Interference Actions' [2010] *Conveyancer and Property Lawyer* 15.

its analysis on the basis of rights, as many of the other chapters in this collection demonstrate.

The main objective of this chapter is to show how a proper understanding of the wrongful interference actions is best achieved through a rights-based, as opposed to a loss-based, approach to the law of torts. Seen from a rights-oriented perspective, these actions appear to be a lot more intuitively acceptable than they do when evaluated in terms of loss. What is more, with a rights-based analysis, it also becomes apparent how each action should be developed in order best to achieve its objectives. Nowhere is this more significant than in relation to negligent interference with property interests, since the true nature of the interests which are the concern of this action are revealed, with intriguing implications for the gist of this particular facet of negligence.

II. THE WRONGFUL INTERFERENCE ACTIONS OUTLINED

Most lawyers (for non-lawyers are rarely familiar with this area of the law) would identify the torts of conversion and/or trespass to goods as being the common law's means of protecting personal property. Whilst these actions do indeed provide a certain degree of such protection, they form only part of the whole. A brief perusal of the Torts (Interference with Goods) Act 1977 reveals that wrongful interference with 'goods' can take several forms: conversion, trespass to goods, negligence in so far as it results in damage to goods or to an interest in goods and 'any other tort so far as it results in damage to goods or to an interest in goods'.[4] A proper evaluation of the wrongful interference actions ought always therefore to take into account *all* of the available actions. Given the relative obscurity of two of these actions in particular,[5] this is not something which usually occurs, meaning that these property torts are often incompletely analysed, and consequently insufficiently understood.

A. Trespass and Conversion[6]

There is some overlap in the coverage of trespass and conversion, and, in order to outline the full range of protection offered by the wrongful interference actions, it is worth clarifying the respective spheres of each. The gist of trespass is direct and wrongful interference with possession,

---

[4] Torts (Interference with Goods) Act 1977, s 1.
[5] Reversionary injury and negligent interference are probably the least well-known.
[6] For a far more detailed account of what amounts to a conversion, see S Green and J Randall, *The Tort of Conversion* (Oxford, Hart Publishing, 2009) ch 3.

but it does not require, as conversion does, any element of appropriation. To use Andrew Tettenborn's example:

> [I]f D takes P's bottle of wine and drinks it, he commits both. But they remain distinct. If D merely moves the bottle from one shelf to another, he commits trespass but not conversion, since there is no appropriation.[7]

The main point at which the two actions diverge, however, is the point at which the defendant's interference crosses the line between acting in relation to another's assets as if they belonged to that other and acting in relation to another's assets as if they were one's own. *Fouldes v Willoughby*[8] is instructive here. In this case, the claimant was attempting to travel, with his horses, on the Birkenhead to Liverpool ferry. The defendant, the proprietor of the ferry, did not want to carry the claimant as a passenger and so, with the intention of encouraging the claimant to disembark, he removed the claimant's horses from the ferry and returned them to the shore. The claimant still refused to leave the ferry and continued on his journey to Liverpool, leaving the horses on the quayside.[9] The fact that the defendant ferryman removed the claimant's horses from his ferry *in order to induce the claimant also to leave* is a material consideration, in that it demonstrates that the defendant was at all times behaving towards the horses in a way which recognised that they were *someone else's* assets rather than behaving as if they were his own:

> It is a proposition familiar to all lawyers, that a simple asportation of a chattel, without any intention of making any further use of it, although it may be a sufficient foundation for an action of trespass, is not sufficient to establish a conversion.[10]

If in *Fouldes*, however, there had there been an accomplice of the defendant waiting at the shore, and had he removed the horses with the intention of having them taken off to the defendant's own stables, the same action would have sufficed to be a conversion of the assets, since there would then have been the requisite evidence of the defendant treating the goods as if they were his own. So, whilst a defendant does not need to *intend to* convert an asset in order to do so, intention is by no means always irrelevant to the ultimate classification of his behaviour. The intentions of the defendant may be relevant insofar as they affect the distinction between the defendant doing something to another's asset and his behaving towards an asset as if it were his own; in other words, they apply only to the *nature*

---

[7] AM Dugdale et al (eds), *Clerk and Lindsell on Torts*, 19th edn (London, Sweet & Maxwell, 2006) (*Clerk and Lindsell on Torts*) para 17-02.

[8] *Fouldes v Willoughby* (1841) 8 M&W 540, 151 ER 1153 (*Fouldes*).

[9] As it happens, what occurred thereafter would, had it been relevant to the case as presented to the court, have complicated matters somewhat, since the horses, abandoned on the turnpike, later turned up at the defendant's brother's inn.

[10] *Fouldes* (1841) 8 M&W 540, 544–45; 151 ER 1153, 1155 (Abinger CB).

of his action, and not the *consequences* of it.[11] It matters why the ferry owner in *Fouldes* removed the horses to the quay, not because of the effect this had on the claimant, but because it tells us what the defendant was doing. For this particular distinction, it is irrelevant whether the defendant's intention was to deal with assets belonging to someone else—that is, whether he knew that someone else had a superior possessory interest in the assets with which he was dealing. All that matters is that he intended to deal with those particular assets as if they were his own.

Despite the overlap between these two actions, therefore, they do in fact protect slightly different rights from different degrees of infringement. In essence, the distinction between the two actions is as follows. The necessary and sufficient elements of a conversion are:

1. A claimant who has the superior possessory right;
2. A deprivation of the claimant's full benefit of that right; and
3. An assumption by the defendant of that right, which includes the right to dispose of the asset in question:

> The very denial of goods to him that has a right to demand them, is an actual conversion, and not only evidence of it, as has been holden; for what is a conversion but an assuming to one's self the property and right of disposing of another's goods ...[12]

The necessary and sufficient elements of a trespass are:

1. A claimant who has the most immediate possessory right (ie, who is in actual possession);[13] and
2. An immediate and direct interference with that right falling short of a full deprivation of the claimant's benefit.

B. Reversionary Injury

Although not referred to explicitly by name in the Torts (Interference with Goods) Act 1977, a significant contribution to this sphere of protection is made by the action of reversionary injury (also known as reversionary damage to goods), a contribution rarely acknowledged on account of its being so little known. The tort of reversionary injury was developed to cover two instances which previously fell outside the common law's protection of personal property: the plight of the co-owner, whose assets have

---

[11] But see the diverging views of J Faust Jr, 'Distinction Between Conversion and Trespass to Chattels' (1958) 37 *Oregon Law Review* 256, 260 and WL Prosser, 'The Nature of Conversion' (1957) 42 *Cornell Law Quarterly* 168, 172. For an account of the same point in relation to trespass, see *Clerk and Lindsell on Torts*, above n 7, at para 17-124.

[12] *Baldwin v Cole* (1704) 6 Mod Rep 212, 212; 87 ER 964, 965 (Holt CJ).

[13] With a few specific exceptions: see *Clerk and Lindsell on Torts*, above n 7, at para 17-28.

been converted by another co-owner, and the problems formerly faced by the owner out of possession.[14] Whilst co-owners can now sue other co-owners in conversion generally,[15] reversionary injury is still a tort of considerable significance for the owner out of possession.

Trespass and conversion are concerned with the position of the person with the most immediate rights in an asset, whilst reversionary injury is an action for the reversioner (ie, the party whose property right in the asset is such that possession will revert to him or her when other possessory rights have expired) to recover for any interference with his or her property right. Although, therefore, the reversioner might be the party with the superior *proprietary* right in an asset, as long as somebody else is lawfully in possession of that asset, he or she is not the one whose right will immediately be affected as a result of a wrongful dispossession:

> The owner of a thing is not necessarily the person who at a given time has the whole power of use and disposal; very often there is no such person. We must look for the person having the residue of all such power when we have accounted for every detached and limited portion of it; and he will be the owner even if the immediate power of control and use is elsewhere.[16]

Tancred v Allgood[17] provides an illustration of how this reversionary action operates. The case concerned an action brought against a sheriff for seizing goods from the possession of an execution debtor, and selling them so that they could not be followed. The claimant had the reversionary right to those assets, which had been let to hire for a term, as yet unexpired, to the debtor from whom they had been seized. The reversioner could not succeed in her action because at that point there had been no infringement of her rights: since the defendant had sold the assets as sheriff under a *fieri facias* and not in market overt, he had not thereby passed title in them so as to affect the claimant's right.[18]

Reversionary injury is a little known action indeed.[19] This is unfortunate, since it has a significant role to play within the wrongful interference actions, by protecting those property rights which are not covered by the better known actions of trespass and conversion. Once it is properly understood, the action of reversionary injury provides an explanation for

---

[14] See ibid, at para 17-138.

[15] Torts (Wrongful Interference with Goods) Act 1977, s 10.

[16] F Pollock, *A First Book of Jurisprudence for Students of the Common Law* (London, Macmillan, 1896) 179.

[17] *Tancred v Allgood* (1859) 4 H&N 438, 157 ER 910.

[18] Although factually it seemed highly improbable that the assets would be recovered before the expiry of the term, legally, the claimant's title remained unimpaired and permanent injury to it had not necessarily arisen. See also *Mukibi v Bhavsar* [1967] EA 473 (Uganda Court of Appeal); *HSBC Rail (UK) Ltd v Network Rail Infrastructure Ltd* [2005] EWHC 403 (Comm), [2005] 2 Lloyd's Rep 343.

[19] See A Tettenborn, 'Reversionary Damage to Chattels' [1994] *Cambridge Law Journal* 326, 326.

what would otherwise be apparently incoherent aspects of those more commonly known torts. For instance, perhaps the most intuitively difficult situation to accept, in terms of the operation of conversion, is that of the term bailor who dispossesses his bailee before the expiration (or termination) of the agreed bailment term. Such a bailor, despite being what laymen and lawyers alike would regard as the 'owner' of the asset, would nonetheless be liable in conversion. This is a factual situation which, prima facie, appears to highlight a potential incoherence within the common law's protection of personal property rights, since it looks as if certain rights are overlooked in favour of those which might be regarded as being inferior. In actual fact, however, such a scenario is a useful and graphic illustration of the respective purposes of each action. Here, conversion allows the bailee to recover against the bailor because the latter interfered with the former's possessory rights, and such an interference generates an entitlement to damages in the law of torts.[20] The bailor, on the other hand, has had no right infringed at this point; his reversionary right is, on these facts, unaffected.[21]

To alter the facts slightly, whilst retaining the element of apparent conceptual difficulty, consider the term bailee who has been dispossessed, this time by a third party. The term bailee, but not his bailor, may sue the dispossessor in conversion.[22] This is because, once more, the term bailor in such a situation has as yet suffered no infringement of her right; only possession has so far been interfered with, and the term bailor had no current right to that anyway. Should the third party do something which affects the bailor's reversionary right, however, such as destroying the asset, permanently reducing its value or absconding with it, then the term bailor may sue. Her action, however, will not be for conversion, but for the injury to her reversion.

The biggest difficulty facing the action of reversionary injury appears to be its apparently esoteric nature and the fact that it so rarely features in evaluations of the common law's protection of personal property rights. This needs to be rectified: only when the crucial role of the reversionary injury action is recognised can the wrongful interference actions be understood as an effective and comprehensive means of protecting the full spectrum of property rights in assets. The necessary and sufficient elements of reversionary injury are:

1. A claimant who has the residual proprietary right; and
2. An interference with the claimant's full benefit of that right.

---

[20] See R Stevens, *Torts and Rights* (Oxford, Oxford University Press, 2007) 66.

[21] Of course, the bailor does not have the right to possession of his asset, but he did not 'lose' this; he voluntarily parted with it when he made the bailment agreement. See also *Brierly v Kendall* (1852) 17 QB 937, 117 ER 1540 for the application of the principle to a mortgagor in possession whose period of credit has not yet expired.

[22] *Gordon v Harper* (1796) 7 TR 9, 101 ER 828.

C. Negligent Interference with Property Rights

Since conversion, trespass and reversionary injury are all predicated on strict liability, one might question why there is any need for negligence within the wrongful interference actions. It might be supposed that a specific negligence action is redundant. Not so. Whilst it is true that the nominate wrongful interference actions employ a strict liability standard, conversion, for instance, requires a 'deliberate' act on the part of the defendant.[23] As Peter Cane has pointed out, however, there is an important distinction to be made here between conduct which is voluntary and that which is deliberate. It is in actual fact *voluntary* conduct which is a requirement of the action of conversion. Such conduct need not be deliberate in the sense that the actor was aware of what its consequences would be, but only in the sense that the actor deliberately performed the act which resulted in the interference with the claimant's assets: 'The fundamental point is that conversion consists of conduct inconsistent with the owner's rights regardless of the intention with which it is done.'[24] The same goes for trespass.[25] Negligence, on the other hand, covers those situations in which there has been conduct on the part of the defendant which cannot be classed as voluntary, and yet which nonetheless interfered with the claimant's rights over his or her assets. It is clear, therefore, why the list of wrongful interference actions, outlined as it was by Parliament in the Torts (Interference with Goods) Act 1977, explicitly includes a separate negligence action.

Crucially, however, the negligence-based element of the wrongful interference actions is more than merely a straightforward application of the general principles of negligence to interests in personal assets. In order to succeed under this head, it is the case that a claimant would need to establish the usual elements of a negligence action: a breach of a duty of care, the existence of actionable damage which is of a type which should have been reasonably foreseeable by the defendant, and a causal link between that breach and the actionable damage suffered. The nature of the damage with which this particular action is concerned is however limited to 'damage to goods *or to an interest in goods*'.[26] Negligent damage to goods is so familiar an action that it requires little attention here. On the other hand, negligent damage to 'an interest in goods' (or, to use the terminology of this chapter, negligent interference with property rights)

---

[23] See *Kuwait Airways Corp v Iraqi Airways Co (Nos 4 and 5)* [2002] UKHL 19, [2002] 2 AC 886 [39] (Lord Nicholls).

[24] P Cane, 'Causing Conversion' (2002) 118 *Law Quarterly Review* 544, 544.

[25] See *Clerk and Lindsell on Torts*, above n 7, at para 17-124. As for reversionary injury, this would seem to encompass the mental states dealt with by all of the possessory wrongful interference actions; that is, both voluntary and negligent actions: at para 17-139.

[26] See Torts (Interference with Goods) Act 1977, s 1 (emphasis added).

needs further analysis, since it does not always look like, or operate in the same way as, standard negligence actions.

A recent High Court decision, *D Pride & Partners v Institute for Animal Health*,[27] illustrates perfectly the function which *ought to be* performed by the action of negligent interference with property rights.[28] Unfortunately for the claimants concerned, it was not pleaded in this case, with the result that they were unable to recover for the interference with their property rights which they suffered as a result of the defendants' negligence. Had they presented their case to the Court as one of negligent interference with property rights (which would have been appropriate), the Court should have granted recovery for the reasons outlined below. The claimants were livestock farmers who were claiming for the losses they had suffered as a result of an outbreak of foot and mouth disease, which they attributed to the negligence of the defendants in allowing the virus to escape from their research facility.[29] The claim was based on the three torts of negligence, private nuisance and the rule in *Rylands v Fletcher*, and Tugendhat J was asked to consider applications by the defendants for the claims to be struck out, either on the grounds that the claims disclosed no good cause of action[30] or on the grounds that the claimants had no real prospect of establishing any liability of the kind for which they claimed.[31]

The interference with the claimants' property rights was constituted by their inability, consequent upon movement restrictions imposed as a result of the outbreak, freely to move and deal with their livestock in a way which was necessary for them to exploit its commercial potential.[32] In losing the capability to move their animals around between farms, and from farms to abattoirs and to locations for export, the claimants had, therefore, suffered an interference with their property rights, because it is, after all, a rudimentary feature of property rights that they enable the holder to *use* the subject matter of those rights.[33] Further, as a result of the movement restrictions imposed pursuant to the Foot and Mouth

---

[27] *D Pride & Partners v Institute for Animal Health* [2009] EWHC 685 (QB), [2009] NPC 56 (*D Pride*).

[28] This is a mouthful, but I cannot think of a more concise term for the action which is both comprehensive and accurate.

[29] There were three defendants to this action: DEFRA; a publicly funded research company; and a company which formulates and distributes foot and mouth disease vaccine. The two latter defendants were licensed by the former to carry out research and production at the Pirbright facility, to which these claims relate. For the statement as to their duty of care, see *D Pride* [2009] EWHC 685 (QB), [2009] NPC 56 [36] (Tugendhat J).

[30] Under CPR pt 3.4(2)(a).

[31] Under CPR pt 24.2.

[32] See H de Soto, *The Mystery of Capital* (London, Black Swan, 2000) *passim*, and especially at 164.

[33] See B McFarlane, *The Structure of Property Law* (Oxford, Hart Publishing, 2008) *passim*, but especially at 4, 22, 145.

Disease (England) Order 2006,[34] the livestock belonging to the claimants suffered either from loss of condition or from welfare problems (or both) because it could not be moved, sold or slaughtered at the optimum time, and because such conditions led, inter alia, to overstocking, stress and overgrazing.[35] Nevertheless, the claims were struck out on the grounds that the claimants had no real prospect of succeeding at trial. The principal reason given for this was that the loss for which they were claiming was classified by Tugendhat J as being relational pure economic loss, not consequent upon any direct harm done to the claimants' assets by the acts of the defendants.[36] As such, it fell under the 'exclusionary rule'[37] as applied to negligence, nuisance and *Rylands v Fletcher*, with the result that it was irrecoverable.

There are two problems with this result, the first of which relates to the judgment of the case as it was pleaded, and the second to its not having been pleaded as a negligent interference action. The first difficulty is that not all of the claimants' loss was, with respect, correctly classified as pure economic loss.[38] This is not a point of direct relevance to the current discussion, although I have discussed it more extensively elsewhere.[39] The second difficulty, which is entirely pertinent to this chapter, is that the claimants' case should have been presented as one of negligent interference with property rights, thereby clearly identifying the nature of the right with which the defendants had interfered. As a result of the defendants' negligence in allowing the foot and mouth disease virus to escape, two of the claimants' property rights were infringed. The content of these two rights, and the distinction between them, will be discussed below. In brief, the first right is the one with which standard negligence actions are familiar,[40] and it was infringed when the claimant's assets suffered physical damage. The second, however, the right which is the specific concern of the wrongful interference actions,[41] was infringed when the claimants were unable to use the subject matter of their property rights as they saw fit. It is the infringement of this latter property right which, without more, constitutes the claimants' damage in an action for negligent

---

[34] SI 2006/182.

[35] Some of the livestock was actually lost through mandatory culling, and the defendants accepted that this was loss of a 'more orthodox kind'. See *D Pride* [2009] EWHC 685 (QB), [2009] NPC 56 [54] (Tugendhat J).

[36] ibid, at [85]–[109].

[37] See *Clerk and Lindsell on Torts*, above n 7, at para 8-115.

[38] A detailed listing of the damage claimed is set out in *D Pride* [2009] EWHC 685 (QB), [2009] NPC 56 [31], [34], [36], [38] (Tugendhat J). Some of this, such as the lost future milk production, could indeed be properly classified as pure economic loss under a standard negligence claim. A substantial element of the damage, however, was the material effects on the livestock, and this does not fall to be viewed correctly as anything other than property damage.

[39] See Green, 'Understanding the Wrongful Interference Actions', above n 3.

[40] Characterised below as a 'derivative right': see text accompanying n 54 below.

[41] Characterised below as an 'original right': see text accompanying n 54 below.

interference with property rights and, as such, should be recoverable.[42] The necessary and sufficient elements of an action for negligent interference with assets are:

1. The standard negligence criteria must be fulfilled in order to establish that there has been an actionable case of negligence;[43] and
2. The defendant's negligence must have interfered with the claimant's current property right in an existing asset. This action covers the whole spectrum of property rights, from the least possessory right to the strongest proprietary right.[44] Crucially, however, in order to sue, a claimant must have had that right at the time of the defendant's negligent act, and that right must have been infringed by the defendant's negligence.[45]

If these criteria have been met, recovery should be allowed to reflect the value of the claimant's infringed property right, regardless of whether this is something for which a conventional negligence claim would allow recovery. The gist of negligent interference with assets is not that which the claimant has lost but that to which he or she is entitled, and what the claimant is entitled to is the right to exercise his or her property rights over the assets in which they vest.

These, then, are the most significant wrongful interference actions. It is clear that there is far more to the common law's protection of personal property rights than just that offered by trespass and conversion. An overview of this nature is a prerequisite of understanding why these actions are, in combination, both comprehensive and effective means of protecting rights over personal property. More is needed, however, to explain why the common law's methods of dealing with these rights are both appropriate and ideally suited to their objective. Such analysis is also necessary to explain why one of these actions in particular, negligent interference with property rights, is an action which needs to be considered as a discrete species of negligence, with special attention directed to the nature of the rights protected by it, in order that its objectives may properly be served.

---

[42] See Stevens, above n 20, at 59–62.

[43] See text accompanying n 26 above.

[44] In this, it is the wrongful interference action which 'catches' negligent interferences with all of the interests protected by the other actions.

[45] *Leigh & Sillivan Ltd v Aliakmon Shipping Co Ltd (The Aliakmon)* [1986] AC 785 (HL); AM Tettenborn, 'The Carrier and the Non-Owning Consignee—An Inconsequential Immunity' [1987] *Journal of Business Law* 12; DG Powles, 'Title to Sue, Problems of Consignees and Others' [1987] *Journal of Business Law* 313.

III. WHY RIGHTS?

For some torts, and negligence is an obvious example, a loss of some form is *constitutive* of the wrong itself, as evidenced by the nature of the right which defines it. In other words, as both Robert Stevens and Allan Beever make clear, people do not have a right that others not behave negligently, but they do have a right *not be injured by* someone so behaving.[46] Perhaps since negligence is often regarded as the paradigm tort, this requirement of *injuria* seems to have pervaded the law of torts as a whole. One result of this has been confusion and a certain degree of incoherence, as identified principally by Stevens.[47] This focus on the factual sequels of wrongs, as opposed to their legal prequels, has particularly problematic implications for those actions dealing with wrongful interference with assets, and is responsible for those actions being generally regarded as mysterious and esoteric. On the other hand, if looked at from the point of view of the legal prequel of wrongs—the right which is constitutive of the wrong—each wrongful interference action can be seen for the effective and appropriate mechanism that it is.

A rights-based analysis achieves this by making it very clear both when the sphere of protection offered by one wrongful interference action ends and another begins, and by explaining why it is important to offer differential protection for different rights. Attempting to reach the same level of understanding by applying a loss-based model is incredibly difficult. This is because the question of what is and is not a right is a qualitative one, whereas the question of what is and is not a loss is a quantitative one. Looked at in the context of loss, for instance, it is hard to explain why an owner out of possession might not be able to sue a wrongful dispossessor in conversion, since, although someone else has lost possession, the owner has still arguably lost something in that a transfer of his asset has occurred without his knowledge and/or consent. Where various individuals have concurrent rights in an asset which has been interfered with, it is always possible to identify some sort of 'loss' suffered by each right-holder, albeit that the extent of such injury may differ considerably depending upon the facts of each case. On a rights-based model, however, qualitative considerations prevail and the answers sought are of a binary nature: either an individual has had a right infringed, or he has not. So, in the example given above, although the owner out of possession might be argued to have suffered some degree of loss by virtue of the dispossession, he will not be able to recover unless and until he has established both that he has an existing right, and that it has been infringed. If he has

[46] See also A Beever, 'A Rights-Based Approach to the Recovery of Economic Loss in Negligence' (2004) 4 *Oxford University Commonwealth Law Journal* 25, 26; D Nolan and A Robertson, 'Rights and Private Law' ch 1 of this book, text accompanying nn 90–97.

[47] Stevens, above n 20, *passim*, but particularly chs 3–4.

the superior possessory right, this will have been infringed and he will be protected by conversion. If, on the other hand, he has the reversionary interest, he might be protected by the action of reversionary injury, but only if his reversion has actually been affected by the dispossession. Loss is no more than a red herring within this, an area of law which is, through necessity, highly discriminating between substantively different property rights.

Such discrimination is crucial since, within the complex matrix of the common law's personal property rules, there needs to be something to protect possession, *independent* of any means of protecting superior proprietary rights. Otherwise, the concept of a possessory right, as distinct from any superior proprietary rights, would be redundant, with profound implications for commercial and economic efficacy. Bailment, for instance, is wholly dependent upon there being a legally enforced distinction between full ownership and lesser (but nonetheless practically valuable) proprietary rights. As Norman Palmer points out:

> The essence of bailment is possession. ... The doctrine is confined to personal property and denotes a separation of the actual possession of goods from some ultimate or reversionary possessory right. ... [T]he central theme of every standard bailment is the carving out, by the bailor, of a lesser interest than his own. That interest is possession, and without possession there can be no relationship of bailor and bailee. Conversely, a transfer that simultaneously confers both possession and ownership upon the grantee cannot create a bailment; and an owner of goods cannot constitute himself their bailee at common law.[48]

In fact, the commercial world relies upon this means of allowing an 'owner' to divide up his property interests amongst other parties, in order to maximise the use and value of his assets.[49] Were the wrongful interference actions not to discriminate so as to protect lesser, possessory rights, possessors would always be liable to dispossession by those with superior proprietary title, despite the fact that this might in turn contravene any prior agreement made between the two parties concerned.[50] Were this to be the case, it would effectively mean that there would be no economic, social or legal value in possession as a discrete right. This is, of course, far from the truth, as Ugo Mattei has made clear:

> [T]he protection of possession against ownership in the domain of movable property is one of the most important institutional evolutions that have guaranteed the development of efficient markets in Western societies. ... The

---

[48] NE Palmer, *Palmer on Bailment*, 3rd edn (London, Sweet & Maxwell, 2009) 2.

[49] See J Gordley, *Foundations of Private Law: Property, Tort and Unjust Enrichment* (Oxford, Oxford University Press, 2008) 61–65.

[50] This is, therefore, in respectful disagreement with Tony Weir's assertion that 'trespass protects possession and conversion protects ownership': T Weir, *An Introduction to Tort Law*, 2nd edn (Oxford, Oxford University Press, 2006) 165.

most important transactions relating to movables lie in their market transfer. Efficient legal institutions therefore are those which facilitate the transfer of movables. Such transfer is motivated by the protection of possession over title and ownership.[51]

Possession, in its peculiar common law incarnation,[52] entails rights of its own. A rights-based analysis of the wrongful interference actions demonstrates both why such rights are worthy of protection and how best this can be achieved.

IV. PROPERTY/TORT TENSION

The wrongful interference actions are sometimes regarded as dysfunctional hybrids of property and tort.[53] This criticism has two dimensions, one conceptual and one practical. The first is apparent and the second real. The conceptual difficulty stems from the assumption that property and tort concerns are necessarily distinct, and should therefore be compartmentalised. The practical difficulty is the attempted maintenance of this distinction when applied to actual factual situations.

The conceptual difficulty is based on an interpretation of the law of torts which does not allow for the protection of what I shall call original property rights. These are the rights in personal property which are protected only by the wrongful interference actions, and so are unfamiliar to the wider law of wrongs. They are the fundamental rights which both introduce and define the relationship between people and assets, whose existence (and consequently infringement) is not tangibly discernible. The content of such rights is independent of the physical state of the phenomena to which they apply, since their concern is with relationships only, and not with the assets themselves. These rights exist all the way along the spectrum of property interests, from bare possession rights through to residual property rights.

On the other hand, there is no such perceived difficulty with the law of wrongs protecting the *subject matter* of those original property rights. It is, for instance, textbook tort law which tells us that claims for property damage are perfectly acceptable in negligence. Of course, the problem here is partly linguistic, a common cause of confusion. The use of the term 'property' to refer to the tangible subject matter of property rights means that the right *to* that subject matter (the original property right), which is infringed when there is an interference with the intangible entitlement, is easily confused with the right *in* that subject matter (the derivative

---

[51] U Mattei, *Basic Principles of Property Law: A Comparative Legal and Economic Introduction* (Westport CT, Greenwood Press, 2000) 88.
[52] See Green and Randall, above n 6, at ch 3.
[53] See the articles and book cited in above n 2.

right), which is infringed when tangible damage occurs to the physical asset. This latter is a derivative right because it is parasitic upon the original right, but nevertheless distinct from it. An individual must have the original right before he or she can have the derivative right. The first right identifies him or her as the individual with the requisite relationship to the asset in question,[54] and the second right invests in him or her *consequent* rights with regard to the subject matter of the original right. The problem is that the original property right is as alien to the law of torts as it is native to the law of property. The law relating to wrongs is more comfortable with having something tangible to remedy, than it is with protecting the very existence of relationships, since the latter is more usually the province of the laws of contract and property.

This discomfort manifests itself in the law of torts' conventional hostility to the recovery of what is referred to as 'pure economic loss'. (Here, we encounter another linguistic aberration, since 'economic' in its true sense actually covers all of the losses with which the law of tort is concerned.[55]) That, however, is an argument for another day. Suffice it to say for present purposes that losses which are intangible, and which can only be measured in pecuniary terms, have not generally been recognised as appropriate concerns of the law of torts. Traditionally, the reasons given for the law of torts' reluctance to grant recovery for 'pure economic loss' are well-known: that such issues are the proper province of the law of contract, and that to allow such claims would be to expose the defendant to potentially indeterminate liability.[56] Stevens has provided us with another explanation: that there is no exclusionary rule as such, but that we do not have a right not to suffer economic loss, and so the infliction of it infringes nothing which the law of torts recognises as worthy of its protection.[57]

None of these arguments, however, is relevant to the wrongful interference actions since, unlike other torts, these actions protect original property rights, the infringement of which will sometimes (if not often) manifest itself as intangible 'loss'. The law of contract is not sufficiently comprehensive in this context to deal with such infringements since there is no necessary contractual basis for such rights. Further, and crucially, there is no problem of indeterminate liability because liability will be limited to those who have an original property right in the asset or assets concerned. Finally, according to Stevens' model, the existence of this original property right means that there is no obstacle to recovering for

---

[54] See, eg, *The Aliakmon* [1986] AC 785 (HL).

[55] A more accurate term would be 'pecuniary' or 'monetary'.

[56] See *The Aliakmon* [1986] AC 785 (HL) 816–17 (Lord Brandon). But see J Stapleton, 'Duty of Care and Economic Loss: A Wider Agenda' (1991) 107 *Law Quarterly Review* 249, 253 for reservations about these arguments.

[57] See Stevens, above n 20, at 21.

infringements of it in the law of torts. If, therefore, the wrongful interference actions are considered through the lens of a rights-based, as opposed to a loss-based, approach, any potential conceptual difficulty with their operation is eliminated. The former model, as espoused by Stevens, can be outlined concisely thus:

> Before a defendant can be characterised as a tortfeasor the anterior question of whether the claimant had a right against him must be answered. The law of torts is concerned with the secondary obligations generated by the infringement of primary rights.[58]

Where the wrongful interference actions are concerned, it is the very infringement of this original property right[59] which amounts to the claimant's cause. There is no need for a claimant to have suffered any loss *consequent upon* his or her right infringement in order to have a successful action in tort, since the 'infringement of rights, not the infliction of loss, is the gist of the law of torts.'[60] On a rights-based interpretation of the law of torts, therefore, there is nothing problematic or heretical about torts addressing original property rights, and dealing with infringements of intangible interests. This already occurs to some extent, but is often masked by the form of the remedy:

> The distinction between damages which are awarded as a substitute for the right and those awarded to compensate for consequential loss can be obscured because in most cases the value attached to the right is precisely the same as the loss suffered, usually financial, by the claimant. If you smash someone else's car the value of the right infringed is the economic cost of fixing it. ... However, it is a mistake to think that where no loss is suffered no claim for damages is available.[61]

What this does mean is that, when negligence claims are made in relation to the infringement of original property rights, claimants will be able to recover for what traditionalists might regard as 'pure economic loss'. By this misleading term is meant, of course, that all a claimant has suffered

---

[58] ibid, at 2.

[59] Both Stevens and Beever distinguish between primary and secondary rights, the former being the anterior right the infringement of which triggers legal action, and the latter the consequent right of the claimant to be compensated for that wrong: Stevens, above n 20, at 287; Beever, above n 46, at 212. It is worth making clear at this point that the original/derivative dichotomy is not interchangeable or commensurable with the primary/secondary dichotomy. The latter differentiates rights from those consequent rights which they necessarily *entail*. The relationship between original and derivative rights, however, is not an automatic one. Although derivative property rights cannot exist without original property rights, the existence of an original property right does not *entail* a derivative right, and original property rights can and do exist without derivative rights as necessary consequences of them. Remove the secondary right from its primary right, on the other hand, and the latter loses its meaning and substance. Both original and derivative rights are, under Stevens' model, primary rights.

[60] Stevens, above n 20, at 2.

[61] ibid, at 61.

as a result of the defendant's negligence is a deterioration in his or her financial position. Where an original property right has been infringed, however, a claimant's injury is not in fact merely financial. By means of a practical illustration of this point, take the oft-cited example of the car manufacturer whose negligence leads to a vehicle breakdown, causing the Dartford Tunnel to be out of operation for a period of time. The financial losses resulting from such an event are generally held to be irrecoverable in negligence because they are indeterminate.[62] Another way of looking at the failure to recover for many of the consequences of such an event is to recognise that no one has a general right not to be delayed or inconvenienced by someone else's careless conduct.[63] Whilst this is indisputable, neither point precludes recovery by any motorists whose particular circumstances mean that they have had a recognised legal right infringed, and in relation to whom there will be no issue of indeterminacy.

Essentially, anyone whose intangible property right has been sufficiently infringed[64] as a result of the delay should be able to claim against the negligent manufacturer. This is because the consequence of having such a property right in something is that 'the rest of the world ... is under a prima facie duty ... not to interfere with [the] use of that thing'.[65] Some degree of interference with others' property is, of course, inevitable in any dynamic society or environment. Every road user, for example, limits the freedom of every other road user to some degree, albeit that those limits will often, in their own right, be infinitesimal, and will only become apparent when aggregated with others (as any rush hour commuter will tell you). Not being able to drive one's car at a satisfying (legal) speed might be regarded by many as an interference with one's property rights in that car. Undoubtedly it is. But it is arguably no more an interference with a right than are the inevitable minor instances of physical contact which occur in, for instance, popular retail sales or unpopular, but necessary, London Underground stations.[66] Just as the reciprocal nature of the risks of such minor 'injury' from shopping and commuting preclude any damage resulting from them being recoverable in tort, so does the reciprocal nature of the risks inherent in exercising one's property rights in a world in which everyone else is trying to do the same.

This of course begs the question of where the line should be drawn between trivial interferences, which are both inevitable in, and necessary for, social interaction and progression, and those interferences which go so far as to erode the function of the law's protection of property inter-

---

[62] See Stapleton, above n 56, at 254.

[63] Imagine the sheer number of claims that would accumulate at least twice daily in most major cities were this to be otherwise.

[64] For an explanation of this, see text accompanying n 72 below.

[65] McFarlane, above n 33, at 22.

[66] See *Re F (Mental Patient: Sterilization)* [1990] 2 AC 1 (HL) 72 (Lord Goff).

ests. In *de minimis non curat lex*, we have a rule but no readily accessible frame of reference for its application. For this, we must look to legal analogy. Fortunately, the law of torts itself can provide this. Whilst the law of wrongs is the source from which springs the duty not to interfere with another's rights, those rights originate from within the law of property.[67] These dual sources of rights and duties, however, have long co-existed comfortably and effectively where the property rights in question relate to real, as opposed to personal, property. As a result, recovery for interference with intangible real property rights has long been accepted in private nuisance.

Nuisance is a tort whose existence depends upon the unreasonableness of the defendant's interference with the property of which the claimant has exclusive possession. Arguably, this context-dependent standard is a natural characteristic of property torts: since there are an inordinate number of different types of property and of different uses of that property, it is impossible to say in advance what will amount to actionable interference on any given set of facts.[68] In many ways, nuisance is to real property what the wrongful interference actions are to personal property. It is, therefore, hard to identify any compelling reason for the latter to be regarded as any more complex than the former, and yet, in relation to nuisance, there appear to be fewer judicial and academic statements of unease than there are in relation to wrongful interference, despite the striking (and unsurprising) parallels between the two actions.

The establishment of an actionable private nuisance depends on the court's finding that the defendant's actions amounted to an unreasonable interference with the claimant's property rights. This is, in any given situation, a question of fact to be determined by the court. As Lord Cooke of Thorndon explained in *Delaware Mansions Ltd v Westminster City Council*:

> I think that the answer to the issue falls to be found by applying the concepts of reasonableness between neighbours (real or figurative) and reasonable foreseeability which underlie much modern tort law and, more particularly,

---

[67] See AP Simester and GR Sullivan, *Criminal Law: Theory and Doctrine*, 3rd edn (Oxford, Hart Publishing, 2007) 474 for an analogous discussion in relation to the law of theft: 'Remove dependence on the law of property, and property offences have no rationale'. That is not to say, however, that the content of such rights is wholly determined by the law of property. See Nolan and Robertson, above n 46, text accompanying n 175 and nn 179–183, and, generally, D Nolan, '"A Tort Against Land": Private Nuisance as a Property Tort' ch 16 of this book, part IX.

[68] Whilst, given the diverse nature of the subject matter of property rights, it is not possible to outline in advance exactly what factual circumstances will amount to an interference for the purposes of any of the property torts, it is not the case that the unreasonableness standard is common to all of these actions. Where direct interferences are concerned, and the trespass torts engaged, for example, a claimant does not have to establish that the interference in question is an unreasonable one in order to succeed. See Nolan, above n 67.

the law of nuisance. The great cases in nuisance decided in our time have these concepts at their heart.[69]

I have made the case for making constructive use of the parallels between unreasonable interference with real property rights and unreasonable interference with personal property rights, in relation to conversion, elsewhere.[70] It is no less valuable here. Despite the obvious physical differences between real and personal property, the nature of the intangible legal interests in them (ie, the original property rights) is identical. There is much to be said, therefore, for approaching their protection in a similar way. In relation to both real and personal property, there can be no static or predetermined level of interference for which recovery can be deemed appropriate. This is because it would be both impossible and undesirable to aim for zero interference with original property rights. Equally, however, it would be socially destructive to fail to regulate any such interference, and thereby to allow it in all forms, and to any extent. There needs, therefore, to be some alternative to these extremes and, where real property is concerned, it has long been recognised that context-dependent reasonableness provides this. Nuisance protects real property rights through the law of wrongs; the wrongful interference actions protect personal property rights through the law of wrongs. If unreasonable interference is the essence of the former, why should it not be of at least comparable significance to the latter?

It would be instructive at this stage to return to the Dartford Tunnel example in order to illustrate the practical importance of this point. A vehicle breakdown, caused by the negligence of the car manufacturer, has meant that traffic congestion has delayed many motorists for a considerable time. The effects on those unfortunate enough to be involved in this congestion are likely to vary considerably in their significance. The situation is doubtless frustrating and boring for all. For some it will also prove expensive if, for instance, they are prevented from getting to a job for which payment depends on their presence, or at least their presence at a certain time. For others, it may mean losing money under other contractual provisions, such as liquidated damages clauses for late delivery. There are still others, however, for whom the consequences will be more significant.

Take, for example, the merchandise supplier on her way to a major stadium event, with a lorry full of clothing emblazoned with the specific details of that evening's one-off performance.[71] If the supplier is prevented by the congestion from reaching the venue, she will lose the profit she would have made by selling her cargo. This causes her undoubted finan-

---

[69] *Delaware Mansions Ltd v Westminster City Council* [2001] UKHL 55, [2002] 1 AC 321 [29].
[70] Green and Randall, above n 6, at 59–65.
[71] With thanks to Roderick Bagshaw for this example.

cial loss, just as it does the plumber who is unable to get to a scheduled job, with the result that her customer enlists the help of an alternative specialist. As outlined above, the law of wrongs does not recognise in anyone the right to make a profit. The merchandise supplier is, however, in a different position to that of the plumber, since her original property right (in the contents of her lorry) has suffered a far more extensive interference. Since the basic content of any (original) property right is the ability to use and exploit the subject matter of that right, preventing the right holder from being able to do this is an interference with that right. Where, as here, the effect of the interference is to negate the core worth of the subject matter of that property right (since the merchandise is now practically worthless), it is clearly an unreasonable interference.

It might be argued, of course, that the plumber has also suffered an interference, in that she is unable to use her tools and equipment as she so desired (ie, on the job for which she was scheduled). This is true, inasmuch as the interference was of the same *type* as that suffered by the merchandiser—that is, an interference with the plumber's original property rights in her tools and equipment. It is harder, however, to describe the interference with the plumber's personal property rights as unreasonable. Although she has been prevented from using the subject matter of her rights on this occasion, their use value has not been exhausted by the delay, meaning that her ability to employ them has not been, given their nature and functionality, severely curtailed. An important distinction needs to be made here, and it relates to financial value. The distinction between the plumber and the merchandiser is not one based on the numerical value of their loss. Indeed, the plumber may have lost more in financial terms on this occasion, because the job from which she was detained would have paid more than the merchandiser lost on missing her gig, both in terms of lost profit and sunk expenditure in stock. This is not decisive, or indeed relevant. What is important is the effect that the delay has had on the intangible original property rights of the respective individuals. The plumber's rights in her equipment were temporarily infringed for the duration of the physical interfering event, but were unaffected beyond this. The plumber will be able to exploit the commercial potential of her tools and equipment many more times. The merchandiser's rights, on the other hand, have been permanently affected in that she no longer has the ability to use or exploit the subject matter of her property rights in any meaningful sense.[72]

---

[72] Of course, the merchandiser may be able to sell the fabric to a rag dealer, but this will be so far removed from the purpose for which she, in this instance, acquired property rights over the material as effectively to negate the worth of that right. After all, if all a property right is intended to give is the ability to put an asset to *some* use, even if that use is not one which the right-holder chooses, then its content is substantially different from what lawyers have come to understand by the existence of such a right.

It will be no easy task for the tort of negligence to recognise the true nature of such rights, and so start to accommodate such claims. Its failure to do so, however, will only serve to perpetuate the current highly inconsistent treatment of comparable legal rights. The law of wrongs has for a long time protected unreasonable interferences with intangible original property rights in real property. It is difficult to see, therefore, why comparable protection should not be afforded to rights which are legally identical in nature, but which relate to a physically different subject matter: personal property. It might be argued that the obvious physical differences between the two might warrant different treatment. For example, real property is not movable, and so there needs to be some form of protection against interferences from neighbours, from whom one cannot remove one's real property. As the Dartford Tunnel example shows, however, such logistical challenges are not limited to real property. Such potential differences can, anyway, be dealt with through the criterion of unreasonable interference; where a claimant has an option to minimise or eliminate the interference him or herself, it is far less likely to be judged to be unreasonable. The fact that a claim will not always (or even often) be needed is no reason at all not to recognise it as a potentially legally valid one.

Unfavourable comparisons with the protection of interests in real property are not, however, the only indicators of the current law's inconsistency on this issue. Possibly harder to defend (and perhaps easier to accept for those who do not regard the analogy with real property as a valid one) is the incoherence *within* the law's protection of original property rights in personal property. Currently, as outlined above, original property rights are protected by the tort of conversion against unreasonable interferences if they are the result of *voluntary* action by another. Whilst this obviously covers deliberate and intentional interferences, it also encompasses entirely 'innocent' interferences[73] in that the interferer only needs to have acted voluntarily towards certain assets, with no requirement that he recognise that those assets belong to another.[74] Here, such an interferer will be liable even if he believed he was acting in relation to his own assets. So, whilst conversion is in one sense an intentional tort, it is strict as to the 'wrongfulness' element.[75] There would seem to be little reason, therefore, for the law to continue to allow negligent interferers to avoid having to compensate those whose property rights they have interfered with, when it already requires 'innocent' interferers to make such redress. The issue has too long been obfuscated by the law of wrongs' unfamiliarity, and

---

[73] For good reason: see part VI below.

[74] See text accompanying n 24 above.

[75] See J Gardner, 'Wrongs and Faults' in AP Simester (ed), *Appraising Strict Liability* (Oxford, Oxford University Press, 2005) 51, 55–56 for the distinction between committing a wrong and acting wrongfully.

consequent misunderstanding, of intangible, original property rights, and its corresponding misuse of the label of 'pure economic loss'. It is to be hoped that a greater understanding of the wrongful interference actions as a whole, together with their inherent key concepts, will serve to clarify this area of the law, and to bring consistency where it is currently lacking.

V. WHY USE THE LAW OF WRONGS TO PROTECT RIGHTS?

It is sometimes argued that the protection of personal property rights should not be achieved through the law of wrongs, and that the common law's practice of so doing is somehow deficient.[76] In fact, however, the converse is true and the common law's means of protecting personal property rights is actually ideally suited to the task. Other than making it harder for academic lawyers to decide what to write about in their books, or to teach on their courses, there would seem to be nothing objectionable about protecting rights in the most effective way possible, regardless of perceived classificatory integrity. After all, such was the common law's story before the advent of the textbook: it is a creature of exigency not design. Indeed, if, as this chapter argues, property rights are best protected through interpreting their infringement as a wrong, then any purported bright line distinction between 'torts' and 'property' as substantively different domains of the law begins to look illusory. Such is the effect of a rights-based analysis.

There are two principal reasons why the law of torts is an appropriate medium through which to protect personal property rights. The first is that it provides a straightforward means of differentiating between differing property rights. The second is that it offers more comprehensive protection for such rights than the law of property could so easily achieve. The rights protected by the wrongful interference actions are rights over assets, a broad category encompassing both proprietary and possessory rights. This is both inevitable and necessary within a system of relative title, such as that which exists in the common law. It is often said that property rights are exigible against the whole world. In reference to the common law world, however, this is of course not strictly true. Common law property rights are exigible against the whole world except those with superior title.

In order to have a right exigible against the whole world without exception, one would have to have a right akin to 'ownership', a concept which is ill at ease in the common law. It was a concept unknown to a younger legal system, and modern use of the term is inconsistent and often unhelpful in a legal context. In a system in which title to property is a

---

[76] See the articles and book cited in above n 2.

purely relative concept, there is no room for what might colloquially be understood as 'ownership' (a term which, in substance, is used to describe various, and dissimilar relationships between persons and things). The layperson's idea of ownership essentially amounts to an absolute entitlement to an asset; being the 'owner' of an asset means that one individual has simultaneously the rights to decide what happens to that asset, how it is used and by whom, to whom it can be transferred temporarily and for how long, to whom it can be transferred permanently and on what conditions, the right to take action against one who appropriates that asset without permission, and the right to reclaim that asset, should the action be successful. The lawyer knows that this concept does not exist as such in the common law. This is largely, however, because it is not needed. Arguably, 'ownership' is an important label to those who regard it as applicable to them, because it signifies that the relationship they have with the asset in question attracts some form of legal protection. Several individuals can, however, each have different relationships concurrently with, and therefore different rights concurrently in, the same asset. Each of these can be sufficiently protected without any need for to a concept of 'ownership'.

According to William Swadling:

> [I]t is title and not ownership which English law protects. Despite what the layman might think, there is no concept of ownership in English law. The proof of that proposition lies in the fact that English law provides no form of protection to anyone we might wish to describe as the 'owner' of goods greater than that provided to someone who simply finds them in the street.[77]

In other words, common law title to assets is nothing more than a practical and relative phenomenon.[78] The protection of personal property rights is not concerned with the safeguarding of absolute entitlements: 'the English law of ownership and possession, unlike that of Roman law, is not a system of identifying absolute entitlement, but of priority of entitlement.'[79]

Somewhat counter-intuitively, these various and relative property rights, which range from immediate possessory rights to reversionary rights, are provided with more robust protection through the law of torts than they would be through the law of property. The law of property is, in principle at least, characterised by a two-dimensional relationship: that between a person (natural or otherwise) and an asset. This principle does not look quite so authentic, however, within the common law system of relative title, in which concurrently held, and yet substantively different, rights can

---

[77] W Swadling, 'Unjust Delivery' in A Burrows and Lord Rodger (eds), *Mapping the Law: Essays in Memory of Peter Birks* (Oxford, Oxford University Press, 2006) 277, 281.

[78] See Gordley, above n 49, at 61–65 and Mattei, above n 51, at 77 for a discussion as to the historical pedigree of this principle.

[79] *Waverley Borough Council v Fletcher* [1996] QB 334 (CA) 345 (Auld J).

exist in relation to the same asset. Here, the two-dimensional model, so paradigmatic of property law, encounters a problem: how does it explain a relationship between person A and an asset, which must accommodate the legitimate rights of both person A and person B?

The multi-dimensional approach of torts, on the other hand, anticipates the involvement, and therefore consideration, of more parties in the legal equation. Not only does this approach recognise the existence and operation of various rights in relation to one asset, but it also accommodates claims against anyone else who has ever interfered with any of those rights. It does not matter, under the tort model, whether the defendant has possession of the asset concerned, nor indeed whether he or she ever had such possession; if the defendant at any point interfered with the claimant's original property right, he or she will be liable to compensate the claimant accordingly. What is important from the point of view of a rights-based law of torts is that the defendant infringed one of the range of rights which exist in relation to that asset.

The same model is also able to accommodate the idea that there are some persons against whom common law property rights are not exigible. A thief, for example, has certain proprietary rights over the assets she has stolen and, as such, can claim for any infringements of those rights.[80] Nevertheless, such rights cannot be infringed by (because they do not exist in relation to) anyone with superior proprietary rights, such as the rightful possessor from whom the assets were wrongfully taken (which would include an earlier thief).[81] These situations demonstrate how the comprehensive protection of rights in personal property cannot, without more, be characterised simply by reference to an asset and a right-holder, but instead require reference to a more complex picture of rights as between persons.

This complex picture is something, however, that even the law of torts struggles to accommodate when operating on the premise of a conventional loss-based model. Owing to the nature of original property rights, the received quantitative concept of a 'loss' will often fail to recognise as a wrong the intangible infringement of those rights. Within a rights-based framework, on the other hand, uninhibited as it is by any quantitative considerations, and concerned only with the qualitative question of whether a right has been infringed, such recognition is paradigmatic. It is only under this latter model, therefore, that the wrongful interference actions can, for perhaps the first time, be regarded as appropriate and coherent elements of both the law of torts, and the common law in its entirety.

---

[80] See, eg, *Costello v Chief Constable of Derbyshire Constabulary* [2001] EWCA Civ 381, [2001] 1 WLR 1437; *Gough v Chief Constable of West Midlands Police* [2004] EWCA Civ 206, [2004] Po LR 164.

[81] For more on this, see Green and Randall, above n 6, at ch 4.

VI. INNOCENT INTERFERERS

The case of the innocent interferer provides another element of the wrongful interference actions which causes some intuitive difficulty.[82] Objections have been levelled against the ability of those whose property rights have been infringed to recover from those who have interfered with their rights innocently. An individual 'innocently' interferes with property rights when he or she does not realise that his or her action, intentional in itself, is inconsistent with anyone else's possessory rights. That such 'innocence' is no excuse for behaviour which amounts to a conversion, for example, was made very clear by the House of Lords in *Hollins v Fowler*.[83] In that case, the defendant cotton brokers had purchased bales of cotton from a third party, who had (unbeknownst to the brokers) obtained the bales fraudulently from the claimants. In taking delivery of the cotton, and transferring it to a customer of theirs, the defendants, despite having earned only commission on the transaction, remained liable to the claimants in conversion. Some justification for such a position was offered by Lord O'Hagan, when he said of the defendants:

> They are innocent of any actual wrongdoing, but those with whom they are in conflict are as innocent as they, and we can only regard the liability attached to them by the law, without being affected in our judgment by its unpleasant consequences. They appear to me to have been guilty of a conversion in dealing with the Plaintiffs' property, and disposing of it to other persons, without any right or authority to do so.[84]

This is, so the argument goes, unfair to hapless defendants, who unknowingly interfere with another's property rights. Arguably, this objection is related to the perceived problem, identified above, with the law of torts protecting original property rights. The liability of innocent defendants looks more uncomfortable within the law of wrongs than it does within the law of property (traditionally regarded as the law of rights). This stems from a perception of the law of wrongs which confuses adjectives and nouns. The relationship between rights and wrongs is a linear one; once a right has been infringed, then a wrong has been committed. The commission of such a wrong, however, does not necessarily equate with the tortfeasor's having done the wrong thing. As John Gardner makes clear:

> The distinction between doing the wrong thing and doing something wrongful is of pervasive importance in most developed legal systems. ... [T]he mere fact that one was justified (= not wrong) in acting wrongfully does not mean that

---

[82] See, eg, Curwen, above n 2, at 577–78.
[83] *Hollins v Fowler* (1875) LR 7 HL 757 (HL). For a more recent consideration of the issue, see *Wilson v Robertsons (London) Ltd* [2006] EWCA Civ 1088, (2006) 150 SJLB 1019.
[84] *Hollins v Fowler* (1875) LR 7 HL 757 (HL) 798–99.

one did not act wrongfully, and does not by itself block one's liability to pay reparative damages to those whom one wronged.[85]

The noun identifies a factual conclusion, and is always relevant. The adjective, on the other hand, makes a normative statement, and is sometimes relevant, since it is not true to say that the law of wrongs is never interested in the normative dimension of behaviour, just that it is not *necessarily* so. When and whether the law of wrongs is interested in the nature, as opposed to the outcome, of behaviour depends upon the right it is protecting, and the existence of justification or excuse has no significance whatsoever for original property rights. Once more, a rights-based analysis clarifies what a loss-based model obfuscates.

So goes the conceptual explanation. The practical explanation is equally forceful and highlights the inherent difficulty in the law's attempts to protect personal property. Whilst there is no need to balance the competing interests of neighbouring property interests, as there is in nuisance, there is a need to balance the competing interests of integrity of personal property with the security of commercial transactions. In holding 'innocent' interferers liable, the law as it stands favours the protection of property interests and, consequently, puts the onus on those dealing with assets to ensure that their actions are not inconsistent with another's rights, rather than requiring possessors actively to exclude others from their assets. Consider the alternative: were claimants not able to sue anyone who had innocently interfered with their property rights, but only those who had done so with full knowledge and intention, this would have the effect of transferring the risk of loss from those who interfere with someone else's rights (albeit without moral blame) to those whose rights have been interfered with (and who will usually also be without moral culpability). As the Law Reform Committee stated in its *Eighteenth Report*:

> The action of conversion has long been established in English law as a vehicle for the protection of proprietary rights. Unlike Roman law, English law achieves this purpose by means of an action *in personam* for damages which, when trover (from which conversion is derived) first appeared in the 15th century, was classified as tortious. But, although so classified, it is and always has been primarily an action for the protection of ownership and it is because of this that questions as to the fault of the defendant are irrelevant, the principle adopted being that 'persons deal with the property in chattels or exercise acts of ownership over them at their peril.' It seems to us that there are sound practical reasons for retaining this principle and that to depart from it would be inconsistent with the view taken by this committee in its 12th Report as to the balance to be struck between sanctity of property on the one hand and, on the other, the commercial advantages to be derived from facilitating transfer of title.[86]

[85] Gardner, above n 75, at 55–56 (footnotes omitted).
[86] Law Reform Committee, *Eighteenth Report (Conversion and Detinue)* (Cmnd 4774, 1971) para 13 (footnotes omitted).

In other words, the sanctity of property takes precedence. Not only is this congruent with the common law's long-established practice of according such precedence to original property rights,[87] but it makes logistical sense. The practical effect of putting the risk of loss on the potential interferer, rather than on the holder of the property right, is that the law also puts on the potential interferer the onus of investigating title to the assets in question. The potential interferer is in a far better position to do this in relation to a specific asset or set of assets with which he or she intends to deal, than is the possessor to protect his or her assets from every potential interferer, of which there might be an indeterminate number.[88] As Cane makes clear, 'in English law, the law of tort plays a major role in protecting property interests. Introducing fault elements into the tort [of conversion] may undermine that function.'[89] It is not immediately obvious why the addition of fault elements needs to be mooted; it would, for the reasons outlined above, add nothing of substance either to the protection of property interests, or to the balance of fairness between right-holder and right-infringer. Moreover, there are other areas of the law of torts in which there are no fault elements, and this seems to create less of a stir.[90] Once more, we see here the arbitrary distinction made (albeit passively at worst, and mostly inadvertently) between real property and personal property, in that innocent interferers with real property rights are rarely identified as being unfairly treated by the common law.

VII. CONCLUSIONS

The main arguments of this chapter can be summarised as follows:

1. There are two main types of property right which need protecting: original rights and derivative rights.
2. It is not only perfectly appropriate, but actually ideal, to protect both of

---

[87] To be contrasted with the civil law tendency to favour the good faith acquirer: see J Bell, S Boyron and S Whittaker, *Principles of French Law*, 2nd edn (Oxford, Oxford University Press, 2007) 279. For a more detailed comparative analysis of the two systems, see CSP Harding and MS Rowell, 'Protection of Property versus Protection of Commercial Transactions in French and English Law' (1977) 26 *International and Comparative Law Quarterly* 354, 355.

[88] Although it must be conceded that in some cases, a defendant may still be liable, despite his or her best efforts at such investigations. Examples of this may be found in the cases where hire purchase companies have not registered their interests in assets and yet still succeed against defendants who checked such registers before dealing with those assets. See, eg, *Moorgate Mercantile Co Ltd v Twitchings* [1977] AC 890 (HL); *Industrial & Corporate Finance Ltd v Wyder Group Ltd* (2008) 152 SJLB 31 (QB).

[89] Cane, above n 24, at 550. See also Mattei, above n 51, at 88 and A Ogus, *Costs and Cautionary Tales: Economic Insights for the Law* (Oxford, Hart Publishing, 2006) 43 for the economic efficiency arguments in favour of protecting possessors.

[90] Trespass to land, for example.

these through the law of wrongs, since this is the most straightforward means of ensuring that each right receives full protection, particularly against those with concurrent property rights in the same asset.

3. In order for the law of wrongs consistently to protect original rights, the intangible nature of their infringement needs to be recognised and accepted. The misapplication of the label 'pure economic loss' has to cease, so that negligent interference with such rights can be appropriately remedied.

4. Such recognition and acceptance is most easily achieved through a rights-based analysis of the wrongful interference actions.

Implicit within these conclusions is another: on a rights-based analysis, any conceptual difficulties associated with torts being used to protect property rights are resolved on two levels. First, such an analysis demonstrates how the protection offered to such rights loses nothing, but actually gains something, by taking the form it does. The second resolution really subsumes the first, by showing how the purported *necessary* distinction between 'property' and 'tort' as discrete areas of the law is both synthetic and unhelpful where the methods of one can serve the interests of the other. After all, classification should be the law's servant, not its master.[91]

---

[91] A point made clearly to me by John Randall QC.

19

Misfeasance in a Public Office: A Justifiable Anomaly within the Rights-Based Approach?

ERIKA CHAMBERLAIN*

I. INTRODUCTION: THE UNEASY PLACE OF MISFEASANCE IN A PUBLIC OFFICE IN MODERN TORT THEORY

T HE TORT OF misfeasance in a public office sits uneasily amidst corrective justice or rights-based approaches to tort law.[1] While the historical misfeasance cases appeared to require the plaintiff to establish an independent rights violation, that requirement has been definitively rejected in the modern form of the tort.[2] In the leading case of *Three Rivers District Council v Governor and Company of the Bank of England (No 3)*, Lord Steyn concluded that no antecedent right is required, 'beyond the right not to be damaged or injured by a deliberate abuse of power by a public officer.'[3] Misfeasance in a public office has thus lost much of the 'correlativity' that is the hallmark of tort law under corrective justice theory. The plaintiff need not establish that the defendant violated a pre-existing right, nor, alternatively, that the defend-

* The author is grateful to Mark Aronson, John Murphy, Jason Neyers, Donal Nolan, Hanna Wilberg, and the participants in the Obligations V Conference for their helpful comments, to Dina Milivojevic for her research assistance, and to Canada's Social Sciences and Humanities Research Council for its financial support.

[1] Although not coterminous, corrective justice and rights-based theories have been grouped together for the purposes of this analysis. As discussed below, these theories share similar core characteristics that appear inconsistent with the structure and purposes of misfeasance in a public office. For the distinction between corrective justice and rights-based approaches, see D Nolan and A Robertson, 'Rights and Private Law' ch 1 of this book.

[2] See generally E Chamberlain, 'The Need for a "Standing" Rule in Misfeasance in a Public Office' (2008) 7 *Oxford University Commonwealth Law Journal* 215.

[3] *Three Rivers District Council v Governor and Company of the Bank of England (No 3)* [2003] 2 AC 1 (HL) (*Three Rivers*) 193, quoting from the trial judgment of Clarke J: [1996] 3 All ER 558 (QB) 584.

ant breached a duty owed to the plaintiff. The gist of the modern tort is that the defendant's unlawful conduct has caused the plaintiff material damage, a formulation that would not justify an order that the defendant pay the plaintiff compensation on the generally-accepted principles of corrective justice. Accordingly, some commentators have described misfeasance in a public office as an anomaly within, or exception to, the rights-based approach.[4]

This chapter seeks to answer two main questions. First, is misfeasance in a public office in fact anomalous, or can it be made to fit within the rights-based paradigm? A review of the historical cases suggests that the modern courts may too hastily have dispensed with the pre-existing right/duty requirement, which had been broadly consistent with rights-based theories. Alternatively, the rights violation involved in claims of public misfeasance is similar in many respects to that involved in the tort of negligence. This is because both rights violations can be framed as entailing the wrongful infliction of a foreseeable loss: whereas the tort of negligence involves the 'right' not to be foreseeably harmed by the defendant's negligent conduct, the tort of misfeasance involves the 'right' not to be foreseeably harmed by a public officer's deliberately unlawful conduct. By analogy to the tort of negligence, misfeasance in a public office may be shown to be consistent with the rights-based approach to private law.

If these arguments fall short, and the misfeasance tort is still found to be an anomaly within the rights-based approach, the second question addressed by this chapter is whether the tort's existence is justifiable on other grounds, such as deterrence, compensation, or vindication for plaintiffs.[5] On account of its unique public law aspects, we may be willing to forgive the anomalous structure of misfeasance in a public office. On the other hand, these unique considerations might mandate that the misfeasance tort be abolished, as the Law Commission has suggested, in favour of a more explicitly public cause of action.[6]

Ultimately, this chapter asks whether misfeasance in a public office, which is ironically the most famous source of the maxim *ubi ius, ibi remedium*,[7] can justify its continued existence within the realm of private law. The answer depends largely on whether private law can legitimately

---

[4] See, eg, R Stevens, *Torts and Rights* (Oxford, Oxford University Press, 2007) 242–43.

[5] Of course, the existence of anomalies may also indicate that rights-based approaches to tort law are flawed: see J Murphy, 'Rights, Reductionism and Tort Law' (2008) 28 *Oxford Journal of Legal Studies* 393, 407.

[6] Law Commission, *Administrative Redress: Public Bodies and the Citizen* (Law Com CP No 187, 2008) para 4.93 ff. In its final report, the Law Commission noted that many consultees disagreed with this proposal and argued that the misfeasance tort should be preserved: see Law Commission, *Administrative Redress: Public Bodies and the Citizen* (Law Com No 322, 2010) (*Final Report*) paras 3.65–3.72.

[7] From Holt CJ's dissenting opinion in *Ashby v White* (1703) 2 Ld Raym 938, 92 ER 126, which was ultimately upheld by the House of Lords in *Ashby v White* (1703) 3 Ld Raym 320, 92 ER 710 (*Ashby*).

be used to promote public law goals, and the extent to which the internal consistency of private law can or should be compromised to achieve those goals. In an era when government action and regulation pervade citizens' lives, the fate of torts like misfeasance in a public office has significant implications for the future scope and role of tort law more generally.

II. CAN MISFEASANCE IN A PUBLIC OFFICE BE RECONCILED WITH THE RIGHTS-BASED APPROACH?

It is not the purpose of this chapter to provide a comprehensive description or defence of rights-based approaches to private law. To be clear, I am neither a proponent nor a detractor of such approaches: I believe that they provide helpful analyses of various tort doctrines, but I do not believe that they have a monopoly over the truth about private law. However, given that rights-based approaches have risen to prominence in recent years, it has become important to test the various specific torts against the rights paradigm, to examine whether it in fact provides the best explanation of tort law. Scholars have accordingly taken pains to show how the torts of negligence, nuisance, defamation and the various economic torts demonstrate (or fail to demonstrate) the coherence of rights-based approaches.[8] Some torts, however, do not readily fit the rights-based mould, and are typically dismissed as being anomalous. Misfeasance in a public office seems to fall within this category of anomalous torts. Before exploring whether this categorisation is correct, I will give a brief overview of the rights-based approach in its various iterations, including corrective justice and civil recourse theories. For my purposes, these theories share three important characteristics: a focus on the relational structure of tort law; a requirement that the defendant violate the plaintiff's rights; and a general rejection of external, instrumentalist or so-called 'policy' justifications for various tort doctrines.

At their core, rights-based approaches to private law seek to explain why the plaintiff can sue the defendant in any given case. It is not enough that the defendant's actions or omissions have caused the plaintiff to suffer loss. The plaintiff can only recover if the defendant has somehow violated the plaintiff's rights or, alternatively, breached a duty owed to the plaintiff. As Ernest Weinrib explains, rights are fundamental to liability in private law because they join the parties in a normative relationship:

> As a determinant of liability, the appropriately relational normative category is that of a right; a right is inherently relational because its existence immediately implies that another is under a duty not to infringe it. Rights mark out legally

[8] See, eg, A Beever, *Rediscovering the Law of Negligence* (Oxford, Hart Publishing, 2007); J Neyers, 'Rights-Based Justifications for the Tort of Unlawful Interference with Economic Relations' (2008) 28 *Legal Studies* 215.

secured spheres of freedom within which the holder of the right can exercise the capacity to pursue self-chosen ends. They also, through the duties that are correlative to them, act as constraints on the actions of others. They are thus the devices through which private law actualises the principle that the action of one party ought not to be inconsistent with the freedom of another.[9]

Under Weinrib's corrective justice theory, rights reflect the equal freedom of the parties, as encapsulated in the notion of Kantian right. Liability in tort is only justifiable where the defendant has acted in a way that is inconsistent with the equal freedom of the plaintiff—ie, where the defendant has breached the plaintiff's rights. Weinrib has described the 'integrating power' of corrective justice in that 'it construes the parties as operating within a coherent normative relationship, the elements of which—the right of the plaintiff and the duty of the defendant—are the correlative articulations of a single juridical norm.'[10] According to Weinrib, the internal coherence of tort law can only be understood through this correlativity of right and duty. It follows that any attempt to explain tort law through factors that are external to, or that focus exclusively on one side of, the bipolar relationship between plaintiff and defendant is inadequate. For instance, a focus on the plaintiff's need for compensation fails to explain why *the defendant* should be the one to provide that compensation. Similarly, a focus on the need to deter the defendant fails to explain why the defendant ought to pay damages *to the plaintiff*. Only by insisting on a right/duty relation between the parties can we explain why *this* defendant is liable to *this* plaintiff.

Similarly, rights theorist Robert Stevens positions rights at the centre of tort law. He explains, 'Before a defendant can be characterized as a tortfeasor the anterior question of whether the claimant had a right against him must be answered. ... The infringement of rights, not the infliction of loss, is the gist of the law of torts.'[11] This structure helps Stevens to explain, for example, why there is generally no liability for omissions: 'we do not have rights good against the rest of the world to compel others to come to our assistance.'[12] Further, while Stevens does not seek to limit the range of rights that we enjoy, he stresses that '[j]udicially created rights are, inevitably, minimalist in content; with a corresponding maximalist approach to liberty of action.'[13] Importantly, the rights created by the private law courts ought not to take into account 'policy' or social considerations, which the courts lack the political legitimacy and technical competence to assess.[14]

---

[9] EJ Weinrib, 'Two Conceptions of Remedies' in CEF Rickett (ed), *Justifying Private Law Remedies* (Oxford, Hart Publishing, 2008) 3, 11.

[10] EJ Weinrib, 'The Juridical Classification of Obligations' in P Birks (ed), *The Classification of Obligations* (Oxford, Clarendon Press, 1997) 37, 42.

[11] Stevens, above n 4, at 2.

[12] ibid, at 9.

[13] ibid, at 339.

[14] ibid, at 308–09.

A blend of Stevens' rights-based analysis and corrective justice theory can be found in Allan Beever's account of the tort of negligence.[15] Like Weinrib, Beever focuses on correlativity or the interpersonal structure of torts: 'a wrong-sufferer has a claim in corrective justice only if the wrong-doer violated *her* right, and she can claim from the wrongdoer only if her right was violated by *that particular wrongdoer*.'[16] Moreover, like Stevens, Beever defines legal wrongs in terms of rights violations. He writes, 'To establish that the defendant committed a wrong, the claimant must show that the defendant damaged something over which she had a right. The law is not interested in loss per se, but only in losses that flow from a violation of the claimant's primary legal rights.'[17] Thus, he explains the general unavailability of recovery for relational economic loss by the fact that plaintiffs in such cases possess no relevant primary rights against the defendant.[18] Moreover, he rejects arguments that recovery may be determined by policy considerations, insisting that his so-called 'principled' approach must eschew any 'policy-based free-for-all.'[19]

Finally, John Goldberg and Benjamin Zipursky have described the normative structure of tort law by using the language of 'civil recourse'.[20] According to Goldberg and Zipursky, a plaintiff can only use the machinery of the state to obtain damages from the defendant if the defendant has interfered with the plaintiff's rights: committing a wrong against a third party will not do. This account of tort law is grounded in the principle that the wrongs of tort are relational. Thus, '[f]raud law enjoins each from deceiving others; negligence law enjoins each from failing to take due care not to injure others; defamation enjoins each from defaming others', and so on.[21] The only person who can sue in tort law is the person who has been wronged—ie, the person whose rights have been infringed. So, for example, a woman cannot sue in defamation merely because her husband was falsely accused of irresponsible conduct.[22] Although the woman might have suffered some loss as a consequence of the false accusation, her claim must fail because none of her rights has been infringed.

The classic illustration of this so-called 'standing' principle is, of course,

---

[15] Beever, above n 8.

[16] ibid, at 45 (emphasis in original).

[17] ibid, at 218.

[18] ibid, at 241–43.

[19] ibid, at 142.

[20] See generally B Zipursky, 'Civil Recourse, Not Corrective Justice' (2002) 91 *Georgetown Law Journal* 695; JCP Goldberg and BC Zipursky, 'Seeing Tort Law from the Internal Point of View: Holmes and Hart on Legal Duties' (2006) 75 *Fordham Law Review* 1563; JCP Goldberg and BC Zipursky, 'Rights and Responsibility in the Law of Torts' ch 9 of this book.

[21] BC Zipursky, 'Rights, Wrongs, and Recourse in the Law of Torts' (1998) 51 *Vanderbilt Law Review* 1, 60.

[22] ibid, at 17, citing *Johnson v Southwestern Newspapers Corp* 855 SW 2d 182 (Tex 7th Ct App 1993).

Cardozo J's opinion in *Palsgraf v Long Island Railroad Co*.[23] The defendant was negligent in having pushed a passenger onto a moving train,
causing the passenger's parcel to become dislodged. The plaintiff suffered
injury when the parcel, which contained fireworks, exploded and caused
some scales on the railway platform to topple on her. Notwithstanding the causal link between the defendant's negligence and the plaintiff's
loss, Cardozo J found that the plaintiff was unable to recover in negligence. The plaintiff's injury was not a reasonably foreseeable result of
the defendant's negligence; accordingly, the defendant did not owe her a
duty of care. In Cardozo J's famous words, 'The risk reasonably to be
perceived defines the duty to be obeyed, and risk imports relation; it is
risk to another or to others within the range of apprehension.'[24] Because
the plaintiff was not within the scope of foreseeable risk, the guard's
negligence was, '[r]elatively to her ... not negligence at all.'[25] Thus, the
plaintiff could not establish that her rights had been violated (or that the
defendant had breached a duty owed to her), and she had no 'standing'
to sue in negligence.[26]

For present purposes, the key aspect of any rights-based approach to
tort law is that a plaintiff can only sue if the defendant has violated his
or her legally-protected rights. It is not sufficient that the defendant has
acted in a way that is blameworthy, and/or that the plaintiff has suffered
loss. Nor is it sufficient that the defendant has breached a duty that he
or she owes to the world at large. The essence of tort law is the bipolar
relationship between plaintiff and defendant, where the plaintiff's right is
the defendant's duty seen from a different vantage point.[27] Tort doctrines
should be determined in terms of these rights-based principles, and not
on the basis of policy or instrumentalist considerations.

In terms of these theories, misfeasance in a public office is viewed as
anomalous because it does not require the plaintiff to show the violation
of some independent right, or the breach of a duty that the defendant
owed specifically to the plaintiff. It is enough, in the modern form of the
tort, that the defendant has acted in a way that is deliberately unlawful,
and that the plaintiff has suffered some (subjectively) foreseeable harm.[28]
In the sections below, I argue that rights-based theorists have prematurely
declared misfeasance in a public office to be anomalous, and that it can
plausibly be squared with rights-based approaches to tort law. First, the

---

[23] *Palsgraf v Long Island Railroad Co* 248 NY 339 (1928) (*Palsgraf*).

[24] ibid, at 345.

[25] ibid, at 341.

[26] Zipursky, 'Rights, Wrongs, and Recourse', above n 21, at 10.

[27] J Feinberg, 'The Nature and Value of Rights' in J Coleman (ed), *Philosophy of Law*
(New York, Garland Publishing, 1994) 243, 249–50.

[28] That is, the defendant must have foreseen that harm to the plaintiff would probably
result, or have been reckless to that fact. Objective, or 'reasonable' foreseeability, is not
sufficient to establish the mental element of misfeasance in a public office: see *Three Rivers*
[2003] 2 AC 1 (HL) 196 (Lord Steyn).

historical misfeasance cases did require the plaintiff to establish a pre-existing right, and recent departures from that requirement should be reconsidered. Secondly, even if misfeasance in a public office does not require a violation of some independent right, it does at least require the violation of the right not to be harmed by the deliberately unlawful actions of a public officer. This right is comparable to the rights-violation entailed in negligence law—ie, the right not to be foreseeably harmed by the negligent actions of the defendant.

A. From *Ashby* to *Three Rivers*

An examination of the early cases indicates that misfeasance in a public office was broadly consistent with the rights-based approach to tort law. Misfeasance is often traced back to *Ashby v White*,[29] where the defendant returning officer wrongfully prevented the plaintiff from voting in an election. The case became a jurisdictional dispute between the House of Commons (which exclusively controlled the franchise) and the House of Lords (which ultimately allowed Ashby's action in the common law courts).[30] The Lords' claim to jurisdiction rested on the classification of the right to vote as a property right belonging to Ashby as a freeholder. The action was accordingly framed in the language of disturbance or nuisance,[31] which meant that the alleged misfeasance in *Ashby* was the deliberate interference with a legal right. Indeed, the basis of Holt CJ's famous dissenting opinion in the Court of King's Bench was that '[i]f the plaintiff has a right, he must of necessity have a means to vindicate and maintain it, and a remedy if he is injured in the exercise or enjoyment of it.'[32] *Ashby* was followed by similar cases in which the plaintiff had been denied the right to vote or run for office.[33] In accordance with *Ashby*, the plaintiff first had to show that he indeed had a right to vote in the relevant election.[34] Thus, the existence of a legal right seemed central to early misfeasance claims.[35]

---

[29] *Ashby* (1703) 3 Ld Raym 320, 92 ER 710.

[30] See E Cruickshanks, '*Ashby v White*: The Case of the Men of Aylesbury, 1701–4' in C Jones (ed), *Party and Management in Parliament, 1660–1784* (Leicester, Leicester University Press, 1984) 87.

[31] JH Baker, *An Introduction to English Legal History*, 4th edn (London, Butterworths, 2002) 432.

[32] *Ashby* (1703) 2 Ld Raym 938, 953; 92 ER 126, 137.

[33] See, eg, *Turner v Sterling* (1726) 2 Vent 25, 86 ER 287; *Drewe v Colton* (1787) 1 East 563, 102 ER 217; *Williams v Lewis* (1797) Peake Add Cas 157, 170 ER 229.

[34] See especially *Cullen v Morris* (1819) 2 Stark 577, 171 ER 741, where there was some dispute over whether the plaintiff had paid the requisite rates in the parish, which was necessary to qualify as a voter.

[35] See also *Rogers v Dutt* (1860) 13 Moo PC 209, 15 ER 78. For more detailed analysis of this requirement, see Chamberlain, 'The Need for a "Standing" Rule', above n 2, at 218–20.

More recently, this requirement has been alternatively framed in terms of the duty owed to the plaintiff. On this approach, it is not enough for the plaintiff to show that the defendant breached some duty owed to the public at large; rather, the plaintiff must show that he or she was within the class of persons to whom the relevant duty was owed.[36] This language of duty is also consistent with rights-based approaches, in that it reinforces the need for correlativity or so-called substantive standing. In order to establish a legal wrong, the plaintiff must show that the defendant breached a duty that was owed *to him or her*.

Nevertheless, the requirement of a pre-existing right or duty was decidedly rejected in *Three Rivers*, which involved a claim by depositors who suffered losses on the demise of the Bank of Credit and Commerce International (BCCI) in the United Kingdom. The plaintiffs alleged that senior officials at the Bank of England had acted in bad faith in licensing BCCI as a deposit-taking institution and in failing to take timely steps to close BCCI. Based on the historical cases, the defendants in *Three Rivers* argued that the plaintiffs should have to establish 'an antecedent legal right or interest' or some form of 'proximity' to bring them into a legal relationship with the relevant public officers. A majority of the Court of Appeal agreed, finding that 'the notion of proximity should have a significant part to play in the tort of misfeasance.'[37] Hirst LJ wrote:

> With the possible exception of [*Bourgoin v Ministry of Agriculture, Fisheries and Food*[38] and *Henly v Lyme*[39]], all the successful claims for misfeasance in public office ... were concerned with a direct and proximate relationship between the plaintiff and the public officer responsible for the acts or omissions complained of. The directness and proximity of the relationship was mirrored in the directness and inevitability, or near-inevitability, of the loss suffered.[40]

The Court of Appeal was careful not to treat the proximity requirement in misfeasance as synonymous with the duty of care in negligence. However, given the facts of the case, they had good reason to insist on some requirement that would restrict the class of plaintiffs who could claim compensation from the defendants. The plaintiffs in *Three Rivers* were some 6000 in number, and had no connection with the Bank of England apart from having deposits in a regulated financial institution. If all those depositors could bring a claim for their economic losses against a regulator that owed a duty only to the public at large, the implications for public authority liability would be far-reaching. As discussed below, the fact that many misfeasance cases involve purely economic interests, which

---

[36] See *Tampion v Anderson* [1973] VR 715.
[37] *Three Rivers* [2003] 2 AC 1 (CA) 55 (Hirst LJ).
[38] *Bourgoin v Ministry of Agriculture, Fisheries and Food* [1986] QB 716 (CA) (*Bourgoin*).
[39] *Henly v Lyme* (1828) 5 Bing 91, 130 ER 995.
[40] *Three Rivers* [2003] 2 AC 1 (CA) 55.

have historically received less protection than physical or property interests, underscores the need for a closer, correlative relationship between
the plaintiff and defendant as a means of limiting liability.

However, the House of Lords concluded that the element of proximity
or 'duty' was not essential to a misfeasance claim, agreeing with the trial
judge that no antecedent right is required, 'beyond the right not to be
damaged or injured by a deliberate abuse of power by a public officer.'[41]
Lord Hobhouse theorised that a requirement of a pre-existing right would
make the tort of misfeasance in a public office superfluous: 'it does not,
and does not need to, apply where the defendant has invaded a legally
protected right of the plaintiff.'[42] Where the defendant has violated a
legally protected right, then the plaintiff will be able to claim through
some other tort. Conversely, if the defendant has innocently caused the
plaintiff loss, the plaintiff has no claim in tort at all. The misfeasance tort,
Lord Hobhouse argued, fills the gap: it applies where the plaintiff has
no legally protected right, but the defendant has wrongfully caused the
plaintiff loss. The necessary 'wrongfulness' is represented by the requirement of malice. This argument has considerable appeal, but should be
examined with caution: it is inconsistent with the traditional structure of
the tort, and has the potential to significantly expand the scope of liability, particularly in the area of economic loss.

(i) The Existence of a Legally Protected Right Does Not Make the Misfeasance Tort Superfluous

It is inaccurate to state that a plaintiff whose legally protected rights have
been violated can always claim through another tort. Axiomatically, this
is only true of rights that are protected *through the law of torts*, such
as bodily integrity, property ownership, or reputation.[43] This ignores that
misfeasance in a public office arose as a hybrid of tort and administrative law, and has historically protected rights of a more civic or political
nature (such as the right to vote, run for office, or be considered for a
licence). While administrative law might assist the plaintiff in enforcing his
or her administrative/procedural rights, only the law of tort can provide
the plaintiff with damages for wrongful interference with those rights.[44]

This division of labour between tort and administrative/constitutional
law still occurs today. For instance, in *Abdelrazik v Minister of Foreign
Affairs*,[45] the plaintiff brought an application under the Canadian Charter

---

[41] *Three Rivers* [2003] 2 AC 1 (HL) 193 (Lord Steyn), quoting [1996] 3 All ER 558
(QB) 584 (Clarke J).
[42] *Three Rivers* [2003] 2 AC 1 (HL) 229.
[43] See *Allen v Flood* [1898] 1 AC 1 (HL) 29 (Cave J).
[44] See, eg, *Harman v Tappenden* (1801) 1 East 555, 102 ER 214.
[45] *Abdelrazik v Minister of Foreign Affairs* [2009] FC 580, [2010] 1 FCR 267 (*Abdelrazik*).

of Rights and Freedoms after government officials left him effectively exiled in Sudan. Abdelrazik, a Canadian citizen, had travelled to Sudan on a valid passport, but was subsequently arrested and detained by the Sudanese authorities, during which time his passport expired. The Canadian government, citing national security concerns, refused to issue Abdelrazik an emergency passport, thereby preventing him from returning home. Zinn J of the Federal Court found that this was a violation of Abdelrazik's right under section 6(1) of the Charter to enter and remain in Canada, and ordered the government to issue an emergency passport and to arrange for Abdelrazik's safe return home.

Since his return to Canada, Abdelrazik has commenced a civil claim against the federal government, including a claim against the Minister of Foreign Affairs for misfeasance in a public office.[46] While the Charter application was necessary to obtain an order for the government to issue an emergency passport, the civil claim is essential if Abdelrazik is to obtain damages for the losses he suffered during his exile. The tort action is, thus, not superfluous.[47] Abdelrazik could enforce his right to enter Canada through the Charter application, but his claim for compensation is framed in the law of tort.[48]

Admittedly, such administrative or constitutional rights are not rights in a Hohfeldian sense, nor are they the kind of rights figured in the leading rights-based approaches to tort law. Nevertheless, their violation can clearly form the basis of a claim for misfeasance in a public office, as long as malice and material damage are established.[49] Moreover, administrative or procedural rights are correlative in the sense that public officers have a duty to comply with them, and that deliberate non-compliance is what makes the officer's conduct 'unlawful' for the purposes of the misfeasance tort. Indeed, in the absence of specific administrative rights, the plaintiff's cause of action in many misfeasance cases would simply collapse. The

---

[46] For a more detailed analysis, see E Chamberlain, '*Abdelrazik*: Tort Liability for Exercise of Prerogative Powers?' (2010) 18 *Constitutional Forum* 119.

[47] This is not to say that Abdelrazik's civil claim should necessarily be successful, just that it is necessary if Abdelrazik is to obtain compensation for any damage he has suffered.

[48] Technically, Abdelrazik could claim damages under section 24(1) of the Charter, which allows a court to order 'such remedy as the court considers appropriate and just in the circumstances.' However, Charter damages are discretionary and must take into account the appropriateness of the remedy for all who might be affected by it, including the community at large. See generally K Cooper-Stephenson, *Charter Damages Claims* (Scarborough, Carswell, 1990) 2. This was affirmed in the recent case of *City of Vancouver v Ward* [2010] SCC 27, [2010] 2 SCR 28 where the Supreme Court of Canada explained that Charter damages must be 'appropriate and just' from the perspectives of both the plaintiff and the defendant. In that case, the court upheld the relatively modest award of $5000 to a plaintiff who had been wrongly strip-searched by police.

[49] For example, in *Ontario Racing Commission v O'Dwyer* [2008] ONCA 446, (2008) 293 DLR (4th) 559 (*O'Dwyer*), the plaintiff successfully claimed in misfeasance for being denied the hearing to which he was statutorily entitled after the termination of his status as an approved horse-racing official.

denial of a hearing, for example, is only 'unlawful' if the plaintiff had a right to such a hearing in the first place.

Finally, in so far as Lord Hobhouse's observations in *Three Rivers* can be taken as rejecting the notion of concurrency between misfeasance in a public office and other torts, his reasoning has not played out in practice. For instance, a survey of modern Canadian cases indicates that misfeasance has been pleaded alongside many torts, including negligence,[50] false arrest,[51] malicious prosecution,[52] and wrongful interference with economic relations.[53] No court has rejected a misfeasance claim based on the impossibility of concurrent actions. Moreover, by adding a claim for misfeasance in a public office, plaintiffs have been able to gain procedural advantages like an expanded scope of recovery and resistance to summary judgment, in addition to the more intangible benefit of tainting the defendant's actions as abusive.[54] Since *Three Rivers*, misfeasance in a public office has become a potentially valuable weapon in a plaintiff's arsenal.

(ii) The Requirement of Malice Is Insufficient to Limit the Ambit of the Tort

Part of the stated justification for dispensing with the right/duty requirement in *Three Rivers* was that the requirement of malice would be sufficient to restrict the scope of misfeasance in a public office. However, the element of malice has been considerably weakened in recent years, and may no longer be able to confine the misfeasance tort in the way that Lord Hobhouse assumed.

The leading historical cases on misfeasance tended to involve some degree of bias or personal ill-will toward the plaintiff, and this has come to be known as 'targeted' malice. For instance, in the prominent Canadian case of *Roncarelli v Duplessis*,[55] the defendant Premier of Québec had a deliberate intention to harm the plaintiff restaurateur because of his involvement with the Jehovah's Witnesses, and ordered the revocation of the plaintiff's liquor licence in order to cause the plaintiff financial loss. However, such targeted actions by public officers are relatively rare.

---

[50] *Uni-Jet Industrial Pipe Ltd v A-G of Canada* [2001] MBCA 40, (2001) 156 Man R (2d) 14; *Odhavji Estate v Woodhouse* [2003] SCC 69, [2003] 3 SCR 263.

[51] *Chartier v A-G of Quebec* [1979] 2 SCR 474.

[52] *Driskell v Dangerfield* [2008] MBCA 60, (2008) 228 Man R (2d) 116; *Miguna v Toronto Police Services Board* [2008] ONCA 799, (2008) 301 DLR (4th) 540. See also *Milgaard v Kujawa* (1994) 118 DLR (4th) 653 (Saskatchewan Court of Appeal), involving one of Canada's most notorious miscarriages of justice.

[53] *Gershman v Manitoba Vegetable Producers' Marketing Board* (1976) 69 DLR (3d) 114 (Manitoba Court of Appeal); *White Hatter Limousine Service Ltd v City of Calgary* [1994] 1 WWR 620 (Alberta Court of Queen's Bench); *Saskatchewan Power Corp v City of Swift Current* [2007] SKCA 27, (2007) 293 Sask R 6.

[54] See generally E Chamberlain, 'What Is the Role of Misfeasance in a Public Office in Modern Canadian Tort Law?' (2010) 88 *Canadian Bar Review* 579.

[55] *Roncarelli v Duplessis* [1959] SCR 121 (*Roncarelli*).

Accordingly, a second 'limb' of the tort has evolved over the years, which covers cases where the public officer knowingly acts in excess of power, with the knowledge that the plaintiff will probably be harmed by that ultra vires action. In such cases, the relevant actions need not be targeted toward the plaintiff, as long as the plaintiff is within the class of persons who will probably be harmed.[56] In turn, the knowledge requirement can be satisfied by recklessness; that is, the officer will be considered to have acted in bad faith if he or she did not have an honest belief in the lawfulness of the impugned actions, and did not care whether the plaintiff would be harmed.[57] This second limb of the tort involves actions that are less obviously abusive or malicious than was historically required.

Nevertheless, it has been contended that even this relaxed test of malice will be a significant hurdle for misfeasance plaintiffs, and that it should keep the tort within reasonable bounds.[58] Admittedly, this is often the stage at which misfeasance claims are struck out. Yet, recent cases indicate that the 'untargeted' form of malice is not altogether difficult to prove;[59] at the very least, even relatively bald allegations of malice increase the odds that a claim will persist beyond the pleadings stage and exert pressure on the defendant to settle.[60] For example, in *Bellan v Curtis*,[61] the plaintiff investors brought a class action after the collapse of the Crocus Investment Fund in Manitoba. The plaintiffs alleged that provincial employees were improperly shielding the fund from investigation and compliance with securities regulations. In claiming misfeasance in a public office against the province, the plaintiffs alleged that the province was aware that its employees were improperly protecting the Fund, and that these actions were likely to injure investors. If these facts could be proved, they would satisfy the element of malice. Accordingly, Hanssen J found that this pleading was sufficient, and refused to strike out the cause of action against the Province.[62]

Thus, while the malice requirement may restrict the ambit of misfeasance in a public office in theory, it may not be sufficiently restrictive in practice. Because malice requires proof of various factual elements, it is unlikely to result in an action being struck out in its early stages. By contrast, as the practice of negligence shows, the element of right or duty is a matter of law which is more conducive to resolution during strike-out or

---

[56] See *Bourgoin* [1986] QB 716 (CA).

[57] *Three Rivers* [2003] 2 AC 1 (HL) 192 (Lord Steyn).

[58] ibid, at 193; H Wruck, 'The Continuing Evolution of the Tort of Misfeasance in Public Office' (2008) 41 *University of British Columbia Law Review* 69. See also Brennan J in *Northern Territory v Mengel* (1995) 185 CLR 307.

[59] See, eg, *McNutt v A-G of Canada* [2004] BCSC 1113; *O'Dwyer* [2008] ONCA 446, (2008) 293 DLR (4th) 559; *McMaster v The Queen* [2008] FC 1158, (2008) 336 FTR 92, affd [2009] FC 937 (*McMaster*).

[60] See generally Chamberlain, 'What Is the Role of Misfeasance', above n 54, at 597–600.

[61] *Bellan v Curtis* [2007] MBQB 221, (2007) 219 Man R (2d) 175.

[62] See also *Miguna v Toronto Police Services Board* [2008] ONCA 799, (2008) 301 DLR (4th) 540.

summary judgment applications. In addition, judicial decisions regarding the existence of a right or duty are more likely to lead to helpful principles and precedents than the more vague, factually-sensitive element of malice. In the long run, such right/duty decisions provide a more certain doctrinal framework for setting the boundaries of liability in misfeasance.

(iii) These Developments May Expand Recovery for Pure Economic Loss

The implications of Lord Steyn's and Lord Hobhouse's statements in *Three Rivers* are most likely to be felt in cases of pure economic loss, and particularly in cases like *Three Rivers*, which involve a large class of depositors or investors. Interestingly, various Commonwealth courts have struck out negligence claims against banking or investment regulators on the grounds that there was insufficient proximity to establish a duty of care.[63] For instance, in *Cooper v Hobart*, the Supreme Court of Canada explained that the duties owed by the Registrar of Mortgage Brokers are owed to the public at large:

> The regulatory scheme governing mortgage brokers provides a general framework to ensure the efficient operation of the mortgage marketplace. The Registrar must balance a myriad of competing interests, ensuring that the public has access to capital through mortgage financing while at the same time instilling public confidence in the system by determining who is 'suitable' and whose proposed registration as a broker is 'not objectionable'. All of the powers or tools conferred by the Act on the Registrar are necessary to undertake this delicate balancing. Even though to some degree the provisions of the Act serve to protect the interests of investors, the overall scheme of the Act mandates that the Registrar's duty of care is not owed to investors exclusively but to the public as a whole.[64]

Thus, while the investors had important interests that could be affected by the actions or omissions of the Registrar, they had no right to enforce the Registrar's obligations. Correlatively, the Registrar owed no duty of care to the investors. There was consequently no liability in negligence.

However, a plaintiff claiming in misfeasance does not have to establish a duty of care, and can thereby avoid some of the 'balancing of interests' discussions that are typically resolved against plaintiffs in negligence actions.[65] This was vividly demonstrated in the Canadian case of *Gran-*

---

[63] See, eg, *Yuen Kun Yeu v A-G of Hong Kong* [1988] 1 AC 175 (PC); *Davis v Radcliffe* [1990] 1 WLR 821 (PC). See generally M Andenas and D Fairgrieve, 'Misfeasance in a Public Office, Governmental Liability, and European Influences' (2002) 51 *International and Comparative Law Quarterly* 757, 776–77.

[64] *Cooper v Hobart* [2001] SCC 79, [2001] 3 SCR 537 [49].

[65] See, eg, *Wynberg v Ontario* (2006) 82 OR (3d) 561 (Ontario Court of Appeal); *Eliopoulos v Ontario* (2006) 82 OR (3d) 321 (Ontario Court of Appeal); *Attis v Canada* [2008] ONCA 660, (2008) 93 OR (3d) 35.

ite Power Corp v Ontario,[66] where a local power supplier was allowed
to continue its misfeasance claim against the Ontario government, while
its negligence claim was struck out. The claims arose out of the provincial government's deregulation of the power industry, which opened up
competition and ultimately undermined the plaintiff's contract to supply
electricity to a small municipality. The negligence claim was struck out for
lack of proximity, since the government was required to balance a variety
of interests and make decisions in the interests of the public as a whole.[67]
Nevertheless, the claim for misfeasance in a public office was allowed to
proceed, because the plaintiff alleged that the province's implementation
of the new energy policy in the relevant municipality allowed competing
companies to gain a foothold. While cases like *Granite Power* are relatively
rare to date, they suggest that plaintiffs may, in some circumstances, be
able to evade the pitfalls involved with bringing negligence claims against
public authorities (such as proximity and policy considerations) by bringing claims in misfeasance instead.

This is particularly troubling in cases of pure economic loss, like *Granite Power* and *Bellan v Curtis*. The malice requirement is not sufficient
to dispense with these claims (at least not prior to trial), and public
authorities may find themselves defending and settling claims that would
not survive the pleadings stage if they were brought in negligence. This
includes a growing number of misfeasance claims against local authorities for municipal planning or zoning decisions, and against provincial
authorities for licensing decisions. These claims almost exclusively involve
pure economic loss. It would be strange if, just as the principles governing such claims in negligence were cohering around limited recovery,[68] the
misfeasance tort reopened the door.

(iv) Summary

The above analysis suggests that the House of Lords might too hastily
have dispensed with the requirement of a pre-existing right or duty in
Three Rivers. The requirement served a useful purpose in keeping the
misfeasance tort within reasonable bounds—something that the weakened
form of the malice requirement may be unable to do. In particular, the
requirement protected public authorities against claims for pure economic
loss based on their exercise of regulatory functions or municipal governance, two areas that have historically been resistant to claims in negligence.
Thus, the requirement of a pre-existing right or duty served both doctri-

---

[66] *Granite Power Corp v Ontario* (2004) 172 OR (3d) 194 (Ontario Court of Appeal)
(*Granite Power*).
[67] ibid, at [23]–[24] (Moldaver JA for Catzman, Moldaver and Goudge JJA).
[68] This is admittedly a generalisation. However, claims regarding planning and zoning
decisions would almost invariably be classed as government policy decisions, and are therefore highly unlikely to form the basis of a successful negligence claim.

nal and practical purposes; the fact that it also rendered misfeasance in a public office consistent with rights-based approaches to tort law is a welcome collateral benefit.

B. The Right Violated by Misfeasance in a Public Office Is Analogous to the Right Violated in the Tort of Negligence

As the above analysis suggests, misfeasance in a public office is consistent with the rights-based approach to tort law because the requirement of a pre-existing right was important to the development of the tort and was too hastily discarded in *Three Rivers*. However, even if this view is incorrect, the misfeasance tort can still be made to fit with rights-based approaches. Specifically, what Lord Steyn described in *Three Rivers* as the right not to be injured by the unlawful actions of a public officer is roughly parallel to the right in negligence law not to be harmed by the careless acts of another. Given that rights theorists have made considerable efforts to explain the tort of negligence[69] (as any general theory of tort law must), this is a promising basis on which to explain the rights foundation of misfeasance in a public office.

Stephen Perry's recent work on the law of negligence provides considerable assistance in developing this line of argument.[70] Perry acknowledges that the 'primary right' implicated by the law of negligence can be difficult to pin down. Whereas many claims involve interference with the protected interests of personal security or tangible property, many other claims do not. Accordingly, at its most basic, Perry has aptly described 'the most fundamental moral right underlying negligence law' as

> a right not to be harmed as a result of someone else acting negligently towards one. The correlative moral duty is a duty not to harm others as a result of acting negligently towards them. Since the idea of acting negligently towards another involves, among other things, subjecting the other to an unreasonable degree of risk, we can describe the qualified underlying moral right as, very roughly, a right not [to] be harmed as a result of having being subjected to a certain unacceptable degree of risk. I say this is 'roughly' what the underlying moral right is because the idea of acting negligently 'towards' another needs to be further unpacked, so as to take account of the distinctive role played by the notion of reasonable foreseeability.[71]

The role of foreseeability in misfeasance in a public office will be discussed

---

[69] See especially Weinrib's pioneering work, EJ Weinrib, *The Idea of Private Law* (Cambridge MA, Harvard University Press, 1995); Beever, above n 8.

[70] See especially S Perry, 'The Role of Duty of Care in a Rights-Based Theory of Negligence Law' in A Robertson and HW Tang (eds), *The Goals of Private Law* (Oxford, Hart Publishing, 2009) 79.

[71] ibid, at 101.

below. For present purposes, I will examine the fundamental moral right that Perry outlines, and compare it to the fundamental right that seems to underlie the misfeasance tort.

Central to Perry's argument is the fact that, in order to breach the duty owed to the plaintiff, a defendant in negligence must not only expose the plaintiff to unreasonable risk, but also cause actual harm. In the language of Arthur Ripstein and Zipursky, the tort of negligence imposes both a duty of non-injuriousness and a duty of non-injury.[72] The duty of care in negligence is a duty of non-injuriousness: it prohibits the defendant from acting in ways that pose a foreseeable risk of harm to the plaintiff. Nevertheless, the defendant will not be liable to the plaintiff unless his or her breach of the duty of care has caused harm to the plaintiff—ie, unless the defendant has breached the duty of non-injury.

This is very similar to the structure of the misfeasance tort, particularly after *Three Rivers*. The duty owed by the defendant is a duty of non-injuriousness: it prohibits a public officer from acting in ways that are deliberately unlawful and that pose a foreseeable risk of harm to the plaintiff (or class of persons to which the plaintiff belongs). However, the defendant will only be liable if he or she breaches the duty of non-injury—ie, if he or she causes material damage. Both torts prohibit defendants from acting in certain ways (carelessly or unlawfully) if those actions pose a risk of harm to the plaintiff. Both torts also mandate that the plaintiff suffer some harm before being permitted to sue; that is, neither tort is actionable per se.

Given that negligence is often used as a paradigm illustration of the rights-based approach to tort law, these structural similarities suggest that misfeasance in a public office may not be as anomalous as is sometimes posited. This argument is supported by the central role of foreseeability in both negligence and misfeasance in a public office. In negligence, reasonable foreseeability helps to define the range of plaintiffs to whom the defendant owes a duty of care and, thus, delimits the overall scope of liability. As *Palsgraf*[73] illustrates, the defendant only owes a duty of care to those persons to whom his or her conduct poses a reasonably foreseeable risk of injury. Correlatively, a plaintiff can only sue if the defendant's negligent conduct posed a reasonably foreseeable risk of injury to him or her. The plaintiff cannot sue if the defendant's conduct posed a foreseeable risk of injury to someone else.

The same reasoning, with slight modification, applies to misfeasance in

---

[72] A Ripstein and BC Zipursky, 'Corrective Justice in an Age of Mass Torts' in GJ Postema (ed), *Philosophy and the Law of Torts* (Cambridge, Cambridge University Press, 2001) 214, 220. The authors explain (at 218): 'If X owes a duty of non-injury to Y, X does not breach that duty unless X has, in fact, injured Y. By contrast, duties of non-injuriousness prohibit persons from acting in certain potentially injurious ways'.

[73] *Palsgraf* 248 NY 339 (1928).

a public office. As far as the law of tort is concerned, the defendant owes a duty to those persons to whom his or her unlawful conduct poses a foreseeable risk of injury. (The difference here is that the harm must be *subjectively* foreseen by the defendant, in terms of actual knowledge or recklessness.) From the plaintiff's perspective, there is a right not to be harmed by the deliberately unlawful actions of a public officer, where the plaintiff is in a class of persons who will foreseeably be harmed. As with the tort of negligence, foreseeability serves to limit the range of plaintiffs who can bring a claim.[74] The plaintiff cannot sue unless he or she belongs to a class that was within the defendant's contemplation when the unlawful conduct took place.

Foreseeability thus serves to provide a relational aspect to both negligence and misfeasance in a public office. As has often been said, there is no such thing as negligence in the air.[75] Negligence is only actionable when it causes harm to a reasonably foreseeable plaintiff. And only that plaintiff has a right to sue the defendant for compensation. Similarly, an unlawful act by a public officer, without more, does not have consequences in the law of tort. It may render the officer subject to disciplinary or other sanctions, but it only gives rise to an action in tort if it causes foreseeable harm to the plaintiff. Further, the only persons who can bring actions in tort are those to whom harm was foreseen by the defendant. This demonstrates the bipolarity of the relationship implicated by the misfeasance tort. The defendant has a duty not to harm foreseeable plaintiffs through his or her unlawful conduct, and the plaintiff has a right not to suffer foreseeable harm as a result of the defendant's unlawful conduct.

Misfeasance in a public office therefore appears consistent with at least one rights-based approach to tort law. Granted, the obvious retort is that Perry's theory of negligence is itself somewhat anomalous, and stands out from the various rights-based theories that were outlined earlier in this chapter. Most notably, Perry's theory does not turn on the existence of some identifiable antecedent right, on which Stevens and Beever would insist. Perry's primary right is simply the right not to be foreseeably harmed by particular kinds of wrongful conduct. Nevertheless, Perry's theory is consistent with the right elucidated in *Three Rivers* (the right not to be harmed by the wrongful conduct of a public officer). Moreover, there is no doubting Perry's overall emphasis on correlativity

[74] Granted, in *Akenzua v Secretary of State for the Home Department* [2002] EWCA Civ 1470, [2003] 1 WLR 741 [19], Sedley LJ (with whom Simon Brown and Scott Baker LJJ agreed) described foreseeability as an expansive rather than a restrictive element of the misfeasance tort, explaining that only the harm suffered by the plaintiff must be of the type foreseen by the defendant. This allows for a large class of potential plaintiffs. Nevertheless, the Court of Appeal still required that the plaintiff's harm fall within the effects that were contemplated by the wrongdoer.

[75] See Cardozo J in *Palsgraf* 248 NY 339 (1928) 341, citing F Pollock, *The Law of Torts*, 11th edn (London, Stevens and Sons, 1920) 455.

and the relational structure of tort law, and Perry clearly labels himself as a corrective justice or rights theorist rather than an instrumentalist.[76] The purpose of this part was to argue that misfeasance in a public office should not be hastily written off as anomalous, and Perry's thesis demonstrates that misfeasance can be plausibly explained through a rights-based approach to tort law.

Before concluding this part, it is worth noting that misfeasance in a public office may also be structurally comparable to the tort of unlawful interference with economic relations. Both torts serve to protect the financial interests of plaintiffs; however, this protection is limited to situations where the defendant has done something that is independently unlawful (in other words, acted ultra vires for the purposes of the misfeasance tort or committed a crime or civil wrong for the purposes of unlawful interference with economic relations).[77] Like misfeasance in a public office, the unlawful interference tort has often been treated as anomalous to the rights-based approach.[78] More recently, Jason Neyers has argued that unlawful interference can be reconciled with the rights-based theory. Though I will not presume to appropriate his arguments here, I would note that several of them have parallels in the tort of misfeasance in a public office,[79] and may therefore provide additional support for the arguments I have presented.

III. IF MISFEASANCE IN A PUBLIC OFFICE IS ANOMALOUS, IS IT STILL A JUSTIFIABLE PART OF PRIVATE LAW?

At this stage, I take an instrumentalist turn and argue that, even if anomalous to the rights-based approach, the existence of misfeasance in a public office is justified on account of that tort's aims and functions. Rights theorists, of course, will find such arguments heretical. But in making them, I am comforted to be in the company of Hanoch Dagan, who has argued that private law is 'neither (wholly) autonomous, nor (purely) instrumental',[80] and of Peter Cane, who has written that 'private law can

---

[76] Perry, above n 70, at 81, though he admits that a 'pluralist' understanding of tort law would ultimately be the most satisfactory view: at 84 n 18.

[77] There is considerable debate about what qualifies as 'unlawful' conduct for the purposes of unlawful interference with economic relations: see JW Neyers, 'The Economic Torts as Corrective Justice' (2009) 17 *Torts Law Journal* 162, 187–95.

[78] ibid, at 164.

[79] For instance, Neyers argues that the unlawful interference tort may be an instance of 'abuse of right,' and that there is a duty not to abusively exercise one's rights with the intention of harming another: ibid, at 184. By analogy, public officers have a duty not to abusively exercise their powers with the intention of harming others: see JW Neyers, 'Explaining the Inexplicable? Four Manifestations of Abuse of Rights in English Law' ch 11 of this book, part III(B).

[80] H Dagan, 'The Limited Autonomy of Private Law' (2008) 56 *American Journal of Comparative Law* 809, 811, 813.

be seen as serving a number of different and sometimes conflicting goals which are reflected in incoherence and inconsistencies in the institution itself.'[81] These statements are particularly apt in light of the uniquely public nature of misfeasance in a public office. In the sections below, I set out three possible justifications for the misfeasance tort, should it be considered out of step with the rights-based approach: that it helps to fulfil the goals of compensation, vindication, and deterrence.

A. Compensation

It is trite that a purpose or at least an effect of tort law is to provide compensation to those who have suffered wrongful losses. But, as rights theorists will quickly point out, this cannot be the sole justification of tort law. Indeed, the right/duty or correlativity requirement of corrective justice is what helps to justify why the plaintiff can claim compensation from a particular defendant. So if, at this stage of my argument, we have concluded that misfeasance in a public office is inconsistent with the rights-based approach, we must explain why its existence is *nevertheless* justifiable within private law. That is, does the plaintiff's need for compensation outweigh the fact that the defendant may not have violated the plaintiff's rights?

It seems clear that misfeasance in a public office cannot be justified simply on the grounds that the plaintiff has suffered losses and is in need of compensation. As Weinrib points out, 'This need ... is unaffected by the way that the injury was produced. The goal of compensation does not in itself embrace the tortfeasor.'[82] The fact that the plaintiff has suffered a loss is not sufficient to justify an order that the defendant pay compensation.

Nevertheless, even if misfeasance in a public office is technically inconsistent with the rights-based approach, it is an overstatement to say that there is no reason to order the defendant to pay damages to the plaintiff. The existing rules for the misfeasance tort require the plaintiff to show that the defendant acted in a way that was deliberately unlawful, that the defendant knew or was reckless as to the fact that the plaintiff would probably suffer harm, and that the plaintiff actually suffered harm. If these elements are proven, it would seem disingenuous for the defendant to argue that damages are not warranted just because there has been, strictly speaking, no violation of the plaintiff's rights. The defendant's wrongdoing is quite clearly implicated in the plaintiff's loss.

---

[81] P Cane, 'Corrective Justice and Correlativity in Private Law' (1996) 16 *Oxford Journal of Legal Studies* 471, 484. See also J Stapleton, 'Evaluating Goldberg and Zipursky's Civil Recourse Theory' (2006) 75 *Fordham Law Review* 1529.

[82] Weinrib, *The Idea of Private Law*, above n 69, at 38.

A more convincing argument against the compensation justification is that the typical misfeasance case involves pure economic loss. As described above, tort law has generally been unwilling to award compensation for such loss except in limited circumstances. Without embarking on a survey of these circumstances, compensation for pure economic loss is generally unavailable unless the defendant has made some undertaking toward the plaintiff or has violated the plaintiff's pre-existing rights (such as by interfering with his or her contractual rights).[83] This puts us back where we started: searching for a rights violation at the heart of the misfeasance tort.

Complementing this concern about awarding compensation for pure economic loss is the reality that compensation for misfeasance in a public office is generally (though not invariably) paid from the public purse.[84] While it may seem justifiable to use public funds to compensate those who suffer physical injuries as a result of government misfeasance, there may be a greater backlash if public funds are used to compensate for pure economic loss. For instance, while the public may sympathise with a business owner who has suffered lost profits on account of a zoning decision or a refusal to issue a licence, it may be unenthusiastic about covering those lost profits from public funds.

In short, it may be difficult to justify the existence of the misfeasance tort based solely on the compensation objective. Further, those cases where compensation seems most warranted are the ones where compensation would already be available through an alternative tort claim: a plaintiff who has been physically abused or wrongfully imprisoned will presumably have good claims in battery, false imprisonment, malicious prosecution, or even negligence.[85] While those plaintiffs might include claims for misfeasance in a public office in their statements of claim, this will normally be for strategic purposes, whether procedural or to colour the defendant's actions as being particularly abusive.[86] The misfeasance claim is not, however, necessary to obtain compensation, and cannot be justified on this basis alone.

---

[83] See generally B Feldthusen, *Economic Negligence: The Recovery of Pure Economic Loss*, 5th edn (Scarborough, Thomson Carswell, 2008).

[84] See the dissenting opinion of Saunders JA in *Ward v British Columbia* [2009] BCCA 23, (2009) 304 DLR (4th) 653 [86], which exhorts caution when awarding damages from the public purse. Saunders JA's opinion not to award damages to a man who had been improperly strip-searched was not, however, upheld by the Supreme Court of Canada: *City of Vancouver v Ward* [2010] SCC 27, [2010] 2 SCR 28.

[85] See, eg, *McNutt v A-G of Canada* [2004] BCSC 1113; *Reynolds v Kingston Police Services Board* [2007] ONCA 166, (2007) 84 OR (3d) 738; *Driskell v Dangerfield* [2008] MBCA 60, (2008) 228 Man R (2d) 116.

[86] See Chamberlain, 'What Is the Role of Misfeasance', above n 54.

B. Vindication

That tort law can serve a vindicatory function was recently affirmed by the House of Lords in *Ashley v Chief Constable of Sussex Police*.[87] The plaintiff had been shot and killed by police in his home, and his family members subsequently brought actions in several torts, including negligence and battery. As the litigation progressed, the defendant admitted liability in negligence, and damages were assessed. However, the defendant denied liability for assault and battery. The question before the House was whether the claim for assault and battery could proceed to trial, notwithstanding that it would have no effect on the quantum of damages. Lord Scott, in finding that the claim could proceed, explained:

> [T]he Ashleys are determined, if they can, to take the assault and battery case to trial not for the purpose of obtaining a larger sum by way of damages ... but in order to obtain a public admission or finding that the deceased Mr Ashley was unlawfully killed by PC Sherwood. They want a finding of liability on their assault and battery claim in order to obtain a public vindication of the deceased's right not to have been subjected to a deadly assault, a right that was infringed by PC Sherwood. They have pleaded a case that, if reasonably arguable on the facts, cannot be struck out as being unarguable in law. Why, therefore, should they be denied the chance to establish liability at a trial?[88]

The vindicatory function of tort law seems particularly valuable to plaintiffs who claim against public authorities. They gain a significant degree of satisfaction from the ability to hold such authorities accountable for their actions.

The vindicatory function of misfeasance in a public office can be illustrated by a recent, if slightly bizarre, case from Canada. In *McMaster v The Queen*,[89] the plaintiff was a federal inmate with very wide feet. Contrary to a Correctional Service Directive, and for reasons that were unexplained, the Acting Chief of Institutional Services at McMaster's prison failed to provide him with properly-fitting shoes. This forced the plaintiff to continue wearing his old shoes, which eventually gave out while he was exercising, causing the knee injury for which he sued. The plaintiff succeeded at trial and won a very modest damage award (CAD$6000).[90] However, according to the plaintiff's lawyer, John Hill, money was not the plaintiff's primary motivation in bringing the misfeasance claim: 'What is really at stake here is not so much that [McMaster] got compensated, but the fact that he has taken public service to task

---

[87] *Ashley v Chief Constable of Sussex Police* [2008] UKHL 25, [2008] 1 AC 962 (*Ashley*).

[88] ibid, at [23].

[89] *McMaster* [2008] FC 1158, (2008) 336 FTR 92.

[90] The plaintiff's injury was assessed at $9000, but the award was reduced by one third for the plaintiff's contributory negligence in wearing worn out shoes.

and exacted some sort of penalty for their not doing their jobs.'[91] Importantly, unlike the tort of negligence, misfeasance in a public office gives an aura of abusiveness or malice to the public officer's actions, and can arguably therefore provide a greater level of psychological vindication to plaintiffs. As Hill explained:

> If we run into situations where people at city hall, or people in the provincial government, or people of the federal government start abusing our rights, or not seeing that we are properly served, ... [the tort of misfeasance in a public office] is something that the average citizen can use to effect some sort of remedy.[92]

The misfeasance tort may thus serve an important vindicatory function for plaintiffs.

Nevertheless, there are certain conceptual difficulties which suggest that vindication cannot be the sole justification for the existence of misfeasance in a public office, particularly if we assume (as we must at this stage of the argument) that misfeasance is inconsistent with the rights-based approach. First, when we use the term 'vindicate' in tort law, we tend to think of it as a transitive verb.[93] That is, if we ask the question 'Vindicate what?', the answer seems to be, 'The plaintiff's rights.'[94] But if the plaintiff had a pre-existing right, then misfeasance would fall squarely within the rights-based approach to tort law, and we would not need independent justification for its existence. Thus, it seems circular to use vindication as a way to explain the anomalous existence of misfeasance in a public office.

Admittedly, vindication can also describe a state of being, as in 'I feel vindicated,' like the plaintiff in *McMaster*. This takes rights out of the equation, and focuses on the psychological benefit the plaintiff gains at having brought the law to bear on the defendant. The plaintiff gains satisfaction from having been proved correct (or more probably, in the case of misfeasance, at the defendant having been proved wrong). Used in this way, vindication may be an independent justification for misfeasance in a public office, even in the absence of a rights violation.

Additionally, the misfeasance tort can serve a vindicatory function for

---

[91] Quoted in C Schmitz, 'Serial Killer Gets $6,000 for Pain and Suffering' *The Lawyer's Weekly* (Ottawa, 7 November 2008).

[92] ibid.

[93] For a more detailed discussion of the meaning of vindication, see N Witzleb and R Carroll, 'The Role of Vindication in the Law of Remedies' (2009) 17 *Tort Law Review* 16.

[94] See, eg, *Merson v Cartwright* [2005] UKPC 38 and *A-G of Trinidad and Tobago v Ramanoop* [2005] UKPC 15, [2006] 1 AC 328, where the plaintiffs claimed damages for breaches of their constitutional rights in situations where they were mistreated and physically abused by police. In the former case, Lord Scott explained, 'The purpose [of the award] is to vindicate the right of the complainant, whether a citizen or a visitor, to carry on his or her life in the Bahamas free from unjustified executive interference, mistreatment or oppression': at [18].

the law itself. In *Kuddus v Chief Constable of Leicestershire Constabulary*, Lord Hutton acknowledged that exemplary damages for the arbitrary use of government power can serve a valid vindicatory purpose: 'the power to award exemplary damages in such cases serves to uphold and vindicate the rule of law because it makes clear that the courts will not tolerate such conduct.'[95] In this way, the tort of misfeasance also serves to vindicate the public interest by censuring public officials who abuse or exceed their powers. As Rand J explained in *Roncarelli*, the denial of a remedy for abuse of power 'would signalize the beginning of disintegration of the rule of law as a fundamental postulate of our constitutional structure.'[96] Thus, the ability to vindicate the rule of law may help to justify the anomalous existence of misfeasance in a public office, particularly given its position as a hybrid of public and private law.

However, a second, and perhaps more difficult problem with a vindicatory justification of the misfeasance tort is that it seems to contradict the requirement that the plaintiff suffer material damage. As indicated, misfeasance in a public office descends from the action on the case, and is not actionable per se.[97] This was affirmed in *Watkins v Secretary of State for the Home Department*,[98] where the claimant inmate unsuccessfully claimed in misfeasance after prison officers wrongly opened and read his private legal correspondence. Although the claimant had a right to confidential communication with his lawyers, his claim failed because he could not establish material damage. As Lord Bingham reasoned, while there 'is an obvious public interest in bringing public servants guilty of outrageous conduct to book ... the primary role of the law of tort is to provide monetary compensation for those who have suffered material damage rather than to vindicate the rights of those who have not.'[99] This seems a rather clear indication that vindication cannot be the sole justification for the existence of the misfeasance tort.

Finally, the vindicatory function of misfeasance in a public office is undermined by its partnership with administrative law, which is better situated to offer pure vindication to plaintiffs. As described above, the traditional pattern of litigation is for plaintiffs to bring administrative proceedings to vindicate their rights or the obligations of public officers. By obtaining mandamus or a declaration, the plaintiff receives official

---

[95] *Kuddus v Chief Constable of Leicestershire Constabulary* [2001] UKHL 29, [2002] 2 AC 122 (*Kuddus*) [79].

[96] *Roncarelli* [1959] SCR 121, 142.

[97] That said, it is not entirely clear what 'material damage' was suffered by the plaintiff in *Ashby* (1703) 3 Ld Raym 320, 92 ER 710. Lord Bingham suggested in *Watkins v Secretary of State for the Home Department* [2006] UKHL 17, [2006] 2 AC 395 (*Watkins*) [14] that, since the right to vote was essentially a property right, the action in *Ashby* was more closely akin to trespass, which is actionable per se.

[98] *Watkins* [2006] UKHL 17, [2006] 2 AC 395.

[99] ibid, at [8]–[9].

confirmation that the public officer must act in a certain way. The plaintiff's claim for misfeasance in a public office is therefore not necessary to vindicate the plaintiff's rights, and instead serves the separate function of compensating the plaintiff for his or her losses.

These conceptual difficulties suggest that, while vindication may provide significant psychological motivation for plaintiffs to bring misfeasance actions, and while exemplary damages may be available to provide a degree of vindication to plaintiffs and the general public, the existence of the misfeasance tort cannot be justified solely on account of its vindicatory purposes. Such a justification is plainly inconsistent with the primary elements and structure of the tort.

C. Deterrence

Perhaps the strongest justification for the existence of misfeasance in a public office lies in its deterrent function. This function can be traced back to the origins of the tort in *Ashby*, where Holt CJ said that '[i]f publick officers will infringe mens rights, they ought to pay greater damages than other men, to deter and hinder other officers from the like offences.'[100] It seems safe to assume that abuse of power and deliberate unlawfulness ought to be discouraged among public officers. Indeed, as Holt CJ's statement suggests, the need for deterrence is sufficiently strong to warrant 'greater damages' than would normally be available.

Holt CJ's suggestion has been endorsed in recent years. In *Kuddus*, misfeasance in a public office was accepted as an appropriate cause of action for which to award exemplary damages. Lord Hutton, explaining the imposition of exemplary awards in cases involving abusive conduct by military or prison officers, commented that they serve 'to deter such actions in future as such awards will bring home to officers in command of individual units that discipline must be maintained at all times.'[101] The decision in *Kuddus* centred almost exclusively on the appropriate interpretation of *Rookes v Barnard*,[102] wherein Lord Devlin set out the limited categories of cases in which exemplary damages would be available. The first category is 'oppressive, arbitrary or unconstitutional actions by the servants of the government.'[103] Exemplary damages are available in these circumstances because 'the servants of the government are also the servants of the people and the use of their power must always be subordinate to their duty of service.'[104]

---

[100] *Ashby* (1703) 2 Ld Raym 938, 956; 92 ER 126, 138.
[101] *Kuddus* [2001] UKHL 29, [2002] 2 AC 122 [79].
[102] *Rookes v Barnard* [1964] 1 AC 1129 (HL).
[103] ibid, at 1226.
[104] ibid.

Lord Devlin's point is crucial to the argument that the misfeasance tort is justifiable in spite of any inconsistencies with the rights-based approach. Exemplary damages themselves pose difficulties in terms of correlativity, because they focus on the need to punish or deter the defendant, and do not explain why the plaintiff should be the beneficiary of the additional damages award.[105] Their availability in misfeasance actions, however, is necessary to express a sense of public outrage at the misuse of the powers that were granted to the official to exercise in the public interest. The need for correlativity between plaintiff and defendant is therefore diminished: the plaintiff simply represents the public interest in deterring the official from misusing his or her powers in the future. This unique public dimension of the misfeasance tort may help to justify any departures from strict correlativity.

Of course, it could be argued that deterrence through private law channels is not necessary because public officials are already subject to other legal processes, such as judicial review, disciplinary procedures, or even the ballot box, which should adequately deter them from abusing their powers or otherwise acting unlawfully. While these alternative procedures are undoubtedly available, experience dictates that they are often insufficient at curbing abuse of power. Electoral processes, by their very nature, are unlikely to deter public officials from abusing individuals; indeed, if the individual happens to be unpopular, the public official could even benefit from abusing his or her powers in such a way that the individual's interests are sacrificed for the good of the majority. For example, in *Roncarelli*,[106] the largely Roman Catholic population of Québec may well have supported the Premier's treatment of the Jehovah's Witnesses. In any event, recourse through electoral processes is likely to be fickle and indirect, and is unlikely to deter public officers in any meaningful way.

Finally, it may be worthwhile to compare the deterrent function of misfeasance in a public office to the strict rules that operate against fiduciaries. In cases where fiduciaries have committed wrongs, such as violating the no-conflicts rule, gain-based remedies may be awarded. These remedies are problematic in terms of corrective justice,[107] because they are not dependent on any corresponding loss to the plaintiff.[108] In many cases, for example, the defendant's gains may have come from a third party or been the result of the defendant's skill and expertise.[109] Instead, it seems

---

[105] But see Stevens, above n 4, at 85–87.

[106] *Roncarelli* [1959] SCR 121.

[107] See generally EJ Weinrib, 'Restitutionary Damages as Corrective Justice' (2000) 1 *Theoretical Inquiries in Law* 1.

[108] Unlike subtractive unjust enrichment, where the defendant's gain equals the plaintiff's loss: see A Duggan, 'Gains-Based Remedies and the Place of Deterrence in the Law of Fiduciary Obligations' in A Robertson and HW Tang (eds), *The Goals of Private Law* (Oxford, Hart Publishing, 2009) 365, 365–66.

[109] See, eg, *Boardman v Phipps* [1967] 2 AC 46 (HL).

that the gain-based remedies awarded in these cases serve to strip the defaulting fiduciary of any gains that were acquired by his or her wrong-doing, on the idea that a fiduciary should not be permitted to profit from a wrong, and with the goal of deterring future wrongful behaviour.[110] As a majority of the Supreme Court of Canada recently explained, stripping the fiduciary of his or her profits 'teaches faithless fiduciaries that con-flicts of interest do not pay. The *prophylactic* purpose thereby advances the policy of equity, even at the expense of a windfall to the wronged beneficiary.'[111]

A useful analogy can be drawn between fiduciaries and public officials. Both are entrusted with fairly substantial powers, which they are expected to use in the best interests of their beneficiaries or the public, respectively. Given the natural temptation to misuse these powers, it is important to have meaningful consequences for any abuse. The law protects the integrity of both the fiduciary relationship and the rule of law by imposing penalties that are sufficiently severe to deter future misuse of power. Of course, a key difference between these relationships is that the consequences of the strict rules are much more likely to be felt by defaulting fiduciaries than by public officers. In misfeasance actions, damages are typically paid not by the public officer, but out of the general state coffers. This seriously undermines the deterrent effect of the misfeasance tort.[112] Still, to the extent that such remedies will motivate public authorities to discipline individuals or enact policies to minimise future misuse of power, the deterrent function of the misfeasance tort may still hold force.

IV. CONCLUSION

The above analysis was intended to show that misfeasance in a public office is not as much of a misfit in tort law as has sometimes been pos-tulated. It can quite plausibly be reconciled with rights-based approaches, and is no less anomalous than the tort of negligence, with which it shares its fundamental structure. But even if misfeasance is inconsistent with the rights-based approach, its utility should not be dismissed. As consultees to the Law Commission's Consultation Paper, *Administrative Redress: Public Bodies and the Citizen* have suggested, misfeasance in a public office serves a vital role in denouncing misconduct by public officials and deterring mis-

---

[110] See *A-G of Hong Kong v Reid* [1994] 1 AC 324 (PC).

[111] *Strother v 3469420 Canada Inc* [2007] SCC 24, [2007] 2 SCR 177 [77] (Binnie J for Binnie, Deschamps, Fish, Charron and Rothstein JJ) (emphasis in original). Bruce Feldthusen has argued that punitive damages may be justifiable in such cases, in addition to disgorge-ment of profits: 'merely stripping the profit from deliberate wrongdoing is arguably not punitive at all' (B Feldthusen, 'Punitive Damages: Hard Choices and High Stakes' [1998] *New Zealand Law Review* 741, 763).

[112] See Feldthusen, 'Punitive Damages', above n 111, at 761.

uses of power.[113] These goals are sufficiently important in modern society that the idiosyncrasies of the misfeasance tort ought to be forgiven. Indeed, it is a tort that underscores the argument that rights-based approaches simply do not provide the entire explanation of tort law.

[113] See Law Commission, *Final Report*, above n 6, at paras 3.66–3.67, 3.69.

20

Unjust Enrichment, Rights and Value

BEN McFARLANE*

I. INTRODUCTION

T HE PURPOSE OF this chapter is to consider how the distinction between rights and other benefits may play a role in defining whether a defendant (D) has been unjustly enriched at the expense of a claimant (C). Robert Chambers has recently drawn attention to the distinction within the law of unjust enrichment between cases involving the receipt of rights and those involving the receipt of other forms of value.[1] On Chambers' approach, the general structure of liability developed by Peter Birks in *Unjust Enrichment*[2] can be applied equally to each category of case: rights and value are two different ways of showing enrichment and, once such enrichment has been established, the same, general model of unjust enrichment liability may apply. The model proposed in this chapter adopts the distinction between the two categories of cases, but gives that distinction a deeper significance. It will be argued that the reasons for, and hence the nature of, D's liability differs between the two categories of cases: it is only in the rights-based cases that D's liability has the strict, unilateral form applying in the core case where D is the innocent recipient of a mistaken payment. It will thus be argued that the distinction highlighted by Chambers undermines his contention that each of the two sets of cases can each be seen as applications of a wider, unified law of unjust enrichment. Indeed, there are strong arguments against

* I am grateful to Lionel Smith and Peter Watts for comments on a draft of this chapter, and to Helen Scott for assistance during a visit to the University of Cape Town in June 2010. The usual disclaimers apply.

[1] R Chambers, 'Two Kinds of Enrichment' in R Chambers, C Mitchell and J Penner (eds), *Philosophical Foundations of the Law of Unjust Enrichment* (Oxford, Oxford University Press, 2009) 242.

[2] P Birks, *Unjust Enrichment*, 2nd edn (Oxford, Oxford University Press, 2005).

using the term 'unjust enrichment' to refer to the strict liability principle operating in the rights-based cases.

II. THE CORE CASE

In *Unjust Enrichment*, Birks sets out to prove the existence, and determine the scope, of an independent principle of liability: an elementary (in the sense that it cannot be reduced or explained by reference to any other simpler principle) reason for which it can be recognised that D has come under a duty to C. To achieve these goals, Birks adopts a very clear strategy: to identify, and determine the scope of, the principle justifying the duty of an innocent recipient to return the value of a unilaterally mistaken payment.[3] This 'core case' is used as, literally, the prime example of a duty dependent on, and thus proving the existence of, the law's recognition of what this chapter will call an independent 'liability principle' based on D's unjust enrichment at C's expense.

The selection of such a starting point has been queried. As Kit Barker has noted, if one is attempting to survey all legal rules relating to the recovery of gains made by D at C's expense, it may seem more natural to begin with a case in which D bears some causal responsibility for the gain, as opposed to a case in which C's mistake is unilateral.[4] The mistaken payment example is, however, central for Birks. A crucial contention of *Unjust Enrichment* is that the scope of the independent liability principle does not include all legal rules having the *effect* of reversing a gain made by D at C's expense;[5] the same response (giving up of a gain) may be justified by different liability principles.[6] The focus on the mistaken payment case is therefore motivated by a desire to locate a case in which the gain-based liability cannot be seen as dependent on, for example, the commission of a wrong, or the entry into a contract.[7]

The strategy adopted by Birks is therefore accepted in this chapter,

---

[3] See ibid, at ch 1.

[4] See K Barker, 'Responsibility for Gain: Unjust Factors or Absence of Legal Ground? Starting Points in Unjust Enrichment Law' in C Rickett and R Grantham (eds), *Structure and Justification in Private Law: Essays for Peter Birks* (Oxford, Hart Publishing, 2009) 47; K Barker, 'The Nature of Responsibility for Gain: Gain, Harm and Keeping the Lid on Pandora's Box' in R Chambers, C Mitchell and J Penner (eds), *Philosophical Foundations of the Law of Unjust Enrichment* (Oxford, Oxford University Press, 2009) 146, 173.

[5] Of course, this view was adopted by Birks long before the publication in 2003 of the first edition of *Unjust Enrichment*: see, eg, P Birks, 'Misnomer' in WR Cornish et al (eds), *Restitution: Past, Present and Future: Essays in Honour of Gareth Jones* (Oxford, Hart Publishing, 1998) 1.

[6] For example, Robert Stevens has noted that D may be under a contractual duty to return a gain made at C's expense: see R Stevens, 'Is There a Law of Unjust Enrichment?' in S Degeling and J Edelman (eds), *Unjust Enrichment in Commercial Law* (Sydney, Lawbook, 2008) 11, 15.

[7] This point is noted by, eg, P Saprai, 'Restitution without Corrective Justice' [2006] *Restitution Law Review* 41, 42–44.

which seeks to determine the nature and scope of the liability principle exemplified by the case of a unilateral mistaken payment. There is a caveat, however: the label 'unjust enrichment' should not immediately be given to that liability principle. Whilst it provides a useful shorthand, it may be premature to assume that it is the most accurate label for the principle under investigation. This is a point which will be returned to in the conclusion of this chapter.

III. GENERALISING FROM THE CORE CASE: BIRKS' APPROACH

Example A1: *C, mistakenly believing that he owes D £50, gives D a £50 note.*

This is the core case of a mistaken payment. Birks identifies the liability principle at play as depending on D's having received and retained a benefit, at the expense of C, in circumstances where there is no basis for D to retain the value of that benefit. Having used the core case to identify an independent liability principle, Birks thus makes three generalisations in determining the scope of that principle.[8] First, the generalisation from D's receipt and retention of money to D's receipt and retention of abstract enrichment, where enrichment is an acquisition measurable in money. As a result, it may be possible for the liability principle to apply, for example, in a case where D mistakenly provides building services for C.[9] Secondly, the generalisation from a transfer by C to a receipt at the expense of C. This means the liability principle may extend, for example, to a case where D receives a benefit which was legally due to, or factually intended for, C: it may thus apply where D makes use of C's property without C's consent.[10] Thirdly, a generalisation from mistakes to other cases where there is no basis for D's retention of an enrichment. This means, for example, that the liability principle may be triggered in a case where C contests the validity of an unlawful tax demand made by D, but nonetheless makes the requested payment.[11]

The extent of these generalisations can be questioned. For example, the focus on the surviving enrichment of D seems inconsistent with the fact that, in Example A1, D's liability arises on receipt of the £50 note;[12] it also adopts a particular, and rather narrow, view of the change of posi-

---

[8] Birks, *Unjust Enrichment*, above n 2, at 9–10.

[9] See, eg, *Pavey & Matthews Pty Ltd v Paul* (1987) 162 CLR 221.

[10] The principle can therefore explain the liability, discussed by Lord Mansfield in *Hambly v Trott* (1776) 1 Cowp 371, 98 ER 1136, to pay a reasonable fee for unauthorised use of another's goods: see the discussion below of Example B3 in part V below.

[11] The principle can therefore explain the liability recognised in *Woolwich Equitable Building Society v Inland Revenue Commissioners* [1993] 1 AC 70 (HL).

[12] See, eg, *Baker v Courage & Co* [1910] 1 KB 56 (KB); *Maskell v Horner* [1915] 3 KB 106 (CA).

tion defence, one that has been persuasively challenged by, for example, Lionel Smith,[13] Ernest Weinrib[14] and Elise Bant.[15] The preference for an 'absence of basis' analysis has attracted still more dissent.[16] The fundamental concern for this chapter, however, is the first generalisation: from D's receipt of money to all cases in which D receives an enrichment measurable by money.

IV. GENERALISING FROM THE CORE CASE: A DIFFERENT APPROACH

On the model proposed in this chapter, the application of the liability principle applying in Example A1 does not depend on D's acquisition of an enrichment measurable by money. Rather, it is founded on the fact that the same event (C's payment) has led both to the loss of a right by C and the acquisition of a right by D.

Example A2: *As a result of a misrepresentation by D, C makes a contract to transfer his title to a car to D for £500. After the sale is completed, and title is transferred to D, C discovers the misrepresentation.*

In such a case, even if £500 is a perfectly fair price for the car, C has a power to rescind the contract and to recover his title to the car. As Peter Watts has noted,[17] this point suggests that the liability principle permitting C to recover his title is not based on the broader question of whether D has, in a general sense, gained from the impugned transaction. A model focused on D's acquisition of an enrichment measurable by money may therefore suggest that the liability principle operating in Example A1 does not operate in Example A2. In contrast, a rights-based model illustrates the underlying similarity of the two examples: in each case, a right has been transferred from C to D.

Chambers relies on cases such as Example A2 to make a different point: liability based on unjust enrichment may arise if D acquires *either* value (as in Example A1) *or* a right (as in Example A2). Further, as Chambers notes, the question of value seems to be irrelevant in the second class of

---

[13] L Smith, 'Restitution: The Heart of Corrective Justice' (2001) 79 *Texas Law Review* 2114.

[14] EJ Weinrib, 'Correctively Unjust Enrichment' in R Chambers, C Mitchell and J Penner (eds), *Philosophical Foundations of the Law of Unjust Enrichment* (Oxford, Oxford University Press, 2009) 31.

[15] E Bant, *The Change of Position Defence* (Oxford, Hart Publishing, 2009).

[16] See, eg, Barker, 'Starting Points in Unjust Enrichment Law', above n 4; A Burrows, 'Absence of Basis: The New Birksian Scheme' in A Burrows and Lord Rodger (eds), *Mapping the Law: Essays in Memory of Peter Birks* (Oxford, Oxford University Press, 2007) 33.

[17] P Watts, 'Restitution—A Property Principle and a Services Principle' [1995] *Restitution Law Review* 49, 49.

case:[18] where D has acquired a right, it is no defence for D to say that he attaches no value to that right, or that D has made no overall gain through its acquisition. Given this, however, it is not immediately obvious why the liability principle operating in the second class of case should be said to depend on any enrichment of D. It is artificial to say that D is enriched, even though D has made no overall gain. If the general liability principle requires a net enrichment of D, then that principle cannot apply where, as in Example A2, C has received a right of equivalent value to the right he has lost. One solution[19] to this problem is to recognise that the distinction between rights and value is not in fact a distinction between two different types of enrichment, each potentially triggering the same form of liability in unjust enrichment, but is rather a distinction between two different liability regimes. On this view, the liability principle applying in Examples A1 and A2, where the impugned transaction involves both the loss of a right by C, and the gain of a right by D, need not depend on D's having made a net gain at C's expense.

Example A3: *C owns a car and holds its valuable registration mark. C instructs auctioneers to sell the car but to retain the mark. D purchases the car from the auctioneers. When selling the car, the auctioneers make clear that the right to the mark is not for sale. The auctioneers, however, fail to comply with the statutory procedure required for retention of the mark. As a result, D is entitled to the mark and successfully applies to be registered as its holder.*

The facts of this example are taken from *Cressman v Coys of Kensington (Sales) Ltd.*[20] Having settled with C, the auctioneers took an assignment of C's rights against D and claimed that D had been unjustly enriched at C's expense. D resisted an unjust enrichment claim by arguing that, as he had acquired the mark consistently with the relevant statutory scheme, his acquisition of it could not be seen as unjust; he also argued that the mark, whilst objectively valuable, was of no benefit to him as he was indifferent to his holding of it and had not profited from it financially. He claimed to have in fact transferred the car, for free, to his partner, without retaining the right to the mark—this gave rise to D's third argument, that if there had been any initial unjust enrichment, he had since changed his position.

The first argument was quickly dealt with by the Court of Appeal. Mance LJ noted that the operation of the statutory scheme was in fact

---

[18] Chambers, above n 1, at 252–54.

[19] Bant notes this difficulty with Chambers' analysis in E Bant, 'Rights and Value in Rescission: Some Implications for Unjust Enrichment' ch 21 of this book. Bant suggests a different solution, consistent with a case such as Example A2 falling within a wider principle of unjust enrichment that does not require a net enrichment of D.

[20] *Cressman v Coys of Kensington (Sales) Ltd* [2004] EWCA Civ 47, [2004] 1 WLR 2775 (*Cressman*).

necessary for there to be any enrichment of D.[21] In dealing with the second argument, Mance LJ considered academic approaches to the question of enrichment, and the meaning of concepts such as free acceptance and incontrovertible benefit. Those concepts are used as means of generalising from the core case of receipt of money to cases involving the receipt of benefits equivalent to money. His Lordship's conclusion was that D had received an incontrovertible benefit, and that the case demonstrated the need for the law to 'recognise as a distinct category of enrichment cases of readily returnable benefit'.[22] Finally, it was held that no change of position defence was available as D knew throughout that the right to the mark was not intended by C to pass to him.

The result of the case is consistent with both the model proposed here and Birks' analysis: the route to that result is, however, different. On Birks' model, the imposition of liability in unjust enrichment depends on D's having received (and still holding) a subjective benefit, equivalent to money. In a case such as *Cressman*, then, C has to show why D can be liable for the value of a benefit that D no longer holds nor claims to subjectively value. On the model suggested here, in contrast, the liability principle exemplified by the core mistaken payment case can apply as the same event (D's registration as holder of the mark) has caused both a legal gain to D (the acquisition of the legal right to the mark) and a legal loss to C (the loss of the legal right to the mark). There is no need to show a subjective benefit to D: liability arises (subject of course to defences such as the change of position defence) simply because of C's lack of consent to a transaction causing C to lose a right and D to gain a right.

The model suggested here thus leads more directly to the result in *Cressman*: such a case falls squarely within the generalisation of the mistaken payment case. It is true that the reasoning of Mance LJ, in particular its detailed discussion of subjective devaluation and incontrovertible benefit, appears to fit more closely with Birks' model. It is, however, important to note that his Lordship prefaced that detailed discussion by noting that

> the parties' submissions failed generally to give due weight to the fact that the academic debate in the passages cited about 'free acceptance' and 'indisputable benefit' relates primarily to situations (typically the supply of services) where any benefit is not readily returnable.[23]

The model proposed here avoids that danger, by distinguishing between, on the one hand, cases where C suffers a legal loss and D makes a legal gain and, on the other, cases (such as those involving the supply of services) where the parties' gains and losses are, instead, merely factual. In the first class of cases, which includes *Cressman*, the question of whether

---

[21] ibid, at [24].
[22] ibid, at [40].
[23] ibid, at [27].

D has made a factual gain is irrelevant when considering D's prima facie liability.

Example B1: *X holds a bank account on trust for C. X, acting in breach of trust, pays £500 to D. D spends the money on his monthly grocery shopping. D first becomes aware of the breach of trust only after the groceries have been consumed.*

On Birks' approach, such a case falls within the logic of Example A1: D has received, and retained, the benefit of money; that enrichment has been acquired at the expense of C, who was entitled to its benefit; and there is no basis entitling D to retain that benefit. It is, however, clear that, in such a case, the law does not currently impose the strict liability recognised in Example A1.[24] Rather, the beneficiary's ability to bring a claim against a recipient of trust assets depends on establishing the recipient's knowledge of the breach of trust at a point when the recipient still held either the right received, or a right counting as a traceable product of that right.[25] There is thus no strict liability claim against the recipient.

It has been argued that the law on this point should be changed.[26] The current state of the law is, however, perfectly explicable if we focus not on the *value* received by D, which can indeed be seen as acquired at the expense of C, but rather on the *right* received by D. For the right acquired by D was formerly held by X, the trustee, not by C. A trust exists because, whilst X holds the right, he is under a duty to C to use that right for C's benefit, not for X's own benefit. The existence of the trust does not, however, alter the fact that the right itself belongs to X: indeed, that is an essential feature of the trust in common law jurisdictions.[27] The absence of a strict liability claim for C against D in Example B1 is compatible with a focus on rights not as an alternative to value, but rather on rights as distinct from value: whilst the value gained by D may have come from C, the *right* acquired by D came from X, not from C. As a result, Example B1 falls outside the principle applied in the core mistaken payment case.

---

[24] See, eg, *Re Montagu's Settlement Trusts* [1987] Ch 264 (Ch); *Bank of Credit and Commerce International (Overseas) Ltd v Akindele* [2001] Ch 437 (CA); *Farah Constructions Pty Ltd v Say-Dee Pty Ltd* [2007] HCA 22, (2007) 230 CLR 89.

[25] Assuming, of course, that D cannot be shown to have dishonestly assisted in X's breach of trust, in which case liability may arise under the so-called 'second limb' of *Barnes v Addy* (1874) LR 9 Ch App 244 (CA).

[26] See, eg, Lord Nicholls, 'Knowing Receipt: The Need for a New Landmark' in WR Cornish et al (eds), *Restitution: Past, Present and Future: Essays in Honour of Gareth Jones* (Oxford, Hart Publishing, 1998) 231.

[27] There are some trust-like structures that do not require the party equivalent to the trustee to hold the subject matter, as it suffices that the trustee has control of that right: the South African *bewind* and Quebecois *fiducie* are examples. See, eg, T Honoré, 'Trusts: The Inessentials' in J Getzler (ed), *Rationalizing Property, Equity and Trusts: Essays in Honour of Edward Burn* (London, LexisNexis, 2003) 7. Such structures fall within the scope of the Hague Convention on the Law Applicable to Trusts and their Recognition, art 2.

Example B2: *C, mistakenly believing that he has a right in particular land, builds on that land. D holds a freehold title to the land.*

On a rights-based analysis, Example B2 also lies outside the model of the core mistaken payment case. First, to the extent that C has spent time and effort in building, C has not thereby lost any right. Secondly, to the extent that C has bought and used building materials, C has lost his right to those materials; but D has not thereby acquired a new right. Anything built by C accedes to D's freehold: as a result, the value of D's freehold may increase, but D acquires no new right.

The fact that a distinction can be made between Example A1 and Example B2 does not, of course, mean that such a distinction should be made. First, however, the law does already make such a distinction. The crucial point is that, in Example B2, C cannot rely on the simple, *unilateral* liability principle available in Example A1.[28] It is clear that, in Example B2, D does not come under a duty to C simply because of D's acquisition of a gain as a result of C's mistake. Some commentators, noting this point, have argued that the liability principle operating in Examples A1 and A2 *should* be applied in a case such as Example B2.[29] The rights-based explanation of Examples A1 and A2, proposed in this chapter, can instead justify the law's current refusal to impose a strict liability on D in a case such as Example B2.

As the law stands, it is necessary for C, in a case such as Example B2, to show that D has some form of responsibility for C's error: D must have created or encouraged a belief in C that C did, or would, have a right in the land; or, at least, that C would receive some reward for his work.[30] It may be that D can come under a duty even without making an express commitment to C: this may occur, for example, if D, knowing of C's belief, simply stands by and fails to correct C's error. In any case, however, liability can only arise if D can bear at least some responsibility for C's decision to spend his time and effort in building: the simple, unilateral model of the core mistaken payment case does not apply.

The absence of liability in a case such as Example B2 is consistent

---

[28] See, eg, *Brand v Chris Building Co Pty Ltd* [1957] VR 625; *Blue Haven Enterprises Ltd v Tully* [2006] UKPC 17 (*Blue Haven*). For an examination of the relevant authorities, see S Degeling and B Edgeworth, 'Improvements to Land Belonging to Another' in LB Moses, B Edgeworth and C Sherry (eds), *Property and Security: Selected Essays* (Sydney, Lawbook, 2010) 277.

[29] See, eg, K Low, 'Unjust Enrichment and Proprietary Estoppel: Two Sides of the Same Coin' [2007] *Lloyd's Maritime and Commercial Law Quarterly* 14, 18; HW Tang, 'An Unjust Enrichment Claim for the Mistaken Improver of Land' [2011] *Conveyancer and Property Lawyer* 8. Degeling and Edgeworth, above n 28, argue in favour of statutory schemes (such as those operating in some Australian jurisdictions) allowing a judge to impose liability on D in certain cases of mistaken improvement; they do not however recommend a direct application of the liability principle operating in Example A1.

[30] See, eg, *Cobbe v Yeoman's Row Management Ltd* [2008] UKHL 55, [2008] 1 WLR 1752.

with Birks' analysis of unjust enrichment, if it is accepted that D can deny that he has benefited from C's work. In distinguishing between the practical effects of Birks' model and that proposed here, therefore, the critical case is one which lies outside the rights-based generalisation of Example A1, but in which D cannot deny that he has benefited from C's work. For example, it may be said that D is 'incontrovertibly benefited' if C can show that the work done on D's land was work which D, in any case, intended to procure at his own expense. As we know that, in such a case, the law does *not* impose a strict liability on D, this is powerful evidence that the law adheres to the rights-based model proposed here, rather than the wider conception of enrichment proposed by Birks. An example is provided by *Blue Haven Enterprises Ltd v Tully*.[31] C established a coffee plantation on D's land, mistakenly believing that C had the best title to that land. Lord Scott, giving the decision of the Privy Council, noted that, as D himself had bought the land in order to develop it as a coffee plantation,

> there is no doubt whatever that [D] has been enriched at [C's] expense. ... The critical question is not whether [D] has been enriched at [C]'s expense but whether the circumstances in which that enrichment came about place [D] under an equitable obligation to compensate [C] accordingly.[32]

In answering that critical question, Lord Scott turned to the law of proprietary estoppel, which requires some 'acquiescence or encouragement or other species of representation by [D]'.[33] This approach is consistent with the model proposed in this chapter: as there has been no event involving both a loss of a right by C and the gain of a right by D, the unilateral liability model of the mistaken payment case cannot apply. Rather, it is necessary for C to show that D has some form of responsibility for C's error: D must have created or encouraged a belief in C that C did, or would, have a right in the land; or, at least that C would receive some reward for his work. The approach of the Privy Council in *Blue Haven*, followed by Judge Kirkham in *JS Bloor Ltd v Pavillion Developments Ltd*,[34] thus provides support for the rights-based model proposed in this chapter.

It is true that in *Blue Haven*, counsel for D, in the words of Lord Scott,

> did not attempt to extend the established jurisprudence. He accepted that for his client to succeed it was necessary to show that [D] had done something, or had just stood by, in circumstances where his actions, or inaction, would

---

[31] *Blue Haven* [2006] UKPC 17.

[32] ibid, at [20].

[33] ibid, at [24].

[34] *JS Bloor Ltd v Pavillion Developments Ltd* [2008] EWHC 724 (TCC), [2008] 2 EGLR 85.

make it unconscionable for him to refuse to re-imburse [C] for the cost of the development.[35]

There is nothing in the decision of the Privy Council, however, to suggest that such an attempt to develop the existing law would have been successful. Indeed, if the simple unilateral liability model could apply in such a case, it would not so much develop the established law as remove its current foundation: the insistence that D's liability depends on D, by his own conduct, bearing some responsibility for C's mistaken belief.

V. THE SCOPE OF THE RIGHTS-BASED GENERALISATION

On the approach taken in this chapter, then, the liability principle exemplified by the core mistaken payment case is significantly narrower in scope than the unjust enrichment principle identified by Birks. The principle does, however, extend beyond the simple case of a transfer of a right from C to D.

Example A4: C, *mistakenly believing that he owes D £50, electronically transfers £50 from C's account at X Bank to D's account at Y Bank.*

In such a case,[36] there is no direct transfer of a right from C to D. The mistaken payment instead consists in the creation a credit to D's account and a correlative debit to C's account. There is no difficulty, however, in extending the logic of Example A1 to this case. In each case, a particular event has both removed a right of C and given D a new right. In Example A1, C's mistake did not prevent the transfer of C's right to D; in Example A4, C's mistake similarly does not imperil the validity of the debit to C's account, and of the credit to D's account. If either (or each) of C and D's account is overdrawn, the logic of Example A1 can again apply. The crucial point is that the event in question involves both: (i) the loss of a right to C *or* the imposition of a duty on C; *and* (ii) the acquisition of a right by D *or* the loss of a duty owed by D.

Example A5: C, *mistakenly believing he is under a duty to do so, pays £5000 to X, thereby discharging a debt owed by D to X. D's debt to X was secured by a charge over D's land.*

As in the case of a payment into D's overdrawn account, C's discharge of a debt owed by D falls within the unilateral liability principle, as D's legal duty has been discharged.[37] Where, as in Example A5, C's payment also causes the release of a security interest, the law generally allows

---

[35] *Blue Haven* [2006] UKPC 17 [25].

[36] See, eg, *Australia and New Zealand Banking Group Ltd v Westpac Banking Corp* (1988) 164 CLR 662.

[37] See, eg, *Exall v Partridge* (1799) 8 TR 308, 101 ER 1405.

that security interest to revive for the benefit of C.[38] This result can be defended on the basis that the event of C's payment has caused not only the discharge of the debt, but also the removal of the security interest. As a result, D has not only lost a duty; he has also lost, in Hohfeldian terms, a liability. It is that loss of a legal liability that distinguishes the removal of a security interest from other cases (such as Example B2) in which D's benefit consists only in an increase to the value of a pre-existing right of D.

In the same way, if Z has a security interest in D's asset, ranked lower than X's security interest, then the release of X's security interest by means of C's payment also involves the release of a liability of Z. Consistently with the approach of the House of Lords in *Banque Financière de la Cité SA v Parc (Battersea) Ltd*,[39] the liability principle applying in a case such as Example A1 can, therefore, also explain why the prejudice caused to Z does not prevent the revival of X's security interest in C's favour. It is important to note, however, that on the model put forward in this chapter, that liability principle cannot be said to mean that, with the removal of X's security right, *all* creditors of D are similarly enriched at C's expense.[40] It is true that any such creditor can be said to gain, in a general, factual sense, from the removal of the security interest. The difference, however, is that there is no specific *legal* gain to an unsecured creditor of D in such a case: both before and after C's payment, an unsecured creditor has a right potentially exercisable in relation to whatever unencumbered assets D may hold.

Example A6: *D usurps an office held by C. As a result, D receives a payment of £50 from X.*

In this case, C has made no payment. If, however, X's payment to D discharges X's duty to pay that sum to C, then the case falls within the logic of Example A1:[41] a particular event has caused both the loss of a right held by C and the gain of a right by D. This analysis only holds, of course, if X's payment *does* operate to discharge X's duty to C. As Smith has convincingly shown, it is the discharge of X's duty, and hence C's loss of a right, which provides the unifying feature of those three-party cases in which D is liable to C.[42] In *An Introduction to the Law of Restitution*, Birks argued instead for a wider principle of 'interceptive subtraction', where a claim may arise if 'the wealth in question would certainly have arrived in [C] if it had not been intercepted by [D] *en*

---

[38] See, eg, *Butler v Rice* [1910] 2 Ch 277 (Ch).

[39] *Banque Financière de la Cité SA v Parc (Battersea) Ltd* [1999] 1 AC 221 (HL).

[40] For the contrary view, see C Mitchell and S Watterson, *Subrogation: Law and Practice* (Oxford, Oxford University Press, 2007) 35–44.

[41] See, eg, *Arris v Stukely* (1677) 2 Mod 260, 86 ER 1060.

[42] See L Smith, 'Three-Party Restitution: A Critique of Birks' Theory of Interceptive Subtraction' (1991) 11 *Oxford Journal of Legal Studies* 481.

route from the third party'.[43] A focus on the legal rights of the parties, as opposed to the wider factual question of benefit, provides a narrower principle which, as Smith has shown, can be used to explain cases of usurpation of office, of unauthorised receipt of rents,[44] and of rights acquired by an unauthorised personal representative.[45]

It can also be argued that there is a further case in which X's payment to D can involve an unjust enrichment of D at C's expense: where X's payment leaves X impecunious and therefore *factually* unable to meet a duty owed to C.[46] This analysis is based on *Re Diplock*,[47] in which executors, under a provision of a will later determined to be void, paid money to charities. The argument certainly explains one of the unusual features of the claim recognised in that case: the next of kin of the deceased (to whom the money paid to the charities should properly have been paid) had a strict liability personal claim against the charities, but the claim was limited to that part of the sum due which the next of kin were unable to recover from the executors.[48] On the model proposed in this chapter, however, there is a deeper problem with the result in *Re Diplock*: if C has neither lost a right, nor acquired a duty or liability, then the mere fact that C has been *factually* impoverished should not be enough to trigger the unilateral liability principle underlying the core mistaken payment case. On this view, the strict liability imposed in *Re Diplock* cannot be seen as justified by the principle applying in the core mistaken payment case; it must instead depend on a narrower principle, dealing with the particular problem of incorrect distribution of estates and based on the courts' supervision of the office held by a personal representative.[49]

Example A7: *C and X agree that, in return for reimbursement from C, X will pay any debts owed by C to D. C and X mistakenly believe that C owes D £50. As a result, X pays £50 to D.*

The agreement between C and X may mean that, as a result of X's payment, C is under a duty to X. If so, the case falls within the principle of Example A1: X's payment to D has led both to D's acquisition of a

---

[43] P Birks, *An Introduction to the Law of Restitution*, rev edn (Oxford, Oxford University Press, 1989) 133–34.

[44] See, eg, *Asher v Wallis* (1707) 11 Mod 146, 88 ER 956.

[45] See, eg, *Lamine v Dorrell* (1705) 2 Ld Raym 1216, 92 ER 303.

[46] See Smith, 'Three-Party Restitution', above n 42, at 498–500.

[47] *Re Diplock* [1948] Ch 465 (CA), affd *Ministry of Health v Simpson* [1951] AC 251 (HL).

[48] *Re Diplock* [1948] Ch 465 (CA) 503–04.

[49] It is important to note that Smith no longer seeks to explain the result in *Re Diplock* as based on the principle applying in the core mistaken payment case; the position adopted in this chapter is consistent with his more recent view that *Re Diplock* must be understood by focusing on 'the policies governing the correct distribution of the estate': see L Smith, 'Unjust Enrichment, Property and the Structure of Trusts' (2000) 116 *Law Quarterly Review* 412, 441–42. This is the approach taken by Lord Goff and G Jones, *The Law of Restitution*, 7th edn (London, Sweet & Maxwell, 2007) paras 30-002–30-003.

right and to the imposition of a duty on C. Such a case may therefore fall within the liability principle applying in the mistaken payment case.[50]

Example A8: *Following an innocent misrepresentation by D, C makes a contract with D that, in a year's time, C will buy 100 barrels of oil from D at a price of $90 per barrel. A month later, C discovers the misrepresentation and rescinds the contract.*

There is a debate as to whether C's power to rescind the executory contract can properly be seen as arising as a result of the same liability principle applying in Examples A1 and A2.[51] It is clear that, as noted by, for example, Graham Virgo,[52] the exercise of the power does not effect restitution from D to C. It is equally clear that, in considering the reasons for which such a power arises, it is very difficult to distinguish such a case from one, such as Example A2, in which C acquires a power to rescind an executed contract.[53] One way to reconcile those points, suggested by Robert Stevens, is to consider the power to rescind an executory contract as based on the same liability principle as applying in Examples A1 and A2, yet not effecting restitution.[54] Smith adopts a different view, by arguing that the liability principle applied in Examples A1 and A2 extends only to cases where a duty is imposed on D. Smith instead analyses C's power as dependent on an inherent defect in D's contractual right against C: due to the misrepresentation, D's right is born subject to C's power to rescind.[55] On the model put forward in this chapter, that very feature of the power to rescind an executory contract may, on the contrary, justify placing the power within the liability principle of the core mistaken payment case.

The argument runs as follows. Where, for example, an agreement is entered into following a misrepresentation made by D to C, the legal conclusion that a contractual duty of C has been created may be justified only on the basis that C has the power to remove that duty. Similarly, in the core case of a mistaken transfer of a right, as in Example A1, D's immediate duty to pay the value of that right to C may be necessary to justify the conclusion that C's right has in fact been transferred to D. D's duty in each of Examples A1 to A8 may thus be justified at one remove: the duty is itself part of the justification for the law's conclusion that a

---

[50] See, eg, *Khan v Permayer* [2001] BPIR 95 (CA), discussed in Birks, *Unjust Enrichment*, above n 2, at 88.

[51] For a useful discussion of the debate, see A Burrows, *The Law of Restitution*, 3rd edn (Oxford, Oxford University Press, 2010) 17–21.

[52] G Virgo, *The Principles of the Law of Restitution*, 2nd edn (Oxford, Oxford University Press, 2006) 29.

[53] See, eg, Birks, *Unjust Enrichment*, above n 2, at 127.

[54] Stevens, 'Is There a Law of Unjust Enrichment?', above n 6, at 14.

[55] L Smith, 'Unjust Enrichment: Big or Small?' in S Degeling and J Edelman (eds), *Unjust Enrichment in Commercial Law* (Sydney, Lawbook, 2008) 35, 40–43.

particular event has both caused C to lose a right (or acquire a duty or liability) and has caused D to gain a right (or lose a duty or liability).

Example A9: *D, a meat supplier, innocently receives cattle stolen from C. D processes the cattle and sells the meat for £500.*

This example is based on a German case, discussed by Smith, in which C's personal claim against D succeeded.[56] The view of the Court was that, whilst D undoubtedly acquired ownership of the meat, he was also under a duty, arising in unjust enrichment, to pay the value of that meat to C. The facts of the example fall within the generalisation of the mistaken payment case as, again, a particular event (in this case, the act of turning one physical thing into a new physical thing) caused C's loss of a right and D's gain of a right. In English law, of course, C also has a claim in conversion against D. Such a claim can arise whenever D physically interferes with goods in which C has a property right. On the model proposed here, an additional claim is available because of the crucial fact that, due to the rules on specification, D's interference also caused C to lose a right, and D to acquire a right.

Example B3: *Whilst C is away on holiday, D, without permission, rides C's horse. D returns the horse safely to its stable, and the horse benefits from the exercise.*[57]

As in Example A9, D is liable in conversion for his interference with a physical thing in which C has a property right. Birks argued that such a case also falls within the liability principle applying in the core mistaken payment case. His analysis was that a form of 'interceptive subtraction' occurs in a case where D makes use of C's property without C's consent.[58] That analysis is controversial. In particular, if one accepts that D's duty to pay a reasonable use fee to C is simply a standard response to D's commission of a wrong against C, there is no need to rely on any other liability principle to explain the result in a case such as Example B3.[59] Certainly, on the model proposed in this chapter, Example B3,

---

[56] The case is set out in BS Markesinis, W Lorenz and G Dannemann, *The German Law of Obligations* (Oxford, Clarendon Press, 1997) vol 1, 786–89. Smith's discussion is in ibid, at 40 n 21. It is not clear whether the case involved hamburgers or, indeed, Hamburgers.

[57] An example given by Lord Mansfield in *Hambly v Trott* (1776) 1 Cowp 371, 98 ER 1136 and used by Lord Shaw in *Watson, Laidlaw & Co Ltd v Pott, Cassels & Williamson* [1914] SC (HL) 18 (HL) 31. The 'Earl of Halsbury's chair' (see *Owners of the Steamship Mediana v Owners, Master and Crew of the Lightship Comet (The Mediana)* [1900] AC 113 (HL) 117 (Lord Halsbury)) fulfils the same exemplary function as Lord Mansfield's horse.

[58] Birks, *Unjust Enrichment*, above n 2, at 81–82.

[59] See, eg, R Stevens, *Torts and Rights* (Oxford, Oxford University Press, 2007) ch 4, especially at 59–69. For a contrary view see A Burrows, 'Are "Damages on the *Wrotham Park* Basis" Compensatory, Restitutionary or Neither?' in D Saidov and R Cunnington (eds), *Contract Damages: Domestic and International Perspectives* (Oxford, Hart Publishing, 2008) 165.

unlike Example A9, falls outside the logic of the mistaken payment case: D has gained no right and C has lost no right (indeed, C has made no factual loss). It has been suggested that Example B3 involves a 'transfer of dominium' from C to D.[60] It is true that D has breached his duty to C not to interfere with a physical thing in which C has a property right; but an introduction of the general notion of dominium does not make it any easier to find a transfer in such a case. D's ability, as a matter of fact, to use C's horse does not mean that D, as a matter of law, acquired a liberty against C to make such use of the horse.

Example B3 can be contrasted with those cases in which D *does* acquire a particular liberty at C's expense. For example, consider a case in which C, in the mistaken belief that he is obliged to do so, gives D a contractual licence, for a nominal sum, to use C's land for a period of six months. Such a case falls squarely within the logic of the mistaken payment case: C has come under a new duty to D; and D has acquired a new right against C. As C's mistake does not render the contract void, then, in the period prior to C's rescission of the contract, D commits no wrong by using the land. Nonetheless, if C does choose to rescind, then the liability principle operating in the mistaken payment case imposes a prima facie duty on D to pay C a reasonable use fee—a sum representing the value of the liberty to use C's land. Similarly, in the core mistaken payment case, the use value of the right acquired by D must be taken into account when determining the extent of D's duty to C. For example, in *Sempra Metals Ltd v Inland Revenue Commissioners*,[61] the House of Lords determined that D's duty, arising as a result of C's payment of tax not due, extended to paying compound interest on the sums received from C. That interest payment can be seen as dependent on the fact that, as a result of C's transfer to D, C lost his liberty (as against D) to make use of the money; and D (as against C) gained that liberty. On the model proposed in this chapter, then, there can be an independent strict liability claim to the use of a right, but only where, in contrast to Example B3, a legal liberty to use that right has been acquired by D.[62]

The debate surrounding Example B3 may seem purely academic; after all, it is clear that, in such a case, D is under a duty to pay a reasonable user fee. If, however, Birks' view is adopted, and the unilateral liability principle can apply where D has made a purely factual gain at C's

---

[60] See, eg, J Beatson, *The Use and Abuse of Unjust Enrichment: Essays on the Law of Restitution* (Oxford, Clarendon Press, 1991) 232; M McInnes, 'Hambly v Trott and the Claimant's Expense: Professor Birks' Challenge' in S Degeling and J Edelman (eds), *Unjust Enrichment in Commercial Law* (Sydney, Lawbook, 2008) 105, 130.

[61] *Sempra Metals Ltd v Inland Revenue Commissioners* [2007] UKHL 34, [2008] 1 AC 561 (*Sempra Metals*).

[62] The analysis here thus supports the view that an *independent* strict liability claim can be made to the use value of money over time. In *Sempra Metals* itself, Lord Nicholls (ibid, at [36]) and Lord Hope (at [112]) each suggested that such a claim is available.

expense, the possibility arises of further, potentially unwelcome liabilities. First, as Mitchell McInnes has pointed out,[63] there is a concern that, in cases where a wrong has undoubtedly been committed, an appeal to the strict liability principle of the mistaken payment case could bypass the broader concerns a court would otherwise consider in deciding if an award of gain-based damages is appropriate. Secondly, the notion of use as involving a factual gain triggering a potential strict liability claim may widen liability beyond cases in which a wrong is committed. For example, if C has a property right in goods, the torts of conversion, trespass and negligence provide him with protection against particular interferences with the physical thing to which his property right relates. It is possible, however, to think of uses of a right that do not involve the physical interference necessary for liability in those torts and so do not constitute wrongs:[64] for example, D may gain a material advantage by pretending to a third party that he has rights in relation to a thing owned by C. It would seem strange if the liability principle operating in the mistaken payment case extended to such a case. Further, the notion of use value must extend to non-proprietary rights, such as a simple contractual right. Given that, as confirmed by the House of Lords in *OBG Ltd v Allan*,[65] the tort of conversion does not impose a strict liability on others not to interfere with such rights, it might seem contradictory for an independent strict liability claim to be available if C can show that D has made a factual benefit from using such a right without C's consent.

VI. CONSEQUENCES OF ADOPTING THE RIGHTS-BASED GENERALISATION

The model proposed here rejects the view that liability in the mistaken payment case can be generalised to all cases involving the receipt of value. In considering the consequences of this analysis, it is useful to examine four features of the competing model, based on or linked to that wider generalisation from rights to value.

First, in the analyses of Birks and Chambers, there is a clear focus on D's *surviving* enrichment.[66] If one seeks to explain the liability in the core mistaken payment case as requiring D to retain an enrichment, one must necessarily focus not on the right acquired by D, but rather on the value of that right. For example, in Example A1, D will be under a duty to C

---

[63] M McInnes, 'Interceptive Subtraction, Unjust Enrichment and Wrongs—A Reply to Professor Birks' [2003] *Cambridge Law Journal* 697.

[64] See, eg, *Club Cruise Entertainment and Travelling Services Europe BV v Department for Transport* [2008] EWHC 2794 (Comm), [2009] 1 All ER (Comm) 955.

[65] *OBG Ltd v Allan* [2007] UKHL 21, [2008] 1 AC 1.

[66] See, eg, Birks, *Unjust Enrichment*, above n 2, at 63; Chambers, above n 1, at 247–49, 261–67.

even if D has spent the £50 note on his weekly grocery shopping, and has consumed that shopping before becoming aware of C's error. In such a case, when C makes his claim, D no longer has the right acquired from C; D does, however, retain the value of that right, as he used it to meet an expenditure that he would, in any case, have incurred. If, therefore, one wishes to explain D's duty as dependent on D's surviving enrichment, that enrichment must take the broader form of value (in Birks' term, an abstract enrichment) rather than the narrower form of a right (what Birks called a discrete enrichment).[67]

Such a case is, however, susceptible to a different explanation. On the model proposed here, D comes under an immediate duty when acquiring the mistakenly-transferred right. The fact that D no longer has that right is relevant only if it allows D to satisfy one of the conditions of a defence to C's claim. In determining the scope of such defences, it is important to note that D's duty is based on a liability principle that makes no reference to the wrongfulness of D's conduct. As Bant has argued, D's duty should not lead to an innocent D's being placed in a worse or substantially different position from that occupied by D before the events giving rise to C's claim.[68] As the purpose of D's duty is to ensure that C is not unjustifiably left in a worse position than that he previously occupied, it must be tempered by a matching concern for D's overall position. That concern is not relevant, however, in the example where D has spent money received from C on an expense which D would, in any case, have incurred. On this view, D's continuing liability in that example depends not on his retention of a factual enrichment, but rather on his initial receipt of a right, and the absence of any reason to remove or reduce his immediate duty to pay C the objective value of that right.

It is true that, when considering whether this countervailing concern applies, our focus is not limited to rights. The example in which D spends mistakenly-transferred money on grocery shopping shows that D's loss of the right acquired from C does not necessarily mean that D's prima facie duty is displaced. The point, however, is that a concern with D's abstract enrichment, manifested in the change of position defence,[69] does not mean that the justification of D's prima facie duty must also depend on such abstract enrichment. There is no inconsistency between the positions that first, D's overall factual gain is not enough to trigger potential liability;

---

[67] See Birks, *Unjust Enrichment*, above n 2, at 69–70.

[68] The formulation of this concern is based on the rationale of the change of position defence set out in Bant, *The Change of Position Defence*, above n 15, at ch 8.

[69] As Bant notes in 'Rights and Value in Rescission', above n 19, the need for *restitutio in integrum*, when applied to rescission, may manifest the same concern, and therefore permit consideration of a subsequent change in value of a right acquired by D: see, eg, *Erlanger v The New Sombrero Phosphate Company* (1878) 3 App Cas 1218 (HL) 1278 (Lord Blackburn); *Campbell v Backoffice Investments Pty Ltd* [2008] NSWCA 95, (2008) 66 ACSR 359.

and secondly, a desire to avoid an overall factual loss to D can temper the prima facie duty arising where D has acquired a right.

Secondly, on the model adopted by Birks and Chambers, the focus is on the surviving *subjective* enrichment of D. This analysis may seem to be supported by the decision of the House of Lords in *Sempra Metals*,[70] recognising that the recipient of a mistaken payment may be under a duty to pay compound interest on the sum received. In that case, the House of Lords set the interest rate by looking to what it would have cost D to borrow the sum received from C—that cost was lower than the market norm, as D could have taken advantage of lower government borrowing rates. This result can be seen as evidence that D is liable only for the subjective value of his surviving enrichment. An alternative view, consistent with the model proposed here, is that D's prima facie duty to pay the objective value of the right acquired is tempered by the need to ensure that the unilateral liability principle does not put D in a worse overall position than the one D occupied before the acquisition of the right from C. As observed by Bant, the rationale underlying the change of position defence may thus be seen to operate beyond the confines of that defence.[71] For example, the same concern has a role to play in the case of C's mistakenly granting D, for a nominal sum, a licence to use C's land. If D would not, in any case, have been willing to pay a higher rate for the use of C's land (or similar land), then, despite D's acquisition of an objectively valuable right, the concern with D's overall position means that D should not be made to pay an additional sum to C. As James Edelman has noted, there are powerful objections to taking a subjective approach to enrichment.[72] The model proposed in this chapter avoids those objections, as the liability principle in the core mistaken payment case imposes a prima facie duty on D to pay the objective value of the right lost (or duty gained) by C. This is because rights and duties, almost by definition, have a value set by the law. If D destroys C's right to a car by destroying that car, D cannot reduce the damages payable to C by showing that the subjective value of the car to C was less than its market value; similarly, if D acquires a right from C as a result of a flawed transaction, D's prima facie duty is to pay the objective value of that right to C.[73]

A third feature of Birks' model, made clear in Chambers' analysis,[74] is the positing of a very close correspondence between the justification for,

---

[70] *Sempra Metals* [2007] UKHL 34, [2008] 1 AC 561.

[71] Bant, 'Rights and Value in Rescission', above n 19.

[72] See J Edelman, 'The Meaning of Loss and Enrichment' in R Chambers, C Mitchell and J Penner (eds), *Philosophical Foundations of the Law of Unjust Enrichment* (Oxford, Oxford University Press, 2009) 211.

[73] Edelman (ibid) usefully draws the parallel between losses and gains in arguing that each should be measured objectively. On the model proposed here, the parallel can be seen as exact as it depends in each case on how the value of a right is to be measured.

[74] See Chambers, above n 1, at 267–76.

and nature of, D's duty. On this view, D's duty is to return the surviving enrichment. Where the enrichment takes the form of an assignable right, that right must be given back; where the enrichment takes the form of surviving value, that value must be given back by the payment of a corresponding sum of money. On this view, if a court, rather than ordering D to transfer a right back to C, has instead ordered D to pay a sum of money to C, it must be inferred that the court has analysed D's enrichment as residing in value, and not in a right. If the standard response in Example A1 is to order D to pay a sum of money to C, D's duty must then be based not on his acquisition of a right, but rather on his receipt of value. As Bant has noted, it is not however necessary to assume such an exact correspondence between the justification for, and the nature of, D's duty.[75] It is perfectly possible to posit a liability principle that is based on, and limited to, cases of receipt of a right, but which generally takes the form of a duty to pay the value of that right.[76] In any case, in a mistaken payment case where D remains solvent, there is no reason why C would wish to claim the return of specific notes, particularly given the procedural complications such a claim involves. The nature of the court's order may therefore owe more to the remedy sought by C than the justification for D's duty.

A fourth feature of Birks' model is the broad interpretation of 'at the expense of' adopted when applying the requirement that D's enrichment be at the expense of C. The concept of interceptive subtraction is vital to that expansive reading of the 'at the expense of' requirement. In discussing Examples A4 and B3, this chapter has already suggested that we need not accept the concept of interceptive subtraction. A further consequence of the model proposed in this chapter can be seen by considering the following example:

Example B4: C, *mistakenly believing that he owes X £50, gives X a £50 note. X knows about C's mistake but, as a result of the payment from C, X gives D, as a gift, £30.*

Birks argued that, in a case such as Example B4, the liability principle applying in the mistaken payment case operates to allow C to bring a claim against D. On his analysis, as C's payment to X is a 'but for' cause of X's payment to D, C can rely on a 'causative' analysis to show that D has been unjustly enriched at C's expense. This does not, however, seem to be the law.[77] This can be explained by applying the rights-based model proposed in this chapter. The liability principle applying in the mistaken

---

[75] Bant, 'Rights and Value in Rescission', above n 19.

[76] This point is developed in part VII below.

[77] See, eg, *Re Byfield* [1982] Ch 267 (Ch). This point is discussed in detail in B McFarlane, 'Unjust Enrichment, Property Rights, and Indirect Recipients' [2009] *Restitution Law Review* 35.

payment case is inapplicable, as the event causing C to lose his right (C's payment to X) is clearly distinct from the event causing D to acquire his right (X's payment to D).

Birks' causative analysis, it is true, would provide a means of understanding the decision of the House of Lords in *Lipkin Gorman v Karpnale Ltd*,[78] and of the Court of Appeal in *Banque Belge pour l'Etranger v Hambrouck*.[79] Those decisions can, however, be analysed as depending on C's assertion of an equitable property right in relation to a specific right received and retained by D.[80] That analysis depends on the fact that, in contrast to Example B4, D received the very right initially acquired by X at C's expense, or a right that counted as a product of that initial right. In each of *Lipkin Gorman* and *Banque Belge*, it can be argued that, as X knew that C did not in fact intend X to acquire the right, X held that right, and its products, on trust for C. In each of those cases, X then transferred such a right, in breach of trust, to D. D was not a bona fide purchaser for value of the right, as D gave no value for it. As a result, when D acquired knowledge of the facts giving rise to C's right under the trust, D came under a duty to hold that right, and its products, for C. Example B4, however, lies outside this analysis: the right received by D is not the same right acquired by X; nor is it a product of that right.

A fifth feature of Birks' analysis—the use of 'absence of basis' as a unifying concept underpinning cases of unjust enrichment—has a more complex relationship with the model proposed here. First, if the liability principle applying in the mistaken payment case is limited by adopting the narrow, rights-based generalisation proposed here, some of the difficulties with the absence of basis model may disappear. This can be seen by considering the following example:[81]

Example B5: *C lives in a flat; D lives in the flat above. C installs central heating and pays for the electricity to heat his flat. D benefits from this heat but refuses to pay C for this benefit.*

In such a case, it is clear that D is under no duty to C. Birks explains that, whilst D has acquired a benefit at C's expense, there is a basis for D to

---

[78] *Lipkin Gorman v Karpnale Ltd* [1991] 2 AC 548 (HL) (*Lipkin Gorman*).

[79] *Banque Belge pour l'Etranger v Hambrouck* [1921] 1 KB 321 (CA) (*Banque Belge*).

[80] See McFarlane, above n 77. See also L Smith, 'Simplifying Claims to Traceable Proceeds' (2009) 125 *Law Quarterly Review* 338, noting that this analysis is not incompatible with C's use of an action for money had and received, as courts had previously permitted such a claim to be brought by a beneficiary for the payment of a sum due from a trustee.

[81] See also the example given by P Watts, 'Book Review: *Unjust Enrichment* by Peter Birks' (2005) 121 *Law Quarterly Review* 163, 165: if C carelessly damages X's car, does C have a claim against D, the panel-beater who makes a profit from repairing X's car? On Birks' model, the 'absence of basis' approach, when combined with the broad interpretation of 'at the expense of', raises the prospect of C's having such a claim. On the model proposed here, no claim is available: see the analysis of Example B4 above.

retain the benefit: C has made a gift to D.[82] As has been pointed out by, for example, Burrows,[83] this explanation is unsatisfactory. It is, perhaps, telling that the difficulty arises from Birks' application of gift: a concept suited to the transfer of rights, but which does not properly apply to a case such as Example B5, where C has transferred no right to B. On the model proposed here, it is precisely because D has acquired no right, and C has lost no right, that the liability principle of the mistaken payment case cannot apply. So, even if C's decision to install central heating was motivated by a mistaken belief that D would have to bear some of the heating costs, so that an 'unjust factor' is present, the unilateral liability principle of the mistaken payment case should not apply.[84]

As pointed out by Charlie Webb,[85] cases such as *Bradford Corp v Pickles*[86] and *Victoria Park Racing and Recreation Grounds Co Ltd v Taylor*[87] may be similarly difficult to explain on Birks' model: in each case, D's acquisition of a factual gain, which could be said to come at C's expense, was insufficient to trigger any duty of D, even in the absence of a specific legal ground for the transfer of value from C to D. On the model proposed here, however, the absence of liability in such cases is easily explained: in each of those cases, C lost no right. In this way, the narrower, rights-based generalisation can meet the concern that the absence of basis analysis, in practice, involves an unacceptable extension of liability.[88]

The theoretical justification of the absence of basis analysis has also been questioned. A particularly strong point, developed by, for example, Barker,[89] is that it is not obvious why a recipient of a gain from another should have to show that the gain has been earned. After all, as a product of necessary human interaction, there are countless situations in which one party acquires a factual benefit at the expense of another, for example by hearing a busker, reading another's newspaper, or taking custom from a competing business. In contrast, in each of Examples A1

---

[82] Birks, *Unjust Enrichment*, above n 2, at 158.

[83] Burrows, 'Absence of Basis', above n 16, at 46.

[84] The presence of an 'unjust factor' (C's mistake) presumably means that, on Burrows' analysis, the liability principle applying in Example A1 *does* apply in such a case: see, eg, ibid, at 44. It seems unlikely, however, that C could bring a successful claim on such facts.

[85] C Webb, 'Property, Unjust Enrichment, and Defective Transfers' in R Chambers, C Mitchell and J Penner (eds), *Philosophical Foundations of the Law of Unjust Enrichment* (Oxford, Oxford University Press, 2009) 335.

[86] *Bradford Corp v Pickles* [1895] AC 587 (HL).

[87] *Victoria Park Racing and Recreation Grounds Co Ltd v Taylor* (1937) 58 CLR 479.

[88] For example, Smith's concern is that cases simply involving infringements of rights should not fall within the liability principle of the core mistaken payment case: see Smith, 'Unjust Enrichment: Big or Small?', above n 55, at 42. That concern can be met by the model proposed in this chapter.

[89] See, eg, Barker 'Starting Points in Unjust Enrichment Law', above n 4; Barker 'The Nature of Responsibility for Gain', above n 4. See also P Jaffey, *The Nature and Scope of Restitution* (Oxford, Hart Publishing, 2000) 17 (benefits are a 'matter of celebration, not regret'); Watts, 'Book Review', above n 81, at 166.

to A9, particular legal rules operate to cause C to lose a right (or acquire a duty or liability) and D to acquire a right (or lose a duty or liability). From C's perspective, those rules, operating as they do to remove a legal entitlement, require justification.

It may therefore seem that the absence of basis model may be more plausible when applied to the narrower, rights-based liability principle proposed in this chapter. There is, however, a difficulty. In a case such as Example A1, there *is* a legal basis for the transfer of C's *right* to D: as C did intend to transfer that particular note to D, D acquires C's right to the note. Similarly, in Example A3, there is a legal basis for D's acquisition of the mark: D acquired that right consistently with, and as a result of, the statutory scheme regulating the holding of such marks. This does not cause a problem for Birks' model: as that model focuses on the abstract value acquired by D at C's expense, it can be argued that, whilst there is a legal basis for the transfer of C's right to D, there is no legal basis on which D can retain the *benefit* of that right. It is very difficult, however, to explain the rights-based liability principle as dependent on an absence of basis for the transfer of C's right to D. An alternative justification of the liability principle must therefore be found.

VII. JUSTIFYING THE LIABILITY PRINCIPLE

The core mistaken payment case exemplifies a liability principle which may cause D to come under a duty to C even though D has no responsibility for a flaw (eg, C's mistake) which has been a cause of C's loss, and D's gain, of a right. On the model proposed in this chapter, the scope of that principle is limited to cases in which the same event involves *both* C's loss of a right (or gain of a duty or liability) *and* D's gain of a right (or loss of a duty or liability). The purpose of the principle is to protect C's initial legal position. As a result, it does not extend to cases where C simply suffers a factual loss, even if that loss correlates to a gain of D. In this way, the principle exists to protect an interest of C that is already recognised as a legally valid entitlement.

The model proposed here thus resembles, in a significant way, models proposed by commentators who have preferred to see the liability principle as based on the need to protect C's property. For example, Watts has argued that many restitution cases can best be seen as depending on a 'property principle': D's strict liability is justified by the general need to ensure an owner of property is not deprived of it, or at least its value, otherwise than as a result of a transfer freely and unqualifiedly consented to.[90] On this view, the liability principle operating in the mistaken payment

---

[90] Watts, 'Restitution—A Property Principle and a Services Principle', above n 17.

case has the same aim as, for example, the tort of conversion: non-tortious restitution and the property torts are thus 'cognate conservators', focused on the protection of C's assets (or at least the value of those assets) and not on the stripping of D's gains.[91] Webb has put forward a similar model, contending that the purpose of the liability principle is to protect C's exclusive entitlement to particular assets.[92] On this view, C's claim in the mistaken payment case can be seen as having its 'basis in the notion of property and [C's] entitlement to the asset or benefit which made its way into [D's] hands.'[93] Webb is therefore sceptical as to the distinction drawn by the law between cases in which a defect in C's consent prevents the transfer of a right and cases, such as Example A1, where a defect in C's consent does not prevent the transfer of a right, but D nonetheless comes under a duty to C.[94]

There are, however, important differences between the rights-based model proposed here and each of the property-based models of Watts and Webb; and, where those differences exist, the law follows the rights-based model. First, that model, unlike the property principle, can explain why the liability principle applied in the mistaken payment case can protect *any* right of C, whether or not that right is one which may correctly be called 'property'. For example, whilst a purely contractual right is not protected by the tort of conversion,[95] it can be protected by the liability principle if, for example, C makes a valid, but mistaken, statutory assignment of such a right to D. Indeed, the liability principle extends to cases where C does not lose a pre-existing entitlement but rather acquires a new duty: so, in Example A4, the liability principle can apply even if C's payment comes from an overdrawn bank account. Similarly, the principle can apply in Example A8 to explain C's power to rescind a purely executory contract: it would be extremely difficult to identify any 'property' of C that is protected in such a case. Secondly, the rights-based model proposed here follows the current law in excluding cases that would, it seems, be covered by a property principle. As noted by Watts, the property principle suggests that the liability principle should apply in a case such as Example B2, at least where it involves C's loss of a property right (as where material used by C in building on D's land accedes to D's land).[96] On the model proposed here, the liability principle does not apply in such a case as D has acquired no right. As seen in the discussion of Example B2 above, the law adopts the latter position.

---

[91] See P Watts, 'Property and "Unjust Enrichment": Cognate Conservators' [1998] *New Zealand Law Review* 151.

[92] Webb, above n 85.

[93] ibid, at 352.

[94] ibid, at 354–59.

[95] *OBG Ltd v Allan* [2007] UKHL 21, [2008] 1 AC 1.

[96] Watts, 'Restitution—A Property Principle and a Services Principle', above n 17, at 62.

Thirdly, it is clear that, contrary to the model proposed by Watts, the liability principle applied in the mistaken payment case does not operate in the same way as a property tort such as conversion. This is explicable on the model proposed here. D can only be liable in the tort of conversion if he has breached a duty not to interfere with a physical thing in relation to which C has a property right. Where D breaches such a duty, however, he is liable even if he has made no legal gain from the breach. Moreover, the change of position defence is not available to D: given that D has breached a duty owed to C, it is justifiable for D to be left worse off as a result of his action. Finally, the model proposed here may assist in dealing with scepticism as to the distinction between, on the one hand, cases where a defect in C's consent prevents the transfer of a right to D and, on the other, cases where a defect does not prevent the transfer of a right, but rather provides the grounds on which the liability principle applies. As was suggested when considering Example A8 (involving rescission of an executory contract), the existence of the liability principle may be necessary to justify the very conclusion that D has acquired a particular right. Certainly, there is nothing self-defeating in legal rules that both recognise that D has acquired a right, and also impose a duty on D to pay C the objective value of that right, for the consequences of recognising D's acquisition of a right (eg, third parties' coming under a duty to D) differ from the consequences of imposing a duty on D, owed to C.[97]

In Example A1, then, the fact that D is under an immediate duty to pay C the value of a right mistakenly transferred from C to D may be seen as a compromise: C's mistake, as it does not change the fact that C intended to transfer that right, and to transfer it to D, does not prevent C from losing, and D from gaining, C's right to the £50. This means, for example, that a third party stealing the £50 note breaches a duty owed to D, and not to C. It also means that, if D were to go into insolvency immediately after receiving the note, then (assuming D had no knowledge of C's mistake[98]), title to the £50 note will be acquired by D's trustee in bankruptcy and so form part of the assets used to meet the claims not only of C, but of all D's creditors. Nonetheless, as C's mistake as to his liability to D was a cause of the transfer of the right to D, D will come under an immediate duty to pay the value of that right to C. This duty

---

[97] This remains true even if D's duty to C gives rise to an equitable property right in C's favour. For example, if D holds a right on trust for C, X can still acquire the right free from any duty to C if X is a bona fide purchaser for value without notice of C's right. In contrast, if the right has remained with C throughout, X, in general, will not be able to rely on the bona fide purchaser defence: see, eg, *Cundy v Lindsay* (1878) 3 App Cas 459 (HL).

[98] Where D has such knowledge, there is a strong argument that D holds his right to the £50 on trust for C: see, eg, *Westdeutsche Landesbank Girozentrale v Islington London Borough Council* [1996] AC 669 (HL) 705–706 (Lord Browne-Wilkinson); *Wambo Coal Pty Ltd v Ariff* [2007] NSWSC 589, (2007) 63 ACSR 429.

arises even though D has no responsibility for C's mistake—the duty is one-sided in the sense that its purpose is to protect C's initial position. D may therefore ask why he should bear the burden of protecting C—the response is that, if D is wholly innocent, D's duty will only exist to the extent that it does not make D factually worse off, as compared to his initial position.

Similarly, in Example A8, D's innocent misrepresentation does not prevent a contract's being formed by the parties: C therefore is subject to a new duty, and D acquires a new right. Again, the validity of the contract has important consequences: it means that, if C chooses to affirm the contract, D will remain under a duty to C. In contrast, if C's mistake were to make a purported contract between C and D wholly void, C would not have that power to enforce any duty of D. Nonetheless, as D's innocent misrepresentation was a cause of C's willingness to enter the contract, D will come under an immediate liability to lose his contractual right against C.

It may be objected that this account offers a description of the liability principle, rather than a justification of it. The account is, however, necessary to reveal the purpose of the principle—to ensure that a deterioration in C's legal position (such as the loss of a right or the gain of a duty) does not unjustifiably leave C in a worse factual position. In none of Examples A1 to A9 can it be said that the deterioration in C's legal position is unjustified or without basis—if that were the case, the legal rules allowing for the transfer of the right to occur in Example A1, or for the validity of the contract in Example A8, would themselves be unjust and ought therefore to be altered. It is, however, possible to state that the factual effect of those legal rules on C's position *as regards D* is unjustified. In cases such as Examples A1 and A8, the factual deterioration in C's position is unjustified as C did not fully consent to it. C's lack of consent is not, however, the only reason for which such a deterioration can be unjust: the invalidity of a tax demand pursuant to which C makes a payment to D can, for example, provide another reason.

The reference to C's factual position may seem to undermine the distinction made here between cases involving rights and cases involving other forms of value. If, in cases such as Examples A1 and A8, our focus is on ensuring that C is not made factually worse off, why is that same concern not triggered in a case such as Example B3, where C mistakenly improves D's land; or in a case such as Example B5, where C mistakenly heats D's flat? The answer suggested by this chapter is that, in Examples A1 and A8, it is the operation of particular legal rules that causes the deterioration in C's factual position. This triggers a particular concern to ensure that C does not unjustifiably suffer as a result of those rules. The duty imposed on D is therefore a necessary part of the justification of the legal rules recognising the transfer of C's right to D, or the existence of the contract between C and D. The extent of D's duty is limited by the same concern to ensure that D does not unjustifiably suffer as a result of the duty's being imposed: this concern, manifested most obviously in the change of position defence, is itself part of the justification for the existence of the liability principle applying in Example A1. In cases such as Examples B3 and B5, in contrast, the deterioration in C's position is caused not by the operation of any legal rules, but rather by the simple fact of C's conduct. There are no relevant legal rules that require, as part of their justification, a duty of D that arises independently of D's conduct. In such cases, as seen above in the discussion of Example B3, a duty can be imposed on D only if D has some responsibility for C's conduct.

VIII. CONCLUSION

With the notable exception of its title and introduction, this chapter has attempted to avoid using the term 'unjust enrichment' as a synonym for the liability principle operating in Example A1, the core case of a unilaterally mistaken payment. In *Unjust Enrichment*, Birks undertakes the important task of identifying, and determining the scope of, that liability principle. Yet it may be that the task is inevitably compromised and complicated by referring to that liability principle as one based on D's unjust enrichment at C's expense. After all, as Barker has persuasively pointed out, if one were beginning with a simple concept of unjust enrichment, and looking for instances of its application, there are many examples of gain-based recovery (such as cases where D is forced to give up profits acquired from the commission of a wrong) that would come to one's attention before the case of a unilaterally mistaken payment.[99] As Barker also suggests, the term 'unjust enrichment' perhaps more naturally refers to a concept that is broader than any one liability principle, and so includes any case where D has to give up or return a gain, whether C's cause of action is based on a wrong, a contract, or some other event.[100] This may be the point captured by the High Court of Australia in referring to unjust enrichment as a 'unifying concept' and not 'a principle which can be taken as a sufficient premise for direct application in particular cases'.[101]

To focus on a 'principle which can be taken as a sufficient premise for direct application in particular cases', we should therefore begin by asking what liability principle explains the duty imposed on D in the case of a unilaterally mistaken payment. In answering this question, we

---

[99] See Barker, 'Starting Points in Unjust Enrichment Law', above n 4.
[100] See Barker, 'The Nature of Responsibility for Gain', above n 4.
[101] *Lumbers v W Cook Builders Pty Ltd* [2008] HCA 27, (2008) 232 CLR 635 [85] (Gummow, Hayne, Crennan and Kiefel JJ). See also *Bofinger v Kingsway Group Ltd* [2009] HCA 44, (2009) 239 CLR 269 [85]–[98] (Gummow, Hayne, Heydon, Kiefel and Bell JJ).

are not determining the scope of unjust enrichment; but we are, and this is the real merit of Birks' approach, discovering the reach of an independent liability principle that can impose a duty on D even where D has committed no wrong, and made no contract. The liability principle is particularly important as it can impose a strict liability on D. On the model proposed here, the scope of the liability principle is limited to cases where the operation of a legal rule involves both: (i) C's loss of a claim right or power[102] *or* C's gain of a duty or liability; and (ii) D's gain of a claim right or power *or* D's loss of a duty or liability. In a subset of such cases, there may be a flaw (for which D may bear no responsibility) that makes the factual deterioration in C's position, caused by the operation of the legal rule, unjustifiable. If so, the justification of the very legal rule that has caused C's legal loss and D's legal gain will require D to come under a duty to C. That duty is to avoid the factual deterioration to C's position, by returning C to his initial position. At least in cases where D bears no responsibility for the relevant flaw, D's duty is limited by the parallel need to ensure that D is not placed in a factually worse position to that occupied by D before the operation of the legal rule.

On the model proposed here, the liability principle is justified at one remove. The function of the principle, as generalised from the core case of a mistaken payment, is to mitigate the effects on C of other legal rules that recognise a particular event as causing both: (i) for C's part, the loss of a right or power, or the imposition of a duty or liability; and (ii) for D's part, the acquisition of a right or power, or the removal of a duty or liability. This means that the liability principle must be understood as part of the logic of the underlying legal rule that has had that effect on C and D. So, in Example A1, part of the justification of the legal rule that C's right to £50 has been transferred to D lies in the fact that, if the transfer has been caused in part by a mistake made by C then, even if D has not contributed to that mistake, D may come under a prima facie duty to pay C the value of the right transferred. Example A8 deals with a different underlying legal rule: one that regulates when C comes under a contractual duty to D. The application of the principle in such a case may therefore differ from its application in a non-contractual case such as Example A1. This can be seen by considering a case in which C's entry into a contract is based on a unilateral mistake, for which D is not responsible. The presence of such a mistake in a simple transfer case, such as Example A1, may suffice to render unjustified the factual deterioration caused to C by the transfer of his right to D. This need not be the case in Example A8: the legal rules about the creation of contractual

---

[102] A case where C mistakenly elects to affirm a voidable contract is one in which the liability principle may be invoked on the basis of an event (C's election) causing both C's loss of a power and D's loss of a liability.

rights may be justified even if C is left to suffer a factual loss as a result of his unilateral mistake.[103]

It has been suggested that, from the perspective latterly adopted by Birks at least, the liability principle operating in the mistaken payment case has an 'apparently second order vacuum filling role'.[104] On the model set out here, the 'second order' flavour comes from the fact that the function of the principle is to justify the operation of *other* legal rules regulating the acquisition and loss of legal rights. A necessary part of the 'event' generating liability (to adopt Birks' terminology) is thus the legal effect of a different event (such as the transfer of a right) falling into a different event-based category (such as consent). On this view it is notable that, whilst Birks' exposition of unjust enrichment was assisted by the use of a classification based on events (facts occurring in the real world and generating legal effects), the crucial event in Examples A1 to A9 consists not only of facts occurring in the real world, but also of the legal effects of those facts, as defined by 'first order' legal rules, such as those regulating the transfer of rights or the creation of contracts.

The model presented here, when compared to that of Birks, depends on a far narrower generalisation of the liability principle exemplified by the case of a unilaterally mistaken payment. It also suggests that a uniformity of function is the only thing binding together the different cases (such as Examples A1 to A9) where the liability principle applies. Whilst it is also possible to say that the principle is a secondary one, this should not be taken to mean that it is unimportant. Indeed, if, as suggested, the principle is an integral part of the justification of *any* legal rule that allows an event to cause both C's loss of a right (or equivalent) and D's gain of a right (or equivalent), then the principle is critical to the functioning of a very wide number of legal rules. It can be seen, for example, as vital to the operation of the law concerning the transfer of rights and of the law concerning the creation of contractual rights: or, as they are sometimes known, property law and contract law.

---

[103] See, eg, *Smith v Hughes* (1871) LR 6 QB 597 (QB).
[104] Stevens, 'Is There a Law of Unjust Enrichment?', above n 6, at 23.

21

Rights and Value in Rescission: Some Implications for Unjust Enrichment

ELISE BANT*

I. INTRODUCTION

R OBERT CHAMBERS HAS recently made a powerful argument that the law of unjust enrichment[1] encompasses two different kinds of enrichment, namely rights and value.[2] The two categories may overlap in many scenarios, but not always. In particular, rights may be actionable enrichments notwithstanding that they have no value. Indeed, in cases of restitution of rights, the value of the enrichment is not relevant because the defendant is not being asked to give up value but to give up a right, regardless of its value. Rescission is given as a key example of restitution of rights, rather than value, and one where the value of rights is not relevant to the question of enrichment.[3]

This chapter uses Chambers' analysis as a springboard to examine more closely the interaction between rights and value in the context of rescission. It demonstrates that the value of rights plays a major, albeit not decisive, role in determining the availability and form of rescission. Indeed, the role of value within rescission sheds considerable light on the nature of primary liability in unjust enrichment and the change of position defence.

* I would like to thank Robert Chambers, Michael Bryan, Jamie Edelman, Birke Häcker and my fellow participants at the Obligations V conference from the Melbourne Law School (Matthew Harding, Ian Malkin, Jeannie Paterson and Andrew Robertson) for their very helpful comments on earlier drafts of this chapter. My thanks go also to my research assistant, Chris Tran, for his assistance with the final draft. All errors and omissions remain mine.
[1] The same division cuts across the law for wrongful enrichment, but will not be the focus of this chapter.
[2] R Chambers, 'Two Kinds of Enrichment' in R Chambers, C Mitchell and J Penner (eds), *Philosophical Foundations of the Law of Unjust Enrichment* (Oxford, Oxford University Press, 2009) 242.
[3] See, eg, ibid, at 254, 256, 259–61.

The main focus of this chapter will be on the requirement of *restitutio in integrum*. This is because changes in the value of rights transferred pursuant to the impugned transaction play a very important role in determining whether that principle is satisfied. This necessarily indicates that the value of the rights at the beginning of the story is also legally significant. However, as will be demonstrated, value does not always play the determining role. Rather, the important overarching principle, itself dictated by the limited purpose of restitution, is that neither party should be placed unjustifiably in a worse (including entirely different) position than they occupied prior to their receipt. This suggests a broader concern at play in the cases and highlights the crucial role of the change of position defence.

II. THE ROLE OF VALUE OUTSIDE ENRICHMENT

The nub of Chambers' thesis is that value is not necessary to establish enrichment where the enrichment constitutes rights, rather than value. However, Chambers also considers that, in such cases, value may nonetheless inform the 'unjust factor' and 'at the expense of' elements of the primary claim. In this way, the defendant's liability to make restitution of rights (rather than value) may still be affected by valuation considerations, albeit not through the element of enrichment. For example, it is trite law that a sale of rights, such as title to land, may be rescinded as a result of (presumed) undue influence if the parties were in a relationship of excessive influence and the transaction was one 'calling for explanation'. Value transferred and received under the impugned transaction will often (although not always) play an important evidential part in determining whether the presumption is attracted. Value plays a similar role in cases of unconscionable dealing,[4] where sale at a gross undervalue is often indicative, albeit not determinative, of exploitation.[5] While this subsidiary role for value can be accepted, its function is precisely that: an incidental, evidential role from which the existence of the relevant unjust factor may be inferred. Value does not itself constitute a necessary element of these unjust factors, nor any other unjust factor.

More contentiously Chambers considers that value may bear on a claimant's entitlement to restitution of rights through the 'at the expense of' requirement of the primary claim in unjust enrichment.[6] He cites *Sprin-*

---

[4] This assumes unconscionable dealing is an unjust factor. For a contrary view, see J Edelman and E Bant, *Unjust Enrichment in Australia* (Melbourne, Oxford University Press, 2006) 32–33.

[5] Chambers, 'Two Kinds of Enrichment', above n 2, at 259–60.

[6] ibid, at 260–61.

gette v Defoe[7] as an example. In that case, the parties purchased property as joint tenants. When their relationship ended, the claimant alleged that they held the property on trust in proportion to their contributions. On Chambers' analysis, the court's subsequent and rigorous valuation of their contributions ('calculated to the penny'[8]) was made not in order to determine the enrichment of the defendant, but to identify the extent to which the defendant's enrichment (in the form of a share of a leasehold estate) was at the claimant's expense.

Clearly, the meaning of the 'at the expense of' requirement is critical to understanding this role for value. Unfortunately, it remains notoriously uncertain. One school of thought is that it signals a requirement that any enrichment to the defendant must be reflected by a corresponding loss to the claimant.[9] But if this interpretation requires a precise correspondence between gain and loss then it must be rejected. James Edelman has recently demonstrated that even if attention is focused solely on the transfer of value between claimant and defendant, so that the gain and loss correspond in kind, the amount of the gain to a defendant will often differ from the claimant's loss.[10] Thus in *Sempra Metals Ltd v Inland Revenue Commissioners*,[11] the government defendant received a benefit in the form of the use of (ie, interest on) money paid to it by mistake. The defendant's gain did not correspond to the corporate claimant's loss of the use of its money. This is because governments are commonly subject to different (lower) government borrowing rates than apply to commercial entities. A reasonable defendant in the position of the government will generally borrow money at lower public sector rates than a reasonable person in the position of the corporate claimant. Thus the measures of loss and gain did not coincide in this case. And the award of restitution in *Sempra Metals* was of the lower government rate of interest.

Chambers' model of the 'at the expense of' element does not appear to require a strict correspondence between types of gain and loss. He explains that, in cases of restitution of rights, the 'enrichment of the defendant is

---

[7] *Springette v Defoe* [2001] UKHL 44; [2002] AC 773. *Foskett v McKeown* [2000] UKHL 29, [2001] 1 AC 102 is similarly analysed.

[8] Chambers, 'Two Kinds of Enrichment', above n 2, at 260.

[9] For principled discussion in favour of this view, see M McInnes, '"At the Plaintiff's Expense": Quantifying Restitutionary Relief' [1998] *Cambridge Law Journal* 472; M McInnes, 'Interceptive Subtraction, Unjust Enrichment and Wrongs—A Reply to Professor Birks' [2003] *Cambridge Law Journal* 697. Cf B McFarlane, 'Unjust Enrichment, Rights and Value' ch 20 of this book, who explores, inter alia, the possibilities inherent in combining a 'correspondence' requirement with a focus on rights (rather than value) as the proper subject of claims in unjust enrichment.

[10] J Edelman, 'The Meaning of Loss and Enrichment' in R Chambers, C Mitchell and J Penner (eds), *Philosophical Foundations of the Law of Unjust Enrichment* (Oxford University Press, Oxford 2009) 211, 232, discussing *Strand Electric and Engineering Co Ltd v Brisford Entertainments Ltd* [1952] 2 QB 246 (CA) and *Sempra Metals Ltd v Commissioner of Inland Revenue* [2007] UKHL 34, [2008] 1 AC 561 (*Sempra Metals*).

[11] *Sempra Metals* [2007] UKHL 34, [2008] 1 AC 561.

the receipt of a right and the expense to the claimant is a corresponding loss of a right or value'.[12] *Springette v Defoe* is employed in this context as an example of a case where enrichment in the form of rights to land was at the expense of the claimant in terms of value. However, even if a strict correspondence is unnecessary, Chambers' model does seem to incorporate the necessity for some linked or countervailing loss to the claimant. This remains problematic for two reasons. First, if loss is relevant, it is not clear why, under Chambers' approach, being enriched by receipt of a right is not necessarily linked to loss of a right, or being enriched by receipt of value does not necessarily correspond to loss of value. One might think that, on this model, there should be some kind of connection between the nature of the enrichment and the nature of the claimant's loss, even if, in 'value' cases, there need not be exact correspondence. Secondly, it is arguable that any loss-based interpretation of the 'at the expense of' requirement, whether or not it is strictly correlative, has been rejected in England and in Australia. In those jurisdictions, restitution for unjust enrichment is about reversing gain: it is both irrelevant and unnecessary in establishing liability that the claimant might have suffered any loss. It is certainly unnecessary to value any loss. It is for this reason that those jurisdictions have rejected a common law defence of passing on.[13]

Finally, if we conclude that the 'at the expense of' requirement does not demand some countervailing loss to the claimant from the defendant's gain, then it becomes difficult to see why considerations of value should ever inform the inquiry. For example, if the 'at the expense of' element is simply a directional requirement to pinpoint who the enrichment was from (and thus who is the correct claimant),[14] why should the amount of any value lost by the claimant be relevant? Value should likewise be unnecessary if the 'at the expense of' element is conceived as a causal requirement.[15]

In summary, any role for value in relation to the 'unjust factor' inquiry is marginal, and its bearing on the 'at the expense of' requirement is highly uncertain. It follows that the primary significance of value must lie in its effects on enrichment and relevant defences, to which we now turn.

[12] Chambers, 'Two Kinds of Enrichment', above n 2, at 258.

[13] The defence is explored in detail in M Rush, *The Defence of Passing On* (Oxford, Hart Publishing, 2006). Cf Ernest Weinrib, who argues that the requirement of a 'corresponding deprivation' is established through the immediate link between the parties as transferor and transferee of net value. It follows that the defendant's liability arising out of a transfer of net value between the parties is not precluded by the passing on defence: see EJ Weinrib, 'Correctively Unjust Enrichment' in R Chambers, C Mitchell and J Penner (eds), *Philosophical Foundations of the Law of Unjust Enrichment* (Oxford, Oxford University Press, 2009) 31, 37.

[14] cf *Re Byfield* [1982] Ch 267 (Ch) 276 (Goulding J).

[15] See, eg, P Birks, *Unjust Enrichment*, 2nd edn (Oxford, Oxford University Press, 2005) 89–98.

III. THE MOTIVATIONS FOR THE RIGHTS/ VALUE DICHOTOMY IN ENRICHMENT

The starting point for the inquiry into the proposed rights/value dichotomy within enrichment is to understand the concerns that inform Chambers' thesis. Two major objectives can be discerned. Both require some preliminary comments.

A. Safeguarding the Corpus of Unjust Enrichment Law

(i) Enrichment as Value and Value Only

First, Chambers is motivated to save vulnerable areas of the law of unjust enrichment from expulsion.[16] He identifies the chief source of the threat as the insistence of some commentators[17] that actionable enrichment must 'have value or be value'[18]—that is, value is not only a sufficient but a necessary element of unjust enrichment. If that is correct, Chambers reasons, a whole host of cases formerly understood as falling under the umbrella of unjust enrichment must belong elsewhere. In particular, he argues that in cases of proprietary restitution, the value of the rights ordered to be restored is either non-existent or irrelevant.[19] It follows that only if rights and value are understood to be independent forms of actionable enrichment can those areas be retained within unjust enrichment.

A core plank in the argument, therefore, is that where restitution of rights is concerned the value of those rights is irrelevant to the claimant's right to restitution. But some care must be taken with this form of statement. It is of course true that if rights are the subject of an order for restitution, then the value of those rights is irrelevant to the remedy. The value of a car is irrelevant to any order for restitution of title to the car to the claimant. However, this is simply an observation of the result, not the process of reasoning that leads to it.[20] That is, the more pertinent question (and the one posed by Chambers) is whether value forms a part of the necessary conditions for the ultimate award of restitution of rights. We have seen that its role is limited at best when it comes to the 'unjust factor' and 'at the expense of' inquiries. Its operation within enrichment and defences will accordingly form the main focus of this essay.

---

[16] Chambers, 'Two Kinds of Enrichment', above n 2, at 243, 261–67, 277. The concern is not merely to retain rescission: if enrichment is limited to value, many property rights to recover assets through rectification, tracing, resulting and constructive trusts are likewise affected.

[17] Namely Peter Birks, Lionel Smith and Weinrib: see ibid, at 261–67.

[18] ibid, at 277.

[19] ibid.

[20] See further text accompanying nn 57–61 below.

(ii) Value as 'an Increase in Net Worth' and the Problem of Exchange Transactions

As a leading instance of proprietary restitution,[21] rescission constitutes one of the endangered species identified by Chambers as requiring a non-value-based analysis of enrichment in order to be retained within unjust enrichment. But its vulnerability is exacerbated by the particular definition of 'enrichment as value' adopted by Chambers. Like Weinrib,[22] Chambers regards value as an increase in net worth.[23] A defendant is only enriched in terms of value by his receipt of an asset if it constitutes a net gain.

This definition presents an obvious problem for rescission cases.[24] Many rescission cases concern the *exchange* of valuable benefits pursuant to a contract.[25] The contract by definition identifies the exchanged benefits as equally valuable. So the defendant's benefit in terms of his receipt of a valuable asset is immediately cancelled out by his own transfer of benefit to the claimant. From this perspective, where is the increase in net value-enrichment that founds the right to rescind? If there is no enrichment, then all rescission cases fall outside the law of unjust enrichment. I agree with Chambers that this seems highly unlikely. As will be explained in the following section, rescission is a restitutionary response that is triggered, inter alia, by a number of established unjust factors. It would be odd if we had to relocate it outside unjust enrichment because of a perceived difficulty in identifying an actionable enrichment.

However, the problem presented by exchange transactions is not solved by shifting, as Chambers does, to a rights-based analysis of enrichment. If, as Chambers argues, enrichment as *value* is seen in terms of an increase in net benefit, then surely enrichment as *rights* must also look to the net increase in benefit received by a defendant.[26] That is, a defendant who has received rights must obtain some net gain by his or her receipt. But in the context of contractual exchanges, even if we accept that the enrichment involved in cases of rescission is rights, not value, we encounter the same problems we saw in the context of value. In contracts, rights are exchanged just like value. Once the exchange of rights is taken into account, parties are left in an enrichment-neutral position, just as they are with value. It is true that, in most cases, the rights exchanged will not be the same rights. So it would be possible to allege that a party to a

---

[21] On the nature of rescission as a proprietary remedy, see text accompanying nn 134–144 below.

[22] Weinrib, above n 13, at 34–39.

[23] Chambers, 'Two Kinds of Enrichment', above n 2, at 251–52.

[24] Weinrib expressly excludes exchange transactions from unjust enrichment for this reason: above n 13, at 36–37.

[25] See, eg, Chambers, 'Two Kinds of Enrichment', above n 2, at 259, discussing rescission of sale transactions made for full market value pursuant to undue influence.

[26] Chambers clearly regards the different forms of enrichment as following similar rules: see below n 66 and accompanying text.

contract has been enriched by a new right. But the party has been simultaneously disenriched by the loss of a right. Indeed, if the transaction is vitiated by some unjust factor, the exchange of rights has also triggered the creation of a new right to rescind on the part of the claimant and a new and corresponding liability on the part of the defendant. If anything, switching to a rights-based analysis underscores that the parties are left in an enrichment-neutral position. The rights-based analysis again makes retention of rescission within unjust enrichment highly problematic.

We will see below that a better approach, more consistent with the operation of rescission and the broader law of unjust enrichment, is to abandon the 'net enrichment' analysis in favour of the traditional approach of identifying actionable enrichment as the benefit received, the right to restitution of which is subject to defences such as change of position.

(iii) A Shift to 'Value Surviving'?

Chambers' conception of value-enrichment as net gain has a secondary consequence: enrichment (as value) becomes a question of 'value surviving' rather than the 'value received' by the defendant.[27] This realignment is said to be consistent with the position in relation to rights, where the right to restitution is always contingent on identification of surviving rights.[28]

Although this seems an innocuous step, the shift has some profound ramifications for the law of unjust enrichment, two of which bear noting here. First, it has a natural tendency to change the point at which the action is complete from (in general) the moment of receipt of a benefit[29] to the moment when restitution is sought (or, perhaps, the date of judgment).[30] It is only then that one can identify the value surviving with any certainty. Secondly, it renders the change of position defence largely redundant.[31] On the 'value surviving' approach, the change of position defence becomes a critical mechanism by which surviving enrichment is identified. Change of position considerations thus feed into the primary

---

[27] Chambers, 'Two Kinds of Enrichment', above n 2, at 247–49, 268.

[28] ibid, at 276.

[29] See, eg, *Guardian Ocean Cargoes Ltd v Banco Do Brasil (No 3)* [1992] 2 Lloyd's Rep 193 (Com Ct); *Coshott v Lenin* [2007] NSWCA 153, followed in *Sharjade Pty Ltd v RAAF (Landings) Ex-Servicemen Charitable Fund Pty Ltd* [2008] NSWSC 1003 (revd on other grounds in *Sharjade Pty Ltd v Commonwealth* [2009] NSWCA 373); *Adamson v Miller* [2008] FMCA 1173. The point when the cause of action is completed may be later, as when the condition or basis upon which a benefit was transferred subsequently fails. It may also be delayed where a defendant only subsequently accepts the benefit: discussed in Edelman, above n 10, at 226.

[30] cf R Stevens, 'Three Enrichment Issues' in A Burrows and Lord Rodger (eds), *Mapping the Law: Essays in Memory of Peter Birks* (Oxford, Oxford University Press, 2007) 49, 53–54, criticised in Edelman, above n 10, at 224–25.

[31] This irresistible tendency is demonstrated in the recent New South Wales Court of Appeal decision in *Heperu Pty Ltd v Belle* [2009] NSWCA 252, (2009) 258 ALR 727.

claim rather than forming a discrete defence.[32] It is only if change of position goes beyond 'disenrichment' that it has any independent role to play.[33]

It has to be said that, at present, this does not reflect the law in England or Australia. In those jurisdictions, the cause of action is complete (usually) at the moment of receipt of the benefit.[34] And the claimant's prima facie right is to restitution of the value of the benefit received, subject to defences such as change of position.[35]

However, support for a 'net value' or 'value surviving' model can be found in other comparative jurisdictions. For example, John Dawson has remarked that the search for the net balance of surviving gain is a major feature of Germany's unjust enrichment jurisprudence.[36] Certainly, it is commonly understood that paragraph 818(3) of the *Bürgerliches Gesetzbuch* (which contains the German change of position defence) reduces every claim to the value surviving in the hands of the defendant, rather than the value received.[37] That is, paragraph 818(3) does not simply contain a defence, but lays down the very measure of restitution.[38]

Given the importance of rescission to Chambers' work, it is also noteworthy that German law restricts restitution following rescission of bilaterally executed contracts voidable for fraudulent misrepresentation, duress and certain types of mistake to the net balance of benefits transferred between the parties (the '*saldo*' theory).[39] This seems to provide further comparative support for a net value or value surviving approach to enrichment within the law of unjust enrichment.[40]

But despite appearances, a deeper comparative analysis of the *saldo* theory ultimately undermines the view that there is anything intrinsically natural or meritorious in a net value or value surviving approach that would favour the development of a similar approach under the common

---

[32] Chambers makes this point explicitly in the context of rights: 'Two Kinds of Enrichment', above n 2, at 276.

[33] The possible role of the defence beyond 'disenrichment' is discussed in the text accompanying nn 130–33 below.

[34] See above n 29.

[35] *Sempra Metals* [2007] UKHL 34, [2008] 1 AC 561; *David Securities Pty Ltd v Commonwealth Bank of Australia* (1992) 175 CLR 353.

[36] J Dawson, 'Erasable Enrichment in German Law' (1981) 61 *Boston University Law Review* 217, 295.

[37] P Birks, 'Change of Position and Surviving Enrichment' in W Swadling (ed), *The Limits of Restitutionary Claims: A Comparative Analysis* (Glasgow, United Kingdom National Committee of Comparative Law, 1997) 36, 58–59.

[38] R Zimmerman and J Du Plessis, 'Basic Features of the German Law of Unjustified Enrichment' [1994] *Restitution Law Review* 14, 38–39; T Krebs, *Restitution at the Crossroads: A Comparative Study* (London, Cavendish Publishing, 2001) 280.

[39] See generally Zimmerman and Du Plessis, above n 38, at 40–42; BS Markesinis, W Lorenz and G Dannemann, *The German Law of Obligations* (Oxford, Clarendon Press, 1997) 764–65; Krebs, above n 38, at 101–04; B Häcker, *Consequences of Impaired Consent Transfers* (Tübingen, Mohr Siebeck, 2009) 71–77.

[40] It was certainly perceived in this way by Birks: see, eg, *Unjust Enrichment*, above n 15, at 225–26.

law. First, it must be recognised that the *saldo* theory is not the only approach historically or presently active in German law[41] and does not command unanimous support.[42] It does not apply where a contract has only been performed by one party and so the element of mutuality of performance is absent.[43] In this case, the original approach to rescission — the *zweinkondiktionentheorie* or 'two claims' theory — applies. This theory regards each party as having an independent unjust enrichment claim against the other to which the change of position defence may apply.[44] Indeed, even in some cases of bilaterally executed contracts, for example those involving fraudulent defendants or claimants who are minors, the two claims theory is still preferred in German law.[45]

Secondly, the *saldo* theory was developed in response to certain perceived injustices of the two claims theory, in particular the perceived injustice of allowing the risk of destruction of an object while in the hands of the rescinding party, and thus over which the defendant has no control, to rest with the defendant following rescission. The difference between the models in this respect is best illustrated through a simple hypothetical.[46] Suppose a claimant purchases title to a car from the defendant pursuant to a voidable contract. The claimant pays £1000 for title to a car worth £800. The claimant later crashes the car. What is the consequence of the car's accidental destruction to the parties' mutual restitutionary liabilities? If a net value approach is applied, the claimant can only recover the difference between the value of what she originally paid and received, that is £200. The subsequent destruction of the car is irrelevant to her right to restitution of that net benefit. If, on the other hand, restitution following avoidance of the contract is a mutual process of restitutionary claim and counter-claim, where the benefit is defined in terms of the value originally received by each party, the claimant's primary claim is for the full purchase price. The defendant then has a counter-claim for the value of title to the car as at the date of transfer. However, the claimant may[47] be entitled to claim a change of position defence to the extent to which her car has diminished in value as a result of the crash. That means that if the

[41] In addition to the 'two claims' theory discussed below, scholars have also suggested modified two claims theories, discussed in Häcker, *Consequences of Impaired Consent Transfers*, above n 39, at 75–77.

[42] Dawson, above n 36, at 295–300; Krebs, above n 38, at 102–03.

[43] Häcker, *Consequences of Impaired Consent Transfers*, above n 39, at 75.

[44] ibid, at 72–73; Zimmerman and Du Plessis, above n 38, at 41; Markesinis, Lorenz and Dannemann, above n 39, at 764–65; Krebs, above n 38, at 101–03.

[45] Markesinis, Lorenz and Dannemann, above n 39, at 765; Häcker, *Consequences of Impaired Consent Transfers*, above n 39, at 74.

[46] Derived from E Bant, *The Change of Position Defence* (Oxford, Hart Publishing, 2009) 97, 103, itself derived from a common example in German scholarship: Zimmerman and Du Plessis, above n 38, at 41–42; Markesinis, Lorenz and Dannemann, above n 39, at 765; Krebs, above n 38, at 102–04.

[47] This will depend on a variety of factors, including any role fault may play in the defence.

car is a complete write-off, she may be able to recover the full measure of the purchase price without being required to make counter-restitution of the car's original value.

The *saldo* theory therefore allocates the risk of destruction of the asset received by a party pursuant to a voidable contract to the party in control of the asset at the time it is destroyed. However, it is not obvious (at least to this commentator) why the mutuality of performance in bilaterally executed contracts should dictate this result. While it could be said, for example, that by entering into the contract the claimant chooses to adopt the risk of possession of the benefit conferred pursuant to the contract, surely that choice is likely to have been vitiated by the same factor that makes the contract voidable? If so, then, normatively speaking, the rescinding claimant is in the same position as the innocent recipient of a mistaken payment that is subsequently stolen or spontaneously devalues (eg, through hyper inflation). There is no doubt that in German law, a defendant in such a position would be entitled to a change of position defence.[48] The analogy suggests that the two claims approach to restitution following rescission, in which the accidental destruction of the received benefit may be taken into account in reducing the claimant's counter-restitutionary liability, may not create such an obviously unjust result after all.[49]

So, the support to be derived for a net value or value surviving model of enrichment from the existence of the *saldo* theory is not as solid as it first might appear. Further, as I have argued at length elsewhere,[50] the English and Australian law of rescission is largely[51] consistent with a two claims model.[52] On this analysis, the rescinding claimant seeks to obtain restitution of the benefit transferred to the defendant, but this is subject to the defendant's counter-entitlement to restitution of benefits transferred to the claimant. The rationale of the requirement of counter-restitution embedded within the requirement of *restitutio in integrum* is to prevent the unjust enrichment of the rescinding party.[53] As Lord Wright explained

---

[48] See, eg, Dawson, above n 36, at 279–80. See also Krebs, above n 38, at 281.

[49] On the application of the change of position defence to 'independent' changes of position under Anglo-Australian law, see the discussion in the text accompanying nn 117–18, 130 below.

[50] Bant, above n 46, at 281.

[51] ibid, at 96–102 discusses the principal deviation, *Kleinwort Benson Ltd v Sandwell Borough Council* [1994] 4 All ER 890 (QB) 941, at length.

[52] For some recent Australian cases characterising the 'defence' of good consideration as a counter-claim for restitution, see *David Securities Pty Ltd v Commonwealth Bank of Australia* (1992) 175 CLR 353, 382 (Mason CJ, Deane, Toohey, Gaudron and McHugh JJ), 400 (Brennan J); *Ovidio Carrideo Nominees Pty Ltd v The Dog Depot Pty Ltd* [2006] VSCA 6, [2006] VConvR 54-713, applied in *R & C Mazzei Nominees Pty Ltd v Aegean Food Import Export Pty Ltd* [2006] VSC 210; [2006] VConvR 54-721 and followed in *Ragi Pty Ltd v Kiwi Munchies Pty Ltd* [2007] NSWADT 108.

[53] The unjust factor is failure of consideration: if required to make restitution, the basis on which the defendant transferred the benefit to the claimant—namely, the benefit of the

in *Spence v Crawford*: 'Though the defendant has been fraudulent, he must not be robbed, nor must the plaintiff be unjustly enriched, as he would be if he both got back what he had parted with and kept what he had received in return'.[54] It follows from this analysis that both parties are potentially entitled to rely upon their changes of position following receipt of the benefit in reduction of their restitutionary or counter-restitutionary liability.[55]

If correct, this analysis wholly undermines rescission as a paradigm for a model of restitution in which enrichment is identified in terms of 'net enrichment' and 'enrichment surviving'. It also requires a severe qualification of any analysis that seeks to explain rescission solely in terms of enrichment as rights. A core task of this chapter is to develop and defend these propositions.

B. The Problem of Proprietary Restitution

The second motivator informing Chambers' right/value thesis is the undoubted need to cast light on the vexed question of proprietary restitution.[56] The flip side of his proposition that there are two kinds of enrichment is that there is only one kind of restitution,[57] namely 'to give up the enrichment itself'.[58] The nature of the enrichment defines the subject (and thus nature) of restitution: 'The event dictates the response'.[59] If the enrichment is value, you get personal restitution; if the enrichment is a right, you get proprietary restitution. The form of the remedy follows the form of the enrichment received. In this way, the proposed bifurcation of enrichment clarifies the availability of proprietary restitution.

There are three things to say about this. First, we have already noted that while it might be true to say that if rights are the subject of an order for restitution, then the value of those rights is irrelevant to the remedy, this is simply an observation of the result, not the process of reasoning that leads to it. An order for restitution of title to a car is what it is: restitution of rights, regardless of value. The important question is how that conclusion (restitution of rights) is reached. Before restitution (and rescission) of rights can occur, there must first occur a complex process of

---

claimant's counter-performance—will fail. In other words, rescission triggers a subsequent failure of consideration.

[54] *Spence v Crawford* [1939] 3 All ER 271 (HL) 288–89.

[55] The traditional insistence of the common law on precise *restitutio in integrum*, designed to protect the defendant's change in position in the absence of machinery to make finer adjustments between the parties, is discussed in the text accompanying nn 95–99 below.

[56] Chambers, 'Two Kinds of Enrichment', above n 2, at 267, 277–78.

[57] ibid, at 267–69.

[58] ibid, at 267.

[59] ibid, at 278.

reasoning in which many considerations—including value—have a part to play. We have seen that Chambers acknowledges that value may impact on the claimant's entitlement to restitution of rights in unjust enrichment through the 'unjust factor' and 'at the expense of' requirements.[60] That is, value properly informs the claimant's entitlement to restitution of rights. There is no reason to think that value (and other considerations) may not likewise impact on the substance, content or form of the remedy that supports and gives effect to the claimant's entitlement as well. They may, for example, dictate that restitution of title to the car must be supplemented by an order for restitution of value for the depreciation of the car,[61] or that the claimant's right to restitution may be better met by an order for restitution of value *simpliciter*. It is no answer, therefore, to the questions of the availability and form of restitution to collapse the enrichment and remedial response inquiries.

Secondly, and leading on from the first point, it is not a matter of logical inevitability that the nature of the restitutionary remedy must follow the nature of the enrichment.[62] A claimant's entitlement to restitution of a right may be validly satisfied through an order for restitution of its value (or vice versa). The instances where pecuniary rescission has been awarded in lieu of proprietary rescission arguably reflect this view.[63] More broadly, it could be argued that the common law is replete with cases (conversion being an obvious example, but perhaps also restitution for *quantum valebat* and the limited availability of specific performance[64]) where pecuniary relief has been thought adequate to meet a claimant's entitlement, even though a specific remedy might have constituted a more perfectly matched response. Further, as again reflection on the common law arguably reveals, the right to specific or pecuniary relief might be influenced by a variety of matters external to the claim, such as the historical form of action through which the claim was traditionally made or the inadequate machinery available to courts to administer specific remedies. The acceptance of a degree of choice in the way a system responds to a claimant's right does not mean that one is forced to adopt the view that rights and remedies are disassociated (the 'basket of remedies' approach). Rather, the simple point is that neither logic nor practice dictates that the form of restitution must always follow the form of enrichment.

Thirdly, so far as arguments from principle are concerned, it was noted earlier that Chambers considers that restitution of rights, like value, must be limited to any 'enrichment surviving'.[65] He argues that 'the most per-

---

[60] Discussed in the text accompanying nn 4–15 above.

[61] Depreciation in rescission is discussed in detail in the text accompanying nn 110–21 below.

[62] cf Chambers, 'Two Kinds of Enrichment', above n 2, at 267–68, 277–78.

[63] Discussed below in the text accompanying nn 98–99 and nn 122–27.

[64] My thanks to Birke Häcker for suggesting these additional examples.

[65] Chambers, 'Two Kinds of Enrichment', above n 2, at 276.

fect form of restitution, and arguably the only justifiable response to unjust enrichment' is to make restitution of the remaining enrichment itself.[66] Given the strict liability imposed on unjust enrichment defendants, the defendant should only be required to give back what survives of the very benefit received, which may be either rights or value. In this way, restricting restitution to extant rights or value assists in preventing unjust enrichment defendants from being returned to a worse position than they occupied prior to their original receipt.[67] On Chambers' analysis, the bifurcation of enrichment into rights and value, and the limitation of restitution to the surviving enrichment, thus serve as crucial pillars supporting the imposition of strict liability in unjust enrichment.

However, there are clear limits to this analysis. Suppose I receive a cheque for $1 million from the lottery and place it on my mantelpiece. It subsequently transpires that I have been paid by mistake. I am in a position easily to make restitution of title to the cheque to the lottery fund when it discovers its error. But suppose further that, in the interim, I donate $500 000 from my account to a charity in reliance on my win, which spends the sum on its charitable works.[68] I can still make restitution of the cheque to the fund. And there has been no change of position relating to the cheque (such as its destruction, for example) which can operate to reduce my restitutionary liability. So unless the change of position defence extends beyond 'disenrichment', an order for restitution of the cheque will no doubt place me in a worse position than I occupied prior to my receipt. In other words, shifting the perspective of the inquiry from restitution of value to specific restitution (or from enrichment received to enrichment surviving) does not help to solve the problem of patrolling the effect of imposing full restitutionary liability in changed circumstances. Nor is the problem limited to pecuniary changes of position. Suppose, in a variation of the problem, I change my position by conceiving a child.[69] Again, there is no doubt that I can make restitution of my rights to the cheque. But that is not really the issue.

Chambers acknowledges that if the change of position defence is to apply in these circumstances, it cannot be solely enrichment-related.[70] He tentatively suggests that the defence can extend to such cases by analogy with the operation of value in the context of the 'at the expense of' requirement: 'Perhaps the defendant's loss of value can operate as a

[66] ibid, at 267.

[67] ibid, at 267–68.

[68] This addition to the hypothetical removes the possibility that the change of position might be reversible by litigation against the charity: Bant, above n 46, at 141–43.

[69] Discussed in detail in ibid, at 132–34. Cf *Hogan v Healy* (1877) 11 IR 119 (Exch Cham) 124 (Palles CB).

[70] Chambers, 'Two Kinds of Enrichment', above n 2, at 276. See generally Bant, above n 46 and the discussion in part V(A) below.

defence corresponding to the claimant's restitutionary rights'.[71] If so, then the defence clearly 'is not limited to disenrichment but includes other forms of detrimental reliance'. Although I wholeheartedly agree with this conclusion, the reasoning adopted to get there is difficult. We saw previously that the idea that rights and loss of value can 'correspond' in a legally relevant way through the 'at the expense of' requirement is highly contentious. But in any event, what is clear is that shifting to a rights/value dichotomy does not of itself determine the nature, form or extent of restitutionary liability. Nor does it supply a complete justification for imposing strict restitutionary liability. The proper form and extent of restitutionary liability demand a much broader inquiry. This is amply supported by the rescission case law, to which we now turn.

IV. RIGHTS AND VALUE IN RESCISSION

A. Rescission and Restitution for Unjust Enrichment

This chapter proceeds on the basis, shared with Chambers, that rescission case law provides valuable insights for the law of unjust enrichment. This is because the relationship between restitution for unjust enrichment and rescission for unjust enrichment is very close. Although they appear to have developed without much, if any, cross-referencing and hence diverge in some important respects,[72] they nonetheless address the same sorts of issues in much the same ways.

'Rescission' is used here to mean the exercise of the power to effect the reversal or unwinding of a transaction (whether it be contract, deed, gift[73] or conveyance[74]) *ab initio* so as to restore the parties to the status quo ante.[75] Rescission effects restitutionary relief in the sense of enabling or

---

[71] Chambers, 'Two Kinds of Enrichment', above n 2, at 276.

[72] Principally, in the election mechanism, which means that the defendant's liability to make restitution of benefits conferred pursuant to a contract, or to make proprietary restitution, arises only from the moment of election: see text accompanying nn 134–144 below. Cf the general position in unjust enrichment, discussed in the text accompanying nn 29–34 above. The operation of the election requirement also has certain consequences for pecuniary rescission. Exploration of these important issues, however, is unfortunately beyond the scope of this essay.

[73] See, eg, *Allcard v Skinner* (1887) 36 Ch D 145 (CA); *Quek v Beggs* (1990) 5 BPR 11,766 (New South Wales Supreme Court); *Louth v Diprose* (1992) 175 CLR 621.

[74] On the operation of rescission on conveyance, independent of contract, see B Häcker, 'Causality and Abstraction in the Common Law' in E Bant and M Harding (eds), *Exploring Private Law* (Cambridge, Cambridge University Press, 2010) 200.

[75] It thus stands in distinction to the confusing use of 'rescission' to indicate a right to terminate a transaction, which discharges the parties from future performance but does not affect accrued rights: see *McDonald v Dennys Lascelles Ltd* (1933) 48 CLR 457; *Johnson v Agnew* [1980] AC 367 (HL).

effecting[76] the return of the benefit received at the expense of the claimant.[77] Although it has been argued that in the case of wholly executory contracts, rescission involves the destruction rather than the giving back of contractual rights,[78] the effect is still to undo the benefit conferred on the other party. The match might not be precise but any distinction seems too fine to be of practical significance.

Turning to the triggers for rescission, it is notable that like restitution, a right to rescind arises both in response to wrongs[79] and in response to claims in unjust enrichment. Thus a limited right to rescind a transaction arises at common law in cases of fraud[80] and duress.[81] A right to rescind also arises in equity in a far wider range of circumstances such as misrepresentation (including innocent misrepresentation),[82] unilateral mistake,[83] duress,[84] undue influence,[85] unconscionable dealing[86] and breach of fiduciary duty.[87]

On its face, therefore, the relationship between rescission for unjust enrichment and restitution for unjust enrichment appears extremely close. For this reason, if no other, the operation of rescission and the role of rights and value within that doctrine call for close scrutiny. Rationality in the law demands that like cases are treated alike.

---

[76] On the effects of rescission, see B Häcker, 'Rescission and Third Party Rights' [2006] *Restitution Law Review* 21, 23–25; B Häcker, 'Rescission of Contract and Revesting of Title: A Reply to Mr Swadling' [2006] *Restitution Law Review* 106. For a critical view of the proprietary consequences of rescission at common law, see W Swadling, 'Rescission, Property, and the Common Law' (2005) 121 *Law Quarterly Review* 123.

[77] P Birks, *An Introduction to the Law of Restitution*, rev edn (Oxford, Clarendon Press, 1989) 163; D O'Sullivan, S Elliot and R Zakrzewski, *The Law of Rescission* (Oxford University Press, Oxford 2008) paras 13.03, 14.02, 15.03.

[78] A Burrows, *The Law of Restitution*, 2nd edn (London, Butterworths, 2002) 57–58. Andrew Burrows appears in the third edition to be slightly more conciliatory towards the restitutionary analysis: see A Burrows, *The Law of Restitution*, 3rd edn (Oxford, Oxford University Press, 2001) 17–20. See also G Virgo, *The Principles of the Law of Restitution*, 2nd edn (Oxford, Oxford University Press, 2006) 29. Cf McFarlane, above n 9, text accompanying nn 51–55.

[79] Such as breach of fiduciary duty: see below n 87.

[80] *Load v Green* (1846) 15 M&W 216, 153 ER 828; *Car and Universal Finance Co Ltd v Caldwell* [1965] 1 QB 525 (HL).

[81] *Universe Tankships Inc of Monrovia v International Transport Workers Federation* [1983] 1 AC 366 (HL) 384 (Lord Diplock), 400 (Lord Scarman), endorsed by McHugh JA in *Crescendo Management Pty Ltd v Westpac Banking Corporation* (1988) 19 NSWLR 40 (New South Wales Court of Appeal) 45; *Dimskal Shipping Co SA v International Transport Workers Federation (The Evia Luck) (No 2)* [1992] 2 AC 152 (HL).

[82] *Redgrave v Hurd* (1881) 20 Ch D 1 (CA); *Alati v Kruger* (1955) 94 CLR 216.

[83] *Taylor v Johnson* (1983) 151 CLR 422.

[84] *Barton v Armstrong* [1976] AC 106 (PC) 118; *Halpern v Halpern* [2007] EWCA Civ 291, [2008] QB 195.

[85] *Allcard v Skinner* (1887) 36 Ch D 145 (CA); *Johnson v Buttress* (1936) 56 CLR 113.

[86] *Louth v Diprose* (1992) 175 CLR 621.

[87] *McKenzie v McDonald* [1927] VLR 134; *Maguire v Makaronis* (1998) 188 CLR 449.

B. *Restitutio in Integrum* and the Role of Value in Counter-Restitution

It is clear that any very broad claim that value is irrelevant to rescission of rights must be qualified. This is because it is a long-standing condition of rescission both at common law and in equity that *restitutio in integrum* must be possible.[88] The condition reflects a concept of rescission as a bipartite process, requiring an unwinding of the transaction on both sides so that the parties are restored substantially to the status quo ante.[89] Part of this 'unwinding' process requires counter-restitution of any benefits received by a claimant as a condition of obtaining rescission and restitution of any benefits conferred on the defendant. If counter-restitution is impossible, then the traditional position is that rescission cannot occur. As discussed below, the requirement of *restitutio in integrum* also encompasses cases where, notwithstanding the ability of the claimant to make counter-restitution, the parties' respective positions have so changed that to permit rescission would place the defendant in an unjustifiably worse (including entirely different) position than he or she occupied prior to the transaction.[90] Thus the requirement may be triggered by irreversible changes of position that have been instigated by the parties in reliance on their receipt of a benefit under the impugned transaction but which do not affect their ability to make full restitution or counter-restitution of received benefits. The next section addresses this second aspect of the *restitutio in integrum* requirement.

A change in the value of a received benefit following transfer often forms an important aspect of rescinding parties' mutual restitutionary and counter-restitutionary liabilities. This is so even in cases where restitution of rights transferred pursuant to the impugned transaction clearly remains possible. The most striking example of this phenomenon is found in the rule that if a benefit received by a rescinding claimant has depreciated due to the act of the claimant, the claimant may be required to make good the difference in value to the defendant as a condition of rescission.[91] To

---

[88] Discussed at length in *Halpern v Halpern* [2007] EWCA Civ 291, [2009] QB 195 [55]–[75] (Carnwath LJ; Sedley and Waller LJJ concurring).

[89] *Newbigging v Adam* (1886) 34 Ch D 582 (CA) 595 (Bowen LJ); *Abram Steamship Co Ltd v Westville Shipping Co Ltd* [1923] AC 773 (HL) 781 (Lord Atkinson); *Spence v Crawford* [1939] 3 All ER 271 (HL) 289 (Lord Wright). Cf O'Sullivan, Elliot and Zakrzewski, above n 77, at para 18.03.

[90] See text accompanying nn 108–29 below. A similar view is taken by O'Sullivan, Elliot and Zakrzewski, above n 77, at paras 18.03–18.07. The learned authors, however, ultimately deny the alignment between *restitutio in integrum*, unjust enrichment and change of position, particularly because they regard the last as solely concerned with disenrichment. On the role of the defence beyond disenrichment, see Part IV(c) and text accompanying n 133 below.

[91] *Erlanger v The New Sombrero Phosphate Company* (1878) 3 App Cas 1218 (HL) 1278 (Lord Blackburn), cited with approval in *Alati v Kruger* (1955) 94 CLR 216, 223–24 (Dixon CJ, Webb, Kitto and Taylor JJ). See also *Brown v Smitt* (1924) 34 CLR 160, 164 (Knox CJ, Gavan Duffy and Starke JJ); *Balfour & Clark v Hollandia Ravensthorpe NL* (1978) 18 SASR 240.

take the earlier example, suppose a claimant purchases title to a car as a result of the defendant's innocent misrepresentation and damages the car in an accident. In equity, she will be required to make a money payment to the defendant to make good the deterioration in value of the title, together with restitution of the title to the car, as a condition of rescission. If the claimant cannot or will not make good that difference so as to make complete counter-restitution, rescission may be denied. This is so notwithstanding that it remains entirely possible to make counter-restitution of title (that is, the right) to the received benefit. This tells us that the value of the right at the time of receipt is not only relevant but crucial to rescission. This is not a model predicated on a prima facie right to restitution of 'enrichment surviving', but on a requirement of restitution of enrichment received, indentified by reference both to the right and its value.

A classic example of the counter-restitution principle at work is contained in the recent New South Wales Court of Appeal decision in *Campbell v Backoffice Investments Pty Ltd*.[92] In that case, Backoffice entered into a share sale agreement to purchase one of two issued shares in a company from Campbell. Other, related agreements were also entered into regarding the future management and directorship of the company, to be shared between Campbell and Weeks, the shareholder and director of Backoffice. The relationship between Weeks and Campbell subsequently deteriorated and Backoffice and Weeks sought rescission of the share purchase contract on statutory grounds. Interestingly, Campbell argued that at best, Backoffice was entitled only to the difference between the value of what was paid for the shares and their actual value at the point of sale—the net gain approach. On this approach, Backoffice would be entitled to nothing. However, Giles JA, with whom Basten JA and Young CJ concurred on this point, preferred an approach that allowed the possibility that Backoffice was entitled to claim restitution of the full value of the purchase price, but made the right subject to the requirements of *restitutio in integrum*. On this approach, the contract of sale could no longer be avoided. By the time Backoffice sought to rescind the contract, although the share right still existed and could be returned to Campbell, it was worthless. Moreover, Giles JA stated, it was 'of course necessary to look beyond the share'.[93] The business run by the company had grossly deteriorated since the sale of the share, in part due to acts of Weeks and Backoffice. In those circumstances, '[r]epayment of $850,000 in return for

---

[92] *Campbell v Backoffice Investments Pty Ltd* [2008] NSWCA 95, (2008) 66 ACSR 359 (revd on other grounds in *Campbell v Backoffice Investments Pty Ltd* [2009] HCA 25, (2009) 238 CLR 304). See also *Chint Australasia Pty Ltd v Cosmoluce Pty Ltd* [2008] NSWSC 635, (2008) 14 BPR 98,336 [127]–[133] (Einstein J).

[93] *Campbell v Backoffice Investments Pty Ltd* [2008] NSWCA 95, (2008) 66 ACSR 359 [107].

a worthless share, even taking into account [Campbell] having got back the much deteriorated business, would not restore the parties to anything like their pre-contracts positions'.[94] Notably, Backoffice had not offered to be subject to an account, even if it had been possible to make financial adjustments to achieve substantial *restitutio in integrum*. This case is just one of many in which considerations of restitution of rights and value are inextricably entwined in determining the claimant's right to rescind. A picture of rescission in such cases that concentrates solely on enrichment as rights and excludes considerations of value is fundamentally incomplete.

Even cases that, on their face, provide considerable support for Chambers' thesis break down on closer analysis. Consider, for example, the seminal case of *Hunt v Silk*.[95] In that case, a tenant sought to 'rescind' (terminate) an agreement to lease and obtain restitution of £10 which he had paid to a landlord pursuant to the agreement. However, the tenant's use of the land under the contract for a matter of a few days meant that *restitutio in integrum* was impossible at common law. Although the case was one of termination rather than rescission proper, it has always been treated as an exemplar of the operation of rescission at common law. On that basis, it is notable that the agreement could be rescinded in the sense that any contractual rights could be returned to the landlord. Counter-restitution of the rights under the agreement was entirely possible.[96] The problem was that the courts were concerned with the tenant's use of the land and the perceived inability of common law courts to make restitution of the value of that use.[97] Times have changed since then. Courts have demonstrated a preparedness to switch from proprietary to pecuniary rescission[98] and regularly make pecuniary allowances for use (as well as deterioration and improvements) as part of the process of rescission.[99] At one level, this development in the law supports Chambers' analysis.

---

[94] ibid.

[95] *Hunt v Silk* (1804) 5 East 449, 102 ER 1142. See also *Blackburn v Smith* (1848) 2 Ex 783, 154 ER 707.

[96] It would be possible to specify the nature of the right with sufficient particularity to preclude this possibility: eg, that it was not possible to make restitution of an unused right to intermediate possession. But this very 'fat' conception of rights simply feeds considerations of value directly into the content of the right.

[97] *Erlanger v The New Sombrero Phosphate Co* (1878) 3 App Cas 1218 (HL) 1278 (Lord Blackburn); *Alati v Kruger* (1955) 94 CLR 216, 225 (Dixon CJ, Webb, Kitto and Taylor JJ). Cf O'Sullivan, Elliott and Zakrzewski, above n 77, at paras 18.23–18.25 who identify the basis of the common law's refusal to order pecuniary adjustments not in any deficiency in the accounting machinery at common law but in the self-help nature of the remedy. Although there is not the space to address this view in detail here, I would simply note that if the claimant's election to rescind does automatically trigger a right in the defendant to counter-restitution, then it would be very odd if that right and the attendant legal consequences were non-justiciable. Cf the very active supervisory role of courts in equitable rescission: see, eg, text accompanying nn 110–27 below.

[98] See, eg, *Hartigan v International Society for Krishna Consciousness Incorporated* [2002] NSWSC 810; *Halpern v Halpern* [2007] EWCA Civ 291, [2008] QB 195.

[99] See the discussion in the text accompanying nn 110–27 below.

There were not simply one but two forms of enrichment received by the tenant in *Hunt v Silk* and both could (and perhaps should)[100] have been addressed independently. But the point is that issues of value intimately affected the availability of relief. If the value of the tenant's occupation did not matter, surely counter-restitution of his contractual rights to the landlord could have taken place automatically. The outcome suggests that value was not irrelevant but decisive. And the fact that pecuniary adjustments and allowances are commonly ordered where the nature or value of rights have been altered only highlights the relevance of value throughout the entire process.

On the other hand, as indicated earlier, *restitutio in integrum* is not solely concerned with issues of value. The focus of the principle is on restoring the parties in substance to the status quo ante. Sometimes, the positions of the parties have so changed that it is impossible to achieve *restitutio in integrum*, whatever issues of rights and values may be involved. Thus in the leading common law cases of *Clarke v Dickson*[101] and *Western Bank of Scotland v Addie*,[102] the claimants were induced to purchase shares in a company by fraudulent misrepresentations. In both cases, by the time the claimant came to know of the fraud and attempted to rescind the transaction, the nature of the company to which the shares related had so changed that rescission was held to be barred. In both cases, the value of the shares had depreciated. But both decisions contemplate that whatever might be the position in relation to restitution of the shares, the change in the nature of the company of itself would suffice to bar rescission.[103] Most explicitly, in *Western Bank of Scotland*, Lord Cranworth stated:

> Assuming that this company, by its directors, fraudulently induced the Respondent to purchase 135 of these shares, so as to entitle him to relief against the company, he cannot insist on *restitutio in integrum* unless he is in a condition to restore the shares which he so purchased. But this is impossible. The purchase was made by him in 1855, and in 1857 he was party to a proceeding whereby the company from which the purchase was made was put an end to. It ceased to be an unincorporated and became an incorporated company, with many statutable incidents connected with it which did not exist before the incorporation. This new company is now in course of being wound up; but even if that were not so, if it still were carrying on the business of bankers, *restitutio in integrum* would have been impossible. The Respondent might in that case have given up 135 shares of the new company, and these

---

[100] cf O'Sullivan, Elliott and Zakrzewski, above n 77, at paras 18.23–18.25.

[101] *Clarke v Dickson* (1858) EB & E 148, 120 ER 463. See also *Capcorn Holding plc v Edwards* [2007] EWHC 2662 (Ch).

[102] *Western Bank of Scotland v Addie* (1867) LR 1 Sc 145 (HL) (*Western Bank of Scotland*).

[103] *Clarke v Dickson* (1858) EB & E 148, 154 (Erle J), 154–55 (Crompton J); 120 ER 463, 467 (Erle J), 467 (Crompton J); ibid, at 159–60.

shares might have been as valuable as, or even more valuable than, the shares which he was induced to purchase, but they would not have been shares in the same company; and unless he was in a position to restore the very thing which he was fraudulently induced to purchase, he cannot have relief by way of restitutio in integrum.[104]

It could be said that the share rights in these cases had changed in nature and thus the original rights could not be restored. The companies to which the share rights related had changed and thus so had the nature of the rights. But that just highlights the fact that thinking in terms of a strict rights/value dichotomy is unhelpful. The ability to identify extant rights and to restore them is not interesting in this context: it is what the rights relate to, their content and value that matters.[105] The hurdle to rescission in these cases was not an inability to restore share rights or their value: rather, the problem was that the company was now simply different from how it had been. Giving the defendant back his share rights, relating as they now did to a fundamentally different type of company, would be returning him to a quite different position than he occupied prior to his receipt. An even clearer example is the Irish case of *Northern Bank Finance Corporation Ltd v Charlton*,[106] where *restitutio in integrum* was impossible because the business of the company had changed from operating licensed premises to substantially a property holding company. Analysing the case in terms of either restitution of rights or value sheds no real light on the reason for the failure to rescind.

The question that arises, therefore, is if (as Chambers argues) rights are inherently enriching and, furthermore, their lack of value is irrelevant to rescission of rights, why do courts then regularly engage in the protracted examination of non-rights related issues?

C. *Restitutio in Integrum* and the Change of Position Defence

A more promising line of inquiry may be revealed through applying a two claims analysis to the case law and, in particular, considering the requirement of *restitutio in integrum* through the lens of the change of position defence. The previous section demonstrated that the requirement of counter-restitution responds to the defendant's 'change in exchange' in conferring a benefit on the claimant. It operates to give effect to the defendant's prima facie right to full counter-restitution from the claimant.[107] However, beyond this requirement, the principle of *restitutio in*

---

[104] *Western Bank of Scotland* (1867) LR 1 Sc 145 (HL) 165–66.

[105] See the comment in above n 96.

[106] *Northern Bank Finance Corporation Ltd v Charlton* [1979] IR 149 (Supreme Court of Ireland) 210.

[107] O'Sullivan, Elliott and Zakrzewski, above n 77, at paras 18.01–18.07, 18.27–18.28.

integrum requires the changes of position of both parties to be taken into account in determining their respective restitutionary liabilities. In the operation of the principle in this aspect, there is a strong analogy to the change of position defence.[108] Adopting a change of position analysis casts fresh light on the very difficult allowance and accounting adjustments that often accompany rescission.[109]

The rescinding claimant's prima facie obligation to make full counter-restitution to the defendant as a condition of rescission is not absolute. The claimant's fault in causing the deterioration is a key factor in determining the extent of his or her counter-restitutionary liability. As explained in the joint judgment of the High Court of Australia in *Alati v Kruger*,[110] even at common law rescission was not barred where the deterioration occurred without fault on the part of the claimant, such as where deterioration was inherent in the nature of the asset or was caused by independent market forces.[111] But the case law is generally silent as to why this should be so.[112] Of the four possible explanations, the best 'fit' with the case law lies with change of position.

First, it is clear that the claimant's good faith cannot of itself constitute the reason for denying the defendant his or her right to counter-restitution or counter-restitution in full. Restitutionary liability in unjust enrichment is notoriously strict. There is no reason to think that counter-restitutionary liability is any different.

Secondly, the 'independent depreciation' rules cannot be explained on the basis that the decline in value was somehow inevitable and thus if the claimant had never received the asset, the defendant would nonetheless have suffered the loss in its value. Particularly in the case of defendants whose conduct did not amount to wrongdoing, it should not be assumed against the defendant that, absent the impugned transaction, the defendant would not have transferred the asset to someone else instead and so again avoided any inevitable decline.[113] Further, there is nothing in the case law to suggest that an independent change in the received benefit caused by a once-off natural calamity (such as a lightning strike killing a

---

[108] The argument is developed most fully in Bant, above n 46, at ch 4.

[109] Even notoriously difficult rules, such as the rule in *Seddon v North Eastern Salt Co Ltd (Seddon's Case)* [1905] 1 Ch 326 (Ch), may be better (though not wholly) understood through the lens of change of position, a thought that appears to have struck Birks in P Birks, 'No Consideration: Restitution after Void Contracts' (1993) 23 *University of Western Australia Law Review* 195, 230 n 137, and morphed into a change of position argument in Birks, *Unjust Enrichment*, above n 15, at 259.

[110] *Alati v Kruger* (1955) 94 CLR 216, 225 (Dixon CJ, Webb, Kitto and Taylor JJ).

[111] cf *Newbigging v Adam* (1886) 34 Ch D 582 (CA) 588 (Cotton LJ); *Adam v Newbigging* (1888) 13 App Cas 308 (HL) 330 (Lord Herschell); *Armstrong v Jackson* [1917] 2 KB 822 (KB) 829–30 (McCardie J).

[112] One exception is the discussion of Cleasby B in *Head v Tattersall* (1871) LR 7 Ex 7 (Exch) 13–14 (risk of depreciation should lie with eventual owner). However, the original premise is unsupported by authority and assumes the very issue in question.

[113] cf O'Sullivan, Elliot and Zakrzewski, above n 77, at para 18.94.

horse transferred to the claimant) would be treated any differently from a sharp decline in value brought about by a change in market forces. Yet in that case, it would not be possible to argue that the benefit (the horse) would have declined in value whoever held it. The lightning might well have missed the horse if it had been in another's paddock.

Thirdly, the defendant's own role in the transaction, or in creating an 'inherent vice' in the benefit that dictates its depreciation, might properly preclude him or her from complaining of the ultimate depreciation of the asset transferred to the claimant. In *Armstrong v Jackson*,[114] a broker sold his shares in a company to his client in breach of his fiduciary duty and as a result of various fraudulent misrepresentations. By the time the client found out and sought to rescind the contract of purchase, the shares had depreciated to a fraction of their original value. The question arose whether *restitutio in integrum* was still possible. In holding that it was, McCardie J emphasised that the shares could still be returned in specie and that it did not lie in the defendant's mouth, having fraudulently induced the claimant to purchase his shares, to complain that if the contract be set aside, he would be left in a worse position than if the contract had never been entered into.[115] The case could be taken as supporting Chambers' view that the value of rights under rescission is irrelevant to restitution of those rights. However, the result is just as consistent with the view that the defendant's fault operated to reduce his right to full counter-restitution, thereby reducing the protection afforded to his change-in-exchange and effectively protecting the claimant from the consequences of his change of position. On this approach, the important overarching principle, itself dictated by the limited purpose of restitution, is that the parties should not be placed unjustifiably in a worse (including entirely different) position than they occupied prior to their receipt. The defendant's fault may rightly bear on this question. Far from showing, therefore, that value is irrelevant, the case forms an important example of fault playing a role in determining the extent of restitutionary liability.

That having been said, it is clear from the cases that the fault of the defendant (whether in inducing the transaction or in causing the inherent defect in the benefit transferred to the claimant) is not the only relevant factor informing the independent depreciation rules. The rules apply beyond fraud to cases of undue influence and innocent misrepresentation and in respect of deterioration suffered entirely independently

---

[114] *Armstrong v Jackson* [1917] 2 KB 822 (KB).

[115] ibid, at 829–30. See also *Northern Bank Finance Corporation Ltd v Charlton* [1979] IR 149 (Supreme Court of Ireland) 18 (O'Higgins CJ; Butler J concurring); *Cheese v Thomas* [1994] 1 WLR 129 (CA) 136 (Sir Donald Nicholls V-C). Cf *Alati v Kruger* (1955) 94 CLR 216. See also *Kellogg Brown & Root Inc v Aerotech Herman Nelson Inc* (2004) 238 DLR (4th) 594 (Manitoba Court of Appeal) [66] (Scott CJM and Steel JA).

of the defendant (such as deterioration caused by independent market forces).[116]

This suggests the final (and best) explanation, namely that the primary focus of the rules is on protecting the claimant making counter-restitution. On this analysis, the rules reflect judicial concern to provide *the claimant* with a *pro tanto* change of position defence.[117] On a two claims analysis, the defendant's counter-claim in unjust enrichment for the benefit conferred on a claimant should be subject to the usual defences, including the change of position defence. Consistently with this approach, the deterioration rules provide that where the benefit received by the claimant has deteriorated due to its inherent qualities or without the fault of the claimant, a change of position defence applies to protect the claimant from full counter-restitutionary liability.

Turning to the other side of the coin, and once more consistently with the two claims analysis, it is generally accepted that a defendant will not be held liable to pay an amount to the claimant reflecting the inherent depreciation of a benefit not due to the fault of the defendant. This rule again operates much like a change of position defence for the defendant. As a matter of practice, however, the concern rarely arises in cases of rescission.[118] As Lord Wright commented in *Spence v Crawford*, the 'plaintiff who seeks to set aside the contract will generally be reasonable in the standard of restitution he requires'.[119]

Interestingly, Lord Wright added that, in cases of deterioration in which the defendant has been fraudulent, the court may order 'compensation to make good the change of position'.[120] That is, where the defendant is fraudulent he cannot rely on the alteration in his position to reduce his liability to return in substance the original benefit received. This is consistent with the modern view that a wrongdoer is precluded from relying on the change of position defence.[121]

Adopting a change of position analysis thus appears to shed considerable light on the reasons underpinning the deterioration rules governing mutual restitution of principal benefits received under a rescinded transaction. Moreover, a change of position analysis may help to explain why parties are sometimes excused from making restitution and counter-restitution of the objective *use value* of a received benefit.[122] The usual

---

[116] See, eg, *Armstrong v Jackson* [1917] KB 822 (KB); *Cheese v Thomas* [1994] 1 WLR 129 (CA) 135 (Sir Donald Nicholls V-C); *Balfour & Clark v Hollandia Ravensthorpe NL* (1978) 18 SASR 240, 258 (Hogarth J).

[117] M Chen-Wishart, 'Unjust Factors and the Restitutionary Response' (2000) 20 *Oxford Journal of Legal Studies* 557, 562; S Worthington, 'The Proprietary Consequences of Rescission' [2002] *Restitution Law Review* 28, 55.

[118] Worthington, above n 117, at 56 n 173.

[119] *Spence v Crawford* [1939] 3 All ER 271 (HL) 289.

[120] ibid, citing *Lagunas Nitrate Co v Lagunas Syndicate* [1899] 2 Ch 392 (CA).

[121] *Lipkin Gorman* [1991] 2 AC 548 (HL) 580 (Lord Goff).

[122] Helpfully discussed in O'Sullivan, Elliott and Zakrzewski, above n 77, at paras 17.09–

position is that parties are required to make restitution ('account for') the reasonable market value of the use of a benefit transferred pursuant to a rescinded transaction, whether it be land, chattels or money. Thus courts have ordered allowances for rent,[123] the value of hiring a motor vehicle,[124] interest[125] and so on. But sometimes recipients have not actually used the benefit, or have not used the benefit to its full market value. Restitution is then restricted to the lesser value actually obtained.[126] Where a party has been fraudulent, however, restitution of the full market value of the use is required. Usually, this rule is analysed as responding to the defendant's wilful default, where the defendant's liability is 'upgraded' because of their wrongdoing.[127] However, this analysis smacks of penalty. An alternative approach is to see innocent defendants as entitled to a change of position defence, where they have changed their position in reliance on receiving the asset (and hence the opportunity to use it) by deciding not to use the asset to its full potential, or by making decisions regarding its use that turned out not to be financially sound. Where a defendant has been fraudulent, he or she has no entitlement to the defence and thus must make full restitution of the objective value of the use benefit received.

In summary, far from demonstrating that value is irrelevant to rescission, an examination of the rescission case law shows that value plays an important informing role in the change of position considerations that shape rescission. Further, Lord Wright's comments regarding the choices open to a rescinding claimant faced with obtaining restitution of a devalued benefit raises an important broader point concerning enrichment as rights and value, and restitution of those enrichments. The comment supports the view that a claimant is entitled to waive his or her right to restitution of value and simply obtain restitution of rights, if those rights are worthless. There is, after all, no harm in requiring a defendant to make restitution of extant but worthless rights.[128] Chambers infers from this that the value of rights in cases of rescission of rights is always irrelevant.

17.20. It is perhaps regrettable that this group of cases was not drawn to the attention of the House of Lords in *Sempra Metals* [2007] UKHL 34, [2008] 1 AC 561. Had it been, much of the discussion of 'subjective devaluation' may have been better directed towards change of position: see the discussion by Bant, above n 46, at 129–30.

[123] See, eg, *Alati v Kruger* (1955) 94 CLR 216. See also *Koutsonicolis v Principe (No 2)* (1987) 48 SASR 328.

[124] See, eg, *F & B Transport Ltd v White Truck Sales Manitoba* (1964) 47 DLR (2d) 419 (Manitoba Court of Queen's Bench).

[125] See, eg, *Maguire v Makaronis* (1996) 188 CLR 449.

[126] See, eg, *Coastal Estates Pty Ltd v Melevende* [1965] VR 433, 440–41 (Sholl J).

[127] O'Sullivan, Elliott and Zakrzewski, above n 77, at paras 17.09–17.12.

[128] Where the right is worthless, a system might rightly consider that it will not expend scarce resources enforcing the claimant's entitlement. However, in the case of rescission, traditionally regarded as a self-help remedy, any policy against trivialities in the law is not so obviously engaged. On the characterisation of rescission as a self-help remedy, see further below n 136 and text accompanying n 143 below.

But the deterioration rules make clear that it is one thing to waive a right to restitution of value; it is another to be forced to accept restitution of valueless or depreciated rights. A defendant will not always be forced to accept counter-restitution of worthless rights that originally had considerable value. Indeed, unless change of position considerations apply to protect the claimant, the defendant to an action of rescission is prima facie entitled to full counter-restitution of the benefit from the claimant and to be protected from any loss in its value.[129]

V. SOME IMPLICATIONS FROM RESCISSION FOR THE LAW OF UNJUST ENRICHMENT

A. For Change of Position

The preceding analysis demonstrates that the rescission case law tells us a good deal about the change of position defence and, inferentially, the law of unjust enrichment. Turning first to its direct implications for change of position, the law of rescission clearly contains a wealth of decisions that provide guidance on difficult and unresolved issues in that defence. For example, we have seen that the requirement of *restitutio in integrum* clearly encompasses cases where the received benefit has naturally deteriorated. That is, it encompasses 'independent' changes in the received benefit as well as broader changes made by a party in reliance on the receipt of the benefit. This has a significant bearing on the ongoing debate over competing 'broad' and 'narrow' versions of the change of position defence.[130] And the corpus of rescission case law also contains numerous examples of, and thus sheds considerable light on, the role of fault in unjust enrichment and in particular the vexed 'wrongdoer' bar to the change of position defence.

Further, it is an interesting feature of the requirement of *restitutio in integrum* that it applies in principle both to rescission for unjust enrichment and rescission for wrongs.[131] To the extent that it incorporates change of position considerations, therefore, the doctrine suggests that the natural focus of the defence is on the remedy of restitution, rather than the particular cause of action in unjust enrichment. This makes some sense. If the aim of restitution is to reverse the transfer of benefit so as

---

[129] Other defences may apply to deny this right, such as laches, limitations periods or estoppel.

[130] *Scottish Equitable Plc v Derby* [2001] EWCA Civ 369, [2001] 3 All ER 818 [30] (Robert Walker LJ) endorsing A Burrows, *The Law of Restitution*, 1st edn (London, Butterworths, 1993) 425–28. See now Burrows, *The Law of Restitution*, 3rd edn, above n 78, at 528–31. For reconciliation of the two versions, see Bant, above n 46, at 143–51.

[131] As can be seen by its application to wrongs-based grounds for rescission, such as breach of fiduciary duty.

to restore the parties to the status quo ante, it is appropriate to consider whether requiring full restitution of rights or value will place the defendant in an unjustifiably worse (including entirely different) position than he or she occupied prior to his or her receipt.[132] In this respect, the company share cases demonstrate that the problem is not simply one of the theoretical possibility of restoring extant rights or value. The inquiry is a broader one, going to the ability to restore the parties substantially to their pre-transaction positions.

This conclusion underscores the point that overly focusing on a rights/value dichotomy may have a tendency to obscure broader considerations that impact on the right to restitution. Indeed, particularly when viewed through the lens of Chambers' rights/value analysis, the rescission authorities clearly support the view that the defence of change of position is not limited to 'disenrichment'. The defence of *'restitutio in integrum* impossible' encompasses consequential and irreversible changes of position that do not directly relate either to the precise right or value received. That is, the defence applies where there is no difficulty in returning the particular benefit received (a company share or its value, a right to a leasehold and so on) but there have been other consequential changes of position that must affect the nature and extent of restitutionary liability. It follows that it (and by analogy, the change of position defence) cannot be solely enrichment-related.[133]

B. Proprietary Powers

Secondly, the rescission cases tell us that sometimes proprietary restitution will be subject to a change of position defence. However, its application underscores the singular nature of rescission as a form of proprietary right. Häcker has convincingly demonstrated, in my view, that the right to rescind is a form of proprietary power. A proprietary power is a kind of inchoate or embryonic proprietary right.[134] The right-holder has the power to create a vested proprietary right to the asset held by the defendant. But prior to the exercise of the power, the holder of the power has no vested proprietary interest such as the beneficiary's interest under an imposed trust.[135] Rather, the holder only has a right or power to pull

---

[132] The rationale of the defence is discussed in Bant, above n 46, at 211–20.

[133] cf Chambers, 'Two Kinds of Enrichment', above n 2, at 275–76, seemingly accepting this proposition. For a full defence of the view that change of position is not concerned solely with 'disenrichment', see Bant, above n 46, at ch 5.

[134] See in particular Häcker, *Consequences of Impaired Consent Transfers*, above n 39, at ch 4; B Häcker, 'Proprietary Restitution after Impaired Consent Transfers: A Generalised Power Model' [2009] *Cambridge Law Journal* 324.

[135] *Daly v The Sydney Stock Exchange Ltd* (1986) 160 CLR 371, 390 (Brennan J; Wilson J agreeing); *Wickham Developments Ltd v Parker* (Unreported, Queensland Court

back legal title (at common law) or bring a trust into existence (in equity). Once the power is exercised,[136] the claimant has a vested proprietary right to the asset held by the defendant and accordingly enjoys the benefit of any increase in its value.

Prior to its exercise, the proprietary power is more fragile than a vested trust right. An equitable power to rescind can be extinguished by the subsequent bona fide purchase of a legal *or* equitable interest in the asset the subject of the power.[137] The comparative fragility of proprietary powers is even starker in the case of common law powers, which are likewise extinguished by the transfer of the impugned property to a bona fide purchaser.[138] This susceptibility stands in marked contrast with the durability of vested common law property rights, in respect of which the defence of bona fide purchase has only had a very limited operation confined, in general terms, to cases of currency and limited instances of 'market overt'.[139] The distinction highlights the difference in durability between vested proprietary rights both at common law and in equity and non-vested, unexercised proprietary powers.

Proprietary powers may be more susceptible to extinction in other respects as well. For example, there is considerable Australian authority to the effect that an unexercised power to rescind a transfer of property is not a 'caveatable interest' under the Torrens system of title registration.[140] This can be justified on the basis that prior to its exercise, the

of Appeal, Fitzgerald P, McPherson and Pincus JJA, 20 June 1995); *Greater Pacific Investments Pty Ltd (in liq) v Australian National Industries Ltd* (1996) 39 NSWLR 143, 152–53 (McLelland AJA, Priestley and Meagher JJA concurring); *Hancock Family Memorial Foundation Ltd v Porteous* [2000] WASCA 29, (2000) 22 WAR 198 [173]–[206] (Ipp, Owen and McKechnie JJ). *Daly* was cited with approval and applied in *Barclays Bank v Boulter* [1999] 4 All ER 513 (HL) 518 (Lord Hoffmann) and *Lonrho plc v Fayed (No 2)* [1991] 4 All ER 961 (Ch) 971 (Millett J). See also *Bristol and West Building Society v Mothew* [1998] Ch 1 (CA) 22–23 (Millett LJ); *Shalson v Russo* [2003] EWHC 1637 (Ch), [2005] Ch 281 [108]–[111] (Rimer J). Against *Westdeutsche Landesbank Girozentrale v Islington London Borough Council* [1996] AC 669 (HL) 716 (Lord Browne-Wilkinson).

[136] There is considerable debate over when this occurs, the candidates including the date of purported exercise by the rescinding party, the date of court order (at which issues of *restitutio in integrum* and defences to rescission are resolved), or a mixture of the two depending on whether rescission occurs in equity or at common law: see text accompanying n 143 below.

[137] *Latec Investments Ltd v Hotel Terrigal Pty Ltd (in liq)* (1965) 113 CLR 265.

[138] *Hunter BNZ Finance Ltd v CG Maloney Pty Ltd* (1988) 18 NSWLR 420.

[139] Discussed in D Fox, '*Bona Fide* Purchase and the Currency of Money' [1996] *Cambridge Law Journal* 547; W Swadling, 'Restitution and *Bona Fide* Purchase' in W Swadling (ed), *The Limits of Restitutionary Claims: A Comparative Analysis* (Glasgow, United Kingdom National Committee of Comparative Law, 1997) 79, 82–89. Note that market overt has been abolished in the United Kingdom, but it still exists in some Australian States.

[140] *Re Pile's Caveats* [1981] Qd R 81; *Swanston Mortgage Pty Ltd v Trepan Investments Pty Ltd* [1994] 1 VR 672; *Wickham Developments Ltd v Parker* (Unreported, Queensland Court of Appeal, Fitzgerald P, McPherson and Pincus JJA, 20 June 1995); *Tanzone Pty Ltd v Westpac Banking Corporation* [1999] NSWSC 478, (2000) 9 BPR 17,287 (revd on other grounds in *Westpac Banking Corporation v Tanzone Pty Ltd* [2000] NSWCA 25, (2000)

holder of a proprietary power has no vested proprietary interest in the asset the subject of the right.[141]

However, authority is by no means uniform.[142] The inconsistency reflects the ongoing uncertainty as to whether rescission is an act of the rescinding party or that of the court. The traditional view has been that rescission is an act of the rescinding party, completed when he or she informs the defendant of his or her intention to reclaim title to the impugned asset.[143] However, the picture is complicated by the undoubted role played by courts in determining whether any purported act of rescission was effective, in particular in determining whether *restitutio in integrum* is possible and determining the conditions on which rescission could, or did, occur in order to enable the parties to be returned to the status quo ante. If the act of rescission is subject to, or conditional upon, judicial approval—itself a process in which discretionary considerations play a leading role—it becomes even more difficult to see that the holder of a proprietary power has a proprietary interest sufficient to support a caveat.[144] It also points to a very different kind of proprietary right than that which arises pursuant to a fixed (vested) trust right.

This difference suggests why rights to rescind might also be fragile in

---

9 BPR 17,521); *Global Minerals Australia Pty Ltd v Valerica Pty Ltd* [2000] NSWSC 1143, (2000) 10 BPR 18,463; *Commonwealth Bank of Australia v Kyriackou* [2003] VSC 175, [2003] V ConvR 54-674; *Vasiliou v Westpac Banking Corporation* [2007] VSCA 113, (2007) 19 VR 229.

[141] The option to purchase, otherwise a strong analogy to the power to rescind, is a caveatable interest: *Laybutt v Amoco Australia Pty Ltd* (1974) 132 CLR 57. However, provided that its terms are identified and certain, the option to purchase is self-executing in the sense that it requires no assistance of the court to be effectively exercised. It is also specifically enforceable in a way that a power to rescind is not. Finally, and most importantly, the option to purchase intentionally gives the optionee the choice whether to exercise it or not over an extended length of time. By contrast, the power to rescind should be exercised promptly on the claimant becoming aware of his or her rights. To caveat a right to rescind may simply run counter to the nature of the right.

[142] *Breskvar v Wall* (1971) 126 CLR 376, 409 (Walsh J), discussed in R Chambers, *An Introduction to Property Law in Australia*, 2nd edn (Pyrmont, Lawbook Co, 2008) 475; *Sinclair v Hope Investments Pty Ltd* [1982] 2 NSWLR 870, 875 (Needham J); *Re McKean's Caveat* [1988] 1 Qd R 524, 525 (Ryan J); *Patmore v Upton* [2004] TASSC 77, (2004) 13 Tas R 95 [61] (Underwood J).

[143] *Alati v Kruger* (1955) 94 CLR 216, 224 (Dixon CJ, Webb, Kitto and Taylor JJ); *AH McDonald & Co Pty Ltd v Wells* (1931) 45 CLR 506, 512-13 (Rich, Starke and Dixon JJ). However, there are important contrary views, particularly regarding equitable rescission operating in its exclusive jurisdiction (ie, equitable rescission in contexts other than fraud and duress): see, eg, RP Meagher, JD Heydon and MJ Leeming, *Meagher, Gummow and Lehane's Equity: Doctrines and Remedies*, 4th edn (Chatswood, LexisNexis Butterworths, 2002) para 24-085; O'Sullivan, Elliott and Zakzrewski, above n 77, at paras 11.49–11.105. Another view is that rescission (whether at common law or in equity) is always the act of the court: see J O'Sullivan, 'Rescission as a Self-Help Remedy: A Critical Analysis' [2000] *Cambridge Law Journal* 509.

[144] It is another thing to take the view that the role of the court provides the defining difference between 'mere equities' and equitable interests: see *Mills v Ruthol Pty Ltd* [2002] NSWSC 294, (2002) 10 BPR 19,381 [118]-[134] (Palmer J); *Westpac Banking Corporation v Ollis* [2008] NSWSC 824 [69]-[77] (Einstein J).

the sense that they are subject to a change of position defence, when vested trust rights do not appear to be similarly exposed. The changes of position that are taken into account for the purposes of the doctrine of *restitutio in integrum* all occur prior to rescission, when the power is inchoate. At this point, the claimant has no vested interest in the asset and so cannot argue that considerations of security of title trump the defendant's entitlement to security of his or her receipt.

C. Rescission, Restitution and Enrichment

Finally, we have seen that rescission does not support any broader move within the law of unjust enrichment from enrichment received to net enrichment or enrichment surviving. The two claims analysis is a good 'fit' with the decided cases and shows rescission to operate in a manner broadly consistent with the usual structural model that applies to restitution for unjust enrichment.[145] That is, the party's prima facie entitlement upon rescission is for restitution of the benefit conferred, subject to defences. The change of position defence is not subsumed within the initial enrichment inquiry to reduce every claim to enrichment surviving. Rather, it is an independent requirement that incorporates, but is not limited to, 'disenrichment' considerations.

Nor would rescission support any argument that the value of received rights is irrelevant to their characterisation as enrichment and thus irrelevant to the corresponding entitlement to restitution. The second conclusion does not follow from the first. A claimant's entitlement to restitution of rights may be greatly affected by issues of value brought in at the point of defences, albeit value does not exhaust all relevant considerations. In other words, even if value is irrelevant in establishing enrichment by receipt of rights, this does not mean value is irrelevant to restitution of those rights. Establishing the prima facie entitlement and establishing the availability and bounds of the remedy are two separate, albeit related steps. It is not possible to avoid the question of the form and extent of the remedy by redefining the enrichment. Nor is it possible to avoid the difficulty by moving the point of determining the enrichment from the point of receipt to the point of rescission (or judgment). Identifying the enrichment is only the starting point, not the end, of the inquiry and the difficulties in determining the availability of proprietary restitution cannot be answered by collapsing the various stages into one.

---

[145] Discussed in the text accompanying nn 34–55 above.

VI. CONCLUSION

This chapter has sought to identify some of the many implications for unjust enrichment that can be derived from the doctrines of rescission. In particular, it has sought to demonstrate that it is neither possible nor desirable to draw a strict division between enrichment as rights and enrichment as value in the law of unjust enrichment. The inquiry is much messier than that elegant dichotomy, but also ultimately more sensitive to the competing rights and interests of the affected parties.

If the law of restitution for unjust enrichment is to develop on secure foundations, with rescission and restitution for unjust enrichment operating as part of a coherent body of law, then the groundbreaking work of Chambers and others in this area must be examined, buttressed where necessary and built upon. This chapter is offered as a small addition to that much larger enterprise. However, much remains to be done, particularly regarding the role and operation of the election requirement and the nature and valuation of pecuniary rescission.[146] It is only once these vital aspects of rescission are examined and understood that crucial questions such as the availability of proprietary restitution, its form and its effect can be properly addressed.[147]

---

[146] See above n 98.

[147] The author, together with Professor Michael Bryan, is the recipient of an Australian Research Council Discovery Grant to support their research project entitled 'The Principles of Proprietary Remedies'. The first stage of the project on the principles of rescission is concerned with precisely these sorts of issues. Scholars interested in engaging with the project are very welcome to contact Elise and Michael at Melbourne Law School.

Index